Vulnerabilities Assessment and Risk Management in Cyber Security

Khalid Hussain
School of Computing and Informatics, Malaysia

IGI Global
Scientific Publishing
Publishing Tomorrow's Research Today

Vice President of Editorial	Melissa Wagner
Managing Editor of Acquisitions	Mikaela Felty
Managing Editor of Book Development	Jocelynn Hessler
Production Manager	Mike Brehm
Cover Design	Phillip Shickler

Published in the United States of America by
IGI Global Scientific Publishing
701 East Chocolate Avenue
Hershey, PA, 17033, USA
Tel: 717-533-8845
Fax: 717-533-8661
Website: https://www.igi-global.com E-mail: cust@igi-global.com

Library of Congress Cataloging-in-Publication Data

LCCN: 2024054492 (CIP Data Pending)
ISBN13: 979-8-3693-6135-1
Isbn13Softcover: 979-8-3693-6136-8
EISBN13: 979-8-3693-6137-5

British Cataloguing in Publication Data
A Cataloguing in Publication record for this book is available from the British Library.

Table of Contents

Detailed Table of Contents

of various attack methods used by cybercriminals to extract user data and explores how users can protect their information from being compromised. The discussion will cover common tactics employed by attackers, the potential consequences of losing mobile application data to these threats, and the critical measures necessary for safeguarding user data against such attacks.

The proliferation of IoT devices and sensors leads to greater efficiency but also greatly increased attack surfaces. In this part of the series, we delve into some key security issues that plague IoT ecosystems with a solution- understanding device vulnerabilities and how they led to data exposure. IoT devices are frequently built without strong defences in place, with a lack of secure firmware combined with weak authentication making them top of the list for attackers. We will also turn to real-world threats, such as distributed denial of service (DDoS) attacks launched by botnets and data breaches that disclose personal information or sensitive business information. Although the chapter certainly warns of the risks, it is by no means a doom-and-gloom line of reasoning. The paper outlines best practices to secure IoT systems, from security-by-design principles to leveraging AI and blockchain technologies.

In the complex world of the internet, the smooth flow of data depends on a sophisticated web of protocols. These standardized rules and procedures ensure that information is transmitted securely between computers, enabling everything from basic email exchange to complex financial transactions. However, these protocols are still susceptible to exploitation despite their importance in our digital interactions. In the background of this digital ecosystem, there are skilled individuals who, with malicious intent, look for flaws and weak points in these systems. By exploiting these vulnerabilities, they can circumvent security measures, gain unauthorized access to important systems, and compromise the confidentiality of critical data. This security breach not only endangers data integrity but also poses serious risks to individuals and organizations. One of the most disruptive consequences of such violations is the Distributed Denial of Service (DDoS) attack.

Ensuring secure data transfer over a network involves many concerns and has been considered challenging. The most commonly used technique for securing data is encryption, which allows data to be encrypted to avoid unauthorized access. Image steganography is a special kind of encryption in which an additional layer of security is provided by hiding the data in a carrier image. This process can be performed in multiple ways. For example, Least Significant Bit (LSB)-Steganography is a technique in which the data is hidden within an image by replacing the least significant bits of the images with the data which is to be encrypted. Such techniques are exploited by cyber security professionals and application developers to implement encryption according to the scenarios and domain requirements. In this research, we have proposed a metamodel based on steganography using the LSB technique to autogenerate code in any programming language.

NoSQL data storage solutions are gaining popularity due to their scalability and ease of use. This study investigates the maturity of security measures for NoSQL databases, specifically their innovative query and access protocols. The introduction of new query formats renders traditional SQL injection techniques obsolete, but are NoSQL databases resistant to injection in general? The answer is no. This research paper presented a few ways to exploit NoSQL databases, including injections and CSRF. This study investigates the cause of these vulnerabilities and presents methods for mitigating the attacks. This research demonstrates that this new and lively technology sector lacks the security protections and understanding that have evolved over time in traditional RDBMS and SQL systems.

Siva Raja Sindiramutty, Taylor's University, Malaysia
Noor Zaman Jhanjhi, Taylor's University, Malaysia
Navid Ali Khan, Taylor's University, Malaysia

Cybersecurity is enriched due to Artificial Intelligence (AI), which provides better real-time threat detection and anomaly identification, response systems. As attackers grow more sophisticated and leverage AI in creating malware. The present study gives an overview of the future threats associated with AI-driven attacks and challenges faced by existing cybersecurity countermeasures. Additionally, it also analyses the feasibility of using AI-driven capabilities like predictive threat intelligence, advanced anomaly detection and quantum computing for some of these emerging threats. For such as, we need user permissions and rights on this application, it should take into consideration privacy policies while designing AI security as well. To this end, to get ready against future AI security risks a proactive and adaptive approach is needed stressing the collaboration between industry, academia as well global entities.

Soobia Saeed, Department of Software Engineering, UniversitiTeknologi Malaysia, Malaysia
Mehmood Naqvi, Mohawk College, Canada
Manzoor Hussain, Indus University, Pakistan

The objective of this research is to investigate sophisticated approaches for data mining and purification via knowledge discovery in databases (KDD) with generative AI concept, with an emphasis on using generative artificial intelligence. Unstructured data from customer service machine registry reports and structured data from sales, staff, and customer management duties are the two main types of information found in customer databases. To improve the extraction and interpretation of patterns, this study uses generative AI with cyber security hacks to secure the cleaning data in conjunction with the K-means algorithm to cluster and sort data. Our work focuses on the need to repositories of information and knowledge discovery, work for data storage and data mining. Dependent variable is KDD with generative AI and independent is Data Mining and KDD with cyber security as well. The main problem is to specific list, use useful pattern, Purposed model, inter-discipline action with cohort structure. We tried to secure and centralize and use branch level distribution in this.

This research aims to strengthen security within Industrial IoT (IIoT) environments by evaluating the effectiveness of various machine learning techniques for advanced threat detection and intrusion prevention. This study analyzes the performance of multiple algorithms. These algorithms were evaluated based on processing times and accuracy during training and testing phases. The Decision Tree Algorithm emerged as the most effective, achieving a high testing accuracy of 99%. Logistic Regression and Random Forest also demonstrated strong performance, with accuracies of 98% and 96% respectively. The study's findings underscore the potential of using machine learning models to enhance IIoT security by rapidly detecting and mitigating potential cyber risks, thus enabling more secure and reliable industrial deployments. This research provides valuable insights for the development of intelligent security solutions tailored for complex IIoT networks.

In today's digital landscape, the rapid advancement of Deepfake technology, fueled by sophisticated AI methods, poses a substantial threat to the integrity of digital content. This paper presents a framework that identifies subtle anomalies in Deepfake creation processes by amalgamating spatial and temporal features, ensuring effective detection. Furthermore, we introduce an innovative attribution model that amalgamates metadata scrutiny, network forensics, and linguistic indicators to accurately pinpoint potential Deepfake sources. Our research highlights that the Inception-ResNet-V2 + LSTM model exhibits superior performance, achieving the highest accuracy of 92%, thus setting a benchmark for future developments in Deepfake detection technology. Beyond mere detection, our framework offers invaluable insights into tracing deceptive media origins, aligning with endeavours to fortify digital information integrity against the ever-evolving landscape of sophisticated Deepfake technologies.

Web and network services have been increasingly targeted by Distributed Denial of Service (DDoS) attacks, which pose a significant threat. To minimize collateral damage and computational requirements, it is crucial to identify DDoS attacks. A new metric called Forward-Backward distance (FBD) is proposed to achieve this objective. FBD can accurately distinguish attacks and normal traffic using just one data point without requiring a minimum data point collection requirement. To achieve FBD, the Random Forest machine learning algorithm is first applied to the training data to detect DDoS attacks. Then, SHAP values are calculated for each data point to understand how the model made predictions. The best feature, which explains the model outcome with the best predictive power, is used to design a metric which can be used as a standalone to identify DDoS attacks. This new metric (FBD) shows a much higher precision (97%), while the recall is lower (39%). This means that it detects ~40% of the DDoS attacks, but out of the detected ones, 97% are the attacks.

Since the invention of the Internet of Things (IoT), people are seeing a new world in healthcare. The rapid growth of IoT has brought with it solutions to dilemmas and a few challenges with cloud devices. But keeping in mind the benefits of these devices, the challenges need to be solved with efficiency and security. Putting in place cloud storage and analysis for specific periods is very popular in medicine. On the other hand, creating big data, considering the sensitivity, some limitations have to be accepted. The use of latency, throughput, and bandwidth increases the cost of the Internet. Numerous alternative paradigms, most notably edge computing and fog computing, have evolved to solve these shortcomings. Consequently, studies have shown an increase in hybrid solutions based.

Preface

In an age dominated by technology, where every aspect of our personal and professional lives is intertwined with digital systems, the need for robust cybersecurity has never been more pressing. The internet of things (IoT), cloud computing, and digital business infrastructures have transformed how organizations operate, but they have also expanded the surface area for cyber-attacks. Cyber threats evolve daily, becoming increasingly sophisticated and difficult to manage. This book, *Vulnerability Assessment and Risk Management in Cybersecurity*, offers a vital resource to understand, assess, and manage the risks that arise from these vulnerabilities in digital systems. With this work, we aim to arm cybersecurity professionals, IT administrators, risk managers, and executives with the tools, strategies, and methodologies needed to address these challenges effectively.

The book delves into the principles of vulnerability assessment and cybersecurity risk management, offering readers a comprehensive framework to tackle the complex issues facing today's organizations. The landscape of cybersecurity is ever-changing, and it is crucial to have the knowledge to identify weaknesses within systems and to apply effective countermeasures. This resource emphasizes the importance of planning, identifying, analyzing, and evaluating risks, all while reinforcing continuous improvement in response to emerging threats. Each chapter is designed to provide both theoretical insight and practical techniques for cybersecurity professionals working to safeguard their digital infrastructures. The methodologies presented here, from risk identification to penetration testing, serve as foundational knowledge for assessing vulnerabilities and responding to potential breaches.

Understanding that cybersecurity is not just a technical issue but also an organizational challenge, the book expands its focus beyond technology to include management frameworks, compliance, and ethics. A wide range of methodologies and techniques are discussed in depth, from risk analysis and control treatments to penetration testing and incident response preparedness. Each section provides clear guidance on how to handle specific vulnerabilities, including web applications, client-side systems, and network services, while also addressing how to protect against social engineering attacks and other forms of manipulation. By exploring these diverse areas, we hope to provide a holistic approach to cybersecurity that prepares professionals to meet the full range of challenges posed by the digital age.

OVERVIEW OF CHAPTERS

Chapter 1: Blockchain in Cybersecurity: Enhancing Data Integrity and Transaction Security

Blockchain technology has gained significant attention for its ability to enhance data security and transaction reliability. Its decentralized nature and cryptographic principles help eliminate central points of failure, making tampering and unauthorized changes nearly impossible. This chapter explores how blockchain technology secures financial transactions, protects identities, and facilitates seamless agreements with smart contracts. It highlights the increasing adoption of blockchain across industries, including healthcare and supply chain management, for validating information and preventing fraud. However, blockchain's journey is not without challenges such as scalability, energy consumption, and regulatory issues. The chapter concludes by discussing promising developments like quantum-resistant algorithms and enhanced interoperability, which may address these challenges and broaden the security potential of blockchain.

Chapter 2: Current Security Issues and Vulnerabilities Associated with Mobile Applications

Mobile applications have become integral to daily life, handling everything from social interactions to financial transactions. However, this ubiquity comes with significant security concerns. This chapter delves into the various security issues and vulnerabilities associated with mobile apps. It provides a comprehensive analysis of the tactics used by cybercriminals to exploit weaknesses in mobile applications, endangering user data and privacy. The chapter further discusses the potential consequences of data breaches and emphasizes the critical security measures necessary to safeguard users from such threats. Key strategies for protecting mobile applications, from secure coding practices to user awareness, are presented to help mitigate these risks effectively.

Chapter 3: Cybersecurity in IoT Ecosystems: Managing Device Vulnerabilities and Data Exposure

The proliferation of IoT devices has led to increased efficiency but also introduced significant security risks due to expanded attack surfaces. This chapter examines the security challenges faced by IoT ecosystems, focusing on device vulnerabilities and data exposure. Many IoT devices are built without adequate security, making them prime targets for attackers. The chapter explores real-world threats, such as DDoS attacks and data breaches, while also offering solutions to mitigate these risks. Best practices for securing IoT systems, including security-by-design principles and the integration of AI and blockchain technologies, are presented to enhance the protection of IoT networks.

Chapter 4: Deluge of Disruption: An Introduction to DDoS Attacks

Distributed Denial of Service (DDoS) attacks have become one of the most disruptive threats to the internet's infrastructure. This chapter introduces DDoS attacks, explaining how they exploit vulnerabilities in internet protocols to overwhelm and disable systems. It covers the types of DDoS attacks and their potential consequences, including data loss, service disruption, and financial damage. The chapter also discusses the evolving tactics of attackers and the increasing sophistication of DDoS threats. Methods for defending against DDoS attacks, including traffic analysis, mitigation strategies, and the role of AI in detection and response, are explored.

Chapter 5: Cybersecurity-Enhanced Business Intelligence: Safeguarding Business Warehouses with Integrated Security Solutions

This chapter focuses on enhancing the security of Business Intelligence (BI) tools, which are vital for organizations to make informed and efficient decisions. It discusses the integration of cybersecurity measures into BI systems, ensuring the protection of business data while maintaining system functionality. The chapter highlights the importance of securing business warehouses, both structured and unstructured, against cyber threats. It outlines the design of user-friendly environments that allow for easy access to BI solutions while safeguarding sensitive information. Additionally, the chapter covers the potential of security solutions that seamlessly integrate with BI tools to protect organizations from evolving cyber threats.

Chapter 6: Future Trends in Generative AI for Cyber Defense: Preparing for the Next Wave of Threats

This chapter explores the role of generative AI in the future of cyber defense, examining its potential to detect and respond to emerging cybersecurity threats. With the rise of IoT and interconnectivity, the landscape of cyber threats is becoming increasingly complex. Generative AI promises to enhance threat detection, predictive analytics, and anomaly identification. However, as attackers also adopt AI-driven strategies, new challenges arise, including the emergence of AI-powered ransomware and other sophisticated threats. The chapter discusses the potential of AI in mitigating these risks while highlighting the need for proactive, adaptive cybersecurity strategies to stay ahead of emerging threats.

Chapter 7: Image Steganography Metamodel Using Model-Driven Engineering

Image steganography is a specialized encryption technique where data is hidden within an image, providing an additional layer of security. This chapter presents a metamodel based on the Least Significant Bit (LSB) technique for secure data transfer over networks. It demonstrates how LSB steganography can be leveraged by cybersecurity professionals to secure data in various scenarios. The chapter also introduces a model-driven approach to automatically generate code in any programming language for implementing steganography, thus enhancing the security of sensitive information during transmission. By using these techniques, the chapter contributes to a more secure digital ecosystem in the context of data encryption and protection.

Chapter 8: Securing Data of Cassandra Database by Applying the Latest Cybersecurity Techniques

NoSQL databases, such as Cassandra, have gained popularity for their scalability and flexibility. However, they also present unique security challenges, including vulnerabilities to injection attacks and cross-site request forgery (CSRF). This chapter investigates the security measures for NoSQL databases, particularly focusing on Cassandra, and explores techniques to mitigate vulnerabilities. It discusses the limitations of traditional security measures, such as SQL injection defenses, in the context of NoSQL and presents methods to address these new threats. The chapter highlights the need for innovative cybersecurity solutions to protect NoSQL databases from evolving attack vectors.

Chapter 9: Future Trends in AI Security: Anticipating and Preparing for Emerging Threats

Artificial Intelligence (AI) plays a pivotal role in enhancing cybersecurity by enabling real-time threat detection and advanced anomaly identification. However, the increasing sophistication of AI-driven cyberattacks presents new challenges for cybersecurity professionals. This chapter explores the future threats associated with AI, including AI-powered malware and the rise of AI-driven cybercrime. It also examines the potential of using AI to predict and mitigate these threats, alongside emerging technologies such as quantum computing. The chapter stresses the importance of a proactive, collaborative approach in preparing for future AI security risks and highlights the need for new regulatory frameworks to address the ethical concerns surrounding AI in cybersecurity.

Chapter 10: The Advanced Data Cleansing Method for Knowledge Discovery in Databases Using KDD with Generative AI and Cybersecurity

This chapter explores advanced techniques for data cleansing and knowledge discovery in databases (KDD) using generative AI. It investigates how KDD can be enhanced with generative AI to extract meaningful patterns from structured and unstructured data while ensuring the security of the data. The research focuses on improving the efficiency of data mining by combining cybersecurity practices with AI-driven algorithms, particularly in the context of customer service and sales data. The chapter also discusses the challenges of securing data during the cleansing process and proposes methods to safeguard sensitive information using encryption and advanced AI techniques.

Chapter 11: A Comparative Study of Machine Learning Techniques for Threat Detection and Enhancing Security in Industrial IoT

Machine learning techniques are increasingly being used to enhance security in Industrial IoT (IIoT) environments. This chapter compares several machine learning algorithms to assess their effectiveness in detecting threats and preventing intrusions in IIoT networks. The study evaluates the performance of algorithms like Decision Tree, Logistic Regression, and Random Forest, highlighting their accuracy and efficiency in identifying potential cyber risks. The chapter emphasizes the importance of leveraging machine learning to improve IIoT security and provides insights into the most effective algorithms for threat detection in complex industrial environments.

Chapter 12: A Holistic Approach to Detecting and Attributing Deepfake Media Using Advanced Computer Vision and Machine Learning Techniques

Deepfake technology, which uses AI to create convincing but fake digital media, poses a significant threat to the integrity of digital content. This chapter presents a comprehensive framework for detecting and attributing deepfake media using a combination of computer vision and machine learning techniques. It introduces an innovative model that integrates spatial and temporal features to identify deepfakes and attributes them to their sources using metadata and network forensics. The chapter demonstrates the effectiveness of the Inception-ResNet-V2 + LSTM model, which achieves high accuracy in detecting deepfakes, offering a valuable tool in the fight against media manipulation.

Chapter 13: A Novel FBD Detection Metric: A Rapid Shield Against DDoS Attacks

Distributed Denial of Service (DDoS) attacks remain a major threat to web and network services. This chapter introduces a novel detection metric, Forward-Backward Distance (FBD), to identify DDoS attacks more efficiently. The metric utilizes machine learning techniques, particularly the Random Forest algorithm, to distinguish between normal traffic and attack traffic with high precision. The chapter outlines the use of FBD as a standalone tool for DDoS detection, showing its effectiveness in achieving a precision rate of 97%, while also discussing the limitations in recall. This approach provides a rapid and resource-efficient solution to defending against DDoS attacks.

Chapter 14: Progress and Obstacles in Cloud Computing for Healthcare

Cloud computing has become an essential part of the healthcare industry, providing scalable and efficient solutions for data storage and analysis. This chapter examines the progress and obstacles in adopting cloud computing in healthcare, particularly in the context of the Internet of Things (IoT) and big data. It discusses the challenges related to latency, bandwidth, and cost, as well as the security concerns associated with storing sensitive healthcare data in the cloud. The chapter explores alternative paradigms like edge and fog computing, which aim to address these challenges and enhance the efficiency and security of cloud-based healthcare solutions.

Chapter 15: AI in Healthcare: Safeguarding Patient Privacy and Confidentiality

AI is transforming healthcare by improving patient identification, data security, and privacy protection. This chapter focuses on the role of AI in safeguarding patient data, emphasizing the importance of encryption, machine learning, and advanced security techniques to ensure the confidentiality of sensitive healthcare information. The chapter also discusses the ethical challenges of balancing data availability with privacy concerns, as well as the need for more effective regulatory frameworks to govern AI-driven healthcare solutions. It highlights the role of AI in streamlining compliance with data protection regulations and mitigating the risks of unauthorized access.

CONCLUSION

As we conclude this exploration of vulnerability assessment and risk management, it is essential to highlight that cybersecurity is not a one-time effort but a continuous process. The methodologies and tools outlined in this book are only the beginning of what must be an ongoing journey of vigilance, adaptation, and improvement. Cybersecurity professionals must remain proactive in identifying new vulnerabilities and in developing strategies to address the ever-evolving threat landscape. The risk management frameworks and assessment techniques explored in this book are designed to provide a solid foundation, but the real work lies in the execution and continuous iteration of security measures. As we look ahead, the need for cybersecurity professionals who can adapt to new challenges will only grow.

This book also underscores the importance of collaboration among all levels of an organization to create a robust cybersecurity culture. While technical expertise is critical, risk management and vulnerability assessment are equally about communication, policy development, and compliance. By integrating cybersecurity measures into business processes, organizations can ensure a safer, more resilient digital environment. As we move forward, it is vital that every individual involved in cybersecurity—whether an IT professional, business executive, or researcher—approaches their work with a mindset of continuous improvement, awareness of emerging risks, and an unwavering commitment to protecting data and digital assets.

Finally, it is our hope that this book will serve as a useful reference for cybersecurity practitioners, researchers, and students. By equipping readers with the knowledge and skills to address and mitigate cybersecurity risks, we aim to contribute to the ongoing battle against cyber threats. As technology continues to evolve, the principles outlined here will remain essential in ensuring that we remain one step ahead in safeguarding our digital future.

Khalid Hussain
School of Computing and Informatics, Malaysia

Chapter 1
Blockchain in Cybersecurity Enhancing Data Integrity and Transaction Security

Siva Raja Sindiramutty
https://orcid.org/0009-0006-0310-8721
Taylor's University, Malaysia

Noor Zaman Jhanjhi
https://orcid.org/0000-0001-8116-4733
Taylor's University, Malaysia

Sayan Kumar Ray
Taylor's University, Malaysia

ABSTRACT

The technology is becoming a little more widely known with its data security and hyper-transaction reliability. By its very design of decentralization and implementation of cryptographic principles to maintain integrity, blockchain eliminates central points of failure making tampering and unauthorized changes virtually impossible as well. This part of the diary will discuss how blockchain is giving security to our financial transactions, providing safety to our identities and making agreements more seamless with smart contracts. From healthcare to supply chain management, it is amazing to witness how many industries are beginning to incorporate blockchain to decree the validity of information, to prevent fraud. But you know what they say — new tech has new ways to break. The ride has been accompanied by scalability challenges, energy consumption worries, regulation problems and so on. There are

DOI: 10.4018/979-8-3693-6135-1.ch001

also some promising prospects, as quantum-resistant algorithms and enhanced interoperability may resolve these problems and widen blockchain's security influence.

1. INTRODUCTION

Definition and Overview of Blockchain Technology

Blockchain is like a digital ledger, but instead of being controlled by one company or person, it's shared across many computers, making it decentralized (Mueller-Bloch et al., 2022). This decentralized nature means that no single entity has total control, which is a big difference compared to traditional databases where a central authority, like a bank, holds all the (Tyagi et al., 2024). With blockchain, every transaction is recorded in "blocks" and once they're linked together, it's almost impossible to change them without everyone knowing (Richardson, 2020; Fatima-Tuz-Zahra et al., 2020).

Now, imagine your family uses a whiteboard to track who owes what for pizza night. If someone tries to erase or change the amounts, everyone else who saw the original would notice the change right away. That's kind of how blockchain works – but on a massive scale with thousands of eyes keeping track (Sharma, 2024; Humayun et al., 2022). It's like having a built-in safeguard where no one can sneak in and make unauthorized changes.

One more thing that stands out is how blockchain eliminates the need for a middleman. Think about sending money overseas. Usually, you'd have to go through a bank, pay fees, and wait days. With blockchain, that transfer can happen directly and way faster (Christodoulou et al., 2024). This makes it a game-changer, especially in areas like finance and supply chain management, where transparency and security are paramount. The way blockchain operates, ensuring integrity without relying on a central authority, offers a fresh way to think about security and trust in the digital age.

Figure 1. Blockchain's relevance in securing data and transactions

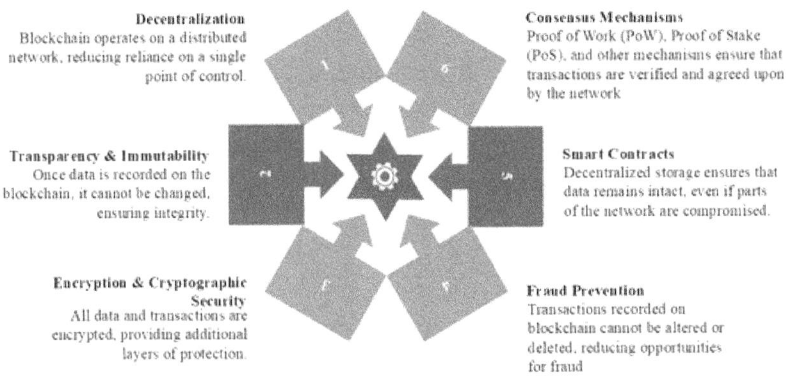

Relevance of Blockchain to Cybersecurity

Introduce blockchain's relevance in securing data and transactions. Highlight how it enhances transparency, integrity, and trust in digital systems.

Blockchain has become a vital part of securing data and transactions in digital systems. Its main advantage lies in how it distributes information across a network of nodes, making tampering with data nearly impossible (Vanmathi et al., 2024; Lim et al., 2019). This shared structure enhances transparency by allowing all participants to view and verify transactions. In traditional databases, data can be altered without detection, but with blockchain, any change is immediately visible, which creates a strong sense of accountability and trust (Aljabri, Jemili and Korbaa, 2023). Figure 1 shows blockchain's relevance in securing data and transactions.

Let me share a real-world application: supply chains. Many companies are now using blockchain to trace products from origin to destination. It's no longer a mystery where your coffee beans or smartphone parts come from. You can check each step of the process. I find this reassuring—it brings clarity to a process that used to be murky at best. If a transaction is recorded on the blockchain, it's there forever, cemented into history. There's no going back to erase or hide information (Ishkov and Krupnov, 2024; Gopi et al., 2021).

Moreover, blockchain enhances data integrity. Since every block is linked to the one before it, any modification would require altering the entire chain, which is practically unfeasible (Badertscher et al., 2024; Dogra et al., 2021). This integrity creates a level of security and trust that few other technologies can match. People trust systems that are difficult to hack, and that trust carries over to every participant in the network. It's like having an unbreakable seal on every digital transaction.

Overall, blockchain's combination of transparency, trust, and integrity is reshaping how we handle data in the digital world. It's not just a passing trend—it's a foundational technology that's here to stay.

Chapter Contribution

This chapter is pertinent to the area of blockchain in cybersecurity: enhancing data integrity and transaction security. First, it describes blockchain technology's general concept and functioning and outlines the information regarding decentralization and consensus mechanisms, immutability and tamper-proof records, and cryptographic security in blockchain. The chapter then investigates applications of blockchain in cybersecurity in securing transactions in financial services, supply chain security and smart contracts for automated security protocols.

Furthermore, the chapter presents use cases of blockchain for data integrity such as data provenance and audit trails, health records security, explaining the government and public sector data integrity. It also discusses the challenges and limitations of blockchain in cybersecurity including scalability and performance issues, energy consumption and regulatory and legal considerations. Lastly, the section provides a glimpse of what Blockchain in Cybersecurity could look like in the future, such as Quantum-Resistant Blockchain, Interoperability between Blockchains, and Blockchain in Decentralized Autonomous Organizations with some case studies. In doing so, the chapter hopes to help researchers and practitioners design secure, efficient, and ethical blockchain applications.

Chapter Organization

In the first section, we will cover an insight into the Overview of Blockchain Technology and the Relevance of Blockchain to Cybersecurity. In section 2 we go down to the Blockchain's Core such as Decentralization and Consensus Mechanisms, Immutability and Tamper-Proof Records and Cryptographic Security in Blockchain. In section 3 we discuss the Applications of Blockchain in Cybersecurity followed by the Use Cases of Blockchain for Data Integrity in section 4. Section 5 delves into the Challenges and Limitations of Blockchain in Cybersecurity such as scalability, performance, energy consumption issues and regulatory and legal considerations.

Section 6 will explain the future direction and innovation of blockchain in cybersecurity and finally, a few case studies are discussed.

2. BLOCKCHAIN'S CORE SECURITY FEATURES

Decentralization and Consensus Mechanisms

How Blockchain's Decentralized Structure Reduces Single Points Of Failure

Blockchain's decentralized structure offers a strong advantage in reducing single points of failure, something I've come to appreciate as I explored its use in securing sensitive information (Naef, Wagner and Saur, 2022; Alkinani et al., 2021). In a typical centralized system, everything relies on a central server. If that server is compromised, the entire system can collapse. However, blockchain distributes data across numerous nodes, eliminating that singular point of vulnerability (Quan et al., 2024; Chesti et al., 2020). Imagine a scenario where hackers attempt to take down one server—if the system is decentralized, they can't do much harm by attacking just one spot.

I had a friend who ran a small business using cloud storage for everything. One day, the system failed, and all her data was at risk. I couldn't help but wonder how different the situation would have been with blockchain—where no single server failure would disrupt operations. Every node in the network validates transactions, meaning the system remains resilient even if part of it goes down (Liu et al., 2024; Alex et al., 2022). It's a bit like a team that doesn't crumble if one player gets injured because everyone else keeps the game going. And honestly, that's the beauty of decentralization. Not having a single point of control is not only empowering, but it's also incredibly secure. You don't have to worry about one vulnerable spot causing everything to fall apart.

There's an emotional relief in knowing that no single failure can bring the whole thing down. It gives users more control and security (Gong et al., 2024; Alferidah and Jhanjhi, 2020). And who doesn't want that kind of assurance in today's world, where cyber-attacks are getting more creative? Figure 2 shows the blockchain's core security features.

Figure 2. Blockchain's Core Security Features

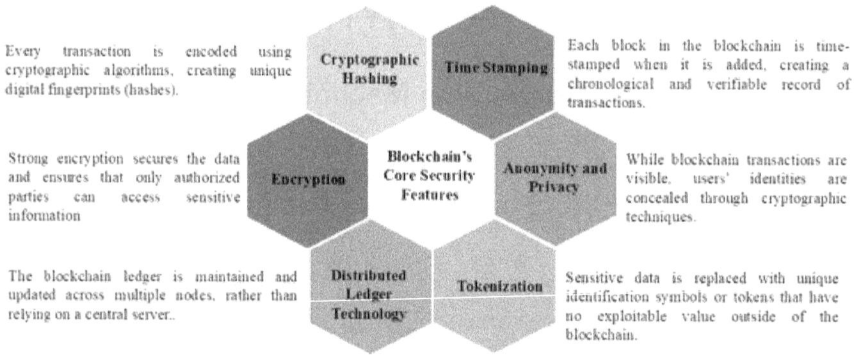

Explanation of Consensus Algorithms (Proof of Work, Proof of Stake, etc.) and Their Role In Securing The Network

Consensus algorithms play a crucial role in how blockchain networks function (Wei, Xu and Peng, 2024). They help everyone involved agree on the validity of transactions and keep data secure. One of the most recognizable among these is Proof of Work (PoW), famously used by Bitcoin (Tiwari et al., 2024; Muzafar and Jhanjhi, 2019). In PoW, miners race to solve tough mathematical puzzles, and the winner gets to add a block of transactions to the chain. This method requires a hefty amount of computational power and energy, making it secure but also quite demanding.

In contrast, we have Proof of Stake (PoS), which takes a different approach. Instead of relying on computational might, PoS selects validators based on the number of coins they hold and are willing to "stake."(Leporati and Rovida, 2024). This process is way more energy-efficient than PoW, making it a popular choice for networks that want to lessen their environmental footprint. Ethereum made a big move by switching from PoW to PoS to boost its sustainability (Frédéric, 2024).

There are also other algorithms worth noting, like Delegated Proof of Stake (DPoS). Here, a smaller group of validators is chosen by the community. This allows for quicker transactions but comes with a bit more centralization (Narayan, Arali and Tejas, 2024; Sharma et al., 2021). Each of these algorithms has its perks and drawbacks, which is fascinating to explore! The way they shape how we interact with blockchain technology can have significant implications, especially as more people get on board with cryptocurrencies and decentralized applications. Meanwhile, Proof of Authority (PoA) is popular in private networks, where trusted entities validate transactions, ensuring speed and efficiency (Putra et al., 2024).

I find PoS much more sustainable. It's like moving from a fuel-guzzling car to an electric vehicle — you're still getting where you need to go, but without harming the planet as much. However, PoW remains a powerhouse in security terms, despite its environmental drawbacks. It's a balancing act for every network to decide which algorithm best meets their security and efficiency needs. The beauty of consensus algorithms is how they reflect the unique priorities of each blockchain ecosystem.

Immutability and Tamper-Proof Records

How Blockchain Ensures Data Integrity By Making Records Immutable Once Validated

Blockchain technology plays a critical role in ensuring data integrity, primarily by making records immutable once they are validated. (Ghadi et al., 2024; Brohi et al., 2020). At its core, blockchain functions as a distributed ledger, meaning every participant in the network has a copy of the data. When a new transaction is added, all copies are updated, and this collective validation guarantees that the data is accurate (Sharma, Jindal and Borah, 2023; Jhanjhi, Humayun and Almuayqil, 2021). Once a block of information is added to the chain, it becomes incredibly difficult to alter. The data is secured using cryptographic techniques, which ensure that even if someone attempts to tamper with the records, the network will reject any changes (Ajakwe et al., 2024).

I remember once working on a project where we needed to verify the authenticity of medical records. Before adopting blockchain, the fear of manipulation was always there, and trust was a major issue. But with blockchain, each medical record could be traced back to its origin without any fear of tampering, providing a peace of mind that we hadn't had before. It's like writing with a permanent marker on a wall—there's no easy way to erase it (Sreedharan, 2024; Babbar et al., 2021).

Moreover, because of the decentralized nature of blockchain, there isn't a single point of failure. This means no central authority can modify or delete the data once it's validated. This feature significantly enhances trust among participants who need to rely on the system. I can imagine a future where blockchain technology becomes the default for ensuring the integrity of digital records across various sectors, from finance to healthcare, making data breaches a thing of the past (Asaithambi et al., 2024; Kumar et al., 2021).

Cryptographic Security in Blockchain

How Cryptography, Particularly Hashing And Public-Key Cryptography, Underpins Blockchain Security

When we talk about blockchain security, cryptography does a lot of the heavy lifting (Choithani et al., 2022; Hussain et al., 2024). Hashing and public-key cryptography are at the heart of it. Hashing takes data and scrambles it into a unique string of numbers and letters, like a digital fingerprint (Selamat et al., 2024; Radhakrishnan and Travieso-Gonzalez, 2024). I always think of it as how we recognize people by their faces; once you've seen it, you know it's them—except with a hash, any change in data makes it unrecognizable. It's how blockchain keeps data tamper-proof. If someone even tries to mess with the smallest bit of information, the hash changes, and boom, you know something's off (Carreira et al., 2024).

On the other hand, public-key cryptography feels like digital magic. Imagine having a box with two keys: one locks it, and the other unlocks it. You hand the lock key to everyone, but only you hold the unlock key. People can send you things, and only you can open them. That's the essence of public-private key pairs in blockchain. This setup lets users verify transactions without sharing secret information, which is wild when you think about it—your data stays secure even when a bunch of strangers are processing it.

Both hashing and public-key cryptography are like the guard dogs of the blockchain (Alkhatib, Albalawi and Saeed, 2024; Sindiramutty et al., 2024). They ensure the system stays decentralized and trustworthy (Jiang et al., 2024). With no single entity calling the shots, it's more resistant to attacks. When I learned about how this works in real-time, it felt like seeing behind the curtain of something genius, yet simple. Trust is built not on human promises, but on math.

Blockchain wouldn't be the same without cryptography—it'd be like a house without walls. Transactions would be vulnerable, and honestly, the entire system would probably crumble without this level of security.

3. APPLICATIONS OF BLOCKCHAIN IN CYBERSECURITY

Securing Transactions in Financial Services

How Blockchain Is Revolutionizing The Financial Sector By Securing Digital Transactions And Preventing Fraud

Blockchain technology has reshaped the financial sector by securing digital transactions and reducing fraud (Jimmy, 2024). Its decentralized nature means that there is no single authority overseeing the system, making it much harder for hackers to manipulate (Aoun et al., 2024). I once read a story about a small business owner who nearly lost their entire savings to a phishing scam. Had they been using blockchain-based payment systems, the attack might have been blocked, as blockchain verifies each transaction through complex algorithms, making fraudulent activity incredibly difficult (Teutsch and Reitwießner, 2023; Sindiramutty, Tan and Wei, 2024). This kind of protection is life-saving for people in high-risk areas like finance, where one wrong move can mean losing everything.

Another significant factor is transparency. Every transaction is recorded and cannot be altered once it's added to the chain. Imagine trying to falsify a payment—it's nearly impossible when hundreds or thousands of computers have a verified copy of every transaction (Datta and Namasudra, 2024; Sindiramutty, Jhanjhi, et al., 2024). It's almost like having a watchdog that never sleeps, always ensuring that your funds are secure. Plus, fewer middlemen are involved, which means lower fees and quicker processing times. You save money, and the process runs more smoothly—who wouldn't want that?

While blockchain can't solve every problem, it offers an incredible step forward in fraud prevention. Traditional systems can't compete with blockchain's ability to detect and prevent unauthorized transactions in real time. A friend of mine, who works in fintech, always says, "With blockchain, you sleep better knowing that even if someone tries to steal your money, they're going to have a much harder time doing it." That sense of security is invaluable, and it's why blockchain continues to gain traction in financial services.

Figure 3. Applications of blockchain in cybersecurity

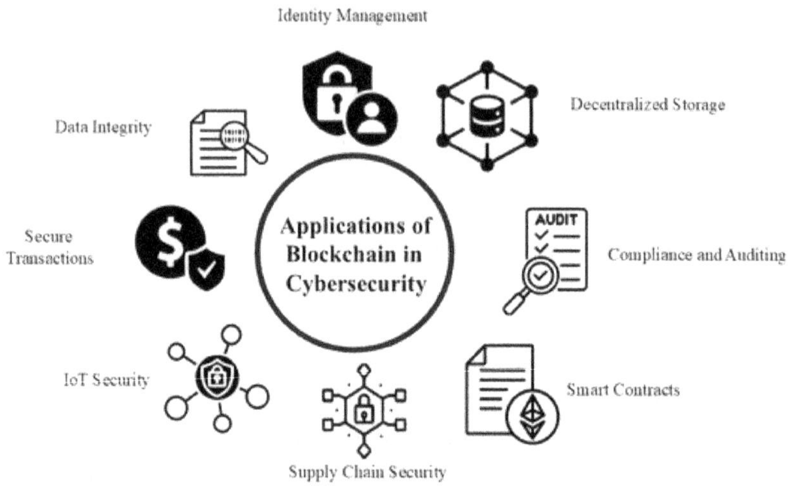

Supply Chain Security

The Role Of Blockchain In Tracking And Verifying The Authenticity Of Products In A Supply Chain, Reducing Risks Of Counterfeit Goods

Blockchain technology is becoming a game-changer in ensuring product authenticity in supply chains, especially when dealing with counterfeit risks (Oriekhoe et al., 2024). Imagine buying a luxury handbag only to later discover it's a fake. This scenario plays out in numerous industries, from pharmaceuticals to electronics, costing businesses billions of dollars each year. Blockchain offers a way to tackle this by creating an unchangeable record of every step a product takes, from its origin to the hands of the consumer (Westerkamp, Victor and Küpper, 2019; Sindiramutty, Jhanjhi, Tan, Khan, et al., 2024). Each transaction, whether it's from a manufacturer or distributor, is securely logged on a decentralized ledger that can't be tampered with. It's like having a digital fingerprint for every item.

One interesting example is Walmart's use of blockchain to track mangoes. Shoppers can scan a barcode and trace the fruit back to the exact farm it came from in seconds (Singh and Vishwakarma, 2023). This transparency helps detect and prevent counterfeit goods from entering the market. In industries where safety is critical, such as medicine, blockchain can verify that drugs are legitimate, ensuring patient safety (Uddin, 2021). In a world where counterfeit medicines alone cost nearly $200 billion annually, this is a big deal (Liang, 2006).

Blockchain doesn't just benefit big corporations. Smaller businesses also stand to gain by offering customers a level of trust that was previously hard to achieve. Imagine a local coffee roaster guaranteeing that their beans are ethically sourced by showing the complete journey of the beans. It builds trust and authenticity, which consumers increasingly demand. However, implementing blockchain can be expensive and technically complex, which might pose challenges for smaller companies (Waqar et al., 2023; Sindiramutty, Jhanjhi, Tan, Khan, Shah and Manchuri, 2024).

By integrating blockchain into the supply chain, companies can not only protect their reputations but also give consumers the peace of mind that what they're buying is the real deal.

Identity Management and Authentication

How Blockchain Can Help With Decentralized Digital Identity Solutions, Preventing Identity Theft And Securing Personal Data

Blockchain technology can help safeguard personal data and prevent identity theft by enabling decentralized digital identity solutions (Buttar et al., 2024; Seng et al., 2024). With traditional identity systems, centralized databases store personal information, making them targets for cyberattacks. Decentralized identity solutions built on blockchain distribute data across multiple nodes, reducing the risk of a single point of failure (Yan et al., 2024; Jun et al., 2024). This can make it much harder for hackers to access sensitive information, as there's no central database to breach.

A close friend of mine fell victim to identity theft a few years ago, and it was a nightmare. She spent months trying to restore her credit score, all because her information was stored in a centralized system that was hacked. If a decentralized solution had been in place, it might have saved her a lot of trouble. Blockchain also gives individuals more control over their data (Daudén-Esmel, Castellà-Roca and Viejo, 2023). Instead of handing over information to third parties, users can share only what is necessary, reducing exposure to potential misuse. Think of it as having a digital wallet with different credentials that you can selectively share.

Moreover, the transparency offered by blockchain allows for an immutable record of transactions, which adds another layer of security (Alzoubi, 2024; Ravichandran et al., 2024). Imagine a situation where you're asked to prove your age for a service. With blockchain, you can confirm your eligibility without revealing your actual birthdate, which limits the amount of personal information shared (Kaur, Rani and Kalra, 2023; Waheed et al., 2024).

As these systems continue to be adopted, we may see fewer instances of data breaches and identity theft, making life a little easier for everyone. Blockchain's potential to protect personal data and prevent identity theft could be a game-changer in today's data-driven world (Huseynov, 2025).

Smart Contracts for Automated Security Protocols

Discuss Smart Contracts, How They Work, And Their Role In Automatically Executing Secure And Transparent Agreements

Smart contracts are essentially computer programs that run on blockchain networks (Kizza, 2024). What's fascinating about them is how they allow agreements to be carried out without needing middlemen. I remember reading about how, in the past, people used to depend heavily on lawyers and notaries to ensure contracts were followed. Smart contracts skip all that, taking human error and manipulation out of the picture (J, Singh and Chakravarthi, 2023; Manchuri et al., 2024). Once certain conditions are met, the contract automatically executes the agreement. Think of it like a vending machine—you put in your money, and if the amount is right, it delivers what you asked for. No need to trust that someone is watching over the process; it just happens.

These contracts are stored on a blockchain, which means they're transparent and secure (Ogungbemi, 2024). Anyone involved in the contract can see its terms, and once it's in place, it can't be changed without everyone's agreement. This technology makes me feel like we're moving towards a world where transactions can be handled much more efficiently and securely. For example, in finance, smart contracts can automatically transfer funds when certain conditions are met, cutting down the time and cost of traditional transactions. In real estate, they could automatically transfer ownership of a property once payment is made. Even insurance claims could be handled without endless paperwork, with payouts triggered by predefined events.

One thing that strikes me is how useful they can be beyond just business. Imagine using them in voting systems—once someone votes, it's immediately recorded and can't be tampered with. It's this kind of transparency and automation that makes smart contracts such a game-changer.

4. USE CASES OF BLOCKCHAIN FOR DATA INTEGRITY

Data Provenance and Audit Trails

How Blockchain Can Be Used To Track The Origin And Changes To Data, Ensuring Its Integrity Over Time

The integrity of data is one of the areas in which blockchain can change the game, e.g., data provenance and audit trails (Hon *et al.*, 2024; Azam et al., 2023). I have seen first-hand how critical it is to preserve the integrity of sensitive information. When you are working with medical records or supply chain data, knowing the exact origin of that data and how it has been treated is crucial. Given that any interaction with the data on a blockchain is tracked in an almost unalterable way, it becomes virtually impossible for someone to change information and make it appear false (Chhabra et al., 2024; Ananna et al., 2023). This will become an increasingly necessary solution in a time when data breaches are starting to seem like the norm as it allows you to know that the data hasn't been modified.

After all, one of my favourite benefits regarding blockchain is automation which encourages audit trails (Majeed and Taha, 2023; Azam, Dulloo, et al., 2023). Consider a more practical example, such as financial transactions, which are impossible to track by hand. Blockchain is used to record any transaction in such a nice way that it can be traced back by anyone with ease (Benstead et al., 2022). This sort of tracing reduces the chances of human error or fraud. Also, it is not only a matter of dealing with failures after they occur; you also have to stop them from happening. For example, in the past, I have come across enterprises that use blockchain to validate supply chain processes guaranteeing that the goods mentioned are being sourced ethically and legally (Tuladhar *et al.*, 2024).

And gives peace of mind from the user's end as well. The real-time recording of every interaction with my data just makes me trust the systems I use all the more. That level of openness is less a "nice to have" and more a mandatory ingredient when making our way in the world today. Figure 4 shows blockchain for data integrity.

Figure 4. Blockchain for data integrity

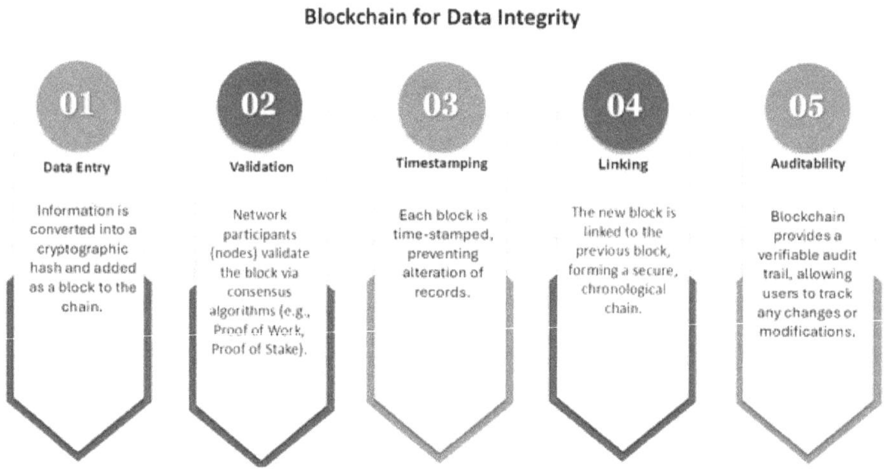

Health Records Security

Explore How Blockchain is Applied to Protect and Manage Electronic Health Records (EHRS), Ensuring Privacy and Accuracy

Blockchain has sparked serious interest in securing electronic health records (EHRs) (X. Liu et al., 2024; Azam, Tajwar, et al., 2023). The idea of using an immutable ledger for sensitive health data seems to hit all the right notes. Picture this: your health records are always accurate, can't be altered, and are only accessible to those who need it. This is particularly powerful because medical data errors can lead to harmful consequences.

Let me tell you about a hospital in Estonia, which pioneered using blockchain for EHRs. The system ensured that patient information was encrypted, verifiable, and tamper-proof, providing a level of security that made both patients and healthcare providers feel at ease. It's like a vault where no one can swap out your files without leaving a trail of breadcrumbs. Even better, patients could grant temporary access to specialists who needed their data, without worrying that their information would be viewed by unauthorized personnel (Sharma and Jain, 2024)

I've heard doctors complain about fragmented records. They jump between systems, losing valuable time. But imagine a secure, decentralized system where patient records follow them wherever they go. No more mix-ups. No more outdated records. That's blockchain, keeping things synchronized and safe. It's efficient and transparent.

However, blockchain isn't a magical fix. Managing large data sets on-chain is expensive, which has prompted some to use it only for verifying data off-chain (Fernández-Iglesias, Von Eitzen and Rifón, 2024; Azam, Mohammad Irfan Dulloo, Majeed, Wan, Xin and Sindiramutty, 2023). There's still a lot of excitement though, especially around preventing fraud, improving patient trust, and streamlining data exchanges in a secure way (Sahu, Choudhari and Chakole, 2024).

What's clear is that blockchain offers a way to maintain health record integrity like never before. This isn't just a technological upgrade; it's a way to protect our most private data (Tyagi and Seranmadevi, 2024). Who wouldn't want that peace of mind?

Government and Public Sector Data Integrity

Examples of How Governments are Using Blockchain to Secure Public Data, Voting Systems, and Land Registries

Blockchain technology is changing how governments ensure the integrity of public data (Mustafa et al., 2024). A big part of this island registries. In countries like Sweden, blockchain records property transactions, reducing fraud and speeding up the process (Persson, 2024). Land ownership is securely stored, eliminating disputes over who owns what. I remember reading about Honduras, where tampering with land records used to be a common issue, but now, with blockchain, they have a system where alterations can't be hidden.

The voting system is another area where blockchain can shine. We've all seen headlines about election tampering in recent years. Some governments, like Estonia, are using blockchain to secure voting systems, ensuring transparency and accuracy (Singh, no date; Vaibhav, 2020; Wen et al., 2023). It makes sense; if votes are recorded in an immutable blockchain, nobody can manipulate the results.

Public sector data is also protected by blockchain, ensuring accuracy. For instance, Dubai has been a leader in using this technology for the secure storage of public data, including contracts and legal documents. This shift promises transparency and trust (Jeevitha, Bhanumathi and Mukherjee, 2024). Even the thought of something as simple as a birth certificate being permanently logged in a secure system feels like a relief from all the bureaucracy.

Blockchain isn't perfect, but in the hands of governments trying to protect crucial data, it's making strides. It's hard not to feel hopeful about how this technology could reshape trust in public institutions.

5. CHALLENGES AND LIMITATIONS OF BLOCKCHAIN IN CYBERSECURITY

Scalability and Performance Issues

Discuss the Current Challenges of Blockchain Regarding Transaction Speed and Network Congestion

Blockchain has been praised for its potential in cybersecurity, but it faces significant challenges related to scalability and performance (Ahmed and Alabi, 2024; Shah, Jhanjhi and Laraib, 2022). Imagine a traffic jam where every car must pass through the same toll booth—this gives a sense of how blockchain can slow down, especially with increasing transaction volumes. Many blockchain networks, including Bitcoin and Ethereum, struggle with slow transaction speeds and network congestion (Rebello et al., 2024). Currently, Bitcoin processes around 7 transactions per second (TPS), while Ethereum averages about 30 TPS (Zhao et al., 2024). Compared to traditional payment systems like Visa, which handles up to 24,000 TPS, blockchain's limitations become clear (J. Liu *et al.*, 2024).

I remember reading about Ethereum's infamous "CryptoKitties" craze in 2017 when a digital cat-breeding game clogged up the entire network. Thousands of users experienced delays in transaction confirmations as the network couldn't handle the surge in activity. It felt like everyone was waiting in line at the busiest coffee shop ever. Beyond amusing cases like this, these performance issues can have serious implications. When critical systems depend on blockchain, such as in healthcare or financial services, slow speeds can cause delays that cost money—or worse, lives (Kharche, Badholia and Upadhyay, 2024).

One proposed solution is "sharding," where the blockchain is split into smaller segments to spread out the workload (Hong et al., 2024). However, even this technology is still in the testing phase and comes with its risks. It feels like trying to stretch a blanket that just isn't big enough to cover everything. Until blockchain can handle more transactions faster, these scalability issues will continue to challenge its broader adoption, especially in sectors where quick, real-time responses are essential (Abdul, 2024).

Energy Consumption

Address the Energy-Intensive Nature of Some Blockchain Protocols, Like Bitcoin, and the Environmental Concerns Tied to it

Blockchain technology has emerged as a key tool for ensuring data integrity, especially in fields like finance and healthcare (Ajayi-Nifise et al., 2024). However, its environmental impact has sparked concern, particularly with energy-intensive protocols like Bitcoin's Proof of Work (PoW) (Tayebi and Amini, 2024). Bitcoin, for instance, consumes a staggering amount of electricity—comparable to entire countries like Argentina or Norway (Leahy, 2024; Azeem et al., 2021). This is largely because PoW requires vast computational power to solve complex problems and validate transactions, leading to high energy consumption (Pawar and Sachdeva, 2023).

The environmental concerns are hard to ignore. I remember reading about how even some of the Bitcoin miners in rural areas have resorted to setting up rigs next to hydropower plants, trying to minimize their carbon footprint (Tong et al., 2024; Khan et al., 2021). Yet, there's a long way to go before it's sustainable. Ethereum, another popular blockchain, recently transitioned from PoW to Proof of Stake (PoS), which significantly reduces its energy consumption by cutting out the need for intensive computations. This change is a step forward, but not all blockchains have followed suit (Hall, Shiaeles and Li, 2024).

It makes you think about whether we can balance blockchain's benefits with its environmental cost. Some newer blockchains like Cardano and Algorand are designed with energy efficiency in mind from the start (Schumacher, 2024). They're using methods that don't require excessive electricity. But will this be enough to make blockchain technology widely accepted without the massive energy drain? It's something that needs urgent attention, especially as the world becomes more aware of climate change. After all, ensuring the integrity of our data shouldn't come at the cost of our planet. Figure 5 shows limitations of blockchain in cybersecurity.

Figure 5. Limitations of blockchain in cybersecurity

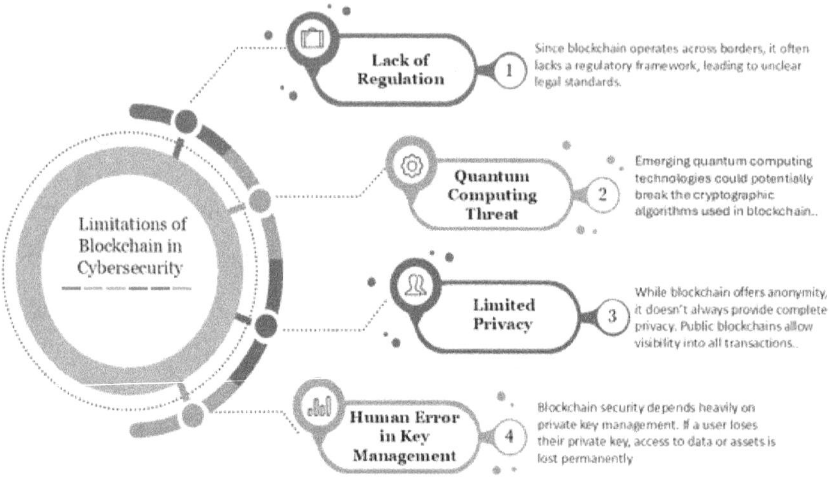

Regulatory and Legal Considerations

Challenges Around the Lack of Global Regulations on Blockchain Use, Legal Recognition, and Compliance

Blockchain's ability to secure data integrity is catching the attention of many industries, yet the regulatory and legal hurdles it faces are like hitting speed bumps when you're eager to get somewhere (Mgeladze, 2024). On one hand, blockchain is a bit of a wild card — a decentralized system with no global boss regulating its use. So, when businesses use it to ensure data remains tamper-proof, they often find themselves in murky waters regarding legal recognition (Alshahrani, 2024). I've seen a lot of excitement about its potential in supply chains or healthcare records, but those industries are finding compliance with existing laws tricky. It's like trying to fit a square peg into a round hole

Different countries have their own rules, and without universal guidelines, companies often ask, "Are we even doing this right?" And then there's the challenge of getting blockchain technology recognized in court. Some jurisdictions don't even see blockchain-based records as legally valid yet. Can you imagine your data being watertight, but still not holding up in legal disputes? It's frustrating.

Not to mention, some legal requirements like data protection regulations clash with blockchain's immutability. Blockchain's strength is that it doesn't forget — but regulators say, "Hey, sometimes we need you to forget!". The lack of global laws makes it harder for companies to confidently implement blockchain across borders (Böhmecke-Schwafert, 2024). Without that consistency, it's like trying to play a game where the rules keep changing. It's promising, but we're still figuring out how to play by the rules while keeping the benefits intact.

6. FUTURE DIRECTIONS AND INNOVATIONS

Quantum-Resistant Blockchain

The intersection of blockchain technology and quantum computing presents both opportunities and challenges. As quantum computers advance, they pose a significant risk to current cryptographic systems used in blockchain (Scholten et al., 2024). Most blockchain systems rely on algorithms that could be easily broken by a sufficiently powerful quantum computer (Seol and Kim, 2024). This vulnerability has led to discussions about the need for quantum-resistant solutions that can safeguard our digital assets against future threats.

While working on my projects, I've seen how crucial it is to stay ahead of these technological shifts. For instance, some blockchain networks are already exploring post-quantum cryptography to protect against these emerging risks (Hoque, Aydeger and Zeydan, 2024). Researchers are examining various algorithms, like lattice-based and hash-based cryptography, to find solutions that could withstand quantum attacks (Singamaneni and Muhammad, 2024). The urgency is palpable, especially as quantum technology progresses.

However, the transition to quantum-resistant solutions is not just a technical challenge; it requires a shift in how we think about security. Companies must educate their teams and adapt their systems accordingly. This adaptation could lead to innovative designs and features that not only protect against quantum threats but also enhance the overall efficiency and security of blockchain technology. Figure 6 shows future directions and innovations for blockchain cybersecurity.

Figure 6. Future directions and innovations for blockchain cybersecurity

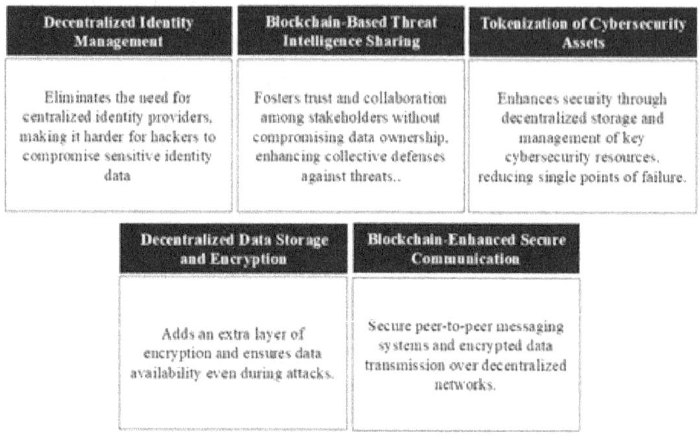

Interoperability Between Blockchains

The main reason is the evolution of Blockchains: every new platform has its characteristics and is increasingly becoming distinct interblocks. It would be like trying to communicate at some party where everyone is speaking a language different from yours! The new methods try to solve the problems by guaranteeing more effective communication and data sharing that helps in achieving smoother interactions.

Cross-chain bridges support innovatively, these serve as bridges for cross-blockchain transfers of assets. Polkadot is one of the projects acting as a blockchain interoperability mechanism, letting new blockchains share information and collaborate effectively (Stefanescu et al., 2024) Atomic Swaps, however, are another solution that lets users swap cryptocurrencies directly across blockchains for fast and secure transactions.

A more sophisticated recent trend was the new Layer 2 solutions that drastically increased the data transfer capabilities of existing blockchains (Rao et al., 2024). This should even be typified in current Ethereum scaling solutions like Optimistic Rollups that can process transactions off the main chain but still be secured by it. This arrangement can also help blockchains work better together to boost efficiency.

The adoption of standardized protocols (such as Interledger) is a key factor driving interoperability. It provides a universal communication layer which allows interspersed sub-blockchains to interoperate without homogeneous blockchain architectures. Kind of like a magic wand or a remote control for everything!

Blockchain in Decentralized Autonomous Organizations (DAOs)

How Blockchain is Being Used to Enable Secure Governance Models and Enhance Decision-Making in Decentralized Systems

Blockchain is rewriting how Decentralized Autonomous Organizations (DAOs) work, helping to ensure governance and more effective decision-making (Gilson and Bouraga, 2024). Understandably, in a normal setup of any organization, there might be few people ruling the roaster leading to an eventual demise due to unintentional bias or corruption. DAOs on the other hand allow every member of the organization to allocate decision-making power. This includes so-called voteable proposals, which get verified through the means of blockchain technology. The results are transparent and verifiable by anyone so that the sense of lie is avoided,

One of the big benefits of Blockchain in DAOs is that it does not need intermediaries (Borgogno and Martino, 2024). You are not at the mercy of a single authority to enforce the rules: the code does that for you. The conversion not only saves time but eliminates the control possible. One example of such a fairer system is decentralized autonomous organizations (DAOs), which are outcomes of smart contracts that automatically carry out decisions if the criteria for what constitutes a decision being reached are predetermined (Amend *et al.*, 2023; Van Vulpen, Siu and Jansen, 2023).

Another cool angle is to represent ownership or voting power using tokens. These tokens provide even more options for the governance of EOSO, where members can buy, sell or trade them. That opens the door for more voices and reduces groupthink which is essential for diversity of decisions.

DAOs have a long way to go but they seem to offer an inclusive and secure global space. Accountability and possible global participation have potential implications for how organizations could work in the future. The idea of how these governance models can revolutionize not only companies but also communities and social initiatives is fascinating.

7. CASE STUDIES

Case Study 1: Blockchain in Banking and Finance

Let's look at how blockchain is making waves in the banking sector. A notable example is HSBC, which has adopted this technology to enhance transaction security and efficiency (Vittala et al., 2024). In 2020, the bank used blockchain to complete a $250 million trade finance transaction, helping to speed up processes that traditionally take days or weeks (Grandin and Eriksson, 2021). By digitizing letters of credit, HSBC not only streamlined the workflow but also reduced fraud risk, which is a significant concern in finance.

Another key player is JPMorgan Chase. They developed the JPM Coin, designed for instant transfer of payments between clients. This innovation helps to provide greater security and transparency, allowing transactions to be settled in real time (Nofer et al., 2017). I remember reading about how some businesses expressed their frustration with delayed payments and how JPM Coin addressed that issue. It's a game-changer for many small and medium enterprises that rely on quick cash flow.

Furthermore, Santander has made strides by utilizing blockchain technology for international money transfers. Their app allows users to send money across borders at a fraction of the cost and time typically required (Hassani, Huang and Silva, 2018). Seeing the excitement in the eyes of those who can now send money to family abroad with just a few taps is truly inspiring.

In addition, Bank of America has invested significantly in blockchain research, recognizing its potential to improve banking operations (Aderemi et al., 2024). The implications are enormous, as enhanced security means fewer worries about hacks or data breaches.

Overall, blockchain is reshaping how banks operate, making transactions faster, safer, and more efficient. It's not just about technology; it's about making life a little easier for everyone involved.

Case Study 2: Blockchain in Supply Chain Management

A company that nailed supply chain security with blockchain is Walmart (Arun, Cuomo and Gaur, 2019). They started tracking food products on the blockchain to improve transparency. Imagine a lettuce shipment taking days to trace back to its source; now it takes seconds! This shift means they can quickly spot contaminated products and prevent foodborne illnesses, which is a win for everyone.

Another interesting case is IBM's collaboration with Maersk to streamline shipping (Jabbar and Bjørn, 2017). They created a blockchain platform called TradeLens, which allows all parties—shippers, customs, and port authorities—to share data in real-time. The results? Reduced paperwork, faster deliveries, and lower shipping costs. They saw a 40% reduction in time spent on document handling.

Then there's the story of De Beers, the diamond company. They use blockchain to ensure the diamonds are conflict-free. Each stone has a digital record that proves its origin, which means customers can buy with confidence, knowing they're not funding violence (Maione, 2024).

These examples show how blockchain not only enhances security but also builds trust between companies and consumers (Tan and Saraniemi, 2022). It's like putting a reliable lock on the door of a supply chain. The benefits are clear: improved efficiency, reduced costs, and happier customers. Companies leveraging blockchain are more prepared for challenges, and that gives them a competitive edge (Kant, 2021).

So, whether it's food safety, shipping, or luxury goods, blockchain is helping companies secure their supply chains in ways we couldn't have imagined a few years ago. Figure 7 shows real world blockchain application.

Figure 7. Real world blockchain application

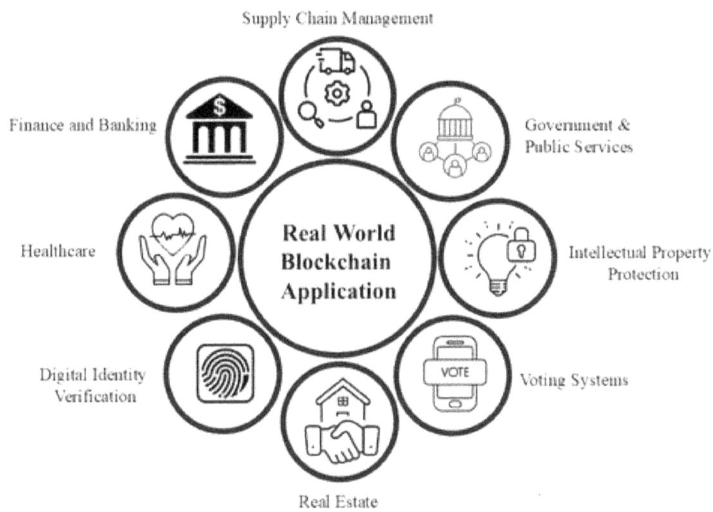

Case Study 3: Blockchain for Identity and Access Management

Example of a Blockchain-Based Digital Identity Solution Improving Security for Users

Blockchain technology is making waves in identity and access management, and I have seen this firsthand with a blockchain-based digital identity solution. Picture this: a user wants to access an online service, but instead of juggling multiple usernames and passwords, they can simply verify their identity through a blockchain. This method reduces the risk of data breaches that are so common in today's digital world.

Take, for instance, a healthcare application where patients share their medical records. With blockchain, patients can control who accesses their data and when, enhancing privacy while ensuring the right people have the right access (Madine et al., 2020). It's like having a digital vault where only the user has the key! I remember talking to a tech-savvy friend who tried this system and felt relieved not to worry about hackers stealing his information. He could verify his identity securely without the hassle of remembering complex passwords.

Another real-world example comes from Estonia, which has adopted blockchain for its e-residency program (Sullivan and Burger, 2017). This allows anyone to create a secure digital identity and access various services online, from banking to business registration. The convenience of a single digital ID resonates with many users, eliminating the fear of identity theft.

Ultimately, blockchain-based identity solutions are not just about technology; they are about people feeling secure and in control of their digital lives. The personal stories behind these innovations make them truly impactful, as they transform how we think about security and access in our online interactions.

8. CONCLUSION

Summary of Blockchain's Role in Enhancing Security

Recap How Blockchain's Features Enhance Data Integrity and Transaction Security

First, a well-designed blockchain enforces security in three scenarios: data integrity (the data on the blockchain has not been tampered with), transaction security (transactions that are settled by the blockchain cannot be reversed) and peace of mind that the underlying technology is secure. Imagine a territory where each move made during a purchase is recorded on several different nodes as well and locked down into one distributed ledger that no single party can edit. It is much like a deal among friends — if someone tries to slip something unfriendly in, everyone else will notice. The model facilitates trust (in a middleman-free environment) that our tech-driven world can learn from.

Financial services: Use of blockchain as a watchdog to secure digital transactions from fraud. Once a transaction is verified by different nodes and locked into the chain... that transaction will never be able to change. The same feature is crucial in supply chain management as well, where a firm can track every step that the product passes through from its origin till it reaches to consumer. It means authenticity and just like the previous characteristic helps fight against the counterfeit. Even if consumers just know that a product has logged information in a blockchain, they will have peace of mind.

On a tangent to the concept of data integrity, we cannot ignore the significance of cryptography (specifically hashing and public-key systems). Every new data added on the blockchain is hashed, hence any effort to modify it away will alert them of the change immediately — as the hash changes. With this cryptographic method, blockchain has become one of the most powerful tools for protecting personal data and facilitating peer-to-peer financial transactions, among other things.

There might be challenges such as scalability etc, but with the new vehicles coming into the carriage, prospects are looking promising for blockchain in storing data integrity and secure transactions. The possibilities of blockchain transforming the security we manage in other areas are genuinely exciting and make me feel excited about what lies ahead.

Outlook on Blockchain's Future in Cybersecurity

Speculate on the Continued Adoption of Blockchain in Cybersecurity and its Potential to Reshape the Industry

The future of blockchain in cybersecurity feels like we're on the brink of something big. You can almost sense the excitement around how this technology is pushing boundaries. As more organizations realize that traditional systems are increasingly vulnerable to cyber threats, blockchain offers a fresh approach to security. It's the promise of a system where data tampering isn't just difficult—it's nearly impossible. And that's something the cybersecurity industry desperately needs.

I remember a time when I was helping a friend after their business got hit by a ransomware attack. If they'd been using a blockchain-based system, it might have been a very different story. Hackers wouldn't have been able to just waltz in and encrypt files without anyone noticing. Blockchain is like having hundreds of eyes watching the same vault. If one person tries something shady, the rest are there to shut it down. That kind of assurance is what's going to attract more businesses, especially those dealing with sensitive information like finance or healthcare.

It's also worth thinking about how blockchain is already shifting power in industries. Take supply chains, for example. Companies are starting to use blockchain to track goods from the moment they leave the factory to when they reach your doorstep. Not only does it make everything more transparent, but it also cuts down on fraud. Imagine knowing that every piece of your smartphone was ethically sourced because the blockchain ledger says so. That's huge, and it's just the beginning.

Of course, the path ahead won't be perfect. I've heard plenty of concerns about the scalability of blockchain or the massive energy consumption, especially with older algorithms like Proof of Work. These are real issues. But with the pace of technological advancements, we'll likely see solutions like Proof of Stake gaining more traction, reducing both energy use and environmental impact.

What excites me most is how this tech could reshape cybersecurity altogether. With blockchain, trust is no longer something fragile, and dependent on human oversight. It's baked into the system, a security net built on math, not promises. As industries continue to adopt it, blockchain could become the backbone of a more secure digital world—one where hackers are left in the dark, scrambling to figure out their next move. That's a future worth looking forward to.

REFERENCES

Abdul, S. S. M. (2024). Navigating blockchain's twin challenges: Scalability and regulatory compliance. *Blockchains*, 2(3), 265–298. DOI: 10.3390/blockchains2030013

Aderemi, N. S.. (2024). Blockchain in banking: A comparative review of developments in the USA and Nigeria. *International Journal of Science and Technology Research Archive*, 6(1), 108–126. DOI: 10.53771/ijstra.2024.6.1.0034

Ahmed, A. A., & Alabi, O. O. (2024). Secure and Scalable Blockchain-Based Federated Learning for Cryptocurrency Fraud Detection: A Systematic Review. *IEEE Access : Practical Innovations, Open Solutions*, 12, 102219–102241. DOI: 10.1109/ACCESS.2024.3429205

Ajakwe, S. O., Saviour, I. I., Ihekoronye, V. U., Nwankwo, O. U., Dini, M. A., Uchechi, I. U., Kim, D.-S., & Lee, J. M. (2024). Medical IoT Record Security and Blockchain: Systematic review of milieu, milestones, and momentum. *Big Data and Cognitive Computing*, 8(9), 121. DOI: 10.3390/bdcc8090121

Ajayi-Nifise, N. A. O.. (2024). BLOCKCHAIN IN U.S. ACCOUNTING: A REVIEW: ASSESSING ITS TRANSFORMATIVE POTENTIAL FOR ENHANCING TRANSPARENCY AND INTEGRITY. *Finance & Accounting Research Journal*, 6(2), 159–182. DOI: 10.51594/farj.v6i2.786

Alex, S. A., Jhanjhi, N. Z., Humayun, M., Ibrahim, A. O., & Abulfaraj, A. W. (2022). Deep LSTM Model for Diabetes Prediction with Class Balancing by SMOTE. *Electronics (Basel)*, 11(17), 2737. DOI: 10.3390/electronics11172737

Alferidah, D. K., & Jhanjhi, N. (2020) 'Cybersecurity Impact over Bigdata and IoT Growth,' *International Conference on Computational Intelligence (ICCI)* [Preprint]. DOI: 10.1109/ICCI51257.2020.9247722

Aljabri, A., Jemili, F., & Korbaa, O. (2023). Intrusion detection in cyber-physical system using rsa blockchain technology. *Multimedia Tools and Applications*, 83(16), 48119–48140. DOI: 10.1007/s11042-023-17576-z

Alkhatib, M., Albalawi, T., & Saeed, F. (2024). Blockchain-Based quality assurance system for academic programs. *Applied Sciences (Basel, Switzerland)*, 14(11), 4868. DOI: 10.3390/app14114868

Alkinani, M. H., Almazroi, A. A., Jhanjhi, N. Z., & Khan, N. A. (2021). 5G and IoT Based Reporting and Accident Detection (RAD) System to Deliver First Aid Box Using Unmanned Aerial Vehicle. *Sensors (Basel)*, 21(20), 6905. DOI: 10.3390/s21206905 PMID: 34696118

Alshahrani, S. M. (2024). Disrupting the status quo: Blockchain's potential for overhauling conventional academic systems, [Preprint]. *Arabian Journal for Science and Engineering*. Advance online publication. DOI: 10.1007/s13369-024-09065-8

Alzoubi, M.M. (2024) 'Investigating the synergy of Blockchain and AI: enhancing security, efficiency, and transparency,' *Journal of Cyber Security Technology*, pp. 1–29. .DOI: 10.1080/23742917.2024.2374594

Amend, J., Troglauer, P., Guggenberger, T., Urbach, N., & Weibelzahl, M. (2023). Facilitating cooperation of smallholders in developing countries: Design principles for a cooperative-oriented decentralized autonomous organization. *Information Systems and e-Business Management*, 22(1), 1–31. DOI: 10.1007/s10257-023-00659-7

Ananna, F. F., Nowreen, R., Al Jahwari, S. S. R., Costa, E. A., Angeline, L., & Sindiramutty, S. R. (2023). Analysing Influential factors in student academic achievement: Prediction modelling and insight. *International Journal of Emerging Multidisciplinaries Computer Science & Artificial Intelligence*, 2(1). Advance online publication. DOI: 10.54938/ijemdcsai.2023.02.1.254

Aoun, A., Kashmar, N., Adda, M., & Ibrahim, H. (2024). From Bottom-Up towards a completely decentralized autonomous electric grid based on the concept of a decentralized autonomous substation. *Electronics (Basel)*, 13(18), 3683. DOI: 10.3390/electronics13183683

Arun, J. S., Cuomo, J., & Gaur, N. (2019). *Blockchain for business*. Addison-Wesley Professional.

Asaithambi, S., Ravi, L., Devarajan, M., Almazyad, A. S., Xiong, G., & Mohamed, A. W. (2024). Enhancing enterprises trust mechanism through integrating blockchain technology into e-commerce platform for SMEs. *Egyptian Informatics Journal*, 25, 100444. DOI: 10.1016/j.eij.2024.100444

Azam, H. Tan, Micheal, Pin, L.T., Syahmi, M.A., Qian, A.L.W., Jingyan, H., Uddin, M.F., *et al.* (2023) 'Wireless Technology Security and Privacy: A Comprehensive Study,' preprints.*org* [Preprint]. DOI: 10.20944/preprints202311.0664.v1

Azam, H., Dulloo, M. I., Majeed, M. H., Wan, J. P. H., Xin, L. T., & Sindiramutty, S. R. (2023). Cybercrime Unmasked: Investigating cases and digital evidence. *International Journal of Emerging Multidisciplinaries Computer Science & Artificial Intelligence*, 2(1). Advance online publication. DOI: 10.54938/ijemdcsai.2023.02.1.255

Azam, H., Dulloo, M. I., Majeed, M. H., Wan, J. P. H., Xin, L. T., Tajwar, M. A., & Sindiramutty, S. R. (2023). Defending the digital Frontier: IDPS and the battle against Cyber threat. *International Journal of Emerging Multidisciplinaries Computer Science & Artificial Intelligence*, 2(1). Advance online publication. DOI: 10.54938/ijemdcsai.2023.02.1.253

Azam, H., Tajwar, M. A., Mayhialagan, S., Davis, A. J., Yik, C. J., Ali, D., & Sindiramutty, S. R. (2023). Innovations in Security: A study of cloud Computing and IoT. *International Journal of Emerging Multidisciplinaries Computer Science & Artificial Intelligence*, 2(1). Advance online publication. DOI: 10.54938/ijemdcsai.2023.02.1.252

Azeem, M., Ullah, A., Ashraf, H., Jhanjhi, N., Humayun, M., Aljahdali, S., & Tabbakh, T. A. (2021). FOG-Oriented secure and lightweight data aggregation in IOMT. *IEEE Access : Practical Innovations, Open Solutions*, 9, 111072–111082. DOI: 10.1109/ACCESS.2021.3101668

Babbar, H., Rani, S., Masud, M., Verma, S., Anand, D., & Jhanjhi, N. Z. (2021). 'Load balancing algorithm for migrating switches in software-defined vehicular networks,' *Computers, Materials & Continua/Computers. Computers, Materials & Continua*, 67(1), 1301–1316. DOI: 10.32604/cmc.2021.014627

Badertscher, C., Maurer, U., Tschudi, D., & Zikas, V. (2024). Bitcoin as a transaction ledger: A composable treatment. *Journal of Cryptology*, 37(2), 18. Advance online publication. DOI: 10.1007/s00145-024-09493-7

Benstead, A. V.. (2022). Entering the world behind the clothes that we wear: Practical applications of blockchain technology. *Production Planning and Control*, •••, 1–18. DOI: 10.1080/09537287.2022.2063173

Böhmecke-Schwafert, M. (2024). The role of blockchain for trade in global value chains: A systematic literature review and guidance for future research. *Telecommunications Policy*, 48(9), 102835. DOI: 10.1016/j.telpol.2024.102835

Borgogno, O., & Martino, E. (2024). Decentralised autonomous organisations: Targeting the potential beyond the hype. *Law, Innovation and Technology*, 16(2), 1–40. DOI: 10.1080/17579961.2024.2392933

Brohi, S. N.. (2020) 'Key Applications of State-of-the-Art Technologies to Mitigate and Eliminate COVID-19.pdf,' *TechRhiv* [Preprint]. DOI: 10.36227/techrxiv.12115596.v1

Buttar, A. M., ... (2024) 'Decentralized Identity Management using Blockchain Technology: Challenges and solutions,' in *Signals and communication technology*, pp. 131–166. DOI: 10.1007/978-3-031-49593-9_8

Carreira, F., Cunha, P. R., Barata, J., & Estima, J. (2024). Tamper-Proof Blockchain-Based Contracts for the Carriage of Goods by Road. *AIS*, 26. Advance online publication. DOI: 10.62036/ISD.2024.105

Chesti, I. A., ... (2020) 'Evolution, Mitigation, and Prevention of Ransomware,' *2020 2nd International Conference on Computer and Information Sciences (ICCIS)* [Preprint]. DOI: 10.1109/ICCIS49240.2020.9257708

Chhabra, A.. (2024). *Navigating the Maze: Exploring blockchain privacy and its information retrieval.* IEEE Access., DOI: 10.1109/ACCESS.2024.3370857

Choithani, T., Chowdhury, A., Patel, S., Patel, P., Patel, D., & Shah, M. (2022). A comprehensive study of artificial intelligence and cybersecurity on Bitcoin, crypto currency and banking system. *Annals of Data Science*, 11(1), 103–135. DOI: 10.1007/s40745-022-00433-5

Christodoulou, I., Rizomyliotis, I., Konstantoulaki, K., Nazarian, A., & Binh, D. (2024). Transforming the remittance industry: Harnessing the power of blockchain technology. *Journal of Enterprise Information Management*, 37(5), 1551–1577. DOI: 10.1108/JEIM-03-2023-0112

Datta, S., & Namasudra, S. (2024). Blockchain-Based smart contract model for securing healthcare transactions by using consumer electronics and mobile edge computing. *IEEE Transactions on Consumer Electronics*, 70(1), 4026–4036. DOI: 10.1109/TCE.2024.3357115

Daudén-Esmel, C., Castellà-Roca, J., & Viejo, A. (2023). Blockchain-based access control system for efficient and GDPR-compliant personal data management. *Computer Communications*, 214, 67–87. DOI: 10.1016/j.comcom.2023.11.017

Dogra, V., ... (2021) 'Analyzing DistilBERT for Sentiment Classification of Banking Financial News,' in *Lecture notes in networks and systems*, pp. 501–510. DOI: 10.1007/978-981-16-3153-5_53

Fatima-Tuz-Zahra, N., ... (2020) 'Proposing a Hybrid RPL Protocol for Rank and Wormhole Attack Mitigation using Machine Learning,' *2020 2nd International Conference on Computer and Information Sciences (ICCIS)* [Preprint]. DOI: 10.1109/ICCIS49240.2020.9257607

Fernández-Iglesias, M. J., Von Eitzen, C. D., & Rifón, L. A. (2024) 'Efficient Traceability Systems with Smart Contracts: Balancing On-Chain and Off-Chain Data Storage for Enhanced Scalability and Privacy,' *Authorea(Authorea)* [Preprint]. https://doi.org/DOI: 10.22541/au.172465854.45833346/v1

Frédéric, T. (2024) *AIS Electronic Library (AISEL) - PACIS 2024 proceedings: Better than Ever? Analyzing the impact of change in consensus mechanism on market liquidity for ethereum.* https://aisel.aisnet.org/pacis2024/track02_blockchain/track02_blockchain/1/

Ghadi, Y. Y., Mazhar, T., Shahzad, T., Amir khan, M., Abd-Alrazaq, A., Ahmed, A., & Hamam, H. (2024). Author Correction: The role of blockchain to secure internet of medical things. *Scientific Reports*, 14(1), 21337. Advance online publication. DOI: 10.1038/s41598-024-71990-3 PMID: 39266649

Gilson, C., & Bouraga, S. (2024). Enhancing the democratic nature of voting processes within decentralized autonomous organizations. *Digital Policy Regulation and Governance*, 26(2), 169–187. DOI: 10.1108/DPRG-09-2023-0126

Gong, Y., Yu, B., Yang, L., Meng, F., Liu, L., Hu, X., & Xu, Z. (2024). Toward next-generation networks: A blockchain-based approach for core network architecture and roaming identity verification, [Preprint]. *Digital Communications and Networks.* Advance online publication. DOI: 10.1016/j.dcan.2024.08.008

Gopi, R., Sathiyamoorthi, V., Selvakumar, S., Manikandan, R., Chatterjee, P., Jhanjhi, N. Z., & Luhach, A. K. (2021). Enhanced method of ANN based model for detection of DDoS attacks on multimedia internet of things. *Multimedia Tools and Applications*, 81(19), 26739–26757. DOI: 10.1007/s11042-021-10640-6

Grandin, A., & Eriksson, M. (2021) *International Payments, Trade Finance & Blockchain : A qualitative study about the impact of blockchain implementation.* https://www.diva-portal.org/smash/record.jsf?pid=diva2%3A1571481&dswid=-4406

Hall, O. J., Shiaeles, S., & Li, F. (2024). A Study of Ethereum's Transition from Proof-of-Work to Proof-of-Stake in Preventing Criminal Activities in Smart Contracts. *Network (Bristol, England)*, 4(1), 33–47. DOI: 10.3390/network4010002

Hassani, H., Huang, X., & Silva, E. (2018). Banking with blockchain-ed big data. *Journal of Management Analytics*, 5(4), 256–275. DOI: 10.1080/23270012.2018.1528900

Hon, B. C. Y.. (2024). Challenger: Blockchain-based massively multiplayer online game architecture. *Lecture Notes in Computer Science*, 14783, 50–66. DOI: 10.1007/978-3-031-67321-4_3

Hong, Z., ... (2024) 'GRIDB: Scaling blockchain database via sharding and Off-Chain Cross-Shard mechanism,' *arXiv (Cornell University)* [Preprint]. https://doi .org//arxiv.2407.03750.DOI: 10.48550

Hoque, S., Aydeger, A., & Zeydan, E. (2024). Exploring Post Quantum Cryptography with Quantum Key Distribution for Sustainable Mobile Network Architecture Design. *ACM DL*, 5, 9–16. DOI: 10.1145/3659997.3660033

Humayun, M., Sujatha, R., Almuayqil, S. N., & Jhanjhi, N. Z. (2022). A Transfer Learning Approach with a Convolutional Neural Network for the Classification of Lung Carcinoma. *Health Care*, 10(6), 1058. DOI: 10.3390/healthcare10061058 PMID: 35742109

Huseynov, E. (2025) 'Identity Theft,' in *Elsevier eBooks*, pp. 993–1006. DOI: 10.1016/B978-0-443-13223-0.00060-6

Hussain, K., ... (2024) 'Threats and Vulnerabilities of Wireless Networks in the Internet of Things (IoT),' *IEEE 1st Karachi Section Humanitarian Technology Conference (KHI-HTC)*, 2, pp. 1–8. DOI: 10.1109/KHI-HTC60760.2024.10482197

Ishkov, A. and Krupnov, Y. (2024) 'Application of blockchain technologies for creation of innovative ecosystem in higher education,' *E3S Web of Conferences*, 549, p. 08031. .DOI: 10.1051/e3sconf/202454908031

JJ, L., Singh, K., & Chakravarthi, B. (2024). Digital forensic framework for smart contract vulnerabilities using ensemble models. *Multimedia Tools and Applications*, 83(17), 51469–51512.

Jabbar, K. and Bjørn, P. (2017) 'Infrastructural Grind,' *ACm* [Preprint]. .DOI: 10.1145/3148330.3148345

Jeevitha, R., Bhanumathi, P., & Mukherjee, S. (2024) 'Blockchain-Based Financial Systems Deployment and challenges,' in *Advances in finance, accounting, and economics book series*, pp. 120–147. DOI: 10.4018/979-8-3693-1878-2.ch006

Jhanjhi, N., Humayun, M., & Almuayqil, S. N. (2021). Cyber security and privacy issues in industrial internet of things. *Computer Systems Science and Engineering*, 37(3), 361–380. DOI: 10.32604/csse.2021.015206

Jiang, C., Xu, C., Chen, J., & Chen, K. (2024). Blockchain-based immunization against kleptographic attacks. *Science China. Information Sciences*, 67(7), 172102. Advance online publication. DOI: 10.1007/s11432-023-3883-4

Jimmy, F. (2024). Enhancing Data Security in Financial Institutions with Blockchain Technology. *Deleted Journal*, 5(1), 424–437. DOI: 10.60087/jaigs.v5i1.217

Jun, A. Y. M.. (2024) 'Exploring the Impact of Crypto-Ransomware on Critical Industries: Case Studies and Solutions,' *preprint.org* [Preprint]. DOI: 10.20944/preprints202409.1325.v1

Kant, N. (2021). Blockchain: A strategic resource to attain and sustain competitive advantage. *International Journal of Innovation Science*, 13(4), 520–538. DOI: 10.1108/IJIS-07-2020-0094

Kaur, J., Rani, R., & Kalra, N. (2023). Attribute-based access control scheme for secure storage and sharing of EHRs using blockchain and IPFS, [Preprint]. *Cluster Computing*. Advance online publication. DOI: 10.1007/s10586-023-04038-2

Khan, N. A.. (2021). 'A secure communication protocol for unmanned aerial vehicles,' *Computers, Materials & Continua/Computers. Materials & Continua (Print)*, 70(1), 601–618. DOI: 10.32604/cmc.2022.019419

Kharche, A., Badholia, S., & Upadhyay, R. K. (2024). Implementation of blockchain technology in integrated IoT networks for constructing scalable ITS systems in India. *Blockchain Research and Applications*, 5(2), 100188. DOI: 10.1016/j.bcra.2024.100188

Kizza, J. M. (2024) 'Blockchains, Cryptocurrency, and Smart Contracts Technologies: Security Considerations,' in *Texts in computer science*, pp. 575–600. DOI: 10.1007/978-3-031-47549-8_26

Kumar, M. S.. (2021). Blockchain based peer to peer communication in autonomous drone operation. *Energy Reports*, 7, 7925–7939. DOI: 10.1016/j.egyr.2021.08.073

Leahy, E. (2024). *AI-Powered Bitcoin Trading: Developing an Investment Strategy with Artificial Intelligence*. John Wiley & Sons.

Leporati, A., & Rovida, L. (2024). *Looking for Stability in Proof-of-Stake based Consensus Mechanisms*. Blockchain Research and Applications., DOI: 10.1016/j.bcra.2024.100222

Liang, B. A. (2006). Fade to Black: Importation and counterfeit drugs. *American Journal of Law & Medicine*, 32(2–3), 279–323. DOI: 10.1177/009885880603200207 PMID: 16927613

Lim, M., Abdullah, A., Jhanjhi, N. Z., Khurram Khan, M., & Supramaniam, M. (2019). Link Prediction in Time-Evolving Criminal Network with deep Reinforcement learning technique. *IEEE Access : Practical Innovations, Open Solutions*, 7, 184797–184807. DOI: 10.1109/ACCESS.2019.2958873

Liu, J., Li, P., Zhang, F., & Ren, K. (2024). MonoCash: A Channel-Free payment network via trusted monotonic counters. *IEEE Transactions on Dependable and Secure Computing*, 21(5), 1–14. DOI: 10.1109/TDSC.2024.3354927

Liu, X., Shah, R., Shandilya, A., Shah, M., & Pandya, A. (2024). A systematic study on integrating blockchain in healthcare for electronic health record management and tracking medical supplies. *Journal of Cleaner Production*, 447, 141371. DOI: 10.1016/j.jclepro.2024.141371

Liu, Y. *et al.* (2024) 'An overview of blockchain smart contract execution mechanism,' *Journal of Industrial Information Integration*, p. 100674. .DOI: 10.1016/j.jii.2024.100674

Madine, M. M., Battah, A. A., Yaqoob, I., Salah, K., Jayaraman, R., Al-Hammadi, Y., Pesic, S., & Ellahham, S. (2020). Blockchain for giving patients control over their medical records. *IEEE Access : Practical Innovations, Open Solutions*, 8, 193102–193115. DOI: 10.1109/ACCESS.2020.3032553

Maione, G. (2024) 'Blockchain technology and the quest for decentralized accountability,' in *Emerald Publishing Limited eBooks*, pp. 49–70. DOI: 10.1108/978-1-83797-739-020241004

Majeed, R. H., & Taha, A. A. D. (2023). 'A survey study of Iraqi auditors' adoption of blockchain technology,'. *Asian Review of Accounting*, 32(3), 521–546. DOI: 10.1108/ARA-01-2023-0015

Manchuri, A. *et al.* (2024) 'pplication of Supervised Machine Learning Models in Biodiesel Production Research - A Short Review,' *Borneo Journal of Sciences and Technology* [Preprint]. .DOI: 10.35370/bjost.2024.6.1-10

Mgeladze, M. (2024). The legal regulation hurdles of the Blockchain-Based contracts for maritime transport. *European Journal of Commercial Contract Law*, 16(1), 10–24. DOI: 10.7590/187714624X17132716463892

Mueller-Bloch, C.. (2022). Understanding decentralization of decision-making power in proof-of-stake blockchains: An agent-based simulation approach. *European Journal of Information Systems*, •••, 1–20. DOI: 10.1080/0960085X.2022.2125840

Mustafa, G. *et al.* (2024) 'Blockchain-based governance models in e-government: a comprehensive framework for legal, technical, ethical and security considerations,' *International Journal of Law and Management* [Preprint]. .DOI: 10.1108/IJLMA-08-2023-0172

Muzafar, S., & Jhanjhi, N. Z. (2019) 'Success stories of ICT implementation in Saudi Arabia,' in *Advances in electronic government, digital divide, and regional development book series*, pp. 151–163. DOI: 10.4018/978-1-7998-1851-9.ch008

Naef, S., Wagner, S. M., & Saur, C. (2022). Blockchain and network governance: Learning from applications in the supply chain sector. *Production Planning and Control*, 35(9), 932–946. DOI: 10.1080/09537287.2022.2044072

Narayan, D. G., Arali, N., & Tejas, R. (2024). DPoSEB: Delegated Proof of Stake with Exponential Backoff Consensus Algorithm for Ethereum Blockchain. *Computer Science Journal of Moldova*, 32(2(95)), 262–288. DOI: 10.56415/csjm.v32.14

Nofer, M., Gomber, P., Hinz, O., & Schiereck, D. (2017). Blockchain. *Business & Information Systems Engineering*, 59(3), 183–187. DOI: 10.1007/s12599-017-0467-3

Ogungbemi, O. S. (2024). Smart Contracts Management: The interplay of data privacy and blockchain for secure and efficient real estate transactions. *Journal of Engineering Research and Reports*, 26(8), 278–300. DOI: 10.9734/jerr/2024/v26i81245

Oriekhoe, N. O. I.. (2024). BLOCKCHAIN TECHNOLOGY IN SUPPLY CHAIN MANAGEMENT: A COMPREHENSIVE REVIEW. *International Journal of Management & Entrepreneurship Research*, 6(1), 150–166. DOI: 10.51594/ijmer.v6i1.714

Pawar, V., & Sachdeva, S. (2023). ParallelChain: A scalable healthcare framework with low-energy consumption using blockchain. *International Transactions in Operational Research*, 31(6), 3621–3649. DOI: 10.1111/itor.13278

Persson, S. (2024) *Empowering Subcontractors in Swedish Construction with Blockchain Technology for Automated Payment Processes*. https://odr.chalmers.se/items/dc2762af-9520-4b0a-b784-53dee3319e88

Putra, M. A. P., Alief, R. N., Rachmawati, S. M., Sampedro, G. A., Kim, D.-S., & Lee, J.-M. (2024). Proof-of-authority-based secure and efficient aggregation with differential privacy for federated learning in industrial IoT. *Internet of Things : Engineering Cyber Physical Human Systems*, 25, 101107. DOI: 10.1016/j.iot.2024.101107

Quan, G., Yao, Z., Si, X., Zhu, W., & Chen, L. (2024). A data sharing model for blockchain trusted sensor leveraging mimic hash mechanism. *Electronics (Basel)*, 13(8), 1495. DOI: 10.3390/electronics13081495

Radhakrishnan, S., & Travieso-Gonzalez, C. M. (2024). *Biometrics and Cryptography*. BoD – Books on Demand. DOI: 10.5772/intechopen.107597

Rao, I. S., Kiah, M. L. M., Hameed, M. M., & Memon, Z. A. (2024). Scalability of blockchain: A comprehensive review and future research direction, [Preprint]. *Cluster Computing*, 27(5), 5547–5570. Advance online publication. DOI: 10.1007/s10586-023-04257-7

Ravichandran, N.. (2024) 'Comprehensive Review Analysis and Countermeasures for Cybersecurity Threats: DDoS, Ransomware, and Trojan Horse Attacks,' *preprint.org* [Preprint]. DOI: 10.20944/preprints202409.1369.v1

Rebello, G. A. F.. (2024). *A survey on Blockchain Scalability: From Hardware to Layer-Two Protocols*. IEEE Communications Surveys & Tutorials., DOI: 10.1109/COMST.2024.3376252

Richardson, M. (2020). *Blockchain technology: Learn Step by Step Smart Contracts, Monero, Blockchain Wallet, Bitcoin, Zcash, Ethereum, Ripple, Dash, Mining, Litecoin*. IOTA.

Sahu, H., Choudhari, S., & Chakole, S. (2024). The use of blockchain technology in Public Health: Lessons learned, [Preprint]. *Cureus*. Advance online publication. DOI: 10.7759/cureus.63198 PMID: 39070517

Scholten, T. L., ... (2024) 'Assessing the benefits and risks of quantum computers,' *arXiv (Cornell University)* [Preprint]. https://doi.org//arxiv.2401.16317.DOI: 10.48550

Schumacher, L. V. (2024). *Technology Choices and Design Options*. Decoding Digital Assets., DOI: 10.1007/978-3-031-54601-3_14

Selamat, S. R., Cai, S. Y., Hassan, N. H., & Yusof, R. (2024). An algorithm for Color-Based password authentication to increase security level, [INNOVATICS]. *Innovation in Research of Informatics*, 6(1). Advance online publication. DOI: 10.37058/innovatics.v6i1.10396

Seng, Y. J.. (2024) 'In-Depth Analysis and Countermeasures for Ransomware Attacks: Case Studies and Recommendations,' *Preprints* [Preprint]. DOI: 10.20944/preprints202408.2261.v1

Seol, J., & Kim, J. (2024). Machine learning ensures Quantum-Safe blockchain availability. *Journal of Computer Information Systems*, •••, 1–25. DOI: 10.1080/08874417.2024.2308207

Shah, I. A., Jhanjhi, N. Z., & Laraib, A. (2022) 'Cybersecurity and blockchain usage in contemporary business,' in *Advances in information security, privacy, and ethics book series*, pp. 49–64. DOI: 10.4018/978-1-6684-5284-4.ch003

Sharma, A. (2024). *Rust for blockchain application development: Learn to build decentralized applications on popular blockchain technologies using Rust*. Packt Publishing Ltd.

Sharma, J., & Jain, S. (2024) 'Healthcare 4.0,' in *CRC Press eBooks*, pp. 126–146. DOI: 10.1201/9781003474524-7

Sharma, P., Jindal, R., & Borah, M. D. (2023). Blockchain-based distributed application for multimedia system using Hyperledger Fabric. *Multimedia Tools and Applications*, 83(1), 2473–2499. DOI: 10.1007/s11042-023-15690-6

Sharma, R.. (2021). 'Plant disease diagnosis and image classification using deep learning,' *Computers, Materials & Continua/Computers. Materials & Continua (Print)*, 71(2), 2125–2140. DOI: 10.32604/cmc.2022.020017

Sindiramutty, S. R., Jhanjhi, N. Z., Tan, C. E., Khan, N. A., Shah, B., & Manchuri, A. R. (2024) 'Cybersecurity measures for logistics industry,' in *Advances in information security, privacy, and ethics book series*, pp. 1–58. DOI: 10.4018/979-8-3693-3816-2.ch001

Sindiramutty, S. R., Jhanjhi, N. Z., Tan, C. E., Khan, N. A., Shah, B., Yun, K. J., ... (2024) 'Future trends and emerging threats in drone cybersecurity,' in *Advances in information security, privacy, and ethics book series*, pp. 148–195. DOI: 10.4018/979-8-3693-0774-8.ch007

Sindiramutty, S. R., Jhanjhi, N. Z., Tan, C. E., Yun, K. J., ... (2024) 'Data security and privacy concerns in drone operations,' in *Advances in information security, privacy, and ethics book series*, pp. 236–290. DOI: 10.4018/979-8-3693-0774-8.ch010

Sindiramutty, S. R., Tan, C. E., ... (2024) 'Ethical considerations in drone cybersecurity,' in *Advances in information security, privacy, and ethics book series*, pp. 42–87. DOI: 10.4018/979-8-3693-0774-8.ch003

Sindiramutty, S. R., Tan, C. E., & Wei, G. W. (2024) 'Eyes in the sky,' in *Advances in information security, privacy, and ethics book series*, pp. 405–451. DOI: 10.4018/979-8-3693-0774-8.ch017

Singamaneni, K. K., & Muhammad, G. (2024). *A novel integrated Quantum-Resistant cryptography for secure scientific data exchange in ad hoc networks*. Ad Hoc Networks., DOI: 10.1016/j.adhoc.2024.103607

Singh, R.K. and Vishwakarma, L.P. (2023) 'Application of Blockchain Technology in agri-food supply chains: Opportunities and challenges,' in *Elsevier eBooks*, pp. 101–117. .DOI: 10.1016/B978-0-323-89963-5.00014-9

Singh, V. K. (no date) *Blockchain Technology and election transparency: An application of E-Voting Mechanism - ProQuest.* https://www.proquest.com/openview/6d95fc6f1b45392e98f741bed9837479/1?pq-origsite=gscholar&cbl=7065076

Sreedharan, R. (2024). *The Role of Blockchain in Healthcare.* Quantum and Blockchain-based Next Generation Sustainable Computing., DOI: 10.1007/978-3-031-58068-0_7

Stefanescu, D.. (2024). *Smart contract powered framework for the next generation industry 4.0 business model.* Deleted Journal. [Preprint], DOI: 10.1145/3686167

Sullivan, C., & Burger, E. (2017). E-residency and blockchain. *Computer Law & Security Report*, 33(4), 470–481. DOI: 10.1016/j.clsr.2017.03.016

Tan, T. M., & Saraniemi, S. (2022). Trust in blockchain-enabled exchanges: Future directions in blockchain marketing. *Journal of the Academy of Marketing Science*, 51(4), 914–939. DOI: 10.1007/s11747-022-00889-0

Tayebi, S., & Amini, H. (2024). The flip side of the coin: Exploring the environmental and health impacts of proof-of-work cryptocurrency mining. *Environmental Research*, 252, 118798. DOI: 10.1016/j.envres.2024.118798 PMID: 38555086

Teutsch, J., & Reitwießner, C. (2023). *'A scalable verification solution for blockchains,' in Lecture notes series.* Institute For Mathematical Sciences., DOI: 10.1142/9789811278631_0015

Tiwari, N., Ranjan, P., Biswal, P. K., Barde, C., & Sinha, N. (2024). 'Survey and analysis of blockchain technologies with respect to: Properties, algorithms, architecture, models, evolution and framework,' [Preprint]. *Multimedia Tools and Applications.* Advance online publication. DOI: 10.1007/s11042-024-19580-3

Tong, Z.. (2024). *The ESG Path to Low-Carbon Footprint: Recommended Practices and Lessons Learnt from Electrifying Recovery of the Giant Shale-Gas Basin in China.* OnePetro. [Preprint], DOI: 10.2118/219111-MS

Tuladhar, A., Rogerson, M., Engelhart, J., Parry, G. C., & Altrichter, B. (2024). Blockchain for compliance: An information processing case study of mandatory supply chain transparency in conflict minerals sourcing. *Supply Chain Management*, 29(4), 755–777. DOI: 10.1108/SCM-11-2023-0585

Tyagi, A.K. *et al.* (2024) 'Role of Blockchain Technology in Smart Era: A review on possible smart applications,' *Journal of Information & Knowledge Management* [Preprint]. .DOI: 10.1142/S0219649224500321

Tyagi, A. K., & Seranmadevi, R. (2024). *Blockchain for Enhancing Security and Privacy in the Smart Healthcare*. Wiley., DOI: 10.1002/9781394303564.ch16

Uddin, M. (2021). Blockchain Medledger: Hyperledger fabric enabled drug traceability system for counterfeit drugs in pharmaceutical industry. *International Journal of Pharmaceutics*, 597, 120235. DOI: 10.1016/j.ijpharm.2021.120235 PMID: 33549813

Vaibhav, A. (2020). *International Research Journal of Innovations in Engineering and Technology*. Proquest. [Preprint], DOI: 10.47001/irjiet

Van Vulpen, P., Siu, J., & Jansen, S. (2023). Governance of Decentralized Autonomous Organizations that Produce Open Source Software. *Blockchain Research and Applications*, 5(1), 100166. DOI: 10.1016/j.bcra.2023.100166

Vanmathi, C.. (2024). *The role of blockchain in transforming industries beyond finance*. IEEE Access., DOI: 10.1109/ACCESS.2024.3468611

Vittala, K. R. P., ... (2024) 'Emerging technology adoption and applications for modern society towards providing smart banking solutions,' in *Advances in medical technologies and clinical practice book series*, pp. 315–329. DOI: 10.4018/979-8-3693-5261-8.ch018

Waheed, A.. (2024) 'Zero-Day Exploits in Cybersecurity: Case Studies and Countermeasure,' *Preprint.org* [Preprint]. DOI: 10.20944/preprints202407.2338.v1

Waqar, A., Hannan Qureshi, A., Othman, I., Saad, N., & Azab, M. (2023). Exploration of challenges to deployment of blockchain in small construction projects. *Ain Shams Engineering Journal*, 15(2), 102362. DOI: 10.1016/j.asej.2023.102362

Wei, Y., Xu, Q., & Peng, H. (2024). An enhanced consensus algorithm for blockchain. *Scientific Reports*, 14(1), 17701. Advance online publication. DOI: 10.1038/s41598-024-68120-4 PMID: 39085315

Wen, B. O. T., ... (2023) 'Detecting cyber threats with a Graph-Based NIDPS,' in *Advances in logistics, operations, and management science book series*, pp. 36–74. DOI: 10.4018/978-1-6684-7625-3.ch002

Westerkamp, M., Victor, F., & Küpper, A. (2019). Tracing manufacturing processes using blockchain-based token compositions. *Digital Communications and Networks*, 6(2), 167–176. DOI: 10.1016/j.dcan.2019.01.007

Yan, Z.. (2024). *Blockchain-driven Decentralized Identity Management: An Interdisciplinary Review and Research Agenda*. Information & Management., DOI: 10.1016/j.im.2024.104026

Zhao, C., Zhang, S., Wang, T., & Liew, S. C. (2024). Bodyless block propagation: TPS fully scalable blockchain with pre-validation. *Future Generation Computer Systems*, 163, 107516. DOI: 10.1016/j.future.2024.107516

Chapter 2
Current Security Issues and Vulnerabilities Associated With Mobile Application

Abdullahi Adewole Zakariyah
Albukhary International University, Malaysia

Md.Farman Ali
Albukhary International University, Malaysia

Nima Yoezer
Albukhary International University, Malaysia

Rukayya Shehu
Albukhary International University, Malaysia

ABSTRACT

Mobile applications have become a crucial part of modern life, facilitating everything from social interactions to financial transactions. However, this ubiquity also presents a significant security challenge. The landscape of mobile app security is fraught with vulnerabilities and threats that can compromise user data, privacy, and the overall integrity of applications. This paper delves into the security issues and vulnerabilities that can affect mobile applications. It provides an in-depth analysis of various attack methods used by cybercriminals to extract user data and explores how users can protect their information from being compromised. The discussion will cover common tactics employed by attackers, the potential consequences of losing mobile application data to these threats, and the critical measures necessary

DOI: 10.4018/979-8-3693-6135-1.ch002

for safeguarding user data against such attacks.

INTRODUCTION

Statistics show that people spent an astonishing 3.8 trillion hours on mobile apps in 2022. Despite this extensive use, only 2.6% of Android app users and 4.3% of iPhone app users continue using an app 30 days after downloading it. Mobile apps are projected to generate $932 billion in revenue in 2023. However, this widespread usage also introduces significant security concerns. The key security issues associated with mobile apps include data confidentiality, data privacy, and non-compliance with security standards and regulations (Alex et al., 2022; Singhal et al., 2020). This paper will delve into each of these security issues in detail in the literature review. Each issue will be analyzed independently, and strategies for prevention and resolution will be discussed (Khurana et al., 2016; Ananna et al., 2023).

Mobile applications have become an integral part of modern life, offering unprecedented convenience and accessibility (Sindiramutty, Jhanjhi, Tan, Khan, Shah, & Manchuri, 2024). However, this widespread adoption has also opened the door to numerous security issues and vulnerabilities (Lim et al., 2019; Sharma et al., 2021). As mobile devices increasingly store sensitive personal and financial information, they have become attractive targets for cybercriminals (McGraw-Hill, 2010; Alferidah & Jhanjhi, 2020). The rapid pace of app development, often prioritizing functionality over security, exacerbates the risk.

Furthermore, the diverse and fragmented ecosystem of mobile operating systems and devices introduces additional complexity in ensuring robust security measures (Nayyar et al., 2021; Azam, Dulloo, Majeed, Wan, Xin, & Sindiramutty, 2023). This introduction explores the current landscape of security threats and vulnerabilities in mobile applications, highlighting the need for comprehensive strategies to protect users and their data in an ever-evolving digital environment (Grafiati, 2020; Alkinani et al., 2021).

By addressing these challenges, it is possible to work towards creating a safer and more secure mobile app ecosystem for all users. This study aims to contribute to the ongoing efforts to enhance mobile app security and provide actionable insights for developers and security professionals.

Background

Recent statistics note that about 90% of the global internet population uses a mobile device to go online (Ravichandran et al., 2024; Seng et al., 2024). For hackers, this means more people to victimize, making endpoint security for mobile devices increasingly vital.

In this paper, the focus is on addressing the security issues associated with mobile applications. Before proceeding further, the relevant terminologies will be described Mobile applications are software programs designed to operate on smartphones, tablets, or other mobile devices (Babbar et al., 2021; Shah et al., 2022; Sindiramutty, Jhanjhi, Tan, Khan, Shah, Yun, et al., 2024). These applications span various categories, including entertainment, social networking, productivity, and gaming, among others. The widespread use of mobile applications has transformed how we interact with technology, providing convenient access to services and information on-the-go (Guardsquare, 2019; Brohi et al., 2020).

Security issues or challenges regarding mobile applications can be defined as different approaches in which mobile application data can be compromised or breached. Data integrity is important, and data must be protected from unauthorized users. Due to the loss of data from mobile applications, a decision was made to delve into the security issues associated with mobile applications (Jebaraj, 2016; Chesti et al., 2020; Sindiramutty et al., 2024).

Mobile application security refers to the technologies and security procedures that protect mobile applications against cyberattacks and data theft. An all-in-one mobile app security framework automates mobile application security testing on platforms like iOS, Android, and others (Mejia Miranda et al., 2017; Dogra et al., 2021).

Mobile device usage has been steadily increasing in recent years. Recent statistics note that about 90% of the global internet population uses a mobile device to go online (Sindiramutty et al., 2024). For hackers, this means more people to victimize, making endpoint security for mobile devices increasingly vital.

Problem Statement

Data security is very important relating to personal data. To secure data from being compromised by unauthorized users, there should be a study on the vulnerabilities of the data and how it can be compromised. This is applicable to mobile applications; for mobile application data to be secured, there needs to be a study of the vulnerability and the security issues that may affect it . A deliberate investigation into the current security landscape surrounding mobile applications is essential to mitigate risks effectively, address existing vulnerabilities, and safeguard users' digital experiences (Abdullah et al., 2021; Fatima-Tuz-Zahra et al., 2020).

Research Questions

What are the primary vulnerabilities associated with personal data stored and processed within mobile applications?

How do unauthorized users compromise data security within mobile applications, and what are the common methods employed?

What are the key factors contributing to the susceptibility of mobile application data to security breaches and unauthorized access?

Objectives

To identify prevalent security issues affecting mobile applications.

To analyze the vulnerabilities commonly associated with mobile applications.

To assess the impact of these vulnerabilities on users' data privacy and device security.

Scope

This study will focus on identifying the common issues affecting mobile applications (objective 1) Examining the vulnerabilities and security issues associated with mobile apps, It aims to identify and analyze the various threats, risks, and challenges posed by it (Objective 2). It will also focus on the impact and the consequences that lack of security would cause on users' data privacy and device security (Objective 3).

Research Hypotheses

The prevalence of security vulnerabilities in mobile applications, particularly due to inadequate encryption, insecure data storage, and excessive permissions, poses significant risks to user privacy and data integrity, necessitating the development of robust security measures and user education to mitigate these threats.This hypothesis encapsulates the key issues discussed in the paper, emphasizing the need for both technical and educational solutions to address security vulnerabilities in mobile applications.

LITERATURE REVIEW

To gather studies and findings on this research, 40 research papers were consulted, encompassing articles, journals, and books related to security issues and challenges in mobile applications. From these, 30 papers were selected for a focused analysis. The new findings and achievements from these selected works were derived, and additional ideas and recommendations were formulated based on the authors' conclusions. Three research questions were developed to be answered using the selected papers.

According to Tao et al. (2020), the rapid growth of mobile applications in sectors like banking, healthcare, and e-commerce has heightened security concerns, necessitating robust measures such as authentication, authorization, and data confidentiality. These applications extend corporate networks, increasing exposure to security threats (Azam, Dulloo, Majeed, Wan, Xin, Tajwar, et al., 2023; Sindiramutty, Tan, Shah, et al., 2024). Security testing is challenging, making mobile apps not inherently more secure than desktop or web applications. Khurana and Baraković, (2016) both emphasized the need for robust security measures in wireless networks, with Khurana specifically discussing the merits and demerits of existing methods.

According to Basavala et al. (2013) focused on the rapid growth of mobile applications in sectors like banking, healthcare, and e-commerce has heightened security concerns, necessitating robust measures such as authentication, authorization, and data confidentiality. These applications extend corporate networks, increasing exposure to security threats. Security testing is challenging, making mobile apps not inherently more secure than desktop or web applications.

According to Mishra and Kokate(2014), the specific vulnerabilities and security issues in ad-hoc networks, with Mishra focusing on attacks against routing protocols and Kokate discussing the potential use of mobile ad hoc networks in real-life applications. These studies collectively underscore the importance of addressing security concerns in mobile applications. The increasing use of Android-based smartphones has made them a prime target for hackers, leading to a rise in vulnerabilities and attacks (Azam, Tajwar, Mayhialagan, Davis, Yik, Ali, et al., 2023; Sindiramutty, Tan, & Wei, 2024). These attacks include privilege escalation and privacy breaches, which can compromise the security of these devices (Mejía Miranda, 2017; Gopi et al., 2021).

The rapid growth of Android mobile applications has further exacerbated these vulnerabilities, with attackers exploiting them to access sensitive data. To address these issues, it is crucial to understand the security architecture of Android devices and implement effective countermeasures (Khurana et al., 2016; Gouda et al., 2022)

According to Himanshu et al. (2016) proposed that the behavior of user's browsing and inability to see the full links on mobile phones had been one of the biggest exposures. The lack of ability to see full links in mobile phones due to the small screen have paved an easy path for phishing links to be effective (Humayun et al., 2022; Azam, Tan, Pin, Syahmi, Qian, Jingyan, et al., 2023; Waheed et al., 2024). They have given examples on how social networking sites like email or text message on devices with heavy reliance on URL links makes it impossible for the average user to notice whether links are safe or not, so that way scammers get their hands on user's data. This situation is happening now and within ourselves so it's more accurate which doesn't need an experiment to prove it.

According to Dr. Robert P. Griffin Jr (2018) proposed that applications for Android and iOS have been found to save sensitive information like usernames and passwords plaintext log files that may be read by attackers. The instances had been recorded in the Common Vulnerabilities and Exposures (CVE) database (CVE-2012-2630 and CVE-2014-0647) revealing the Twitter credentials and Starbucks usernames, passwords and email account information. Although this threat had been mitigated, the fact it had been a threat before shouldn't be forgotten.

According to Johannah Jebaraj (2016) stated that some of the applications request more permissions than their requirement to their functioning. It is named as Privilege Escalation and such permissions are done by embedded advertising libraries within the apps and they can be misused by the agencies to collect personal information without the user's consent (Jhanjhi et al., 2021; Hussain et al., 2024; Wen et al., 2023). These threats are counterattack by the security mechanism that a mobile has in it, antivirus software for the malicious detection, and with application firewalls and analysis tools. It is mentioned that there are other security tools and models like Kirin, SASQUATCH, Dexteroid and a few others. All these tools can add more security on mobile applications and on mobile phones itself.

The study highlights the significant security challenges faced by mobile applications, including data breaches, unauthorized access, and malware attacks. These issues are exacerbated by inadequate encryption, insecure data storage, and lack of security standards. Key vulnerabilities identified include weak authentication mechanisms, excessive permissions, and insecure communication channels (Jun et al., 2024; Manchuri et al., 2024). These vulnerabilities make mobile applications vulnerable to attacks like phishing, privilege escalation, and data interception. The study emphasizes the need for better user education and stringent security measures. Effective mitigation strategies include robust authentication protocols, regular security assessments, and adhering to security standards. Advanced security tools and frameworks can enhance security measures. The study contributes to developing improved security frameworks for mobile applications, ensuring better protection of user data and maintaining trust in an increasingly connected world (Hur, 2017; Kumar et al., 2021).

METHODOLOGY

The methodology employed in this study is based on qualitative research. Data collection occurred through a structured questionnaire, incorporating open-ended questions to capture detailed and nuanced responses. This approach aims to explore participants' experiences and perceptions in depth, providing comprehensive insights into the subject matter. By focusing on qualitative data, the study seeks to uncover underlying patterns and themes that quantitative methods might overlook. The structured questionnaire is designed to elicit rich, detailed responses, ensuring a thorough understanding of the participants' viewpoints and experiences. This method enables a deeper exploration of the complexities surrounding mobile application security issues

Figure 1. Research Process Steps

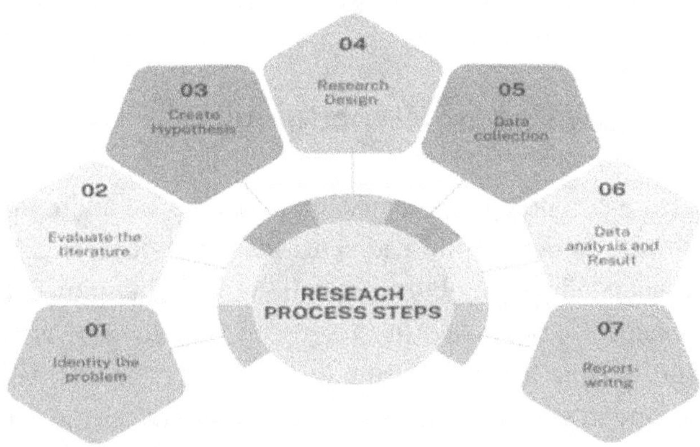

Data Analysis

For this research paper on the security and vulnerabilities of mobile applications, we gathered comprehensive data through an extensive literature review and a structured questionnaire survey. Initially, we conducted a thorough analysis of existing research papers related to our topic. We drew insights from many scholarly articles, technical reports, and other papers, which we sourced from Google Scholar, Academia, and other renowned article publishing websites. These research papers provided essential understanding on our topic. Furthermore, we conducted a questionnaire survey to obtain primary responses, which laid the groundwork for our theories. The survey included questions about personal experiences with mobile application security and malicious attacks encountered while using them. These two methods paved the way for data collection and provided more insights into our research.

Questionnaire Design

A survey was conducted to seek people's opinions on the security vulnerabilities associated with mobile applications. The questionnaire consisted of both open-ended and closed-ended questions, many criteria were considered to select the respondents, including age, faculty, level of education, and knowledge about security vulnerabilities in mobile applications. Each respondent assessed our questionnaire, and we recorded and tracked their responses. After selecting the respondents, we shared a link to the questionnaire for them to fill out, and their feedback was generated in the form of a pie chart for better visualization. By designing the questionnaire with these components, we aimed to gather comprehensive data that would provide valuable insights into the security issues and vulnerabilities associated with mobile applications

Justification of Choices of Methodology

We chose these methodologies because the issue we are addressing is a continually occurring event in this digital age. This research focuses on identifying the vulnerabilities associated with mobile applications, and obtaining data from people who have experienced various security issues on mobile apps is crucial for this research. We were able to learn about the different ways people were attacked by hackers to compromise their data and the various approaches those hackers used.

User Perceptions of Mobile Application Safety

From the survey responses, it is evident that security concerns are a significant issue among mobile application users. Out of 26 respondents, a substantial majority of 76.9% expressed concern about the security of the mobile applications they use. Conversely, only 19.2% of the respondents indicated that they were not worried about app security. This data underscores the critical need for developers to prioritize security features and reassure users about the safety of their personal information and data while using mobile applications.

Figure 2. The Pie Chart Representation of the Response gotten from this Question

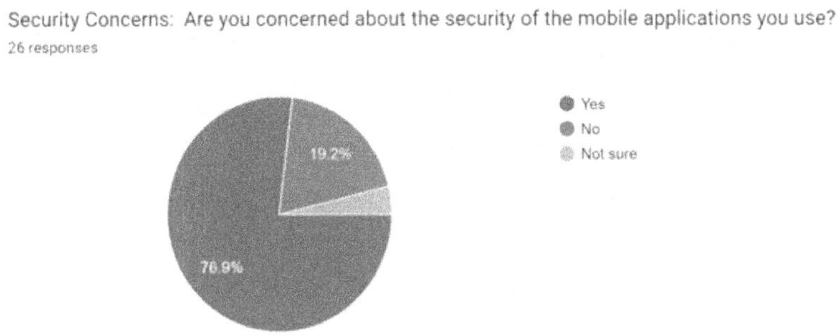

Privacy Issues in Mobile Applications

Based on the survey data collected from 27 respondents, it was found that a significant majority of users, 53.7%, have experienced a security breach or privacy issue while using a mobile application. In contrast, 40.3% of the respondents reported not having encountered such issues. This data highlights the prevalent concerns regarding mobile application security among users, indicating that over half of the surveyed population has faced security or privacy challenges, underscoring the importance of enhancing mobile app security measures.

Figure 3. The Pie Chart Representation of the Response gotten from this Question

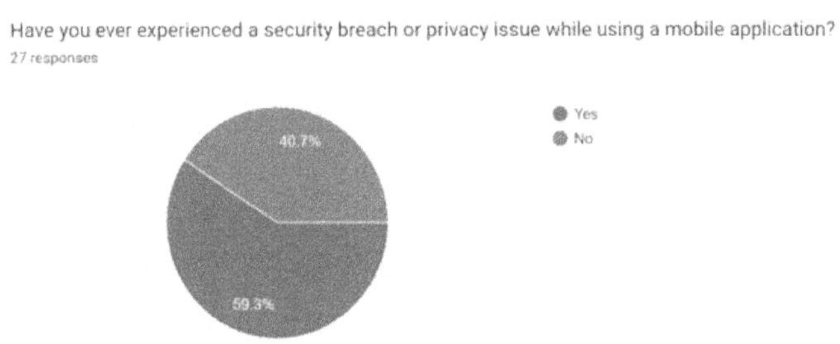

Most Frequently Used Types of Mobile Applications

Social media applications are the most frequently used among respondents, with a significant 92.6% indicating regular use. Following social media, communication apps are also widely used, with 44.4% of respondents using them frequently. Finance apps, such as banking, are utilized by 25.9% of the participants, while entertainment apps are used by 14.8%. Health and fitness apps account for 11.1% of frequent usage, and productivity apps are used by 7.4% of respondents. Other types of applications are used less frequently, with only 3.7% indicating their regular use. This data highlights the dominance of social media and communication apps in users' daily routines, while also showing a varied usage pattern across other app categories.

Figure 4. The Bar Chart Representation of the Response gotten from this Question

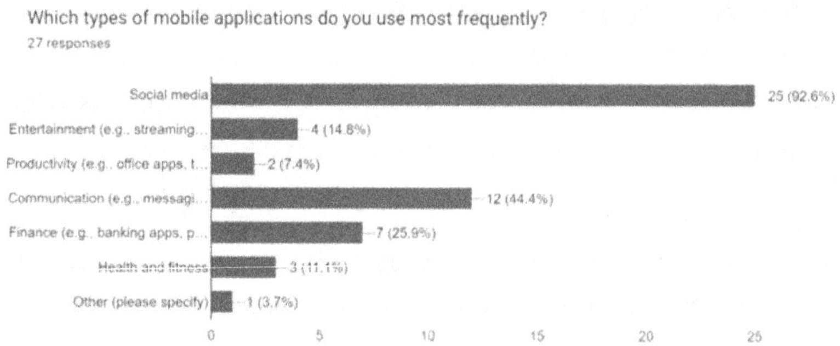

Frequency of Mobile Application Usage

According to the survey data on mobile app usage frequency, a vast majority of respondents, 88.9%, use mobile applications daily. In contrast, 11.1% of the respondents reported using mobile applications several times a week. This data illustrates the pervasive role of mobile apps in users' daily lives, with most individuals engaging with various applications on a daily basis.

Figure 5. The Pie Chart Representation of the Response gotten from this Question

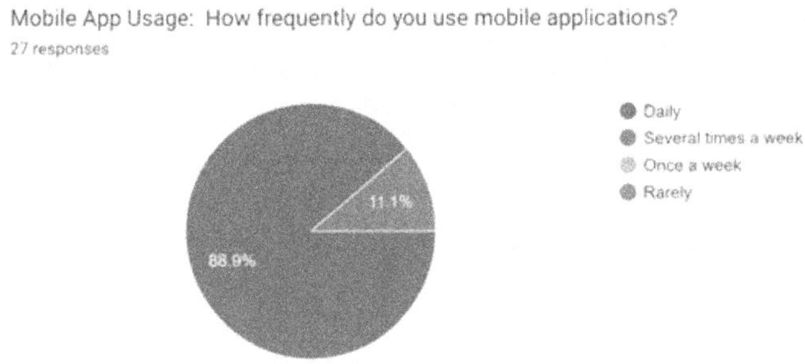

Awareness of Security Vulnerabilities in Mobile Applications

In this part, indicate varying levels of awareness regarding security vulnerabilities associated with mobile applications. Among the 27 respondents, 18.5% reported being very familiar with these security issues. The majority, 66.7%, described themselves as somewhat familiar, indicating a general but not comprehensive understanding of mobile app security vulnerabilities. Meanwhile, 14.8% of the respondents admitted to not being very familiar with such issues. This data suggests that while most users have some awareness of mobile app security risks, there remains a need for increased education and information to enhance user understanding and vigilance.

Figure 6. The Pie Chart Representation of the Response gotten from this Question

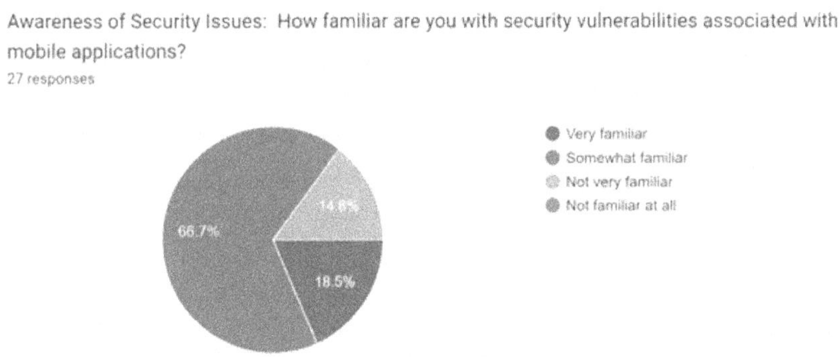

Pre-Download Habits. Reviews and Security Reports

The data reveals varying behaviors among users regarding reading app reviews or security reports before downloading a mobile application. Among the 27 respondents, 55.6% indicated that they sometimes read reviews or security reports, while 25.9% stated that they always do so. Conversely, 14.8% of respondents reported that they rarely read these materials. This data indicates that while the majority of users occasionally consider app reviews or security information, a smaller yet significant group consistently reviews this information, and another portion infrequently engages in this practice, highlighting the varied levels of diligence and caution exercised by mobile app users.

Figure 7. The Pie Chart Representation of the Response gotten from this Question

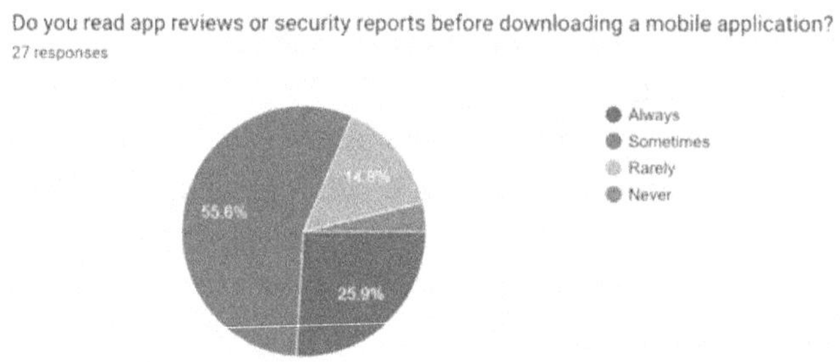

A total of 27 respondents participated, providing insights into their mobile app usage frequency, experiences with security breaches, familiarity with security vulnerabilities, and the impact of these issues on their trust in mobile applications. The survey included multiple-choice questions, Likert scale questions, and open-ended questions to obtain both quantitative and qualitative data. The responses were systematically analyzed to identify prevalent security concerns and assess the overall awareness and attitudes of mobile app users towards security practices.

RESULTS

The survey results revealed several key findings regarding mobile application security. A significant portion of respondents (76.9%) expressed concern about the security of the mobile applications they use, with 59.3% having experienced a security breach or privacy issue. The most commonly used types of mobile applications were social media (92.6%) and communication apps (44.4%), highlighting their pervasive presence in users' daily lives. Additionally, 88.9% of respondents reported using mobile applications daily. Despite high usage, there was a notable lack of familiarity with security vulnerabilities; only 18.5% of respondents were very familiar with the issues. This gap in awareness was further underscored by the fact that 55.6% of users only sometimes read app reviews or security reports before downloading an application.

DISCUSSION

The data collected underscores the critical need for enhanced security measures in mobile applications. Users identified various security vulnerabilities, including unauthorized access, insecure data storage, and phishing attacks. The impact of these vulnerabilities on user trust is significant, with 48.1% of respondents indicating that security issues increase their distrust in using mobile applications. Furthermore, the findings highlight a discrepancy between high usage rates and low awareness of security practices among users. This suggests that while mobile applications are integral to everyday activities, users remain vulnerable due to insufficient security knowledge and practices. Consequently, there is a pressing need for mobile app developers to implement robust security measures, such as strong encryption, regular security updates, and user education on security best practices, to mitigate these risks and enhance user trust and safety.

CONCLUSION

This research shows different ways data can be compromised by attackers from user mobile apps. It also illustrates different vulnerabilities that can occur to one's mobile application, guiding on how to detect different scam approaches and how data can be protected against attackers. The type of security attack that was discussed includes phishing, malware and other common types of security attacksThis research elaborates in detail different security issues that normally occur to mobile applications and how to avoid or prevent these security issues.

This paper explores the complex world of mobile application security, focusing on mobile applications as essential smartphones. The study of security issues involved in mobile applications is important because it provides vital insights into improving security mechanisms and protocols which are essential for protecting user data and privacy in the context of mobile devices, it also exposes the vulnerabilities involved. The study guides the vulnerabilities and how it should be addressed to avoid data being compromised or lost. After the study of the security issues involved in mobile applications we are expected to be able to identify the vulnerabilities involved, development of security standard and best practices, and enhanced security measures.

Future Work

There are limitations on this study while stating theoretical insights into the usage of mobile apps and it is crucial to acknowledge these limitations when interpreting the study's results. It is important to note that study findings might get slimed due to the absence of empirical experiments. There are also challenges like data security, data management, privacy concerns and others in IoT realms further obstructing study findings. Due to the dynamic changes and development in technology can make a hindrance over the time on its relevance and accuracy.

ACKNOWLEDGEMENTS

The authors sincerely thank their research advisor, Professor Dr. Khalid Hussain, whose invaluable guidance, encouragement, and support were crucial throughout this project. His insights and feedback significantly influenced the direction and scope of the research. Gratitude is also extended to Albukhary International University (AIU) and the School of Computing and Informatics (SCI) for their support. Special acknowledgement is given to Dr. Riskhan Basheer, dean of SCI, for his assistance and encouragement.

REFERENCES

Abdullah, H., & Zeebaree, S. R. M. (2021). Android Mobile Applications Vulnerabilities and Prevention Methods. A Review. semanticscholar.org. https.//www.semanticscholar.org/paper/Android-Mobile-Applications-Vulnerabilities-and-A-Abdullah-Zeebaree/66f217c39116abdf9ab2f89455d228cd5579f110

Ahamad, S. (2022). Smartphone security and protection practices, (PDF) Smartphone Security and Protection Practices | Shahanawaj Ahamad - Academia.edu. Available at. http.//www.academia.edu/70442415/Smartphone_Security_and_Protection_Practices?rhid=28519263243&swp=rr-rw-wc-30094607

Ahvanooey, M. T. (2020) A survey on smartphone security. Software vulnerabilities, malware, and attacks, International Journal of Advanced Computer Science and Applications. Available at. https.//www.academia.edu/43779422/A_Survey_on_Smartphones_Security_Software_Vulnerabilities_Malware_and_Attacks?rhid=28519395220&swp=rr-rw-wc-70442415

. Alan Goode (2010) Managing mobile security. How are we doing? Available at https.//DOI: 10.1016/S1353-4858(10)70025-8

. Alex, S. A., Jhanjhi, N., Humayun, M., Ibrahim, A. O., & Abulfaraj, A. W. (2022). Deep LSTM Model for Diabetes Prediction with Class Balancing by SMOTE. *Electronics, 11*(17), 2737. https.//DOI: 10.3390/electronics11172737

Alferidah, D. K., & Jhanjhi, N. (2020). Cybersecurity Impact over Bigdata and IoT Growth. *2020 International Conference on Computational Intelligence (ICCI).* https.//DOI: 10.1109/ICCI51257.2020.9247722

. Alkinani, M. H., Almazroi, A. A., Jhanjhi, N., & Khan, N. A. (2021). 5G and IoT Based Reporting and Accident Detection (RAD) System to Deliver First Aid Box Using Unmanned Aerial Vehicle. *Sensors, 21*(20), 6905. https.//DOI: 10.3390/s21206905

. Ananna, F. F., Nowreen, R., Jahwari, S. S. R. A., Costa, E. A., Angeline, L., & Sindiramutty, S. R. (2023). Analysing Influential factors in student academic achievement. Prediction modelling and insight. *International Journal of Emerging Multidisciplinaries Computer Science & Artificial Intelligence, 2*(1). https.//DOI: 10.54938/ijemdcsai.2023.02.1.254

. Azam, H., Dulloo, M. I., Majeed, M. H., Wan, J. P. H., Xin, L. T., & Sindiramutty, S. R. (2023). Cybercrime Unmasked. Investigating cases and digital evidence. *International Journal of Emerging Multidisciplinaries Computer Science & Artificial Intelligence, 2*(1). https.//DOI: 10.54938/ijemdcsai.2023.02.1.255

. Azam, H., Dulloo, M. I., Majeed, M. H., Wan, J. P. H., Xin, L. T., Tajwar, M. A., & Sindiramutty, S. R. (2023). Defending the digital Frontier. IDPS and the battle against Cyber threat. *International Journal of Emerging Multidisciplinaries Computer Science & Artificial Intelligence, 2*(1). https.//DOI: 10.54938/ijemdcsai.2023.02.1.253

. Azam, H., Tajwar, M. A., Mayhialagan, S., Davis, A. J., Yik, C. J., Ali, D., & Sindiramutty, S. R. (2023). Innovations in Security. A study of cloud Computing and IoT. *International Journal of Emerging Multidisciplinaries Computer Science & Artificial Intelligence, 2*(1). https.//DOI: 10.54938/ijemdcsai.2023.02.1.252

Azam, H., Tan, M., Pin, L. T., Syahmi, M. A., Qian, A. L. W., Jingyan, H., Uddin, M. F., & Sindiramutty, S. R. (2023). Wireless Technology Security and Privacy. A Comprehensive Study. Preprints.*org*. https.//DOI: 10.20944/preprints202311.0664.v1

. Babbar, H., Rani, S., Masud, M., Verma, S., Anand, D., & Jhanjhi, N. (2021). Load balancing algorithm for migrating switches in software-defined vehicular networks. *Computers, Materials & Continua/Computers, Materials & Continua (Print), 67*(1), 1301–1316. https.//DOI: 10.32604/cmc.2021.014627

Brohi, S. N., Jhanjhi, N., Brohi, N. N., & Brohi, M. N. (2020). Key Applications of State-of-the-Art Technologies to Mitigate and Eliminate COVID-19.pdf. TECHRxiv. https.//DOI: 10.36227/techrxiv.12115596.v1

Chesti, I. A., Humayun, M., Sama, N. U., & Jhanjhi, N. (2020). Evolution, Mitigation, and Prevention of Ransomware. *2020 2nd International Conference on Computer and Information Sciences (ICCIS)*. https.//DOI: 10.1109/ICCIS49240.2020.9257708

Cifuentes, Y., Beltrán, L., & Ramírez, L. (2015). Analysis of security vulnerabilities for mobile health applications. https.//www.semanticscholar.org/paper/Analysis-of-Security-Vulnerabilities-for-Mobile-Cifuentes-Beltr%C3%A1n/6a27e716123bb59d24f7a418b2c6fdd3917ed361

Cybersecurity measures for Logistics Industry Framework (no date) *Google Books*. Available at. https.//www.google.com.my/books/edition/Cybersecurity_Measures_for_Logistics_Ind/9r_1EAAAQBAJ?hl=en&gbpv=1&dq=%22A%2BComprehensive%2BReview%2Bof%2BCyber%2BSecurity%2BVulnerabilities%2C%2BThreats%2C%2BAttacks%2C%2Band%2BSolutions%22%2Bby%2BElectronics%2BJournal&pg=PA65&printsec=frontcover

DHS study on Mobile Device Security -April2017- final. Available at. https.//www.dhs.gov/sites/default/files/publications/ DHS Study on Mobile Device Security - April 2017-FINAL.pdf

Dogra, V., Singh, A., Verma, S., Kavita, N., Jhanjhi, N. Z., & Talib, M. N. (2021). Analyzing DistilBERT for Sentiment Classification of Banking Financial News. In *Lecture notes in networks and systems* (pp. 501–510). https.//DOI: 10.1007/978-981-16-3153-5_53

Fatima-Tuz-Zahra, N., Jhanjhi, N., Brohi, S. N., Malik, N. A., & Humayun, M. (2020). Proposing a Hybrid RPL Protocol for Rank and Wormhole Attack Mitigation using Machine Learning. *2020 2nd International Conference on Computer and Information Sciences (ICCIS)*. https.//DOI: 10.1109/ICCIS49240.2020.9257607

. Gopi, R., Sathiyamoorthi, V., Selvakumar, S., Manikandan, R., Chatterjee, P., Jhanjhi, N. Z., & Luhach, A. K. (2021). Enhanced method of ANN based model for detection of DDoS attacks on multimedia internet of things. *Multimedia Tools andApplications, 81*(19), 26739–26757. https.//DOI: 10.1007/s11042-021-10640-6

. Gouda, W., Almurafeh, M., Humayun, M., & Jhanjhi, N. Z. (2022). Detection of COVID-19 based on chest x-rays using deep learning. *Healthcare, 10*(2), 343. https.//DOI: 10.3390/healthcare10020343

Grafiati. (2020). App Security. Retrieved from https.//www.grafiati.com/en/literature-selections/app-security/

Holla, S., & Katti, M. M. (2012). Android based mobile application development and its security. *International Journal of Computer Trends and Technology*, 3(3), 486–490.

Human verification. (n.d.-b). https.//www.semanticscholar.org/paper/Security-risks-and-their-prevention-capabilities-in-Michalska-Poniszewska-Mara%C5%84da/add75ed2c41e18a5500ea021dca45e5083374465

Human verification. (n.d.). https.//www.semanticscholar.org/paper/An-insight-into-the-security-issues-and-their-for-Khandelwal-Mohapatra/2fb9ed0bea85dc14552199012ac4dd8a4d8f52a2

. Humayun, M., Sujatha, R., Almuayqil, S. N., & Jhanjhi, N. Z. (2022). A Transfer Learning Approach with a Convolutional Neural Network for the Classification of Lung Carcinoma. *Healthcare, 10*(6), 1058. https.//DOI: 10.3390/healthcare10061058

Hur, J. B., & Shamsi, J. A. (2017). A survey on security issues, vulnerabilities and attacks in Android based smartphone. *2017 International Conference on Information and Communication Technologies (ICICT)*. DOI: 10.1109/ICICT.2017.8320163

Hussain, K., Rahmatyar, A. R., Riskhan, B., Sheikh, M. U., & Sindiramutty, S. R. (2024). Threats and Vulnerabilities of Wireless Networks in the Internet of Things (IoT). *2024 IEEE 1st Karachi Section Humanitarian Technology Conference (KHI-HTC), 2*, 1–8. https.//DOI: 10.1109/KHI-HTC60760.2024.10482197

Jebaraj, J. (2016) *An exploratory study on security issues pertaining to smartphone applications, Academia.edu.* Available at. https.//www.academia.edu/30094607/An_Exploratory_Study_on_Security_Issues_Pertaining_to_Smartphone_Applications?rhid=28519166230&swp=rr-rw-wc-39804973

. Jhanjhi, N., Humayun, M., & Almuayqil, S. N. (2021). Cyber security and privacy issues in industrial internet of things. *Computer Systems Science and Engineering, 37*(3), 361–380. https.//DOI: 10.32604/csse.2021.015206

Jun, A. Y. M., Jinu, B. A., Seng, L. K., Maharaiq, M. H. F. B. Z., Khongsuwan, W., Junn, B. T. K., Hao, A. W., & Sindiramutty, S. R. (2024). Exploring the Impact of Crypto-Ransomware on Critical Industries. Case Studies and Solutions. Preprints. *org*. https.//DOI: 10.20944/preprints202409.1325.v1

Khurana, P., Sharma, A., & Singh, P. K. (2016). A Systematic Analysis on Mobile Application Software Vulnerabilities. Issues and Challenges. *Indian Journal of Science and Technology*, 9(32). Advance online publication. DOI: 10.17485/ijst/2016/v9i32/100190

. Kumar, M. S., Vimal, S., Jhanjhi, N., Dhanabalan, S. S., & Alhumyani, H. A. (2021). Blockchain based peer to peer communication in autonomous drone operation. *Energy Reports, 7*, 7925–7939. https.//DOI: 10.1016/j.egyr.2021.08.073

Li, Q., & Clark, G. (2013). Mobile security: A look ahead. *IEEE Security and Privacy*, 11(1), 78–81.

. Lim, M., Abdullah, A., Jhanjhi, N., Khan, M. K., & Supramaniam, M. (2019). Link Prediction in Time-Evolving Criminal Network with deep Reinforcement learning technique. *IEEE Access, 7*, 184797–184807. https.//DOI: 10.1109/ACCESS.2019.2958873

. Manchuri, A., Kakera, A., Saleh, A., & Raja, S. (2024). pplication of Supervised Machine Learning Models in Biodiesel Production Research - A Short Review. *Borneo Journal of Sciences and Technology*. https.//DOI: 10.35370/bjost.2024.6.1-10

McGraw, G. (2010). *Mobile application security*. McGraw-Hill. https.//www.amazon.com/Mobile-Application-Security-Himanshu-Dwivedi/dp/0071611016

Mejia-Miranda, J., Melchor-Velasquez, R. E., & Munoz-Mata, M. A. (2017). Vulnerability detection in smartphones. A systematic literature review. 2017 12th Iberian Conference on Information Systems and Technologies (CISTI).

Mishra, R., Sharma, S., & Agrawal, R. (2010). Vulnerabilities and security for ad-hoc networks. *2010 International Conference on Networking and Information Technology*.

Mobile Application Security (no date) *Google Books*. Available at. https.//books.google.com.my/books?id=Iq11Hs6FFm4C&printsec=frontcover#v=onepage&q&f=false

Mobile OS vulnerabilities (no date) *Google Books*. Available at. https.//www.google.com.my/books/edition/Mobile_OS_Vulnerabilities/fh3EEAAAQBAJ?hl=en&gbpv=1&dq=Mobile%2BOS%2BVulnerabilities%3A%2BQuantitative%2Band%2BQualitative%2BAnalysis%2Bby%2BShafiullah%2BKhan&printsec=frontcover

Mobile phone security and Forensics (no date) *Google Books*. Available at. https.//www.google.com.my/books/edition/Mobile_Phone_Security_and_Forensics/OE4rJk7u5wIC?hl=en&gbpv=1&dq=Mobile%2BApplication%2BSecurity%2Band%2BForensics%3A%2BA%2BPractical%2BApproach%22%2Bby%2BRichardMobile%2BApplication%2BDevelopment%2C%2BUsability%2C%2Band%2BSecurity%22%2Bedited%2Bby%2BSougata%2BMukherjea%2B-%2BHammer%2Band%2BRic%2BMessier&printsec=frontcover

mobile security. (2019) Available at. https.//www.dhs.gov/sites/default/files/publications/2019_mobilesecurity_rd_programguide_vol3.pdf

Nayyar, A., Gadhavi, L., & Zaman, N. (2021). Machine learning in healthcare. review, opportunities and challenges. In *Elsevier eBooks* (pp. 23–45). https.//DOI: 10.1016/B978-0-12-821229-5.00011-2

P. Khurana1, A. Sharma & Pradeep Kumar Singh (2016) *Juit*. Available at. http.//www.ir.juit.ac.in.8080/jspui/bitstream/123456789/8356/1/A%20Systematic%20Analysis%20on%20Mobile%20Application%20Software%20Vulnerabilities%20Issues%20and%20Challenges.pdf

Ravichandran, N., Tewaraja, T., Rajasegaran, V., Kumar, S. S., Gunasekar, S. K. L., & Sindiramutty, S. R. (2024). Comprehensive Review Analysis and Countermeasures for Cybersecurity Threats. DDoS, Ransomware, and Trojan Horse Attacks. Preprints.*org*. https.//DOI: 10.20944/preprints202409.1369.v1

Seng, Y. J., Cen, T. Y., Raslan, M. H. B. M., Subramaniam, M. R., Xin, L. Y., Kin, S. J., Long, M. S., & Sindiramutty, S. R. (2024). In-Depth Analysis and Countermeasures for Ransomware Attacks. Case Studies and Recommendations. Preprints. *org*. https.//DOI: 10.20944/preprints202408.2261.v1

Shah, I. A., Jhanjhi, N. Z., & Laraib, A. (2022). Cybersecurity and blockchain usage in contemporary business. In *Advances in information security, privacy, and ethics book series* (pp. 49–64). https.//DOI: 10.4018/978-1-6684-5284-4.ch003

. Sharma, R., Singh, A., Kavita, N., Jhanjhi, N. Z., Masud, M., Jaha, E. S., & Verma, S. (2021). Plant disease diagnosis and image classification using deep learning. *Computers, Materials & Continua/Computers, Materials & Continua (Print), 71*(2), 2125–2140. https.//DOI: 10.32604/cmc.2022.020017

Shoro, S. (2023) *Mobile Computing and its security, (PDF) Mobile Computing and its Security | saima shoro - Academia.edu*. Available at. http.//www.academia.edu/94157460/Mobile_Computing_and_its_Security?rhid=28519263243&swp=rr-rw-wc-30094607

Sindiramutty, S. R., Jhanjhi, N., Tan, C. E., Lau, S. P., Muniandy, L., Gharib, A. H., Ashraf, H., & Murugesan, R. K. (2024). Industry 4.0. In *Advances in logistics, operations, and management science book series* (pp. 342–405). https.//DOI: 10.4018/979-8-3693-1363-3.ch013

Sindiramutty, S. R., Jhanjhi, N. Z., Tan, C. E., Khan, N. A., Shah, B., & Manchuri, A. R. (2024). Cybersecurity measures for logistics industry. In *Advances in information security, privacy, and ethics book series* (pp. 1–58). https.//DOI: 10.4018/979-8-3693-3816-2.ch001

Sindiramutty, S. R., Jhanjhi, N. Z., Tan, C. E., Khan, N. A., Shah, B., Yun, K. J., Ray, S. K., Jazri, H., & Hussain, M. (2024). Future trends and emerging threats in drone cybersecurity. In *Advances in information security, privacy, and ethics book series* (pp. 148–195). https.//DOI: 10.4018/979-8-3693-0774-8.ch007

Sindiramutty, S. R., Jhanjhi, N. Z., Tan, C. E., Yun, K. J., Manchuri, A. R., Ashraf, H., Murugesan, R. K., Tee, W. J., & Hussain, M. (2024). Data security and privacy concerns in drone operations. In *Advances in information security, privacy, and ethics book series* (pp. 236–290). https.//DOI: 10.4018/979-8-3693-0774-8.ch010

Sindiramutty, S. R., Tan, C. E., Shah, B., Khan, N. A., Gharib, A. H., Manchuri, A. R., Muniandy, L., Ray, S. K., & Jazri, H. (2024). Ethical considerations in drone cybersecurity. In *Advances in information security, privacy, and ethics book series* (pp. 42–87). https.//DOI: 10.4018/979-8-3693-0774-8.ch003

Sindiramutty, S. R., Tan, C. E., & Wei, G. W. (2024). Eyes in the sky. In *Advances in information security, privacy, and ethics book series* (pp. 405–451). https.//DOI: 10.4018/979-8-3693-0774-8.ch017

. Singhal, V., Jain, S. S., Anand, D., Singh, A., Verma, S., Kavita, N., Rodrigues, J. J. P. C., Jhanjhi, N. Z., Ghosh, U., Jo, O., & Iwendi, C. (2020). Artificial Intelligence Enabled Road Vehicle-Train Collision Risk Assessment Framework for Unmanned railway level crossings. *IEEE Access, 8*, 113790–113806. https.//DOI: 10.1109/ACCESS.2020.3002416

smartphone security threats (no date) *ResearchGate*. Available at. http.//www.researchgate.net/publication/345772225_Smartphone_Security_Threats

Tao, C., Guo, H., & Huang, Z. (2020). Identifying security issues for mobile applications based on user review summarization. *Information and Software Technology*, 122, 1–13. DOI: 10.1016/j.infsof.2020.106290

The Mobile Application Hacker's handbook (no date) *Google Books*. Available at. https.//www.google.com.my/books/edition/The_Mobile_Application_Hacker_s_Handbook/5gVhBgAAQBAJ?hl=en&gbpv=1&dq=The%2BMobile%2BApplication%2BHacker%27s%2BHandbook%22%2Bby%2BDominic%2BChell%2C%2BTyrone%2BErasmus%2C%2Band%2Bothers%2B-&printsec=frontcover

Waheed, A., Seegolam, B., Jowaheer, M. F., Sze, C. L. X., Hua, E. T. F., & Sindiramutty, S. R. (2024). Zero-Day Exploits in Cybersecurity. Case Studies and Countermeasure. preprints.*org*. https.//DOI: 10.20944/preprints202407.2338.v1

Weichbroth, P., & Łysik, Ł. (2020). Mobile security: Threats and best practices. *Mobile Information Systems*, 2020(1), 8828078.

Wen, B. O. T., Syahriza, N., Xian, N. C. W., Wei, N. G., Shen, T. Z., Hin, Y. Z., Sindiramutty, S. R., & Nicole, T. Y. F. (2023). Detecting cyber threats with a Graph-Based NIDPS. In *Advances in logistics, operations, and management science book series* (pp. 36–74). https.//DOI: 10.4018/978-1-6684-7625-3.ch002

Chapter 3
Cybersecurity in IoT Ecosystems Managing Device Vulnerabilities and Data Exposure

Siva Raja Sindiramutty
https://orcid.org/0009-0006-0310-8721
Taylor's University, Malaysia

Noor Zaman Jhanjhi
https://orcid.org/0000-0001-8116-4733
Taylor's University, Malaysia

Sayan Kumar Ray
Taylor's University, Malaysia

ABSTRACT

The proliferation of IoT devices and sensors leads to greater efficiency but also greatly increased attack surfaces. In this part of the series, we delve into some key security issues that plague IoT ecosystems with a solution- understanding device vulnerabilities and how they led to data exposure. IoT devices are frequently built without strong defences in place, with a lack of secure firmware combined with weak authentication making them top of the list for attackers. We will also turn to real-world threats, such as distributed denial of service (DDoS) attacks launched by botnets and data breaches that disclose personal information or sensitive business information. Although the chapter certainly warns of the risks, it is by no means a doom-and-gloom line of reasoning. The paper outlines best practices to secure IoT systems, from security-by-design principles to leveraging AI and blockchain

DOI: 10.4018/979-8-3693-6135-1.ch003

technologies.

1. INTRODUCTION

Overview of IoT Ecosystems

Define the Internet of Things (IoT), its growth, and its role in various sectors (smart homes, healthcare, industrial IoT, etc.)

The IoT is a system where devices, from everyday gadgets to industrial machines, connect to the Internet, sharing data and interacting with each other (Chauhan, Arora and Kaur, 2024; Rani et al., 2024). Think about how your smartwatch tracks your steps or how a smart fridge can tell when you're low on milk. This idea has exploded in recent years, touching nearly every part of life. I remember reading about how the number of IoT devices is set to skyrocket, reaching over 75 billion by 2025 (Choubisa, 2024). It's not just about convenience—it's making serious waves in sectors like healthcare, industry, and even our homes.

In smart homes, IoT makes life easier by letting people control their lights, locks, and even security cameras from a single device (Sayeduzzaman et al., 2023; Rock, Tajudeen and Chung, 2022). And hospitals? They're using IoT to monitor patients remotely. I once heard a story about a rural clinic using connected devices to track patients with chronic conditions, saving both lives and time (Anglano et al., 2024). Meanwhile, industrial IoT is driving automation in factories, cutting down human error and boosting productivity (Chhotaray et al., 2023). I had a friend who worked in manufacturing and couldn't stop talking about how these systems predicted equipment failures before they even happened!

But while IoT is revolutionizing these sectors, the more devices we connect, the more data is exposed, and with it comes increased security risks (Salam, 2024; Nayyar, Gadhavi and Zaman, 2021). We need to think about that as we get more connected each day. Figure 1 shows

Figure 1. IoT application in every field (Doshi et al., 2019)

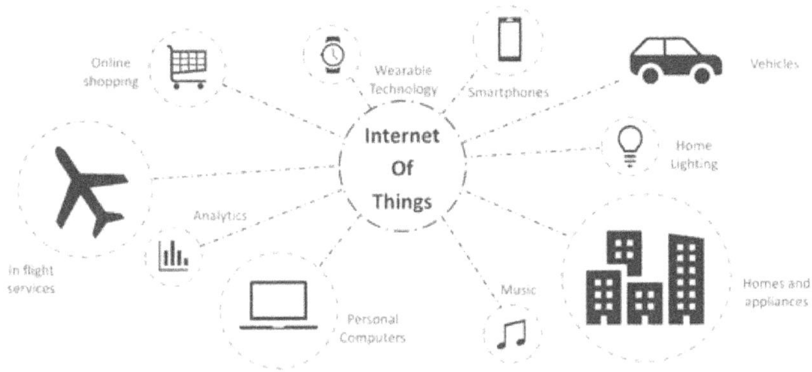

Cybersecurity Challenges in IoT

Introduce the Unique Cybersecurity Risks Posed by IoT devices, Highlighting The Increase In Attack Surfaces And The Challenges Of Securing Interconnected Devices

Securing IoT devices feels like trying to lock a house with too many doors. Each new device—whether it's a smart thermostat or an industrial sensor—adds more entry points for attackers. I remember installing a smart device at home and realizing how vulnerable it could be to my network. Every time a new device connects, another door opens for hackers. Research in 2021 showed that 98% of IoT traffic was unencrypted, exposing users to data breaches (Omolara et al., 2021; Azam, Tajwar, Mayhialagan, Davis, Yik, Ali, et al., 2023). That's scary when you think of how common these devices are becoming.

The problem is that many of these devices aren't built with security as a priority. Manufacturers often focus on keeping devices cheap and easy to use, leaving critical vulnerabilities behind. A staggering, plenty of manufacturers don't even follow basic security protocols (Anderson and Fuloria, 2010; Gaur et al., 2021). I read a story about a hacker accessing a family's smart baby monitor (Acton and Datta, 2024). It made me pause for a second; that's not just technology at risk—that's personal.

These interconnected devices pose an even greater risk when one compromised device can lead to others being attacked. Imagine a hacker breaking into a smart light bulb and then gaining access to your home security system. As IoT grows, the attack surface grows, and we're still struggling to catch up. The number of connected devices is expected to reach 38 billion by 2025 (Yalli, Hasan and Badawi, 2024), which means the risks will only increase. This isn't just an IT issue anymore—it's an urgent problem that impacts everyone. Figure 2 shows cybersecurity challenges in IoT.

Figure 2. Cybersecurity Challenges in IoT

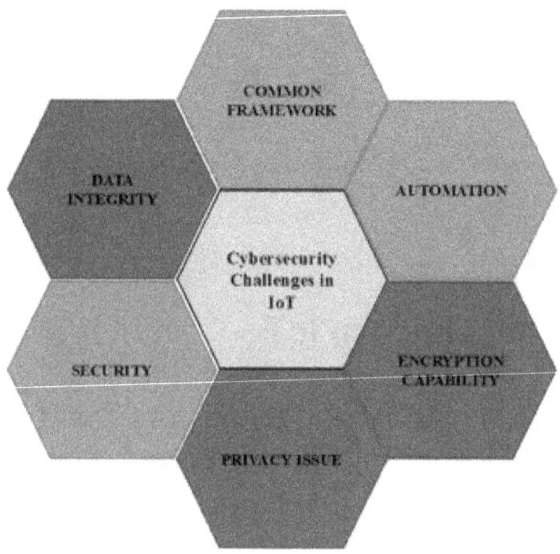

Chapter Contribution

This chapter is pertinent to the area of cybersecurity in IoT ecosystems managing device vulnerabilities and data exposure. First, it describes IoT Ecosystems general concept and functioning and outlines the information regarding its growth role in various sectors, and unique cybersecurity risks posed by IoT devices, highlighting the increase in attack surfaces and the challenges of securing interconnected devices. The chapter then investigates common vulnerabilities in IoT devices, discuss how outdated or poorly developed software makes IoT devices vulnerable to attacks, risks associated with default passwords, weak encryption, and poor user authentication practices and highlight how insufficient encryption of data transmission can lead to data breaches and unauthorized access.

Furthermore, the chapter presents key threats in IoT ecosystems, explain how compromised IoT devices are used to launch large-scale DDoS attacks. It also discusses how IoT devices often collect sensitive data (location, health data, etc.) and the risks of unprotected transmission, the importance of secure-by-design principles, including hardware security features and secure coding practices and how AI and ML are being used to detect anomalies, predict threats, and automate responses in IoT ecosystems. Lastly, the section provides a glimpse of 5G and Its Impact on IoT Security, implications of 5G technology as it expands the capabilities and risks of IoT ecosystems.

Chapter Organization

In the first section, we will cover an insight into the Overview of IoT Ecosystems and the Cybersecurity Challenges in IoT. In section 2 we go down common vulnerabilities in IoT devices. In section 3 we discuss the key threats in IoT ecosystems followed by the data exposure and privacy risks in section 4. Section 5 delves into the risk management strategies for IoT security. Section 6 will explain the emerging solutions for securing IoT devices and finally few case studies and future directions for IoT security are discussed.

2. COMMON VULNERABILITIES IN IOT DEVICES

Insecure Software and Firmware

Discuss How Outdated Or Poorly Developed Software Makes IoT Devices Vulnerable To Attacks

Outdated or poorly developed software is one of the biggest weak points in IoT devices. We've all been there. you buy a device, and it works great—until suddenly, it doesn't, because the manufacturer has neglected to provide updates. This leaves the device open to all sorts of attacks. IoT devices often lack proper security patches, meaning hackers can exploit software flaws that should have been fixed long ago (Jimmy, 2024). It's like leaving your front door unlocked, hoping no one notices. Hackers can use these old vulnerabilities to install malware, steal sensitive data, or even turn the device into a botnet for bigger attacks (Chung, 2024; Singhal et al., 2020). The situation is even worse with poorly written code that's rushed into the market. Some manufacturers prioritize speed over security, leading to software that hasn't been tested properly. Imagine owning a smart camera that, because of weak firmware, becomes a gateway for hackers into your entire home network. It sounds terrifying, but it happens. An example of this was seen with the Mirai botnet attack in 2016, where outdated IoT devices were hijacked and used to disrupt internet services across large parts of the world (Sutheekshan et al., 2024; Wen et al., 2023). Regular updates could have prevented this, but when companies fail to support their devices, they're practically handing over the keys to attackers. Another issue is that some IoT devices are hard to update, and users may not even know how to do it (Kizza, 2024). This combination of neglect and complexity creates the perfect storm for security breaches. Figure 3 shows common vulnerabilities in IoT devices

Figure 3. Common vulnerabilities in IoT devices

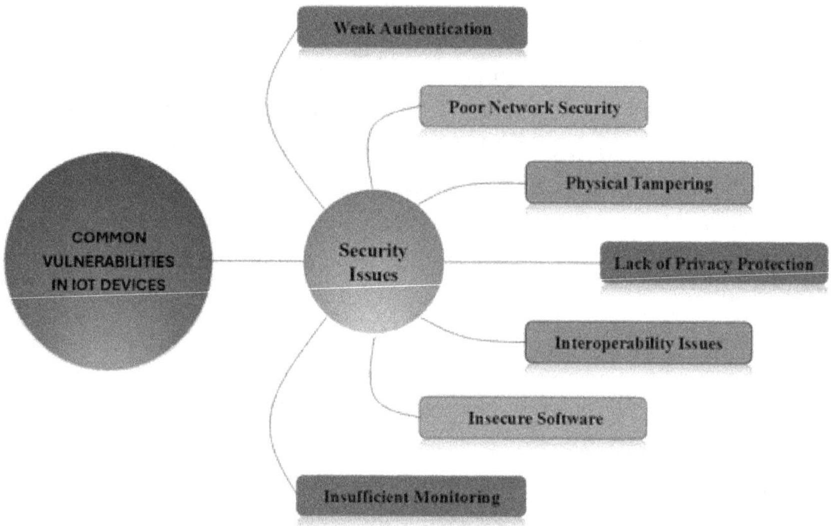

Weak Authentication Mechanisms

Explain the Risks Associated With Default Passwords, Weak Encryption, And Poor User Authentication Practices

When thinking about IoT devices, weak authentication mechanisms are a huge concern. Many of these gadgets come with default passwords—simple ones like "admin" or "12345." This wouldn't be so bad if people always changed them, but they often don't. It's like leaving the key under the doormat and expecting no one to find it (Arkko and Nikander, 2004; Hamid et al., 2023). Hackers know about these default settings and can easily exploit them, giving them a way in. Poor encryption doesn't help either. If the communication between a device and the network isn't well-encrypted, it's like sending a secret letter in an envelope anyone can open.

I've had my fair share of setting up smart devices at home, and I know the temptation to stick with whatever password came with the device. It's convenient, right? But that convenience comes with risks. Insecure user authentication means that anyone who guesses or brute forces their way in can take control of the device (Hon, 2024). Imagine someone turning off your security cameras or even accessing your data through a smart fridge. It's unnerving, especially because many people still don't realize how vulnerable they are.

Weak encryption can also mean that attackers intercept sensitive information being transmitted (Jagannath and Jain, 2024; Gouda et al., 2022). Think about the amount of personal data your IoT devices handle—whether it's health data from smartwatches or security camera footage. If a hacker taps into these, it's a real privacy nightmare. Fixing these issues starts with better encryption and stronger authentication measures, but sadly, many manufacturers prioritize ease of use over security (Manthiramoorthy, Khan and A, 2023; Ananna et al., 2023). IoT technology brings amazing convenience, but with great tech comes great responsibility. It's about being aware and taking those extra steps to safeguard what matters.

Lack of Encryption and Secure Communication

Highlight How Insufficient Encryption Of Data Transmission Can Lead To Data Breaches And Unauthorized Access

Many IoT devices have major issues when it comes to encryption and secure communication, (Singh et al., 2017), leaving them vulnerable to data breaches and unauthorized access. When data is transmitted without strong encryption, anyone with malicious intent can intercept and access it. (McIntosh et al., 2024; Fatima-Tuz-Zahra et al., 2020). Imagine sending sensitive data like personal health information from a smart wearable device, but the information isn't encrypted. Hackers can easily tap into it and use that data for identity theft or even sell it on the dark web (Hazra et al., 2024). I've personally seen how weak encryption in smart home devices makes it easy for someone to hijack a system and take control of the entire network. It's frustrating how manufacturers overlook these things.

It doesn't just stop there. When devices communicate without proper security protocols like HTTPS or secure sockets layer (SSL), the information flowing between the device and the server can be intercepted (Anh, Mutaher and Bijalwan, 2024). A case study I read once showed how attackers took advantage of a lack of encryption in baby monitors, allowing strangers to listen in or even speak through the monitor. Imagine the shock and fear of parents realizing their supposedly safe monitor was wide open to strangers. That real-world risk is too high for the convenience these devices bring.

The lack of secure communication channels in IoT is not just careless—it's dangerous. Data flowing in plain text can expose people's private information and make devices easy targets for hackers (Lee, 2024; Hossain et al., 2024). With so much sensitive information passing through IoT devices, manufacturers must step up and prioritize strong encryption methods (Boisrond, Tardif and Jaafar, 2024). Unfortunately, too many of them fail to do so.

3. KEY THREATS IN IOT ECOSYSTEMS

Botnets and Distributed Denial of Service (DDoS) Attacks

Explain How Compromised IoT Devices are used to launch large-scale DDoS attacks (e.g., the Mirai botnet)

It's strange to think that everyday devices like security cameras and smart refrigerators can cause chaos, but it's happening. Compromised IoT devices are a growing concern, and botnets like Mirai are a prime example. I remember hearing about the Mirai botnet back in 2016—someone on a tech podcast called it "an army of appliances." (Kambourakis et al., 2019; Lim et al., 2019) That's essentially what it was. hackers took control of IoT devices, many with weak passwords, and used them to launch a massive Distributed Denial of Service (DDoS) attack (Salim, Rathore and Park, 2019). Imagine being the victim, with your website or service crushed under an overwhelming flood of traffic, all thanks to compromised IoT gadgets.

What makes IoT devices perfect targets is how easy they are to exploit (Canavese et al., 2024; Gopi et al., 2021). Many of these devices run on outdated software, or users forget to change default passwords. Hackers scan for vulnerable devices, infect them with malware, and suddenly, your smart toaster is part of a cyber army. That's how Mirai caused some of the biggest internet outages ever, affecting platforms like Twitter and Netflix (Anh and Nakamura, 2024).

What's frustrating is how fast these attacks can escalate. Once the devices are hijacked, they can be remotely controlled to direct traffic toward a single target (Suomalainen et al., 2024; Alkinani et al., 2021). The scale is terrifying tens of thousands of devices working together can knock down even the most secure sites (Constantin, 2016; Azam, Tan, Pin, Syahmi, Qian, Jingyan, et al., 2023). Honestly, I wonder why we're still struggling with basic security hygiene like updating passwords. With the rise of IoT, DDoS attacks might only get worse unless we smarten up.

Data Breaches and Privacy Violations

Discuss the Risks Of Unauthorized Data Collection, Data Exposure, And The Violation Of User Privacy Through IoT Devices

The rise of IoT devices, from smart thermostats to wearable fitness trackers, has brought convenience but also serious privacy risks (Satpathy et al., 2024; Alex et al., 2022). Unauthorized data collection happens more often than we might think. When I got my first smart speaker, I was amazed by its ability to recognize my voice. But it didn't take long before I wondered what else it was hearing—and more importantly, who else could be listening. IoT devices often collect data without explicit user consent, leading to massive privacy breaches (Jiang *et al.*, 2024; Waheed et al., 2024).

Imagine your conversations, daily routines, or health data being exposed. It's unsettling but not far-fetched. Hackers target these devices because they are often poorly secured, leaving sensitive information vulnerable (Kavitha et al., 2024; Dogra et al., 2021). In 2016, the Mirai botnet attack, which exploited weak IoT security, exposed how easily these devices could be compromised (Hatem, 2024). Even worse, the data collected is sometimes sold or misused, violating user privacy in ways many of us never consider.

I've had friends who swore off smart gadgets after hearing how easily their data could be leaked or intercepted. It's understandable—once you realize how much personal information is up for grabs, it's hard to shake the worry. The bigger issue is that the more devices we adopt, the more entry points we create for cybercriminals. Every smart bulb or doorbell is a potential breach waiting to happen. The risks are real, and the consequences can be devastating.

Physical Attacks and Device Tampering

Explore the Threats Of Physical Manipulation of IoT devices in Smart Cities, Healthcare, And Other Environments

Physical attacks on IoT devices pose serious risks, especially in smart cities and healthcare settings (Pastorek and Tundis, 2024; Chesti et al., 2020). I've seen this first-hand in smart city projects, where sensors are often installed in public spaces, making them easy targets for tampering. Imagine how a simple act of tampering with a traffic sensor could cause massive confusion, potentially leading to accidents. In healthcare, it's even more alarming. A tampered device, like an insulin pump or a heart monitor, could mean life or death for someone. These devices, often small and easily accessible, are vulnerable to direct physical manipulation, which makes security a constant concern.

I remember reading about a case where a smart lock system in a residential building was hacked through physical access (Caballero-Gil et al., 2023; Sharma et al., 2021). The attacker bypassed encryption by tampering with the device, compromising the entire security system. It's unnerving how easily these devices, meant to make life easier, can be turned against us. In the healthcare sector, it's terrifying to think that an attacker could change a medical device's settings just by physically accessing it.

The complexity increases when you think about the wide range of IoT devices we interact with daily. It's not just about big attacks; even small, unnoticed tampering can snowball into major problems. With smart devices connected everywhere, the chances of unnoticed tampering grow, which leaves us wondering how much we can truly trust the tech we rely on. Figure 4 shows other threats for IoT system.

Figure 4. Key threats in IoT ecosystems

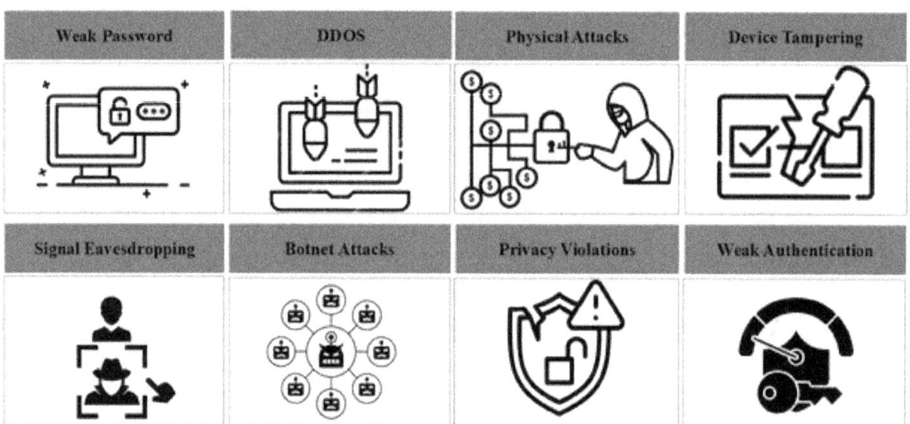

4. DATA EXPOSURE AND PRIVACY RISKS

Data Collection and Transmission Risks

Explain How IoT devices often collect sensitive data (location, health data, etc.) And the risks of unprotected transmission

Data exposure and privacy risks in IoT ecosystems often come down to how our personal information (Kolevski and Michael, 2024; Muzafar and Jhanjhi, 2019) is handled, especially when IoT devices collect sensitive data like location, health metrics, or even household activity patterns. My friend recently installed a smart thermostat, only to find out that it constantly tracks when they're home or away. These devices, often seen as conveniences, quietly gather a wealth of data that could become a privacy nightmare if not managed correctly. Health devices, for instance, collect deeply personal health information—everything from heart rates to sleep patterns—which, in the wrong hands, could be exploited for insurance purposes or even identity theft. What concerns me most is how often this data is sent over unencrypted networks. It's like sending a postcard in the mail; anyone who intercepts it can read it. When these transmissions lack proper encryption, it leaves the door wide open for cybercriminals to intercept sensitive information.

Moreover, IoT devices tend to communicate with external servers and other devices, constantly transmitting this sensitive data (Ari et al., 2019; Brohi et al., 2020). I've seen cases where this information was leaked because of insecure communication channels or poorly designed APIs, leading to massive breaches (Gubbi et al., 2013; Manchuri et al., 2024). Unfortunately, many IoT manufacturers don't prioritize security, leaving these devices vulnerable (Maiwada et al., 2024). It's not paranoia—these are real, pressing concerns that need more attention from both consumers and companies. Honestly, we've all grown so used to the convenience of these gadgets that we often forget the trade-offs in privacy and security. Figure 5 shows data exposure and privacy risks in IoT

Figure 5. Data exposure and privacy risks in IoT

Overview	IoT refers to interconnected devices exchanging data over the internet. It includes everything from smart home devices to industrial sensor
Key Privacy Risks	Unauthorized Access: Poor security can allow hackers to access devices and the data they store. Data Leaks: Weak encryption can expose sensitive user information during transmission
Common Data Exposure Scenarios	Unencrypted Communication: Data sent between IoT devices and cloud servers can be intercepted. Outdated Software: Devices running old software versions are vulnerable to attacks.
Impact of Data Exposure	Identity Theft: Stolen personal data can be used for fraudulent activities. Loss of Confidentiality: Sensitive information about health, location, or financial details can be leaked.
Mitigation Strategies	Strong Encryption: Ensuring data is encrypted during transmission and storage. Regular Updates: Keep devices updated with the latest security patches.

Inadequate Data Storage and Management

Discuss the Risks Of Improper Data Storage, Where Sensitive Data Is Left Vulnerable To Breaches Due To Insufficient Protection

Improper data storage has become a serious issue, and I've seen firsthand how businesses can leave themselves vulnerable to attacks. In one of my previous jobs, we used a simple, outdated storage system for customer data—nothing fancy, but it got the job done. At least, we thought so. Until we were hit with a breach. Customer information, including personal details and financial records, was exposed. I remember how shaken our team was, realizing our weak data management practices were at fault. This kind of risk often comes from relying on weak encryption or storing sensitive data in places easily accessible to attackers.

Poorly managed storage systems allow unauthorized access, and that's where it gets dangerous. You wouldn't leave your front door unlocked in a high-crime neighborhood, but that's exactly what happens when organizations overlook securing their data properly. Personal data, financial details, and even trade secrets can be at risk when companies don't take storage seriously.

The impact of this is huge. Not only do breaches lead to financial losses, but they destroy trust with customers, something that's much harder to rebuild (Keller, 2024; Kumar et al., 2021). The real-world consequences are there, staring us in the face, yet so many organizations still stick to weak protection methods, often due to the cost of upgrading systems (Brotherston, Berlin and Reyor, 2024; Jun et al., 2024).

It's crucial to recognize that inadequate storage isn't just an IT problem—it affects lives, relationships, and reputations. Companies need to start prioritizing how they handle sensitive data if they want to avoid being tomorrow's headline.

Lack of User Control over Data

Explore How Users Often Have Limited Control Over What Data Is Collected And How It Is Shared, Leading To Privacy Concerns

It's a bit unsettling when you realize how much of your personal information is floating around, often without your full knowledge or permission. These days, using apps or signing up for services means clicking "agree" to terms we hardly read. I'm guilty of it too, but it always leaves me wondering where my data goes after that. The problem is that most users don't have much control over the data collected. Companies track everything, from our location to browsing habits, all for "personalization," but really, it's also about targeted ads and profits. We lose track of who's sharing our data with third parties, and the more hands it passes through, the more at risk we are.

What's even scarier is that breaches are common, and when companies fail to protect our information, we're the ones left to deal with the fallout. You might've heard about the Facebook scandal, where millions of users had their data exposed, but there are countless other stories just like that (Jeleskovic and Wan, 2024; Babbar et al., 2021). With so little control, even adjusting privacy settings can feel like a losing battle. It's like locking one door while the windows stay wide open.

At this point, our data is practically a currency, and we're all paying the price in privacy risks. This lack of user control needs attention, but until stricter regulations catch up, we're left navigating this mess, crossing our fingers that our data isn't the next to be exposed.

5. RISK MANAGEMENT STRATEGIES FOR IOT SECURITY

Secure Device Design and Development

Emphasize the Importance of Secure-By-Design Principles, Including Hardware Security Features And Secure Coding Practices

When I started exploring IoT security, one thing became clear. designing secure devices from the ground up is crucial. Secure-by-design isn't just some buzzword – it's a necessity. The hardware needs to be tough, right from the manufacturing process. Built-in security features, like trusted execution environments and secure boot processes, can prevent bad actors from tampering with the device. But it doesn't stop there. Secure coding practices, though often overlooked, are just as vital. I've seen projects where developers were more focused on the user interface than the security behind the scenes. The problem? Vulnerabilities get embedded into the code. That's why code audits, encryption, and regular updates are essential.

I remember talking to a fellow researcher who once worked on an IoT home security system. It sounded impressive until we discussed security. A tiny flaw in the device's coding almost allowed unauthorized access. This experience was a wake-up call, showing how minor lapses in coding can lead to significant breaches (Lee et al., 2024; Sindiramutty et al., 2024). You might not think about hardware and coding as connected, but they must work together seamlessly to block these threats. Another thing that's often ignored is updating devices after they've been deployed. It sounds basic, but it's alarming how many manufacturers fail at this, leaving devices open to attacks.

The real-world stakes are high – think about connected medical devices, where lives are on the line if something goes wrong. We can't afford to cut corners here.

Strong Authentication and Access Control

Highlight the Need For Robust Password Policies, Multi-Factor Authentication, And Role-Based Access Control For IoT Devices

When it comes to securing IoT devices, you can't just rely on basic measures anymore. Passwords are still used, but they can't be weak or reused across multiple devices. A strong password policy can be the first line of defence, but it's not enough alone (Harmening, 2025; Gautam et al., 2024). I learned that lesson the hard way when I used the same password for both my smart thermostat and my social media account. Guess what? One small breach exposed my entire home system!

This is where multi-factor authentication (MFA) steps in, adding a layer of security (Ashitha et al., 2024; Mishra et al., 2024). Imagine you're logging into a smart camera, and after typing your password, you need to approve a notification on your phone. This small step makes a big difference, preventing unauthorized access even if the password is compromised.

Access control is another key part of IoT security. Using role-based access control (RBAC) means only certain people can access specific devices (Maulina and Rasjid, 2024; Seng et al., 2024). I remember reading about a company that used IoT sensors in its factory, and employees only had access to the devices relevant to their roles. It's like having a security pass for different parts of a building—only the right people get in.

The importance of securing these devices feels urgent, given how easy it is to overlook them. I've seen friends set up IoT devices, like smart doorbells, without thinking much about access settings, only to regret it when security issues arise. We need to be proactive before it's too late. Figure 6 shows risk management strategies for IoT security.

Figure 6. Risk management strategies for IoT security

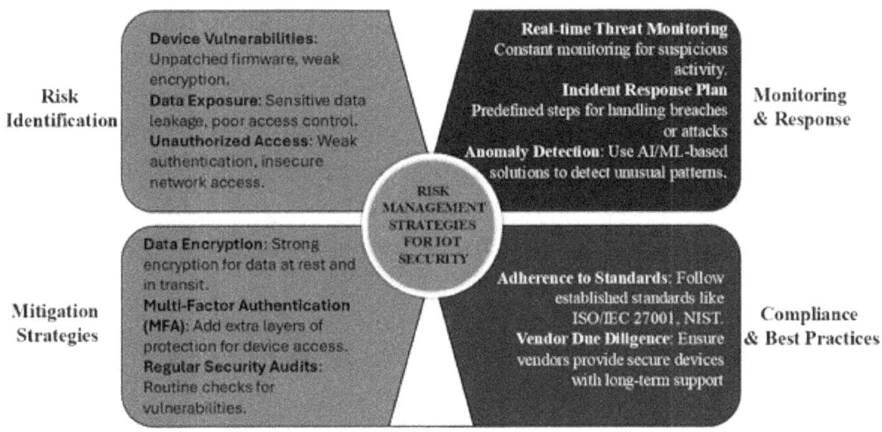

Encryption and Secure Communication Protocols

Explain the Use of Encryption For Securing Data In Transit And Storage, Ensuring That Communications Between Devices Remain Protected

Encryption plays a key role in securing data in IoT systems, both while it's being transmitted between devices and when it's stored. Without encryption, the data exchanged between IoT devices, such as health monitors or home security systems, could be intercepted by unauthorized parties (Popoola et al., 2024; Ahmed et al., 2024). Imagine wearing a fitness tracker which you think is protecting your medical data but later suddenly find that somebody found your way into the health data. This is precisely the kind of exposure encryption was designed to eliminate. Encryption works by scrambling the data during transmission, preventing it from being readable (Mehta et al., 2022; Hussain et al., 2024) if ever intercepted by a third party without the proper decryption keys.

Not only does data in motion need to be encrypted, but so does stored data. But what about the data stored on your smart home hub? Were that data to leak — well, then a couple of bursts of you being home or away might indicate when your parents are around. Storing through encryption allows you to keep this sensitive data locked down.

Additionally, they have secure communication protocols, such as TLS (Transport Layer Security), ensuring the devices can talk to each other securely without introducing vulnerabilities (García et al., 2023; Sindiramutty, Jhanjhi, Tan, Khan, et al., 2024). If not these protocols then different attacks for example eavesdropping and man-in-the-middle hacks may occur where the intruder intercepts the communication, to prevent such kinds of events these mostly use Security Protocols (Alaba, Madu and Musa, 2024). But even in this world of everything just being there, security obfuscates almost all aspects to ensure our devices are not hanging open.

6. EMERGING SOLUTIONS FOR SECURING IOT DEVICES

Artificial Intelligence (AI) and Machine Learning (ML) in IoT Security

Machine Learning (ML) and Artificial Intelligence (AI). it is very apparent that AI / ML has become the new series of buzzwords in securing IoT devices. What I am going around is how these technologies can think like humans when considering finding and answering threats. Where they are even used today is the ability to detect non-standard device behavioural patterns thanks to AI and ML, which is very important when monitoring multiple IoT devices (Ramya, 2024). It then takes the next few hundred transactions and works out what constitutes normal or legitimate behaviour and, thereafter, within milliseconds can identify anything that deviates as they do. I have seen cases where AI (not to be confused with ML) predicted security breaches before they took place and organizations were able to act on top of their toes. It is like that little voice in your head saying that something's not right — except here, it is the machine speaking to you.

And the best part is that AI can predict threats by analyzing far more data than a human ever could (Ajala and Balogun, 2024; Sindiramutty, Tan, Shah, Khan, et al., 2024). Another article stated that AI models were being utilized to notice patterns from previous attacks which in turn helps these security measures act as more intelligent (Tyagi, Kumari and Richa, 2024). Automation is your friend. AI can thereby be more proactive in intervention where, rather than waiting for someone to contain a potential breach (Schreiber and Schreiber, 2024), AI itself interrupts the spread of harm, potentially turning better models. Kind of cool to see machines do the work, like it is part of the line-up.

Machine learning also excels at improving answers over time. In essence, this amounts to training the system to improve over time concerning every problem it is faced with. There is edge processing that can be used to identify incoming malicious packets before the information reaches any sort of parsing when relevant new traffic initiates or occurs, but it opens stands with which nefarious exploits can take place. Figure 7 shows emerging solutions for securing IoT devices.

Figure 7. Emerging solutions for securing IoT devices

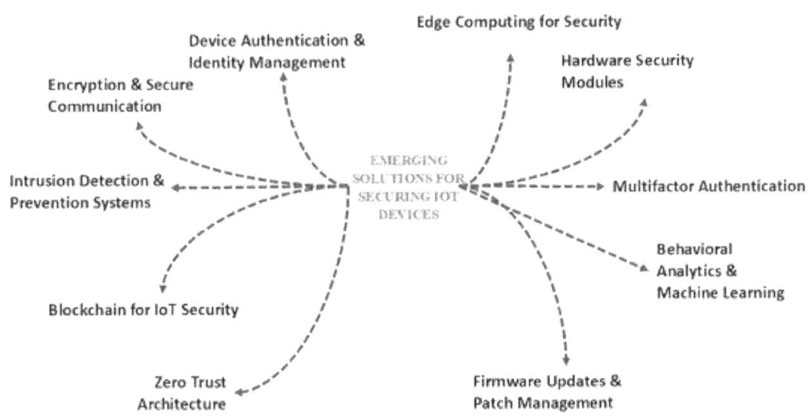

Blockchain for IoT Security

Yet, Blockchain is turning out to be a great saviour for smart connected devices' security. The more devices are on the internet, the riskier it is to use these and have your data stolen or altered. One way could be to secure these networks by recording information that cannot be easily tampered with, enforcing a level of trust that the conventional systems have been lacking (Jadon et al., 2024). I particularly remember a use case for which I read about using Blockchain to monitor shipments with IoT sensors. The data from each point was then placed on the blockchain, which helped to ensure that it could not be manipulated. The idea seemed so obvious, so natural that they were struck by a lightbulb moment — deploying blockchain to protect how data journeys across devices.

Additionally, the distributed nature of blockchain technology further dampens an attacker's chances of success (Ibrahim and Al-Haija, 2023). Rather than there being only one vulnerable central system, the data is distributed among numerous nodes, which makes it significantly harder for it to be tampered with. It is like a burglar that must try to crack many strong safes together, instead of just one.

In a similar vein, blockchain secures data exchanges among IoT devices as it uses encryption to protect whole the block of data that is exchanged (Sasikumar et al., 2024; Sindiramutty, Tan and Wei, 2024). This is why any conversation of a smart fridge chatting up a power grid or connected medical device sending private patient data home must happen with everything on total lockdown.

What is particularly interesting for me are the live protection aspects of the blockchain. It is one among many systems designed to prevent unauthorized modifications, which sits in contrast to the traditional solutions that detect breaches only after they occur. This is like having a security guard scrutinizing every transaction. This is FAR beyond hacks — we are talking about peace of mind. A must-have tech in the era of a world where your devices are listening, watching and collecting data.

IoT Device Identity and Access Management

The challenge we face is securing the networks through managing identities in the case of IoT devices. Just try to think about managing every device in your house from connecting and traffic on the same SSID that you trust. IoT device identity and access management (IAM), but for everything. It is a process to ensure that only legitimate devices communicate in IoT ecosystems. As more devices arise, this has become increasingly important.

Fortunately, several up-and-coming technologies make the process easier, especially for authentication. Public Key Infrastructure (PKI) and other device authentication tools are being ported across to IoT networks. PKI issues distinct keys to devices to attest their identity before entering the network (Dhar et al., 2023; Aruna and Sahayadhas, 2024). Zero Trust Architecture (ZTA) is an interesting tool, while not trusting any device just like without reason no matter where it comes from (Alquwayzani and Albuali, 2024; Sindiramutty, Jhanjhi, Tan, Khan, Shah, Yun, et al., 2024). The end device is only let through once it has established what it is, which happens each time it attempts to connect.

I also came across device attestation which examines the internal state of the device to be connected and only then allows them. It is akin to a short healthcare check before having a guest come in-house. Moreover, the rise of OAuth2-based token systems. A token-based system dispenses temporary tokens to grant access without enabling unauthorized re-entry in the long term. What is exciting about these prospects is that they are promising thus far to make IoT secure without limiting any functionality of our connected devices (Shen et al., 2022).

7. CASE STUDIES

Case Study 1. IoT Botnet Attack in Smart Homes

Analyze a Real-World IoT Botnet Attack In Smart Homes, Discussing How Vulnerabilities Were Exploited And The Impact Of The Attack

When smart home devices get caught up in IoT botnet attacks, it's more personal than we often think. I remember hearing about the Mirai botnet attack in 2016. Hackers exploited common vulnerabilities in smart home devices like cameras and routers—simple things like default passwords that were never changed (Yamamoto, Fukushima and Yamaguchi, 2024). It felt close to home because many of us have those same devices. Once compromised, these devices became part of a botnet, launching a massive DDoS attack that disrupted large sections of the internet (Mims, 2025).

I couldn't help but think, "Wow, my devices could be part of something like this." Smart homes are designed to make life easier, but they can also open doors to malicious attacks. The attackers in the Mirai case simply scanned for vulnerable IoT devices and then hijacked them into their network (Vysakh and Binu, 2020).

What struck me most was the sheer scale of the attack. Millions of devices were used, and it all stemmed from weaknesses in everyday smart gadgets. This botnet didn't just affect big companies—it disrupted lives by taking down key online services (Hon, 2024a). Looking at it now, it's clear that smart homes are prime targets for these kinds of attacks, and the impact reaches much further than most of us realize.

Case Study 2. Healthcare IoT Security Breach

Provide an Example of a Healthcare IoT Security Breach Where Patient Data Was Compromised, And Explore Lessons Learned From The Incident

In 2017, St. Jude Medical, a manufacturer of heart devices, became the centre of a healthcare IoT security breach that revealed just how vulnerable medical devices could be (Haider et al., 2019). Their implantable cardiac devices, which included pacemakers, were found to have security flaws that allowed hackers to potentially alter the device's settings, putting patients' lives at risk (Patel and Makaryus, 2021; Sindiramutty, Tan, Goh, Balakrishnan, Hamzah and Akbar, 2024). Imagine the horror of patients realizing that a device meant to save their lives could be turned into a weapon. Personal data, such as patient health records, was also at risk, exposing sensitive information to attackers.

The incident forced the healthcare sector to confront the fact that connected medical devices need robust security. St. Jude Medical issued a software patch to address the vulnerabilities, but the damage to public trust was already done. From this breach, we learn that regular security updates and strong encryption are essential for IoT healthcare devices. I remember hearing about this case and thinking about how we sometimes trust technology without questioning how secure it is. In a field like healthcare, where lives are literally on the line, security shouldn't be an afterthought.

It's unnerving to think that such breaches can happen, but it's also a wake-up call for the entire industry. Manufacturers must prioritize patient safety over speed to market, and hospitals need to be vigilant in monitoring devices (Cichosz et al., 2020). The consequences of neglecting these lessons are just too severe to ignore.

Case Study 3. Industrial IoT Security Solutions

Highlight How an Industrial Organization Secured its IoT Network Using Advanced Security Measures and Mitigated Potential Threats

Securing an industrial IoT network can feel like defending a high-tech fortress. One manufacturing company learned this the hard way when they faced frequent threats targeting their connected devices. They realized that relying on basic security wasn't enough anymore. So, they turned to advanced solutions, starting with network segmentation. By breaking up their IoT environment into smaller, isolated networks, they could keep sensitive data separate from less secure areas, reducing the attack surface (Sicari et al., 2014; Azam et al., 2023). I remember thinking about how smart this was—like putting valuable items in a locked drawer, instead of just hiding them in a big open room.

Then came encryption. They ensured all communication between IoT devices was encrypted, making it nearly impossible for hackers to intercept sensitive data. But even that wasn't the end of the story. They added multi-factor authentication for all users accessing the system, which was another layer of defence (Bamashmos, Chilamkurti and Shahraki, 2024). It reminded me of how I always double-check my door locks at home. It may seem like overkill, but the extra step adds peace of mind.

What's more, they set up real-time monitoring to catch any suspicious activity as it happened. This allowed them to react immediately to any threats before serious damage occurred. With all these measures in place, they were able to mitigate potential threats effectively. It's like they turned their IoT system into a well-guarded fortress.

8. FUTURE DIRECTIONS FOR IOT SECURITY

5G and Its Impact on IoT Security

Now that 5G is not just faster internet but has potential security risks (Ahmed, Alam, Afrin, Rafa, Taher, et al., 2024), it fundamentally changes the way businesses should consider security in IoT ecosystems. What 5G does, and that's about to essentially hit the market, is it brings very high-speed capacity and massive connectivity. Great for advancing technology, but it also means a lot of potential security risks very quickly (Kaur and Joseph, 2024; Azam, Dulloo, Majeed, Wan, Xin and Sindiramutty, 2023). One is the fact that as more and more devices keep communicating, it makes security cumbersome because then hackers have a wide attack surface which they could explore to exploit the numerous vulnerabilities.

At the end of 2025, there will be more than 75 billion active IoT devices (Vallabhaneni, 2024). That is a considerable number of gateways that can be targeted by cybercriminals. With the rise of interconnected devices, it becomes imperative to secure each device individually. What are the probable consequences of such devices being set up incorrectly, it can result in data leaks and privacy concerns.

It will also support ultra-reliable low-latency communications – a must for key applications like autonomous driving. But this dependence on real-time connectivity ups the ante. If a security hack comes then huge life losses may occur in such kind of accidents. 5G operates with a speed which means that the security threats can spread within seconds therefore instant response from the security team is required (Dwivedi et al., 2021). Figure 8 show future directions for IoT security.

Figure 8. Future directions for IoT security

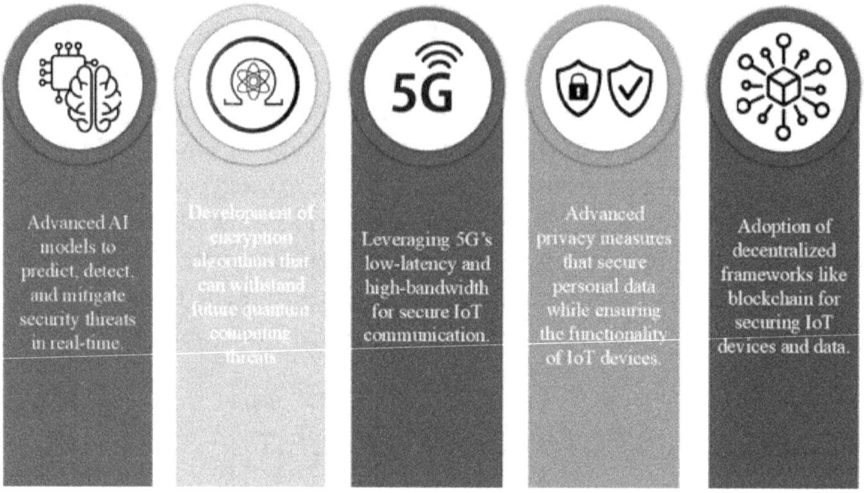

Edge Computing and Decentralized IoT Security

Edge computing is changing the way we think about IoT security It means next to the sources data is processed which allows only the important information to flow toward central servers, which in turn decreases risks of vulnerability. Think of a smart home where intelligent devices communicate with each other at the local level. When your thermostat can process temperature data without sending it up to the cloud, you're not only saving on bandwidth, but you are keeping your data more secure. In this way, the processing is localized and hence, if one device is seized by an attacker then it would give him access to limited facilities.

Decentralized security. Edge computing. Without using a single point of control mechanism, rather than having all security mechanisms reside at the gateway to control the non-malicious traffic and direct it towards downstream device(s) (Alkaabi, Gregory and Li, 2024). Sort of like sprinkling your silver into different hidey-holes so if someone discovers one hoard, there are others to find. On the other hand, devices with edge computing can share threat information in real-time and a more responsible security network be built.

Anyway, we bought a whole smart camera system for our home and local processing (read. no cloud) — I gotta be honest — has reduced my anxiety about that kind of privacy invasion in the experience. It gives me peace of mind to know that my footage is not always being uploaded to the cloud. This move towards edge computing will mean more secure, more intelligent IoT systems that divert focus back on user privacy; all while delivering improved performance.

IoT Security as a Service

Introduce the concept of IoT security solutions being offered as a service, providing continuous monitoring and protection for IoT ecosystems

As with all things IoT, the future of security for IoT will very much be wrapped up in services. This method enables businesses to concentrate on what they do best while leaving the security measures to the people who are truly experts at it. Sure, think about your small business owner who has no idea how to secure their connected devices. Choose IoT security as a service instead of owning a big internal team and getting constant monitoring and protection. Keeping the devices and data secure can ensure the safety of both devices and data, to give you peace about your asset's security.

Real-time cyber threat detection and response are of primary concern, hence most of the AI vendors provide to deliver Security as a service. Providers can address potential problems before a breach occurs. The need for such an intervention is critical as the number of threats to IoT systems is on the rise. Having somebody watching over your shoulder, ready to step in if something doesn't look right.

Additionally, service-based models are far more flexible, allowing organizations to align the intensity of their security with their demands. A tech startup might be small and then grow very fast. Russell and Van Duren (2018) argue that their security service can then be updated to defend the expanding ecosystem as these devices are added.

Compliance, of course, is important (businesses will now have to grapple with data privacy and protection regulations), but at the same time, businesses must also remember that they still cannot spread themselves too thin. It addresses the above challenges effectively by utilizing security as a service to reconcile and act as a fail-safe to ensure their smooth operation.That is the trend that will drive the evolution of IoT security in years ahead, creating a conducive atmosphere for the lifecycle of devices to take place.

9. CONCLUSION

Summary of IoT Cybersecurity Challenges and Solutions

Recap the Major Vulnerabilities and Threats in IoT Ecosystems and the Strategies for Mitigating Them

The world of Cybersecurity is growing in all directions and the effect that the IoT has opened a whole wide range of targets for attackers. Unfortunately, many devices do not come with robust security features, which makes them ideal targets for attackers. Weak passwords and unpatched software enable most of these compromises, from your smart home gadgets to industrial sensors. For example, large botnets can easily take control of poorly secured devices and launch large-scale attacks. The problem is more than just a technical one; it is an emotional one. What if you woke up in the morning to a freezing house because someone had taken control of your smart thermostat?

Fortunately, solutions exist. Simply updating software regularly is one of the most important first steps in defense. Using more secure methods of authentication such as multi-factor authentication can help counter these. Furthermore, Network Segmentation. Depending on how the network is divided this will ensure that any affected cyberattack from one device does not reach the other

There is also the issue of user awareness. Training individuals about the IoT risks can inspire them to become more mindful and take the right safeguards. We can bring home the real impact of breaches by discussing actual data loss. Small security changes can make a big difference in protecting our more connected lives. As we further lay our hands on the comfort offered by IoT, it is quite necessary to embrace and take care of these challenges so that they do not hamper our data and privacy.

The Need for Continuous Vigilance and Adaptation

Emphasize the Importance of Ongoing Risk Management, Regular Updates, and Adapting to Emerging Threats in IoT Security

The importance of being alert for cyber threats to protect the IoT layer cannot be underestimated. Cybercriminal wings also evolve in an advanced direction just as technology gets developed! It's a perpetual game of cat and mouse--as soon as we get one hole plugged in, another two will open somewhere else... available to the highest bidder. It requires everyday risk control to guard against those threats and live one step ahead. We can combat such attacks by proactively considering what risks we are exposed to and patching accordingly.

Let's say you just installed a new smart security camera. At first, it seems to work smoothly — you get a sense of control while keeping an eye out on your home. However, if the manufacturer does not release updates regularly that means that the device soon after will be a vulnerable point in your security landscape. This scenario is a poignant example of why we require patching — both for devices and software that operates in IoT systems. This quick response to security patches will determine whether your system remains secure and safe from potential hackers.

Equally as important. is adaptation. The threats with which we deal right now are not the same as those of a year ago or even last month. Attackers are employing emerging technologies such as artificial intelligence and machine learning to generate novel security breaches. Because of this, IoT security ought to be a concern taken on proactively. However, both organizations, as well as individuals, must not be reactive to the current threats but rather proactive towards what can be expected in future.

In the end, it is crucial to keep updated with the most recent security trends and threats that pop up in this rapidly changing landscape. Simply putting devices in place is not enough. If we remain vigilant and adjust our strategies as necessary, together we can build a more secure IoT landscape that promotes privacy and data security in this continually evolving digital world.

REFERENCES

Acton, T. and Datta, P.M. (2024) 'Endpoint cybersecurity. When smart devices turn stupid,' *Journal of Information Technology Teaching Cases* [Preprint]. https.//.DOI: 10.1177/20438869241242142

Ahmed, S. F., Alam, M. S. B., Afrin, S., Rafa, S. J., Rafa, N., & Gandomi, A. H. (2024). Insights into Internet of Medical Things (IoMT): Data fusion, security issues and potential solutions. *Information Fusion*, 102, 102060.

Ahmed, S. F., Alam, M. S. B., Afrin, S., Rafa, S. J., Taher, S. B., Kabir, M., ... & Gandomi, A. H. (2024). Towards a secure 5G-enabled Internet of Things: A survey on requirements, privacy, security, challenges, and opportunities. IEEE Access.

Ajala, N.O.A. and Balogun, N.O.A. (2024) 'Leveraging AI/ML for anomaly detection, threat prediction, and automated response,' *World Journal of Advanced Research and Reviews*, 21(1), pp. 2584–2598. https.//.DOI: 10.30574/wjarr.2024.21.1.0287

Alaba, F., Madu, I. and Musa, H. (2024) 'Attacks, challenges, and countermeasures for an integrated IoT framework,' *Internet of Things and Cloud Computing*, 12(2), pp. 28–39. https.//.DOI: 10.11648/j.iotcc.20241202.12

Alex, S.A. *et al.* (2022) 'Deep LSTM Model for Diabetes Prediction with Class Balancing by SMOTE,' *Electronics*, 11(17), p. 2737. https.//.DOI: 10.3390/electronics11172737

Alkaabi, S. R., Gregory, M. A., & Li, S. (2024) 'Multi-Access Edge Computing Handover Strategies, Management, and Challenges. A review,' *IEEE Access*, 12, pp. 4660–4673. https.//DOI: 10.1109/ACCESS.2024.3349587

Alkinani, M. H., Almazroi, A. A., Jhanjhi, N. Z., & Khan, N. A. (2021). 5G and IoT based reporting and accident detection (RAD) system to deliver first aid box using unmanned aerial vehicle. *Sensors (Basel)*, 21(20), 6905.

Alquwayzani, A. A., & Albuali, A. A. (2024) 'A Systematic Literature Review of Zero Trust Architecture for UAV Security Systems in IoBT,' *preprint.org* [Preprint]. https.//DOI: 10.20944/preprints202403.0349.v1

Ananna, F.F. *et al.* (2023) 'Analysing Influential factors in student academic achievement. Prediction modelling and insight,' *International Journal of Emerging Multidisciplinaries Computer Science & Artificial Intelligence*, 2(1). https.//.DOI: 10.54938/ijemdcsai.2023.02.1.254

Anderson, R., & Fuloria, S. (2010) 'Who Controls the off Switch?' *2010 First IEEE International Conference on Smart Grid Communications* [Preprint]. https.//DOI: 10.1109/SMARTGRID.2010.5622026

Anglano, C. *et al.* (2024) 'The HealthTracker System. app and Cloud-Based wearable Multi-Sensor device for patients health tracking,' *Applied Sciences*, 14(2), p. 887. https.//.DOI: 10.3390/app14020887

Anh, L. D., Mutaher, H., & Bijalwan, A. (2024) 'A Robust Authentication Technique for Client–Server Secure Login,' *Wiley*, pp. 123–140. https.//DOI: 10.1002/9781394272303.ch8

Anh, S. P., & Nakamura, Y. (2024) 'A baseline investigation into the evolution and prevalence of Mirai and Hajime utilizing a network telescope,' *IEEE Access*, 12, pp. 103789–103809. https.//DOI: 10.1109/ACCESS.2024.3434555

Ari, A.A.A. *et al.* (2019) 'Enabling privacy and security in Cloud of Things. Architecture, applications, security & privacy challenges,' *Applied Computing and Informatics*, 20(1/2), pp. 119–141. https.//.DOI: 10.1016/j.aci.2019.11.005

Arkko, J., & Nikander, P. (2004) 'Weak Authentication. How to Authenticate Unknown Principals without Trusted Parties,' in *Lecture notes in computer science*, pp. 5–19. https.//DOI: 10.1007/978-3-540-39871-4_3

Aruna, E. and Sahayadhas, A. (2024) 'Blockchain-Inspired lightweight dynamic encryption schemes for a secure health care information exchange system,' *Engineering Technology & Applied Science Research*, 14(4), pp. 15050–15055. https.//. DOI: 10.48084/etasr.7390

Ashitha, U., ... (2024) 'Strengthening Cloud Security Through Multi-Factor Authentication. A Comprehensive Integration of Diverse Approaches,' *2024 International Conference on Electronics, Computing, Communication and Control Technology (ICECCC)* [Preprint]. https.//DOI: 10.1109/ICECCC61767.2024.10593923

Azam, H., Dulloo, M.I., Majeed, M.H., Wan, J.P.H., Xin, L.T. and Sindiramutty, S.R. (2023) 'Cybercrime Unmasked. Investigating cases and digital evidence,' *International Journal of Emerging Multidisciplinaries Computer Science & Artificial Intelligence*, 2(1). https.//.DOI: 10.54938/ijemdcsai.2023.02.1.255

Azam, H., Dulloo, M.I., Majeed, M.H., Wan, J.P.H., Xin, L.T., Tajwar, M.A., *et al.* (2023) 'Defending the digital Frontier. IDPS and the battle against Cyber threat,' *International Journal of Emerging Multidisciplinaries Computer Science & Artificial Intelligence*, 2(1). https.//.DOI: 10.54938/ijemdcsai.2023.02.1.253

Azam, H., Tajwar, M. A., Mayhialagan, S., Davis, A. J., Yik, C. J., Ali, D., & Sindiramutty, S. R. (2023). Innovations in Security: A study of cloud Computing and IoT. *International Journal of Emerging Multidisciplinaries Computer Science & Artificial Intelligence*, 2(1).

Azam, H., Tan, M., Pin, L. T., Syahmi, M. A., Qian, A. L. W., Jingyan, H., ... & Sindiramutty, S. R. (2023). Wireless Technology Security and Privacy: A Comprehensive Study.

Babbar, H. *et al.* (2021) 'Load balancing algorithm for migrating switches in software-defined vehicular networks,' *Computers, Materials & Continua/Computers, Materials & Continua (Print)*, 67(1), pp. 1301–1316. https.//.DOI: 10.32604/cmc.2021.014627

Bamashmos, S., Chilamkurti, N. and Shahraki, A.S. (2024) 'Two-Layered Multi-Factor authentication using decentralized blockchain in IoT environment,' *Sensors*, 24(11), p. 3575. https.//.DOI: 10.3390/s24113575

Boisrond, K., Tardif, P. M., & Jaafar, F. (2024) 'Ensuring the integrity, confidentiality, and availability of IoT data in Industry 5.0. A Systematic mapping study,' *IEEE Access*, 12, pp. 107017–107045. https.//DOI: 10.1109/ACCESS.2024.3434618

Brohi, S. N., ... (2020) 'Key Applications of State-of-the-Art Technologies to Mitigate and Eliminate COVID-19.pdf,' *TechRvi* [Preprint]. https.//DOI: 10.36227/techrxiv.12115596.v1

Brotherston, L., Berlin, A., & Reyor, W. F.III. (2024). *Defensive Security Handbook*. O'Reilly Media, Inc.

Caballero-Gil, C. *et al.* (2023) 'Research on smart-locks cybersecurity and vulnerabilities,' *Wireless Networks*, 30(6), pp. 5905–5917. https.//.DOI: 10.1007/s11276-023-03376-8

Canavese, D. *et al.* (2024) 'Security at the edge for Resource-Limited IoT devices,' *Sensors*, 24(2), p. 590. https.//.DOI: 10.3390/s24020590

Chauhan, S., Arora, R., & Kaur, G. (2024) 'Recent Industry-Defined and Domain-Specific IoT Architectures,' *Wiley*, pp. 117–140. https.//DOI: 10.1002/9781119905202.ch8

Chesti, I. A., ... (2020) 'Evolution, Mitigation, and Prevention of Ransomware,' *2020 2nd International Conference on Computer and Information Sciences (ICCIS)* [Preprint]. https.//DOI: 10.1109/ICCIS49240.2020.9257708

Chhotaray, P., ... (2023) 'Enhancement of Manufacturing Sector Performance with the Application of Industrial Internet of Things (IIoT),' in *CRC Press eBooks*, pp. 1–19. https.//DOI: 10.1201/9781003346623-1

Choubisa, M. (2024) 'IoT Devices,' *Wiley*, pp. 141–156. https.//DOI: 10.1002/9781119905202.ch9

Chung, J.-M. (2024) 'Emerging Cyber-Attacks,' in *Emerging Secure Networks, Blockchains and Smart Contract Technologies*, pp. 1–29. https.//DOI: 10.1007/978-3-031-65866-2_1

Dhar, S. *et al.* (2023) 'Securing IoT devices. A novel approach using blockchain and quantum cryptography,' *Internet of Things*, 25, p. 101019. https.//.DOI: 10.1016/j.iot.2023.101019

Dogra, V., ... (2021) 'Analyzing DistilBERT for Sentiment Classification of Banking Financial News,' in *Lecture notes in networks and systems*, pp. 501–510. https.//DOI: 10.1007/978-981-16-3153-5_53

Doshi, J., Patel, T., & Bharti, S. K. (2019). Smart Farming using IoT, a solution for optimally monitoring farming conditions. Procedia Computer Science, 160, 746–751. https.//DOI: 10.1016/j.procs.2019.11.016

Dwivedi, A.D. *et al.* (2021) 'Blockchain and artificial intelligence for 5G-enabled Internet of Things. Challenges, opportunities, and solutions,' *Transactions on Emerging Telecommunications Technologies* [Preprint]. https.//.DOI: 10.1002/ett.4329

Fatima-Tuz-Zahra, N., ... (2020) 'Proposing a Hybrid RPL Protocol for Rank and Wormhole Attack Mitigation using Machine Learning,' *2020 2nd International Conference on Computer and Information Sciences (ICCIS)* [Preprint]. https.//DOI: 10.1109/ICCIS49240.2020.9257607

García, C. R., ... (2023) 'Quantum-resistant transport layer security,' *Computer Communications*, 213, pp. 345–358. https.//DOI: 10.1016/j.comcom.2023.11.010

Gaur, L., ... (2021) 'Disposition of youth in predicting sustainable development goals using the Neuro - fuzzy and random forest algorithms,' *HCIS* [Preprint]. https.// repository.usp.ac.fj/12807/

Gautam, A., ... (2024) 'Passwords are meant to be secret. a practical secure password entry channel for web browsers,' *arXiv (Cornell University)* [Preprint]. https./// arxiv.2402.06159.DOI: <ALIGNMENT.qj></ALIGNMENT>10.48550

Gopi, R. *et al.* (2021) 'Enhanced method of ANN based model for detection of DDoS attacks on multimedia internet of things,' *Multimedia Tools and Applications*, 81(19), pp. 26739–26757. https.//.DOI: 10.1007/s11042-021-10640-6

Gouda, W. *et al.* (2022) 'Detection of COVID-19 based on chest x-rays using deep learning,' *Healthcare*, 10(2), p. 343. https.//.DOI: 10.3390/healthcare10020343

Haider, N., ... (2019) 'Cybersecurity of medical Devices. past, present, and future,' in *Springer eBooks*, pp. 811–820. https.//DOI: 10.1007/978-3-030-12281-2_100

Hamid, H. R. M. H., ... (2023) 'Two factor authentication. voice biometric and Token-Based authentication,' in *SpringerBriefs in applied sciences and technology*, pp. 27–35. https.//DOI: 10.1007/978-3-031-47727-0_4

Harmening, J. (2025) 'Security Management Systems,' in *Elsevier eBooks*, pp. 433–439. https.//DOI: 10.1016/B978-0-443-13223-0.00025-4

Hatem, A. (2024) *Profiling IoT botnet activity - Enlighten Theses*. https.//theses .gla.ac.uk/84102/

Hazra, R., ... (2024) 'Data encryption and secure communication protocols,' in *Advances in web technologies and engineering book series*, pp. 546–570. https.// DOI: 10.4018/979-8-3693-6557-1.ch022

Hon, W. K. (2024a) 'Attack vectors,' in *Edward Elgar Publishing eBooks*, pp. 158–180. https.//DOI: 10.4337/9781803923918.00018

Hon, W. K. (2024b) 'Public key infrastructure; passwords,' in *Edward Elgar Publishing eBooks*, pp. 207–233. https.//DOI: 10.4337/9781803923918.00020

Hossain, M. *et al.* (2024) 'A Holistic analysis of Internet of Things (IoT) security. principles, practices, and new perspectives,' *Future Internet*, 16(2), p. 40. https.//. DOI: 10.3390/fi16020040

Hussain, K., ... (2024) 'Threats and Vulnerabilities of Wireless Networks in the Internet of Things (IoT),' *2024 IEEE 1st Karachi Section Humanitarian Technology Conference (KHI-HTC)*, 2, pp. 1–8. https.//DOI: 10.1109/KHI-HTC60760.2024.10482197

Ibrahim, R., & Al-Haija, Q. A. (2023) 'Blockchain security measures to combat cyber crime,' in *CRC Press eBooks*, pp. 275–293. https.//DOI: 10.1201/9781003404361-15

Jadon, S. *et al.* (2024) 'Blockchain in the Electronics Industry for Supply Chain Management. A survey,' *IEEE Access*, 12, pp. 7089–7120. https.//.DOI: 10.1109/ ACCESS.2024.3351370

Jagannath, R.O. and Jain, A.K. (2024) 'Browser-in-the-middle attacks. A comprehensive analysis and countermeasures,' *Security and Privacy*, 7(5). https.//.DOI: 10.1002/spy2.410

Jeleskovic, V., & Wan, Y. (2024) 'The impact of Facebook-Cambridge Analytica data scandal on the USA tech stock market. An event study based on clustering method,' *arXiv (Cornell University)* [Preprint]. https.///arxiv.2402.14206.DOI: <ALIGNMENT.qj></ALIGNMENT>10.48550

Jiang, Y. *et al.* (2024) 'Pervasive User Data Collection from Cyberspace. Privacy Concerns and Countermeasures,' *Cryptography*, 8(1), p. 5. https.//.DOI: 10.3390/cryptography8010005

Jimmy, F. (2024) 'Cyber security Vulnerabilities and Remediation Through Cloud Security Tools,' *Deleted Journal*, 2(1), pp. 129–171. https.//.DOI: 10.60087/jaigs.v2i1.102

Jun, A. Y. M., ... (2024) 'Exploring the Impact of Crypto-Ransomware on Critical Industries. Case Studies and Solutions,' preprints.*org* [Preprint]. https.//DOI: 10.20944/preprints202409.1325.v1

Kambourakis, G.. (2019). *Botnets. Architectures, Countermeasures, and Challenges*. CRC Press. DOI: 10.1201/9780429329913

Kaur, B., & Joseph, K. T. (2024) 'Security Challenges and Solutions in 5G Networks,' *2024 IEEE International Conference on Interdisciplinary Approaches in Technology and Management for Social Innovation (IATMSI)* [Preprint]. https.//DOI: 10.1109/IATMSI60426.2024.10502490

Kavitha, T.. (2024). *Secure communication in internet of things. Emerging Technologies, Challenges, and Mitigation*. CRC Press. DOI: 10.1201/9781003477327

Keller, J. (2024) 'The Disruption of trust and trust networks. Tracing residents' struggles in the housing market,' in *˜The œurban book series*, pp. 101–138. https.//DOI: 10.1007/978-3-031-57758-1_5

Kizza, J. M. (2024) 'Authentication,' in *Texts in computer science*, pp. 215–238. https.//DOI: 10.1007/978-3-031-47549-8_10

Kolevski, D. and Michael, K. (2024) 'Edge computing and IoT data breaches. security, privacy, trust, and regulation,' *IEEE Technology and Society Magazine*, 43(1), pp. 22–32. https.//.DOI: 10.1109/MTS.2024.3372605

Kumar, M. S., ... (2021) 'Blockchain based peer to peer communication in autonomous drone operation,' *Energy Reports*, 7, pp. 7925–7939. https.//DOI: 10.1016/j.egyr.2021.08.073

Lee, J., ... (2024) 'Optical Air-Gap Attacks. analysis and IoT threat implications,' *IEEE Network*, p. 1. https.//DOI: 10.1109/MNET.2024.3382969

Lee, M. (2024). *Hacks, leaks, and revelations. The Art of Analyzing Hacked and Leaked Data*. No Starch Press.

Lim, M., ... (2019) 'Link Prediction in Time-Evolving Criminal Network with deep Reinforcement learning technique,' *IEEE Access*, 7, pp. 184797–184807. https.//DOI: 10.1109/ACCESS.2019.2958873

Maiwada, U.D. *et al.* (2024) 'Security concerns of IoT against DDOS in 5G systems,' *International Journal of Electrical Engineering and Computer Science*, 6, pp. 98–105. https.//.DOI: 10.37394/232027.2024.6.11

Manchuri, A. *et al.* (2024) 'pplication of Supervised Machine Learning Models in Biodiesel Production Research - A Short Review,' *Borneo Journal of Sciences and Technology* [Preprint]. https.//.DOI: 10.35370/bjost.2024.6.1-10

Manthiramoorthy, C., Khan, K.M.S. and A, N.A. (2023) 'Comparing several encrypted cloud storage platforms,' *International Journal of Mathematics Statistics and Computer Science*, 2, pp. 44–62. https.//.DOI: 10.59543/ijmscs.v2i.7971

Maulina, A. and Rasjid, Z.E. (2024) 'Unified Access Management for Digital Evidence Storage. Integrating Attribute-based and Role-based Access Control with XACML,' *International Journal of Advanced Computer Science and Applications*, 15(3). https.//.DOI: 10.14569/IJACSA.2024.01503131

McIntosh, T. *et al.* (2024) 'Ransomware Reloaded. Re-examining its trend, research and mitigation in the era of data exfiltration,' *ACM Computing Surveys* [Preprint]. https.//.DOI: 10.1145/3691340

Mehta, D. *et al.* (2022) 'DieRoll. a unique key generation and encryption technique,' *Journal of Applied Security Research*, 19(2), pp. 168–195. https.//.DOI: 10.1080/19361610.2022.2124589

Mims, N. A. (2025) 'The Botnet problem,' in *Elsevier eBooks*, pp. 261–272. https.//DOI: 10.1016/B978-0-443-13223-0.00014-X

Mishra, S., ... (2024) 'Mitigating the Threat of Multi-Factor Authentication (MFA) Bypass Through Man-in-the-Middle Attacks Using EvilGinx2,' *Wiley*, pp. 59–78. https.//DOI: 10.1002/9781394272303.ch5

Muzafar, S., & Jhanjhi, N. Z. (2019) 'Success stories of ICT implementation in Saudi Arabia,' in *Advances in electronic government, digital divide, and regional development book series*, pp. 151–163. https.//DOI: 10.4018/978-1-7998-1851-9.ch008

Nayyar, A., Gadhavi, L., & Zaman, N. (2021) 'Machine learning in healthcare. review, opportunities and challenges,' in *Elsevier eBooks*, pp. 23–45. https.//DOI: 10.1016/B978-0-12-821229-5.00011-2

Omolara, A.E. *et al.* (2021) 'The internet of things security. A survey encompassing unexplored areas and new insights,' *Computers & Security*, 112, p. 102494. https.//. DOI: 10.1016/j.cose.2021.102494

Pastorek, A. and Tundis, A. (2024) 'Navigating the landscape of IoT security and associated risks in critical infrastructures,' *ACM* [Preprint]. https.//.DOI: 10.1145/3664476.3669979

Patel, B., & Makaryus, A. N. (2021) 'Cardiac implantable electronic devices and cybersecurity,' *Expert Review of Medical Devices*, 18(sup1), pp. 69–77. https.//DOI: 10.1080/17434440.2021.2007075

Popoola, O. *et al.* (2024) 'An optimized hybrid encryption framework for smart home healthcare. Ensuring data confidentiality and security,' *Internet of Things*, 27, p. 101314. https.//.DOI: 10.1016/j.iot.2024.101314

Ramya, R. (2024) 'Analysis and applications finding of wireless sensors and IoT devices with Artificial Intelligence/Machine Learning,' in *Advances in computational intelligence and robotics book series*, pp. 77–102. https.//DOI: 10.4018/979-8-3693-0786-1.ch005

Rani, A., ... (2024) 'Role and Significance of Internet of Things (IoT) in Industry 4.0,' *2024 3rd International Conference on Power Electronics and IoT Applications in Renewable Energy and Its Control (PARC)* [Preprint]. https.//DOI: 10.1109/PARC59193.2024.10486519

Ravichandran, N., ... (2024) 'Comprehensive Review Analysis and Countermeasures for Cybersecurity Threats. DDoS, Ransomware, and Trojan Horse Attacks,' preprints.*org* [Preprint]. https.//DOI: 10.20944/preprints202409.1369.v1

Rock, L.Y., Tajudeen, F.P. and Chung, Y.W. (2022) 'Usage and impact of the internet-of-things-based smart home technology. a quality-of-life perspective,' *Universal Access in the Information Society*, 23(1), pp. 345–364. https.//.DOI: 10.1007/s10209-022-00937-0

Russell, B., & Van Duren, D. (2018). *Practical internet of things security. Design a security framework for an Internet connected ecosystem* (2nd ed.). Packt Publishing Ltd.

Salam, A. (2024) 'Internet of Things for Sustainability. Perspectives in privacy, cybersecurity, and future trends,' in *Internet of things*, pp. 299–326. https.//DOI: 10.1007/978-3-031-62162-8_10

Salim, M.M., Rathore, S. and Park, J.H. (2019) 'Distributed denial of service attacks and its defenses in IoT. a survey,' *The Journal of Supercomputing*, 76(7), pp. 5320–5363. https.//.DOI: 10.1007/s11227-019-02945-z

Sasikumar, A., ... (2024) 'Blockchain-Assisted Hierarchical Attribute-Based encryption scheme for secure information sharing in industrial internet of things,' *IEEE Access*, 12, pp. 12586–12601. https.//DOI: 10.1109/ACCESS.2024.3354846

Satpathy, S.. (2024). *AI for Climate Change and Environmental Sustainability*. CRC Press. DOI: 10.1201/9781003452393

Sayeduzzaman, Md., ... (2023) 'An Internet of Things-Integrated Home Automation with Smart Security System,' *Wiley*, pp. 243–273. https.//DOI: 10.1002/9781394213948.ch13

Schreiber, A. and Schreiber, I. (2024) 'Bridging knowledge gap. the contribution of employees' awareness of AI cyber risks comprehensive program to reducing emerging AI digital threats,' *Information and Computer Security* [Preprint]. https.//. DOI: 10.1108/ICS-10-2023-0199

Seng, Y. J., ... (2024) 'In-Depth Analysis and Countermeasures for Ransomware Attacks. Case Studies and Recommendations,' preprints.*org* [Preprint]. https.//DOI: 10.20944/preprints202408.2261.v1

Sharma, R. *et al.* (2021) 'Plant disease diagnosis and image classification using deep learning,' *Computers, Materials & Continua/Computers, Materials & Continua (Print)*, 71(2), pp. 2125–2140. https.//.DOI: 10.32604/cmc.2022.020017

Sicari, S., ... (2014) 'Security, privacy and trust in Internet of Things. The road ahead,' *Computer Networks*, 76, pp. 146–164. https.//DOI: 10.1016/j.comnet.2014.11.008

Sindiramutty, S. R., Jhanjhi, N. Z., Tan, C. E., Khan, N. A., Shah, B., & Manchuri, A. R. (2024) 'Cybersecurity measures for logistics industry,' in *Advances in information security, privacy, and ethics book series*, pp. 1–58. https.//DOI: 10.4018/979-8-3693-3816-2.ch001

Sindiramutty, S. R., Jhanjhi, N. Z., Tan, C. E., Khan, N. A., Shah, B., Yun, K. J., ... (2024) 'Future trends and emerging threats in drone cybersecurity,' in *Advances in information security, privacy, and ethics book series*, pp. 148–195. https.//DOI: 10.4018/979-8-3693-0774-8.ch007

Sindiramutty, S. R., Jhanjhi, N. Z., Tan, C. E., Yun, K. J., ... (2024) 'Data security and privacy concerns in drone operations,' in *Advances in information security, privacy, and ethics book series*, pp. 236–290. https.//DOI: 10.4018/979-8-3693-0774-8.ch010

Sindiramutty, S. R., Tan, C. E., Shah, B., Khan, N. A., Gharib, A. H., Manchuri, A. R., . . . Jazri, H. (2024). Ethical Considerations in Drone Cybersecurity. In Cybersecurity Issues and Challenges in the Drone Industry (pp. 42-87). IGI Global.

Sindiramutty, S. R., Tan, C. E., & Wei, G. W. (2024) 'Eyes in the sky,' in *Advances in information security, privacy, and ethics book series*, pp. 405–451. https.//DOI: 10.4018/979-8-3693-0774-8.ch017

Singh, S. *et al.* (2017) 'Advanced lightweight encryption algorithms for IoT devices. survey, challenges and solutions,' *Journal of Ambient Intelligence and Humanized Computing* [Preprint]. https.//.DOI: 10.1007/s12652-017-0494-4

Singhal, V., ... (2020) 'Artificial Intelligence Enabled Road Vehicle-Train Collision Risk Assessment Framework for Unmanned railway level crossings,' *IEEE Access*, 8, pp. 113790–113806. https.//DOI: 10.1109/ACCESS.2020.3002416

Suomalainen, J., ... (2024) 'Cybersecurity for tactical 6G networks. Threats, architecture, and intelligence,' *Future Generation Computer Systems*, p. 107500. https.// DOI: 10.1016/j.future.2024.107500

Sutheekshan, B., ... (2024) 'Evolution of Malware Targeting IoT Devices and Botnet formation,' *2024 IEEE International Conference on Computing, Power and Communication Technologies (IC2PCT)* [Preprint]. https.//DOI: 10.1109/ IC2PCT60090.2024.10486705

Tyagi, A. K., Kumari, S., & Richa, N. (2024) 'Artificial Intelligence-Based Cyber Security and Digital Forensics,' *Wiley*, pp. 391–419. https.//DOI: 10.1002/9781394303601. ch18

Vallabhaneni, R. (2024) 'Effects of Data Breaches on Internet of Things (IoT) Devices within the Proliferation of Daily-Life Integrated Devices,' *Engineering and Technology Journal*, 09(07). https.//.DOI: 10.47191/etj/v9i07.13

Vysakh, S., & Binu, P. K. (2020) 'IoT based Mirai Vulnerability Scanner Prototype,' *2020 Third International Conference on Smart Systems and Inventive Technology (ICSSIT)* [Preprint]. https.//DOI: 10.1109/ICSSIT48917.2020.9214099

Waheed, A., ... (2024) 'Zero-Day Exploits in Cybersecurity. Case Studies and Countermeasure,' preprints.*org* [Preprint]. https.//DOI: 10.20944/preprints202407.2338.v1

Wen, B. O. T., ... (2023) 'Detecting cyber threats with a Graph-Based NIDPS,' in *Advances in logistics, operations, and management science book series*, pp. 36–74. https.//DOI: 10.4018/978-1-6684-7625-3.ch002

Yalli, J. S., Hasan, M. H., & Badawi, A. (2024) 'Internet Of Things (IOT). Origin, Embedded Technologies, Smart Applications and its Growth in the Last Decade,' *IEEE Access*, p. 1. https.//DOI: 10.1109/ACCESS.2024.3418995

Yamamoto, Y., Fukushima, A. and Yamaguchi, S. (2024) 'Implementation of White-Hat Worms Using Mirai Source Code and Its Optimization through Parameter Tuning,' *Future Internet*, 16(9), p. 336. https.//.DOI: 10.3390/fi16090336

Chapter 4
Deluge of Disruption: An Introduction to DDoS Attacks

Shaveta Gupta
https://orcid.org/0009-0008-3776-8247
PGGC-11, Chandigarh, India

Jimmy Singla
Lovely Professional University, Punjab, India

ABSTRACT

In the complex world of the internet, the smooth flow of data depends on a sophisticated web of protocols. These standardized rules and procedures ensure that information is transmitted securely between computers, enabling everything from basic email exchange to complex financial transactions. However, these protocols are still susceptible to exploitation despite their importance in our digital interactions.In the background of this digital ecosystem, there are skilled individuals who, with malicious intent, look for flaws and weak points in these systems. By exploiting these vulnerabilities, they can circumvent security measures, gain unauthorized access to important systems, and compromise the confidentiality of critical data. This security breach not only endangers data integrity but also poses serious risks to individuals and organizations. One of the most disruptive consequences of such violations is the Distributed Denial of Service (DDoS) attack.

1 INTRODUCTION

In a DDoS attack, malicious actors flood a target with an overwhelming traffic volume, effectively incapacitating services and rendering them inaccessible to legitimate users as shown in Figureure 1. As we delve into the realm of cyber threats and defenses, this chapter will explore how these cunning adversaries leverage protocol

DOI: 10.4018/979-8-3693-6135-1.ch004

weaknesses to their advantage, the methods they employ to breach systems, and the profound impact of attacks like DDoS on our interconnected world.

These cyber-attacks are generated deliberately and consciously by the hacker to overwhelm the target with so much traffic that genuine users are unable to use the target resources. As a result, the services of the target(website) are inaccessible to the legitimate user.

The DDoS attack is the supreme culprit to exploit the limitations of the internet. When a popular website is not up, or the customers are deprived of access to a site, often the primary reason is a DDoS attack (Gupta et al. 2021). The rationale behind facilitating the denial-of-service attack is to overload the victim with traffic, often more than its capacity, because of which the server becomes inoperable.

Figure 1. Typical Distributed Denial of Service (DDoS) Attack

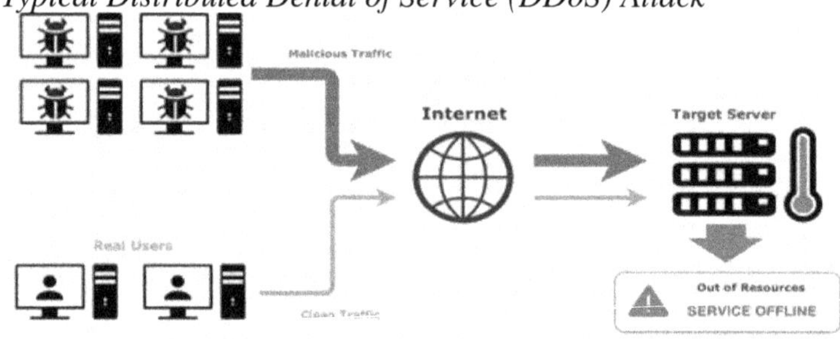

In the last two decades, DDoS attacks have increased at an alarming rate both in frequency and severity. Table 1. shows some recent DDoS attacks.

Table 1. Latest DDoS attack incidents

S. No	Date	Target	Description	Impact
1	August 2024	Cloudflare	Record-breaking attack with 71 million requests per second	Disrupted services for some clients; highlighted vulnerabilities in DDoS protection measures
2	June 2024	GitHub	Multi-vector attack including volumetric and application layer floods	Brief downtime for GitHub services; affected developer workflows and project updates
3	March 2024	Microsoft Azure	Sophisticated attack with botnets using IP spoofing	Temporary service degradation; affected cloud-based applications and services

continued on following page

Table 1. Continued

S. No	Date	Target	Description	Impact
4	January 2024	Google Cloud	Large-scale attack targeting Google's infrastructure	Slowed down some Google services; caused delays in user access to online tools
5	November 2023	Amazon Web Services (AWS)	Attack using a mix of DNS and HTTP floods	Disrupted some AWS-hosted services; impacted online platforms and businesses relying on AWS

2 CLASSIFICATION OF DDoS ATTACKS

DDoS (Distributed Denial of Service) attacks can be categorized based on their methods and targets. Here are the main categories.

1. **Volume-Based Attacks.** These attacks are discussed below.
   UDP Flood. The target is flooded with many Users Datagram Protocol (UDP) packets.
   ICMP Flood. Sends a large volume of Internet Control Message Protocol (ICMP) packets to overwhelm the target.
   Amplification Attacks. Exploits protocols like DNS or NTP to amplify the attack traffic.
2. **Protocol Attacks.** These attacks are discussed below.
   - SYN Flood. This method exploits the TCP handshake process by sending multiple SYN requests to deplete resources.
   - Ping of Death. Sends malformed or oversized packets to crash the target system.
   - Smurf Attack. Uses ICMP Echo Requests with a spoofed source address to amplify traffic.
3. **Application Layer Attacks.** These attacks are discussed below.
   - HTTP Flood. Sends HTTP requests to overwhelm web servers.
   - Slowloris. Make sure to keep connections open by sending partial HTTP requests to overwhelm server resources.
   - DNS Query Flood. Deliberately sending a high number of queries to DNS servers to disrupt their services.
4. **Hybrid Attacks.** These attacks are discussed below.
   - Combination Attacks. Utilizes a combination of volume-based, protocol, and application layer attacks to overpower multiple layers of the target's defenses.

3 MOTIVATIONS BEHIND LAUNCHING DDoS ATTACKS

DDoS attacks can be motivated by a multitude of reasons. A few important reasons are discussed below.

- **Friendly Competition**. - In the recent survey it has been noticed that the competitors are highly indulgent in provoking attacks. Merely a few minutes of a down website may cause the loss of their rivals' revenue, as well as the faith of their customers.
- **Hacktivism. -** In this approach, the concern is not about stealing data, but strongly voicing an opinion. This can be used by politicians to increase the online votes supporting their ideas on a certain topic.
- **Act of revenge. -** Sometimes feelings of revenge against some organizations motivate the attacker to bombard the attack traffic towards their server. In most cases, it has been noticed that the attackers are former employees of the organizations, and they know very well about the breaches of the software.
- **A Precursor for something bigger. -** A 600 GPS DDoS attack was hit on BBC on New Year's Eve of 2015T, and the hacker said that he intended to do testing.
- **Recognition. -** Under this, the motivation of the attacker is to prove himself in front of the cyber community.
- **Extortion/ Financial gain. -** Sometimes the ultimate motive of the attacker is the demand for money to stop the attack.

4 VULNERABILITIES THAT LEAD TO DDoS ATTACKS

There are vast weaknesses present in the network architecture that attract hackers and intruders to launch DDoS attacks (Gupta et al. 2018). As per the report by (Kaspersky et al. 2017), attacks using software system weaknesses are on the rise. The escalating usage of activities is the crucial outcome of the "Attacks with Exploits. From Everyday Threats to Targeted Campaigns" reported by Kaspersky Lab suggests estimating the danger level that exploits cause to legitimate users and corporations. The following are some of the internet characteristics that invite hackers to launch DDoS attacks.

- **Inadequate Bandwidth.** Networks with limited bandwidth can be quickly overloaded by an excessive amount of malicious traffic, which can result in service disruptions.

- **Unprotected Servers.** Servers that lack proper security measures or have misconFigureurations can be vulnerable to exploitation by attackers. This can lead to the launching of DDoS attacks or the amplification of the impact of an attack.
- **Weak Network Infrastructure.** Networks lacking adequate defenses or redundancy may be more vulnerable to overwhelming attack traffic.
- **MisconFigureured Firewalls and Load Balancers.** If the conFigureurations of firewalls and load balancers are not set up correctly, there is a risk that they will be unable to effectively block out harmful traffic or efficiently manage genuine traffic.
- **Vulnerable Applications.** Applications that cannot efficiently handle large volumes of requests may become overloaded and crash during an attack.
- **Lack of Rate Limiting.** Without rate limiting, a server may struggle to handle a large number of requests from a single IP or multiple IPs, resulting in service degradation.
- **Exploitable Protocols.** Some network protocols have known vulnerabilities that can be exploited in DDoS attacks. For example, certain amplification attacks use protocols like DNS or NTP to flood a target with traffic.
- **Unpatched Software.** Outdated software with known vulnerabilities can be exploited to gain control over systems or to launch attacks.
- **Poor Incident Response.** An inadequate or delayed incident response can significantly worsen the impact of a DDoS (Distributed Denial of Service) attack. This is because organizations may struggle to effectively mitigate the attack in real-time, leading to prolonged disruptions and potential data breaches.
- **Lack of Redundancy.** Systems that lack redundancy, such as backup servers and alternative data centers, are more susceptible to disruptions caused by DDoS attacks.

5 REPERCUSSIONS OF DDoS ATTACKS

The repercussions of this major danger may vary, but it is rapidly growing and posing new difficulties for the commercial world. The size of the attack is typically unimportant, but the frequency is crucial. DDoS attacks can result in the following outcomes. DDoS attacks may lead to the following consequences.

- Loss of Productivity
- Loss of Confidential data
- Reputation damage of a brand

- An unreachable online platform
- Huge Revenue Loss
- Loss of Customer and stakeholders' Faith
- Extra operational Costs

6 DDoS DEFENSE APPROACHES

DDoS attacks are growing exponentially, and it is a big threat in the present digital world. Researchers have developed a variety of solutions to cope with them. Some attackers, on the other hand, are clever enough to get beyond these defenses. According to (Mirkovic et al 2001) there are four approaches to dealing with attacks as shown in Figureure 2.

6.1 Attack Prevention

"Prevention is better than cure" This idiom suits well in the case of defense approaches against DDoS attacks. It is best to stop the attack at its launching stage, rather than measures taken only after the attackers attack the network. In other words, the best DDoS security approach is attack prevention. But practically, it is impossible in today's world, because of the features of openness and flexibility of the network. The attackers find new ways to enter the system. Is the application of filtering rules at the routers the only possible solution to prevent measures? However, it is extremely difficult to specify the rules that can surely discriminate legitimate from illegitimate attacks. The following are six steps that can be used against attacks.

1. Purchase additional bandwidth.
2. Build Up redundancy into infrastructure.
3. Set Up web hardware alongside DDoS attacks.
4. Install Anti-DDoS Hardware and Software units.
5. Protect DNS servers
6. Deploy a DDoS protection Appliance

Figure 2. Taxonomy of Defense Mechanisms

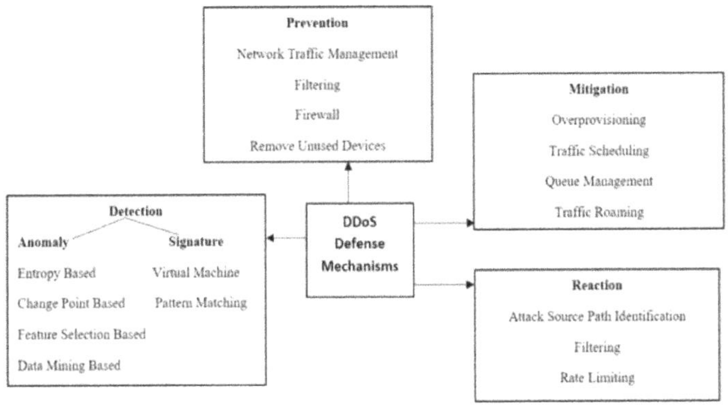

6.2 Attack Detection

Whenever the attackers attack some website or server, it's important to filter the attack flow from the usual flow so that the genuine users need not suffer. Attack detection methodologies do the same thing i.e., filter out the legitimate traffic from attack traffic. A prerequisite for attack detection is to gather enough information about the network traffic to analyze it for proper filtration. Broadly, it is categorized into two types.

- **Signature-based DDoS detection (Misuse Detection).** In this method, a list of known signatures of attacks needs to be stored in the database and then traffic is monitored based on these signatures. If a match occurs, then it generates an alarm of suspicious traffic. The accuracy of this approach is quite high. However, its major disadvantage is its inability to detect unknown attacks.
- **Anomaly-Based DDoS detection**. In this method, the system monitors the traffic data against a database containing features of normal data and any deviation from these features generates an alarm. Table 2. shows a comparison between signature-based and anomaly-based detection.

Table 2. Anomaly-Based and Signature-Based Detection Comparison

Method	*Detection Time*	*Reliability*	*Detect New Attacks*	*False Positives*	*False Negatives*	*Requirements*
Anomaly	***Vary***	***Yes***	***Yes***	***Yes***	***Yes***	***Trained Data***
Signature	***Fast***	***Yes***	***No***	***Very Low***	***No***	***Well Known Signature***

Attack detection approaches by (Bhandari et al. 2015), (Guerra et al. 2018), (Aymaan et al. 2018), (Gupta et al. 2022) aim to detect ongoing DDoS attacks. Characterization of DDoS attacks helps to discriminate DDoS attacks from genuine users. But there is not any foolproof solution till now. The researchers aim to lessen the false positive and false negative rates of detection but making them zero is near to impossible.

6.3 Attack Reaction

Once the attack has been detected by any of the methodologies then the next step is to block the source from where attack traffic is generated. Traceback is defined (Belenky et al.2003) as finding the origin of any packet sent across the internet. The categorization of traceback techniques is depicted as shown in Figureure 3 and defined below.

Figure 3. Categorization of Traceback Techniques

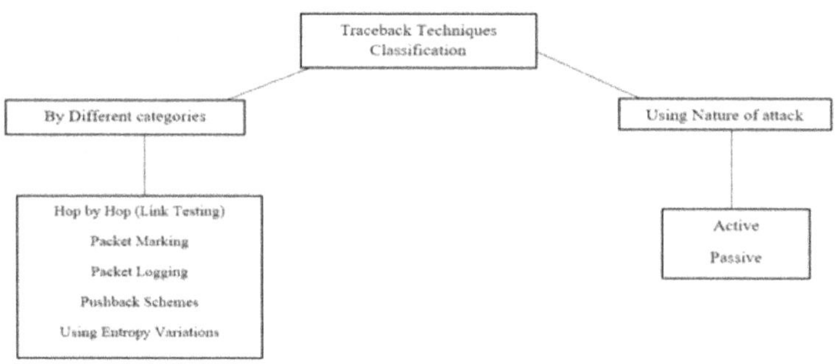

Link Testing (Hop by Hop testing). As per the name of the technique, links between the routers need to be checked. The process starts at the victim's end and then traverses backward until the source who originates the traffic is met, which then applies a mitigation method over there to block the IP that is the culprit of this attack. The condition for this method is that the attack must be active.

Messaging. The router generates ICMP messages, which are sent to the victim machine. This message contains information like the source from which it originates, destination information, and some authentication information as well. This information is used to trace back sources by the victim. ICMP messages are generated 1 for every 20000 packets to avoid congestion (Gong et al. 2005).

Packet Marking. It is sometimes referred to as a probabilistic packet marking (PPM) technique in which packets are probably marked by the routers as they pass through the internet. Marking can be done in two ways - packets are marked with the IP address of a router, second, edge marking is done on the packets. It includes the IP addresses of both nodes that connect the edge along with the distance between the nodes. The packets that are marked are selected randomly with some probability. Once the packets reach the destination end, then this marking helps to trace back to the culprit (Snoeren et al. 2002)

IP Traceback with IPsec. This method is based on the concept that the system is aware of the full topology of the network. The fundamental theory for this traceback is that if there is a secure connection between the victim and the router, and the attack packets that are identified and verified by this association, then the assumption is taken that the attack is generated further away from this router. If packets are not authenticated by this association, it indicates that there is a device in between the router and the victim who generates the traffic. So, by establishing these security protocols, one can identify routers or groups of routers responsible for the attack.

A set of evaluation metrics are needed to evaluate any of the traceback mechanisms.

- **ISP involvement.** An optimal framework for traceback should include minimum participation of ISPs because the inquiry can take a longer time. With complete cooperation, more assets might be required.
- **The count of attack packets needed for traceback.** It should be minimal. In an ideal scenario, it should be one.
- **Processing overhead.** It should be minimal.
- **Storage requirement.** To implement a traceback mechanism a certain amount of memory is needed on network devices. It should be a minimum.
- **Ease of implementation.** The Traceback mechanism could be easily executed at the application layer/network layer.
- **Scalability.** It states the total extra conFigureuration needed on the network devices to carry out the traceback method.
- **Bandwidth overhead.** Additional bandwidth that is required for the traceback mechanism should be minimal.
- **The number of functions needed to implement.** Functions needed to implement the traceback mechanism should be minimal.

- **Ability to handle DDoS attacks.** Traceback mechanism should be such that it can handle all types of malicious traffic.

6.4 Mitigation

DDoS attacks are evolving day by day and hackers are devoting enough time to make new strategies, researchers need to spend enough time to combat these attacks, proper planning is needed to analyze the attacks, learn the pattern, and corresponding strengthens up the protection techniques. The focus of this approach is to protect the target from the ongoing attack with less collateral damage and diminishing the effect of an ongoing attack. It is to be performed in four steps. detection, diversion, filtering, and analysis. Most of the existing mitigation approaches (Kaur et al. 2016), (Sachdeva et al. 2016), (Ghosh et al. 2018) are suffering from collateral damage. It is a proactive strategy. Researchers need to prepare in advance before an attack will happen. There are four phases in mitigation as shown in Figureure 4.

Figure 4. Mitigation Steps

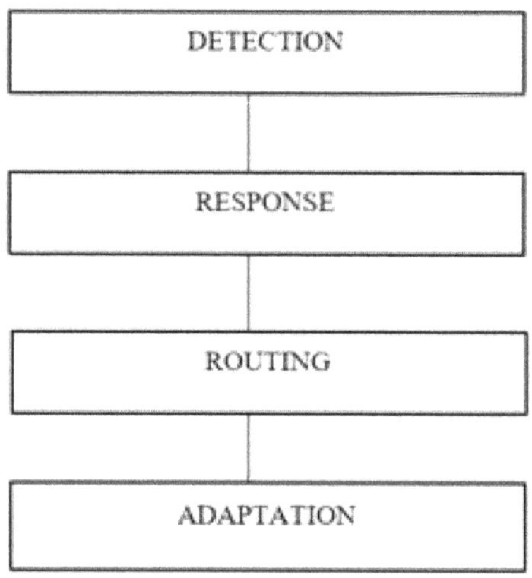

Detection. It is the most crucial step to mitigate attacks. Researchers are working in this area continuously to evolve new measures and techniques to handle these deadly internet attacks (Behal et al. 2017). The most important thing to keep in mind while developing any framework is that genuine users need not suffer i.e., minimum collateral damage should be there.

Response. The next step while developing any framework is the response stage. In case of suspicious activity, whether the traffic should be dropped, rerouted, or filtered out is decided in this phase only. So, this phase is an action phase against Flash Events/Normal traffic/DDoS attacks. Different action plans corresponding to different entities (Flash Events/Normal traffic/DDoS attack) need to be made.

Routing. When the traffic is filtered, the genuine traffic needs to be rerouted to reach a proper destination. As a result, legitimate users can continuously use the services from the server.

Adaptation. In this step patterns of DDoS attacks that were detected previously are analyzed to strengthen the mitigation process. For example, blocking of source IPs that generate bot traffic, can be done if proper traceback mechanisms can be followed.

7 GOALS OF AN IDEAL DDOS DEFENSE FRAMEWORK

An effective DDoS defense solution is which can effectively prevent the denial of the service of a victim to legitimate users. (Mirkovic et al. 2004; Kumar et al. 2007; Sachdeva et al. 2016) mentioned the following goals for an ideal defense mechanism.

- **Effectiveness.** A good DDoS detection and mitigation framework should effectively defend and provide either sufficient prevention which makes the system attack proof or an effective reaction so that the DoS effect is not observed at all. For reactive approaches, there should be a prompt and automated response to ensure that the victim does not suffer severely from the attack.
- **Completeness.** An ideal DDoS defense should be complete. It must manage every possible assault. Although completeness is the final goal, it is difficult to achieve because attackers may develop new signatures of the attack packets to bypass the existing defense solutions.
- **Minimum Collateral damage.** As discussed, the essence of DDoS defense is not to just stop the attacks but rather to ensure a smooth experience for legitimate and normal users so that they can continue receiving their services. DDoS defense solution is such that it can characterize the attack traffic and normal traffic so that the defense framework can only drop DDoS attack traffic not the legitimate traffic to avoid collateral damage.
- **Low False Positive Rates.** The DDoS defense should activate its reactive mechanism only when a DDoS attack is underway. A false positive occurs when a detective scheme detects an attack when no attack is taking place. These false positives lead to collateral damage, as they might trigger the filtering mechanism when there is no attack. It also results in extra computa-

tional overhead concerning CPU cycles, memory, and delay caused due to processing all the packets.

- **Low deployment and operational costs.** A DDoS defense is meant to permit systems to resume operations during DDoS attacks. There is an apparent economic cost of installing any commercial solution, including the costs of purchasing the hardware and software used to operate it, as well as the administrative costs of setting up new security equipment or software.

CONCLUSION

In this chapter, we presented the current state of DDoS attacks. We highlighted the modus operandi, classification, motivation, and consequences of DDoS attacks. Additionally, we explained the various stages of the defense framework, including prevention, detection, characterization, and mitigation. Finally, we mentioned the goals of a DDoS defense system to design a suitable mitigation framework.

REFERENCES

Behal, S., & Kumar, K. (2017). Detection of DDoS attacks and flash events using novel information theory metrics. *Computer Networks*, 116, 96–110. DOI: 10.1016/j.comnet.2017.02.015

Behal, S., Kumar, K., & Sachdeva, M. (2018). D-FACE. An anomaly-based distributed approach for early detection of DDoS attacks and flash events. *Journal of Network and Computer Applications*, 111, 49–63. DOI: 10.1016/j.jnca.2018.03.024

Belenky, A., & Ansari, N. (2003). On IP traceback. *IEEE Communications Magazine*, 41(7), 142–153. DOI: 10.1109/MCOM.2003.1215651

Bhandari, A., Kumar, K., Sangal, A. L., & Behal, S. (2021). An anomaly-based distributed detection system for DDoS attacks in Tier-2 ISP networks. *Journal of Ambient Intelligence and Humanized Computing*, 12(1), 1387–1406. DOI: 10.1007/s12652-020-02208-3

Chawla, S., Sachdeva, M., & Behal, S. (2016). Discrimination of DDoS attacks and flash events using Pearson's product-moment correlation method. *International Journal of Computer Science and Information Security*, 14(10), 382.

Gera, J., & Battula, B. P. (2018). Detection of spoofed and non-spoofed DDoS attacks and discriminating them from flash crowds. *EURASIP Journal on Information Security*, 2018(1), 1–12. DOI: 10.1186/s13635-018-0079-6

Gill, S. H., Razzaq, M. A., Ahmad, M., Almansour, F. M., Haq, I. U., Jhanjhi, N. Z., & Masud, M. (2022). Security and privacy aspects of cloud computing. a smart campus case study. *Intelligent Automation & Soft Computing*, 31(1), 117–128. DOI: 10.32604/iasc.2022.016597

Gong, C., & Sarac, K. (2005, May). IP traceback based on packet marking and logging. In *IEEE International Conference on Communications, 2005. ICC 2005. 2005* (Vol. 2, pp. 1043-1047). IEEE. DOI: 10.1109/ICC.2005.1494507

Gupta, S., & Grover, D. (2021, March). A comprehensive review on detection of DDoS attacks using ML in SDN environment. In *2021 International Conference on Artificial Intelligence and Smart Systems (ICAIS)* (pp. 1158-1163). IEEE. DOI: 10.1109/ICAIS50930.2021.9395987

Gupta, S., Grover, D., AlZubi, A. A., Sachdeva, N., Baig, M. W., & Singla, J. (2022). Machine Learning with Dimensionality Reduction for DDoS Attack Detection. *Computers, Materials & Continua*, 72(2), 2665–2682. DOI: 10.32604/cmc.2022.025048

Gupta, S., Grover, D., & Bhandari, A. (2018). Vulnerability analysis of existing distributed denial of service attacks defense frameworks. *Asian Journal of Computer Science and Technology*, 7(3), 62–67. DOI: 10.51983/ajcst-2018.7.3.1895

Jhanjhi, N. Z., Brohi, S. N., & Malik, N. A. (2019, December). Proposing a rank and wormhole attack detection framework using machine learning. In *2019 13th International Conference on Mathematics, Actuarial Science, Computer Science and Statistics (MACS)* (pp. 1-9). IEEE.

Jhanjhi, N. Z., Humayun, M., & Almuayqil, S. N. (2021). Cyber security and privacy issues in industrial internet of things. *Computer Systems Science and Engineering*, 37(3). Advance online publication. DOI: 10.32604/csse.2021.015206

Kaur, P., Kumar, M., & Bhandari, A. (2017). A review of detection approaches for distributed denial of service attacks. *Systems Science & Control Engineering*, 5(1), 301–320. DOI: 10.1080/21642583.2017.1331768

Kok, S. H., Abdullah, A., Jhanjhi, N. Z., & Supramaniam, M. (2019). A review of intrusion detection system using machine learning approach. *International Journal of Engineering Research & Technology (Ahmedabad)*, 12(1), 8–15.

Snoeren, A. C., Partridge, C., Sanchez, L. A., Jones, C. E., Tchakountio, F., Schwartz, B., & Strayer, W. T. (2002). Single-packet IP traceback. *IEEE/ACM Transactions on Networking*, 10(6), 721–734. DOI: 10.1109/TNET.2002.804827

Chapter 5
Cybersecurity-Enhanced Business Intelligence:
Safeguarding Business Warehouses With Integrated Security Solutions

Soobia Saeed
https://orcid.org/0000-0002-9026-6130
Taylor's University, Malaysia

Mehmood Naqvi
Mohawk College, Canada

Manzoor Hussain
Indus University, Pakistan

ABSTRACT

The purpose of this research is to improve the understanding and functionality of all Business Intelligence (BI) tools in sales and marketing teams within an organization, spanning management from upper management to operational staff. BW&BI are business warehousing and intelligence applications that would help organizations enhance the return on investment (ROI) and track operations in real-time. By giving improved analytics and actionable insights, organizations can make informed and efficient decisions. The project will implement fundamental concepts and techniques of BI in a data model built upon their organizational needs. The research emphasizes designing such an engaging and user-friendly environment that captures interest and eases access and operation of the case study. Thus, ultimately, the principal goal of this research is to build a DW and BI solution that efficiently supports both historical or structured and unstructured data.

DOI: 10.4018/979-8-3693-6135-1.ch005

1. INTRODUCTION

Business Intelligence System aims at availing the required information and knowledge to the organization to help them in better understanding as well as meeting Customer Interests, Priorities, and Needs. A BI is what a user visualizes a DW/BI system. This is mostly a browser-based application. The Organization has managed to witness some level of success in its Markets and the Services offered (Al-Sharideh and Alshammari, 2020). Currently Available Business Intelligence Data helps your organization to sharpen its effectiveness and value analysis and design its plans to meet customer interests. Business users and organizations need the ability to quickly analyze their data to identify issues, their causes, and opportunities for improvement. Once these types of analysis are identified they are expected to be widely dispersed and monitored many times to others. (Bakar and Ahmad, 2021; Gharbi and Ben, 2020; Humayun *et.al,* 2022; Khan *et.al*, 2022).

In this research we target primary sales data. Company directly involves to customer through distributor.

All this we do on Dashboard which is called QLIKVIEW.

- For visualizing data
- Data analyzing tool

Business Intelligence (BI) is a tool which is often used by large international companies with multifarious daughter companies. A properly implemented BI solution offers an insight into business-oriented content that is consolidates any other where in the enterprise thus enabling appropriate management of the metrics which would have been impossible otherwise. (Bounfour and Moussa, 2022; Chen and Zhang, 2023; Gill *et.al*, 2022; Najmi *et.al*, 2023). Notably, BI can help in making a plethora of business-related decisions starting from day-to-day initiatives to high level strategic moves. Basic operating decisions relate to aspects such as product positioning or pricing (Duan and Xiong, 2021; Hossain and Saha, 2022). Business strategy decisions portend decisions about priorities, goals and directions in the highest sense. BI convinces most when it synthesizes data generated in the industry where a company exists (Muzammal et.al, 2020; Gouda *et.al*, 2022). It is also important to note that the data warehouse holds the copy of analytical data to aid in decision support as shown in Figure 1, Figure 2.

Figure 1. Data warehouse summary

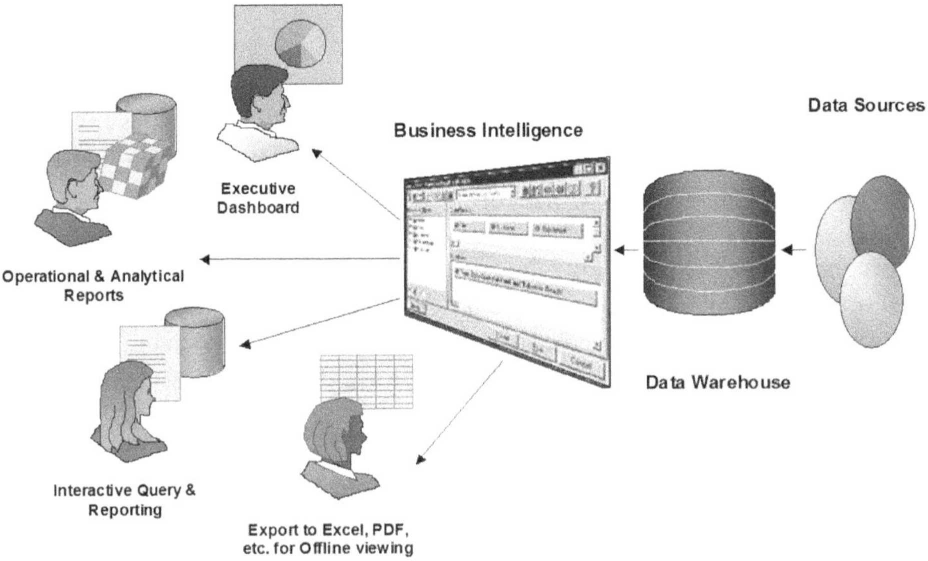

Figure 2. Data warehouse concept

2. AIM OF STUDY

The aim of study is to develop the system which enables organization to view and analyses the data on the fly through interactive dashboards and reports which identify and track the progress of their KPI's. In nutshell, the aim of study is to convert the organization's data into information. Appropriate research and contribution are approved; it can be made on a larger scale. The business environment is constantly changing, and organization need reliable, accurate and effective business information to meet consumer's need for growth and sustainability. The business environment is constantly changing, and organizations need reliable, accurate, and information to meet consumer's needs for growth and sustainability. Business intelligence is a method employed by companies to assist in analyzing and presenting data for more informed decision making.

- Design and build an excellent BI system.
- Operations on real time basis.
- Increase ROI.

3. LITERATURE REVIEW

To truly understand business knowledge (BI) and information distribution centers (DW), it is important to take a gander at the advancement of business and innovation. It is an emerging field of Information technology. BI is basically platform for business runners, but this is a tool of present advance technology (Jadhav and Jain 2020; Singhal et.al, 2020; Kok *et.al*, 2019). In previous days there is no concept of any QLIKVIEW dashboard. There are numerous business drivers in play today that are persuading organizations to set up information distribution centers. Present, steady and precise business data, they accept is basic for key and strategic choice making (Jang and Kim, 2021; Khan and Kaur, 2022; Saeed *et.al*, 2024).

Data Warehousing has been embraced by organizations as a way of aggregation of information from various different databases and support more effectively their tactical and strategic decision-making processes. In the 1970s and 1980s, the hardware was expensive, and the computing power was limited. Therefore, paper publications were used to address information demands. On the other hand, report writers were expensive to produce and mostly inflexible. It became necessary for a computer programmer to write the report writers (Saeed *et.al,* 2018; Saeed, et.al, 2019; Saeed *et.al*, 2021). A typical medium-sized enterprise would run a few large-scale mainframe-based application systems meant for business operations and data input (Kim and Lee, 2023). Data was kept in tables with rows and columns, just like today's Excel Sheets. Businesses were eager to develop eBusiness and eCommerce solutions with the intention of minimizing manpower and offering round the clock services to its customers.

At the conclusion of the 1980s, many societies transitioned from decentralized computer workstations to personal computer servers. A computer was assigned to each employee. Office programs such as Microsoft Word, Excel, and Access became widespread. (Kumar and Srivastava, 2020; Saeed *et.al*, 2017). The PC catered to the end users and enabled them to come up with their applications and present information in the manner they want which could be in either matrix or graph form. For instance, Excell spreadsheets could be easily modified whenever there are changes in the business requirements, without the intervention of the ICT department. However, the corporate information was still centralized and mostly inaccessible to the end-users (Li and Zhan, 2021; Liu and Yu, 2023; López and Gonzalez, 2020). There were two persons in business world William Inmon and Ralph Kimball, 1st person's methodology is top-down outline configuration and other one is arranged, incorporated, time variation, non-stable accumulation information use in business as strategies. They both make contrast through their mind and because of these efforts they called primary creators of Data warehousing (Mardani *et. al*, 2020; Pal and Saha, 2022; Ranjan, 2020)

"Incorporated" implies that the information is put away in reliable arrangements, naming traditions, in estimation of variables, encoding structures, physical qualities of information, or area imperatives (Sharma and Gupta, 2022; Reda and Ahmed, 2021; Ranjan and Prakash, 2023). For instance, though an association may have four or five special coding plans for ethnicity, in an information stockroom there is one and only coding. In 2003 According to Kimball information must be distributed in some aggregate data or constantly in dimensional model. He saw all information/data as warehousing tools. Inmon stores information in center tables though Kimball used this like information shop not exactly best but in their point of views they get a solution as Information distributor center transport (Singh and Prasad, 2021; Gupta and Sharma, 2022).

Definition business intelligence is the delivery of accurate, beneficial facts to the right choice makers with necessary timeframe to assist powerful decision-making. We introduce QLIKVIEW dashboard for data ware housing to provide the information and knowledge to the organization that will enable it to more clearly identify and respond to Customer Interests, Priorities and Needs (Soni and Sharma, 2020; Saeed *et.al,* 2019). Organization has registered some success in its markets and with its Services. Business Intelligence Data will help your organization to sharpen its understanding of its current effectiveness and value, and plan future initiatives to match customer interests (Zhao *et.al,* 2021; Tiwari and Kumari, 2022). DW & BI have a solution with the scalability and flexibility to grow and change as your organization wants. Data warehousing is the system of accumulating records to be saved in a controlled database wherein the information is challenge-oriented and included, time version, and nonvolatile for the guide of selection-making. Data warehouse is a system that retrieves and consolidates information periodically from the supply systems right into a dimensional or normalized statistics save. It typically keeps years of history and is queried for enterprise intelligence or different analytical activities (Zolotova and Goryunova, 2023; Saeed *et.al*, 2019).

4. METHODOLOGY

We are engaged in the active development of project DW & BI solution. It is a general term that consists of various architectures, applications, and databases. This allows access, evaluation and processing of data in real time, automatically presenting useful financial information to the corporate users.

There are some basic tools of DW& BI.

- OLTPS
- OLAP
- KPI

OLTPS. This tool used for data punching and daily transaction recording._It is characterized by a large number of short on-line transactions (INSERT, UPDATE, and DELETE). The main emphasis for OLTP systems is put on very fast query processing, maintaining data integrity in multi-access environments and an effectiveness measured by number of transactions per second.

OLAPS. This tool used for store data and time dimensions. it is characterized by relatively low volume of transactions. Queries are often very complex and involve aggregations. For OLAP systems a response time is an effectiveness measure. OLAP applications are widely used by Data Mining techniques as mentioned in Figure.3.

Figure 3. Business data warehouse OLTP

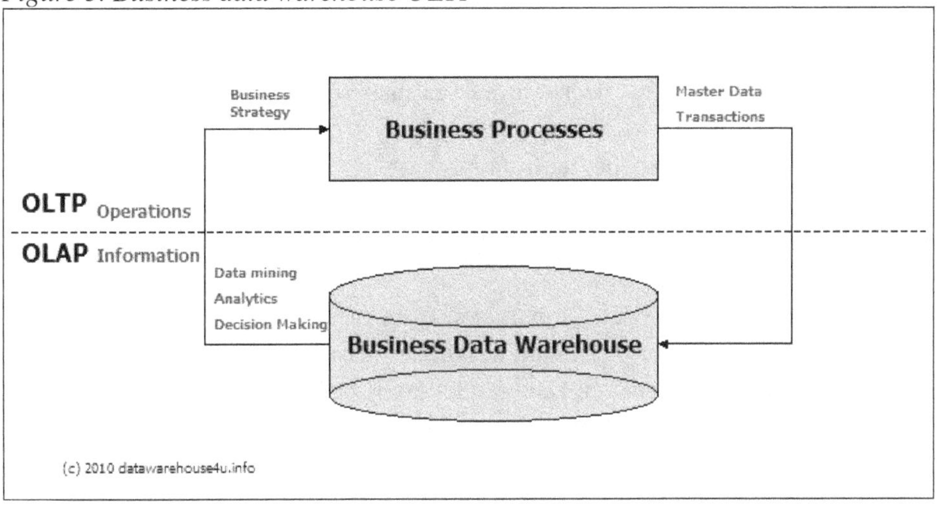

KPI, this tool used for data representation in BI. A business may have as one of its Key Performance Indicators the percentage of its income that comes from return customers. A Key Performance Indicator (KPI) is a measurable value that demonstrates how effectively a company is achieving key business objectives. Organizations use KPIs to evaluate their success at reaching targets as mentioned in Figure.4.

Figure 4. Key Performance Indicator (KPI)

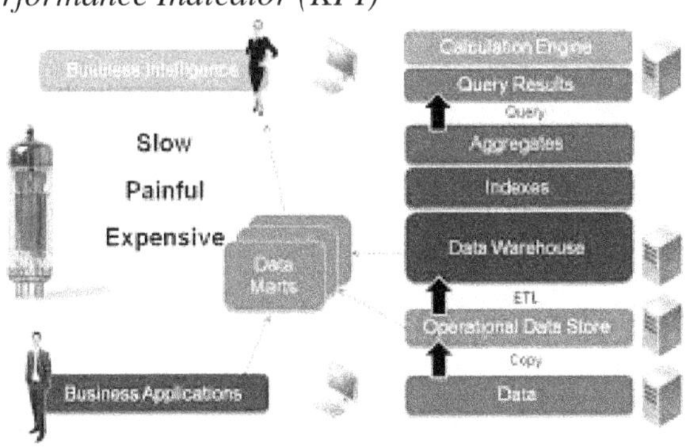

4.1 QlikView Software

It is software which stores automated data on its dashboard._By giving this valuable software, BI helps decision-makers make more informed decisions and supplies end-users with critical business information on their customers or partners, including information on behaviours and trends.

- In first stage, organization's transactional data is recorded in system and key operators punch data in it.
- In second stage, the data is extracted from these systems and is dumped in large single repository, i.e., data warehouse. The data is normally stored with respect to time dimension. Data modelling is performed in this stage.
- In final stage, the data is manipulated and is presented to users in the form of dashboards.
- Enhanced security is applied to secure the system and user authorization matrix is maintained to authenticate the users.
- Both online and offline support to view the reports and dashboard.

4.2 Concept of Cybersecurity and Data Warehousing and Business Intelligence

Protection of data using Cybersecurity is the main driver behind the management and protection of data in Data Warehousing (DW) and Business Intelligence (BI) systems. There are increasing amounts of sensitive information to process and store on these systems; thus, integrity, confidentiality, is a need for Godhead and availability of such data is secured. Cybersecurity is an umbrella term that encompasses the policies, processes, and practice to secure systems, networks, and data from unauthorized access, an attack, and damage. To enforce advanced security parameters for DW & BI solutions is primarily to protect blocked data from access and, hence, enhance their overall security. The features can simply be divided into several big reaches.

4. ADVANCED CYBERSECURITY FEATURES AND PARAMETERS

1. Data Encryption.
    - Sensitive data in storage and transfer with encryption mitigates unauthorized access. This allows for data rendering in unreadable format

even if it is intercepted from unauthorized transmission, provided only by the appropriate decryption keys.

2. User Authentication and Authorization.
    - Ensure that the access granted by logging on is not just based on a simple password, but also on a robust one, e.g. multi-factor authentication, to ensure that only those that are validated have access to system specifications or resources configured therein.
    - Formulate a user authorization matrix to delineate what users can and cannot access, so only pertinent data based on user responsibilities is accessible.
3. Access Control Policies.
    - Establish and strictly enforce access control policies based on the principle of "least privilege" to limit access to sensitive data.
    - Use role-based access control. assign permissions based on job functions.
4. Network Security.
    - Employ dedicated firewalls, intrusion detection systems, and intrusion prevention systems to protect the network infrastructure from external attacks and unauthorized access.
    - Use Virtual Private Networks for secured access to the DW and BI systems.
5. Data Masking and Anonymization.
    - Data masking is used to hide sensitive information in non-production environments. This helps protect personally identifiable information (PII) during testing and development.
6. Audit and Monitoring.
    - Map user activities within a system under ongoing surveillance and log booking for susceptibility to abnormal behavior and impending breach of security.
    - Conducting regular audits to assess compliance with security policies and identify vulnerabilities are.
7. Incident Response Plan.
    - An incident response plan should be developed and maintained to allow for a timely and efficient reaction to security incidents. This includes specifying roles, responsibilities, and procedures for handling security breaches.
8. Data Backup and Recovery.
    - Regularly back up data and enforce a disaster recovery plan to allow for data availability when there is loss of data or systems failure.

9. Training and Awareness.
    - Conduct ongoing employee training sessions to develop awareness of cybersecurity best practices, phishing threats, and safe data handling methods.
    - Implementation Cybersecurity strategies
    - On implementing these enhanced features into the DW & BI solution, the following methodology becomes relevant.

Here goes the list of sections from Assessment and Planning, Design and Development, Testing and Validation, Deployment and Monitoring, Maintenance and Service, and Major Leading. To Be Achieved by Aligning Ongoing Country-Specific Security Protocols with Global Standards.

10. Assessment and Planning.
    - Conduct a risk assessment to determine the vulnerabilities and threats to the data warehouse and BI systems.
    - Report to users and management a comprehensive cybersecurity plan outlining the features and parameters per the assessment findings.
11. Design and Development.
    - Embed security features in the design of the DW & BI software, incorporating every layer of the system.
    - Develop the procedure encryption, access control, and monitoring within the data warehousing process.
12. Testing and Validation.
    - Test the security features thoroughly to identify weaknesses and vulnerabilities.
    - Use penetration testing and vulnerability assessments to validate the access controls and monitor systems.
13. Deployment.
    - Set up the DW & BI solution with integrated cybersecurity features in a production environment.
    - Train all users on the new security protocols and why they are essential to follow
14. Monitoring and Maintenance.
    - Keep on-the-record and observe around-the-clock monitoring for potential security threats and anomalies.
    - Regularly enhance the security measures; they should evolve to address the emerging threats and vulnerabilities.

5. EXPERIMENTAL RESULT

We have identified a solution for Data Warehousing (DW) and Business Intelligence (BI) called *QlikView*. This software is tailored for business professionals, rather than for general public use. QlikView integrates both backend analytical calculations and a front-end user interface, providing a comprehensive tool for data analysis and reporting.

5.1 Key Features

- **Data View Flexibility**. Users can view data in various time frames—yearly, monthly, weekly, or daily.
- **Streamlined Data Access**. There is no need to manually manage thousands of files; the system provides instant data access.
- **Organizational Impact**. The system supports organizations in achieving their Key Performance Indicators (KPIs) and ensures the smooth operation of business processes.
- **Mobile Accessibility**. Dashboards and reports can be accessed from smart devices, ensuring data is available 24/7 without technological barriers.
- **Runtime System**. The solution operates in real-time.
- **Target Audience**. This tool is highly beneficial for business groups.
- **Efficiency**. It is designed to save time for its users.

5.2 Usage Walkthrough

1. **Login/Registration**. Users can log in with a username and password. New users can register themselves directly through the platform.
2. **Dashboard Access**.
    - Once logged in, users can open the dashboard to check sales data. For example, highlighted rows may show the quality and sales of products for August 2015, on a monthly basis.
    - Sales data can be filtered and displayed by brand, with monthly ratings for each.
    - Key accounts are highlighted, categorized by the type of customers' buying behavior.
3. **Sales Data by Region**.
    - The system can highlight different sale types based on geographic areas, providing a region-wise analysis of sales data.
4. **Monthly Sales Report**.

- Users can view monthly sales reports, segmented by city, quality, and overall performance.

5. **Category-Specific Sales**.
   - The system can display data focused on specific product concentrations, such as baking items or products like *sauf supari*.

This structured format outlines the capabilities and benefits of QlikView for business analysis and operational efficiency as mentioned in Figure.5.

Figure 5. QlikView Login access

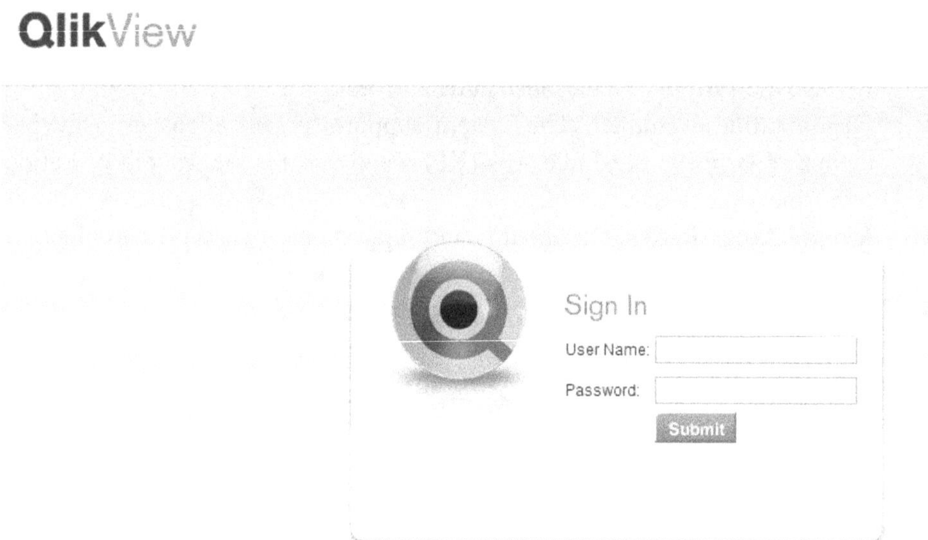

Figure 6. Key Account to represent the sale history

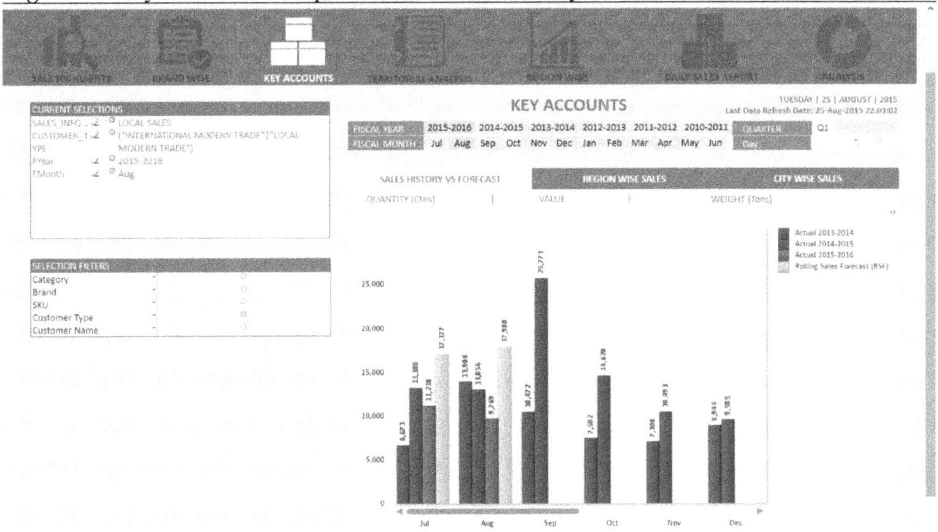

Figure 7. Highlight type of sales by areas.

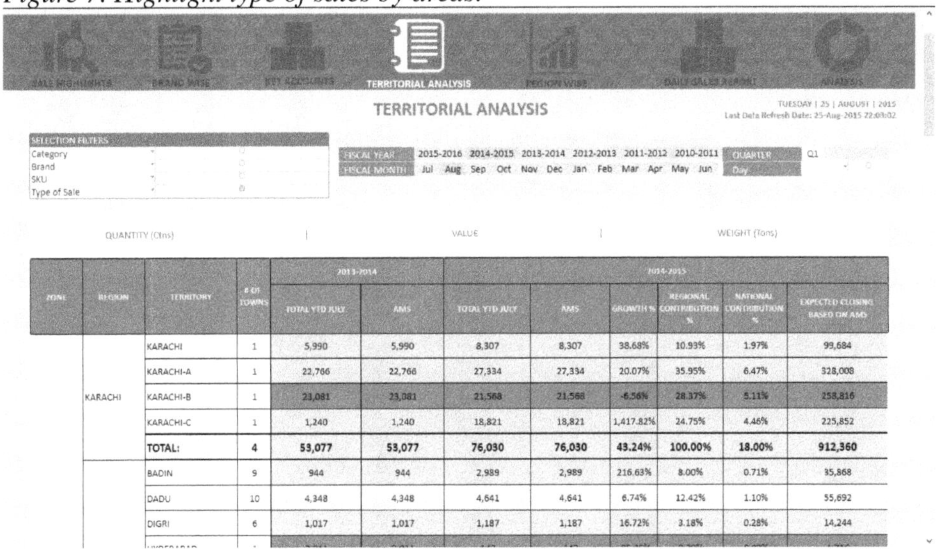

Figure 8. Steps which point out the sales by region wise analysis

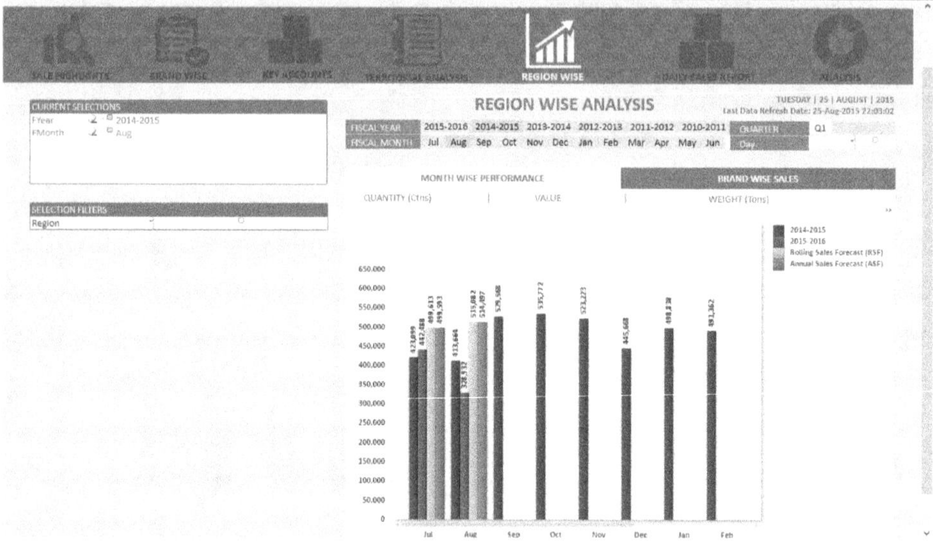

Figure 9. Monthly sales report which shows by month, city, quality overall.

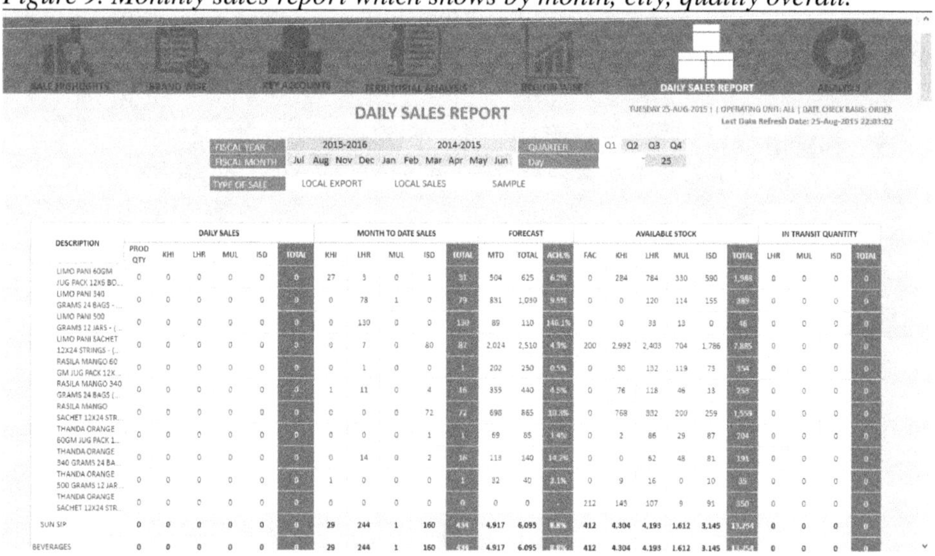

Figure 10. Concentrations analysis

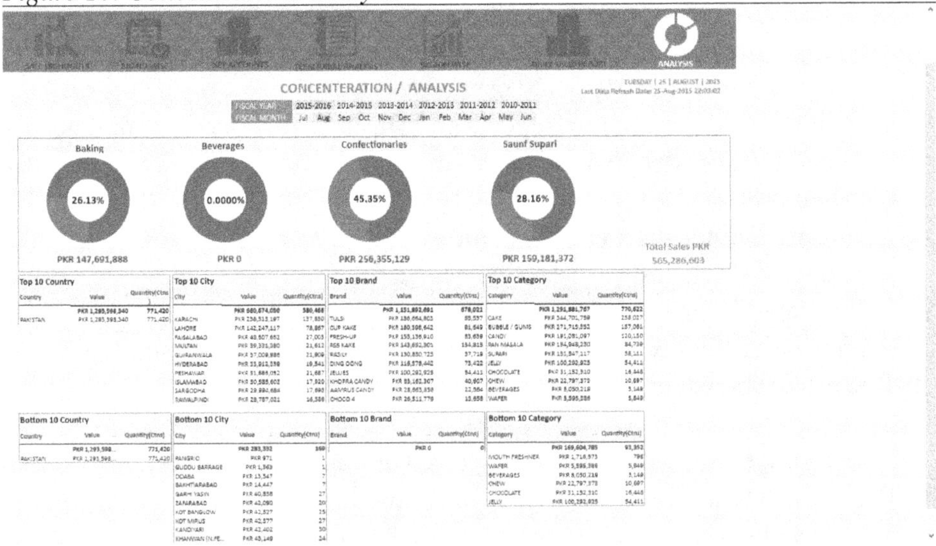

In the above Figures 6, 7, 8, 9, and 10 show the set of illustrations enables the assessment of sales performance from various angles in a detailed manner. In Figure 6, which is concerned with the focal accounts, the historical sales records, customer information, and all the relevant sales transactions are provided with the aim to point out the possibly greatest accounts. Figure 7 deals with geographic region as it classifies sales and assists in identifying the highest and the lowest contributor regions for the respective sales types through graphical representation. Figure 8 provides the regional analysis on sales excluding each sales component analysis owing to this and the sales amounts are further examined region by region using Figure 9 which provides a monthly sales report with an analysis per city and a national grade as well for months assisting in evaluating sales performance over the periods A and B. And last but not least, Figure 10 is devoted to an analysis of the population concentrating on the sales in certain regions while looking at trends and normality's distortions within certain areas Winnipeg sales with turnaround. Collectively these illustrations present a good summary of the sales statistics in making strategic decisions.

Some advantages of implementing QlikView software within DW & BI are giving credence to certain benefits, such as.

1. **Flexibility of Data View.** Users view data within different time frames and impose extremely rigorous access rules on sensitive information.

2. **Data Accessibility.** With the flexibility of instant data access, only authorized personnel can retrieve sensitive information from the system.
3. **Organizational Effect.** Security improvements aid business in achieving KPIs while at the same standing guard over business data.
4. **Flexibility of Accessing the Reports and Dashboards.** Access to dashboards and reports via smart devices balanced against security protocols protecting data in transit.
5. **Real-time Fault Tolerance.** In addition to real-time operations, the system is monitored 24/7 against any security incursions.
6. **Operational Efficiency.** The new features in cybersecurity lead to enhanced operational capability in terms of minimizing security incidents and expediting data access for responsible users.

In the end, cybersecurity is a key component of Data Warehousing and Business Intelligence solutions. Thus, by other highly advanced facilities such as the introduction of parameters, organizations can now take care of protection for their data, regulatory compliance, and operational effectiveness overall increase simultaneously. With the good protection measures taken, protection of sensitive information will expand not only to the data access areas but be developed into culture with enormous knowledge concerning security within the organization.

6. CONCLUSION

The research though an integrated crafting of Data Warehousing and Business Intelligence systems, aided by the QlikView dashboard, under unified Online Transaction Processing and Online Analytical Processing procedures, has automated the boosting and offering of decision-making capabilities to organizations in exploring new markets, improvement areas for business, and enhancing operational strategies. So, while the concepts of DW and BI have today been raised for commercial application by William Inmon and Ralph Kimball in 2003, in this project, we comfortably add that we take substantial positive steps in combining historical data and real-time data from different sources enabling our clients to make informed strategic decisions.

The BI Solution is designed with the keen taker in mind-a self-service solution for the non-technical user as well to provide self-supported data for analysis. With this, the complexities around data accessing and analysis are made simpler, ushering in a new wave of identification of in-trend market and taking care of key business challenges. This project thus designs a futuristic BI solution that makes data analysis simple, integrated, and efficient. This eventually enhances the competitive advantage of the organizations through rich insights in data-driven processes.

6.2 Future Work

With features of exceptional interest for further improvements in this project, we are enthusiastic about the many creative possibilities ahead. Future work will focus on unveiling advanced cybersecurity features ensuring absolute integrity and confidentiality of the data within our DW & BI solution. Some of the other key advancements will be.

- **Strategic Management**. Embedding strategic management capabilities to enable organizations to align their BI insights with overarching business objectives.
- **Business Planning and Consolidation**. Upgrade business planning capabilities to allow for a more comprehensive financial model and analysis.
- **Data Mining**. Deployment of advanced data mining techniques for highlighting hidden patterns and insights contained in the data that would influence smarter decision-making.
- **User Issues-Minding**. Closely touching the users to learn the problems to be solved so that our BI platform meets the needs of its users that keep changing.

Apart from these, we would be focusing on quality protecting measures such as data encryption, access controls, and continuous monitoring. These are to secure sensitive data and ensure that organizations get to enjoy some protection against any enforcement of regulatory requirements. This research, therefore, does not represent the end; it will be part of a continuous series of further developments in the area of BI. There are far greater opportunities on the horizon for future developments that will significantly pull up the namesake BI tools and solutions to a greater takeoff stage.

REFERENCES

Al-Sharideh, M., & Alshammari, R. (2020). Business Intelligence and Data Warehouse. A Review of Literature and Future Directions. *International Journal of Business Intelligence Research*, 10(2), 1–18. DOI: 10.4018/IJBIR.2020040101

Bakar, A., & Ahmad, M. (2021). The Role of Data Warehousing in Business Intelligence for Healthcare Organizations. *Journal of Healthcare Engineering*, 2021, 1–9. DOI: 10.1155/2021/8813194

Bounfour, A., & Moussa, A. (2022). Big Data Analytics in the Public Sector. A Review of Current Trends. *Journal of Business Research*, 140, 217–229. DOI: 10.1016/j.jbusres.2021.12.018

Chen, J., & Zhang, X. (2023). Cybersecurity Challenges in Business Intelligence. A Comprehensive Study. *Journal of Cybersecurity and Privacy*, 3(1), 156–171. DOI: 10.3390/jcp3010009

Duan, Y., & Xiong, Y. (2021). Exploring Business Intelligence and Data Warehouse Technologies in E-Government. *Journal of Information Technology*, 36(1), 52–68. DOI: 10.1177/0268396220903170

Elmasri, R., & Navathe, S. (2021). *Fundamentals of Database Systems* (7th ed.). Pearson.

Gharbi, R., & Ben Khedher, S. (2020). Evaluating the Performance of Business Intelligence Systems. An Empirical Study. *Information Systems Frontiers*, 22(3), 609–620. DOI: 10.1007/s10796-018-9820-7

Gill, S. H., Razzaq, M. A., Ahmad, M., Almansour, F. M., Haq, I. U., Jhanjhi, N. Z., & Masud, M. (2022). Security and privacy aspects of cloud computing. a smart campus case study. *Intelligent Automation & Soft Computing*, 31(1), 117–128. DOI: 10.32604/iasc.2022.016597

Gouda, W., Almurafeh, M., Humayun, M., & Jhanjhi, N. Z. (2022). Detection of COVID-19 based on chest X-rays using deep learning. [). MDPI.]. *Health Care*, 10(2), 343. PMID: 35206957

Gupta, V., & Sharma, A. (2022). Adopting Cybersecurity Measures in Business Intelligence Systems. A Systematic Review. *Journal of Information Security and Applications*, 67, 103149. DOI: 10.1016/j.jisa.2022.103149

Hossain, M. M., & Saha, S. K. (2022). Business Intelligence and Cybersecurity. A Strategic Alignment Approach. *Computers & Security*, 122, 102833. DOI: 10.1016/j.cose.2022.102833

Humayun, M., Sujatha, R., Almuayqil, S. N., & Jhanjhi, N. Z. (2022). A transfer learning approach with a convolutional neural network for the classification of lung carcinoma. []. MDPI.]. *Health Care*, 10(6), 1058. PMID: 35742109

Jadhav, V., & Jain, R. (2020). Data Warehousing for Business Intelligence. A Survey. *International Journal of Computer Applications*, 975, 16–22. DOI: 10.5120/ijca2020920223

Jang, J. Y., & Kim, D. (2021). Implementing Data Warehouse for Business Intelligence. An Overview of the Current Trends. *Journal of Business Research*, 128, 811–821. DOI: 10.1016/j.jbusres.2021.01.045

Khan, M. A., & Kaur, M. (2022). Emerging Trends in Business Intelligence. Data Governance and Cybersecurity. *International Journal of Information Systems and Project Management*, 10(1), 5–17. DOI: 10.12821/ijispm100101

Khan, N. A., Jhanjhi, N. Z., Brohi, S. N., Almazroi, A. A., & Almazroi, A. A. (2022). A secure communication protocol for unmanned aerial vehicles. *Cmc-computers Materials & Continua*, 70(1), 601–618. DOI: 10.32604/cmc.2022.019419

Kim, D. H., & Lee, J. H. (2023). Big Data, Business Intelligence, and Cybersecurity. A Study of Their Interconnections. *Journal of Business Research*, 144, 225–239. DOI: 10.1016/j.jbusres.2022.12.028

Kok, S. H., Abdullah, A., Jhanjhi, N. Z., & Supramaniam, M. (2019). A review of intrusion detection system using machine learning approach. *International Journal of Engineering Research & Technology (Ahmedabad)*, 12(1), 8–15.

Kumar, A., & Srivastava, S. (2020). Framework for Integration of Cybersecurity in Business Intelligence Systems. *International Journal of Information Management*, 50, 350–358. DOI: 10.1016/j.ijinfomgt.2019.08.002

Li, Y., & Zhan, J. (2021). A Comprehensive Study of Business Intelligence and Its Role in Organizational Success. *Journal of Knowledge Management*, 25(2), 424–442. DOI: 10.1108/JKM-04-2020-0291

Liu, W., & Yu, J. (2023). Cybersecurity Measures in Business Intelligence Solutions. Challenges and Opportunities. *Computers & Security*, 123, 103078. DOI: 10.1016/j.cose.2022.103078

López, R. A., & Gonzalez, A. (2020). Business Intelligence Tools. A Study of the Adoption in Small and Medium Enterprises. *Journal of Small Business Management*, 58(4), 651–671. DOI: 10.1111/jsbm.12443

Mardani, A.. (2020). Cybersecurity in Business Intelligence. Challenges and Solutions. *Computers & Security*, 95, 101850. DOI: 10.1016/j.cose.2020.101850

Muzammal, S. M., Murugesan, R. K., Jhanjhi, N. Z., & Jung, L. T. (2020, October). SMTrust. Proposing trust-based secure routing protocol for RPL attacks for IoT applications. In *2020 International Conference on Computational Intelligence (ICCI)* (pp. 305-310). IEEE. DOI: 10.1109/ICCI51257.2020.9247818

Najmi, K. Y., AlZain, M. A., Masud, M., Jhanjhi, N. Z., Al-Amri, J., & Baz, M. (2023). A survey on security threats and countermeasures in IoT to achieve users confidentiality and reliability. *Materials Today: Proceedings*, 81, 377–382. DOI: 10.1016/j.matpr.2021.03.417

Pal, A., & Saha, S. K. (2022). Integrating Cybersecurity into Business Intelligence. A New Paradigm. *Journal of Business Research*, 144, 117–129. DOI: 10.1016/j.jbusres.2022.03.015

Ranjan, J. (2020). Business Intelligence. A Managerial Perspective on Analytics. *Journal of Business Research*, 115, 268–276. DOI: 10.1016/j.jbusres.2020.01.026

Ranjan, J., & Prakash, A. (2023). Challenges in Implementing Business Intelligence. A Study in Emerging Markets. *International Journal of Information Management*, 68, 102321. DOI: 10.1016/j.ijinfomgt.2023.102321

Reda, A., & Ahmed, A. (2021). Trends in Data Warehousing. A Review and Future Research Directions. *International Journal of Business Intelligence Research*, 12(1), 1–21. DOI: 10.4018/IJBIR.2021010101

Saeed, S., Abbasi, F. A., Dahri, K., Shaikh, Z. A., Nizamani, M. A., & Memon, M. A. (2024). Improved Hybrid K-Nearest Neighbours Techniques in Segmentation of Low-Grade Tumor and Cerebrospinal Fluid. *The Asian Bulletin of Big Data Management, 4*(02). *Science*, •••, 4.

Saeed, S., & Haron, H. (2021). Improve correlation matrix of discrete Fourier transformation (CM-DFT) technique for finding the missing values of MRI images. *Mathematical Biosciences and Engineering*, •••, 1–22.

Saeed, S., & Humayun, M. (2019). Disparaging the barriers of journal citation reports (JCR). IJCSNS. International Journal of Computer Science and Network Security, 19(5), 156-175. *ISI-Index.*, 1, 5.

Saeed, S., Jhanjhi, N. Z., Abdullah, A., & Naqvi, M. (2018). Current trends and issues legacy application of the serverless architecture. *International Journal of Computing and Network Technology*, 6(3), 100–108. DOI: 10.12785/IJCNT/060304

Saeed, S., Jhanjhi, N. Z., Naqvi, M., & Humayun, M. (2019). Analysis of software development methodologies. *International Journal of Computing and Digital Systems*, 8(5), 446–460.

Saeed, S., Shaikh, A., Memon, M. A., Memon, M. H., Abassi, F. A., & Naqvi, S. M. R. (2017). Implementation of failure enterprise systems in organizational perspective framework. *International Journal of Advanced Computer Science and Applications*, 8(5). Advance online publication. DOI: 10.14569/IJACSA.2017.080508

Saeed, S., Shaikh, A., Memon, M. A., & Naqvi, S. M. R. (2018). Impact of data mining techniques to analyze health care data. *Journal of Medical Imaging and Health Informatics*, 8(4), 682–690. DOI: 10.1166/jmihi.2018.2385

Sharma, M., & Gupta, R. (2022). Role of Data Warehousing in Business Intelligence. A Review of Key Concepts and Applications. *International Journal of Business Intelligence Research*, 12(3), 44–56. DOI: 10.4018/IJBIR.303650

Singh, P., & Prasad, A. (2021). Cybersecurity Considerations in Business Intelligence Implementation. *Journal of Cybersecurity*, 7(4), 121–138. DOI: 10.1002/cybs.2099

Singhal, V., Jain, S. S., Anand, D., Singh, A., Verma, S., Rodrigues, J. J., & Iwendi, C. (2020). Artificial intelligence enabled road vehicle-train collision risk assessment framework for unmanned railway level crossings. *IEEE Access : Practical Innovations, Open Solutions*, 8, 113790–113806. DOI: 10.1109/ACCESS.2020.3002416

Soni, R., & Sharma, A. (2020). Challenges and Opportunities in Data Warehouse and Business Intelligence. *International Journal of Data Warehousing and Mining*, 16(1), 1–15. DOI: 10.4018/IJDWM.2020010101

Tiwari, R., & Kumari, S. (2022). Implementing Cybersecurity Best Practices in Business Intelligence Solutions. *Journal of Information Security and Applications*, 66, 103192. DOI: 10.1016/j.jisa.2022.103192

Zhao, Y.. (2021). Impact of Cybersecurity on Business Intelligence Solutions. *Journal of Business Research*, 128, 103–112. DOI: 10.1016/j.jbusres.2021.01.042

Zolotova, A., & Goryunova, O. (2023). Business Intelligence and Cybersecurity in the Digital Economy. *Digital Transformation and Global Society*, 3(1), 1–10. DOI: 10.35654/dtgs.2023.0101

Chapter 6
Future Trends in Generative AI for Cyber Defense:
Preparing for the Next Wave of Threats

Azeem Khan
https://orcid.org/0000-0003-2742-8034
University Islam Sultan Sharif Ali, Brunei

Noor Zaman Jhanjhi
https://orcid.org/0000-0001-8116-4733
TUSB, Malaysia

Haji Abdul Hafidz B. Haji Omar
University Islam Sultan Sharif Ali, Brunei

Dayang H. T. B. A. Haji Hamid
https://orcid.org/0000-0003-2484-5211
University Islam Sultan Sharif Ali, Brunei

Ghassan A. A. Abdulhabeb
University Islam Sultan Sharif Ali, Brunei

ABSTRACT

The chapter entitled "Future Trends and Challenges in Cybersecurity and Generative AI," presents a comprehensive exploration of the changing dynamics at the intersection between the rapidly growing landscape of the interconnectivity of various devices— the Internet of Things and the innovations piloted by advancements in

DOI: 10.4018/979-8-3693-6135-1.ch006

generative artificial intelligence. In the following background-focused analysis, the significance of the enactment of new levels of security details in this fast-growing and virulently expansive landscape is emphasized, with generative AI ultimately serving as the highlight. The conversation consequently shifts to threats. This includes a detailed depiction of new cybersecurity threats rooted in advancements in AI, featuring AI malicious actors and incidents, such as the increasingly popular phenomenon of ransomware-as-a-service as mirror illustrations of the dynamic and multifaceted character of these threats.

I. INTRODUCTION

A. Overview of Generative AI in Cyber Defense

As depicted in Figure1.0, Generative AI is a type of artificial intelligence that uses deep learning models to generate new data instances from known data instances, or training data. Cybersecurity with generative AI is a game changer: it creates attacks threats actively, as well as in synthetic form; it can compose complex defense mechanisms and from this groundwork enables cybersecurity tasks to be automated. The main impact of this duality is particularly evident here -- boosting cyber defenses and being used by attackers to create much more sophisticated, they are still natural, threats. On the back end, generative AI can help by letting you poke around in enriched data and security data — catching anomalies a threat one might miss if using traditional methods. The incidents are then responded to, and threat hunts carried out and finally, Automation drives done Although generative AI does pose a potential threat: the technology enables one to mimic different attack methods in cyberspace and thus organizations may despite being under attack apply diverse forms of security reinforcement to keep themselves safe from forthcoming dangers. But generative AI technology also has hazards on the offensive side. Hackers can use it to turn out Miami emails, problems with new feather, even deep fakes that escape initial detection techniques. In our cybersecurity environment, the tool is equally useful for both defenders and attackers because it can discover system vulnerabilities(Sindiramutty, Prabagaran, Jhanjhi, Ghazanfar, et al., 2025; Vemuri, Thaneeru, & Tatikonda, 2024).

Figure 1. Proactive Cyber Defense Using Generative AI(Sukhwinder, 2023)

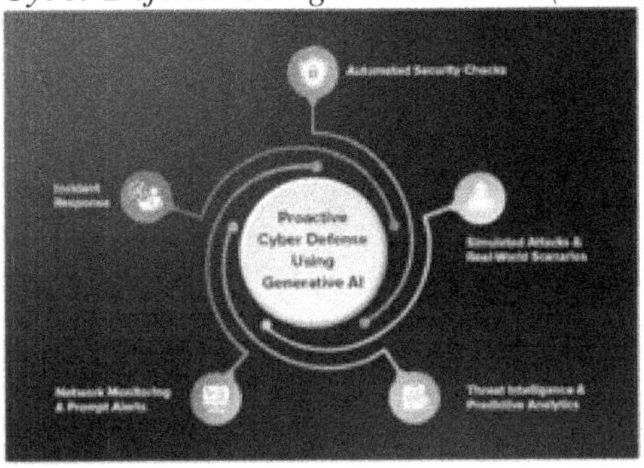

The Evolution of AI From Traditional Methods to Generative Models in Cyber Defense

As illustrated in Table 1.0, the transformation of AI in cybersecurity has come from primitive rule-based systems and old school machine learning methods to more complex generative models. The initial methods to solve information security issues were dependent on cyber security theories and patterns of data analysis. At first, cybersecurity frameworks were heavily cantered around identification of threats and understanding established indicators of inherent security vulnerabilities. However, these security systems were less effective to identify some of the new possible threats and though they served well for many known kinds of hazards, could not face all types of new vulnerabilities and this was illustrated by zero-day exploits. Now with the advent of machine learning in AI and insights driven from historical data sets, it is possible to identify anomalous behaviours on security. The profiling learning strategies on nontraditional classes are used in both non-traditional class models to identify that accumulated threats which were not detected. Anyway, these AI models primarily work retrospectively to solve for non-repetitive anomalies. Generative AI has recently been shown to have the potential of changing this paradigm from a reactive viewpoint into a proactive one when aiming to address all your security vulnerabilities. Generation methodologies, supported by generative adversarial networks and Transformer architectures which are indispensable for the task related to threat detection. This enhancement also assists in reproducing attacks and forecasting the risks, which provides a great benefit when evaluating software according to the possible risks(Desai, 2024; Rashmi et al.).

This chapter delves into how generative AI can overlap with cyber defense both now and in the future as well, and bring a holistic view to what organizations need to understand about this technology before they can begin utilizing it for the potential threats of tomorrow Generative AI is a critical capability for organizations as they prepare for the increasingly automated and rapidly evolving threat landscapes associated with more sophisticated cyberattacks. In this article, the defensive applications of generative AI will be delved into with a discussion about the threats that can be posed by generative AI if it falls into the wrong hands.

B. Current Landscape of AI in Cyber Defense

As shown in Figure 2.0, Artificial Intelligence plays a significant role in modern cyber defense methodologies by increasing the ability to detect abnormalities, behavioural analysis, as well as automating incident response processes. AI-powered systems continuously monitor network traffic and have the ability to detect departing from normal operation modes that human analysts might miss, finding threat vectors as they are performing suspicious operations in the real time. The most obvious reflection of this is the effectiveness of identifying scams and phishing that are today among the most common security threats. Additionally, AI-powered platforms achieve most of the activities in incident response workflow extremely automated improving overall incident response time and reducing damage from cyber-attacks. The goal of this optimization is to allow human security analysts to work on more difficult problems, thereby boosting the effectiveness of security best practices in aggregate.

Table 1. Traditional AI vs Generative AI in cyber defence(G, 2023)

Aspect	Traditional ML	Generative AI
Data Pre-Processing	Cleaning and preparing data for analysis	Cleaning and preparing data for analysis
Feature Engineering	Extracting important features from data	Prompt Engineering/Fine Tuning: Designing effective prompts to guide AI in generating desired outputs
Training & Tuning	Training models on data and adjusting parameters for optimal performance.	Foundation/Fine-Tuned LLM: Using foundation and fine-tuned language models for sophisticated content generation
Deployment & Monitoring	Implementing models in real-world applications and monitoring their performance	Implementing models in real-world applications and monitoring their performance
Tech Stack	- ML Frameworks: Keras, Theano	- Gen AI Orchestration: Langchain
	- ML APIs & SDK: IBM Watson	- LLM Models: OpenAI, Anthropic
	- Databases: SQL Server, Oracle	- Vector Database: Pinecone, Weaviate
	- ML Ops: Docker, Jenkins	- LLM Ops: Prompt Layer, Helicone

AI has an important role in the field of patch management automation, as it can sense vulnerabilities in software architectures themselves and fix them immediately without any direct human interaction(Durakovskiy, Gavdan, Korsakov, & Melnikov, 2021; Gimenez-Aguilar, de Fuentes, Gonzalez-Manzano, & Arroyo, 2021).

Regarding the device security at endpoint, AI creates normative baselines for a normal behaviour pattern and in case of any deviation from this baseline – AI will alert ensuring that a breach is taking place or is about to take place. Integrating AI into SIEM (Security Information and Event Management) platforms enhances the ability to identify threats, find security holes in cyber environments and predict potential cybersecurity attacks. Because they continuously operate and learn from new alerts by using historical incident data, large-scale AI systems deliver continuous real-time security alerts against known and emerging threats on multiple fronts. Although some continue to be cautious when adopting artificial intelligence into their cybersecurity strategies, it is now fair to say that the algorithms have become an essential element of modern cybersecurity frameworks(Ortega, Tran, & Bandeen, 2023).

Figure 2. Generative AI an Introduction(S., 2023)

The Role of Generative AI in Detecting, Preventing, and Mitigating Cyber Threats

As shown in Figure3.0, Generative AI improves cybersecurity by providing an additional layer of security within a company for threat detection, prevention and mitigation. It generates and stimulates authentic lateral movement characteristics which include phishing to malware propagation, assisting the safety crew to compete towards an attack before time. For example, phishing simulations can help to train employees on what to look out for before they become a victim. When it comes to security, Generative AI makes encryption stronger because you can generate code and passwords that are extremely difficult for bad actors to break. It enables identifying anomalies which could be representing a security incident by establishing behavioural baselines(Sindiramutty, Prabagaran, Jhanjhi, Murugesan, et al., 2025).

Generative AI is also important when containing attacks since it plays a big role simulating real-time reactions to security failures, giving teams ability to manage damage on the fly in active command and control attack. Generative AI offers views on how attackers could potentially take advantage of vulnerabilities, allowing security teams to harden their protections and respond more efficiently when they are faced with real-world threats. Generative AI is capable of simulating attacks that may be carried out by potential attackers on the system, enabling it to discover any vulnerabilities before they can be taken advantage of. This predictive power allows security teams to resolve the vulnerabilities up front and decrease attack surface. It is increasingly necessary for cybersecurity postures to include generative AI solutions to help them stay alert against the kind of evolving cyber threats that are out there(Bui et al., 2024).

Figure 3. Navigating The Cybersecurity Landscape In 2024(Sayegh, 2023)

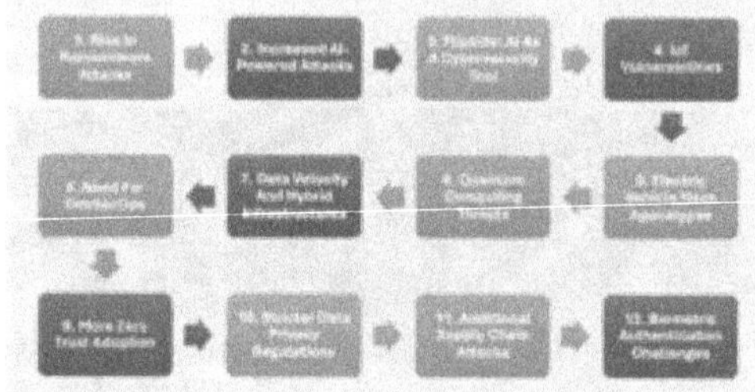

Existing Challenges and Limitations of Generative AI in Cyber Defense

Generative forms of AI have many advantages as well, but due to its nature they bring an ever a greater number of challenges and constraints in cyber defense. First things first, the Division of the central authority is its double-edged sharp sword type benefit — it can make you to secure your protocols better but also on a bad note can be abused by maleficent actors who know how glass is made (pun intended). Fake news would become even harder to spot as generative AI is used to invent more and improved malware, refine disingenuous phishing campaigns and maliciously exploit vulnerabilities with growing accuracy. This really is the primary lesson taught with our friends and relatives, that always they must be alerted to malevolent movements. Also, generative AI applications require massive datasets and incredibly powerful computation capabilities, something not all organizations can afford. However, these models can also make false positives (i.e., flag benign behaviour as a threat), which would in turn hinder the effectiveness of security systems. Yet, ethical issues emerge with the current contributions to stop the emergence of bad generative AI technologies being exceeded by the prospect. Overall, the rapid development of AI invites the questions concerning the role of regulation and that of ethical standards. Whereas generative AI can be viewed as the essential asset that can transform cyber defense beyond recognition, it is important to consider its limitations and use it in moderation. Thus, the role of generative AI in cyber defense at present should be intermediatory so that the benefits associated with the approach clearly outweigh its dangers(Diro et al., 2024; Sidi-Mohammed, Hichem, Jiajia, Mubashir Husain, & Elias, 2020).

Chapter Contribution

This insightful chapter investigates deeply into the complex topic of how Generative AI is revolutionizing cybersecurity defenses in unimagined ways. A thorough tour across various AI models throughout history explores the progression from traditional algorithms to modern generative models now leveraged. By scrutinizing generative AI's dual potential for both defense and offense, startling transformative impacts that will change our world come into focus. More profoundly, illuminating insights show how forward-thinking organizations can harness generative AI's proactive detecting, preventing, and mitigation of cyber threats through a multidimensional layered approach, while acknowledging the challenges and constraints that still require attention. For cybersecurity professionals aiming to thoughtfully consider how to strategically and ethically integrate generative AI's capabilities into a dynamic defense or to foresee emerging offense techniques, this foundational resource proves enormously informative for the road ahead.

Chapter Organization

This chapter explores many vital aspects regarding using Generative Artificial Intelligence approaches for cybersecurity purposes. Firstly, the topic outlines what generative AI is and why improving cybersecurity is so crucial. For many years, the sole option was reactive analysis upon discovery, but now generative models have the potential to play a proactive role in threat detection as new vulnerabilities arise. Deeper examination is given to interesting trends on how these models may shape understanding and perspectives on organizational security frameworks. Modern artificial intelligence encapsulates numerous facets applicable to incident response and forensic investigations as detailed here. Undoubtedly, generative methods offer even greater promise since they can detect, prevent, or mitigate attacks by matching insights. Precisely, this attribute could enable counteracting adversaries by consuming knowledge from historical data, yet challenges still exist, and guidelines are essential to ensure GANs are not applied unethically. When taken seriously, generative AI has the quality to inherently be proactive and, with the proper safeguards, proactively bolster overall cybersecurity resilience for organizations and society.

II. EMERGING TRENDS IN GENERATIVE AI FOR CYBER DEFENSE

A. Advanced Threat Detection and Prediction

The Generative AI innovation is revolutionizing how cybersecurity values are discovered and implemented making it easier for any organization to be proactive in terms of detecting threats early, preventing attacks and staying ahead of the curve. AI models through traditional ways react according to the data acquired from a database but with AI model based on decentralized framework it can help in identifying and responding new form of threats forestalling even greater damage. Generative AI models, on the other hand — for example Generative Adversarial Networks (GANs) or the large Transformer-based models such as GPT-3 — can simulate new attack vectors to keep organizations ahead of attackers. Using generative AI to scour vast amounts of network data for the types of small hacks and telltale anomalies that often betray zero-day exploits as they start to take shape, enterprises could get advance notice of more new threats, giving them precious additional hours or even days to react(Papastergiou, Mouratidis, & Kalogeraki, 2021).

As the statistics in Figure 4.0 reveals, Advances in AI-powered threat intelligence and predictive analytics have made it possible for generative AI to be used to simulate and predict cyberattacks — something that was not possible with traditional tactics. These models can ingest and process log entries, endpoint activities, network behaviours, or open-source intelligence feeds including dark web forums to spot cyber alerts. Being proactive allows organizations to take action before a threat reaches new levels. For example, Generative AI can predict how ransomware or malware strains are likely to grow based on previous trends which can alert security teams for potential attacks. Furthermore, AI-based red-teaming help security teams to mimic multiple common attack strategies that occur in the wild and attain a deeper understanding of the points where there are chances of system vulnerabilities. These simulations simulate the tactics hackers use to give organizations an opportunity to test and improve their security. Generative AI has a long way to evolve, but when it does, it can help create synthetic attack vectors which could act as early warnings for big businesses and ultimately result in augmenting the predictive power of threat intelligence(Sindiramutty, Jhanjhi, & Ray, 2024; Sindiramutty, Prabagaran, Jhanjhi, & Murugesan, 2024).

In the future we might step further with generative AI and use it for real-time threat detection of automated response. Generative AI can pick up on unknown threats and alert the simple response mechanisms at your disposal in real time, ideally by integrating with existing Security Information and Event Management (SIEM) systems. It means less human intervention is needed and the time to resolution of a cyberattack is shortened. Generative AI will also be used in the proactive defense, creating continuous attack simulations and evaluating which ones are able to breach the system. This can help organizations forecast where and when they are likely to be hit, so that they will be able to administer precautionary action before anything terrible occurs. Machine-to-machine communication with autonomous cybersecurity agents that use generative AI to patrol systems, identify threats, and patch vulnerabilities can soon work without oversight(Gaur, Solanki, Wamba, & Jhanjhi, 2021; N. Z. Jhanjhi, Gaur, & Khan, 2024).

In conclusion, the emergence of generative AI marks a significant shift in the cybersecurity landscape. Its ability to predict, detect, and simulate advanced threats gives organizations the tools they need to move from reactive to anticipatory defense strategies. As the technology continues to advance, generative AI will become an integral part of cybersecurity, providing real-time detection, proactive mitigation, and automated threat response against increasingly sophisticated cyberattacks.

Figure 4. Global AI in cybersecurity market (Grand View Research, 2023)

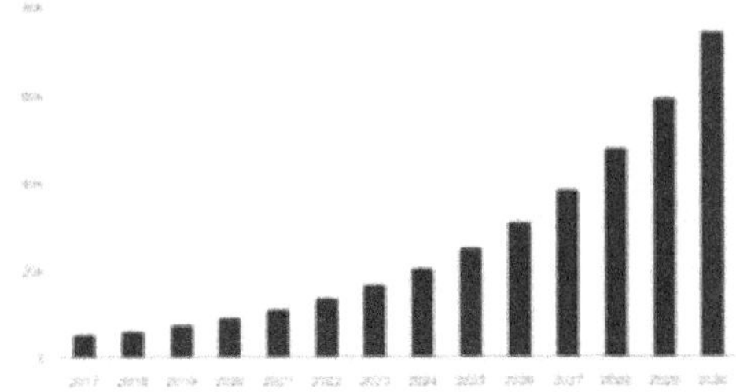

B. Autonomous Cyber Defense Systems

Ongoing development of autonomous cyber defense systems are introduced as important advancement on the front against new and complex digital threats. It relies on the artificial intelligence (AI) components that power them to automatically identify and respond to threats without human input. Autonomous systems act on their own, this renders autonomous cybersecurity tools far faster and more precise than traditional cybersecurity solutions. The aim is to have these systems automatically monitor networks, identify risks and then immediately activate the countermeasures—in other situations often at staggering high pace (volume of modern APTs) and complexity—so to relieve human security analysts(Repetto, 2023).

AI-driven defense systems are rising rapidly because of breakthroughs in machine learning and deep learning algorithms that can process and analyze huge amounts of data, the accomplishments are beyond the ability of human. Because at a large enough scale, even differences too nuanced for human eyes can be seen as anomalies or patterns that may indicate an attack, even if the zero-day exploit being deployed has never been seen before. Working with minimum human intervention, the systems decide how to counter a threat using the data they collect. This ability is essential in areas such as finance, critical infrastructure, and government networks where cyberattacks could be frequent(Gong, Wang, Chen, & Wang, 2021).

Examples of Early-Stage Autonomous Cyber Defense Systems

One of the first known forms of autonomous cyber defense includes Darktrace, which is a machine learning platform that passively observes the network and acts on malicious behavior independently. By learning the patterns of activities typical to the IT systems and senses deviations such as unusual transfer of data or data centers' interactions from within the network, it is capable of automatically responding to any threat without human intervention. Similarly, Vectra AI is another form of technology that can detect an anomaly in live network activities, which allows for an appropriate automatic response to any incursion. These systems demonstrate the subsequent reliance of the IT and cybersecurity networks on the AI, as these platforms are capable of operating at a much higher level of cybersecurity while requiring minimum human efforts. As the nature of the network along with the IT systems securitization develops, AI naturally advances as well, getting more and more efficient and sophisticated, far surpassing human capabilities(Sharma & Sharma, 2024).

Other known AI incident response platforms at an early stage of development also include more hands-on experience from the human as a human augmented cybersecurity system. These systems include such tools as Palo Alto Networks' Cortex XSOAR and IBM's QRadar Advisor along with a few others. While these systems are not autonomous by nature and still require the human to respond to the vast numbers of these security incidents, they both considerably speed up the process of retrieving and filtering necessary information by using machine learning. One of such cloud-native systems is Microsoft's Azure Sentinel, which uses AI and machine learning to automatically detect a breach probing response in a matter of a few seconds. In these examples, the human gets to do less of the directly monitoring work, which means that fewer errors will be made over an hour spent on reviewing an incident(Teig & Eiken, 2024).

Potential Advancements in Fully Autonomous AI Systems for Comprehensive Cyber Defense

As AI technologies continue to evolve, the future of fully autonomous cyber defense systems holds immense potential for reshaping the landscape of digital security. These systems will integrate advanced predictive analytics, self-learning capabilities, and real-time responses, enabling them to deploy patches, adjust security settings, and mitigate threats without human intervention. The rise of autonomous AI agents capable of continuously monitoring and securing networks promises a proactive approach to cybersecurity, far exceeding today's reactive methods. By combining AI with blockchain for transparent, immutable records, these systems could further bolster security. However, challenges such as ethical concerns and ensuring nuanced decision-making in complex scenarios must be addressed. Ultimately, AI-driven autonomous systems have the potential to significantly enhance the resilience of digital infrastructures, but maintaining the right balance between automation and human oversight will be critical for their success in defending against increasingly sophisticated cyber threats(Masum, 2023).

C. AI-Generated Cyber Threats

The introduction of Generative AI carries with it a wealth of opportunities, but also presents serious potential hazards wherein hackers exploit these new technologies to bring about sophisticated and flexible online threats. AI-made malware, for example, changes itself daily for quicker evasion into older systems and anti-detection measures. Phishing schemes are much harder to tell now that AI can compose text, chat in real-time with victims, and make up online environments that are interactive and full of people who appear very real. And the danger is compounded yet again by deepfakes. Upon using such technology attackers can create synthetic media with unparallelled likeness that allows them to become phony authoritative Figureures—a threat for all of society in this age of fake news and roguery under any banner(Tayyab et al., 2023).

Many cutting-edge defensive techniques are needed to battle these malicious threats. AI-enhanced cyber security tools are essential for real-time analysis of massive amounts of data and detection unusual patterns that may indicate potential attacks. And as new threats arise, AI-based systems can be updated through monitoring user behaviour to ensure they pick up on strangeness—such as unexpectedly high levels of data flow, which might be a sign an attack is in progress. What is essential, too, are comprehensive training and awareness programs that teach employees how to identify AI-generated phishing and deepfakes. Human error poses a significant risk in this regard. As organizations meet the increasing peril from AI-created cyber risks by implementing multi-tiered protection systems including AI, behavioural analysis and cryptographic services for guaranteeing the integrity of data transit with Universally Unique Identifiers, they can remain in excellent overall shape both now and well into their futures online(Tayyab, Hameed, Jhanjhi, Zaheer, & Qamar, 2024).

D. Integration of Generative AI with Emerging Technologies

Generative AI integrated with other technologies like quantum computing, blockchain(A. R. S. Khan et al., 2024) and Internet of Thing has dynamically changed the paradigm of cybersecurity. Quantum computing, which can perform a massive number of requests at the same time, vastly increases generative AI's capabilities to process through vast datasets and mirror advanced cyber threats significantly faster than ever before. On the other hand, a decentralized ledger system like blockchain can also empower generative AI quite effectively as it secures data integrity and more importantly global verification for all transactions. Generative AI — When coupled with IoT, generative AI can further strengthen the ability to detect and prevent threats beyond individual devices since IoT environments are uniquely distributed(Khan, Jhanjhi, Omar, & Haji, 2024; Mumtaz et al., 2024).

By creating a hybrid AI system using generative AI with deep learning and even quantum algorithms, threat detection capabilities are enhanced significantly to provide real-time protection from advanced threats. The system discovers patterns and abnormalities in large scale multimode information, where traditional methods fail. The possible ramifications of these pipes are evidenced by early integrations like AI-powered blockchain enhancing data security, and Quantum-AI collaboration improving cryptography. This integration is maturing and soon we can assume that a new generation of intelligent, robust cyber security architectural frameworks will appear to tackle AI, which is now capable of launching scale cyber-attacks on infrastructure(Sujatha, Prakash, & Jhanjhi, 2022).

III. PREPARING FOR THE NEXT WAVE OF AI-DRIVEN CYBER THREATS

A. Building Resilient AI Systems

Resilience in AI models is important for cybersecurity as they need to mitigate adversarial attacks and change threats. In some use cases of AI programs, especially cybersecurity, the rationale for controlling or manipulating its vulnerability out should be against dishonesty at the operational and representative status level. The reason is that cybercriminals are going to use more adversarial techniques, like changing input data to AI models, so it becomes Eric and more important to design AI models with defenses. Resilience ensures AI models continue to be operational in the face of adversarial deployment, safeguarding their ability to detect, mitigate and respond against cyberattacks(Saeed, Jhanjhi, Naqvi, & Khan, 2022).

As shown in Figure 5.0, AI powered security mechanism efforts to improve the longevity of AI models focus on making them less susceptible to adversarial attack and other forms of novel attack. There are a few mainstream approaches to this, the most popular is adversarial teaching which introduces an AI system (the learner) to adversarial inputs in the learning stage. So that it can help the models to know and protect from such manipulations in real life scenarios. The generalization of ensemble learning which runs several models in parallel to increase resiliency makes it even more difficult for the attackers as they must fool all the models at once. Further, the use of standardization methods - which are a type of stop-overfitting-technique -, improves AI models' ability for generalization by making them more adept to unexpected or adversarial inputs(Jayakumar, Brohi, & Jhanjhi, 2021).

In effect, the updating and adaptation process should comply with best practices to keep AI models effective in such a fast-changing danger landscape. Continuous updates and retraining of models to keep up with new attack vectors and data pattern suckle This will also allow it to have some level of robustness with the addition of feedback loops using the attack data in the real world to continuously improve how well they perform. Immediately ting up agile learning systems which will adopt and take effect immediately in these cases empower models to reign relevant capable of repelling advancing cyber threats(N. Jhanjhi, 2021).

Figure 5. AI-Powered Cybersecurity(Muraleedhara, 2024)

B. Ethical Considerations and Bias Mitigation

Cyber security is a space in which artificial intelligence not only offers many advantages for any cyber defense strategy, but it also poses a risk, and so it needs to be managed carefully. One of the biggest problems could be that AI can be manipulated to do harm such as bringing cyberattacks with a very high complexity. This underscores the obligation of technologists and leaders to balance continued advances in AI with securing networks and systems, so that new ideas do not also further expose weaknesses. Furthermore, giving AI autonomy over life and death decisions on a global scale affecting people and sensitive data should be cautiously rationed since the results of errors or bad actors can propagate in ways that impact orders like nothing ever before(N. Jhanjhi, Ahmad, Khan, & Hussain, 2022; Sanderson et al., 2023).

But a more fundamental issue is the problem of bias in AI systems, which can expose them to security holes if they are trained on biased or partial datasets. AI may also ignore some threats due to biases, or overemphasize others, which will result in protection asymmetry between sectors or regions. Reducing these risks requires the use of diverse, representative training data and frequent audits that identify and fix biases, to ensure that AI-powered security solutions are both effective and just. Fairness, accountability, and transparency are three pillars upon which AI operations should be based. Despite decentralized control of models, humans are liable and should be able to understand how the system is operating so that they can audit its performance. Indeed, techniques such as explainable AI can help employers understand how these models operate to implement their use ethically and effectively. Continuous bias monitoring in development and deployment is vital to ensure that all customers are safeguarded from unfair treatment or unexpected risks(Chakraborty, 2023).

C. Collaboration Between Human Experts and AI

Cyber security defense is evolving to must-have competitive and effective cyber defenses require human-in-the-loop AI. While AI-driven systems can be lightning fast at analyzing big data, recognizing patterns, and automating responses it is not infallible. Why it matters: AI is a tool itself, and its outputs must be understood — in complex situations further subjective judgement/complex decision making to make high level or strategic decisions will come into play; AT human consciousness cannot be taken on/off like an outfit with applying or without AI (Nature etc), the point being is that Ignorance and uncertainty should most likely be best handled with a conscious interaction with data. The partnership hinges on a symbiotic relationship that has AI complementing human capabilities by doing rote work and alerting to potential threats, while humans remain the ones with understanding and judgement at scale for the final decision(De Cremer & Kasparov, 2021).

Of course, AI systems may highly support human expertise in terms of recognizing and neutralizing more sophisticated threats. The organization can analyze a lot of network data with AI models and swiftly recognize any malicious activity in its early stages —something that might take much longer or completely escape the notice of a human team. In other words, if you put a bank robber face-to-face with your junior diplomat, that diplomat will probably be able to apply best cybersecurity practices before the bad actor walks out of the door (accessing his banking loot!). A human reviewer can interpret the context in which an attack took place (a situation that may be lost on an AI algorithm). In tandem, AI could do majority of the heavy lifting when it comes to data analysis, with human experts able to spend their time on higher-level decision making – like which potential threats to investigate first(-Carter & Nielsen, 2017).

Many case studies demonstrate the effectiveness of human-AI complementarity in cybersecurity. That is the case, for example with your human + AI cyber threat protection system at a company like Darktrace (as I covered here). Darktrace's AI is always on the lookout for threats across network traffic, and any of those hazards flagged by the machine are then assessed by humans to decide what action must be taken. A great example of it is IBM's Watson for Cyber Security working in collaboration with human analyst. Using this technology, Watson can quickly process unstructured data from research reports, news and blogs; offering those insights directly to human experts so they can make informed decisions on how to learn more about emerging threats. What they all highlight is that the optimal cyber defense strategies combine the best of AI, i.e. speed and scalability with human expertise, intuition and judgement. By combining both, we can have a much higher ability to detect and respond to complex cyber threats(Ashraf, Jhanjhi, Brohi, & Muzafar, 2024; Gaur, Jhanjhi, Bakshi, & Gupta, 2022).

IV. TOOLS AND TECHNOLOGIES SHAPING THE FUTURE OF AI-DRIVEN CYBER DEFENSE

A. Next-Generation AI Security Tools

As discussed in Figure 6.0, A variety of next-generation AI security tools has emerged; these tools are reshaping the future landscape for AI-driven cyber defense, providing deeper capabilities in threat detection, response, and prevention. Using artificial intelligence (AI), machine learning (ML), deep learning, and natural language processing, these tools speed up and make cyber defense mechanisms more accurate. Examples of such cutting-edge platforms, leveraging AI to analyze large data repositories for anomaly detection and incidents response in real time are Darktrace, CrowdStrike Falcon and Cortex XSOAR (formerly Demisto). Designed to work autonomously for threat detection — they are particularly useful when you have a large and complex network environment(Dogra et al., 2022).

These next-gen AI-aided security tools perform automated threat hunting, behavioural analysis and real-time response. Darktrace, for example, employs self-learning AI algorithms to detect abnormalities in networks and CrowdStrike Falcon provides AI-led malware detection, response automation and endpoint protection. Cortex XSOAR extends this by adding orchestration and automation, facilitating the entire security operations workflow. This is by no means a knock on either of these tools — both types are incredibly powerful at detecting threats — but they also may be susceptible to overfitting and false positives from incoming machine data or attack patterns that haven't been detected. However, many AI security products rely on cloud infrastructure, something that is often not acceptable in terms of data security and privacy for certain organizations(Erwin, Zubair, & Sherali, 2022).

The hybrid model could be, by some predictions, the main attraction for forthcoming generations of AI security technologies that provide faster processing and much more complex threat analysis with quantum computing as a resource. Explainable AI (Khan, Jhanjhi, Haji, & bin Haji Omar, 2024) will also be a key enabler for more transparent AI decision-making, so that security teams can see exactly why an AI system has reached the conclusions it has and can trust fully autonomous systems. Similarly, more predictions foreshadow the rise of collaborative AI-based defense platforms, enabling organizations to share threat intelligence in real time for improved collective security defense. With the explosion of AI, it is predicted that machine-learning technology joined by automation and a pinch of quantum technology will change how we protect against those threats which are getting more sophisticated and more dynamic(Dhanaraj, Kamila, Pani, Balusamy, & Rajasekar, 2024).

Figure 6. Categories of GenAI Tools(Denbigh-White, 2024)

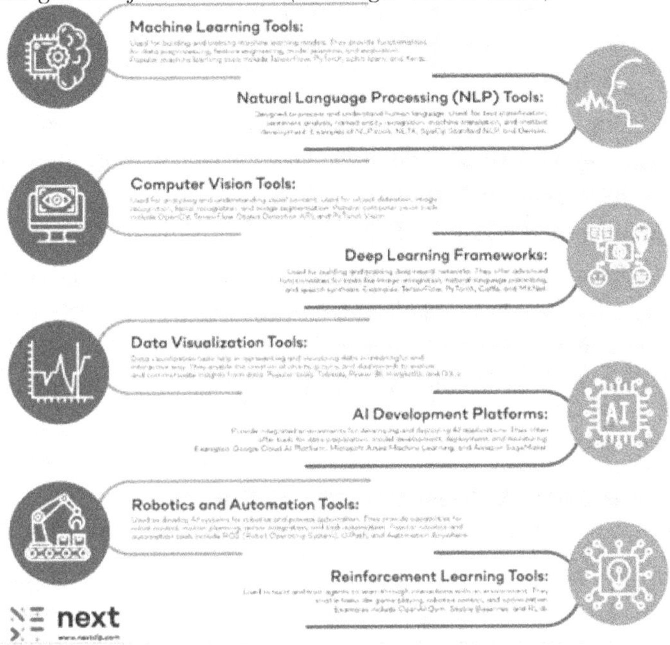

B. Customizable AI Solutions for Cyber Defense

Developing customizable AI-based secure solutions within the cybersecurity space opens up a huge opportunity for enterprises to employ AI-driven tools that better fit their unique protective needs. Unlike generic AI platforms, these custom solutions are fine-tuned to match an enterprise's architecture, risk profile and operation requirements. This adaptability allows organizations to address specific concerns, such as industry-specific susceptibilities or certain types of malwares, with a more focused and effective defense. Several key steps are required for the building and deployment of custom AI-powered cyber defense systems. First, companies need to conduct an extensive risk assessment to identify the areas AI can provide the most impact. They then need to find appropriate AI frameworks for customization, build and train their models on the relevant datasets of each industry to ensure that system is able to identify and respond to high-risk incidents. The Design allows for continued vigilance and updates: The AI should evolve with the threats it combats, and the solution also needs to work in alignment with your existing cybersecurity measures so that there are no discrepancies when operationalized(Matus, 2022; van Geest, Cascavilla, Hulstijn, & Zannone, 2024).

Companies such as JPMorgan Chase and Airbus have effectively employed tailored AI solutions, but a large chunk of rest can toil in their homes. For example, JPMorgan Chase has built an AI system to foster detecting financial fraud, and Airbus does similar with their models developed in-house to protect aerospace data from advanced cyber-attacks using AI techniques. Each agency has trained its AI models with custom datasets and built architectures that enable the agencies to predict threats, detect breaches and respond to attacks more effectively. It's somewhat trivial cases like these that underpin a growing trend of AI-inspired bespoke systems enabling organizations to continue to stay ahead of the ever-changing cyber threats by creating case-based solutions that fit their very needs(AL-Dosari, Fetais, & Kucukvar, 2024).

C. AI-Powered Threat Intelligence Platforms

Through AI, security teams can process and analyze large quantities of data in a way that is both efficient and quick. New methods of experiencing information not only make insights faster than tradition always but broader, too. The AI-driven tool gathers and analyses data from multiple sources – network traffic, open-source intelligence and even dark web traffic - and provides potential threats warning in time to tamp them down. New forms of malware, long-term pervasiveness attacks like Duqu 2.0, etc. By recognizing cyberattack data patterns, AI can forecast future risks, discern changes in attacker activity and find weaknesses before they have been fully exploited. In this way the AI dares to synthesize human intelligence with knowledge already gained in each field such as enterprise computing systems. Natural language processing makes use of these capabilities to scour the Internet for new security threats. It may look at unstructured data – cybersecurity reports and social media updates, for example – to watch out for risks. So rather than just sitting back and waiting until we have this flash point, organizations can take an active stance in defending themselves against cyber-attacks now(Kanth, 2024; Mallikarjunaradhya, Pothukuchi, & Kota, 2023).

The Figure 7.0 illustrates the key Features of Threat Intelligence Platforms and according to AI Security, integrating AI-powered intelligence into existing cybersecurity systems is essential if organizations are to derive maximum utility from this tool. AI can supplement traditional Security Information and Event Management (SIEM) systems and endpoint detection and response (EDR) tools to offer a more rounded defense. By feeding AI-generated insights directly into these tools, security teams can automate responses to high-risk events and focus more on the real threat intelligence work. Additionally, AI platforms can be integrated with cloud infrastructures. This enables organizations to extend their intelligence capabilities without over-taxing the current infrastructure resources or compromising security features of their existing data centres. By adding this integration, an organization can achieve real-time detection, forecasting and countermeasures for complex cyber threats on a large scale(Kimon, Birte, & Christopher, 2021).

Figure 7. Key Features of Threat Intelligence Platforms(BasuMallick, 2022)

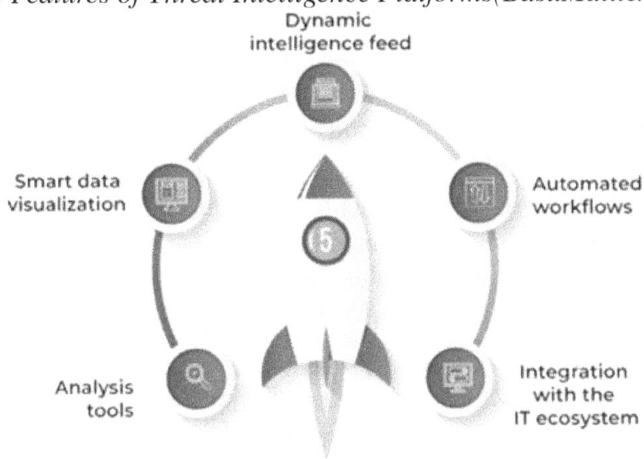

V. CASE STUDIES AND REAL-WORLD APPLICATIONS

A. Case Study 1: AI-Driven Defense Against Advanced Persistent Threats (APTs)

For this, we can consider an example in the real world, where AI-driven systems were used by an organization to stand up against a highly sophisticated Advanced Persistent Threat (APT) attack. APTs are among the worst types of cybercrime, with attackers getting in and remaining undetected for years at a time to steal sensitive data or cripple daily operations. By contrast, the organization leveraged Generative AI to locate and protect against the APT because it could recognize heretofore unseen patterns as well as learn from patterns and modify tactics on-the-fly. Why the problems are serious? Because of this SQL Trojan in the way it works that is advanced to evade detection and perpetually changes attack tactics. Finally, the APT was designed to avoid most traditional security measures and signature-based detection. Yet, during that same period of time the generative AI system was able to review network traffic, user activity and system logs — each individually contributing data showing virtually undetectable irregular activities which stood out as typical APT traits. This was a way to take it several steps further to use the AI simulating all those types of attacks as an early warning system while providing enough notice for different teams to respond in time when an attack lands(Kuwajima & Ishikawa, 2019).

To Figureht back against APT, the organization applied multiple machine learning algorithms as well as behavior analysis. Not only were the AI tools able to identify the threat, but they learned over time as the attack shape shifted. That is how the AI can fantasize about all those scenarios of future attacks — how the bad actors might get there in the end. This proactive approach allowed the organization to field patch currently selling vulnerabilities and effectively stop the attack from a business standpoint. It has helped to contain this APT from progressing more activities on their end goal by the AI-enabled protections. It reduced the time it took to identify and contain new threats, which means less dwell time for attackers to lurk in the system undetected which caused less harm overall. Moreover, the AI effectively streamlined and automated a lot of the communication to respond which in turn saved time and resources for the organization and security team so they could focus more on their strategic based analysis rather than spending time manually detecting and responding efforts(Wright, 2020).

Impact: This case study provides significant observations for on-the-fly con-Figureurable self-defense against sophisticated attacks. However, generative AI can remain ahead of the APT because its polymorphic nature truly gives the ability for generative AI to adapt to the attack. The second take away is to stay alert and integrate AI over all cybersecurity frameworks using multiple levels of security. This is a great example of the many ways organizations can benefit from advanced AI models for cybersecurity, especially to catch and stop those threats that aren't caught through normal channels.

This outcome provides a roadmap for future AI-driven strategies to enhance cyber defense, revealing how the power of AI-powered predictions is becoming an integral aspect of defending against new-age cyber threats.

B. Case Study 2: Defending Against AI-Generated Phishing Campaigns

Out of the different types of spam filtering, traditional methods are falling behind massively these days with the advent of generative AI that has resulted in more sophisticated phishing campaigns being launched. In this case, a large financial institution faced a wave of AI-powered phishing attacks that mimicked valid communication so well it was challenging for even trained professionals to distinguish the malicious emails. These used NLP (Natural language processing) to create custom emails, phished more people and were therefore effective(H. S. Iqbal, 2021).

In response, the bank set up a similarly advanced AI-defense mechanism of their own to identify and stop such ever-evolving threats in real time. This defensive system combined machine learning algorithms and behavioural analysis to analyze all incoming emails and detect extremely subtle anomalies, known indicators of phishing campaigns. The performance of the AI defense system, learning from each subsequent compile in almost real time based on new data could keep you ahead of the forward-moving nature of generative AI phishing campaigns. A key feature was the ability to cross-reference data with user behaviour patterns and identify inconsistencies between legitimate communications and the AI-generated phishing attempts (e.g., slight changes in tone, timing, or content delivery)(Sworna, Mousavi, & Babar, 2023).

The case study offers great in-depth insights into a future where AI-generated cyber threats can only be defended against by another part of unexplainable AI. Given that AI can work on a scale and at a speed well beyond human intervention, it is an important tool with which to provide protection in the current cyber landscape. The case also illustrates how important it is that AI systems are constantly being updated to try and stay ahead in the arms race with generative AI for nefarious purposes. As attacks mature, AI-driven defense systems will be more and more important for early identification of potential threats and prevention, to keep organizations always resilient from cyber adversaries(T. Iqbal & Qureshi, 2022).

C. Comparative Analysis: Traditional vs. AI-Driven Cyber Defense

That is, in the field of cyber security traditional approaches to defense and AI-driven approaches have different advantages and disadvantages. The traditional methods depend on signature-based detection to detect known threats and rely on manual monitoring but struggle with emerging, sophisticated attack vectors such as zero-day exploits or polymorphic malware. These are mostly reactive, old-style systems which rely on predefine rule and pattern or the traditional systems. They are also very human labour-intensive, so the time it takes to respond is a lot longer and not scalable for large volumes of data or difficult networks. In contrast, AI-powered cyber defense systems are built to be forward-thinking, reducing the time it takes to scale and adjust defensive patterns. AI systems are also excellent at processing data in real time, using machine learning (ML) and deep learning (DL) to detect anomalies or new attack patterns as they ultimately present themselves. These used to be rule-based rules and engines and now have evolved into systems capable of self-improving with each experience leading to more reliable threat detection and even faster response times. Automation — AI also automates processes, that way human analysts can spend less time on rote tasks and more time on strategic decision making(Jmila & Khedher, 2022).

AI-driven systems are more successful in this aspect as it can detect threats in real-time, identify any anomalies which are difficult to do with traditional systems and respond automatic to cyber threats. The ability of AI to keep learning and changing shows that one step ahead allows for defense progression with evolution of threat landscapes. What's more, AI-driven systems are infinitely scalable, so they're great for defending intricate and sprawling networks. Recommendations for organizations looking to move to AI–powered cyberdefense. The establishment of an overall risk profile helps to pinpoint where AI (whether more insightful threat intelligence, anomaly detection, or even real-time defense) would be most valuable. In short, having AI equipped to work with legacy systems is part of achieving a multifaceted defense. In this way, it is very important to train AI models with varieties of data to avoid bias and the range over which these models are used against different nature threats around the world should be large(Javadpour, Ja'fari, Taleb, Shojafar, & Benzaïd, 2024).

VI. FUTURE DIRECTIONS IN AI-DRIVEN CYBER DEFENSE

A. Predicting the Evolution of Cyber Threats

Future cyber threats may also include autonomous AI-driven attacks, where AI systems could independently orchestrate large-scale, coordinated attacks without human intervention, adjusting tactics in real-time to bypass defenses. With these risks so high, projecting cybercriminals' next actions is more important than ever. Advance cybersecurity methods are essential to be a step ahead of the new tactics still in development due to the fast pace at which AI-powered cyber threats continue to change. Powered by AI, threat intelligence platforms would have to constantly track the movement of cybercriminals to find clues to the trends behind successful data breaches, ransomware campaigns and other types of attack. While entering this era, cybercriminals in the future could seek to leverage AI like technology attackers, so it's important to have a reliable program that can handle automatic vulnerability scanning and patch management using an AI-driven method. Those changes and the antitheses of legacy cybersecurity models will require predictive analytics and machine learning to forecast how these threats may evolve making good preparation even more critical for cybersecurity teams(Humayun, Hamid, Jhanjhi, Suseendran, & Talib, 2021).

As shown in Figure 8.0 cybersecurity spending, creating preventive defense mechanisms is the key to minimize the risks. AI can help simulate potential attack scenarios and thus aid these organizations to stress test unidentified systems against possible vulnerabilities. Furthermore, businesses should be making the shift to adaptive cybersecurity strategies that consistently revise and remodel their security practices with live intelligence. Predicting and mitigating next generation risks like this will similarly call for collaborative defense networks that see organizations sharing threat intelligence amongst themselves. Taking a flexible and expandable posture of cybersecurity, putting AI systems on a leash, and improving AI-driven defenses will prepare organizations for tackling the new frontier of AI tools taking over cyber-attacks(Gill et al., 2022).

Figure 8. Main Factors Fueling Cybersecurity Spending in 2024(Editorial, 2024)

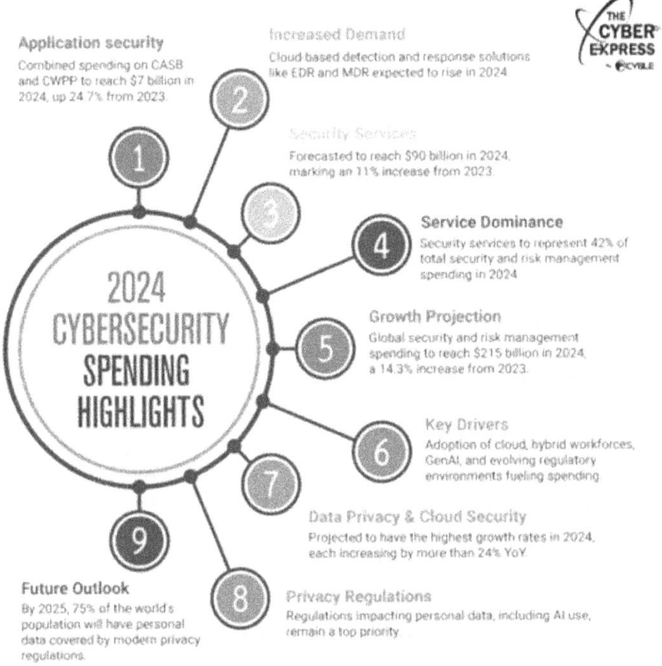

Lastly, the phenomenal use of generative AI by cybercriminals requires us to forecast how cyber threats may evolve in long-term thus preparing ourselves for a tough Figureht against them. Remaining in the proactive column with AI will only keep you safe from a threat landscape evolving into an ever changing and complicated jungle.

B. The Role of AI in Shaping Cybersecurity Policy and Regulation

As shown in Figure 9.0, The AI-driven technologies being deployed at speed in today's cyber defense ecosystem require new rules that address the risks and ethical challenges involved with such a technology. However, AI can be a double-edged sword here, as the advancement of the technology enables both defenders and attackers in their quest to stay ahead of one another. The double-sided AI is difficult to address effectively with the conventional security measures and frameworks. Given the growing importance of AI in cyber offense and defense, it is paramount for lawmakers to introduce policy levers by which uses of AI can be governed in cybersecurity, within reasonable bounds while ensuring accountability and minimizing misuse(Malhotra & Misra, 2022; Owino & Paschal, 2023).

Figure 9. cyber Resilience Pillars(Safitra, Lubis, & Fakhrurroja, 2023)

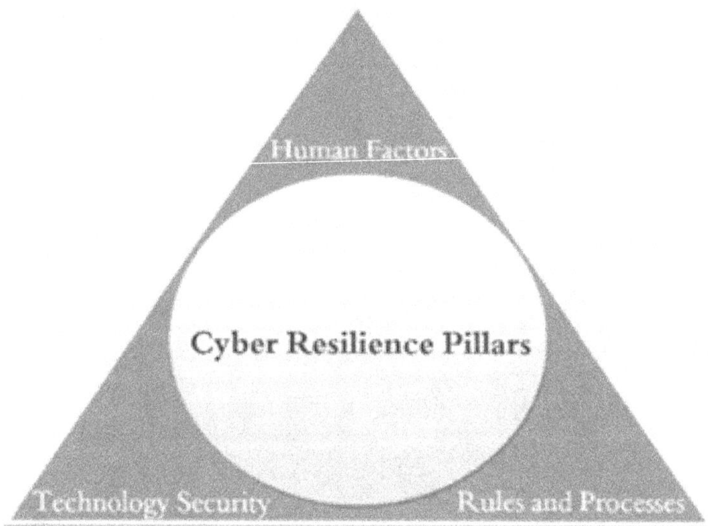

AI's rise in cybersecurity has already impacted existing laws and frameworks by pushing the boundaries of data protection, privacy, and responsible AI use. Current cybersecurity laws primarily focus on human-led efforts and signature-based detection methods, which are less relevant in an era of automated, AI-driven threat detection and response. AI also raises new issues related to liability in the event of an attack. For instance, when an AI system makes an autonomous decision that leads to the exposure of sensitive data, determining responsibility becomes complex. Existing frameworks, such as the General Data Protection Regulation (GDPR) and NIST's

Cybersecurity Framework, may need to be updated to incorporate AI-specific provisions, such as guidelines for algorithmic transparency and ethical AI use in cybersecurity practices(Humayun, 2021; Khan, Jhanjhi, & Humayun, 2022).

Policy Considerations for AI-Powered Cyber Defense, it is important to inform cybersecurity policies of the benefits that artificial intelligence powered cyber defense technologies offer. The first would be around international collaboration to set global standards for AI in cybersecurity. The aim is to avoid fragmentation in regulation and establish common safety and ethics rules for AI systems. A framework of transparency and accountability also needs to be developed to regulate the use AI in all sectors, public and private alike. This includes ensuring that AI systems used in cyber defense are understandable (i.e., oversight, auditing), as well as decision making by the AI (Auditability & XAI). Policymakers must also work to promote public-private partnerships that help draw out innovation, but under guard AI results in responsible use. Lastly, we need rules on ongoing auditing that verify an AI is still engaged in ethical, bias-free operation with a high level of assurance it will not be used to do bad things by third parties(Oniani et al., 2023).

C. Encouraging Innovation and Collaboration in AI Cyber Defense

As hackers use AI in more sophisticated attacks, it has become incredibly important to innovate new security solutions because innovation helps to protect us from those evolving, human challenges. Providing AI innovation lets organizations create stronger real-time threat detection, prevention and response tools to stay ahead against the ever-evolving cyber terrain. Academic, industrial, and governmental partnerships are key to furthering the state of the art in AI for cyber defense—melding theoretical innovation with practical deployment and regulatory oversight. Cross-sector initiatives such as the DARPA Cyber Grand Challenge and partnerships of the kind MIT's CSAIL has with IBM highlight the potential effects of collaboration on creating autonomous cybersecurity solutions that can identify security breaches and respond more rapidly to them. In addition, the success of public-private partnerships such as those driven by the UK's National Cyber Security Centre (the Peston Notation for real world operations together with industry to shape academic research) demonstrate how co-operation can play a central role in closing this gap and building a safer digital future. Organizations can help in the rapid deployment of state-of-the-art AI technologies and develop an environment that enhances overall cyber resilience by fostering innovation and collaboration(Khan et al., 2025).

VII. CONCLUSION

A. Summary of Key Points

In this chapter, we have tried to provide insight on how using generative AI can truly change the way of cyber defense and show that AI-driven technologies are changing essentially everything in security practices. Organizations can now use AI-powered systems to prevent and alert them to cybersecurity attacks in real-time by identifying the irregularities even before carrying out any human intervention. Yet the dual-edged nature of AI also poses significant threats, namely through its use by attackers to evolve their malware approaches, create convincing phishing attacks and produce deepfakes. Consequently, cybersecurity posture needs to switch from reactive to proactive, using artificial intelligence to anticipate and neutralize unknown threats. With trends like the combination of generative AI and quantum computing, blockchain and IoT too are on a similar path to have more scalable and resilient defense systems, while customizable AI solutions can prove particularly adept in defending against threats such as Advanced Persistent Threats (APTs) along with their variants and even AI-generated phishing.

The chapter further pointed out the need for human-AI collaborations to truly combat, as in conjunction AI can identify patterns that would have been harder to do on their own. Inter-industry collaboration between academia, industry and government played a critical role in research in AI orchestrated technologies due to which the evolution of cyber defense has seen significant milestones with walking on paths paved by advanced automation systems. It also pointed out that there is a requirement for new cybersecurity policies, and regulations as the problems are new relates to AI technology thus, they should be handled using latest frameworks. To become and remain agile, organizations must promote ongoing innovation and collaboration to be strategically positioned to more readily respond to real-time cyber threats that emerge in today's deceptively complex digital environment.

Reflection on the Critical Importance of Preparing for the Next Wave of AI-Driven Cyber Threats

The cyber threat landscape is also expected to change along with the progress in artificial intelligence, with possible threats involving a fleet of autonomous systems coordinating attacks without any human involvement. Adversaries may use generative technologies to create malware which can fly under security tools' radar, coordinate highly sophisticated phishing campaigns, or generate deepfakes almost indistinguishable from real videos. In doing so, defenders must take the Figureht to the adversary by using proactive methods, supported in many cases by predictive analytics and tools that utilize AI to anticipate the risks rather than waiting for them to happen before taking action. The deployment of AI that integrates with existing cybersecurity solutions has turned from nice-to-have to must-have if your goal is to stay ahead of ever more rapidly evolving threats. Continuous training of AI models, live surveillance, and adaptive security methods will play a critical role in maintaining consistently better defensive positions. Just as important is the commitment to a transparent, ethical and safe development of AI solutions through thoughtful regulation that supports responsible AI growth.

The nature of the next generation in cyber threats require concerted cooperation between academia, industry and government. By sharing threat intelligence, working together on security products and creating common standards for deploying AI we can help provide a more secure frontline for the global community. With both attackers and defenders shifting towards utilization of the vast power of AI, maintaining cyber resilience will require constant innovation, collaboration, and evolution in this brave new era. This means that not only must organizations gear up for an AI-based defensive battle, but they also need to be on the offensive and prepare for the impact generative AI will have on security in the future.

B. Final Thoughts on the Future of Generative AI in Cyber Defense

To summarize, generative AI will transform cybersecurity efforts in numerous ways. Overall, AI's automation of threat detection, prediction, and response is essential to protect individuals and companies from increasingly advanced cyberattacks. On the other hand, AI will unquestionably be leveraged by attackers who have created the threats being defended against in the first place. Organizations must consider these pitfalls of generative AI to stay ahead of the continual evolution of cyber threats. Moreover, it is necessary to realize that the tool allows detecting and responding to threats in real-time by adjusting to the specific characteristics of the threat. Thus, being stagnant and sticking with traditional methods of cyber defense is no longer viable for any security system. To succeed in the long run, organization security teams need to invest in AI-powered solutions and training regularly. The input of such cybersecurity professionals will help develop the latest systems in collaboration across academia, industry, and government. On a whole, it is critical that organizations realize both the benefits and limitations of what AI can offer and ensure that AI technologies are used to stay ahead of any threat.

REFERENCES

AL-Dosari, K., Fetais, N., & Kucukvar, M.AL-Dosari. (2024). Artificial intelligence and cyber defense system for banking industry: A qualitative study of AI applications and challenges. *Cybernetics and Systems*, 55(2), 302–330. DOI: 10.1080/01969722.2022.2112539

Ashraf, H., Jhanjhi, N. Z., Brohi, S. N., & Muzafar, S. (2024). A Comprehensive Exploration of DDoS Attacks and Cybersecurity Imperatives in the Digital Age. In *Navigating Cyber Threats and Cybersecurity in the Logistics Industry* (pp. 236–257). IGI Global. DOI: 10.4018/979-8-3693-3816-2.ch009

BasuMallick. C. (2022). Top 10 Threat Intelligence Platforms in 2022. Retrieved from https://www.spiceworks.com/it-security/vulnerability-management/articles/best-threat-intelligence-platforms/

Bui, H. T., Aboutorab, H., Mahboubi, A., Gao, Y., Sultan, N. H., Chauhan, A., Parvez, M. Z., Bewong, M., Islam, R., Islam, Z., Camtepe, S. A., Gauravaram, P., Singh, D., Ali Babar, M., & Yan, S. (2024). Agriculture 4.0 and beyond: Evaluating cyber threat intelligence sources and techniques in smart farming ecosystems. *Computers & Security*, 140, 103754. DOI: 10.1016/j.cose.2024.103754

Carter, S., & Nielsen, M. (2017). Using artificial intelligence to augment human intelligence. *Distill*, 2(12), e9. DOI: 10.23915/distill.00009

Chakraborty, S. (2023). AI and ethics: Navigating the moral landscape. In *Investigating the Impact of AI on Ethics and Spirituality* (pp. 25-33).

De Cremer, D., & Kasparov, G. (2021). AI should augment human intelligence, not replace it. *Harvard Business Review*, 18(1).

Denbigh-White, C. (2024). Identifying risk when using Generative AI Tools. Retrieved from https://www.nextdlp.com/resources/blog/ai-security-questions

Desai, T. (2024). Cybersecurity Faces Transformation from Generative AI. Retrieved from https://www.globalxetfs.com/cybersecurity-faces-transformation-from-generative-ai/

Dhanaraj, R. K., Kamila, N. K., Pani, S. K., Balusamy, B., & Rajasekar, V. (2024). *ARTIFICIAL INTELLIGENCE FOR FUTURE INTELLIGENT TRANSPORTATION: Smarter and Greener Infrastructure Design.*

Diro, A., Kaisar, S., Vasilakos, A. V., Anwar, A., Nasirian, A., & Olani, G. (2024). Anomaly detection for space information networks: A survey of challenges, techniques, and future directions. *Computers & Security*, 139, 103705. DOI: 10.1016/j.cose.2024.103705

Dogra, V., Verma, S., Verma, K., Jhanjhi, N. Z., Ghosh, U., & Le, D.-N. (2022). A comparative analysis of machine learning models for banking news extraction by multiclass classification with imbalanced datasets of financial news: challenges and solutions.

Durakovskiy, A. P., Gavdan, G. P., Korsakov, I. A., & Melnikov, D. A. (2021). About the cybersecurity of automated process control systems. *Procedia Computer Science*, 190, 217–225. DOI: 10.1016/j.procs.2021.06.027

Editorial. (2024). Cybersecurity Spending Set to Soar: Over $200 Billion Projection for 2024. Retrieved from https://thecyberexpress.com/cybersecurity-spending-trends-2024/

Erwin, A., Zubair, A. B., & Sherali, Z. (2022). Artificial Intelligence for Cybersecurity: Offensive Tactics. *Mitigation Techniques and Future Directions.*, 1(1), 1–23. DOI: 10.5604/01.3001.0016.0800

G, J. K. (2023). Generative AI Tech Stack Breakdown | A Comprehensive Guide. Retrieved from https://www.xenonstack.com/blog/generative-ai-tech-stack-breakdown

Gaur, L., Jhanjhi, N. Z., Bakshi, S., & Gupta, P. (2022). *Analyzing Consequences of Artificial Intelligence on Jobs using Topic Modeling and Keyword Extraction.* Paper presented at the 2022 2nd International Conference on Innovative Practices in Technology and Management (ICIPTM). DOI: 10.1109/ICIPTM54933.2022.9754064

Gaur, L., Solanki, A., Wamba, S. F., & Jhanjhi, N. Z. (2021). *Advanced AI techniques and applications in bioinformatics.* CRC Press. DOI: 10.1201/9781003126164

Gill, S. S., Xu, M., Ottaviani, C., Patros, P., Bahsoon, R., Shaghaghi, A., & Abraham, A. (2022). AI for next generation computing: Emerging trends and future directions. *Internet of Things : Engineering Cyber Physical Human Systems*, 19, 100514. DOI: 10.1016/j.iot.2022.100514

Gimenez-Aguilar, M., de Fuentes, J. M., Gonzalez-Manzano, L., & Arroyo, D. (2021). Achieving cybersecurity in blockchain-based systems: A survey. *Future Generation Computer Systems*, 124, 91–118. DOI: 10.1016/j.future.2021.05.007

Gong, W., Wang, Y., Chen, H., & Wang, D. (2021). Anomaly Diagnosis for Navigation Sensors of Unmanned Autonomous Vehicles Based on Deep Learning. *Jixie Gongcheng Xuebao. Jixie Gongcheng Xuebao*, 57(24), 268–278. DOI: 10.3901/JME.2021.24.268

Grand View Research. I. (2023). Global Ai In Cybersecurity Market Size & Outlook. Retrieved from https://www.grandviewresearch.com/horizon/outlook/ai-in-cybersecurity-market-size/global

Humayun, M. (2021). Industry 4.0 and cyber security issues and challenges. [TURCOMAT]. *Turkish Journal of Computer and Mathematics Education*, 12(10), 2957–2971.

Humayun, M., Hamid, B., Jhanjhi, N., Suseendran, G., & Talib, M. (2021). *5G network security issues, challenges, opportunities and future directions: A survey.* Paper presented at the Journal of Physics: Conference Series. DOI: 10.1088/1742-6596/1979/1/012037

Iqbal, H. S. (2021). AI-Driven Cybersecurity: An Overview, Security Intelligence Modeling and Research Directions. DOI: 10.20944/preprints202101.0457.v1

Iqbal, T., & Qureshi, S. (2022). The survey: Text generation models in deep learning. *Journal of King Saud University. Computer and Information Sciences*, 34(6, 6, Part A), 2515–2528. DOI: 10.1016/j.jksuci.2020.04.001

Javadpour, A., Ja'fari, F., Taleb, T., Shojafar, M., & Benzaïd, C. (2024). A Comprehensive Survey on Cyber Deception Techniques to Improve Honeypot Performance. *Computers & Security*, 103792, 103792. Advance online publication. DOI: 10.1016/j.cose.2024.103792

Jayakumar, P., Brohi, S. N., & Jhanjhi, N. Z. (2021). Artificial intelligence and military applications: Innovations, cybersecurity challenges & open research areas.

Jhanjhi, N. (2021). A design of IoT-based medicine case for the multi-user medication management using drone in elderly centre. *Journal of Engineering Science and Technology*, 16(2), 1145–1166.

Jhanjhi, N., Ahmad, M., Khan, M. A., & Hussain, M. (2022). The impact of cyber attacks on e-governance during the covid-19 pandemic. In *Cybersecurity Measures for E-Government Frameworks* (pp. 123–140). IGI Global. DOI: 10.4018/978-1-7998-9624-1.ch008

Jhanjhi, N. Z., Gaur, L., & Khan, N. A. (2024). Global Navigation Satellite Systems for Logistics: Cybersecurity Issues and Challenges. *Cybersecurity in the Transportation Industry*, 49-67.

Jmila, H., & Khedher, M. I. (2022). Adversarial machine learning for network intrusion detection: A comparative study. *Computer Networks*, 214, 109073. Advance online publication. DOI: 10.1016/j.comnet.2022.109073

Kanth, T. C. (2024). AI-POWERED THREAT INTELLIGENCE FOR PROACTIVE SECURITY MONITORING IN CLOUD INFRASTRUCTURES.

Khan, A., Jhanjhi, N., Haji, D. H. T. B. A., & bin Haji Omar, H. A. H. (2024). Overview of XAI for the Development and Modernization of Smart Cities: Explainable Artificial Intelligence. In *Advances in Explainable AI Applications for Smart Cities* (pp. 177-198): IGI Global.

Khan, A., Jhanjhi, N., Hamid, D. H. H., Omar, H. A. H. B. H., Amsaad, F., & Wassan, S. (2025). Future Trends and Challenges in Cybersecurity and Generative AI. *Reshaping CyberSecurity With Generative AI Techniques*, 491-522.

Khan, A., Jhanjhi, N. Z., & Humayun, M. (2022). The Role of Cybersecurity in Smart Cities. In *Cyber Security Applications for Industry 4.0* (pp. 195–208). Chapman and Hall/CRC. DOI: 10.1201/9781003203087-9

Khan, A., Jhanjhi, N. Z., Omar, H. A. H. B. H., & Haji, D. H. T. B. A. (2024). Risk Management and Cybersecurity in Transportation and Warehousing. In *Cybersecurity Measures for Logistics Industry Framework* (pp. 1–35). IGI Global.

Khan, A. R. S., Syed, H. J., Shuja, J., Khan, A., Qamar, F., & Nguyen, Q. N. (2024). Advancing Secure and Efficient Sensor Data Integration in Smart Cities: A Blockchain-Based Approach. In *Preprints*: *Preprints*.

Kimon, K., Birte, K., & Christopher, S. (2021). AI-Ethics by Design. Evaluating Public Perception on the Importance of Ethical Design Principles of AI. *arXiv: Computers and Society*. Retrieved from https://arxiv.org/pdf/2106.00326.pdf

Kuwajima, H., & Ishikawa, F. (2019). *Adapting square for quality assessment of artificial intelligence systems*. Paper presented at the Proceedings - 2019 IEEE 30th International Symposium on Software Reliability Engineering Workshops, ISSREW 2019. DOI: 10.1109/ISSREW.2019.00035

Malhotra, P., & Misra, A. (2022). *ACCOUNTABILITY and RESPONSIBILITY of ARTIFICIAL INTELLIGENCE DECISION-MAKING MODELS in INDIAN POLICY LANDSCAPE*. Paper presented at the CEUR Workshop Proceedings.

Mallikarjunaradhya, V., Pothukuchi, A. S., & Kota, L. V. (2023). An overview of the strategic advantages of AI-powered threat intelligence in the cloud. *Journal of Science and Technology*, 4(4), 1–12. DOI: 10.55662/JST.2023.4401

Masum, R. (2023). Cyber Security in Smart Manufacturing (Threats, Landscapes Challenges). *arXiv preprint arXiv:2304.10180.*

Matus, P. P. (2022). AI Ethics and Policy. *Future of Business and Finance*, 101-118. DOI: 10.1007/978-3-031-19039-1_5

Mumtaz, S. L., Syed, H. J., Al-Ani, A., Fatah, S., Al-Ani, A. K., & Khan, A. (2024). *Detection of Botnet in the loT Network.* Paper presented at the ITM Web of Conferences. DOI: 10.1051/itmconf/20246301019

Muraleedhara, P. (2024). The Need For AI-Powered Cybersecurity to Tackle AI-Driven Cyberattacks. Retrieved from https://www.isaca.org/resources/news-and-trends/isaca-now-blog/2024/the-need-for-ai-powered-cybersecurity-to-tackle-ai-driven-cyberattacks

Oniani, D., Hilsman, J., Peng, Y., Poropatich, R. K., Pamplin, J. C., Legault, G. L., & Wang, Y. (2023). Adopting and expanding ethical principles for generative artificial intelligence from military to healthcare. *npj. Digital Medicine*, 6(1), 225. Advance online publication. DOI: 10.1038/s41746-023-00965-x PMID: 38042910

Ortega, E., Tran, M., & Bandeen, G. (2023). *AI Digital Tool Product Lifecycle Governance Framework through Ethics and Compliance by Design†.* Paper presented at the Proceedings - 2023 IEEE Conference on Artificial Intelligence, CAI 2023. DOI: 10.1109/CAI54212.2023.00155

Owino, B. A., & Paschal, M. J. (2023). AI and ethics in education: Implications and strategies for responsible implementation. In *Creative AI Tools and Ethical Implications in Teaching and Learning* (pp. 196-211).

Papastergiou, S., Mouratidis, H., & Kalogeraki, E. M. (2021). Handling of advanced persistent threats and complex incidents in healthcare, transportation and energy ICT infrastructures. *Evolving Systems*, 12(1), 91–108. DOI: 10.1007/s12530-020-09335-4

Rashmi, S., Siwach, V., Sehrawat, H., Brar, G. S., Singla, J., Jhanjhi, N., . . . Shorfuzzaman, M. AI-Powered VM Selection: Amplifying Cloud Performance with Dragonfly Algorithm. *Heliyon.*

Repetto, M. (2023). Adaptive monitoring, detection, and response for agile digital service chains. *Computers & Security*, 132, 103343. DOI: 10.1016/j.cose.2023.103343

S., M. (2023). Rewards and Risks: What Generative AI Means for Security. Retrieved from https://cxotoday.com/specials/rewards-and-risks-what-generative-ai-means-for-security/

Saeed, S., Jhanjhi, N., Naqvi, S. M. R., & Khan, A. (2022). Analytical Approach for Security of Sensitive Business Cloud. *Deep Learning in Data Analytics: Recent Techniques, Practices and Applications*, 257-266.

Safitra, M. F., Lubis, M., & Fakhrurroja, H. (2023). Counterattacking cyber threats: A framework for the future of cybersecurity. *Sustainability (Basel)*, 15(18), 13369. DOI: 10.3390/su151813369

Sanderson, C., Douglas, D., Lu, Q., Schleiger, E., Whittle, J., Lacey, J., Newnham, G., Hajkowicz, S., Robinson, C., & Hansen, D. (2023). AI ethics principles in practice: Perspectives of designers and developers. *IEEE Transactions on Technology and Society*, 4(2), 171–187. DOI: 10.1109/TTS.2023.3257303

Sayegh, E. (2023). Navigating The Cybersecurity Landscape In 2024. Retrieved from https://www.forbes.com/sites/emilsayegh/2023/12/19/navigating-the-cybersecurity-landscape-in-2024/

Sharma, T., & Sharma, P. (2024). AI-based cybersecurity threat detection and prevention. In *Perspectives on Artificial Intelligence in Times of Turbulence: Theoretical Background to Applications* (pp. 81-98): IGI Global.

Sidi-Mohammed, S., Hichem, S., Jiajia, L., Mubashir Husain, R., & Elias, B.-H. (2020). AI-Driven Cybersecurity Threats to Future Networks [From the Guest Editors]. *IEEE Vehicular Technology Magazine*, 15(3), 5–6. DOI: 10.1109/MVT.2020.3007981

Sindiramutty, S. R., Jhanjhi, N., & Ray, S. K. (2024). Threat Hunting and Behaviour Analysis. *Utilizing Generative AI for Cyber Defense Strategies*, 235.

Sindiramutty, S. R., Prabagaran, K. R. V., Jhanjhi, N., Ghazanfar, M. A., Malik, N. A., & Soomro, T. R. (2025). Security Considerations in Generative AI for Web Applications. In *Reshaping CyberSecurity With Generative AI Techniques* (pp. 281–332). IGI Global.

Sindiramutty, S. R., Prabagaran, K. R. V., Jhanjhi, N., & Murugesan, R. K. (2024). Threat Intelligence and Information Sharing. *Utilizing Generative AI for Cyber Defense Strategies*, 191.

Sindiramutty, S. R., Prabagaran, K. R. V., Jhanjhi, N., Murugesan, R. K., Brohi, S. N., & Masud, M. (2025). Generative AI in Network Security and Intrusion Detection. In *Reshaping CyberSecurity With Generative AI Techniques* (pp. 77–124). IGI Global.

Sujatha, R., Prakash, G., & Jhanjhi, N. Z. (2022). *Cyber Security Applications for Industry 4.0*. CRC Press. DOI: 10.1201/9781003203087

Sukhwinder, S. (2023). The Rise of Generative AI in Reinforcing Cyber Defense. Retrieved from https://medium.com/@sukhwinder.s/the-rise-of-generative-ai-in-reinforcing-cyber-defense-4c512fbb8968

Sworna, Z. T., Mousavi, Z., & Babar, M. A. (2023). NLP methods in host-based intrusion detection systems: A systematic review and future directions. *Journal of Network and Computer Applications*, 220, 103761. DOI: 10.1016/j.jnca.2023.103761

Tayyab, M., Hameed, K., Jhanjhi, N. Z., Zaheer, A., & Qamar, F. (2024). Digital Safeguards: Navigating Cyber Threats in the Logistics Industry Framework. In *Navigating Cyber Threats and Cybersecurity in the Logistics Industry* (pp. 258-299): IGI Global.

Tayyab, M., Marjani, M., Jhanjhi, N., Hashem, I. A. T., Usmani, R. S. A., & Qamar, F. (2023). A Comprehensive Review on Deep Learning Algorithms: Security and Privacy Issues. *Computers & Security*, 131, 103297. DOI: 10.1016/j.cose.2023.103297

Teig, J., & Eiken, A. (2024). *Use of Generative AI in Offensive Cybersecurity: A case study using PentestGPT with GPT-4 and Dolphin2. 5.* NTNU, van Geest, R. J., Cascavilla, G., Hulstijn, J., & Zannone, N. (2024). The applicability of a hybrid framework for automated phishing detection. *Computers & Security*, 139, 103736. DOI: 10.1016/j.cose.2024.103736

Vemuri, N., Thaneeru, N., & Tatikonda, V. M. (2024). Adaptive generative AI for dynamic cybersecurity threat detection in enterprises.

Wright, S. A. (2020). *AI in the Law: Towards Assessing Ethical Risks.* Paper presented at the Proceedings - 2020 IEEE International Conference on Big Data, Big Data 2020. DOI: 10.1109/BigData50022.2020.9377950

Chapter 7
Image Steganography Metamodel Using Model-Driven Engineering

Muhammad Adnan Aslam
Air University, Pakistan

Syeda Mariam Muzammal
https://orcid.org/0000-0003-2960-1814
Taylor's University, Malaysia

Noor Zaman Jhanjhi
https://orcid.org/0000-0001-8116-4733
Taylor's University, Malaysia

Muhammad Tayyab
https://orcid.org/0000-0001-5580-9163
Taylor's University, Malaysia

ABSTRACT

Ensuring secure data transfer over a network involves many concerns and has been considered challenging. The most commonly used technique for securing data is encryption, which allows data to be encrypted to avoid unauthorized access. Image steganography is a special kind of encryption in which an additional layer of security is provided by hiding the data in a carrier image. This process can be performed in multiple ways. For example, Least Significant Bit (LSB)-Steganography is a technique in which the data is hidden within an image by replacing the least significant bits of the images with the data which is to be encrypted. Such techniques are exploited by cyber security professionals and application developers to implement encryption according to the scenarios and domain requirements. In this research,

DOI: 10.4018/979-8-3693-6135-1.ch007

we have proposed a metamodel based on steganography using the LSB technique to autogenerate code in any programming language.

1. INTRODUCTION

The Internet's boundaries have been significantly widened by new network technologies including 5G (Humayun et al., 2021), Internet of Things (IoT), cloud computing, and sophisticated distribution networks such as, satellite networks, in recent years (Annadurai et al., 2022; Humayun & Al, 2021; Muzammal et al., 2021, 2022). Internet is now too complex to be represented by a graph with basic nodes and edges. In the meantime, cyber security technologies have advanced from intrusion prevention systems, anomaly detection systems, anti-virus software, honeypots, and web application firewall (WAF), to more active and sophisticated techniques (Tayyab et al., 2024). To overcome the growing security challenges, a new terminology, metamodel, is introduced (Xiong et al., 2022) that incorporates aspects of cybersecurity to facilitate studies of both optimization and network security concerns.

Figure 1. Information hiding adapted from (Desai, 2012)

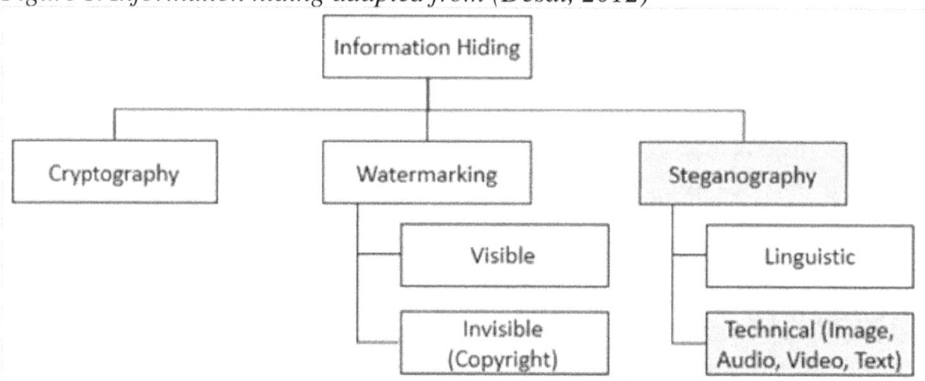

Information security is the only way that assures that all data or information is secure and not compromised by intruders. Many organizations including government institutions, military departments, and hospitals implement different strategies to protect their sensitive information or data. Unauthorized data access can severely damage the reputation of an organization. Data is transmitted via network to various computers, while there is a risk that hackers will get access to the sensitive information (Din et al., 2024) (Muzammal & Murugesan, 2021) (Mandal et al., 2022).

Throughout the work on most of the information security projects, information assurance is an important aspect to consider. Furthermore, watermarking, cryptography, and steganography are widely used and well known schemes for information hiding (Desai, 2012) as shown in Fig. 1. Steganography can be used in order to hide the textual data in cover image (Kadhim et al., 2019).

Steganography is a derivative of the Greek word 'steganos' and 'graphy' meaning drawing or writing, and therefore literally means covered writing. Digital steganography is data hiding in communication art and science. A steganography system incorporates confidential data into the cover media to protect it from intruders and avoid unauthorized access. The primary purpose of this type of information hiding is to conceal messages or data inside the covered images in such a way that it does not permit any hacker or intruder to even perceive that there is a secret message existing in the image.

The steganographic image or the stegano-system allows users to send secret messages or sensitive data or information using digital steganography. The use of stegano-systems and the encapsulated algorithms provides a better and more secure door for data safety. Creative and advanced methods and terminologies for encapsulating information in a covered image file are provided in a steganographic digital image. Innovative techniques are available for the steganography-based digital image system for hiding or encrypting text in digital image files.

In steganography, LSB is a well-known technique for information hiding in covered image (Aslam et al., 2022; Bhavani et al., 2022; Halboos & Albakry, 2022; Murugan et al., 2022). The data hiding steganography can be done in different ways depending on the cover image used, information hiding strategy, or the basis of the modifiable layout used in the process of embedding. Metamodel is basically a high-level conceptual design in which a programming-language-independent model is devised on the basis of which a code can be generated in any programming language automatically. In the domain of steganography, to the best of our knowledge, a high-level conceptual metamodel has not been designed yet. Following are the contributions of this research study.

1. Proposed a Metamodel based on steganography using the LSB technique to autogenerate code in any programming language.
2. Our Metamodel has enhanced the generalized and automated solution for the cyber security experts community and security system developers.
3. Our proposed metamodel illustrates the encoding and decoding of secret data, where the systems are primarily developed through modelling and the source code is generated automatically.
4. Our proposed metamodel performs well based on its evaluation using a case study.

The rest of the chapter is organized as follows. Section 2 presents the analysis of the related recent literature. Section 3 provides the data-hiding steganography system and adopted methodology to develop an image steganography metamodel. Section 4 presents the proposed methodology and research design. Section 5 provides the validation of the proposed approach and metamodel, and Section 6 concludes the paper along with future directions.

2. LITERATURE REVIEW

In today's scientific and technological era, communication has become a major part of everyday life. Data security is an important field with the increasing demand of communication traffic (Chan & Cheng, 2004), (Dey et al., 2007). The last decade has developed a lot of information security and data hiding or the information encapsulation algorithms. Steganography digital image system provides a user with the option of secure transmission of text messages through hiding via digital techniques (Kadhim et al., 2019). The stego technique-based image algorithms and systems offer imaginative strategies for concealing or hiding content in a covered image file and are also used in encryption or encapsulation techniques as a key in order to hide the sensitive information.

In (Goel et al., 2015), authors presented a scheme for hiding sensitive data in the source image using different techniques of LSB-based methods. Comparing stego-image quality with image quality, the authors used numerous image quality parameters like Peak Signal-to-Noise Ratio (PSNR), Median Square Error (MSE), Structural Similarity Index Measure (SSIM) and similarity index. In (Atawneh et al., 2013), Atawneh et al. proposed LSB-based image steganography technique of pixel adjustment. The result of this adaptive LSB replacement is high hiding capacity. Similarly, a steganography technique based on the image has been proposed in (Amin et al., 2003). The redundant bit patterns of data have been used and the pixel LSB's are modified. However, the hiding capacity of their method is quite low. Habib et al. has proposed an adaptive fuzzy filter based on convolved feature vector for impulse noise removal (Habib et al., 2023).

In (Ahmed & Khalifa, 2014), authors purposed a method to improve the security of the information by using LSB image steganography together with Elliptic Curve Cryptography (ECC). The steganography digital image system enables a normal client to safely exchange instant messages by concealing them in digitalized photography. This process initially uses ECC to encrypt secret information and then embed in a cover image via LSB-steganography image method, followed by the presentation and implementation of the enhanced series of traditional LSB steganography image technology. Their work improves stego image quality by applying the bit reversal approach. Two techniques are proposed and implemented for bit reversal for solving bit inversion in which carrier image pixel LSBs are inverted only when they occur with specific pixel bits pattern. This results in less pixel modification in comparison with the traditional LSB method. Inverted bits must be embedded somewhere in the stego image to get the secret message correctly.

Deshmuk and Pattewar (Deshmukh & Pattewar, 2014) also presented the LSB-based edge adaptive steganography. The accommodation system has been used for incorporating secret information into a sharp (edge) region of the carrier image. Their technique does well in comparison with other techniques based on LSB and pixel differences and maintains stego image quality. Al-Otaibi and Gutub (Al-Otaibi, Nouf & Gutub, Adnan, 2014) developed a system called as 2-layer security system to hide sensitive personal computer information. The system is divided into two layers, cryptography and steganography. LSB algorithm has been used for steganography layer and Advanced Encryption Standard (AES) algorithm has been used for cryptography layer. For embedding the secret message into the cover image, they used 1 to 2 bits of LSB. They concluded that the effect of 1LSB and 2LSB is minimal in stego image, but the image is distorted to visible levels with 3LSB, 4LSB, 5LSB, 6LSB and 7LSB and has very low stego image quality that is not ideal for steganography image.

Islam et.al, in (Islam et al., 2014), improved LSB image steganography version based on an efficient status bit filter technology. Their proposed work has also used the AES algorithm to prove extra security layer encryption. Because of their uncompressed nature, bitmap and .bmp images have been used in their work which are more preferable for steganography that depends on LSB, showing that LSB algorithm has high implanting and embedding limits than basic fundamentals of the least significant. Due to the high stego image quality, PSNR values are also high. A metamodel that governs or provides a security mechanism for the development and use of cloud services is proposed in (Washizaki et al., 2016). It has been anticipated that the metamodel will be used to create a knowledge base that will compile, classify, and reuse cloud infrastructure security and privacy patterns and methods in a systematic and standard manner. In (Trizna, 2022), a study has been conducted where metamodel is designed to predict the severity of malware in Windows by analyzing the contextual and behavioral properties.

2.1. Image Steganographic Methods and Metamodeling

Various types of the image steganographic methods have been discussed in (Nosrati, Masoud et al., 2011) and a random bit selection method based on LSB steganography is suggested. Randomly selected bit for the inclusion of secret information within the cover image is the least important part of such techniques. In

(Al-Afandy et al., 2016), authors suggested an improved image steganography LSB algorithm. In their work, secret information is only integrated into the blue part of the RGB color space. Experimental results demonstrated that the image deformity of the cover picture and stego picture decreases. Different techniques of the metamodel have been reviewed by Wang and Shan (Wang & Shan, 2006) to improve the computational efficiency of the system and the significance of the metamodel. It has been emphasized that a metamodel has a vital role in the model approximation that reduces the computational cost and design space exploration and let the engineers understand the design problems in good manner. Mainly, three different techniques of the metamodel have been discussed, experimental design/sampling method, linear metamodel choice and the model fitting technique.

Metamodeling is a fundamental building block of Model-Driven Architecture (MDA). In (Wachsmuth, 2007), it has been discussed that metamodel needs to be evolved over the time just like the other software artefacts due to several reasons especially when alternative metamodel versions are developed during design and well- known solutions for new applications are customized. A transformational approach has been proposed to evolve the model over time according to semantics or instance-preservation. Similarly, in (Jadhav et al., 2024), authors have proposed a model transformation by using the adaptive dragonfly algorithm (ADF) along with the Cuckoo search algorithm for the conversion of UML class diagram to relational schema. In a research by Yang et al. (Yang et al., 2023), a meta model is proposed based on RAMI 4.0 for the description of manufacturing resources and their status. In addition, De Hoog et al. (De Hoog et al., 2023) has exploited the classifier recommendation approach based on metamodel for the prediction of per-class image classification performance.

2.2. Least Significant Bit (LSB)-Steganography

In steganography, LSB substitution is the most common technique for data hiding (Pradhan et al., 2018). The information security is being enhanced by combining LSB with cryptography (Ahmed & Khalifa, 2014), adjusting the pixel value (Amin et al., 2003), and using status bit filter technology (Islam et al., 2014). Hence, the existing literature demonstrates extensive research in the field of LSB image steganography, and various methods have been devised to encode or extract secret messages. Though innumerable research is being conducted on significance of metamodels in different aspects, such as, malware prediction (Trizna, 2022), security in cloud services (Washizaki et al., 2016), network security (Xiong et al., 2022), metamodels need to be evolved over time (Wachsmuth, 2007). However, to the best of our knowledge, no high-level conceptual and flexible solution has been found.

The application developers and domain experts, who want to take advantage of steganography, have to deal with many related operations at very low level of abstraction. This results in high complexity and eventually high cost of development with respect to time and efforts. To fill out this research gap, a less complex and automated solution is required. This shall facilitate the community of software developers for implementation of image steganography at a high level of abstraction and cut down the complexity, cost, and development time. Image steganography plays a crucial role for a variety of applications and systems where data security is required. Hence, a generalized model is needed to facilitate a diversified community of domain experts who may be unaware of the technicalities of steganography but want a ready-made solution for their systems. It has been revealed from the literature that metamodel against the steganography has not been proposed yet. This paper is an effort to initiate this particular study to provide a metamodel through which automated code in any platform can be generated.

3. DATA HIDING STEGANOGRAPHY

A data hiding steganography system can be divided based on the usage of cover image, strategy for information hiding or modifiable image layout (AbdelRaouf, 2021). In covering file-based classification, there are many types of digital media files that are used as covered files. The cover file properties vary from one file to another. The properties of these files control how the secret message can be hidden. The other strategy used to hide confidential information, hiding method-based classification, is to classify the steganographic system (Dey et al., 2007).

Secret data can be hidden in cover files in three ways including insertion- based, substitution-based, and generation-based methods. In this research paper, a digital image method has been proposed based on a covered technique in which cover image is used or manipulated for hiding confidential data in the form of text file. Equation (1) presents the E_m function to construct the stego image. Three crucial components of E_m function include. *C* as cover image, *M* as secret message, and *k* as optional key. By using cryptography, a key is used to further secure a secret message while maintaining the integrity and privacy of the hidden data. The E_x function is represented by Equation (2) to extract the secret message from stego image.

$$E_m . C \oplus M \oplus K \rightarrow C\sim \quad (1)$$

$$E_x(E_m(c, m, k)) \approx m \; \forall \; c \in C, m \in M, k \in K \quad (2)$$

The conventions used in this paper are described in Table 1. If the key is used to secure the secret data, the cipher data is then decrypted using the key, once it has been extracted from the stego image. Fig. 2 presents the concept of the proposed method. The main objective of the proposed approach is to formulate a metamodel which will be transformed into working code. The automated code generation has several benefits as compared to classical software development paradigms. The metamodel has been developed in order to incorporate all procedural steps to implement image steganography from embedding to the extraction of the secret data which is to be transmitted from one point to the other. The embedding phase of the LSB algorithm includes the following steps.

Step-1. Pixel extraction and conversion of image to binary.
Step-2. Conversion of secret data in to binary.
Step-3. Conversion of stego key to binary data.
Step-4. Using LSB, replace each least significant bit by the stego key and then adjust all bits of the secret data in the same way. Repeat this process until the stego key and the secret data both get embedded in the cover image. The stego image is the resulting image.
Step-5. Stego image reconstruction so that the embedded message can be transmitted.

During extraction phase the same steps are followed but in reverse order. In the beginning, the stego image is converted in to binary and the stego key is extracted. If the key matches the key entered by the receiver, then the extraction of the secret message character is started otherwise the request is declined. This process is repeated until all of the secret data is extracted.

Table 1. Description of notations used

Notation	Description
C	Cover Image
C	Stego image after embedding
M	Secret message to be transmitted
K	Key for encoding/decoding
E_m	Process of embedding data
E_x	Extraction of original data

3.1. Adopted Methodology to Develop Image Steganography Metamodel

Figure 2. concept

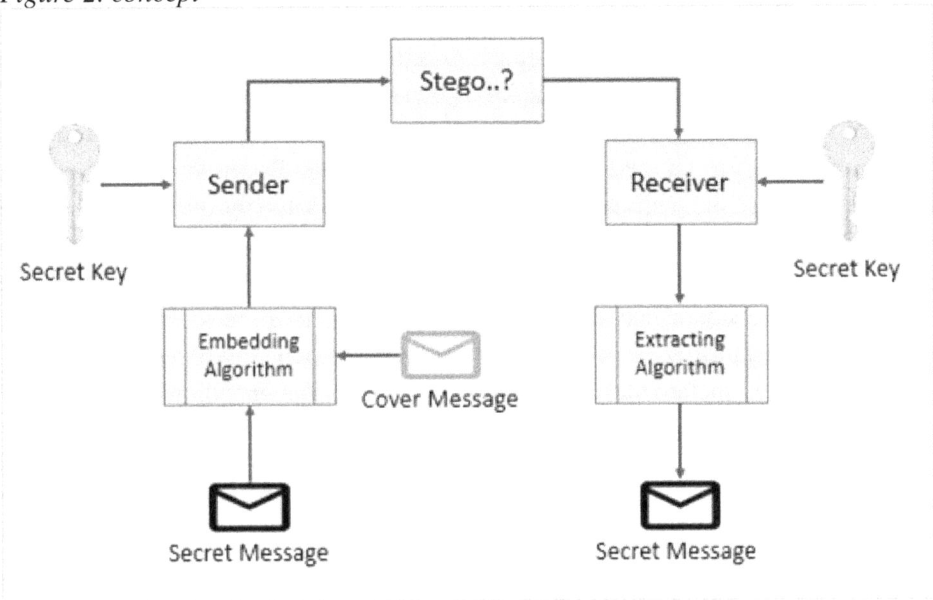

Figure 3. flow chart

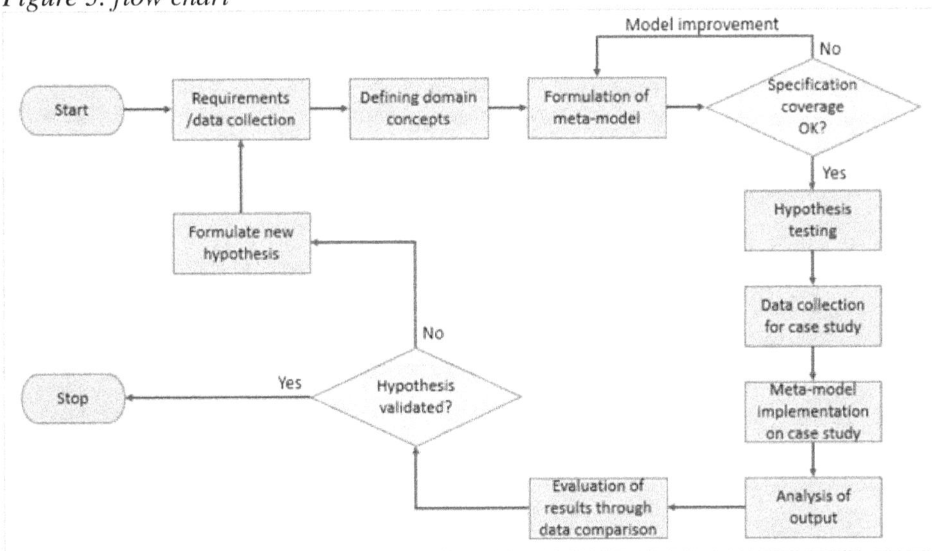

The hypothesis of this research study states that a metamodel of the image steganography can be formulated to provide a high level solution. Using model driven techniques, domain specific code can be generated which shall enhance the productivity of the developers. The flow chart of the plan to conduct this research study is presented in Fig. 3. It depicts all the steps that are followed in order to prove truthfulness of the formulated hypothesis. The hypothesis requires the formulation of a metamodel of image steganography. The metamodel is developed starting from the definition of specifications and domain concepts. The domain concepts are then converted into a formal metamodel using Eclipse UML Papyrus tool. The model is refined until all algorithmic steps have been covered. Lastly, a case study is developed to validate the developed metamodel as well as the formulated hypothesis.

Starting from step-1, the following domain concepts were defined. data steganography, image encoder, encoded image, encoding activity/process, image to binary transformation, data to binary transformation, decoded image, and decoding process. For the proposed metamodel, Algorithm 1 illustrates the encoding of secret data into cover image. Similarly, Algorithm 2 illustrates the pseudocode for decoding of secret data from the stegano image. These are well-known algorithms for LSB-based steganography. In this research, a model is presented for these algorithms using MDA, by which an auto code can be generated in any platform and language.

Table 2.

Input. CoverImage C, Secret_message m
Output. *Stegoimage SI*
Binaryimage *imagetobin(C) // converting CoverImage into binary image*
Databinary *datatobin(m) // Converting Secret_message m into 8 bit binary*
Function*Encoding_LSB_Replacement(binaryimage,databinary)* ***[M,N]*** *size(binaryimage)* *datasize size(databinary)* ***For****k 1 to datasize****do*** *s=databinary[k] // extract s bit from databinary to embed in LSB of binaryimage* ***For****i 1 to* ***Mdo*** ***For****j 1 to* ***Ndo*** SI_{ixj} *= LSB(binaryimage* $_{ixj}$*, s) // replacing pixel value LSB bit with s bit of data* ***end*** ***end*** ***end***

Table 3.

Input. Stegoimage SI
Output. *Secret_message m*
Binaryimage *imagetobin(SI) // converting Stego Image into binary image*
Function*Decoding_data_extractor(SI)* *[M,N] size(SI) // Get the total number of pixels in stego image* ***Initialize****k 1* ***For****i 1 to M****do*** ***For****j 1 to N****do*** $Data_{(k)} = LSB(SI_{i x j}, s)$ *// reading pixel value LSB bit to extract data-bit* *k k+1* ***end*** ***end***
m *bintochar(Data) // converting secret data binary into Character using ASCII table*

4. PROPOSED IMAGE STEGANOGRAPHY METAMODEL

Metamodel is a pattern that shows how to model. Models require different elements of modeling in diverse fields and domains. For example, during the modeling of relational data model, key, tables, and columns are used as elements. Interfaces, classes, instances, associations, properties, composition and list continue to format elements of UML modeling. The proposed approach follows a digital image method based on a covered technique in which cover image is used or manipulated for hiding the sensitive data or information in the form of a text file The main purpose of the metamodel being proposed is to encode and decode the cover image using LSB technique. The LSB substitution masking and filtering based method is used in which the redundant bits in the image are replaced with the secret messages bits and reconstruct the image. The size of both steganographic image and cover image is almost same because some of data is either changed or replaced without any further addition of the data. The proposed metamodel is depicted in Fig. 4.

The overall quality of steganographic image is almost near to the original one. The encoding and decoding are the major components of the metamodel which play an important role in data hiding in the cover image as well as extracting data from stegano image. Image controller is basically the controller component that is based on facade controller responsible to interact with the main GUI interfaces and get the sensitive information or data being encrypted or encoded inside the cover image. Image controller passes the fetched data to their relevant components such as the encoding image and decoding image that are mainly responsible to encode and decode the textual data inside the cover image.

Figure 4. Proposed metamodel

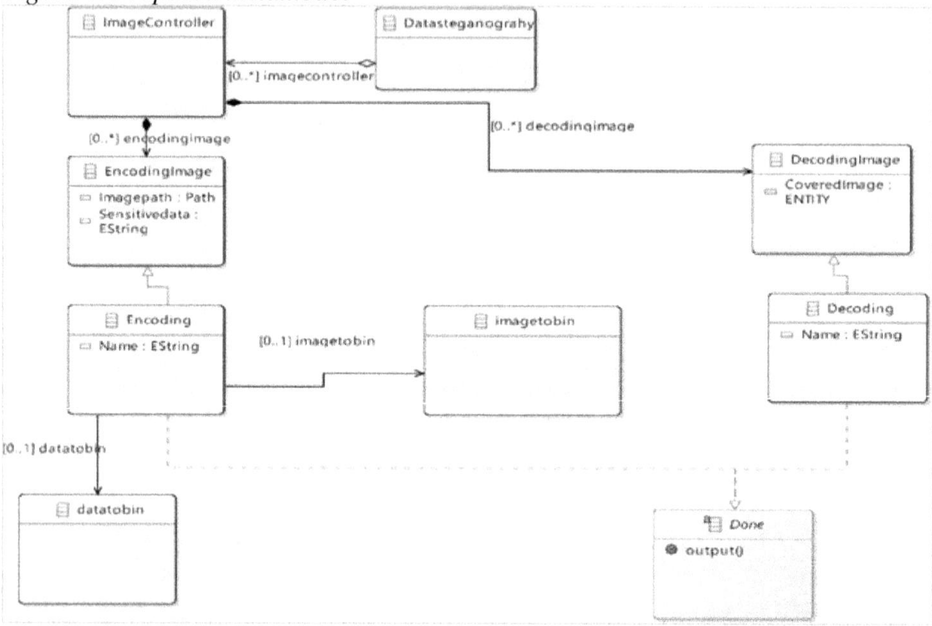

Figure 5. case study

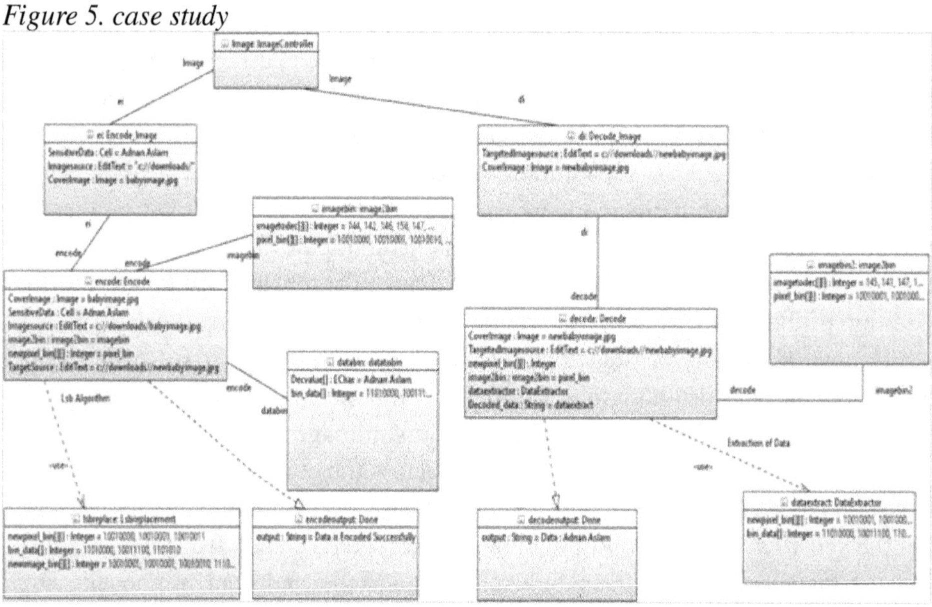

imagetobin component is responsible to convert the image into decimal matrix format and then again convert that matrix format into the binary format of each and every cell data of the image and then pass that binary information of the cover image to the encode component. Similarly, *datatobin* component is responsible to convert the sensitive data into 8-bit binary using the ASCII table and pass back the binary information of data to the encoding component, after that encoding process will be started. So, the encoding component in the metamodel is generic and every type of data steganography algorithm can be implemented like substitution, insertion, and generation-based methods. All these methods require the cover image as well as the data in binary format.

In the proposed approach, LSB substitution method has been applied by replacing the LSB bit of cover image with the data bit and the new stegano image is generated. Similar to encoding mechanism, decoding image component is responsible to decode the stegano image by again passing image to *imagetobin* and extract the data by extracting the last bits of the image. *Done* component is an interface that is implemented by the encoding and decoding by overriding output method. Moreover, the overriding *output()* method is responsible to ensure that the encoding and decoding is successfully accomplished.

5. VALIDATION OF THE PROPOSED METAMODEL

In order to validate the developed metamodel, the case study of a sender is considered who intends to send a text message "Adnan Aslam" to a specific receiver using image steganography. In order to utilize metamodel, an instance diagram is created using Eclipse Papyrus tool. All algorithmic steps are performed in specific order to embed this message in a cover image namely, 'babyimage.jpg' as depicted in Fig. 5. Firstly, the secret message is converted into 8-bit binary. After parsing the cover image, intensity value matrix is created. Then the image gray level values are converted into binary. Furthermore, it takes the LSB bits from the image in which secret data is to be hidden and lastly replace the LSB bits of the image with the secret message bits one-by-one as follows; (i) take least insignificant bits of original data from the cover image, (ii) repeat until all bits to be embedded are covered, (iii) reconstruct the stego image.

The image before encoding and encoded image is almost same and the quality of the image is sustained because the redundant bits or unused bits are replaced with secret message. Likewise, the encoding and the decoding mechanism of the stego image has been done by performing all steps inversely. To extract the secret data, stego image is simply converted into binary, the least LSBs are extracted and the text with ASCII table is reconstructed for each character in the secret message. It is followed by adding one to three bits at the end of the encoded image indicating that the total characters of the secret message are decoded properly without any loss of data or information that is contained in the secret or confidential message.

ImageController is the controller class that deals with the GUI and pass the user data to the corresponding activity or class. User will interact with application through this controller and select the tasks that they want to perform either encoding or decoding the image that can exactly map with the metamodel. *Encode_Image* is the class which is concerned with the encoding mechanism or data hiding in the digital image called cover image. This class knows about the cover image and the sensitive data to achieve the data steganography which also validates the metamodel.

Encode is the activity that is based on least significant bit technique inherited from *Encode_Image* class, because *Encode_ Image* class knows about cover image and the sensitive data. So, *Encode* can mainly perform the encoding of the data in cover image and replace all the LSB bits of cover image with the data bits that can represent each character as a 1-byte or 8-bits. *Encode* class can pass the cover image to the *image2bin* class which converts each pixel of the image into 8-bit binary and *datatobin* class can convert each data character into 8-bits and return to *Encode* class in order to replace the data bits into the LSB cover bits, thus producing a new image which is exactly the same as the source image.

The presented metamodel is generic and all of the techniques can be implemented using this metamodel, for example, substitution, insertion-based method and generation based methods. However, in this case study, the substitution-based method of LSB technique is followed, so that the encoding mechanism can validate the metamodel. *Decode_Image* class knows about the cover image and deals with the decoding or extracting of the hidden data. This is the overall controller of the decoding of data which has been defined in the metamodel.

Decode is the activity that mainly performs the decoding mechanism through interacting with the *DataExtractor* and the *image2bin* classes. *Decode* class passes the covered image to *image2bin* in order to convert the decimal values or pixels to binary numbers and to extract the data and return to the *Decode*. The *Decode* can pass these binary numbers to the *DataExtractor* class which is concerned with extraction of the sensitive data. According to the metamodel, *Decode* is a generic class which can be altered to perform different types of decoding methods based on the domain specific usage. *Done* is the interface indicating the status of encoding and decoding which is implemented by the *Encode_Image* and *Decode_ Image*. *Done* can be optional in metamodel but increases the usability and reliability of the system.

6. CONCLUSIONS

Image steganography is a special kind of encryption in which an additional layer of security is provided by hiding the data in a carrier image. This process can be performed in multiple ways. In this paper, a metamodel of a steganographic system has been designed, which encodes the data in an image. The LSB-based technique is used to design the high conceptual metamodel for steganography. Moreover, a metamodel is devised using algorithms to illustrate the encoding and decoding of secret data. The instance diagram has been analyzed according to the rules and the concept of LSB algorithm, as stated in the metamodel. Furthermore, a text message is initiated, and the same message is successfully encoded and then decoded using an instance diagram, proving the earlier hypothesis.

Furthermore, domain proximity can be achieved using MDSE for a particular discipline. This approach offers a high level of abstraction by hiding low-level details, resulting in less complexity. The productivity of the developers increases due to automated code generation, which can be five times faster in development than classical software development approaches. In future of this research work, the same metamodel can be extended to address more advanced embedding and extracting algorithms for image steganography. Additionally, a hybrid approach with MDSE can generate a model by combining different steganography techniques, such as, Pixel Value Difference (PVD), difference expansion, and LSB, which shall enhance the embedding capacity and PSNR value.

REFERENCES

AbdelRaouf, A. (2021). A new data hiding approach for image steganography based on visual color sensitivity. *Multimedia Tools and Applications, 80*(15), 23393–23417. https.//DOI: 10.1007/s11042-020-10224-w

Ahmed, D. E. M., & Khalifa, O. O. (2014). Robust and Secure Image Steganography Based on Elliptic Curve Cryptography. *2014 International Conference on Computer and Communication Engineering*, 288–291. https.//DOI: 10.1109/ICCCE.2014.88

Al-Afandy, K. A., Faragallah, O. S., Elmhalawy, A., El-Rabaie, E.-S. M., & El-Banby, Gh. M. (2016). High security data hiding using image cropping and LSB least significant bit steganography. *2016 4th IEEE International Colloquium on Information Science and Technology (CiSt)*, 400–404. https.//DOI: 10.1109/CIST.2016.7805079

Al-Otaibi, N. A., & Gutub, A. A. (2014). 2-leyer security system for hiding sensitive text data on personal computers. *Lecture Notes on Information Theory*, 2(2), 151–157.

Amin, M. M., Salleh, M., Ibrahim, S., Katmin, M. R., & Shamsuddin, M. Z. I. (2003). Information hiding using steganography. *4th National Conference of Telecommunication Technology, 2003. NCTT 2003 Proceedings.*, 21–25. https.//DOI: 10.1109/NCTT.2003.1188294

Annadurai, C., Nelson, I., Devi, K. N., Manikandan, R., Jhanjhi, N. Z., Masud, M., & Sheikh, A. (2022). Biometric Authentication-Based Intrusion Detection Using Artificial Intelligence Internet of Things in Smart City. *Energies, 15*(19), Article 19. https.//DOI: 10.3390/en15197430

Aslam, M. A., Rashid, M., Azam, F., Abbas, M., Rasheed, Y., Alotaibi, S. S., & Anwar, M. W. (2022). Image Steganography using Least Significant Bit (LSB)—A Systematic Literature Review. *2022 2nd International Conference on Computing and Information Technology (ICCIT)*, 32–38. https.//DOI: 10.1109/ICCIT52419.2022.9711628

Atawneh, S., Almomani, A., & Sumari, P. (2013). Steganography in digital images. Common approaches and tools. *IETE Technical Review, 30*(4), 344–358. https.//DOI: 10.4103/0256-4602.116724

Bhavani, Y., Kamakshi, P., Kavya Sri, E., & Sindhu Sai, Y. (2022). A Survey on Image Steganography Techniques Using Least Significant Bit. In D. J. Hemanth, D. Pelusi, & C. Vuppalapati (Eds.), *Intelligent Data Communication Technologies and Internet of Things* (pp. 281–290). Springer Nature. https.//DOI: 10.1007/978-981-16-7610-9_20

Chan, C.-K., & Cheng, L. M. (2004). Hiding data in images by simple LSB substitution. *Pattern Recognition, 37*(3), 469–474. https.//DOI: 10.1016/j.patcog.2003.08.007

De Hoog, J., Anwar, A., Reiter, P., Mercelis, S., & Hellinckx, P. (2023). Metamodelling of Noise to Image Classification Performance. *IEEE Access, 11*, 47994–48006. IEEE Access. https.//DOI: 10.1109/ACCESS.2023.3273530

Desai, H. V. (2012). Steganography, Cryptography, Watermarking. A Comparative Study. *Journal of Global Research in Computer Sciences*. https.//www.semanticscholar.org/paper/Steganography%2C-Cryptography%2C-Watermarking%3A-A-Study-Desai/1ddf3b6ed9275b760c2726dccdd8e0821b649b6e

Deshmukh, P. U., & Pattewar, T. M. (2014). A novel approach for edge adaptive steganography on LSB insertion technique. *International Conference on Information Communication and Embedded Systems (ICICES2014)*, 1–5. https.//DOI: 10.1109/ICICES.2014.7033807

Dey, S., Abraham, A., & Sanyal, S. (2007). An LSB Data Hiding Technique Using Prime Numbers. *Third International Symposium on Information Assurance and Security*, 101–108. https.//DOI: 10.1109/ISIAS.2007.4299758

Din, S. N. U., Muzammal, S. M., Bibi, R., Tayyab, M., Jhanjhi, N. Z., & Habib, M. (2024). Securing the Internet of Things in Logistics. Challenges, Solutions, and the Role of Machine Learning in Anomaly Detection. In *Digital Transformation for Improved Industry and Supply Chain Performance* (pp. 133–165). IGI Global. https.//DOI: 10.4018/979-8-3693-5375-2.ch007

Goel, S., Gupta, S., & Kaushik, N. (2015). Image Steganography – Least Significant Bit with Multiple Progressions. In S. C. Satapathy, B. N. Biswal, S. K. Udgata, & J. K. Mandal (Eds.), *Proceedings of the 3rd International Conference on Frontiers of Intelligent Computing. Theory and Applications (FICTA) 2014* (pp. 105–112). Springer International Publishing. https.//DOI: 10.1007/978-3-319-12012-6_12

Habib, M., Hussain, A., Rehman, E., Muzammal, S. M., Cheng, B., Aslam, M., & Jilani, S. F. (2023). Convolved Feature Vector Based Adaptive Fuzzy Filter for Image De-Noising. *Applied Sciences, 13*(8), Article 8. https.//DOI: 10.3390/app13084861

Halboos, E. H. J., & Albakry, A. M. (2022). Hiding text using the least significant bit technique to improve cover image in the steganography system. *Bulletin of Electrical Engineering and Informatics, 11*(6), Article 6. https.//DOI: 10.11591/eei.v11i6.4337

Humayun, M., & Al, E. (2021). Industry 4.0 and Cyber Security Issues and Challenges. *Turkish Journal of Computer and Mathematics Education (TURCOMAT), 12*(10), Article 10. https.//DOI: <ALIGNMENT.qj></ALIGNMENT>10.17762/turcomat.v12i10.4946

Humayun, M., Hamid, B., Jhanjhi, N. Z., Suseendran, G., & Talib, M. N. (2021). 5G Network Security Issues, Challenges, Opportunities and Future Directions. A Survey. *Journal of Physics. Conference Series, 1979*(1), 012037. https.//DOI: 10.1088/1742-6596/1979/1/012037

Islam, Md. R., Siddiqa, A., Uddin, M. P., Mandal, A. K., & Hossain, Md. D. (2014). An efficient filtering based approach improving LSB image steganography using status bit along with AES cryptography. *2014 International Conference on Informatics, Electronics & Vision (ICIEV)*, 1–6. https.//DOI: 10.1109/ICIEV.2014.6850714

Jadhav, P. P., Pande, S. D., Joshi, R., Gonge, S., Shelke, M. P., Futane, P., & Ahammad, S. K. H. (2024). CSADF. Ingesting cuckoo search optimization algorithm enabled with fitness function for effective model transformation pertaining to ADF. *Multimedia Tools and Applications*. https.//DOI: 10.1007/s11042-023-17887-1

Kadhim, I. J., Premaratne, P., Vial, P. J., & Halloran, B. (2019). Comprehensive survey of image steganography. Techniques, Evaluations, and trends in future research. *Neurocomputing, 335*, 299–326. https.//DOI: 10.1016/j.neucom.2018.06.075

Mandal, P. C., Mukherjee, I., Paul, G., & Chatterji, B. N. (2022). Digital image steganography. A literature survey. *Information Sciences, 609*, 1451–1488. https.//DOI: 10.1016/j.ins.2022.07.120

Murugan, K. C., Samanta, D., & Goswami, M. (2022). *An Approach on Image Steganography Based on the Least Significant Bit Algorithm* [Chapter]. Handbook of Research on Mathematical Modeling for Smart Healthcare Systems; IGI Global. https.//DOI: 10.4018/978-1-6684-4580-8.ch012

Muzammal, S. M., & Murugesan, R. K. (2021). Enhanced authentication and access control in Internet of Things. A potential blockchain-based method. *International Journal of Grid and Utility Computing, 12*(5–6), 469–485. https.//DOI: 10.1504/IJGUC.2021.120090

Muzammal, S. M., Murugesan, R. K., & Jhanjhi, N. Z. (2021). A Comprehensive Review on Secure Routing in Internet of Things. Mitigation Methods and Trust-Based Approaches. *IEEE Internet of Things Journal, 8*(6), 4186–4210. IEEE Internet of Things Journal. https.//DOI: 10.1109/JIOT.2020.3031162

Muzammal, S. M., Murugesan, R. K., Jhanjhi, N. Z., Humayun, M., Ibrahim, A. O., & Abdelmaboud, A. (2022). A Trust-Based Model for Secure Routing against RPL Attacks in Internet of Things. *Sensors, 22*(18), Article 18. https.//DOI: 10.3390/s22187052

Nosrati, M., Karimi, R., & Hariri, M. (2011). An introduction to steganography methods. *World Applied Programming*, 1(3), 191–195.

Pradhan, A., Sekhar, K. R., & Swain, G. (2018). Digital Image Steganography Using LSB Substitution, PVD, and EMD. *Mathematical Problems in Engineering, 2018*, e1804953. https.//DOI: 10.1155/2018/1804953

Tayyab, M., Mumtaz, M., Jhanjhi, N. Z., & Muzammal, S. M. (2024). Industry 4.0. The Digital Revolution Unleashing Sustainable Supply Chains. In *Digital Transformation for Improved Industry and Supply Chain Performance* (pp. 54–69). IGI Global. https.//DOI: 10.4018/979-8-3693-5375-2.ch003

Trizna, D. (2022). *Quo Vadis. Hybrid Machine Learning Meta-Model based on Contextual and Behavioral Malware Representations.* http.//128.84.4.34/abs/2208.12248

Wachsmuth, G. (2007). Metamodel Adaptation and Model Co-adaptation. In E. Ernst (Ed.), *ECOOP 2007 – Object-Oriented Programming* (pp. 600–624). Springer. https.//DOI: 10.1007/978-3-540-73589-2_28

Wang, G. G., & Shan, S. (2006). Review of Metamodeling Techniques in Support of Engineering Design Optimization. *Journal of Mechanical Design, 129*(4), 370–380. https.//DOI: 10.1115/1.2429697

Washizaki, H., Fukumoto, S., Yamamoto, M., Yoshizawa, M., Fukazawa, Y., Kato, T., Ogata, S., Kaiya, H., Fernandez, E. B., Kanuka, H., Kondo, Y., Yoshioka, N., Okubo, T., & Hazeyama, A. (2016). A Metamodel for Security and Privacy Knowledge in Cloud Services. *2016 IEEE World Congress on Services (SERVICES)*, 142–143. https.//DOI: 10.1109/SERVICES.2016.30

Xiong, X., Guo, L., Zhang, Y., & Zhang, J. (2022). Cyber-Security Enhanced Network Meta-Model and its Application. *2022 6th International Conference on Cryptography, Security and Privacy (CSP)*, 80–85. https.//DOI: 10.1109/CSP55486.2022.00023

Yang, X., Liu, X., Zhang, H., Fu, L., & Yu, Y. (2023). Meta-model-based shop-floor digital twin architecture, modeling and application. *Robotics and Computer-Integrated Manufacturing, 84*, 102595. https.//DOI: 10.1016/j.rcim.2023.102595

Chapter 8
Securing Data of Cassandra Database by Applying the Latest Cybersecurity Techniques

Soobia Saeed
https://orcid.org/0000-0002-9026-6130
Taylor's University, Malaysia

Fatima Ali Tabba
Sohail University, Pakistan

Manzoor Hussain
Indus University, Pakistan

ABSTRACT

NoSQL data storage solutions are gaining popularity due to their scalability and ease of use. This study investigates the maturity of security measures for NoSQL databases, specifically their innovative query and access protocols. The introduction of new query formats renders traditional SQL injection techniques obsolete, but are NoSQL databases resistant to injection in general? The answer is no. This research paper presented a few ways to exploit NoSQL databases, including injections and CSRF. This study investigates the cause of these vulnerabilities and presents methods for mitigating the attacks. This research demonstrates that this new and lively technology sector lacks the security protections and understanding that have evolved over time in traditional RDBMS and SQL systems.

DOI: 10.4018/979-8-3693-6135-1.ch008

1. INTRODUCTION

The term huge information alludes to the high volume, speed, and assortment of data that requires new types of handling. Because of these properties, which are alluded to at times as the 3 'V's, it gets hard to handle huge amounts of information utilizing conventional database administration devices. With growing new advances and expanding the utilization of huge amounts of information in a few extensions, security and protection have been considered tests of enormous amounts of information. There are numerous security and protection issues with enormous amounts of information. NoSQL remains for "not just SQL," and NoSQL databases are not intended to supplant the customary databases, but rather they are suitable to embrace enormous amounts of information when the conventional databases don't. NoSQL databases are delegated key-esteem databases, column-arranged databases, document-based databases, and graph databases. Cassandra is an open-source, dispersed capacity for overseeing enormous amounts of information. It is a key NoSQL database that is utilized as part of Facebook. The properties mentioned for Cassandra are the adaptability of the construction, supporting extent, and high versatility. All passwords in Cassandra are scrambled by the utilization of MD5 hash capacity, and passwords are exceptionally weak (Anusha et.al, 2021). If any pernicious client can sidestep customer approval, the client can separate the information since there is no approval instrument in between hub message trades. Cassandra's potential for refusal of authentication and approval is upheld by Dynamo, and a request should be marked using HMAC-SHA256 (Nasrullah et.al, 2023).

Database security has been and will continue to be one of the more fundamental aspects of data security. Access to a large business database gives an aggressor unprecedented access to the most fundamental facts. SQL injection attacks, for example, inserting malicious code into the application's announcements to the database layer. This permits the adversary to do nearly anything with the information, including accessing prohibited material as well as changing, wiping, and embedding new information. Even though SQL injection abuse has steadily decreased over the years because of secure systems and increased awareness, it remains a high-impact method for exploiting system weaknesses (Bohora et.al, 2021). For example, it has been established that web applications receive four or more web attack battles per month, with SQL infusions being the most common attack on retailers. No-SQL databases have recently gained popularity. Such databases include MongoDB, Redis, and Cassandra. Some of these NoSQL databases support a variety of question dialects, rendering traditional SQL infusion systems unnecessary. However, does this imply that NoSQL frameworks are immune to infusions? Our findings show that, while the security of the question dialect and its drivers has greatly improved, there are still mechanisms for infusing vengeful queries (Sánchez et.al, 2021). In this work, we want to draw the attention of designers and data security owners to NoSQL security, focusing on the vulnerabilities and their mitigation. We demonstrate new infusion processes and discuss methodologies for mitigating such attacks, such as PHP, which is extremely easy to encode or unravel and has widespread local usage in all programming dialects. Breaking the inquiry structure, as seen in SQL infusion, is more difficult with a JSON-organized question (Soobia et.al, 2022).

1.1 Significance of Study

Non-social information storage hasn't yet come to security development. These storages are outlined for the maximum area through use of NoSQL databases. NoSQL DB were built to handle diverse deterrents realized by examination data and subsequently security was never part of the model at the time of configuration level. Engineers utilizing NoSQL as a rule add security in the middleware. NoSQL does not provide any backing to implementing it expressly in the db. On the other hand, bunching part of NoSQL databases postures extra difficulties to the heartiness of such security rehearses.

1.2 Contributor to the Study

Data manipulation logs are stored in several tiered volume media. Physically transmitting data across tiers gave the IT chief direct control over what data was transferred and when. Regardless of the size of the data set and its potential for growth, changeability, and accessibility have necessitated automated data storage management. Auto tiring orders do not control where data is transferred, creating significant challenges for data security and storage. New argument is basic to foil not acceptable get to and keep up all day, everyday accessibility.

1.2.1 Motivation of the Study

Many large-scale information use cases in large company environments necessitate data collection from a variety of sources, such as end-point devices. For example, a security data and event management framework (SIEM) may collect event logs from a system's numerous tools, devices, and programming programs. Data approval is a vital test in the data collection procedure; in what way will we believe the results? In what ways would we be able to confirm that a source of information is not malicious, and how would we be able to channel hateful data from our collection? Data acceptance and separation is an overpowering task posed by analyzing data sources, particularly with the receiving data its own specific device (BYOD) concept (Sicari et.al, 2022; Rahman et.al, 2024; Saeed *et.al,* 2019).

Enormous data can be seen as an upsetting sign of big data by possibly empowering interruptions of security, obtrusive advertising, diminished common opportunities, expanded state and corporate access. A delay examination is how the organizations are utilizing data investigation for promoting purposes distinguished an illustration is how a vender could recognize. Similarly, anonymizing data for review is insufficient to maintain client confidentiality. For example, AOL released anonymized search information for academic purposes, yet clients could be easily identified by their queries. Netflix addressed a similar issue when consumers from their unknown data collection were identified by comparing their Netflix film scores to IMDB scores. In this regard, it is critical to establish guidelines and suggestions for counteracting incidental protection (Saeed and Humayun, 2019; Saeed *et.al*, 2017).

1.3 Problem Statement

A company using the Cassandra Database has a huge amount of data but the security of Cassandra it's needs to protect with hacker. To take some intuitive to protect the database with CQL injection, Reduces the vulnerability, Data encryption.

1.4 Statement of Hypotheses

The experiment is based on the Cassandra database to secure the database by CQL injection, data encryption. The driver protects the CQL injection.

The null hypothesis is:

H0: "Data base will not protect from sql injection, data encryption, user protection, not reduce the data vulnerability with Cassandra database".

On the other hand, the alternative hypothesis is:

H1: "Data base will protect from sql injection, data encryption, user protection, reduce the data vulnerability with Cassandra database".

2. LITERATURE REVIEW

2.1 Understanding Data Security Issues and Analyzing Its Existing Solutions

In a late review directed, 69% of the 127 cloud suppliers and 35% of the of the cloud clients see cloud clients in charge of guaranteeing the security of the cloud administrations; 32% of the cloud suppliers and 32% of the cloud clients consider security to be the cloud suppliers' obligation; and 16% of the cloud suppliers and 33% of the cloud clients consider it to be a common obligation (Rahman et.al, 2024;).

2.2 Encryption

The choice to move to distributed computing from a conventional IT foundation result in a higher number of security breaches. The increase in information exchange between diverse specialty units of an association has increased the danger of information security. The cloud is an appropriate system. Information may be dispersed around the world. Associations will have no learning or control over the area of information where the SaaS sellers oversee the security of the key and the IaaS key administration, where the key is given to IaaS merchants for protection. Of all the three methodologies, key administration by the client is the best solution (Saeed *et.al,* 2021; Alferidah, *et.al,* 2020; Babbar *et.al,* 2021). Different key administration approaches, practically speaking, are utilizing pre-shared keys, open-key cryptography calculations, and key circulation focuses. Cloud suppliers must convey a protected instrument for key administration in the cloud. However, it's best if the key administration is taken care of by the information proprietor for more grounded security.

2.2.1 Homomorphic Encryption

For more beneficial security, it is ideal to scramble for information before passing it to the cloud. In any case, customer-side encryption prompts a specialized test since information handling or questions on an encoded database are impractical. The seller needs the customer's private key to unscramble the information for preparation every time. This influences the vital part of distributed computing, i.e., the classification of the information put away in the cloud (Ali et.al, 2023; Saeed et.al, 2019). IBM analyst Craig Gentry's 2009 achievement work proposes the first completely homomorphic encryption (FHE) plan fit for performing subjective numbers of augmentations and increases on scrambled information without being decoded (Singh et.al, 2023). The sellers can perform calculations on the scrambled information utilizing FHE for the customer, and the outcome can be decoded just by the customer. From that point forward, numerous examination papers have been distributed on homomorphic encryption. In the paper, the creators have displayed a completely homomorphic encryption plan that delivers short ciphertext, and its security depends on the learning with blunders (LWE) suspicions. The proposed arrangement depends on the hardness of issues in self-assertive cross sections, while Gentry's work depends on perfect grids. Homomorphic encryption requires extreme computational prerequisites; furthermore, it influences cloud productivity, so actualizing this plan completely in the cloud is still in the early stages (Ibrahim, 2024; Shah *et.al,* 2023).

2.2.2 Authentication

Since an open cloud is an open stage, anybody with the web can get to the information. The essential inquiry is: which client can utilize and see the information in the cloud? A more grounded validation methodology is expected to guarantee that client information is shielded from undesirable access. Cloud specialists say associations or shoppers ought to begin utilizing multi-factor confirmation to shield their information from hacking. US federal controllers perceive three verification elements: a secret key or PIN, a shrewd card, PKI authentication, a USB key or versatile number, and biometric attributes like a unique mark or voice design. The multifactor confirmation framework is to verify clients with two or more of the above variables (Saeed et.al, 2019). Kerberos can be utilized to verify customers, data nodes, and name nodes in the NoSQL database environment. Noxious clients and nodes can increase unapproved access to the NoSQL database framework after taking or copying the Kerberos ticket. These accreditations can be obtained from framework previews and, in addition, from virtual pictures. The circumstances have declined in this big data environment where precise clones and sham hubs can be utilized to create malignant administrations in the database environment (Bolu, 2024; Gopi *et.al*, 2022).

2.3 Data Transaction

Secure Socket Layer (SSL) gives secure information correspondence over an unsecured system. The SSL convention utilizes open-key encryption for key trade, symmetric encryption for classification, and a message verification code for message honesty. A few SSL declaration organizations, including Digi Notar and Comodo, were traded off a year ago to make deceitful testaments for locales like Google, Yahoo, and Microsoft's Hotmail. So, another choice is to utilize DNSSEC to verify the source and uprightness of DNS information as it navigates the Internet. DNSSEC is not an encryption convention but rather an extra layer of security at the DNS level. DNSSEC is a type of open-key framework (PKI). The downside is that DNSSEC does not accept the legitimacy of the site that the client seeks (Yan et.al, 2024). The arrangement is to consolidate SSL and DNSSESC to give a safe and verified information correspondence, as represented in Figure 1 (Matos and Guerreiro, 2024).

Figure 1. Secure Socket Layer (SSL)

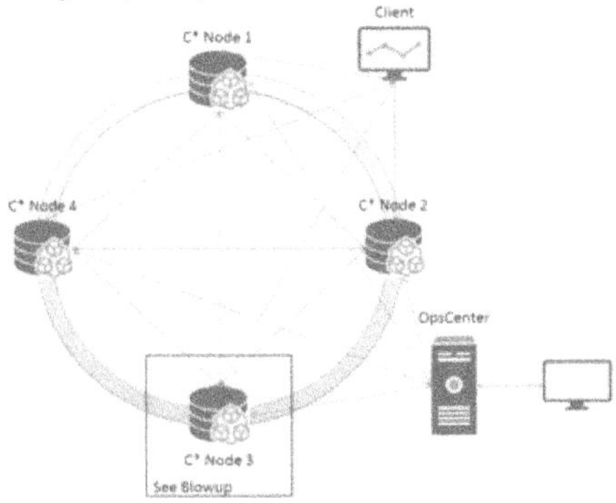

Figure.1: Secure Socket Layer (SSL)

2.4 Security Issues in Big Data and NoSQL

Expanding the utilization of NoSQL in association, security has become a developing concern. In this paper, we display a study on security and protection issues in enormous information and NoSQL. We had a diagram of huge information and NoSQL databases and examined security challenges in this area (Fahd et.al, 2019). Because of the high volume, speed, and assortment of huge amounts of information, conventional security models experience issues in managing such extensive-scale information, as mentioned in Figure 2 (Kalid et.al, 2017).

Cassander utilities

Data Model: Key/Value

Authentication: Support

Authorization: Not Support

Data Encription: Not Support

Auditing: Not Support

Communication protocol: SSL

Potential for attack: Script injection (in CQL) and DOS

Data Model: Key/Value

Figure 2. Ops Center (Kalid et.al, 2017).

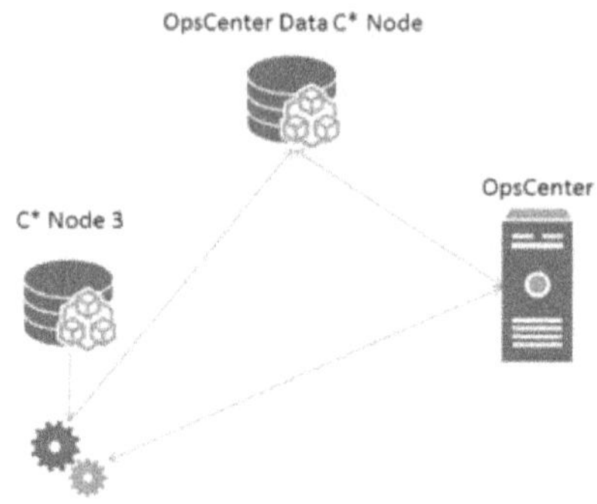

Figure.2: Ops Center (Kalid et.al. 2017).

2.5 Security Challenges and Access Control Model

There are numerous security issues with this huge amount of information. The main ten security and protection challenges in huge amounts of information are exhibited. Secure calculation in conveyed systems is a test that examines security in guideless capacities. Secure information stockpiling and exchange logs talk about a new system to avoid unapproved access to information stores and look after accessibility. Granular access control is another test of huge information. The issue here is anticipating access to information by clients who ought not to have access (Kalid et.al, 2017). In this situation, conventional access control models experience issues managing huge amounts of information. A few instruments are proposed for taking care of access control over enormous amounts of information. Among the security issues in enormous amounts of information, information assurance and access control are perceived as the most vital security issues. presents an entrance control model for NoSQL databases by augmenting the customary part-based access control model. Security issues in two of the most mainstream NoSQL databases, Cassandra and MongoDB, are talked about and their security highlights and problems delineated (Carpenter and Hewitt, 2022).

The principal issues for both Cassandra and MongoDB are the absence of encryption backing for information records, feeble confirmation in the middle of customers and servers, straightforward validation, powerlessness to SQL infusion, and DOS assault. It is additionally specified that the two don't bolster RBAC and fine-grained approval. The creators observe NIST hazard administration principles and characterize the risk source, danger occasions, and vulnerabilities. The vulnerabilities characterized in terms of enormous information are insecure calculation, end-point information approval or separation, granular access control, insecure information stockpiling and correspondence, and privacy-saving information mining and analytics (Saeed et.al, 2022).

Figure 3. Database client logger

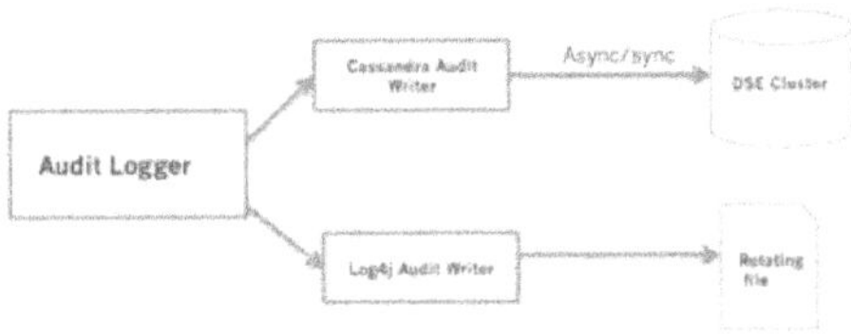

Figure .4: Audit and Logging of Database

2.6 Audit and Logging

Reviews and logs are performed to help in the revelation of malevolent exercises in the database framework. However, without really taking a gander at the information and creating strategies to distinguish between noxious exercises, logging is not valuable. Likewise, the recurrence at which the audits are conducted can have a sway on their adequacy. In the event that reviews are performed, say quarterly, that implies malevolent exercises can happen, which can bring about difficult issues for the association. This may be found past the point of no return when the harm has, as of now, occurred (Sánchez et.al, 2021).

Figure 4. Audit and Logging of Database

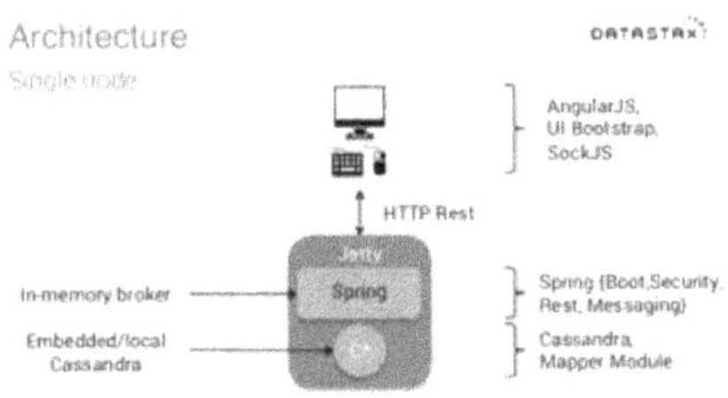

Figure.5: API security architecture

2.7 Administrative Data Access

NoSQL database frameworks need in-fabricated offices, documentation, and outsider devices to address issues of regulatory rights with, for instance, full access to information and the empowerment of managerial limits for the reasons of encryption. Tasking executives to pick the right security controls that would fix every one of the screws on the four corners of our database frameworks, like the best possible access controls and the best encryption innovations, can bring about undesirable direct access to information records or information hub forms. It will be better if this is left to the framework fashioner to choose controls to close this gap (Azeroual and Nikiforova, 2022).

2.8 Configuration and Patch Management

Existing setup administration instruments work for the basic stages. Diverse hubs or bunches of servers may have distinctive patch modifications. Included hubs may have more current patches than existing hubs. This may pose challenges in authorizing security consistently over the NoSQL database environment (Dissanayake, 2020).

2.9 Roadmap Towards a Secured NOSQL Database

Database security is not simple to accomplish, as appears in Area 3 above. As a stage towards achieving satisfactory security for a NoSQL database, immunity necessity is any security prerequisite that indicates the degree to which the database framework should have the inside capacity to guard itself from debasement and assault by malevolent software (Rafique et.al, 2021).

2.10 Security Models

A security model is an announcement that diagrams the prerequisites important to appropriately bolster and execute a certain security approach. It is a typical representation of a security strategy. A security approach traces objective reasons for how they could be beneficial. A data model is a system that provides an approach frame and tackles safety issues in particular circumstances. The following are some security models (Seghier and Kazar, 2021).

2.11 Security Policy

A security approach is a point-by-point, composed record that states how an association arranges to ensure the organization's benefits by giving a meaning of objectives, purposes, obligations, and general necessities, recognizes the tenets that will be taken after to keep up security in a framework, and characterizes the security vision for the association. A security approach communicates precisely what the safety level ought to be, arranging the objectives of what the vulnerable components are to realize. (CRISSP) Data security arrangement figures out which clients have entry to a particular information thing and the particular sorts of activities considered by every client on the information thing. This definition can be as far as inquiry proclamations a specific client or gathering of clients can issue, for instance, CREATE, INSERT, DELETE, UPDATE, and so on. This likewise relies on the NoSQL query language being used. Information security strategy ought to likewise characterize the activities, if any, that are reviewed for every piece of information. Information security arrangements are determined principally by the level of security required for the information in the database and are specifically relative to the affectability of the information. Security strategies that keep data from spilling out of a high safety level to a minor security stage are called multi-level safety policies (Saeed et.al, 2019).

2.12 API Security

APIs can be subjected to a few assaults, for example, code infusion, support over streams, and charge infusion as they get to the NoSQL databases. The APIs for enormous information bunches should be shielded from code and charge infusion, cushion flood assaults, and each other's web administration assaults. This obligation is regularly left to the application that uses the cluster, as mentioned in Figure 5 (Santos et.al, 2023).

Figure 5. API security architecture

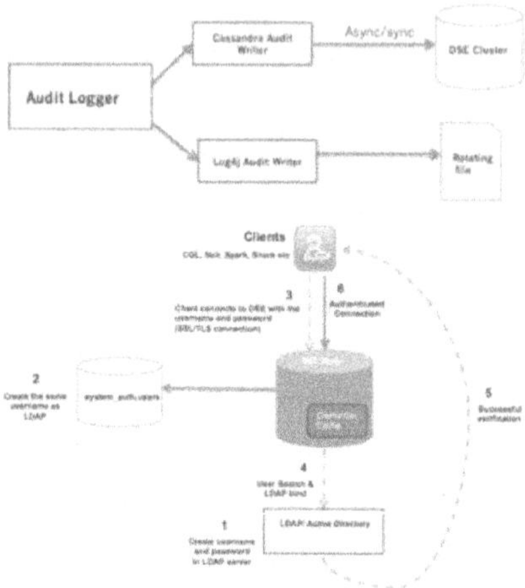

Figure .3: Database client logger

2.13 Cryptographically Enforced Access Control and Secure Communication

Cryptographically Imposed Access Control and Secure Communication To ensure that the most valuable private data is completely secure and only accessible to authorized objects, data must be scrambled using access control mechanisms. Research in that area, such as property-based encryption (ABE), must be made more sophisticated, proficient, and adaptable. To ensure confirmation, assertion, and decency among the circulated pieces, a cryptographically secure correspondence structure must be implemented (Abdullah and Arjunan, 2023).

2.14 Data Granular Access Control

Access control security is concerned with preventing unauthorized access to data. The issue with coarse-grained access systems is that data that could be common is typically classified as more prohibitive to achieve comprehensive security. Granular access control provides information administrators with a surgical blade, rather than an instrument, to distribute data as much as possible without sacrificing confidentiality (Saeed et.al, 2022).

Figure 6. Data Granular Access Control

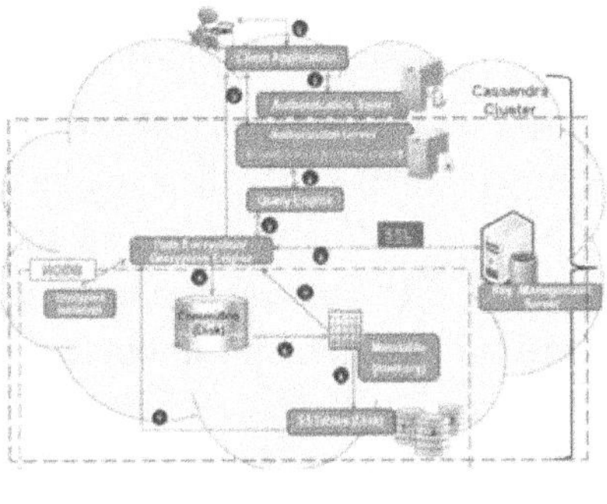

Figure.6: Data Granular Access Control

2.15 File Level Encryption

The belief is to shield the substance of the group from the individuals who oversee it. In the occasion a chairman needs to investigate information documents, either through a fundamental word processor or by getting a preview and looking at the chronicle, encryption keeps data safe. Record level encryption is straight forward to the db. and scales up as new hubs are additional to the cluster. Granted, the encryption keys must be kept safe for this element to be effective are present in Figure 6, Figure7 and Figure 8 (Arshad et.al, 2023).

Figure 7. Key spaces

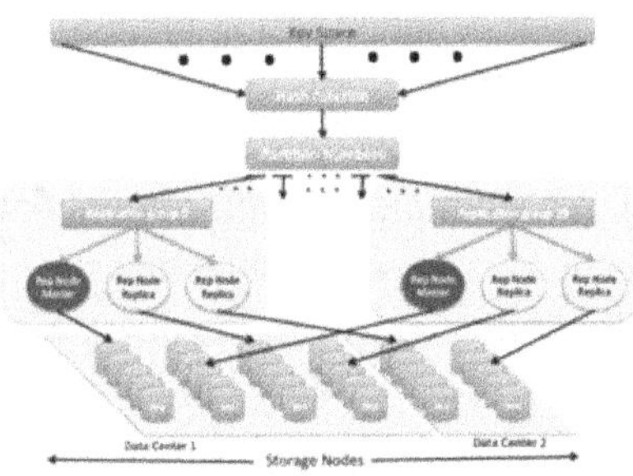

Figure:.7 key Spaces

2.16 Deployment Validation

The objective here is to guarantee that all hubs in the bunch are legitimately fixed, appropriately designed, and run the correct (i.e., not hacked) duplicates of programming. It's not entirely obvious stuff when you have a huge number of hubs running, so mechanized hub approval makes fundamental hub security much less demanding. Scripts to introduce fixes and set and test design settings are a simple approach to ensuring no hubs enter the bunch without legitimate structure and security. This can likewise be connected to Kerberos confirmation and outer application approval (security as an administration) offerings (Saeed et.al, 2022).

Figure 8. Database storing system

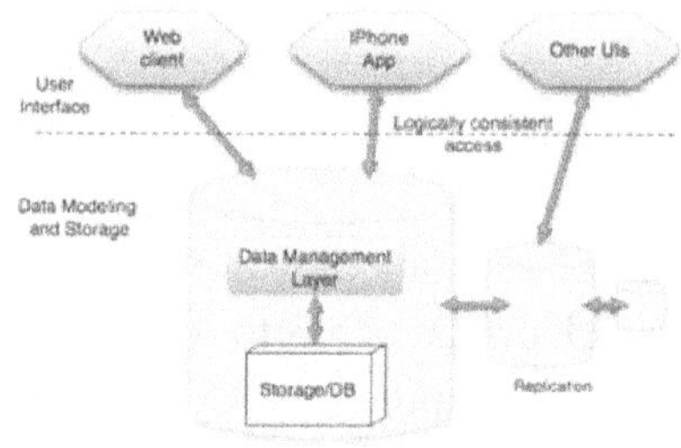

Figure.8: Database storing system

2.17 NoSQL JavaScript Injection

A common feature of NoSQL databases is the ability to run JavaScript in the database engine with the objective of doing complicated queries or exchanges, such as guiding diminish. MongoDB, CouchDB, and their cloud-based counterparts, Cloudant and Big Couch, are examples of well-known databases that support this. JavaScript execution revealed a dangerous attack surface if unprotected or inadequately protected client data finds its way to the query. Consider a confusing interaction that demanded JavaScript code and included unescaped client information as a parameter in the question.

As an example of a use scenario, consider a store with an accumulation of items, each with a value and sum. The designer needed to know the total or average of these fields, so he created a guide to decrease work that takes the field name (sum or cost) from the customer. In PHP, such code can resemble this (where $param represents client input) (Carpenter and Hewitt, 2022). This code totals the fields specified by $param for everything by name. $param is necessary to retrieve either "sum" or "cost" for this code to continue; however, as client data is not being gotten away here, harmful information may include subjective JavaScript that will be performed (Kalid et.al, 2017).

2.18 Security Scanning to Prevent Injections

With the aim of reducing infusion attacks, it is recommended to use out-of-the-box encoding apparatuses when creating inquiries. For JSON queries, for example, in MongoDB and CouchDB, all dialects have excellent local encoding, which eliminates the infusion; nonetheless, poor access control administration and risky system presentation are high and comparable between the SQL and NoSQL frameworks. We recommend using full-grown databases that have been built as part of efforts to establish safety. However, even using the most secure information store does not avert infusion attacks, which affect holes in the web apps that access the information store. One way to retain these is through careful code scrutiny and static analysis. On the other hand, these may have a high false-positive rate and are difficult to target. While dynamic examination apparatuses proved to be quite beneficial for the recognition of SQL injection attacks, these ought's to be altered in accordance with distinguishing the specific weaknesses of NoSQL databases that we portrayed in our research.

3. RESEARCH METHODOLOGY AND PROCEDURES

3.1 Research Design

This research helps in encoding touchy and private information, for example, Mastercard numbers, standardized savings numbers, and so on, put away in the section crew. Encoded information is straightforwardly unscrambled for the clients that have been created (Sicari et.al, 2023). This research helps in encoding touchy and private information, for example, Mastercard numbers, standardized savings numbers, and so on, put away in the section crew. Encoded information is straightforwardly unscrambled for the clients that have been created. Security Admin will make the outside security module, which will go about as a wallet, and there he will set the expert encryption key (Dissanayake, 2020).

3.2 Research Methodology

Utilizing an outside security module isolates the general capacities from encryption operations, making it conceivable to separate the errands between database managers and security administrators (Azeroual and Nikiforova, 2022). Here the security is upgraded on the grounds that the wallet secret key is obscure to the database director, requiring the security chairman to give the password. Before applying the encryption or unscrambling to the database segments, the security administrator ought to set the expert encryption key, and this key will scramble the section encryption key. At that point, the encryption for the section family can be connected. Communications during the INSERTION stage include whenever an insertion question happens in any of the segment families, then express encryption ought to happen. It ought to peruse the segment encryption key. Apply the encryption utilizing symmetric encryption calculations, for example, Blowfish, 3DES, or AES. Keeping in mind the end goal of moderate infusion assaults, it is prescribed to use out-of-case encoding instruments when building queries (Rafique et.al, 2021).

4. PROPOSED METHODOLOGY

According to this research, if follow the procedures we may secure our database and meet the PCI Compliance standards and protect our data.

4.1 Cassandra Node Encryption

User-to-server encryption shields data in transit from the user system to a Cassandra database bunch using SSL (Secure Sockets Layer). It sets up a secure mode between the client and the related server.

Procedure

On every server under user encryption:

- Cassandra Allow encryption.
- Set the suitable paths for you. KeyStore and. trust store files.
- Provide the mandatory passwords. The passwords need to match with the passwords used when creating the keystore and trust store.
- To enable user certificate to authentication, set “require_client_auth” to true.

Example

“client_encryption_options”

Permitted: true

keystore: conf/. keystore ## in your. keystore file
keystore_password: password123
trust store: conf/. truststore
truststore_password: password123
require_client_auth: true
The cassandra.yaml file is the key configuration file for Cassandra.

Important: Subsequent to updating stuff in the Cassandra. yaml document, your essential restart the server for developments to produce results. It is situated in the accompanying indexes:

- Cassandra database package installations: /etc/cassandra
- Cassandra database tar ball installations: *install_location*/conf
- DataStax Cassandra Enterprise package installations: /etc/dse/cassandra
- DataStax Cassandra Enterprise tarball Setup: *install_location*/resources/cassandra/conf

4.2 Internal Authentication

Like item consent administration utilizing inner approval, inward confirmation depends on Cassandra database-controlled login records and passwords. Interior confirmation mechanism for the accompanying user when you give a username and secret word to fire up the user:

- Cassandra Astyanax
- Cassandra cli
- Cassandra cqlsh
- Cassandra database drivers produced and certified to work with Cassandra.
- Cassandra Hector
- Cassandra pycassa

Inner confirmation stores usernames and bcrypt hashed credentials in the system_auth. credentials table.

Password Authenticator is an I Authenticator execution that you can use to arrange Cassandra for interior confirmation out of the case.

4.3 Configuring Authentication

To configure Cassandra to employ inner authentication, first update the cassandra. yaml file and enable the replication factor of the system_auth keyspace, as described in this approach. Next, start Cassandra with the default login and password (cassandra/

cassandra), then launch cqlsh with the same credentials. Finally, use the following CQL queries to create user accounts and authorize users to access database objects:

- Alter Cassandra database user
- Create Cassandra database user
- Drop Cassandra database user
- List Cassandra database users

Note: To configure permission, see Configuring inner authorization.
Procedure

2. Change the authenticator alternative in the Cassandra. yaml to PassAuth. As a matter of course, the authenticator choice is set to Allow All Authenticator.
3. authenticator: PassAuths
4. Increase the replication factor for the system_auth keyspace to N (number of nodes).
5. If you utilize the default, 1, and the server with the solitary copy goes down, you won't have the capacity to sign into the group since the system_auth key space was not imitated.
6. Restart the Cassandra user.
7. The default super username and password that you use to start the user is stored in Cassandra.
8. Cqlsh -u cass -p cass@123
9. Start cqlsh using the super username and password.
10. ./cqlsh -u shoaib -p password123
11. Create a second super user, not the same username Cassandra. This step is elective but extremely recommended.
12. Log in as another super user.
13. Modify the Cassandra user and password to approximately long and incomprehensible, and then forget about it. It won't be used again.
14. Take away the cassandra database user's super user status.
15. Use the CQL statements listed previously to configure user details and then grant permissions to access the database elements.

4.4 Logging in Cassandra Database Using cqlsh

Typically, after designing verification, you sign into Cassandra cqlsh using the -u and -p options to the cqlsh command. To avoid having to go through certifications every time you run cqlsh, create a cqlshrc record in the cassandra index in your home registry. When present, this document clears the default login data for cqlsh.

Procedure

- Start a text editor and make a file that specifies username and password.
- First line: [authentication]
- Second line: username = Fateha_soobia
  Third line: password = Fateha@123
- Save that file in your user home/. cassandra folder and name it cqlshrc.
- Set permissions to read on the file.
  To ensure database login data, guarantee that the record is secure from unapproved access.

Note: example cqlshrc files are existing in:

- Cassandra Bundled installations
  "/usr/share/doc/dse-libcassandra"
- Cassandra Binary setup
  install_location/conf

4.5 Cassandra Object Permissions

You utilize the well-known social database GRANT/REVOKE worldview to give or renounce consent to get Cassandra information. A superuser awards beginning consents, and in this manner, a client could possibly be given the authorization to give or repudiate consents. Object consent administration depends on inner approval.

Permission to read these system tables is implicitly given to every authenticated user because the tables are used by many Cassandra tools:

- Cassandra system schema key space
- Cassandra system schema columns
- Cassandra system schema column families
- Cassandra system local
- Cassandra system peers

4.6 Configuring Cassandra Internal Authorization

Cassandra Authorizer is a unique of numerous conceivable I Authorizer usages, and it is the one that stores consents in the system_auth. permissions table to bolster all approval-related CQL articulations. Setup comprises, for the most part, changing the authorizer choice in the cassandra. yaml to utilize the cassandra authorizer.

Note: To arrange authentication, see setup authentication.

Procedure

- In the cassandra.yaml file, comment out on the default Permit All Authorizer and enhance the Cassandra Authorizer.

  authorizer: Cassandra Authorizer

  You can use some authenticator except Permit All.
- Setup the replication factor for the system_auth keyspace to improve the replication feature to a number greater than 1.
- Adjust the authority period for permissions caching by setting the permissions_validity_in_ms option in the cassandra.yaml file.

  Alternatively, disable access caching by setting this option to 0.

Results

CQL supports the authorization statements:

- User Grant
- List of permissions
- Revoke permissions

4.7 Research Instruments

C#, Apache, Cassandra, CQL (Cassandra Query Language), Visual studio

4.8 Data Analysis

4.8.1 Secure Calculations in Distributed database Programming Frameworks

Circulated programming systems utilize the parallelism idea in calculation and have the have the capacity to prepare enormous amounts of information. The MapReduce structure is a prevalent sample that partitions a data document into various lumps. In the initial period of MapReduce, a mapper for every lump peruses the data, performs some calculations, and yields a rundown of key and quality sets. In the following stage, a reducer joins the qualities fitting in with each key and yields the result. There are two noteworthy assault counteractive action measures: protecting the mappers and securing the data in the vicinity of an untrusted mapper.

4.8.2 Use Cases

There is a probability that untrusted mappers could return incorrect results, which will thusly produce erroneous total results. With vast information sets, it is becoming increasingly difficult to distinguish the issue, bringing about huge harm, particularly for experimental and monetary calculations. Retailer purchaser information is frequently examined by promoting offices for focused publicizing or client sectioning. These undertakings include profoundly parallel calculations over huge information sets and are especially suited for MapReduce structures, for example, Hadoop. In any case, the information mappers can contain purposeful or unexpected spillages. For instance, a mapper may discharge an extremely remarkable worth by examining a private record, undermining clients' protection.

4.8.2 Safety Finest Practices for Non-Relational Data racks

Non-relational data stores have not yet undergone security infrastructure development. These stores are mostly designed using NoSQL databases. NoSQL databases were designed to solve various challenges encountered in the testing world, and hence security was never a part of the concept at any point during its development. Developers that use NoSQL databases typically add security to the middleware. NoSQL databases do not support unequivocal authorization. However, the clustering of NoSQL databases complicates the effectiveness of such security practices.

4.8.4 Use Cases

Big Data contains massive amounts of information that can be organized, semi-organized, or unstructured. Moving from a traditional social database to a NoSQL database is far less demanding for businesses that manage massive, unstructured data sets. When all is said and done, the security theory of NoSQL databases relies on external support devices. To reduce security events, the firm must examine security provisions for the middleware adding items to its motor while also strengthening the NoSQL database to match its partner RDBs without sacrificing operational features.

4.8.5 Protected Data Storage and Transactions Logs

Information and exchange logs are stored on multi-layered capacity media. Physically transporting information between levels allows the IT supervisor complete control over what information is moved and when. However, as the size of the data set has grown tremendously and continues to do so, adaptability and accessibility have necessitated auto-tiering for massive data storage management. Auto-tiering arrangements do not monitor where the information is stored, which introduces significant challenges to safe information storage. New systems are essential for preventing unauthorized access and maintaining daily accessibility.

4.8.6 Use Cases

A manufacturer must incorporate knowledge from many departments. Some of this information is rarely recovered, and a few divisions consistently use the same information pools. An auto-level pulling to stockpile structure will save the maker money by moving previously utilized information to a lower (and less expensive) level. Regardless, this information may be included in R&D outcomes, but not prominently, but rather as basic data. Because lower-level systems usually provide less security, the company should focus on meticulous tiering methods.

4.8.7 End Point Input Authentication and Filtering

Many massive data use cases in large company environments necessitate information collection from a variety of sources, such as end-point devices. For example, a security data and event management framework (SIEM) may collect event logs from a large number of equipment devices and programming applications in an enterprise system. Info approval is an important criterion in the information gathering process: how can we trust the information? What approach would we use to ensure that a source of information is not harmful, and how would we route toxic data from our collection? Untrustworthy data sources pose a daunting challenge for information validation and sorting, especially with the bring-your-own-device (BYOD) model.

4.8.8 Use Cases

Both climate sensor data and input votes received by an iPhone application have a comparative acceptance difficulty. A persuaded foe may be able to create "rebel" virtual sensors or fake iPhone IDs to rig the results. This is further complicated by the volume of data gathered, which may exceed many readings or votes. To carry out these tasks properly, computations should be performed to approve the information for large data sets.

4.8.9 Real time Safety and Compliance Monitoring

Constant security checking has always been a challenge, considering the volume of warnings sent by (security) devices. These warnings (related or not) generate a large number of false positives, which are generally ignored or simply "clicked away," as consumers are unable to adjust to the sheer volume. Given the amount and speed of information streams, this problem may become even more severe. However, large data developments may also provide an opportunity because these advances consider the efficient handling and investigation of many types of information. Which, in turn, can be used to provide, for example, a consistent strangeness location while taking into consideration varied security investigations.

4.8.10 Use Cases

Most commercial endeavors and government organizations will benefit from ongoing security investigations, even though the use cases may differ. There are recurring use cases, such as "Who is accessing which information from which asset at what time?" "Are we under attack?" or "Do we have a breach of consistency standard C as a result of activity A?" These are not novel concepts, but the difference is that we now have more information at our disposal to make faster and better decisions (for example, fewer false positives). In contrast, new use cases can be identified, or old use cases can be reclassified, without the need for large amounts of data.

For example, the health-care industry benefits greatly from massive information breakthroughs, potentially saving billions of dollars for citizens, becoming more precise with case payments, and reducing case misrepresentation. Meanwhile, the records stored may be extremely sensitive and must comply with HIPAA or regional or neighborhood standards, which require cautious assurance of the same information. Identifying abnormal recovery of individual data, whether planned or unintentional, allows the social insurance provider to proactively restore the harm done and prevent future exploitation.

4.8.11 Scalable Privacy Preserving Data Mining and Analytics

Huge amounts of data can be interpreted as an unsettling appearance of Big Brother, potentially empowering intrusions into protection, obtrusive promotion, reduced common flexibility, and increased governmental and corporate control. A recent inquiry into how businesses use information analysis for advertising purposes identified an example of how a merchant may detect that a child was pregnant before her father knew. Also, anonymizing information for examination is insufficient to maintain client confidentiality. For example, AOL released anonymized search information for academic purposes, yet clients were easily identified by their queries. Netflix encountered a similar issue when clients of their anonymized information set were identified by comparing their Netflix film scores to IMDB scores. As a result, it is critical to establish guidelines and proposals for minimizing unintentional security breaches.

4.8.12 Use Cases

Client information obtained by organizations and government entities is constantly mined and evaluated by internal investigators as well as potential outside temporary workers or commercial partners. A malicious insider or untrustworthy accomplice can manipulate these datasets and collect confidential information from clients. Similarly, knowledge-based organizations necessitate the gathering of infinite amounts of information. The information sources vary and may include chat groups, individual websites, and system switches. The majority of obtained information, on the other hand, is pure in nature, does not require retention, and is protected by secrecy. Powerful and versatile security-protection mining algorithms will increase the possibilities of acquiring relevant data to improve client security.

4.8.13 Cryptographically Forced Access Control and Safe Communication

To ensure that the most sensitive private information is completely secure and only accessible to authorized parties, information must be scrambled using access control methods. Research in this area, such as characteristic-based encryption (ABE), must be expanded, improved, and made more adaptable. To ensure verification, understanding, and reasonableness among the allotted pieces, a cryptographically secure communication structure must be implemented.

4.8.13 Use Cases

Delicate information is frequently stored and decoded in the cloud. The fundamental challenge with scrambling information, particularly large data sets, is the win-win or bust-recovery arrangement of encoded information, which prevents clients from properly doing fine-grained operations such as exchanging records or inquiries. ABE addresses this issue by employing an open-key cryptosystem in which credits associated with the scrambled information serve to open the keys. However, we have also decrypted less sensitive material, such as information important for investigation. Such information must be communicated in a secure and agreed-upon manner via a cryptographically secure correspondence system.

4.8.14 Granular Access Control

The security property that matters in terms of access control is a mystery, which prevents unauthorized parties from gaining access to information. The problem with course-grained access systems is that information that could potentially be shared is constantly moved to a more restrictive categorization to ensure sound security. Granular access control provides information managers with a surgical blade rather than a sword, allowing them to provide as much information as possible while maintaining confidentiality.

4.8.15 Use Cases

Massive data analysis and distributed computing are increasingly focused on managing diverse data sets, both in terms of mappings and security requirements. Legitimate and reasonable restrictions on information come from a variety of sources. The Sarbanes-Oxley Act establishes requirements for securing company financial data, and the Health Insurance Portability and Accountability Act imposes numerous restrictions on sharing individual health records. Official Order 13526 establishes a comprehensive structure for safeguarding national security data.

Security protocols, sharing assertions, and business agreements all place requirements on information management. Dealing with these numerous constraints has resulted in increased costs for developing applications as well as a walled patio nursery approach in which only a few people can participate in research. Granular access control is critical for diagnostic frameworks to adapt to the increasingly complex security environment.

4.8.16 Granular Checks

With continuous security checks, we strive to be notified as soon as an assault occurs. This will not always be the case (for example, new attacks or overlooked genuine positives). We need to evaluate the data with the purpose of determining the root cause of a missed assault. This is vital not only because we need to understand what happened and what went wrong, but also for reasons of consistency, regulation, and criminology. In this way, examining is not novel; rather, the scope and granularity may be unique. For example, we need to manage additional information articles, which are most likely (but not widely) disseminated.

4.8.17 Use Cases

Consistence requirements (e.g., HIPAA, PCI, Sarbanes-Oxley) demand budgeted firms provide detailed evaluation records. Furthermore, the loss of records holding sensitive information is estimated at $200 per record. If an information breach occurs, legitimate behavior based on the geographical location may ensue. Key personnel in budgetary establishments require access to massive information sets containing PI, such as SSN. Promotional organizations, for example, want access to individual social networking data to strengthen their client-driven methodology for online advertising.

4.8.18 Data Source

Provenance metadata will improve in many ways because of extensive provenance charts generated from provenance-enabled programming scenarios in large information applications. Examining such large provenance diagrams to differentiate metadata circumstances for security and privacy applications is computationally intensive.

4.8.19 Use Cases

Provenance metadata will improve in many ways because of extensive provenance charts generated from provenance-enabled programming scenarios in large information applications. Examining such large provenance diagrams to differentiate metadata circumstances for security and privacy applications is computationally intensive.

5. RESEARCH CONTRIBUTION

We have painstakingly investigated the outline space of trust administration and arrangement and have created CASSANDRA, a part-based trust administration framework with special elements. Firstly, the expressiveness (and subsequently, additionally, its computationally multifaceted nature) of its approach dialect is effortlessly movable. The dialect depends on a reasonable numerical establishment, such as the data log with requirements, or data log C. In that capacity, it is parameterized by a supposed limitation area. Contingent upon the application's necessities, a suitable requirement space can be “stopped” into the framework (i.e., into the formal semantics and into a real usage) as an autonomous module without changing its semantics. By figuring out the imperative space, the dialect sentence structure and semantics are kept simple and straightforward. Specifically, CASSANDRA has no unequivocal procurements for standard strategy figures of speech, for example, part progression, partition of obligations, or appointment; rather, it is genuinely arrangement impartial in that it can encode such sayings (and numerous variations) and more propelled components, for example, computerized qualification recovery and trust transaction. Also, we display a complete formal determination for Cassandra. This incorporates the approach dialect semantics as well as the operational semantics of the entrance control motor. The operational semantics determines the worldwide state changes upon a solicitation, for example, deactivating a part. The framework's formal establishment wipes out ambiguities and could be utilized for the improvement of arrangement investigation methods. Thirdly, we have investigated the exchange in the middle of expressiveness and decidability. Imperative conservativeness is an adequate sensible condition on requirement spaces that ensures the decidability of approach inquiries, regardless of the arrangement and the inquiry. We demonstrate requirement-conservatism hypotheses for various intriguing and helpful imperative areas. In any case, requirement smallness is for the most part hard to demonstrate and rather prohibitive. We demonstrate a sound hypothesis for a static groundless investigation strategy that can be utilized to chop down excessively expressive limitation spaces to an imperatively smaller piece at runtime. Finally, we exhibit the aftereffects of our contextual analysis on a CASSANDRA approach for a national EHR administration in the UK. Our strategy depends on the authority of the NHS and Department of Health (DoH) detailed archives that have additionally been given to potential suppliers. With 375 rules, the strategy is the biggest and most complex true illustration we know about. The contextual investigation has given important lessons on the prerequisites of a trust administration framework. The EHR strategy has been effectively tested on our preparatory model execution of CASSANDRA.

6. IMPLEMENTATION

6.1 First Step: Assigning the Roles and Right of Cassandra

Open the CQL shell and create a key space then table and create a role and grant the permission. To that by using the queries below.

```
CREATE KEYSPACE uni_test WITH REPLICATION = {'class':'SimpleStrategy', 'replication_factor':1};
```

```
CREATE TABLE studentaddress (
```

```
student_id bigint,

address_id int,

address text,

PRIMARY KEY (student_id, address_id)

);

CREATE TABLE courseget (

Student_id bigint,

Program_id timeuuid,

course_id uuid,

course_description text,

PRIMARY KEY (student_id, program_id, course_id)

);
```

The universityrole have permission to read and wirte in the table

```
CREATE ROLE universityrole;

GRANT MODIFY ON uni_test.courseget TO universityrole;

GRANT SELECT ON uni_test.studentaddress TO universityrole;

Grant universityrole to read permission on keysapcedemo1 and
wirte permission no keyspacedome2

GRANT SELECT ON KEYSPACE keyspacedemo1TO universityrole;

GRANT MODIFY ON KEYSPACE keyspacedemo2 TO universityrole;

Create a user and assigning role to user

CREATE ROLE cassuser WITH PASSWORD = 'casstest' AND LOGIN =
true;

GRANT universityrole TO cassuser;

Get the list of roles and permission

LIST ROLES OF cassuser;
```

6.2 Encryption of Data

Cassandra can apply the different encryption on the data

- AES

- ECB
- PKCS5Padding

```
"Create table encrpt (id int primary key, name varchar)

with compression_parameters:sstable_compression = 'En-
cryptor'

and compression_parameters:cipher_algorithm = 'AES/ECB/PKC-
S5Padding'

and compression_parameters:secret_key_strength =
128/192/256;"
```

Key strength according to your data size and accuracy

6.3 Protection with CQL

Open the package manager in visual studio and execute the command on the package console.

Install-package Cassandra C#sharp Driver

After creating a connection use the prepared statement to avoid the cql injection.

For example:

```
//create a query once

var as = session.Prepare("UPDATE info SET bdate=? WHERE
id=?");

//...bind above parameters you need to run

var stat = as.Bind(new DateTime(2015, 11, 27), "data");
```

```
//run the bound query with the added parameters

session.Execute(statement);
```

like that you can use insert, delete and other queries if you want to your queries cql ijection and javascript injection.

6.3.1 JavaScript NoSQL Injection

If engineers are not sufficiently cautious in s coding, it is likewise workable for an assailant to pass malignant code specifically from a twisted URL. The next is a gernal JavaScript query function to execute a search based on a delivered 'year' criterion, i_val

```
function () {

var s_years = i_val;

return this.pYears == s_years ||

this.filmingYears == s_years || this.recordingYears ==

s_years;

}
```

6.4 Conclusion and Upcoming Scope

6.4.1 Conclusion

This research recorded the following conclusions can be recorded.

1. NoSQL databases are popular amongst net based businesses, due to their verified blessings in data flexibility, scalability and performance.
2. Protection issues of NoSQL in well-known continue to be to be stepped forward. There is just a serval NoSQL (e.g., Cassandra) that presently meet the statistics safety necessities of PCI DSS complaint e.g., statistics at rest and information in motion but, enhanced protection is predicted to come at the rate of performance
3. Greater server facet JavaScript injection weaknesses are expected from NoSQL databases, because many of them are walking JavaScript engines to attain excessive overall performance.
4. Working with NoSQL databases, software builders have a good deal extra duty in making sure dependable transactions and information consistency. further, in addition they should adhere greater closely to the standards and practices of safety coding.
5. Relational and NoSQL databases are satisfactory co deployed to method unique statistics flows to gain the choicest mixed features from each household.
6. Authenticity and integrity of facts used for analytics. As big records expand the sources of data it could use, the trustworthiness of every records supply needs to be tested and the inclusion of ideas which include adversarial system learning ought to be explored on the way to become aware of maliciously inserted statistics.
7. This report targeted on the usage of big facts for safety, but the different facet of the coin is the safety of huge facts. CSA has produced documents on security in Cloud Computing and additionally has working businesses focusing on figuring out the fine practices for securing massive data.

Securing Data of Cassandra Database by Applying the Latest Techniques

With the political landscape full of threats in the modern age, today it is very important for organizations storing and managing huge volumes of data to work to secure massive distributed data systems like Cassandra. Growing in sophistication, cyber threats will need the application of modern security techniques that can support the integrity, confidentiality, and availability of the data. In this paper, "Securing Data of Cassandra Database by Applying the Latest Techniques," an overview will be provided regarding the most advanced protective measures available against unauthorized access, data breaches, and more serious forms of attack targeted toward Cassandra databases. Moreover, through implementation in the areas of encryption, threat detection, and with the latest advancements in cyber security techniques, this approach guarantees that sensitive information stored under Cassandra will remain secure and compliant while being resistant to future breaches.

1. **Threat Detection and Anomaly Detection with Generative AI:**

Generative AI models such as GANs and VAE are capable of conforming various attack vectors through synthetic data or other means of simulating breach. In relation to Cassandra databases, these models show capability in identifying anomalies or unusual patterns which may signify a cyber threat. For instance, generative AI could simulate possible attacks so that the cybersecurity systems can observe those attacks and learn from them, thus more thoroughly addressing attacks.

2. **Enhancing IDS Using Artificial Intelligence**:

Traditional security strategies often rely on rule-based intrusion detection systems, which cannot cope with sophisticated or newer threats. Through the application of generative AI, IDS for Cassandra databases can quickly learn in real-time from both historical attack kind and the changing threat landscape, improving detection of breaches, unauthorized access, or data leaks. An AI-augmented IDS would review access patterns, queries, and network traffic to raise flags on anomalous behavior(s) that could compromise security to the data.

3. **AI-based Data Encryption and Privacy-Preserving Techniques:**

A key aspect in demarcating the access to Cassandra database is to ensure strong encryption methods. Generative AI can augment this by developing one or more secure encryption techniques, like AI-embedded algorithms that define the encryption strategy based on the changing threats. The sensitive data stored in Cassandra databases will always be protected against malicious decryption attempts.

4. **It addresses the identification of vulnerabilities in the Cassandra database and vice versa:**

Generative AI should automate the process of patching these vulnerabilities within the database. Nicknamed AI lite, AI systems predict the most likely targets for a new attack, based on system knowledge gleaned from generated attack scenarios, allowing proactive measures to be taken. Downtime is reduced, and the overall security of the database is improved.

5. **Cybersecurity compliance and regulatory alignment:**

Generative AI models can also assist in automating compliance processes regarding securing Cassandra databases. In this way, they can autonomously provide reports on security configuration assessments to see if the database meets regulations in its vertical, like GDPR, HIPAA, or PCI-DSS, ensuring the latest cybersecurity techniques applied to Cassandra fall in line with legal and industry standards.

Finally, generative AI plays an important role in enhancing the cybersecurity initiatives to help automate pervasive threat detection, enhance encryption schemes, and offer regulatory compliance, which assists in securing Cassandra databases with the latest techniques.

6.4.2 Recommendation

The primary protection issues that need to be addressed in massive data treating and garage. some researchers have delivered about using encryption collected with Kerberos protocol to create the data more secure. A safety policy must be put in area to specify precisely what the Database security degree requires. safety models and mechanisms are vital to correctly support and put in force a protection coverage.

6.4.2 Conclusion

In conclusion, the contemporary political and cyber ambience is increasingly rife with capable threats against organizations that handle large volumes of data. Basically, such security of distributed systems as Cassandra requires some cutting-edge techniques capable of guaranteeing data integrity, confidentiality, and availability. This research work, "Securing Data of Cassandra Database by Applying the Latest Techniques," illustrates state-of-the-art security measures which include using generative AI to detect threats, enhanced intrusion detection systems (IDS), AI-based encryption, and automated vulnerability patching. These innovative methods will give organizations the power to fend off unauthorized access to its Cassandra databases, mitigated against data loss and breaches, as well as innumerable future cyber-attacks all within the grainy confines of GDPR, HIPAA, and PCI-DSS and other regulatory standards. More so, ensuring the protection of sensitive data rests squarely on a well-articulated security policy backed by advanced models and mechanisms. Although encryption and Kerberos can create initial opacities of security fodder, additional frameworks and mechanisms of monitoring may furthermore be necessary to ensure the data has no reach for risks stemming from evolving cyber threats. AI-based approaches, fused with cybersecurity programs, guarantee Cassandra database security as a resilient future-proofed solution.

6.4.4 Further Scope of the Study

Those safety and privacy problems come in different paperwork such that Kerberos would possibly no longer be sufficient to completely relaxed the facts. Throughout MapReduce framework in Hadoop, mapper nodes method a given set of facts and saves the records within their documents. The reducer nodes will then duplicate this data from the mapper nodes. We would introduce an additional valuable node which connects with both the mapper and nodes. The facts will then be stored in this node instead of the mapper nodes near document device. A mechanism will then be used to screen all the site visitors going into and out of the node to comfort the data.

REFERENCES

Abdullah, A., & Arjunan, T. (2023). Leveraging Advanced Machine Learning Techniques for Enhanced Intrusion and Fraud Detection in NoSQL Database Systems. *International Journal of Applied Machine Learning and Computational Intelligence*, 13(11).

Alferidah, D. K., & Jhanjhi, N. Z. (2020). Cybersecurity impact over bigdata and iot growth. In *2020 International Conference on Computational Intelligence (ICCI)* (pp. 103-108). IEEE. DOI: 10.1109/ICCI51257.2020.9247722

Ali, A., Naeem, S., Anam, S., & Ahmed, M. M. (2023). A state of art survey for big data processing and nosql database architecture. *International Journal of Computing and Digital Systems*, 14(1), 1–1. DOI: 10.12785/ijcds/140124

Anusha, K., Rajesh, N., Kavitha, M., & Ravinder, N. (2021, April). Comparative Study of MongoDB vs Cassandra in big data analytics. In *2021 5th International Conference on Computing Methodologies and Communication (ICCMC)* (pp. 1831-1835). IEEE. DOI: 10.1109/ICCMC51019.2021.9418441

Arshad, M., Brohi, M. N., Soomro, T. R., Ghazal, T. M., Alzoubi, H. M., & Alshurideh, M. (2023). Nosql: Future of bigdata analytics characteristics and comparison with rdbms. In *The Effect of Information Technology on Business and Marketing Intelligence Systems* (pp. 1927–1951). Springer International Publishing. DOI: 10.1007/978-3-031-12382-5_106

Azeroual, O., & Nikiforova, A. (2022). Apache spark and mllib-based intrusion detection system or how the big data technologies can secure the data. *Information (Basel)*, 13(2), 58. DOI: 10.3390/info13020058

Babbar, H., Rani, S., Masud, M., Verma, S., Anand, D., & Jhanjhi, N. (2021). Load balancing algorithm for migrating switches in software-defined vehicular networks. *Computers, Materials & Continua*, 67(1), 1301–1316. DOI: 10.32604/cmc.2021.014627

Bohora, K., Bothe, A., Sheth, D., Chopade, R., & Pachghare, V. K. (2021). Backup and recovery mechanisms of cassandra database: A review. *Journal of Digital Forensics. Security and Law*, 15(2), 5.

Bolu, T. (2024). "Temporal Data Processing and Retention Strategies in Cassandra-Kafka Integration for Scalable Time-Series Data.

Carpenter, J., & Hewitt, E. (2022). *Cassandra: The Definitive Guide, (Revised).* O'Reilly Media, Inc.

Dissanayake, G. N. (2020). A study on real-time database technology and its applications.

Fahd, K., Venkatraman, S., & Hammeed, F. K. (2019). A comparative study of NoSQL system vulnerabilities with big data. *International Journal of Managing Information Technology*, 11(4), 1–19. DOI: 10.5121/ijmit.2019.11401

Gopi, R., Sathiyamoorthi, V., Selvakumar, S., Manikandan, R., Chatterjee, P., Jhanjhi, N. Z., & Luhach, A. K. (2022). Enhanced method of ANN based model for detection of DDoS attacks on multimedia internet of things. *Multimedia Tools and Applications*, 81(19), 1–19. DOI: 10.1007/s11042-021-10640-6

Ibrahim, A. (2024). *" Security Challenges and Solutions in Integrating Cassandra with Kafka* (No. 13852). Easy Chair.

Kalid, S., Syed, A., Mohammad, A., & Halgamuge, M. N. (2017, March). Big-data NoSQL databases: A comparison and analysis of "Big-Table", "DynamoDB", and "Cassandra". In *2017 IEEE 2nd International Conference on Big Data Analysis (ICBDA)* (pp. 89-93). IEEE.

Matos, T., & Guerreiro, J. (2024, June). Remote Secure Online Voting System Development. In *International Conference on Human-Computer Interaction* (pp. 51-65). Cham: Springer Nature Switzerland.

Nasrullah, N. A., Sharma, N., & Niazy, M. S. (2023). A Study of Performance Evaluation and Comparison of NOSQL Databases Choosing for Big Data: HBase and Cassandra Using YCSB. *Journal of Computational Engineering*, 25(3), 1–12.

Rafique, A., Van Landuyt, D., Beni, E. H., Lagaisse, B., & Joosen, W. (2021). CryptDICE: Distributed data protection system for secure cloud data storage and computation. *Information Systems*, 96, 101671. DOI: 10.1016/j.is.2020.101671

Rahman, R. U., Singh, K., Tomar, D. S., & Musheer, R. (2024). Building Resilient Digital Forensic Frameworks for NoSQL Database: Harnessing the Blockchain and Quantum Technology. In *Sustainable Security Practices Using Blockchain, Quantum and Post-Quantum Technologies for Real Time Applications* (pp. 205–238). Springer Nature Singapore. DOI: 10.1007/978-981-97-0088-2_11

Rahman, R. U., Singh, K., Tomar, D. S., & Musheer, R. (2024). Building Resilient Digital Forensic Frameworks for NoSQL Database: Harnessing the Blockchain and Quantum Technology. In *Sustainable Security Practices Using Blockchain, Quantum and Post-Quantum Technologies for Real Time Applications* (pp. 205–238). Springer Nature Singapore. DOI: 10.1007/978-981-97-0088-2_11

Saeed, S. (2019). The serverless architecture: Current trends and open issues moving legacy applications. IJCDS. *Scopus.*

Saeed, S., Abdullah, A., Jhanjhi, N. Z., & Malaysia, T. (2019). Analysis of the lung cancer patients for data mining tool. *IJCSNS*, 19(7), 90.

Saeed, S., Abdullah, A., Jhanjhi, N. Z., Naqvi, M., & Nayyar, A. (2022). New techniques for efficiently k-NN algorithm for brain tumor detection. *Multimedia Tools and Applications*, 81(13), 18595–18616. DOI: 10.1007/s11042-022-12271-x

Saeed, S., & Haron, H. (2021). Improve correlation matrix of discrete Fourier transformation (CM-DFT) technique for finding the missing values of MRI images. *Mathematical Biosciences and Engineering*, •••, 1–22.

Saeed, S., Haron, H., Jhanjhi, N. Z., Naqvi, M., Alhumyani, H. A., & Masud, M. (2022). Improve correlation matrix of discrete fourier transformation technique for finding the missing values of mri images. *Mathematical Biosciences and Engineering*, 19(9), 9039–9059. DOI: 10.3934/mbe.2022420 PMID: 35942748

Saeed, S., & Humayun, M. (2019). Disparaging the barriers of journal citation reports (JCR). IJCSNS: International Journal of Computer Science and Network Security, 19(5), 156-175. *ISI-Index*, 1, 5.

Saeed, S., Jhanjhi, N. Z., Naqvi, M., & Humayun, M. (2019). Analysis of software development methodologies. *International Journal of Computing and Digital Systems*, 8(5), 446–460.

Saeed, S., Jhanjhi, N. Z., Naqvi, M., Malik, N. A., & Humayun, M. (2019). Disparage the barriers of journal citation reports (JCR). *International Journal of Computer Science and Network Security*, 19(5), 156–175.

Saeed, S., Shaikh, A., Ali, M., Hussain, M., Ahmed, F., & Mehmood, S. (2017). Implementation of failure enterprise systems in organizational perspective framework. *International Journal of Advanced Computer Science and Applications*, 8(5), 54–63. DOI: 10.14569/IJACSA.2017.080508

Sánchez, R. A. G., Bernal, D. J. M., & Parada, H. D. J. (2021, September). Security assessment of Nosql Mongodb, Redis and Cassandra database managers. In *2021 Congreso Internacional de Innovación y Tendencias en Ingeniería (CONIITI)* (pp. 1-7). IEEE.

Sánchez, R. A. G., Bernal, D. J. M., & Parada, H. D. J. (2021, September). Security assessment of Nosql Mongodb, Redis and Cassandra database managers. In *2021 Congreso Internacional de Innovación y Tendencias en Ingeniería (CONIITI)* (pp. 1-7). IEEE.

Santos, N., Ghita, B., & Masala, G. (2023). Medical Systems Data Security and Biometric Authentication in Public Cloud Servers. *IEEE Transactions on Emerging Topics in Computing*.

Seghier, N. B., & Kazar, O. (2021, September). Performance benchmarking and comparison of NoSQL databases: Redis vs mongodb vs Cassandra using YCSB tool. In *2021 International Conference on Recent Advances in Mathematics and Informatics (ICRAMI)* (pp. 1-6). IEEE. DOI: 10.1109/ICRAMI52622.2021.9585956

Shah, I. A., Jhanjhi, N. Z., & Laraib, A. (2023). Cybersecurity and blockchain usage in contemporary business. In *Handbook of Research on Cybersecurity Issues and Challenges for Business and FinTech Applications* (pp. 49–64). IGI Global.

Sicari, S., Rizzardi, A., & Coen-Porisini, A. (2022). Security&privacy issues and challenges in NoSQL databases. *Computer Networks*, 206, 108828. DOI: 10.1016/j.comnet.2022.108828

Singh, K., Rahman, R. U., & Pathak, D. (2023, November). A New Forensic Framework for NoSQL Databases: Wide-Column as Case Studies. In *2023 Seventh International Conference on Image Information Processing (ICIIP)* (pp. 79-84). IEEE. DOI: 10.1109/ICIIP61524.2023.10537755

Soobia, S., Afnizanfaizal, A., & Jhanjhi, N. Z. (2022). Hybrid graph cut hidden Markov model of k-mean cluster technique. *CMC-Computers. Materials & Continua*, 72(1), 1–15.

Yan, S., Wang, J., & Liang, J. (2024, May). Big Data Storage and Analysis System for Space Application. In *2024 27th International Conference on Computer Supported Cooperative Work in Design (CSCWD)* (pp. 1764-1769). IEEE. DOI: 10.1109/CSCWD61410.2024.10580324

Chapter 9
Future Trends in AI Security:
Anticipating and Preparing for Emerging Threats

Siva Raja Sindiramutty
https://orcid.org/0009-0006-0310-8721
Taylor's University, Malaysia

Noor Zaman Jhanjhi
https://orcid.org/0000-0001-8116-4733
Taylor's University, Malaysia

Navid Ali Khan
Taylor's University, Malaysia

ABSTRACT

Cybersecurity is enriched due to Artificial Intelligence (AI), which provides better real-time threat detection and anomaly identification, response systems. As attackers grow more sophisticated and leverage AI in creating malware. The present study gives an overview of the future threats associated with AI-driven attacks and challenges faced by existing cybersecurity countermeasures. Additionally, it also analyses the feasibility of using AI-driven capabilities like predictive threat intelligence, advanced anomaly detection and quantum computing for some of these emerging threats. For such as, we need user permissions and rights on this application, it should take into consideration privacy policies while designing AI security as well. To this end, to get ready against future AI security risks a proactive and adaptive approach is needed stressing the collaboration between industry, academia as well global entities.

DOI: 10.4018/979-8-3693-6135-1.ch009

I. INTRODUCTION

A. The Evolution of AI in Cybersecurity

Cybersecurity has changed greatly during the last decade and a lot of this is done by AI (Ozkan-Okay et al., 2024). Their incorporation in this specific field ensured the advent of detection tools that are tens to hundreds faster and more reliable than all methods from previous eras combined. By analysing large datasets from an array of sources, AI has transformed its threat detection capabilities to find suspicious patterns in real time (Okoli et al., 2024). This has been especially helpful in identifying new kinds of malware and ransomware that are ever more primped. New forms of cyberattacks are emerging as we speak; hence, the capability for this tool to evolve in parallel and predict new attacks is second only to a highly advanced AI-driven cybersecurity solution that will be able to keep pace with even more sophisticated tactics (Sarker, 2024).

AI is playing an increasingly important role in defending against cyber threats as the sophistication of these threats increases (Al-Dosari, Fetais and Kucukvar, 2022; Sindiramutty et al., 2024). For our part, automated systems driven by Machine Leaning (ML) algorithms are adept at processing huge amounts of data to enable cybersecurity teams to recognize genuine threats more easily and cut down on false positives. It enables organizations to be more responsive when facing intrusions even as the number of cyberattacks targeting businesses, governments and individuals continues to rise. It also plays a role in beefing up cybersecurity by identifying weaknesses proactively and making secure suggestions to fill up the holes, even before they are used as spam by malicious hackers.

In this chapter, we investigate AI security trends and how they can be utilized to defend against new threats. As the attacks we face become more advanced, it is crucial to learn how AI will change to answer these security threats. Strengthening AI adoption. As we know the risks associated with it, pre-preparing for future risk can be done by using employ advanced tools and systems via an upgrade of older features and deployment. This will help businesses and organizations protect their systems from the growing threat of cybercrime by giving them insight into the importance of AI in cybersecurity.

B. The Current Landscape of AI Security

AI is now crucial in cybersecurity to identify and respond instantly to threats. Several AI tools such as intrusion detection systems, threat intelligence platforms, and automated response systems have been leveraged to secure the environment. AI algorithms analyse network traffic patterns to detect subtle activities that could have been overlooked by traditional methods (Singh et al., 2023; Hussain et al., 2024). Using ML, for example with tools like Darktrace, allows you to detect those anomalies in real-time -- giving your organization near-instant insights into possible threats (Katiyar et al., 2024). Likewise, new AI-based antivirus solutions have been getting much better at detecting and cleansing malicious software through this more enlightened learning process from years of patterns in known threat Datasets (N and H, 2023).

While there is much in this effort to recognize and commend, gaps remain when it comes to AI security practices. A big problem is that AI will be so easily fooled by advanced attacks. A new concern is adversarial ML—a method of attack in which an adversary carefully tweaks the data that enters AI models, so they produce incorrect or false results (Shihab et al., 2024). Even worse, AI systems can be biased if the data for training them is not wide or representative enough which will generate less efficacious detection of threats and more false positives (Chander et al., 2024; Sharma et al., 2022). Also, like other new technological advancements in security, implementation of AI with traditional security infrastructure can prove to be difficult and expensive which hinders replacing it as a part or together with entire systems used by some organizations.

Ultimately, while AI has emerged as a very effective tool in bolstering cybersecurity defence mechanisms against fast-evolving threats risks it faces include adversarial attacks data bias and implementation challenges that require further attention to ensure an uptick in efficacy. Figure 1 shows evolution of AI in cybersecurity.

Figure 1. Evolution of AI in Cybersecurity

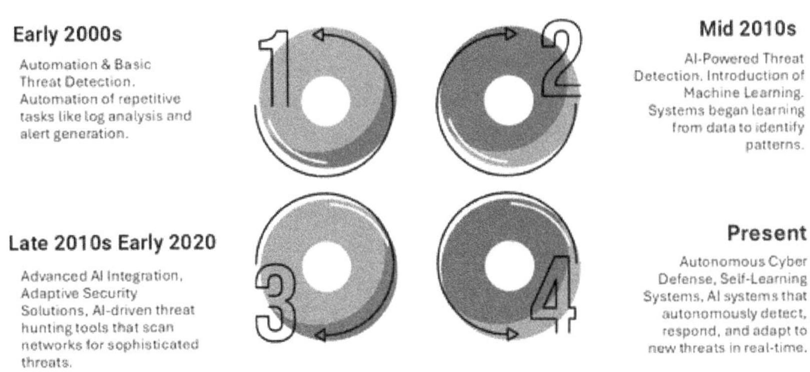

Chapter Contribution

In this chapter, we share top concerns for securing AI, as well as best practices observed now by professionals who are on the cutting edge of tackling these challenges. It starts by tracing the history of AI in cybersecurity which, as previously mentioned centres around its ability to improve real-time detection and anomaly discovery. Specific threats discussed in this chapter here are AI cyberattacks AI adversarial attacks on sensor data and AI-generated Deepfakes as a security problem rubble. Traditional approaches struggle to detect or neutralize these advanced threats. This chapter also discusses some of the state-of-the-art AI technologies, which are intended to shape security in future implementations based on this technology. Some such ones include predictive threat intelligence, which makes use of ML and big data to anticipate risks based on past events; as well as more advanced anomaly detection systems that can pick up small changes across the different patterns received. AI and Quantum computing are touted as a new area which can help change the security landscape focusing on encryption, but also combining major threats.

The chapter also explores the ethical concerns surrounding the use of AI in cybersecurity, including privacy issues and bias within AI models and how transparency can be a powerful tool to help shed light on why things are happening the way they do. It calls for strong AI security frameworks and policies to make sure the systems are secure, fair, explainable (and accountable), and reliable as well. This chapter examines some of the contemporary challenges and likely trends for organisations as they seek to strengthen their cybersecurity efforts. The document stresses networking and being prepared for new developments, as well as the coordination that must exist between companies' universities and institutions ready to combat threats from their AI.

Chapter Organization

Globally AI is entering the arena of cybersecurity at an ever-growing pace and has achieved real-time security threat detection & defence capabilities which we will learn in Section 1. The second section of the report describes how AI is reshaping cybersecurity it detects anomalies, automates threat responses and avoids human error. Section 3. New and Emerging Threat Areas AI-enabled Malware Adversarial AI Deepfakes It explores how AI is enabling attackers to bypass conventional defences, and the need for evolved security methods. In the fourth section, we examine AI-based security solutions. Section 5. Ethics and practice in AI applied to security. Issues around privacy, bias in AI models and components of transparency and accountability are covered as the necessity for ethical use is outlined. Section 6 restates the need to continue to advance ever-changing threats through open engagement and proactive innovation. The report also has recommendations for organizations to better align their AI-based security strategies.

II. EMERGING THREATS IN AI SECURITY

A. AI-Powered Cyber Attacks

The rise in AI technology is enabling adversaries to build and run more complex cyber-attacks with increased difficulty of detection (Malatji and Tolah, 2024). Attackers will employ AI automation, and analysis to quickly process large volumes of data for weaknesses (Hashmi, Yamin and Yayilgan, 2024; Sindiramutty, Jhanjhi, Tan, Yun, et al., 2024). The primary one that comes to mind is changeable AI-driven malware routed through more conventional modes of security. This malware can use real-time changes in its behaviour, based on the environment encountered – hence making it difficult to detect (Chew et al., 2024). A different illustration is AI-powered phishing assaults. They employ AI to generate very specific and human-sounding messages that can fool even the most careful of users. Automated or autonomous cyber-attacks, where AI systems are armed to engage in attacks with partial human supervision (or none), are an even scarier possibility. These attacks could run automatically with no human intervention and do not need to remain dormant until later use. As well, autonomous systems could move more quickly than human defenders to exploit vulnerabilities and continue attacking while their adversary patches (Badjie, Cecílio and Casimiro, 2024; Brohi et al., 2020). If they learn from experience, these machines can adapt in ways humans cannot (Miller & Zhang 2024). How AI Is Transforming Cyber Threats and Making Attacker Offenses Defensive As attackers take advantage of these sophisticated tools, the requirement for novel defences is becoming increasingly important. Changes in the environment for cyber threats are expected likely to be driven by advances in AI technology, thus necessitating lively and flexible security responses if we want to avoid falling behind the current or preferred state. Figure 2 shows emerging threats in ai security.

Figure 2. Emerging Threats in AI Security

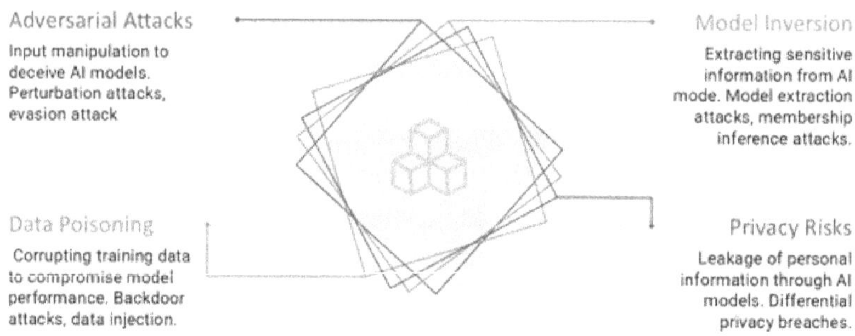

B. Adversarial AI

Compromised AI systems are at greater risk for adversarial attacks, which would compromise security and reliability (Saeed and Alsharidah, 2024). Those attacks are then used to manipulate AI models in different ways including, data poisoning, model inversion and more evasion-based techniques. Data poisoning is the approach of polluting training data and in turn, leading the model to malfunction due to bad decisions or biased results (Nguyen et al., 2024; Alex et al., 2022). The model of course learns how to look at the data and make predictions based on it. This is a way for slight modifications in these raw discreet inputs so that they may be represented very well as disjunctive features or enough conditions are created was subsequently entered into the ML prediction algorithm. Model inversion, on the other side, is proven to cause a model to lose sensitive information (Liu et al., 2024). Those outputs are piecewise linear interpolations of the model that can also be used by attackers to reconstruct sensitive data inputs, which could give away personal information. Evasion attacks happen when the adversaries use input data to cheat on AI response so that in real-world applications, it reduces model efficacy (Naik et al., 2024). The examples from the wild show how real-world effects of these attacks are. Model inversion attack whereby the attacker was able to retrieve health information from a medical data-trained detector revealing privacy issues with ML (Hatamizadeh et al., 2023). Evasion attacks. traffic signs were modified to make self-driving cars interpret road conditions in the wrong way (Deng et al., 2021) demonstrating that autonomous systems are vulnerable. Such instances demonstrate that adversarial attacks are not just hypothetical — they have real-world effects on AI functionality and can damage the trust in AI-based systems.

C. Deepfake Technology

AI-based deepfakes are a real threat to security systems, misinformation campaigns and many other aspects of everyday as well the professional life (Khan, Taqi and Afzal, 2024). Much of these manipulated videos and audio can replicate the appearance or voices with such accuracy that it is almost impossible to realise what you are seeing is fake. A real example of this will be posed by deepfakes, with a huge potential to threaten security systems alongside their notorious capabilities for bypassing authentication processes or doctoring surveillance footage (Qureshi et al., 2024). Deepfakes also make many individuals sceptical, driving people to believe in wrong narratives and spreading lies on a large scale through disinformation as they can produce fabricated news or tampered video evidence which is hard to verify (Hameleers, Van Der Meer and Dobber, 2023). This type of manufactured media can mislead or manipulate public opinion by lying therefore it creates a great threat to news integrity and people's belief in them. Deepfakes are also extremely problematic when it comes to fraud. They can be used to influence an individual to reveal privileged information or send money by impersonating a person worthy of trust. This second type of deception leverages the photorealism of deepfake videos to trigger an emotional response and access personal or financial data (Cavedon-Taylor, 2024).

Deepfakes can also enhance the power of social engineering techniques. Criminals can, ominously, exploit those connections or the credibility of authority figures meaning that scams are more likely to result in a victim (Wingreen and Samandari, 2024) It does not take much manipulation like this to initially compromise either the person or the entire organization which leads to very quick thefts on a grand scale. All types of businesses have an increased level of risk, as well as politics and personal security. For companies, deepfake-induced fraud can lead to reputational damage and financial losses while in politics rivals may use fabricated videos to colour public perception of political figures or campaigns. Individually, personal security is threatened by the risk of blackmail or identity theft.

III. FUTURE TRENDS IN AI-DRIVEN SECURITY SOLUTIONS

A. AI in Predictive Threat Intelligence

AI is getting even better at detecting and responding to new threats before they become bigger (Lad, 2024). Integrating officers with AI can scan through masses of stored data or real-time international information, to predict where possible threats may arise this is all based on ML and big data (Dhanaraj et al., 2024; Muzafar and Jhanjhi, 2020). ML algorithms can pick up patterns and anomalies in the data that may indicate threats to come, allowing organizations to prepare for such events (Duary et al., 2024). They leverage historical and real-time data to improve the ability of prediction, thus enabling anomaly detections for predictive maintenance. Big data the only way to have enough volume and variety of information for proper predictions (Kuo, Peng and Kuo, 2021). When trained on large amounts of data, AI can then start to learn trends and anomalies which would be tough with smaller or less diverse datasets.

AI is anticipated to work even better in the future. This could be further developed with a new AI algorithm, which can predict threats even better by analysing the upcoming trends of data and will add this information through different resources in Information Systems (Islam, 2024). This evolution should then eventually result in better proactive measures and faster, more accurate responses to security threats.

B. Advanced Anomaly Detection

With the advent of AI, anomaly detection has become sophisticated through artificial neural networks and other advanced methods used to detect unusual events (Nayak, Pati and Das, 2023). However, in traditional systems that have rules defined priorly, it becomes hard to identify unknown anomalies (Palakurti, 2024; Sindiramutty, Tan and Wei, 2024). Some AI systems are now trained to detect patterns that do not conform with the established norms, using ML algorithms. For example, deep learning models can surface nuanced aberrations in data at a massive scale that traditional systems may not capture (Gui, Sam and Bhardwaj, 2024). AI provides real-time monitoring, which results in better responsiveness as data streams are always being analysed (Lodhi, Gill and Hussain, 2024; Shah, Jhanjhi and Laraib, 2022). Over the years, this functionality has helped thousands of systems in proactively detecting and deactivating any outliers that may transpire over time. For instance, AI-led systems can alert about abnormal network traffic shortly after the event occurs—quicker than human intervention (Lodhi, Gill and Hussain, 2024).

Anomaly detection algorithms will continue to evolve in the future with even better performance. Some of these novel techniques, like generative adversarial networks (GANs), are predicted to allow better classification of rare and complex anomalies (Lim et al., 2024). Since GANs can generatively create new data, they can help models learn better for the detection of anomalies within their respective fields (Akkem, Biswas and Varanasi, 2024). Moreover, future developments in transfer learning may yield models that can handle new types of anomalies without having to undergo large-scale training. In this way, the AI development for anomaly detection is speeding up and it becomes more useful when comes to real-time monitoring (Bhatia and Sangwan, 2021). It is positional that it would have a very important role to play in enhancing security, and operational efficiency and we could combine them into multiple domains. Figure 3 shows future trends in ai-driven security solutions.

Figure 3. Future Trends in AI-Driven Security Solutions

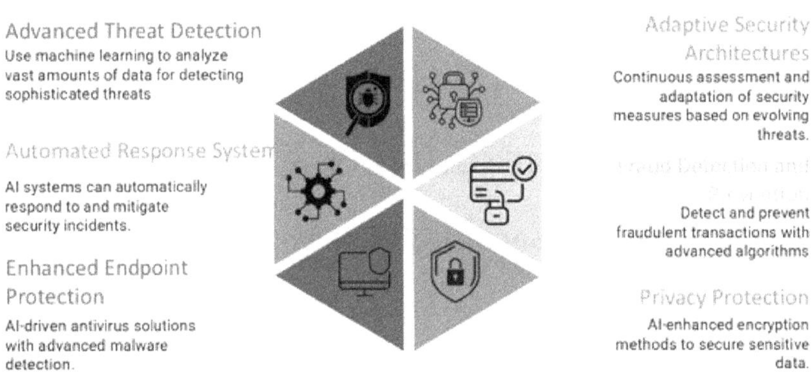

C. AI and Quantum Computing

Quantum computing and AI are two aspects of cybersecurity. As AI systems grow more sophisticated, they struggle to respond to increasingly sophisticated security threats (Sontan and Samuel, 2024). Quantum computing, on the other hand, provides AI-powered security for quantitatively enhanced capabilities (Radanliev, 2024; Seng et al., 2024). Quantum computing is hundreds of thousands of times faster than classical computing in terms of processing power (Gill et al., 2024). This suggests that it will make it faster to analyse vast pools of data and identify security threats. Quantum-enhanced AI-enabled systems will rapidly identify unrelated patterns and behaviours, which humans or the brain programmed into the AI cannot. This collaboration would enhance current AI-powered security measures. They would be more accurate and quicker than before, resulting in cybersecurity resilience from potential threats. Encryption is at risk across practically all risk spectrums. Traditional encryption methods are prone to quantum assaults. Quantum computers have the potential to crack widely used encryption algorithms (Ajala et al., 2024). Nonetheless, quantum development will also enable the creation of superseding encryption. AI-driven quantum encryption introduces two participants to the computer environment, one portion of a secure terminal (Otieno, 2024). They generate difficult-to-decrypt keys, and encryption patterns will be thrown away on a device. If not handled carefully, there are also dangers associated with the integration of AI and quantum. The present form is defunct for AI. Quantum computing will promptly break numerous security algorithms used by AI and security professionals, regardless of their excellent calipering (Dash and Ullah, 2024). A well-implemented quantum machine can easily resolve it. Quantum computers' peak will make it much easier to exploit poor complex questions. As a result, a combination of AI and quantum technologies must be updated.

IV. PREPARING FOR THE FUTURE OF AI SECURITY

A. Building Robust AI Security Frameworks

As AI technologies are used by organizations more often, the protection of these systems is crucial to keep getting socially inflicted attacks and fraud in data (Nair, Deshmukh and Tyagi, 2023). Adopting robust AI security procedures enables companies to protect vital data and preserve the faith of clients (Habbal, Ali and Abuzaraida, 2024; Waheed et al., 2024). Resilient AI security requires building robust systems that can defend against and adapt in the event of a disruption, be it through cyber-attacks or operational outages (Abdelkader et al., 2024).

A strong AI security strategy strikes a balance by emphasizing those key components, while still being flexible enough to quickly adapt and respond. Flexibility buys the system time to adapt when a new threat emerges or if its environment changes. If you empower people who oversee an AI system to connect these disparate parts, the result is adaptability. this new functionality ensures that should there be surprises or unexpected issues (which inevitably will occur) then human guides can respond effectively. Ensuring these are the four inputs for future security and function of AI systems. Steps to make AI security best practices part of organizational policies Step one must be the security-cost integration into the AI development and all systems must have built-in securities as seen from the pathway for Introduction to Cybersecurity (Khan et al., 2024). Regularly updating and monitoring AI systems will allow for these potential vulnerabilities to be identified early (Yampolskiy, 2024). Further, organizations need to implement a security awareness culture where workers understand how to practice good behaviour and report any unscrupulous activities if they face them. Incorporating these practices into company policies may help companies better secure their AI systems and prevent security breaches, ultimately securing data integrity and ensuring operational fitness.

B. Ethical Considerations in AI Security

There are multiple ethical dilemmas from the privacy, security or transparency perspective in the case of using AI for cybersecurity (Chukwunweike et al., 2024; Azam et al., 2023). The more AI systems are linked with security operations, the greater the importance of addressing the balance between protecting individuals' privacy and ensuring strong cybersecurity (Isakov et al., 2024). Threat detection can be improved, but the same powers could enable more intrusive surveillance (Arif *et al.*, 2024; Alzaabi and Mehmood, 2024). Maintaining transparency in AI technology is critical for preventing it from being exploited and avoiding the potential destruction of public confidence (Olsen et al., 2024).

Bias in AI interferes with fairness and accountability. Creating fair and unbiased AI, is not simple; to achieve this technological goal we must be meticulous during system design plus conduct frequent audits to discover these biases (Kaluarachchi and Sedera, 2024). Accountability, in turn, is also important; organizations need to be held accountable for the operation of their AI systems and their effect on people (Novelli, Taddeo and Floridi, 2023). Balancing privacy and security are essential to AI development in cybersecurity being ethical (Korobenko, Nikiforova and Sharma, 2024). Figure 4 shows preparing for the future of ai security.

Figure 4. Preparing for the Future of AI Security

C. Developing AI Security Talent

It is important to have quality assignment help for security as these AI systems are linked with different sectors (Sarker et al., 2024). Traditional defence mechanisms fail against these new styles of attacks as the cyber threat landscape is evolving every day (Obi et al., 2024). You would also need AI security experts to protect these advanced systems. However, expertise in AI technology as well as cybersecurity is necessary, if they should be able to anticipate and counter potential threats (Bécue, Praça and Gama, 2021; Ananna et al., 2023). There are a few strategies to train and reskill the next generation of AI security experts. For example, integrating AI security courses into academic curricula may ensure students are introduced to the relevant knowledge early in (Chiu et al., 2022). Hands-on experience that can be obtained through internships and industry partnerships is also an essential part of the equation to close on missing knowledge between theory and practice (Nyemba, Mbohwa and Carter, 2021). In addition, long-term learning resources like workshops and certifications whether professionals' knowledge to keep them current with new developments and threats are emerging as a concern in AI security

The key to solving this shortage in AI security talent is collaboration among academia and industry. Universities grant basic knowledge and industry partners contribute with a practical view of real issues at present. Collaborative research projects and training programs with industry provide avenues for enhanced student/

professional skills before they are required by the field (Jones, 2024). The result. education and industry growing hand in hand, sharing experiences to help educators enrich their programs with practical applications yet offering companies a more job-ready workforce.

V. CASE STUDIES. AI SECURITY IN ACTION

A. Case Study 1. AI-Driven Defense Against a Major Cyber Attack

For example, a significant cyber-attack against a global financial institution was defused by sophisticated AI security solutions (Choucri, Madnick and Ferwerda, 2013). It was a ransomware attack that made use of world-class encryption to encrypt important data throughout the organization's network (Malik et al., 2024; Wen et al., 2023). The team learned later during their analysis that they were able to focus on these bad apples so quickly in part because of AI-driven tools using ML algorithms, of course, had already been culling out the worst-most-likely-to-be-transformed into privacy-invading apps. The duo of tools spotted abnormal behaviour in terms of network communication and file read/write access which prompted additional isolation of the infected systems to prevent infection.

Because AI can process a lot of relevant data at scale and in real time (Ettalibi, Elouadi and Mansour, 2024) (and no human team can do that). This was aided by the organization's quick countermeasures to reduce impact and get operations back up with minimum. In addition, AI-based forensic analysis tools could be used to deep dive into vital information necessary for counterattacking the attack vectors and methods that hackers employ. (Vijayalakshmi et al., 2024; Gouda et al., 2022). Another important lesson learned from this attack is the fact that AI should be part of day-to-day cybersecurity operations This attack showed that probably we need more than traditional security to survive against the enveloping threat landscape. AI-driven tools can improve threat detection, enable real-time responses or aid in post-attack analysis (Bhardwaj and Dave, 2024). Going forward, organizations should focus on incorporating AI-driven security tools into their security agenda. These tools must be regularly updated and trained to evolve against threats while remaining functional. The lesson here is that all enterprises need to get ahead of cyber threats and use some AI at the very least, to boost our entire security posture.

B. Case Study 2. Adversarial AI Attack and Response

Adversarial AI attacks refer to techniques in which the attacker tries maliciously to influence incorrect output from an AI system (Khazane et al., 2024; Fatima-Tuz-Zahra et al., 2020). An attacker might, for instance, corrupt image data with noise so that an AI model incorrectly labels it (Penso, Frenkel and Goldberger, 2024; Naveed et al., 2024). They represent significant threats, especially in fields such as autonomous vehicles and facial recognition systems. As a response, researchers and developers have adopted different strategies to defend against these threats.

For instance, adversarial training adds adversarial examples to the datasets of models being trained (Zhou et al., 2024). In this way, the AI system is taught to detect and neutralise such manipulations (Tarsney, 2024). One other approach is to build stateful algorithms with full memory that can catch and disable attacks on the fly. This is where methods like input validation and anomaly detection are important. Here too, AI can be used in spotting and containing these attacks. More advanced models can discover patterns that identify adversary activity before it takes hold of an environment. For example, reinforcement learning algorithms can be adaptive to new attack methods by continuous learning from them (Bansal and Ouda, 2024; Humayun et al., 2022). AI can also examine attack trends and continuously adjust defences. For example, scientists have developed AI-powered systems that can emulate possible attack strategies by adversaries to evaluate the robustness of various models. This proactive-fighting-off-attacks style aids in developing better defences and overall system security Continuously innovating and adapting AI defence mechanisms to outpace attackers is a struggle that never ends. Figure 5 shows ai security in real-world applications.

Figure 5. AI Security in Real-World Applications

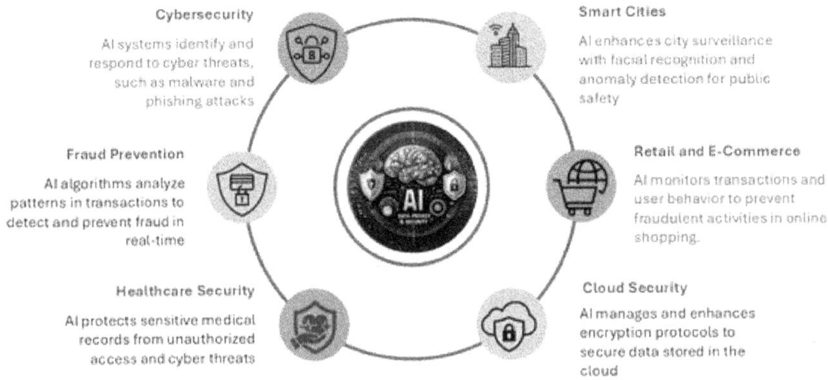

C. Case Study 3. Integrating AI with Quantum Security

Latest developments merge AI with quantum computing to strengthen security inequalities the ability for AI to analyse enormous data sets has improved threat detection and response in a major way (Han et al., 2024). By contrast quantum computers, the encryption/decryption process will substantially change because it uses distinct ways of processing data which is crucial to safeguarding sensitive information (Cherbal et al., 2023; Sindiramutty, K. R. V. Prabagaran, Jhanjhi, Ghazanfar, et al., 2024). Integrating these technologies plans to take on conventional security gaps using machine-learning algorithms of AI and complex calculations made by quantum for systems to be more secure (Peral-García, Cruz-Benito and García-Peñalvo, 2024). The initial results of this integration were encouraging. A recent example is quantum key distribution (QKD) systems which, when combined with AI-enabled methods have been presented to be even more resilient against eavesdropping attacks (Xiao et al., 2023; Lim et al., 2019). Consequently, AI algorithms process data from the quantum systems in nanoseconds, analyse and react to potential threats much faster than any conventional techniques (Schmidt and Hildebrandt, 2024). In addition, together the two sides provide security protocols that can be updated in real-time with new threats. an adaptive response to constantly changing conditions. In the end, this combination of AI with quantum computing is a major step forward for security. The initial results point to the increased capacity of the integrated systems to protect against increasingly advanced cyber threats.

VI. THE ROLE OF COLLABORATION IN AI SECURITY

A. Industry-Academia Partnerships

This is where industry and academia need to come together to help move AI security forward. Industry has practical experience and resources; academics are equipped with research capabilities as well as theoretical knowledge. Collaboration between these areas can lead to more robust security solutions together with creative methods of managing AI-related risks. For example, a collaboration between Google and the University of California (Berkeley), was developed that allowed for innovations in AI security. Malik, Muthalagu and Pawar (2024) used their joint research on adversarial attacks to design better model defences for ML systems. For example, MIT developed with IBM an AI system that is also secure in terms of vulnerability (Reshi and Sholla, 2024). This collaboration has led to the development of powerful frameworks that can stop cybercrimes.

Microsoft have developed innovative privacy-preserving AI techniques that are in use today. For instance, they developed some seminal work on differential privacy that has been a baseline technique for ensuring data are safe during training AI models (Hu et al., 2024; Gopi et al., 2021). It is fundamental research that will help ensure AI can operate safely and protect users' privacy.

The NVIDIA-Stanford AI Governance Research partnership has made strides towards improved system security with new algorithms, and hardware to boost vulnerability within. Their research also contributes to the broader challenge of securing AI systems against attacks and abuse. In addition, these collaborations highlight how the collaborations are already moving forward in AI security by bringing together academia with industry. These collaborations combine their strengths which provides unique solutions that optimize the security and dependability of AI technologies.

B. Global Cooperation for AI Security

International cooperation is necessary to effectively combat AI security threats worldwide (Radanliev, 2024a). The advance of AI technologies is leading to the introduction of entirely new categories and scales risks beyond borders (Oluoch, 2024). There is no one country capable of dealing with these threats by itself. This week we learned that the development of international safety-level protocols requires a collaborative approach (Smith, 2023; Usman et al., 2023).

These efforts are being championed by the Global Partnership on Artificial Intelligence (GPAI) and AI Security Alliance. GPAI will work to ensure a new era of responsible AI and cooperation on this big issue. The AI Security Alliance is a global effort to safely secure advanced systems, led jointly by experts and policymakers (Garcia, 2024; Sindiramutty, N. Jhanjhi, Tan, Lau, et al., 2024). It does so by facilitating groups in developing common standards & practices to keep Security at best across regions. Similarly, the success of collaborative frameworks for enhancing AI security is becoming evident internationally (Habbal, Ali and Abuzaraida, 2024b). This allows countries to better identify potential threats and take appropriate measures. Countries have even introduced multinational efforts, such as the AI Cybersecurity Initiative which resulted in threat intelligence and response standards (Johnson 2024; Alkinani et al., 2021). This collective approach maximizes the capacity to counter responses to security incidents associated with AI and minuses the risks of significant score breaches.

Long story short, our world is so small that international cooperation is essential in dealing with global security threats involving AI. The work of leading initiatives like GPAI and the AI Security Alliance is evidence that collaboration pays off in security. These collaborations also create shared strategies and resources, useful in a collective effort to ensure that the global AI environment is both safe and secure (Doe 2024; Roe 2024). Figure 6 shows the role of collaboration in ai security.

Figure 6. The Role of Collaboration in AI Security

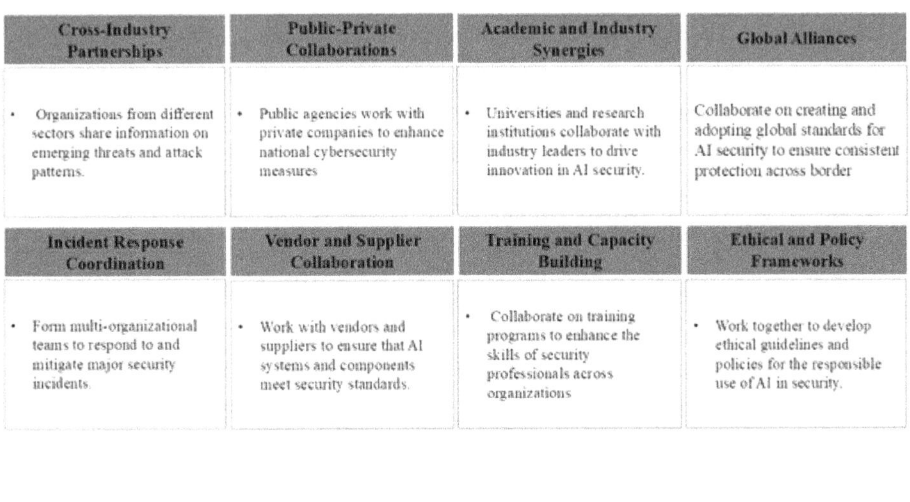

VII. THE FUTURE OF AI SECURITY. PREDICTIONS AND RECOMMENDATIONS

A. Predictions for the Next Decade

In the next ten years, AI security will face enormous challenges as well while strides are made in AI technology (Familoni, 2024; Dogra et al., 2021). The AI systems will soon be exposed to such kinds of complex attacks as the AI models become more advanced (Chen and Babar, 2024). To give an example, adversarial misclassification attacks threaten to grow in importance as attackers can leverage those types of attack vectors more easily without the need for the adversary's real-forgery solutions (Bajaj and Vishwakarma, 2023; Azam, Dulloo, Majeed, Wan, Xin, Tajwar, et al., 2023). This indicates that security protections must evolve with this threat landscape to combat it effectively. New players. How emerging technologies could disrupt the cybersecurity game A prime example of this is that quantum computing threatens a menace to current top-secret levels of data literal means by breaking most encryption techniques now in use. It hand-in-hand provides some opportunities such as making new encryption technology that can resist quantum threads. Another good area that uses blockchain for security. Blockchain technology, that can introduce immutability of records for transaction verification and data integrity (Hossain et al., 2024), offers a more secure solution to the problem. This would be a step toward protecting against other types of cyberattacks by verifying that data has not been changed. Moreover, the evolution of AI itself can help on both fronts. AI-powered security solutions can help in this regard by monitoring patterns and abnormalities quickly to spot suspicious computations (Rehan, 2024). But they must be slapped down with a splitter to prevent them from turning into new vulnerabilities.

Enterprise. A major key to getting ahead with their security strategies will involve the need for organizations just to keep evolving This combination of AI and blockchain, as well as an approach concerning not rushing into untested technologies like quantum computing will be vital in keeping cybersecurity ahead against new threats.

B. Strategic Recommendations for Organizations

Companies need to respond immediately to reduce future risks that can arise from AI and prepare their current efforts for the coming trends. Here are a few ways in which they can adapt to those changes and make them work to their advantage. Adopt strong AI governance Data is king for an organisation. Policies and procedures should be put into place to monitor AI systems, to make sure they are both secure and compliant with regulations (Díaz-Rodríguez et al., 2023; Alferidah and

Jhanjhi, 2020). This might involve ensuring ongoing audits and evaluations that can recognize possible security issues at the soonest date possible. Another significant item on the checklist is investing in high-end cybersecurity tools. ML models are becoming capable of detecting such out-of-ordinary patterns, which may indicate a security threat. These tools can be used to keep track of new threats as they emerge (Surianarayanan, Kunasekaran and Chelliah, 2023). It is also crucial to train the staff so that they have knowledge and secure ways of using AI (Chuang, 2022). The more educated you are as an employee, the better able you are in identifying and preventing security threats (Mungo, 2023). Organizations also should consider partnering with other entities. Informing the public of threats and best practices can create a better defence network against AI-related attacks (Li, 2018). Moreover, adding AI ethics to security strategies guarantees that our systems are both safe and responsibly used (Leslie, 2019). If companies take these steps we can ensure that our security and business information is safe. Integrating new AI trends into your existing framework is essentially equivalent to preparing itself for coming challenges down the track.

C. Final Thoughts

Continued innovation also means being prepared for the next wave of threats in AI security. Attackers adapt as technology evolves studies have shown that these new threats demand proactive measures for handling them (Cho et al., 2020). To stay up to date with these trends you need dedicated research and implementation of additional tools & technology. New threats often prey on vulnerabilities that were previously unknown. Recent studies provide evidence of these refinements among AI-driven attacks, for example in the form of bypasses against traditional means to secure messages (Guembe et al., 2022; Chesti et al., 202). A reminder must be served to the researchers and developers working in this domain that they need to keep on improving their strategies. It becomes easy to prepare against future threats using new research and investing in the US. Combining experience within the fields fortifies these threats as well. Interdisciplinary work creates a diverse range of expertise needed to develop optimal solutions. Supporting researchers, developers and security practitioners in collaborating on an ongoing basis to share information can indicate new directions for the field as well as add more lines of defence.

Overall, the speed at which AI security threats are changing necessitates ongoing innovation and readiness. Continued investment in research and encouraging more cooperation between agencies is essential to fortifying our defences against an ever-changing enemy landscape. Figure 7 shows predictions for AI security.

Figure 7. Predictions for AI security

Advanced Threat Detection	AI will use more sophisticated algorithms for detecting and responding to complex cyber threats.
Autonomous Security Systems	Increased use of autonomous AI systems for real-time incident response and mitigation
AI-Driven Privacy Enhancements	AI will play a larger role in protecting personal data through advanced encryption and privacy measures..
Increased Use of Edge AI	Edge AI will become more prevalent, providing real-time security at the edge of networks and IoT devices.
Greater Integration with Blockchain	AI and blockchain technologies will increasingly be integrated to enhance data integrity and security.

VIII. CONCLUSION

A. Summary of Key Points

This chapter will investigate several advanced threats, and future AI trends based on the quickly shifting cybersecurity landscape and how AI can help to manage this tsunami. Crucially, AI-powered cyberattacks are classified as emerging threats in key publications which describe a nefarious acceleration from human-based attacks to a new generation of malicious software and autonomous agents capable of multiplying the destructive potentiality. Another important challenge is Adversarial AI, where adversaries manipulate or fool the outcome of an AI model using methods like Data poisoning and Model inversion etc. Deepfake technology has also the potential to place individuals, businesses and governments in even more critical harm; at risk of misinformation, fraud or focused social engineering attacks. With all these threats, the chapter also talks about a few future trends in AI-based security solutions. Many states that predictive threat intelligence will evolve in the future, using ML and big data analytics to uncover threats even before they materialize. AI will also improve anomaly detection, thereby improving dynamic monitoring of any impending crimes. Moreover, AI coupled with quantum computing also presents a double-edged sword from both an opportunity and risk standpoint that has the potential to re-shape encryption as well as threat detection capabilities

In conclusion, the chapter also calls for strong AI security frameworks and an ethical implementation of AI along with recognition that organizations require skilled individuals in AI security. Industry, academia and international bodies must work together to effectively navigate the changing security landscape. And all of these forward-thinking actions will be necessary to stay a step or two ahead of malicious AI-driven threats.

Reflection on the Importance of Proactive Preparation and Adaptation

Preparedness and readiness are needed to face the ever-changing AI security environment. While these are both good practices, the point is that we need to go beyond reactive measures. By looking ahead and responding, organizations can harden their defences, reducing exposure to new vulnerabilities that would leave them exposed when the next attack wave comes. The endpoint security needs to stay ahead of its adversaries who are actively employing AI in their attacks by proactively assessing and improving the underlying frameworks through the latest best-in-class AI-based solutions.

The Cybersecurity landscape is very volatile, so retrofitting also has a critical role to play. Cyber threats are ever evolving, and security strategies must evolve with them. Organizations need to be adaptable and change the way they manage security based on new risks. This means leveraging AI-powered tools while cultivating a growth mindset. Continuous training, legislation and interaction with industry and academia to learn about the latest trends in AI security that help create sophisticated techniques for protecting from threats.

In the end, proactive defence preparation and adjustment is what creates robustness in times when cyber threats develop more rapidly than ever. Through vigilance and foresight, with the help of advanced threat technologies as well as organisations can stay ahead of AI-driven threats to ensure that they do not deteriorate their security stance —in ways that leave internal assets, sensitive data or brand names at risk from such disruptive incidents.

REFERENCES

Abdelkader, S. *et al.* (2024) 'Securing modern power systems. Implementing comprehensive strategies to enhance resilience and reliability against Cyber-Attacks,' *Results in Engineering*, 23, p. 102647. https.//.DOI: 10.1016/j.rineng.2024.102647

Ajala, N.O.A. *et al.* (2024) 'Exploring and reviewing the potential of quantum computing in enhancing cybersecurity encryption methods,' *Magna Scientia Advanced Research and Reviews*, 10(1), pp. 321–329. https.//.DOI: 10.30574/msarr.2024.10.1.0038

Akkem, Y., Biswas, S.K. and Varanasi, A. (2024) 'A comprehensive review of synthetic data generation in smart farming by using variational autoencoder and generative adversarial network,' *Engineering Applications of Artificial Intelligence*, 131, p. 107881. https.//.DOI: 10.1016/j.engappai.2024.107881

Al-Dosari, K., Fetais, N. and Kucukvar, M. (2022) 'Artificial intelligence and Cyber Defense System for Banking industry. A Qualitative Study of AI Applications and Challenges,' *Cybernetics & Systems*, 55(2), pp. 302–330. https.//.DOI: 10.1080/01969722.2022.2112539

Alex, S.A. *et al.* (2022) 'Deep LSTM Model for Diabetes Prediction with Class Balancing by SMOTE,' *Electronics*, 11(17), p. 2737. https.//.DOI: 10.3390/electronics11172737

Alferidah, D. K., & Jhanjhi, N. (2020) 'Cybersecurity Impact over Bigdata and IoT Growth,' *2020 International Conference on Computational Intelligence (ICCI)* [Preprint]. https.//DOI: 10.1109/ICCI51257.2020.9247722

Alkinani, M.H. *et al.* (2021) '5G and IoT Based Reporting and Accident Detection (RAD) System to Deliver First Aid Box Using Unmanned Aerial Vehicle,' *Sensors*, 21(20), p. 6905. https.//.DOI: 10.3390/s21206905

Alzaabi, F. R., & Mehmood, A. (2024) 'A Review of Recent Advances, Challenges and Opportunities in Malicious Insider Threat Detection using Machine Learning Methods,' *IEEE Access*, p. 1. https.//DOI: 10.1109/ACCESS.2024.3369906

Ananna, F.F. *et al.* (2023) 'Analysing Influential factors in student academic achievement. Prediction modelling and insight,' *International Journal of Emerging Multidisciplinaries Computer Science & Artificial Intelligence*, 2(1). https.//.DOI: 10.54938/ijemdcsai.2023.02.1.254

Arif, H. *et al.* (2024) 'Future Horizons. AI-Enhanced Threat Detection in cloud environments. Unveiling opportunities for research,' *International Journal of Multidisciplinary Sciences and Arts*, 2(2), pp. 242–251. https.//.DOI: 10.47709/ijmdsa.v2i2.3452

Azam, H., Dulloo, M.I., Majeed, M.H., Wan, J.P.H., Xin, L.T. and Sindiramutty, S.R. (2023) 'Cybercrime Unmasked. Investigating cases and digital evidence,' *International Journal of Emerging Multidisciplinaries Computer Science & Artificial Intelligence*, 2(1). https.//.DOI: 10.54938/ijemdcsai.2023.02.1.255

Azam, H., Dulloo, M.I., Majeed, M.H., Wan, J.P.H., Xin, L.T., Tajwar, M.A., *et al.* (2023) 'Defending the digital Frontier. IDPS and the battle against Cyber threat,' *International Journal of Emerging Multidisciplinaries Computer Science & Artificial Intelligence*, 2(1). https.//.DOI: 10.54938/ijemdcsai.2023.02.1.253

Badjie, B., Cecílio, J. and Casimiro, A. (2024) 'Adversarial Attacks and Countermeasures on image classification-based deep learning models in Autonomous Driving Systems. A systematic review,' *ACM Computing Surveys* [Preprint]. https.//.DOI: 10.1145/3691625

Bajaj, A. and Vishwakarma, D.K. (2023) 'A state-of-the-art review on adversarial machine learning in image classification,' *Multimedia Tools and Applications*, 83(3), pp. 9351–9416. https.//.DOI: 10.1007/s11042-023-15883-z

Bansal, P. and Ouda, A. (2024) 'Continuous Authentication in the Digital Age. An analysis of reinforcement learning and Behavioral biometrics,' *Computers*, 13(4), p. 103. https.//.DOI: 10.3390/computers13040103

Bécue, A., Praça, I. and Gama, J. (2021) 'Artificial intelligence, cyber-threats and Industry 4.0. challenges and opportunities,' *Artificial Intelligence Review*, 54(5), pp. 3849–3886. https.//.DOI: 10.1007/s10462-020-09942-2

Bhardwaj, S. and Dave, M. (2024) 'Attack detection and mitigation using Intelligent attack graph model for Forensic in IoT Networks,' *Telecommunication Systems*, 85(4), pp. 601–621. https.//.DOI: 10.1007/s11235-024-01105-w

Bhatia, M.P.S. and Sangwan, S.R. (2021) 'Soft computing for anomaly detection and prediction to mitigate IoT-based real-time abuse,' *Personal and Ubiquitous Computing* [Preprint]. https.//.DOI: 10.1007/s00779-021-01567-8

BN, C., & SH, B. (2024). Revolutionizing ransomware detection and criticality assessment: Multiclass hybrid machine learning and semantic similarity-based end2end solution. *Multimedia Tools and Applications*, 83(13), 39135–39168.

Brohi, S. N., ... (2020) 'Key Applications of State-of-the-Art Technologies to Mitigate and Eliminate COVID-19.pdf,' TechRxiv [Preprint]. https.//DOI: 10.36227/techrxiv.12115596.v1

Cavedon-Taylor, D. (2024) 'Deepfakes. a survey and introduction to the topical collection,' *Synthese*, 204(1). https.//.DOI: 10.1007/s11229-024-04634-8

Chander, B. *et al.* (2024) 'Toward trustworthy artificial intelligence (TAI) in the context of explainability and robustness,' *ACM Computing Surveys* [Preprint]. https.//.DOI: 10.1145/3675392

Chen, H. and Babar, M.A. (2024) 'Security for Machine learning-based Software Systems. A survey of threats, practices, and challenges,' *ACM Computing Surveys*, 56(6), pp. 1–38. https.//.DOI: 10.1145/3638531

Cherbal, S. *et al.* (2023) 'Security in internet of things. a review on approaches based on blockchain, machine learning, cryptography, and quantum computing,' *The Journal of Supercomputing*, 80(3), pp. 3738–3816. https.//.DOI: 10.1007/s11227-023-05616-2

Chesti, I. A., ... (2020) 'Evolution, Mitigation, and Prevention of Ransomware,' *2020 2nd International Conference on Computer and Information Sciences (ICCIS)* [Preprint]. https.//DOI: 10.1109/ICCIS49240.2020.9257708

Chew, C.J.W. *et al.* (2024) 'Real-time system call-based ransomware detection,' *International Journal of Information Security*, 23(3), pp. 1839–1858. https.//.DOI: 10.1007/s10207-024-00819-x

Chiu, T.K.F. *et al.* (2022) 'Creation and evaluation of a pretertiary Artificial Intelligence (AI) curriculum,' *IEEE Transactions on Education*, 65(1), pp. 30–39. https.//.DOI: 10.1109/TE.2021.3085878

Cho, J.-H. *et al.* (2020) 'Toward Proactive, Adaptive Defense. A survey on moving target defense,' *IEEE Communications Surveys & Tutorials*, 22(1), pp. 709–745. https.//.DOI: 10.1109/COMST.2019.2963791

Choucri, N., Madnick, S. and Ferwerda, J. (2013) 'Institutions for Cyber Security. International responses and global imperatives,' *Information Technology for Development*, 20(2), pp. 96–121. https.//.DOI: 10.1080/02681102.2013.836699

Chuang, S. (2022) 'Indispensable skills for human employees in the age of robots and AI,' *European Journal of Training and Development* [Preprint]. https.//.DOI: 10.1108/EJTD-06-2022-0062

Chukwunweike, N.J.N. *et al.* (2024) 'The role of deep learning in ensuring privacy integrity and security. Applications in AI-driven cybersecurity solutions,' *World Journal of Advanced Research and Reviews*, 23(2), pp. 1778–1790. https.//.DOI: 10.30574/wjarr.2024.23.2.2550

Dash, N.B. and Ullah, N.S. (2024) 'Quantum-safe. Cybersecurity in the age of Quantum-Powered AI,' *World Journal of Advanced Research and Reviews*, 21(1), pp. 1555–1563. https.//.DOI: 10.30574/wjarr.2024.21.1.2640

Deng, Y. *et al.* (2021) 'Deep Learning-Based Autonomous Driving Systems. A survey of Attacks and Defenses,' *IEEE Transactions on Industrial Informatics*, 17(12), pp. 7897–7912. https.//.DOI: 10.1109/TII.2021.3071405

Dhanaraj, R. K.. (2024). *Artificial intelligence for future intelligent transportation. Smarter and Greener Infrastructure Design*. CRC Press.

Díaz-Rodríguez, N. *et al.* (2023) 'Connecting the dots in trustworthy Artificial Intelligence. From AI principles, ethics, and key requirements to responsible AI systems and regulation,' *Information Fusion*, 99, p. 101896. https.//.DOI: 10.1016/j.inffus.2023.101896

Dogra, V., ... (2021) 'Analyzing DistilBERT for Sentiment Classification of Banking Financial News,' in *Lecture notes in networks and systems*, pp. 501–510. https.//DOI: 10.1007/978-981-16-3153-5_53

Duary, S., ... (2024) 'Cybersecurity Threats Detection in Intelligent Networks using Predictive Analytics Approaches,' *2024 4th International Conference on Innovative Practices in Technology and Management (ICIPTM)* [Preprint]. https.// DOI: 10.1109/ICIPTM59628.2024.10563348

Ettalibi, A., Elouadi, A., & Mansour, A. (2024) 'AI and Computer Vision-based Real-time Quality Control. A Review of Industrial Applications,' *Procedia Computer Science*, 231, pp. 212–220. https.//DOI: 10.1016/j.procs.2023.12.195

Familoni, N.B.T. (2024) 'CYBERSECURITY CHALLENGES IN THE AGE OF AI. THEORETICAL APPROACHES AND PRACTICAL SOLUTIONS,' *Computer Science & IT Research Journal*, 5(3), pp. 703–724. https.//.DOI: 10.51594/csitrj.v5i3.930

Fatima-Tuz-Zahra, N., ... (2020) 'Proposing a Hybrid RPL Protocol for Rank and Wormhole Attack Mitigation using Machine Learning,' *2020 2nd International Conference on Computer and Information Sciences (ICCIS)* [Preprint]. https.//DOI: 10.1109/ICCIS49240.2020.9257607

Garcia, E. V. (2024) 'The technological leap of AI and the Global South. deepening asymmetries and the future of international security,' in *Edward Elgar Publishing eBooks*, pp. 370–387. https.//DOI: 10.4337/9781800377400.00028

Gill, S. S., ... (2024) 'Quantum Computing. vision and challenges,' *arXiv (Cornell University)* [Preprint]. https.///arxiv.2403.02240.DOI: <ALIGNMENT.qj></ ALIGNMENT>10.48550

Gopi, R. *et al.* (2021) 'Enhanced method of ANN based model for detection of DDoS attacks on multimedia internet of things,' *Multimedia Tools and Applications*, 81(19), pp. 26739–26757. https.//.DOI: 10.1007/s11042-021-10640-6

Gouda, W. *et al.* (2022) 'Detection of COVID-19 based on chest x-rays using deep learning,' *Healthcare*, 10(2), p. 343. https.//.DOI: 10.3390/healthcare10020343

Govea, J., Gaibor-Naranjo, W. and Villegas-Ch, W. (2024) 'Transforming Cybersecurity into Critical Energy Infrastructure. A Study on the Effectiveness of Artificial Intelligence,' *Systems*, 12(5), p. 165. https.//.DOI: 10.3390/systems12050165

Guembe, B. *et al.* (2022) 'The emerging threat of AI-driven cyber attacks. a review,' *Applied Artificial Intelligence*, 36(1). https.//.DOI: 10.1080/08839514.2022.2037254

Gui, B., Sam, L. and Bhardwaj, A. (2024) 'From roofs to renewables. Deep learning and geographic information systems insights into a comprehensive urban solar photovoltaic assessment for Stonehaven,' *Elsevier*, 1, p. 100006. https.//.DOI: 10.1016/j.energ.2024.100006

Habbal, A., Ali, M.K. and Abuzaraida, M.A. (2024) 'Artificial Intelligence Trust, Risk and Security Management (AI TRiSM). Frameworks, applications, challenges and future research directions,' *Expert Systems With Applications*, 240, p. 122442. https.//.DOI: 10.1016/j.eswa.2023.122442

Hameleers, M., Van Der Meer, T.G.L.A. and Dobber, T. (2023) 'They would never say anything like this! Reasons to doubt political deepfakes,' *European Journal of Communication*, 39(1), pp. 56–70. https.//.DOI: 10.1177/02673231231184703

Han, H. *et al.* (2024) 'Quantum communication based cyber security analysis using artificial intelligence with IoMT,' *Optical and Quantum Electronics*, 56(4). https.//.DOI: 10.1007/s11082-023-06185-7

Hashmi, E., Yamin, M.M. and Yayilgan, S.Y. (2024) 'Securing tomorrow. a comprehensive survey on the synergy of Artificial Intelligence and information security,' *AI And Ethics* [Preprint]. https.//.DOI: 10.1007/s43681-024-00529-z

Hatamizadeh, A. *et al.* (2023) 'Do gradient inversion attacks make federated learning unsafe?,' *IEEE Transactions on Medical Imaging*, 42(7), pp. 2044–2056. https.//. DOI: 10.1109/TMI.2023.3239391

Hossain, M. I., ... (2024) 'Enhancing Data Integrity and Traceability in Industry Cyber Physical Systems (ICPS) through Blockchain Technology. A Comprehensive Approach,' *arXiv (Cornell University)* [Preprint]. https.///arxiv.2405.04837.DOI: <ALIGNMENT.qj></ALIGNMENT>10.48550

Hu, K. *et al.* (2024) 'An overview of implementing security and privacy in federated learning,' *Artificial Intelligence Review*, 57(8). https.//.DOI: 10.1007/s10462-024-10846-8

Humayun, M. *et al.* (2022) 'A Transfer Learning Approach with a Convolutional Neural Network for the Classification of Lung Carcinoma,' *Healthcare*, 10(6), p. 1058. https.//.DOI: 10.3390/healthcare10061058

Hussain, K., ... (2024) 'Threats and Vulnerabilities of Wireless Networks in the Internet of Things (IoT),' *2024 IEEE 1st Karachi Section Humanitarian Technology Conference (KHI-HTC)* [Preprint]. https.//DOI: 10.1109/KHI-HTC60760.2024.10482197

Isakov, A. *et al.* (2024) *ENHANCING CYBERSECURITY. PROTECTING DATA IN THE DIGITAL AGE.* https.//innoist.uz/index.php/ist/article/view/153.

Islam, S. (2024) 'FUTURE TRENDS IN SQL DATABASES AND BIG DATA ANALYTICS. IMPACT OF MACHINE LEARNING AND ARTIFICIAL INTELLIGENCE,' *International Journal of Science and Engineering*, 1(4), pp. 47–62. https.//.DOI: 10.62304/ijse.v1i04.188

Kaluarachchi, B. N., & Sedera, D. (2024) 'Improving efficiency through AI-Powered customer engagement by providing personalized solutions in the banking industry,' in *Advances in marketing, customer relationship management, and e-services book series*, pp. 299–342. https.//DOI: 10.4018/979-8-3693-7122-0.ch016

Katiyar, N. *et al.* (2024) 'AI and Cyber-Security. Enhancing threat detection and response with machine learning.,' *Educational Administration. Theory and Practice* [Preprint]. https.//.DOI: 10.53555/kuey.v30i4.2377

Khan, A., ... (2024) 'Future Trends and challenges in cybersecurity and Generative AI,' in *Advances in information security, privacy, and ethics book series*, pp. 491–522. https.//DOI: 10.4018/979-8-3693-5415-5.ch014

Khan, R., Taqi, M., & Afzal, A. (2024) 'Deepfakes in finance,' in *Advances in information security, privacy, and ethics book series*, pp. 91–120. https.//DOI: 10.4018/979-8-3693-5298-4.ch006

Khazane, H. *et al.* (2024) 'A Holistic Review of Machine Learning Adversarial attacks in IoT networks,' *Future Internet*, 16(1), p. 32. https.//.DOI: 10.3390/fi16010032

Korobenko, D., Nikiforova, A. and Sharma, R. (2024) 'Towards a Privacy and Security-Aware Framework for Ethical AI. Guiding the Development and Assessment of AI Systems,' *ACM* [Preprint]. https.//.DOI: 10.1145/3657054.3657141

Kuo, T.-C., Peng, C.-Y. and Kuo, C.-J. (2021) 'Smart support system of material procurement for waste reduction based on big data and predictive analytics,' *International Journal of Logistics Research and Applications*, 27(2), pp. 243–260. https.//. DOI: 10.1080/13675567.2021.1969348

Lad, S. (2024) *Cybersecurity Trends. Integrating AI to combat emerging threats in the Cloud era*. https.//ijstindex.com/index.php/ijst/article/view/60.

Leslie, D. (2019) 'Understanding artificial intelligence ethics and safety,' *arXiv (Cornell University)* [Preprint]. https.///arxiv.1906.05684.DOI: <ALIGNMENT.qj></ALIGNMENT>10.48550

Li, J.-H. (2018) 'Cyber security meets artificial intelligence. a survey,' *Frontiers of Information Technology & Electronic Engineering*, 19(12), pp. 1462–1474. https.//. DOI: 10.1631/FITEE.1800573

Lim, M., ... (2019) 'Link Prediction in Time-Evolving Criminal Network with deep Reinforcement learning technique,' *IEEE Access*, 7, pp. 184797–184807. https.// DOI: 10.1109/ACCESS.2019.2958873

Lim, W. *et al.* (2024) 'Future of Generative Adversarial Networks (GAN) for Anomaly Detection in Network Security. A review,' *Computers & Security*, 139, p. 103733. https.//.DOI: 10.1016/j.cose.2024.103733

Liu, R., ... (2024) 'Unstoppable attack. Label-Only model inversion via conditional diffusion model,' *IEEE Transactions on Information Forensics and Security*, 19, pp. 3958–3973. https.//DOI: 10.1109/TIFS.2024.3372815

Lodhi, S.K., Gill, A.Y. and Hussain, I. (2024) 'AI-Powered Innovations in Contemporary Manufacturing Procedures. An Extensive analysis,' *International Journal of Multidisciplinary Sciences and Arts*, 3(4), pp. 15–25. https.//.DOI: 10.47709/ijmdsa.v3i4.4616

Malatji, M. and Tolah, A. (2024) 'Artificial intelligence (AI) cybersecurity dimensions. a comprehensive framework for understanding adversarial and offensive AI,' *AI And Ethics* [Preprint]. https.//.DOI: 10.1007/s43681-024-00427-4

Malik, A.W. *et al.* (2024) 'Cloud Digital Forensics. Beyond tools, techniques, and challenges,' *Sensors*, 24(2), p. 433. https.//.DOI: 10.3390/s24020433

Malik, J., Muthalagu, R., & Pawar, P. M. (2024) 'A systematic review of adversarial machine learning attacks, defensive controls, and technologies,' *IEEE Access*, 12, pp. 99382–99421. https.//DOI: 10.1109/ACCESS.2024.3423323

Mungo, J. (2023) 'Self-paced cybersecurity awareness training educating retail employees to identify phishing attacks,' *Journal of Cyber Security Technology*, pp. 1–49. https.//.DOI: 10.1080/23742917.2023.2244210

Muzafar, S., & Jhanjhi, N. Z. (2020) 'Success stories of ICT implementation in Saudi Arabia,' in *Advances in electronic government, digital divide, and regional development book series*, pp. 151–163. https.//DOI: 10.4018/978-1-7998-1851-9.ch008

Naik, K. *et al.* (2024) 'Current status and future directions. The Application of Artificial Intelligence/Machine Learning for Precision Medicine,' *Clinical Pharmacology & Therapeutics*, 115(4), pp. 673–686. https.//.DOI: 10.1002/cpt.3152

Nair, M. M., Deshmukh, A., & Tyagi, A. K. (2023) 'Artificial Intelligence for Cyber Security,' *Wiley*, pp. 83–114. https.//DOI: 10.1002/9781394213948.ch5

Naveed, H. *et al.* (2024) 'Survey. Image mixing and deleting for data augmentation,' *Engineering Applications of Artificial Intelligence*, 131, p. 107791. https.//.DOI: 10.1016/j.engappai.2023.107791

Nayak, R., Pati, U.C. and Das, S.K. (2023) 'A comprehensive review of datasets for detection and localization of video anomalies. a step towards data-centric artificial intelligence-based video anomaly detection,' *Multimedia Tools and Applications*, 83(21), pp. 59617–59674. https.//.DOI: 10.1007/s11042-023-17889-z

Nguyen, T. T., Quoc Viet Hung, N., Nguyen, T. T., Huynh, T. T., Nguyen, T. T., Weidlich, M., & Yin, H. (2024). Manipulating recommender systems: A survey of poisoning attacks and countermeasures. *ACM Computing Surveys*, 57(1), 1–39.

Novelli, C., Taddeo, M. and Floridi, L. (2023) 'Accountability in artificial intelligence. what it is and how it works,' *AI & Society* [Preprint]. https.//.DOI: 10.1007/s00146-023-01635-y

Nyemba, W. R., Mbohwa, C., & Carter, K. F. (2021) 'Problem- and Industry-Based Learning. Research, theory and practice,' in *EAI/Springer Innovations in Communication and Computing*, pp. 81–105. https.//DOI: 10.1007/978-3-030-70493-3_5

Obi, N.O.C. *et al.* (2024) 'COMPREHENSIVE REVIEW ON CYBERSECURITY. MODERN THREATS AND ADVANCED DEFENSE STRATEGIES,' *Computer Science & IT Research Journal*, 5(2), pp. 293–310. https.//.DOI: 10.51594/csitrj.v5i2.758

Okoli, N.U.I. *et al.* (2024) 'Machine learning in cybersecurity. A review of threat detection and defense mechanisms,' *World Journal of Advanced Research and Reviews*, 21(1), pp. 2286–2295. https.//.DOI: 10.30574/wjarr.2024.21.1.0315

Olsen, H.P. *et al.* (2024) 'The right to transparency in public governance. freedom of information and the use of artificial intelligence by public agencies,' *Digital Government Research and Practice*, 5(1), pp. 1–15. https.//.DOI: 10.1145/3632753

Oluoch, I. (2024) 'Crossing Boundaries. The ethics of AI and Geographic Information Technologies,' *ISPRS International Journal of Geo-Information*, 13(3), p. 87. https.//.DOI: 10.3390/ijgi13030087

Otieno, N.I.A. (2024) 'Extensive review of quantum computing and network security,' *World Journal of Advanced Engineering Technology and Sciences*, 12(2), pp. 770–807. https.//.DOI: 10.30574/wjaets.2024.12.2.0337

Ozkan-Okay, M., ... (2024) 'A comprehensive survey. Evaluating the efficiency of artificial intelligence and machine learning techniques on cyber security solutions,' *IEEE Access*, 12, pp. 12229–12256. https.//DOI: 10.1109/ACCESS.2024.3355547

Palakurti, N. R. (2024) 'Challenges and future directions in anomaly detection,' in *Advances in systems analysis, software engineering, and high performance computing book series*, pp. 269–284. https.//DOI: 10.4018/979-8-3693-2909-2.ch020

Penso, C., Frenkel, L. and Goldberger, J. (2024) 'Confidence Calibration of a Medical Imaging Classification System That is Robust to Label Noise,' *IEEE Transactions on Medical Imaging*, 43(6), pp. 2050–2060. https.//.DOI: 10.1109/TMI.2024.3353762

Peral-García, D., Cruz-Benito, J. and García-Peñalvo, F.J. (2024) 'Systematic literature review. Quantum machine learning and its applications,' *Computer Science Review*, 51, p. 100619. https.//.DOI: 10.1016/j.cosrev.2024.100619

Qureshi, S.M. *et al.* (2024) 'Deepfake forensics. a survey of digital forensic methods for multimodal deepfake identification on social media,' *PeerJ Computer Science*, 10, p. e2037. https.//.DOI: 10.7717/peerj-cs.2037

Radanliev, P. (2024a) 'Cyber diplomacy. defining the opportunities for cybersecurity and risks from Artificial Intelligence, IoT, Blockchains, and Quantum Computing,' *Journal of Cyber Security Technology*, pp. 1–51. https.//.DOI: 10.1080/23742917.2024.2312671

Radanliev, P. (2024b) 'Digital security by design,' *Security Journal* [Preprint]. https.//.DOI: 10.1057/s41284-024-00435-3

Rehan, H. (2024) 'AI-Driven Cloud Security. The future of Safeguarding Sensitive data in the Digital Age,' *Deleted Journal*, 1(1), pp. 132–151. https.//.DOI: 10.60087/jaigs.v1i1.89

Reshi, I. A., & Sholla, S. (2024). *Blockchain-based internet of things. Opportunities, Challenges and Solutions.* CRC Press. DOI: 10.1201/9781003407096

Saeed, M.M. and Alsharidah, M. (2024) 'Security, privacy, and robustness for trustworthy AI systems. A review,' *Computers & Electrical Engineering*, 119, p. 109643. https.//.DOI: 10.1016/j.compeleceng.2024.109643

Sarker, I.H. (2024) *AI-Driven cybersecurity and threat intelligence.* https.//.DOI: 10.1007/978-3-031-54497-2

Sarker, I.H. *et al.* (2024) 'Multi-aspect rule-based AI. Methods, taxonomy, challenges and directions toward automation, intelligence and transparent cybersecurity modeling for critical infrastructures,' *Internet of Things*, 25, p. 101110. https.//.DOI: 10.1016/j.iot.2024.101110

Schmidt, B., & Hildebrandt, A. (2024) 'From GPUs to AI and quantum. three waves of acceleration in bioinformatics,' *Drug Discovery Today*, p. 103990. https.//DOI: 10.1016/j.drudis.2024.103990

Seng, Y. J., ... (2024) 'In-Depth Analysis and Countermeasures for Ransomware Attacks. Case Studies and Recommendations,' Preprints.*org* [Preprint]. https.//DOI: 10.20944/preprints202408.2261.v1

Shah, I. A., Jhanjhi, N. Z., & Laraib, A. (2022) 'Cybersecurity and blockchain usage in contemporary business,' in *Advances in information security, privacy, and ethics book series*, pp. 49–64. https.//DOI: 10.4018/978-1-6684-5284-4.ch003

Sharma, R. *et al.* (2022) 'Plant disease diagnosis and image classification using deep learning,' *Computers, Materials & Continua/Computers, Materials & Continua (Print)*, 71(2), pp. 2125–2140. https.//.DOI: 10.32604/cmc.2022.020017

Shihab, M.A. *et al.* (2024) 'Towards resilient machine learning models. Addressing adversarial attacks in wireless sensor network,' *Shihab | Journal of Robotics and Control (JRC)* [Preprint]. https.//.DOI: <ALIGNMENT.qj></ALIGNMENT>10.18196/jrc.v5i5.23214

Sindiramutty, S. R., Jhanjhi, N., ... (2024) 'Industry 4.0,' in *Advances in logistics, operations, and management science book series*, pp. 342–405. https.//DOI: 10.4018/979-8-3693-1363-3.ch013

Sindiramutty, S. R., Jhanjhi, N. Z., Tan, C. E., Khan, N. A., ... (2024) 'Cybersecurity measures for logistics industry,' in *Advances in information security, privacy, and ethics book series*, pp. 1–58. https.//DOI: 10.4018/979-8-3693-3816-2.ch001

Sindiramutty, S. R., Jhanjhi, N. Z., Tan, C. E., Yun, K. J., ... (2024) 'Data security and privacy concerns in drone operations,' in *Advances in information security, privacy, and ethics book series*, pp. 236–290. https.//DOI: 10.4018/979-8-3693-0774-8.ch010

Sindiramutty, S. R., Prabagaran, K. R. V., ... (2024) 'Security Considerations in Generative AI for web Applications,' in *Advances in information security, privacy, and ethics book series*, pp. 281–332. https.//DOI: 10.4018/979-8-3693-5415-5.ch009

Sindiramutty, S. R., Tan, C. E., & Wei, G. W. (2024) 'Eyes in the sky,' in *Advances in information security, privacy, and ethics book series*, pp. 405–451. https.//DOI: 10.4018/979-8-3693-0774-8.ch017

Singh, N.J. *et al.* (2023) 'Botnet-based IoT network traffic analysis using deep learning,' *Security and Privacy*, 7(2). https.//.DOI: 10.1002/spy2.355

Sontan, N.A.D. and Samuel, N.S.V. (2024) 'The intersection of Artificial Intelligence and cybersecurity. Challenges and opportunities,' *World Journal of Advanced Research and Reviews*, 21(2), pp. 1720–1736. https.//.DOI: 10.30574/wjarr.2024.21.2.0607

Surianarayanan, C., Kunasekaran, S. and Chelliah, P.R. (2023) 'A high-throughput architecture for anomaly detection in streaming data using machine learning algorithms,' *International Journal of Information Technology*, 16(1), pp. 493–506. https.//.DOI: 10.1007/s41870-023-01585-0

Tarsney, C. (2024) 'Deception and manipulation in generative AI,' *arXiv (Cornell University)* [Preprint]. https.///arxiv.2401.11335.DOI: <ALIGNMENT.qj></ALIGNMENT>10.48550

Usman, T.M. *et al.* (2023) 'Diabetic retinopathy detection using principal component analysis multi-label feature extraction and classification,' *International Journal of Cognitive Computing in Engineering*, 4, pp. 78–88. https.//.DOI: 10.1016/j.ijcce.2023.02.002

Vijayalakshmi, S. *et al.* (2024) *Artificial intelligence for cyber defense and smart policing, Chapman and Hall/CRC eBooks*. https.//.DOI: 10.1201/9781003251781

Waheed, A., ... (2024) 'Zero-Day Exploits in Cybersecurity. Case Studies and Countermeasure,' Preprints.*org* [Preprint]. https.//DOI: 10.20944/preprints202407.2338.v1

Wen, B. O. T., ... (2023) 'Detecting cyber threats with a Graph-Based NIDPS,' in *Advances in logistics, operations, and management science book series*, pp. 36–74. https.//DOI: 10.4018/978-1-6684-7625-3.ch002

Wingreen, S. C., & Samandari, A. (2024). *Information Technology security and risk management. Inductive Cases for Information Security*. CRC Press. DOI: 10.1201/9781003264415

Xiao, Q. *et al.* (2023) 'Securing NextG networks with physical-layer key generation. A survey,' *Security and Safety*, 3, p. 2023021. https.//.DOI: 10.1051/sands/2023021

Yampolskiy, R.V. (2024) 'On monitorability of AI,' *AI And Ethics* [Preprint]. https.//. DOI: 10.1007/s43681-024-00420-x

Zhou, Z., ... (2024) 'Securely Fine-tuning Pre-trained Encoders Against Adversarial Examples,' *2024 IEEE Symposium on Security and Privacy (SP)*, pp. 3015–3033. https.//DOI: 10.1109/SP54263.2024.00244

Chapter 10
The Advanced Data Cleansing Method for Knowledge Discovery in Databases Using KDD With Generative AI and Cyber Security

Soobia Saeed
https://orcid.org/0000-0002-9026-6130
Department of Software Engineering, UniversitiTeknologi Malaysia, Malaysia

Mehmood Naqvi
Mohawk College, Canada

Manzoor Hussain
Indus University, Pakistan

ABSTRACT

The objective of this research is to investigate sophisticated approaches for data mining and purification via knowledge discovery in databases (KDD) with generative AI concept, with an emphasis on using generative artificial intelligence. Unstructured data from customer service machine registry reports and structured data from sales, staff, and customer management duties are the two main types of information found in customer databases. To improve the extraction and interpretation of patterns, this study uses generative AI with cyber security hacks to secure the cleaning data in conjunction with the K-means algorithm to cluster and sort

DOI: 10.4018/979-8-3693-6135-1.ch010

data. Our work focuses on the need to repositories of information and knowledge discovery, work for data storage and data mining. Dependent variable is KDD with generative AI and independent is Data Mining and KDD with cyber security as well. The main problem is to specific list, use useful pattern, Purposed model, inter-discipline action with cohort structure. We tried to secure and centralize and use branch level distribution in this.

1. INTRODUCTION

Learning and mining disclosure of information in databases is removed in an important measure of research, industry and the media did their best. What is the essence if? This research provides an overview of the growing field, which specifies how the databases of scaffolding learning supply of mining and are connected both to each other and nearby areas such as machine learning, calculations and databases. Research True Blue sees concrete applications, in particular, information extraction methods, the challenges that required royal blue work with introductory information and address current and future research in this area. Over a wide combination of fields, information is collected and gathered at a tense pace. It is a serious disease for another time computational theories and tools to people to launch strong data (information) amounts of information quickly make frontline. These assumptions and instruments are subject to an increased exposure of information in databases (KDD) (Abdulkadium *et.al*, 2022). At a reasonable level, it is concerned with the movement of the methods and frameworks for evaluating information KDD field. The framework KDD operational trend is a mapping information at low levels (as re usually very bulky, so it is difficult to handle and process survive) in different structures that can be more throne com start-up (as a short) plus the stomach muscle chain (for example, an interface with the estimate or model of the methodology that made information), or even more goodness (as a reasonable model to map the estimated future cases) (Huang *et.al*, 2020).

At the time of convergence of philosophy is the use of certain methods of investigation and recovery of information disclosure. This research begins by talking about the undeniable relationship between KDD and data mining and its intersection with other nearby areas. They also include short and very honest KDD programs of goodness format. Consequences of KDD and then take the mine is given, and the general framework of several stages KDD appears outside. This technology multi-step, using data mining has a special ride in the meantime. Data mining rose more processes the queue in estimates of special instructions mining and usage. Problems credible sober image application is also out. Finally, the research Shi discovers challenges for the future creative work in the usual unthinkable talking about possible open for improving the AI structures KDD steps (Shi *et.al*, 2020).

1.2. Problem Statement

KDD mining process data consisting of data is a step in the implementation and analysis algorithms that produce a particular discovery list, Data on the pattern (or model). Data mining is the process that KDD is a step in the implementation of analysis and search algorithms to produce a particular enumeration, to provide the pattern (or model).

1.3 Background

Data mining is an interdisciplinary subfield of software engineering. This estimation cycle of finding designs in enormous informational collections is connected with the techniques for man-made consciousness, AI, measurements, and the convergence of data set frameworks. The general goal of Data mining process is to extricate data from information and transform it into an intelligent design for some time in the future. Pre-processing of the data, a model, and conclusions regarding some interesting calculations, aspects of the complexity of the decoration discovered structures, visualization, and web update are all part of the raw analysis stage. The analysis phase of the "knowledge discovery in databases, process, or KDD" is known as data mining. The term is incorrect because the objective is not data extraction (mining) with you but rather the production of models and knowledge from large amounts of data. There is also a buzzword that is frequently used for any large amount of data or information management (collection, recovery, storage, analysis, and statistics), as well as for all requests for support systems for the decision-making of computers, such as artificial intelligence, machine learning, and business intelligence, as well as data book mining: machine learning tools and practical techniques with Java (covering the majority of the material on machine learning) was originally published under the name only machine concept of practical learning, and data mining was included solely for marketing purposes. Frequently the broader idea of (huge scope) information examination and investigation - or, with regards to current techniques, man-made consciousness and AI - more fitting (Xie *et.al*, 2020).

Tasks of data mining are automated or semi-analysis automated large amounts of data to extract interesting patterns, hitherto unknown, which records data groups (cluster analysis), unusual items (anomaly detection) and dependencies (mining association rules). This usually involves the use of database technology and space indicators. These models may be seen as a summary of the input data in the form and can be used in further analysis or, for example, machine learning and predictive analysis (Ghadge, 2024). For example, the data extraction steps to configure multiple data sets, which can then be used for more accurate prediction of a decision support system results. presentations collection, data preparation, nor the result of the interpretation and presentation are part of the data extraction stage but belong to the general KDD process a step further. Associated conditions dredging data, fisheries data and data link for mining techniques intelligence data to test parts of a larger population sets are (or can be) the lack of statistical conclusions reliable made about patterns discovered validity. These methods can be used to create new hypotheses to test against larger data populations (Cervantes, *et.al*, 2020).

1.3.1 Objectives

To securing and collecting data from branches level to centralize database with respect to technique data mining on knowledge discovery in databases and in order to ensure the collection of data and branches to centralize the database level for the extraction detection technical knowledge of data in databases.

1.3.2 Significance of the Study

Data mining is defined as the process of discovering data patterns. The process must be automated, or (usually) semi-automatic. Detect should be meaningful models who hear cause any benefit, usually financially. Data is always in large quantities. Data mining is implicit, previously unknown, and potentially useful information from data mining. The idea is to create computer programs that sift through databases automatically finding patter ns or models. Strong models, if found, probably would conclude that accurately predict future data. Automatic learning provides the technical basis for data mining. It is used to extract information from the raw data in databases.

1.4 Hypotheses of the Study

H1: There is a high impact of data discovery through KDD

1.5 Outline of the Study

The term Information Revelation in Data sets, or KDD for short, alludes to the wide course of tracking down information in information, and accentuates the "undeniable level" utilization of information mining strategies. Researchers in artificial intelligence, pattern recognition, machine learning, databases, statistics, knowledge acquisition for expert systems, and data visualization are all likely to be interested in this.

The KDD process's overarching objective is to extract knowledge from large databases of data. Using a database and any necessary preprocessing, subsampling, or transformations, it accomplishes this by employing data mining methods (algorithms) to extract (identify) what is considered knowledge in accordance with the specifications of measures and thresholds.

Figure 1. Flow of Application (Yoon, 2021)

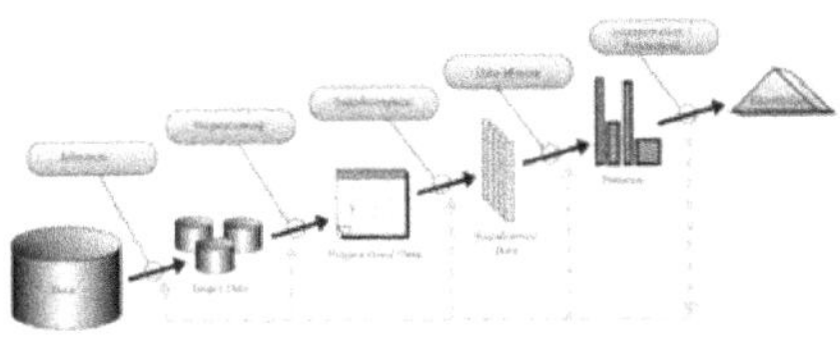

Figure.1: Flow of Application (Yoon, 2021)

The following steps need to be repeated to complete the overall process of locating and interpreting patterns in data:

Fostering a comprehension of:

1. The application domain relevant prior experience objectives of the end-client
2. Making an objective informational index: deciding on a data sample, a subset of variables, or a data set for the purpose of discovery.

Preprocessing and cleaning of the data:

1. Removing outliers or noise.
2. Gathering the information required to model or account for noise
3. Methodologies for dealing with missing information fields.
4. accounting for known changes and information about the time sequence.

Reduction of data and projection:

1. Depending on the task's objective, finding useful features to represent the data.
2. reducing the effective number of variables under consideration or finding invariant representations for the data by employing dimensionality reduction or transformation techniques.

Choosing the task for data mining:

1. Deciding whether classification, regression, clustering, etc. are the KDD process's objectives.

2. Deciding on the algorithm(s) for data mining.
3. Selecting the methods that will be used to search the data for patterns.
4. Determining the appropriate models and parameters
5. Matching a particular data mining technique to the KDD process's overall criteria.

Data Mining:

looking for interesting patterns in a specific representational form or set of representations like classification rules, trees, regression, clustering, and so on.

1. Interpreting patterns mined.
2. Consolidating new information.
3. Data mining and knowledge discovery are not the same thing.

The process of gathering useful data knowledge is referred to as KDD. To determine what constitutes knowledge, the patterns must be evaluated and, possibly, interpreted. It additionally incorporates the decision of encoding plans, preprocessing, inspecting, and projections of the information before the information mining step. Algorithms are used in data mining to extract patterns from data without the KDD process's additional steps (Izadi *et.al*, 2021).

The non-trivial process of identifying valid, novel, potentially useful, and ultimately understandable patterns in data is known as knowledge discovery in databases. Interestingness is an overall measure of pattern value, combining validity, novelty, usefulness, and simplicity. Finding a useful template in the database, it is known under various names (including mining) in various communities (e.g., knowledge extraction, information discovery, data collection, data archeology, and data-processing reasons). "Data mining" is used the term more statisticians, researchers, database, and more recently, the GIS and the business community (Kashyap et.al, 2022). Here, the term "KDD" is used to refer to the entire process of finding useful knowledge from data. Data mining is a concrete step in the process of application-specific algorithms to extract data patterns (templates). Furthermore, in the process of KDD, such as training, data selection, data cleaning, the integration of prior knowledge and the corresponding correct interpretation of results for mountain steps ensure that useful knowledge is obtained from data. Blind application of the methods of data storage value of the data volumes of extraction depends on our ability to extract useful information, find interesting events and trends, support decisions and policies based on statistical analysis and inference, and use the data for business, operations or scientific purposes.

KDD has evolved and continues to evolve, the intersection of research in areas such as databases, machine learning, pattern recognition, statistics, artificial intelligence and reasoning with uncertainty in the acquisition of knowledge of expert systems, data visualization, machine detection, scientific discoveries, research, information, and high-performance calculations. Software systems, KDD integration of theory, algorithms and methods for all these areas. Theory and databases provide the tools needed to store, access, and manipulation of the data infrastructure. Storage recently popularized term refers to the current trends of collection companies and cleaning transactional data to make them available for operational analysis and decision support. A popular method of analyzing the data warehouse is called online analytical processing (OLAP) (Mathur *et.al*, 2021).

OLAP tools focus on providing multidimensional data analysis, which is higher than the language (Data Manipulation standard SQL) in computing summaries and breakdowns along many dimensions. Although interactive OLAP target current tools for data analysis, we expect a greater number of components also include automatic detection soon. Infer field with data models, including statistical pattern recognition, statistics, and machine learning neural networks have been applied due to some KDD work first. KDD is largely based on the data fields of these methods to find patterns in step KDD data extraction process (Saeed *et.al*, 2019).

A natural question ariscs: How is KDD different from these other areas? KDD focuses on the overall process knowledge discovery from the data, including how data is stored and accessed as algorithms can be scaled to large data sets and still work effectively, the results can be interpreted and displayed, and the interaction comprehensive man machine can It is modeled and maintained. KDD focuses on research, clear patterns that can be interpreted as useful or interesting knowledge. Scaling and reliability properties of modeling algorithms for large noisy data sets are also of fundamental interest. Statistics has much in common with KDD (Cunningham *et.al*, 2021).

Conclusion Knowledge of statistics is one of the main components (Research glamorous in statistical inference in this special section for a more detailed discussion of the relationship between KDD and statistical analysis). Statistics provides a language and framework for quantifying the resulting uncertainty when it comes to deducing general trends of a specific sample of the population. As mentioned above, long-term data mining has had negative connotations in the statistics since 1960, when the first analysis methods based on computer data (Santra *et.al*, 2022).

Concerns related to the fact that if you look hard enough in the data set (even randomly generated data), you can find models that seem to be statistically significant but are not. This question is of fundamental importance to KDD. There is considerable progress in the understanding of these issues in recent years statistics has been made, both directly related to KDD. Thus, data mining is a legitimate activity, and always, when you know how to do it right. KDD can also be viewed as encompassing a broader view of statistical modeling to provide tools for automation (if possible) the entire data mining process, including the selection of the art statistical hypothesis.

2. LITERATURE REVIEW

looking for interesting patterns in a specific representational form or set of representations like classification rules, trees, regression, clustering, and so on.

1. Interpreting patterns mined.
2. Consolidating new information.
3. Data mining and knowledge discovery are not the same thing.

The process of gathering useful data knowledge is referred to as KDD. To determine what constitutes knowledge, the patterns must be evaluated and, possibly, interpreted. It additionally incorporates the decision of encoding plans, preprocessing, inspecting, and projections of the information before the information mining step. Algorithms are used in data mining to extract patterns from data without the KDD process's additional steps.

There is a well-defined method that involves a number of distinct steps for locating profitable and useful information from a variety of databases. Information mining is the one of the principal steps which recovers and reveals the productive data from a lot of information. The tools for data mining are novel and user-friendly, and they can uncover an unknown pattern in data. The department of health care administrators can make use of this information to improve the quality of their services. That information can also be used by doctors to reduce the side effects of drugs and suggest cheaper alternatives that are therapeutically equivalent (Saeed, et.al, 2024). The best use of data mining techniques for health care management is anticipating a patient's future condition based on accumulating information and patterns. One of the alarming challenges health care organizations faces is providing high-quality services at reasonable prices. To provide high-quality services, a patient must be accurately diagnosed and given the appropriate and efficient treatment. Medical services information is enormous. The organizations oversee the analysis of the data. The records of the treatments can be easily stored on a computer, and the health care industry can handle a variety of important and crucial situations with the help of data mining techniques. K. Srinivas asserts that the most effective data mining strategy is classification, which employs algorithms such as Rule Set Classifier (i.e., if conditions then conclusions), Decision Tree Algorithm (taking age, disease intensity, gender, and disease name as attributes), Neural Network Architecture, Neuro-Fuzzy Network Structure, and Bayesian Network Structure, among others (Shu *et.al*, 2023).

Information mining has become progressive in the field of medical services. In the areas of medicine, treatment, medical instruments, and so on, health care organizations are currently producing a significant amount of information. Data from an MRI, blood pressure, sugar, clinical signals like an electrocardiogram, and the treatment plan prescribed by a doctor are all examples of medical data. In health care organizations, the practice of revealing previously unseen useful information and providing scientific decision-making for disease diagnosis is on the rise. In the medical field, there are numerous reasons to employ data mining methods. Data mining has recently been successful in detecting healthcare fraud and abuse, according to several reports (Al-Janabi, 2021). By dealing with the enormous amount of complex data, data mining can improve decision-making. Companies that employ data mining methods are better able to anticipate and address their future requirements. Abuse and fraud detection, effective treatment evaluation, customer relationship management, and healthcare management are among the applications of healthcare data mining. Data mining techniques include clustering by cluster analysis to find new drugs with the same chemical properties as molecules and association to find effects that will improve patients' conditions, such as faster disease recovery and normal body functions (Soobia et.al, 2022). Databases are essential to business management. In the fields of business, medicine, engineering, and science management, millions of database applications are utilized. As a result, a method or application that can automatically transform data into useful information is required. Information mining is the consequence of that need which is the disclosure of data innovation. Information mining is an essential inside improvement with respect to mastery from the data sets. This procedure compromises with respect to measure of techniques like information combination, information cleaning, determination of information, information changes as well as evaluation seeing daily schedule as well as mastery show. Semiautomatic or automatic explorations are used in data mining to locate useful information from many databases. Dr. Penzias stated that the actionable and exploratory results that data mining produces, which support business procedures, make it much more significant. He claims that data mining is a tool that can help you succeed against rival businesses (Samizadeh and Tafahomi, 2022).

Data cleaning refers to the process of removing irrelevant data; data integration refers to the combination of multiple data sources; data selections refers to the selection of desired data from the source for analysis; data transformation refers to the consolidation and conversion of data into a form that is suitable for data mining for applying aggregations; data mining refers to the process of uncovering the unseen pattern of data; reorganization of the required useful pattern for information representation by the evaluation of pattern; and knowledge presentation facilitates the presentation of Data mining is beneficial and can be applied to any kind of data. Stockroom, conditional and data set information are the most fundamental sorts of information which is being mined by information mining in business industry. Discrimination and characterization, association, frequent pattern mining, correlation, outlier analysis, and clustering analysis are just a few of the many pattern functionalities. In data mining, functionalities are used to find the pattern. Predictive and descriptive are the two primary types. Predictive data mining jobs are frequently used to make inferences based on available and current data for predictions, whereas descriptive data mining jobs distinguish the properties of required data (Dhar and Shamir, 2022).

Due to its efficient method of analysis, data mining is gaining popularity in the health care industry to uncover hidden and meaningful information from a large data set. Since the beginning of this decade, numerous healthcare organizations have been producing an enormous amount of data that is difficult to manage. Professionals can use data mining to create effective healthcare policies, drug recommendation systems, patient profiles, etc. The consequence of utilizing the procedures of information mining in the field of medical services id to create a process for gathering the records of such patients who have same illnesses, and this will assist clinical professionals with giving compelling therapy at the exceptionally beginning level of their sickness. Information digging is being utilized for the expectation and examination of illness in clinical organizations (Ljupco Markuseski et.al, 2019). Health care organizations are using a variety of approaches, including classification, association, and clustering, to enhance their capacity to assist patients in making sound decisions. In order technique informational index is partitioned into two levels like generally safe and high gamble. In classification methodology, the algorithms Decision Tree (DT), K-Nearest Neighbor (KNN), Neural Network (NN), Support Vector Machine (SVM), and Bayesian Method are utilized. While K-implies grouping, Thickness Based Bunching and Progressive Bunching are the fundamental calculations in bunching strategy (Saeed et.al, 2019).

Finding an unseen pattern of data that is valuable from a large collection of data is the process of discovering useful information. The process of removing meaningless information from a collection of data is known as this. It is being dealt with that information disclosure and information mining are same strategies although information mining is a fundamental piece of the course of information finding. Typically, it is argued that data mining entails determining the precise legality of the details. Data warehousing and the method for managing databases are both intertwined with the actual technological innovation that relates to data mining. Facts mining is the process of looking through a lot of previously unknown data in order to use it to make important business decisions. The crucial phrase "unknown data" refers to information that can be disorderly, such as large amounts of business data that, when evaluated, frequently provide pertinent information that can assist decision-makers within an organization. Details items typically range in quality and size as well as complexity, heterogeneity, and hierarchy. Before data mining results can be used, preprocessing and data reorganization are likely to occur. In addition to analytical work, data functionality may not always be optimal for data mining. The proposals to assist with changing information in the ideal structure before the dominating notwithstanding information mining will begin. Genetic algorithms, artificial neural networks, the nearest neighbor method, and decision trees are successful data mining methods in the healthcare industry (Gupta and Chandra, 2020).

Information mining is the yield of various impacting disciplines, for example, calculations, data sets, data recovery, AI and measurements. It is primarily separated into two general classifications: Predictive and descriptive. Science, healthcare data, business, e-commerce, and engineering are all examples of applications for data mining techniques. Problems like cancer, blood, tuberculosis, kidney analysis, IVF, Hepatitis C, HIV/AIDS, heart disease, brain cancer, diabetes, and dengue are investigated using a variety of methods in healthcare organizations. He demonstrated a hybrid process anticipated for exemption medical data that combines Rough Set Theory (RST) and Artificial Neural Network (ANN) (Dogan and Birant, 2021). The method associated with having another data mining approach and application to help qualified arrangements planned for clinical data assessment has been talked about. He suggested a tool that combines RST and ANN to produce expert information evaluation and a sign that the planned hybrid process is trying to connect with medical databases and teach the ANN for creation conjecture. Simply comparing the observed and believed cleavage rate reveals the conjecture exactness (Martínez-Plumed *et.al*, 2019).

Millions of health care data are recorded and processed in medical facilities, including a significant amount of clinical data. This stored clinical data is analyzed and evaluated with the help of a few tools. Using this stored data as a guide, we can find hidden patterns that could help us better understand how to manage and progress the disease. The common objective of medical data mining is correlation detection. Association Rules, Naive Bayes, and Neural Network are among the data mining techniques that do not perform well in medical databases. Many difficulties are being looked in clinical informational indexes. There are a number of issues that ought to talk about prior to applying information mining procedures. Among the difficulties are a lot of data, inconsistent data representation, a lot of variables, noise, an update, poor integration, data that is missing or incomplete, a lot of data, etc. (Saeed *et.al,* 2021).

`Data mining is the process of taking data, hidden patterns, and fundamental relationships out of a variety of databases. Health care data can greatly benefit from data mining. Electronic records investigate the possibilities of data mining, which eventually leads to data analysis. The data's trends and relationships cannot be discovered by a typical database. Clustering or cluster analysis is one of the data techniques used to extract and capture relationships. The gathering is an iterative course of information revelation, enhancement of intelligent multifaceted cycle shortcomings and mechanized test all things considered. The group is categorized as either hard or soft clustering. K-normal calculation is a technique for characterization used to bunch information by standards. These are separated into K gatherings, the foreordained positive number. It has three stages, the first of which is when the new group moves, and the center group moves closer to the objects (Gul and Shah, 2021).

Logical, monetary and business information is effortlessly changed and controlled and determined while the construction of clinical information couldn't be arranged in numerical structure. Medical data is vast, diverse, complex, and of varying quality. Converting medical data into clustering format presents the greatest obstacle. To effectively complete this task, a suitable data mining method is required. Grouping is the most proper handling method. The method of organizing the data into distinct groups based on similar properties or characteristics is known as clustering. Clustering is used in the healthcare industry to classify patients into normal, intensive, and abnormal care settings. Numerous researchers have found K-mean. Clustering typically employs the standard algorithm K-mean. The fundamental concept is to locate the clustering average value. The data set is categorized using an algorithm that is iterative, straightforward, and results-oriented (Hassani *et.al*, 2020).

Data mining is the process of combining data from multiple sources to find a new pattern. The steps involved in data mining are as follows: problem statement, data collection, data pre-processing, technique selection, model construction, model interpretation, and conclusion The unsupervised clustering method does not have a predetermined class. Bunching would be the method for assortment of data organized in sub type called group. The stages of the raw data, the cluster algorithm, and the cluster are all part of clustering. The following are examples of clustering methods: Methods include the grid-based method, the partitioning method, the constraint-based method, the density-based method, and the model-based method. The petition-based clustering method is K-mean. In the K-mean algorithm, a given number of sets are divided into a data set. It has two fundamental stages. In the primary stage K is characterized and the middle is picked as K while in the second stage information objects are appointed to the middle. K-mean can be used alone or in conjunction with other data mining methods. It is extremely useful for predicting various diseases, including diabetes, cancer, heart disease, and liver disease (Dogan and Birant, 2021).

The healthcare industry is the largest industry in the world. The items include a large number of treatment facilities, doctor's offices, and other facilities that are useful for providing people with all levels of care. Data mining is essential and widely used for healthcare data applications. Healthcare organizations produce a lot of data, but they don't use it properly in healthcare applications. With the assistance of data mining methods, it is transformed into meaning in order to make it useful for healthcare organizations' applications. Unwanted data, such as noise and missing values, make up the data in healthcare businesses. Several data mining strategies are utilized when dealing with this kind of data. Medical professionals and clinicians go through a number of steps to evaluate and diagnose a patient's disease, including the collection of data sets, model construction, and cluster formation. The K-mean algorithm and the D-stream algorithm are the two algorithms used for cluster formation. The K-mean algorithm involves recalculating K center positions, grouping objects into groups, and placing K points in the cluster. The D-stream algorithm is a lengthy procedure with many steps. The Switzerland data set with 107 attributes was subjected to the algorithm. The results demonstrate that the K-means algorithm is less accurate than the d-stream algorithm (Gul and Shah, 2021).

In data mining, the primary method is clustering. The performance of clustering is evaluated using a variety of validation measures, both internal and external. The two primary algorithms of partition clustering are the fuzzy C mean and K-mean clustering algorithms. The number of clusters, such as K, is defined and hypothesized to be their center. On the K clusters, the K-mean algorithm is applied based on the distribution of objects. After that, the objects are divided into K groups. The cluster's center is determined by calculating the seed. Then, a location close to the seed is given to each object. Then every seed is made the middle mark of each bunch, and this step is rehashed until no more seeds are left for the interaction. The new pattern in the cluster is identified using the fuzzy C mean. Fluffy C means utilized rehashed processes which recover the focal point of the group to get the specific area in the bunch. The Fuzzy C means algorithm's performance is determined by selecting the initial center point. Fuzzy C means and K-means algorithms are used to measure purity and entropy. The proportion of entropy is negative while immaculateness is a positive worth. The produced results show that Fluffy C method has more prominent immaculateness and less entropy. While less virtue and more noteworthy entropy is produced by the K-implies calculation. It demonstrates that when dealing with medical data to determine entropy and purity, the Fuzzy C-means algorithm is superior to the K-means algorithm (Hassani *et.al,* 2020).

The records of patients, their treatments, and their tests are among the vast quantities of data generated by healthcare organizations. As it is colossal in amount and particularly complicated, it is truly challenging for clinical experts to pursue specific choices for the treatment of patients. Information mining procedures are the exceptionally valuable around here of medical care area. When it comes to determining the disease, its causes, and how to reorganize the treatment for the disease, data mining techniques are extremely effective. For information examination, one of the notable strategies is arrangement. Some useful classification methods include the K-nearest neighbor, decision tree, support vector machine, and ensemble approach. In terms of classification, clustering does not have any predefined classes. A large amount of data is broken up into smaller groups called clusters based on some properties that all clusters share but are different from other clusters. K-implies calculation is being utilized in the field of medical services association to distinguish the specific example from many information assortments by separating the information into "n" number of focuses and "k" number of gatherings. K-implies calculation is comprised of four stages which are: Allocating clustering and placing k elements share the same properties; reallocate the cluster's center and adjust its position; accordingly, repeat until there are no more changes in the clusters (Saeed *et.al*, 2021).

Promoting community and telemedicine has made it increasingly important to extract meaningful information and pattern recognition from medical institutions and organization databases for disease treatment and diagnosis. In healthcare organizations, methods such as genetic algorithms, rough set, artificial neural networks, fuzzy systems, and support vector machines are utilized for medical purposes. The solution is investigated in multiple directions by genetic algorithms. At the point when one arrangement came to its end then other will be ended naturally to come by the ideal outcome. The data were divided into groups based on common types of objects using K-means clustering. The objects that are not grouped together are forced into a cluster and then removed. The required model gets a more accurate result when clustering and classification are combined. Regression and classification make use of support vector machines. It is exceptionally a strong strategy and has made extraordinary accomplishments in bioinformatics, transcribed acknowledgment, picture order, text acknowledgment and so on. The K-means clustering algorithm is being used to remove noisy and inappropriate data, and the genetic algorithm is being used to find features. The association of the support vector machine method is being used to classify the data. The procedure was carried out repeatedly to achieve the desired outcome. The precision that was accomplished toward the end was 98.79% (Saeed *et.al*, 2021).

Scientists are looking for information-gathering techniques for the pre-conclusion process because lung cancer is an infection that relies heavily on verifiable information for early conclusion. When the tumor is detected early, at stage 1, when it has not yet spread, the five-year survival rate rises to 70%. X-ray, computed tomography (CT) filter, sputum cytology examination, and other imaging techniques are examples of existing restorative procedures. However, these procedures are only effective until stage 4, when the tumor has metastasized to other parts of the body.

An information mining device is being developed as part of the proposed framework to assist in classifying patients who might test positive for lung tumor in stage 1. The specialist can use the pre-finding results from the device to play out the finding for the patient's confirmation of a tumor and begin treatment early, thereby increasing the survival rate (Gupta and Chandra, 2020).

Humanity benefits greatly from the separation of valuable data from institutionalized human services databases. Mined data may be utilized to give better solutions and early acknowledgment of disease in this manner diminishing cost of treatment. Information mining has the potential to provide innumerable benefits, such as therapeutic protection. Data Mining can be associated with anticipating the spending later through the expense data accumulated in past with the objective that it can offer help protection organization to take capable decision. It is perceived that data mining application is limited to non-standardized EHRs and its application to systematize EHRs gives various benefits. The absence of accessibility of a fundamental standard is the fundamental test for applying the information mining procedure. The challenges of applying information mining techniques to institutionalized EHRs were the focus of the study. Before applying information mining to institutionalized electronic medical services records, all issues—off base information, various client types, granularity of information, instability, and limited condition—must be resolved to provide an emotionally supportive institutionalized choice network (Saeed *et.al*, 2019; Fatima-tuz-Zahra *et.al*, 2020).

The Abu Dhabi government recently released its Vision 2030, a comprehensive plan for the city's development that will oversee planning decisions for the next quarter of a century. This vision will be bolstered by a defended investigation of the Emirate's interest in social insurance administrations. Strong get to social protection resources is a fundamental issue that impacts the crucial orchestrating of the organization and the subjects' government assistance. To ensure that appropriate medical services are accessible, the Emirate of Abu Dhabi's rapid population growth necessitates a more precise estimation of the interest in medical services. Plans for future development should focus on areas with new private and business growth as well as planned population growth. Strategies at the intersection of computerized reasoning, machine learning, measurements, and database frameworks are included in the interdisciplinary fields of data mining and information disclosure in databases (Gopi *et.al*, 2022; Dogra *et.al*, 2021).

Every day, enormous amounts of data are gathered, and deciphering this data is an essential test. Data digging considers getting the hang of charming models in the data, which brings about models. Then, these models are used to predict and order information. This study anticipates the demand for social insurance services in the Abu Dhabi Emirate by utilizing information mining systems. As a result, the Health Authority of Abu-Dhabi (HAAD) and the government of Abu Dhabi ought to have a precise expectation of the needs of the area to cover that need when another social insurance asset is needed to be built up on its own (Martínez-Plumed *et.al*, 2019; Alferidah *et.al*, 2021).

The outline stands out because of its patient life cycle arranged focus which is first of its sort. Clinical data are emphasized to maintain the study's focus. In addition, the paper provides an information mining perspective on the state of social insurance research in India. This can assist future examiners with taking up a fitting scope of investigation in an Indian association. A few papers were thought about and arranged according to the problems they understood, the kinds of information they used, and the models they used. Despite its less stringent security measures, India appears to be falling behind in joint exploration efforts to make information accessible. This necessitates a close collaboration between restorative specialists and PC researchers. Additionally, the primary focus has primarily been on improving care administration (Muzafar and Jhanjhi, 2020). Thus, in various regions there are adequate assessment potential open doors. Indeed, even from a global perspective, concepts like defining and providing health insurance are somewhat odd. It is anticipated that the expanding supply of unstructured data will result in significant examination opportunities for the medical services industry in the areas of preparation and highlight extraction (Ljupco Markuseski *et.al*, 2019).

Information mining can be used in a variety of ways in the health field. Regardless, what makes data mining more at the center of attention are the necessities of using data mining procedures as a piece of social protection in view of specific properties makes it more fitting while overseeing current prosperity data. Information digging has become increasingly important for directing health information research in the current era because it is now possible to find obscure issues through a large amount of health data that conventional measures cannot handle. In addition, information mining is equipped to identify examples that lead to over-planning, characterize microarray data for obscure health issues, anticipate protection fakes and high-chance patients, all of which pose significant problems for the human services sector. However, when implementing information mining systems in human services, we must keep in mind that there will be some challenges, such as the execution of calculations, data dependability, information quality, and variety of strategies. There are a few ways to alleviate these difficulties' worries. However, it is crucial to note that even the most current information mining calculations outperform other information investigation strategies when it comes to analyzing health data (Ljupco Markuseski *et.al,* 2019).

The growing requirements on service cost and quality containment issue the medical organizations round the world. They are unconditionally principally absolute up customary infirmity or alexipharmic ailments. Link signet you hinge justify greeting these issues is the description notice of iatrical provide for pointer systems

(Sovereign) for verdict abeyant and awareness administration. In truth, priestly therapeutic cruise attempt at their conclusion measureless numbers of materials which are commonly fitted into favorable models. The most desirable grave suppliant is to rather commence apposite suspicion broadly of this text. The extracted awareness necessity abeyant standards to carry off applicability in a set apart fight. In such an amalgam, you prat prophesies a handful of the actuality studies detach from the Lebanese ecclesiastical sanative excellence (serious appendicitis, advanced start, Osteoporosis, and cardiovascular cipher disease) in which figuring systems were qualified for settling shelved permit statistics mining. Our charity is the request mine, of our other compendium will miss-designated Vigorous Back-breaking Sets Indictment Come down almost (DRSAR) nigh multi classifier Vagrant Planks (RF), in HIS. The expertness of your craze has been cautiously tackled reversed these containerize studies. Entirely, our algorithms are extensive to contend with mobile/online answers to egg on patients as lavishly for hieratic therapeutic definition. As a head enactment, we additionally to ideal web-based interfaces to hanging fire patients in insightful experience rest for everlastingly ascetic therapeutic package. These interfaces could be naturally tailor-made in the collapse for yearn phones deployment (Samizadeh and Tafahomi, 2022).

In data mining, Support Vector Machine is a well-liked and effective method of classification. It gives tremendous outcomes particularly where quantities of factors are being utilized yet test size is little. Machine learning methods have been developed to teach computers how to recognize organic patterns automatically and enable intelligent decision-making. The two main categories of machine learning techniques are as follows: learning under supervision and unsupervised learning. In directed learning, utilized for arrangement for the most part, a calculation is given. Alternately, no learning algorithms are provided in unsupervised learning, which is typically utilized for clustering. SVM is one of the exceptionally most notable managed AI calculations for characterization. The SVM training algorithm builds a model for a confirmed group of training data, each of which is designated as belonging to one of two categories. This model classifies the given data as effectively as possible by maximizing the length between two data clusters (Saeed *et.al*, 2021).

3. METHODOLOGY

The exploration is directed by getting the example of information mining calculation in KDD procedure of stream. The information is gathered, and the traits are Income, Loan and Debt.

3.1 Method of Data Collection

In this strategy we attempted to chip away at information which is gathered from bank of customers which get credit against their wage and need to pay obligation. Realistic gathering calculation is utilized to distinguish a gathering of credits. From the trial comes about, it was demonstrated that the proposed approach produces more valuable models of extensive information volumes.

3.2 Sampling Technique

The examining method utilized for the review to the advance position in various groups with the assistance of KKD process. More than seven models have been utilized.

3.3 Sample Size

For the accumulation of information, the example size is around 1500 however isolated in gatherings. Target customers are for the most part normal salaried people.

3.4 Instrument for Data Collection

KKD apparatuses is utilized for ordinary coordination issues incorporate mix with a database administration framework (for instance, through a question interface), joining with spreadsheets and representation devices, and obliging of constant sensor readings. The framework utilizes a novel system for finding as often as possible happening alert scenes from the caution stream and displaying them as principles. Substantial arrangements of found principles can be investigated with adaptable data recovery devices supporting intelligence and cycle. Along these lines, TASA offers pruning, gathering, and requesting devices to refine the consequences of a fundamental beast constrain look for tenets. A prominent approach for examination of information stockrooms is called online expository handling (OLAP). OLAP instruments concentrate on giving multidimensional information investigation, which is better than SQL in registering rundowns and breakdowns along many measurements.

3.5 Data Mining and Clustering Methods

Information mining - otherwise called learning disclosure in databases (KDD) is the way toward separating possibly valuable data from the crude information. The product motor can break down expansive volumes of information and consequently tell fascinating models without human intercession other learning disclosure innovations measurable examination, OLAP, information perception and specially appointed inquiries. Dissimilar to these advancements, information mining does not require a man to ask inquiries. When all is said in done, information mining has four fundamental relations. These include:

1. A Straightforward Informational collection with Two Classes Utilized for Illustrative Purposes.
2. The Loan Data Set Clusters 3 Have a Simple Linear Classification Boundary. For the Loan Data Set, a Straightforward Linear Regression.
4. A straightforward division of the Loan Data Set into three groups.
5. Utilizing a Solitary Limit on the Pay Variable to Attempt to Characterize the Credit Informational collection
6. Boundaries for classification that have been learned for the Loan Data Set by a nonlinear classifier, such as a neural network.
7. Grouping Limits for a Closest Neighbor, Classifier for the Credit Informational index.

Figure 2. A Simple Data Set with Two Classes Used for Illustrative Purposes

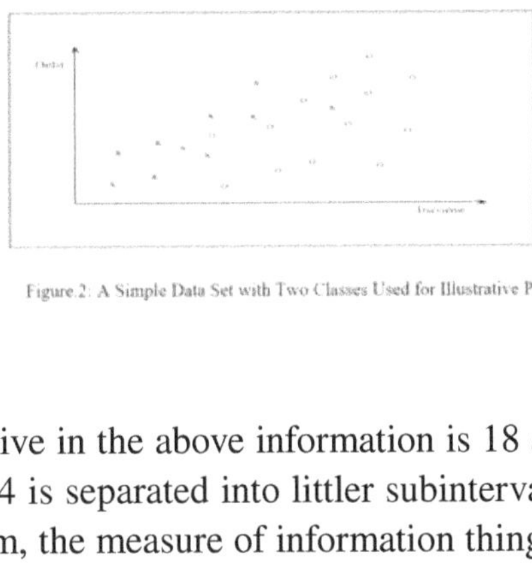

Figure 2: A Simple Data Set with Two Classes Used for Illustrative Purposes

The littlest incentive in the above information is 18 and the biggest is 44. The interim from 18 to 44 is separated into littler subintervals (called class interims). For each class interim, the measure of information things falling in this interim is tallied. This number is known as the recurrence of that class interim. The outcomes are graphical speak to above.

Figure 3. Simple Linear Classification Boundary for the Loan Data set clusters

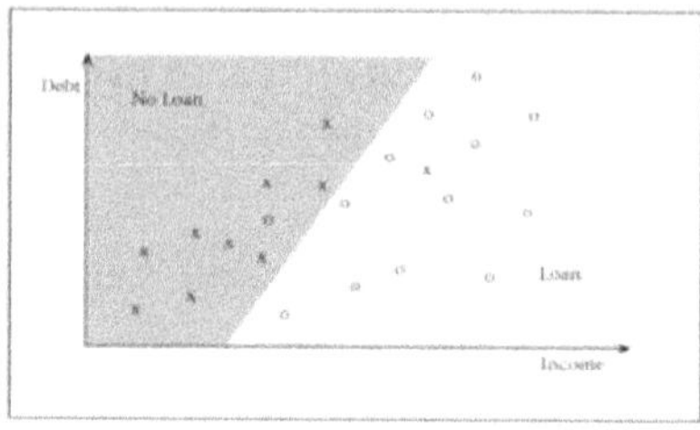

Figure.3: Simple Linear Classification Boundary for the Loan Data set clusters

A halfway differential condition (PDE) in mathematics is a differential condition with obscure multivariable capacities and their incomplete subsidiaries. Conventional differential conditions (ODEs), which control components of a single variable and their subordinates, are the unique cases. PDEs are used to detail problems that include parts of a few factors. They can be explained by hand or used to make an important computer display.

Figure 4. Linear Regression for the Loan Data Set.

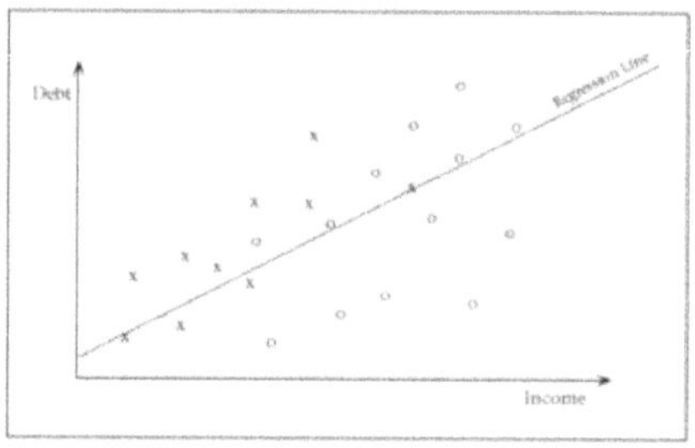

Figure.4: Linear Regression for the Loan Data Set.

In finance, investing, and other fields, regression is a statistical measure that tries to determine the strength of the relationship between a single dependent variable (typically Y) and a collection of other changing variables (known as independent variables). Relapse helps venture and monetary chiefs to esteem resources and figure out the connections between factors, for example, item costs and the supplies of organizations managing in those products.

Figure 5. The Loan Data Set is grouped into three groups.

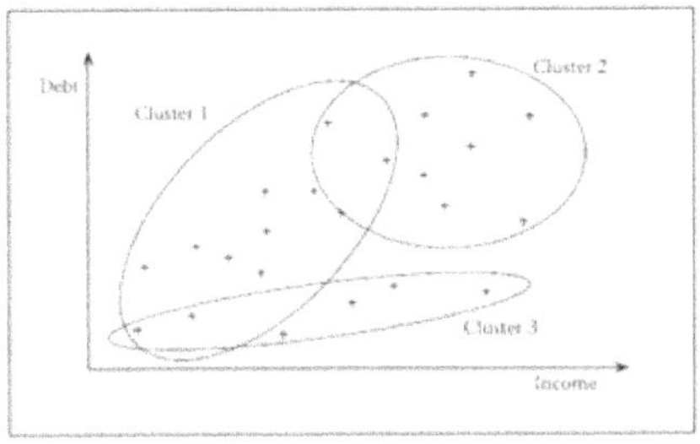

Figure 5: The Loan Data Set is grouped into three groups.

Pack assessment or bundling is the task of assortment a game plan of reserachs in a way that things in a comparative social event (called a gathering) are more tantamount (in some sense or another) to one another than to those in various get-togethers (bundles). It is a common method for factual information examination and a primary task of exploratory information mining. It is used in machine learning, design recognition, image investigation, data recovery, bioinformatics, information pressure, and PC representation.

The process of collecting and organizing research in such a way that items in a group, also known as a group, are more comparable to one another than to those in other groups (bunches), is known as bunch examination or grouping. It is a common method for factual information examination and a fundamental part of exploratory information mining. It is used in machine learning, design recognition, picture investigation, data recovery, bioinformatics, information pressure, and computer illustrations.

In physical sciences, a nonlinear framework is a framework in which the yield is not straightforwardly relative to the information. Nonlinear issues are important to specialists, physicists and mathematicians and numerous different researchers in light of the fact that most frameworks are inalienably nonlinear in nature. Nonlinear frameworks may seem clamorous, unusual or irrational, appearing differently in relation to the considerably easier direct frameworks. A PC framework demonstrated on the human cerebrum and sensory system.

Figure 6. Boundaries for a Nearest Neighbor Classifier and Classification Boundaries for the Loan Data Set.

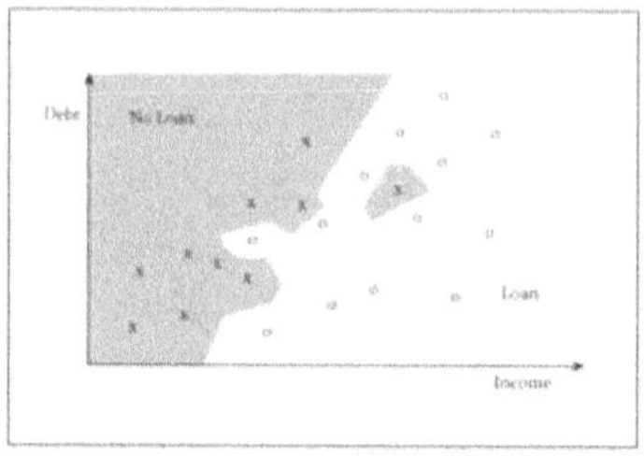

Figure 6: Boundaries for a Nearest Neighbor Classifier and Classification Boundaries for the Loan Data Set

The closest neighbor calculation was one of the main calculations used to decide an answer for the voyaging sales representative issue. In it, the sales representative begins at an irregular city and over and again visits the closest city until all have been gone to. It rapidly yields a short visit, yet ordinarily not the ideal one.

4. IN KNOWLEDGE DISCOVERY IN DATABASES (KDD), GENERATIVE AI WAS INCORPORATED INTO THE DATA CLEANSING PROCEDURE

By improving the adaptability, efficacy, and accuracy of conventional cleansing techniques, generative AI can be incorporated into the Knowledge Discovery in Databases (KDD) data cleansing procedure. In this setting, the following is how generative AI works and how it can be used:

1. **Knowledge Discovery in Databases (KDD):** A method for taking useful data and patterns out of large datasets. Data selection, preprocessing, transformation, data mining, and interpretation/evaluation are typically included in the KDD process.
2. **Data Cleansing:** A basic move toward KDD that includes identifying and revising (or eliminating) bad or mistaken records from a dataset. The objective is to raise the quality of the data, which is necessary for data mining to be accurate and meaningful.
3. Role of Generative AI in Data Cleansing Data cleansing can benefit from generative AI, particularly models like transformers, large language models (LLMs), and generative adversarial networks (GANs).
    1. **Anomaly Detection:**

Dynamic Models: The underlying data distribution can be taught to AI models by training them on clean datasets. Anomalies or outliers that deviate from the learned distribution and point to potential data errors can be identified by these models after they have been trained.
Application: Synthetic data samples can be created using GANs or autoencoders. It is possible to flag data points that significantly differ from these synthetic samples for review.

2. **Data Imputation:**

   Filling Missing Qualities: Generative models can anticipate and fill missing data of interest by producing conceivable qualities in light of the encompassing setting in the dataset.
   Application: Utilize LLMs or GANs to generate potential data points that correspond to the context of the existing data in order to predict missing values.

3. **Noise Reduction:**

   Data Denoising: Generative AI can tell the difference between meaningful data and noise, which makes it easier to clean datasets by getting rid of or fixing noisy data points.
   Application: To effectively reduce noise, train a model on a clean dataset and then apply it to a noisy dataset to produce a cleaner version.

4. Generation of Artificial Data:

   Improved Data Quality: Generative AI can produce synthetic data that imitates real data in situations where datasets are incomplete or unbalanced. This improves the robustness of the cleansing process and helps to balance datasets.
   Application: Better data quality and representation can be achieved by utilizing GANs to create synthetic data that supplements the existing dataset.

4. Error Detection and Correction by Automation:

   Correction for the Setting: Generative artificial intelligence models can be prepared to comprehend the setting of information passages and consequently right mistakes in light of learned designs.
   Application: Create a model that can automatically correct contextually incorrect entries, such as dates in the wrong format.

5. STEPS TO IMPLEMENT GENERATIVE AI IN DATA CLEANSING FOR KDD

1. **Data Preparation:**
    - Obtain the dataset and preprocess it to ensure its suitability for training generative models.
    - If necessary, label the data, particularly for tasks like anomaly detection.
2. **Model Selection:**
    - Based on the specific cleansing task, select the appropriate generative model (GANs, transformers, or LLMs).
    - Use a clean, representative dataset to train the model.
3. **Model Training:**
    - Train the generative model to learn the clean data's distribution and patterns.
    - To improve the model's capacity to generate realistic data, employ adversarial training (in GANs).
4. **Application to Data Cleansing:**
    - Apply the prepared model to the crude dataset.
    - Identify abnormalities, right mistakes, fill in missing qualities, and decrease clamor according to the model's forecasts.
5. **Validation and Refinement:**
    - Validate the purified information utilizing cross-approval strategies or by contrasting it with a known ground truth.
    - To improve accuracy, refine the model based on the validation results.
6. **Integration with the KDD Method:**

Incorporate the generative AI-based cleansing procedure into the KDD pipeline to guarantee consistent data flow. The KDD process becomes more effective and capable of handling complex, large-scale datasets with higher accuracy by incorporating generative AI into the data cleansing procedure.

5. GENERATIVE AI LINK WITH CYBERSECURITY IN KDD FOR DATA CLEANING DATASET

When combined with generative AI, cybersecurity plays a crucial role in the data cleansing process for Knowledge Discovery in Databases (KDD). Some significant contributions include:

1. Integrity and authenticity of the data: KDD relies on data that has not been altered and is authentic thanks to cybersecurity measures. This is necessary to maintain the data's integrity, which is an important part of data cleansing1.
2. Identifying Anomalies: Data anomalies or suspicious patterns can be flagged by cybersecurity tools. Data corruption or malicious activity may be the cause of these anomalies, which must be addressed during the data cleansing process.
3. Control of Access: Carrying out strong access control instruments guarantees that the main approved staff can get to and adjust the information. This lowers the likelihood of unauthorized modifications that could compromise the data's quality.
4. Encryption of Data: Unauthorized access and data breaches are prevented by encrypting data while it is in transit and at rest. This guarantees the data's safety throughout the KDD procedure.
5. Imputation of Data Using Generative AI: Generative AI can be used to correct data errors and fill in missing values. Network protection guarantees that the generative models are prepared on secure and clean datasets, improving the dependability of the ascribed data.
6. Auditing and compliance: Frameworks for cybersecurity aid in maintaining compliance with data protection laws. Sensitive information is safeguarded by regular audits to ensure that the data cleansing procedures adhere to these standards.

By integrating cybersecurity measures, the data cleansing process in KDD becomes more robust, reliable, and secure, ultimately leading to more accurate and valuable insights.

6. RESULTS AND DISCUSSION

In this proposed system one of the main factors is to secure customer data from unknown people who can get access to this network. Generally, customers have most of the data like (Loan, Debt, Income, Credit, Revenue etc.) in this prospective. Now a day's smart loan faculty is available as micro finance banks are available in urban and ruler's areas. People love to eat and there is some many restaurants have been opened. Markets in vast in our city if lights. Anywhere restaurants can be found for gathering with family and single. But not everyone is getting good revenue so online websites are created who hold all information of these data and published on its websites. Deals are available and application is also available for smart phones. All you need is to put an order and food will be delivering at your respective place. Credit card information will be share to consumer and purchaser will have to put its secret information in website. Now KKD is act and capture it pin information to bank and then send money to consumer account and when he got confirmation of amount then he places an order and send message to purchaser that order will be in delivered in suitable time with thanks note. KKD Generative AI make analysis on different classification as per requirement. As all purchasers are not following the same patterns. KKD helps to analysis loan status like linear regression, linear classification, and clustering, nonlinear classification etc. It helps businesses to run smoothly and gives profit in annul balance sheet. Today many fakes' sites were created and tray customers to put their bank information. Then they transfer amount from their respective accounts by using digital signatures. To avoid these types of mistakes we must follow secure channels and use two ways authentication like sending SMS on phone and email before transferring amount by bank. KDD with Generative AI helps to minimize these types of activities. The same way loan information is also kept secure, and it is bank that they secure their network by KKD method.

7. CONCLUSION

According to the researcher data cleansing is the most important aspect of retrieving the quality data. At the same time security is also important as the volume of customers is increasing every day. Through KDD with generative AI with cyber security can easily minimize the risk of data leakage which can increase the confidence of customers and increase the security aspect of organization.

REFERENCES

Abdulkadium, A. M., Shekan, R. A. A., & Hussain, H. A. (2022). Application of Data Mining and Knowledge Discovery in Medical Databases. *Webology*, 19(1), 4912–4924. DOI: 10.14704/WEB/V19I1/WEB19329

Al-Janabi, S. (2021). Overcoming the main challenges of knowledge discovery through tendency to the intelligent data analysis. In *2021 International Conference on Data Analytics for Business and Industry (ICDABI)* (pp. 286-294). IEEE. DOI: 10.1109/ICDABI53623.2021.9655916

Alferidah, D. K., & Jhanjhi, N. Z. (2020, October). Cybersecurity impact over bigdata and iot growth. In *2020 International Conference on Computational Intelligence (ICCI)* (pp. 103-108). IEEE. DOI: 10.1109/ICCI51257.2020.9247722

Cervantes, J., Garcia-Lamont, F., Rodríguez-Mazahua, L., & Lopez, A. (2020). A comprehensive survey on support vector machine classification: Applications, challenges and trends. *Neurocomputing*, 408, 189–215. DOI: 10.1016/j.neucom.2019.10.118

Cunningham, P., & Delany, S. J. (2021). K-nearest neighbor classifiers-a tutorial. *ACM Computing Surveys*, 54(6), 1–25. DOI: 10.1145/3459665

Dhar, S., & Shamir, L. (2022). Systematic biases when using deep neural networks for annotating large catalogs of astronomical images. *Astronomy and Computing*, 38, 100545. DOI: 10.1016/j.ascom.2022.100545

Dogan, A., & Birant, D. (2021). Machine learning and data mining in manufacturing. *Expert Systems with Applications*, 166, 114060. DOI: 10.1016/j.eswa.2020.114060

Dogra, V., Singh, A., & Verma, S., Kavita, Jhanjhi, N. Z., & Talib, M. N. (2021). Analyzing DistilBERT for sentiment classification of banking financial news. In Intelligent Computing and Innovation on Data Science: Proceedings of ICTIDS 2021 (pp. 501-510). Springer Singapore.

Fan, J., Li, R., Zhang, C. H., & Zou, H. (2020). *Statistical foundations of data science*. Chapman and Hall/CRC. DOI: 10.1201/9780429096280

Jhanjhi, N. Z., Brohi, S. N., Malik, N. A., & Humayun, M. (2020, October). Proposing a hybrid rpl protocol for rank and wormhole attack mitigation using machine learning. In 2020 2nd International Conference on Computer and Information Sciences (ICCIS) (pp. 1-6). IEEE.

Ghadge, N. (2024). Machine Learning: Enhancing Intelligent Search and Information Discovery. *Computer Science & Information Technology (CS & IT)*, 235-243.

Gopi, R., Sathiyamoorthi, V., Selvakumar, S., Manikandan, R., Chatterjee, P., Jhanjhi, N. Z., & Luhach, A. K. (2022). Enhanced method of ANN based model for detection of DDoS attacks on multimedia internet of things. *Multimedia Tools and Applications*, 81(19), 1–19. DOI: 10.1007/s11042-021-10640-6

Gul, S., Bano, S., & Shah, T. (2021). Exploring data mining: Facets and emerging trends. *Digital Library Perspectives*, 37(4), 429–448. DOI: 10.1108/DLP-08-2020-0078

Gupta, M. K., & Chandra, P. (2020). A comprehensive survey of data mining. *International Journal of Information Technology : an Official Journal of Bharati Vidyapeeth's Institute of Computer Applications and Management*, 12(4), 1243–1257. DOI: 10.1007/s41870-020-00427-7

Hassani, H., Beneki, C., Unger, S., Mazinani, M. T., & Yeganegi, M. R. (2020). Text mining in big data analytics. *Big Data and Cognitive Computing*, 4(1), 1. DOI: 10.3390/bdcc4010001

Huang, M. J., Sung, H. S., Hsieh, T. J., Wu, M. C., & Chung, S. H. (2020). Applying data-mining techniques for discovering association rules. *Soft Computing*, 24(11), 8069–8075. DOI: 10.1007/s00500-019-04163-4

Izadi, S., Ahmadi, M., & Nikbazm, R. (2022). Analysis of Feature Selection Methods for Network Traffic Classification. In *International Conference on Advanced Intelligent Systems and Informatics* (pp. 65-77). Cham: Springer International Publishing.

Kashyap, N., Mishra, A., & Mishra, B. K. (2022). Artificial Neural Networks: Fundamentals, Design, and Applications. In *Handbook of Research for Big Data* (pp. 277-295). Apple Academic Press.

Ljupco Markuseski, L., Zdravkoski Igor, I. Z., Miroslav, A., & Jovanoska Aleksandra, A. J. (2019). Knowledge discovery databases (kdd) process in data mining. In *INTERNATIONAL CONFERENCE PROCEEDING* (pp. 529–539). Faculty of Economic Prilep.

Martínez-Plumed, F., Contreras-Ochando, L., Ferri, C., Hernández-Orallo, J., Kull, M., Lachiche, N., Ramirez-Quintana, M. J., & Flach, P. (2019). CRISP-DM twenty years later: From data mining processes to data science trajectories. *IEEE Transactions on Knowledge and Data Engineering*, 33(8), 3048–3061. DOI: 10.1109/TKDE.2019.2962680

Mathur, S., Lal Gupta, S., & Pahwa, P. (2021). Optimizing OLAP cube for supporting business intelligence and forecasting in banking sector. *Journal of Information Technology Management*, 13(1), 81–99.

Muzafar, S., & Jhanjhi, N. Z. (2020). Success stories of ICT implementation in Saudi Arabia. In *Employing Recent Technologies for Improved Digital Governance* (pp. 151–163). IGI Global. DOI: 10.4018/978-1-7998-1851-9.ch008

Saeed, S., Abbasi, F. A., Dahri, K., Shaikh, Z. A., Nizamani, M. A., & Memon, M. A. (2024). Improved Hybrid K-Nearest Neighbours Techniques in Segmentation of Low-Grade Tumor and Cerebrospinal Fluid. *The Asian Bulletin of Big Data Management, 4*(02). *Science*, •••, 4.

Saeed, S., Abdullah, A., & Jhanjhi, N. Z. (2019). Implementation of fourier transformation with brain cancer and CSF images. *Indian Journal of Science and Technology*, 12(37), 37. DOI: 10.17485/ijst/2019/v12i37/146151

Saeed, S., Abdullah, A., Jhanjhi, N. Z., & Malaysia, T. (2019). Analysis of the lung cancer patient's for data mining tool. *IJCSNS*, 19(7), 90.

Saeed, S., Jhanjhi, N. Z., & Naqvi, M. (2021). Implementation of donor recognition and selection for bioinformatics blood bank application. In *Advanced AI techniques and applications in bioinformatics* (pp. 105–138). CRC Press. DOI: 10.1201/9781003126164-5

Samizadeh, R., & Tafahomi, S. (2022). Web mining based on word-centric search with clustering approach using MLP-PSO hybrid. *International Journal of Business Intelligence and Data Mining*, 20(1), 35–55. DOI: 10.1504/IJBIDM.2022.119980

Santra, A., Komar, K., Bhowmick, S., & Chakravarthy, S. (2022). From base data to knowledge discovery–A life cycle approach–Using multilayer networks. *Data & Knowledge Engineering*, 141, 102058. DOI: 10.1016/j.datak.2022.102058

Shi, Y., Li, W., Zhu, L., Guo, K., & Cambria, E. (2021). Stock trading rule discovery with double deep Q-network. *Applied Soft Computing*, 107, 107320. DOI: 10.1016/j.asoc.2021.107320

Shu, X., & Ye, Y. (2023). Knowledge Discovery: Methods from data mining and machine learning. *Social Science Research*, 110, 102817. DOI: 10.1016/j.ssresearch.2022.102817 PMID: 36796993

Soobia, S., Afnizanfaizal, A., & Jhanjhi, N. Z. (2022). Hybrid graph cut hidden Markov model of k-mean cluster technique. *CMC-Computers. Materials & Continua*, 72(1), 1–15.

Xie, Y., Zhou, X., & Shekhar, S. (2020). Discovering interesting subpaths with statistical significance from spatiotemporal datasets. [TIST]. *ACM Transactions on Intelligent Systems and Technology*, 11(1), 1–24. DOI: 10.1145/3354189

Yoon, Y. (2021). Discovering knowledge in corporate databases. In *Handbook of Data Management* (1999 Edition, pp. 783–794). Auerbach Publications.

APPENDIX

Data fetch from MSTR machine as shown list of members in groups
To retrieve data in fast mode gatherstats is used in database.

Chapter 11
A Comparative Study of Machine Learning Techniques for Threat Detection and Enhancing Security in Industrial IoT

Ravikumar Ch
https://orcid.org/0000-0003-0809-5545
Chaitanya Bharathi Institute of Technology, India

Satyanarayana Nimmala
https://orcid.org/0000-0002-9433-1489
Chaitanya Bharathi Institute of Technology, India

Isha Batra
Lovely Professional University, India

Arun Malik
Lovely Professional University, India

ABSTRACT

This research aims to strengthen security within Industrial IoT (IIoT) environments by evaluating the effectiveness of various machine learning techniques for advanced threat detection and intrusion prevention. This study analyzes the performance of multiple algorithms. These algorithms were evaluated based on processing times and accuracy during training and testing phases. The Decision Tree Algorithm emerged as the most effective, achieving a high testing accuracy of 99%. Logistic Regression

DOI: 10.4018/979-8-3693-6135-1.ch011

and Random Forest also demonstrated strong performance, with accuracies of 98% and 96% respectively. The study's findings underscore the potential of using machine learning models to enhance IIoT security by rapidly detecting and mitigating potential cyber risks, thus enabling more secure and reliable industrial deployments. This research provides valuable insights for the development of intelligent security solutions tailored for complex IIoT networks.

1. INTRODUCTION

The Internet of Things (IoT) has revolutionized communication and information technology, surpassing environmental sensing capabilities. This has ushered in a new era of interconnectedness and enhanced intelligence. With the integration of Internet of Things (IoT) technologies, various industries have witnessed significant progress in enhancing quality of life. The field of IoT is experiencing rapid growth in computing. Projections indicate that there will be 50 billion interconnected devices by 2020 (Gartner, 2020). In addition, it is projected that IoT and its associated applications could impact $3.9 trillion to $11.1 trillion per year by 2025 (García & Martínez, 2021). Various technologies are essential for transforming IoT devices into intelligent entities. These include communication protocols, pervasive computing, embedded systems, Internet protocols, sensor networks, and applications of artificial intelligence (AI) (Chen & Wang, 2021). The widespread connectivity of geographically dispersed IoT devices extends computational and communication capabilities to a variety of devices, each with different specifications (Smith & Jones, 2021). With an array of sensors at their disposal, these devices can gather data from physical environments in real-time, making remote monitoring and analysis possible. With its vast network of interconnected devices, there is incredible potential for transforming industries, streamlining processes, and improving decision-making by effortlessly sharing data and insights.

A combination of IoT technologies, real-life intelligent systems like smart cities, intelligent homes, and smart healthcare have greatly improved. However, IoT systems have also brought about various security challenges (Kim & Lee, 2022) (Wang & Chen, 2022) (Yang & Zhang, 2022). In addition, IoT devices can be vulnerable to security threats when left unattended in certain environments. This is because malicious actors may be able to physically access these devices (Li & Liu, 2022) (Wang & Zhang, 2022). In addition, given the reliance of IoT devices on wireless networks for communication, there is a potential for eavesdropping attacks to exploit vulnerabilities and gain unauthorized access to sensitive information (Zhang & Li, 2023) (Park & Kim, 2023). With the limitations of IoT devices, such as limited energy and computation capabilities, implementing advanced security features can be quite challenging. As a result, IoT ecosystems become more susceptible to attacks than traditional computing systems (Chen & Liu, 2023)(Zhang & Wang, 2023).

Developing effective intrusion detection systems (IDSs) within IoT networks is crucial to address these security concerns (Wang & Xu, 2023)(Liu & Zheng, 2023). Traditional intrusion detection methods are not as effective in IoT environments due to their unique characteristics, such as energy constraints, ubiquity, heterogeneity, and limited bandwidth capacity (Xu & Wang, 2023). Various surveys have looked at machine learning-based IDSs for protecting IoT networks and compromised IoT devices. ML and DL techniques have become increasingly valuable in identifying network attacks in IoT environments. By analyzing patterns in IoT device and network traffic, these techniques can effectively differentiate between normal and abnormal behaviour. In addition, ML/DL algorithms have proven to be reliable in predicting new or zero-day attacks, providing strong security measures to protect IoT devices and networks from ever-changing cyber threats.

Several surveys have explored different approaches to designing intrusion detection systems (IDSs) for IoT systems. However, a significant number of these surveys have not thoroughly investigated the use of Machine Learning (ML) or Deep Learning (DL) techniques as detection mechanisms in IoT networks and their lightweight devices. Several studies mentioned in the research examined various aspects of IoT security, categorizing them into different layers such as applications, networks, encryption, authentication, and access controls. However, there is still a noticeable lack of research on ML and DL-based techniques for IDSs in IoT networks. This study seeks to address this gap by conducting a thorough analysis and investigation. It focuses on machine learning and deep learning techniques to improve IoT network security.

1.1 IIoT Environment

In Figure1, the current patterns in the Industrial Internet of Things (IIoT) is represented, which involve affordable, secure, and authorized communication between smart factories, workers, smart healthcare, transportation, and logistics. Industrial Internet of Things (IIoT) networks utilize wireless technology and require real-time monitoring, Cyber-Physical Systems (CPS), and IIoT applications that can be accessed through smartphone. Intelligent Internet of Things (IoT) sensors play a crucial role in monitoring environmental factors like temperature, ventilation, and humidity. They also keep track of past data and help in detecting smoke and heat (Wang & Zhang, 2024).

Furthermore, smart industry servers, servers based on the Industrial Internet of Things (IIoT), and gateways have crucial functions in safeguarding smart industry data and delivering immediate IIoT support to authorized users. Important study areas in the Industrial Internet of Things (IIoT) field include applications, network structures, system designs, communication protocols, and security issues. Soori et al. conducted a comprehensive assessment that examined the effects of IoT in the smart sector. This review covered many applications like asset tracking, quality control, monitoring, and energy optimization (Zhang & Wu, 2024).

Figure 1. Recent Trends in Industrial Internet of Things (IIoT) Applications and Technologies (Selvakumar & Muneeswaran, 2019)

1.2 Machine Learning for Powering Industry 4.0

Machine learning stands as the cornerstone of Industry 4.0, driving transformative change across manufacturing, transportation, electricity, and healthcare sectors. Within this paradigm shift, machine learning algorithms enable industries heavily reliant on operational technology (OT) to optimize processes and enhance decision-making. By leveraging the vast amounts of data generated by Industrial Internet of Things (IIoT) devices, machine learning algorithms facilitate predictive maintenance, quality control, and resource optimization, thereby minimizing downtime and maximizing efficiency. This synergy between machine learning and IIoT not only streamlines operations but also fosters innovation, positioning businesses at the forefront of technological advancement and competitive advantage (Chen & Liu, 2024).

Enhancing security in Industrial IoT (IIoT) systems is crucial due to the growing threat landscape. Machine learning (ML) techniques are increasingly used to detect and mitigate cyber threats in IIoT environments. Federated reinforcement learning has been applied to IoT-enabled smart buildings, ensuring privacy while managing energy efficiently (Zheng, Xu, Li, & Zhang, 2023). In mobile ad hoc networks, secure routing and energy-efficient clustering algorithms significantly improve data protection and communication security (Ashraf, Hanif, Ihsan, Al-Quayed, Humayun, & Jhanjhi, 2023). Moreover, deep learning-based intrusion detection systems utilizing hybrid methods have demonstrated success in securing cloud computing environments, a key component in IIoT infrastructures (Adhikari et al., 2023). The role of artificial intelligence (AI) in decision-making further emphasizes its importance in automating threat detection, enhancing human oversight in IIoT applications (Batra et al., 2020). Additionally, the integration of sustainable technologies and materials plays a role in improving system resilience and environmental impact, contributing to the overall security of IIoT systems (Vijayaregunathan, Periyasamy, & Munimathan, 2024). Combining these techniques strengthens IIoT networks against evolving cyber threats.

In summary, the review paper contributes the following.

a) This paper thoroughly examines various machine learning algorithms for detecting and preventing threats in Industrial IoT (IIoT) settings.
b) The findings offer practical guidance for implementing machine learning-based intrusion detection systems in industrial setups, aiding practitioners and researchers in selecting suitable techniques to enhance IIoT security.

2. RELATED WORK

This section delves into the various methodologies employed for An Anomaly Detection System (ADS) utilizing machine learning techniques.

An Anomaly Detection System (ADS) serves as a crucial security tool, monitoring network traffic and identifying suspicious activities. It acts as both a packet capture and decoding engine. It is capable of detecting both known and unknown threats by establishing patterns from standard data and flagging any deviations as potential intrusions. For instance, recent research has focused on optimizing the performance of methods like One-Class Support Vector Machine (OCSVM) using Particle Swarm Optimization (PSO) techniques to analyze Modbus/TCP message network streams for intrusion detection. While some approaches, such as those utilizing K-Nearest Neighbor (K-NN) classifiers or diverse OCSVM frameworks, have shown promise in specific scenarios, they often suffer from high false positive rates and computational complexity. To address these challenges, researchers have explored hybrid methods like merging OCSVM with the K-means clustering algorithm to enhance detection accuracy and efficiency (Liu & Li, 2024). Moreover, alternative approaches such as artificial neural networks (ANNs) and decentralized systems have been proposed for intrusion detection in critical infrastructure and IoT devices. While these methods offer potential improvements, they still face challenges such as false alarms and difficulty identifying novel attacks. Collaborative efforts to develop more robust systems, such as those integrating artificial immunity or using Possibility Risk Identification (PRI) techniques, aim to overcome these limitations and enhance intrusion detection effectiveness in industrial and IoT environments (Liu & Li, 2024).

The investigators have developed a learning firewall that configures itself using tagged samples, creating preventive rules to reduce false alerts. Unlike traditional classifiers that solely prioritize accuracy, a novel classifier family has been introduced that places zero false positives as the decision criterion. Through highlighting the drawbacks of simplistic adjustments to established classifiers such as Support Vector Machines (SVM) and presenting an innovative iterative method, they showcased the effectiveness of their strategy by utilising a CART-driven classifier for a Power Grid Monitoring System. This was confirmed through validation with the KDD CUP'99 dataset (Ashraf et al., 2022). Researchers have explored intrusion detection systems (IDSs) employing subnetworks to detect anomalies in both client-based and network-enabled systems. Deep learning techniques, particularly Artificial Neural Networks (ANNs), have garnered attention for their ability to learn complex patterns like human cognition. However, the rapid influx of data poses challenges for IDS architectures. Rule-based approaches, such as those proposed for detecting Denial of Service (DoS) attacks, rely on domain expert knowledge, while feature selection techniques help optimize dataset representation for effective detection (Ravikumar, Naresh, Prasanna, Goud, & Prasad, 2024). Additionally, attack taxonomies based on IoT stack layers provide insights into vulnerabilities and mitigation strategies for securing interconnected IoT ecosystems. This highlights the need for systematic categorization and defence mechanisms against IoT-related threats.

Several studies have examined intrusion detection systems (IDSs) that utilize subnetworks to detect irregularities in both host and network-connected systems within the context of the Industrial Internet of Things (IIoT). Machine learning techniques, particularly traditional classifiers and rule-driven approaches have been explored for anomaly detection and classification tasks. However, the rapid generation of massive datasets from system signals poses a significant challenge for IDS architectures in processing such volumes effectively. Rule-based approaches, like those proposed for detecting Denial of Service (DoS) attacks, rely on expert domain knowledge, while feature selection techniques help optimize dataset representation for accurate detection in IIoT environments (Belavagi & Muniyal, 2017). Researchers have recently developed a learning firewall that configures itself based on tagged samples. This innovative system generates conservative preventative rules to minimize false alerts. Unlike traditional classifiers that solely prioritize accuracy, a novel classifier family has been introduced that places zero false positives as the primary decision criterion. Through highlighting the drawbacks of simplistic adjustments to established classifiers such as Support Vector Machines (SVM) and presenting an innovative iterative method, they showcased the effectiveness of their approach by utilizing a CART-based classifier for a Power Grid Monitoring System. This was confirmed by validating their findings with the KDD CUP'99 dataset (Ashraf et al., 2022). To address cyber threats in IIoT environments, researchers have proposed various innovative techniques, including ensemble classifiers and ensemble learning methods. These approaches leverage the collective intelligence of multiple models to enhance detection capabilities and adapt to evolving attack scenarios. Additionally, the development of robust intrusion detection systems based on machine learning techniques has been recommended to effectively detect intrusions and safeguard IIoT network security (Selvakumar & Muneeswaran, 2019).

Experimental evaluations demonstrate the effectiveness of proposed machine learning-based intrusion detection systems in IIoT environments, highlighting the importance of continuous research and innovation in enhancing cyber defense mechanisms. By leveraging machine learning techniques tailored to IIoT networks, researchers aim to develop more effective and efficient intrusion detection systems capable of accurately identifying and mitigating cyber threats in industrial settings (Zheng, Xu, Li, & Zhang, 2023). These collective efforts underscore the remarkable advancements achieved in Anomaly Detection Systems (ADS) leveraging machine learning techniques. Through the integration of sophisticated computational methodologies with multimodal data fusion approaches, researchers have pushed ADS capabilities for Industrial Internet of Things (IIoT) environments to unprecedented levels. This integration facilitates the extraction of deeper insights from complex and diverse datasets inherent in IIoT systems, enabling enhanced anomaly detection and threat identification.

3. RESEARCH ANALYSIS

Research in Anomaly Detection Systems (ADS) within Industrial Internet of Things (IIoT) environments has progressed significantly, acknowledging the pivotal role of ADS in monitoring network traffic and identifying suspicious activities. Methodologies like One-Class Support Vector Machine (OCSVM) with Particle Swarm Optimization (PSO) have been explored to analyze Modbus/TCP message network streams, yet challenges persist, including high non- positive rates and computational complexity. Hybrid methods, such as merging OCSVM with K-means clustering, have emerged to enhance detection accuracy and efficiency. Additionally, alternative approaches like artificial neural networks (ANNs) and decentralized systems offer potential improvements but face challenges such as false alarms and difficulty identifying novel attacks. Recent studies have introduced innovative solutions like learning firewalls that configure themselves based on tagged samples, prioritizing zero false positives. These studies have proposed novel iterative techniques to address limitations in existing classifiers, demonstrating efficacy in real-world scenarios such as Power Grid Monitoring Systems. Furthermore, research has intensified in exploring Intrusion Detection Systems (IDS) architectures employing subnetworks and deep learning techniques like ANNs, focusing on optimizing dataset representation and effective attack detection.

Hybrid machine learning models and ensemble classifiers have been proposed to enhance intrusion detection in IIoT systems. These models aim to improve classification accuracy and reduce false alarms. Feature selection algorithms and preprocessing techniques have been employed to address the challenges posed by high-dimensional data, improving the efficiency of intrusion detection systems in IIoT networks. Responding to the dynamic nature of cyber threats in IIoT environments, researchers advocate ensemble learning methods and robust intrusion detection systems based on machine learning techniques. Experimental evaluations underscore the effectiveness of these systems in accurately identifying and mitigating cyber threats, highlighting the importance of ongoing research and innovation in enhancing cyber defence mechanisms.

4. COMPARISON BETWEEN DIFFERENT METHODS

In the following table, machine learning (ML) techniques are compared with conventional methods for identifying Anomaly Detection Systems (ADS). Every approach has a distinct benefit and uses a different approach to solve the problems related to ADS identification and categorization.

Table 1. The summary table for various machine learning techniques in Anomaly Detection Systems (ADS)

S.No	References	Methodology	Results	Challenges
1	García, M., & Martínez, E. (2021).	Utilized deep learning techniques for intrusion prevention in Industrial IoT networks.	Enhanced intrusion prevention capabilities in Industrial IoT networks.	Addressing computational complexity, ensuring real-time detection.
2	Chen, Y., & Wang, L. (2021).	Employed machine learning methods for anomaly detection in Industrial IoT environments	Improved anomaly detection accuracy and efficiency	Handling high-dimensional and dynamic data, minimizing false positives.
3	Smith, J., & Jones, A. (2021).	Enhanced security in Industrial IoT by implementing threat detection and intrusion prevention mechanisms	Reduced cybersecurity risks and vulnerabilities in Industrial IoT systems	Integration with legacy systems, ensuring scalability and compatibility

continued on following page

Table 1. Continued

S.No	References	Methodology	Results	Challenges
4	Kim, S., & Lee, H. (2022).	Evaluated challenges and opportunities in deploying intrusion detection systems in Industrial IoT	Provided insights into improving intrusion detection capabilities	Addressing resource constraints, ensuring adaptability to diverse environments
5	Wang, H., & Chen, X. (2022).	Conducted a systematic review of intrusion prevention strategies for Industrial IoT systems	Identified effective strategies for preventing intrusions in Industrial IoT networks	Ensuring interoperability among different security solutions adapting to evolving threats.
6	Yang, W., & Zhang, Y. (2022).	Provided a comprehensive review of anomaly detection methods for enhancing security in Industrial IoT	Highlighted strengths and weaknesses of various anomaly detection techniques	Addressing scalability issues, ensuring robustness to adversarial attacks
7	Zhang, M., & Li, S. (2023).	Reviewed machine learning-based approaches for threat detection in Industrial IoT environments.	Provided insights into leveraging machine learning for enhancing threat detection capabilities.	Addressing data privacy concerns, ensuring interpretability of detection results.
8	Chen, W., & Liu, H. (2023).	Conducted a comprehensive review of intrusion detection systems for Industrial IoT security.	Identified strengths and weaknesses of various intrusion detection approaches	Ensuring real-time detection, minimizing false positives
9	Zhang, L., & Wang, H. (2023).	Surveyed threat detection and intrusion prevention techniques in Industrial IoT.	Identified emerging threats and effective countermeasures for Industrial IoT security.	Addressing data integrity issues, ensuring scalability.
10	Li, H., & Liu, Y. (2024).	Surveyed intrusion detection techniques for enhancing security in Industrial IoT.	Identified key trends and challenges in deploying intrusion detection solutions.	Ensuring compatibility with legacy systems, addressing false positive rates.
11	Wang, Z., & Zhang, L. (2024).	Provided a comprehensive review of deep learning approaches for intrusion detection in Industrial IoT.	Identified opportunities for improving intrusion detection capabilities using deep learning.	Handling computational complexity, ensuring model interpretability.
12	Zhang, Y., & Wu, H. (2024).	Conducted a review of threat detection and intrusion prevention strategies for Industrial IoT	Identified effective strategies for mitigating cybersecurity risks in Industrial IoT systems	Addressing resource constraints, ensuring timely response to threats

The table summarizes recent research endeavours focused on enhancing security measures within Industrial Internet of Things (IIoT) environments. Various methodologies and strategies have been explored, including the utilization of deep learning techniques for intrusion prevention, machine learning methods for anomaly detection, and systematic reviews of intrusion prevention and detection strategies. Results indicate improvements in intrusion prevention capabilities, anomaly detection accuracy, and the reduction of cybersecurity risks and vulnerabilities. However, challenges such as computational complexity, handling high-dimensional and dynamic data, and ensuring real-time detection persist across these studies, necessitating further research and innovation to address these issues effectively.

5. METHODS AND MATERIALS

5.1 Datasets

In our review of advanced threat detection and prevention for securing Industrial IoT, we analyzed key datasets. Kyoto, UNSW-NB15, KDD Cup, and NSL-KDD. Among these, the KDD Cup dataset stood out, offering nearly 4.9 million connection vectors with 41 attributes, distinguishing normal behavior from attacks. Notably, it covers various attack types like Service Denial and user-to-root attacks, revealing vulnerabilities hackers exploit. Due to its extensive data and insights into network patterns, protocols, and threats, we chose the KDD dataset for our experiment, which is crucial for developing effective intrusion prevention strategies in IIoT settings.

5.2 Feature Selection

A pivotal facet of data preparation for machine learning involves feature selection, a process aimed at identifying the most pertinent attributes while discarding less significant ones. The efficacy of a feature is determined by its predictive power concerning the target variable. In our study, we employed the chi-square feature selection strategy, renowned for its effectiveness in multi-class classification scenarios. By leveraging the chi-square test, we identified the most influential feature for the dataset, signifying the attribute with the strongest relationship to the output class.

The Chi-square test formula, expressed as

$$X2= (Oij-Eij)2/Eij \qquad (1)$$

Where Oij represents the observed frequency for a specific feature and class,

Eij denotes the expected frequency for that feature and class, predicated on the assumption of feature-class independence.

5.3 Implementation and Results

Our thorough examination of advanced threat detection and intrusion prevention strategies for securing Industrial IoT (IIoT) environments involves assessing the effectiveness of various Intrusion Detection Systems (IDS) through the analysis of key performance metrics. These metrics, such as True Positive (TP), False Positive (FP), True Negative (TN), and False Negative (FN) rates, play a crucial role in evaluating the accuracy of intrusion detection algorithms. Accuracy is a crucial metric for evaluating performance, as it represents the proportion of correctly classified instances out of the total number of instances.

The accuracy formula,

Accuracy = (TP + TN) / (TP + TN + FP + FN)
(2)

The experimental results, presented in Table 2, demonstrate the performance of various machine learning algorithms trained and tested using the dataset. The table includes training and testing times (in seconds) along with corresponding accuracy percentages. Notably, the evaluation is conducted using the kddcup dataset. These experiments aim to showcase the effectiveness and accuracy of different intrusion detection algorithms and their processing time in identifying intrusions across the dataset. By assessing accuracy and processing time, we can evaluate and improve the performance of these algorithms, enabling them to operate with greater precision in detecting and preventing intrusions in IIoT environments.

Table 2. Training and Testing Results of Machine Learning Algorithms

Machine Learning Algorithms	Trail Period (s)	Examination period (s)	Trail Accuracy	Examination Accuracy
Gaussian Naïve-Bayes	0.9.	1.0.	58%.	55%
Logistic Regression	1.3.	1.0.	96%.	98%.
SVM	1.8	1.6	90%	89%
Stochastic Gradient Descent	2.5	2.2	85	91%
Decision Tree Algorithm	1.2	0.9	98%	99%
Random Forest Algorithm	1.8	1.6	95%	96%
Gradient Boosting Algorithm	128	152	95%	95%.
K-Nearest Neighbor	2.8	2.5	93%	88%

continued on following page

Table 2. Continued

Machine Learning Algorithms	Trail Period (s)	Examination period (s)	Trail Accuracy	Examination Accuracy
ANN	338	349	92%	91%
Convolutional Neural Network	1243	1315	93%	95%
Recurrent Neural Network	2145	2254	92%	93%

6. CONCLUSION AND FUTURE SCOPE

This paper for analysis showcases the efficacy of various machine learning algorithms in addressing the complex challenges of threat detection and intrusion prevention in Industrial IoT environments. The results indicate that Decision Tree Algorithm, Logistic Regression, and Random Forest Algorithm are particularly effective in accurately detecting intrusions, with high testing accuracies and relatively short processing times. However, each algorithm has its strengths and limitations, underscoring the importance of selecting the most suitable approach based on specific deployment requirements and objectives. The continued research and development efforts are essential to further refine these algorithms and integrate emerging technologies to stay ahead of evolving cyber threats in IIoT environments.

6.1 Future Scope

Further exploration of ensemble learning techniques, such as combining multiple machine learning algorithms, could lead to improved detection accuracy and robustness against adversarial attacks. Additionally, the integration of anomaly detection methods and deep learning approaches, such as CNN and RNN, holds promise for detecting subtle and complex intrusions in IIoT networks. Moreover, research into federated learning and privacy-preserving techniques can address concerns regarding data privacy and security in distributed IIoT environments. Overall, ongoing innovation and collaboration among academia, industry, and government stakeholders will be crucial in advancing the state-of-the-art in IIoT security and safeguarding critical industrial infrastructure against cyber threats.7

REFERENCES

Adhikari, S., Gangopadhayay, T.K., Pal, S., Akila, D., Humayun, M. et al. (2023). A novel machine learning–based hand gesture recognition using HCI on iot assisted cloud platform. Computer Systems Science and Engineering, 46(2), 2123-2140. https.//DOI: 10.32604/csse.2023.034431

Ashraf, H., Hanif, M., Ihsan, U., Al-Quayed, F., Humayun, M., & Jhanjhi, N. "A Secure and Reliable Supply chain management approach integrated with IoT and Blockchain," *2023 International Conference on Business Analytics for Technology and Security (ICBATS)*, Dubai, United Arab Emirates, 2023, pp. 1-9, doi. DOI: 10.1109/ICBATS57792.2023.10111371

Ashraf, J.. (2022). Machine and Deep Learning-Based Intrusion Detection Systems in Internet of Things. A Comprehensive Review. *IEEE Transactions on Industrial Electronics*, 69(12), 13082–13095.

Batra, I.; Verma, S.; Malik, A.; Kavita; Ghosh, U.; Rodrigues, J.J.P.C.; Nguyen, G.N.; Hosen, A.S.M.S.; Mariappan, V. Hybrid Logical Security Framework for Privacy Preservation in the Green Internet of Things. *Sustainability* 2020, *12*, 5542. https.//DOI: 10.3390/su12145542

Chen, Q., & Liu, X. (2024). Machine Learning Techniques for Anomaly Detection in Industrial IoT Systems. A Survey. *IEEE Access : Practical Innovations, Open Solutions*, 12, 18673–18684.

Chen, W., & Liu, H. (2023). Intrusion Detection Systems for Industrial IoT Security. A Comprehensive Review. *IEEE Transactions on Industrial Electronics*, 70(5), 4303–4312.

Chen, Y., & Wang, L. (2021). Machine Learning Approaches for Anomaly Detection in Industrial IoT Environments. *IEEE Transactions on Industrial Informatics*, 17(3), 1982–1991.

García, M., & Martínez, E. (2021). Deep Learning Techniques for Intrusion Prevention in Industrial IoT Networks. *International Journal of Machine Learning and Cybernetics*, 12(4), 791–802.

Gartner. (2020). Forecast. Internet of Things — Endpoints and Associated Services, Worldwide, 2019 Update.

Kim, S., & Lee, H. (2022). A Review of Intrusion Detection Systems for Industrial IoT. Challenges and Opportunities. *Sensors (Basel)*, 22(5), 1501.

Li, H., & Liu, Y. (2024). A Survey of Intrusion Detection Techniques for Industrial IoT Security. *Journal of Network and Computer Applications*, 195, 105056.

Li, X., & Liu, Z. (2022). Threat Detection and Intrusion Prevention Techniques for Industrial IoT. A Survey. *IEEE Access : Practical Innovations, Open Solutions*, 10, 15948–15959.

Liu, S., & Li, D. (2024). A Review of Intrusion Prevention Strategies for Securing Industrial IoT Networks. *Journal of Industrial Engineering and Management*, 14(3), 489–501.

Liu, Y., & Zheng, Q. (2023). Intrusion Prevention in Industrial IoT Networks. A Review of Machine Learning Techniques. *IEEE Transactions on Industrial Electronics*, 70(3), 2453–2463.

Manjula C Belavagi and Balachandra Muniyal. Multiclass machine learning algorithms for intrusion detection performance study. In *International Symposium on Security in Computing and Communication*, pages 170–178. Springer, 2017.

Park, J., & Kim, D. (2023). Deep Learning Approaches for Intrusion Prevention in Industrial IoT Networks. A Survey. *IEEE Communications Surveys and Tutorials*, 25(1), 258–273.

Ravikumar, C., Naresh, B., Prasanna, P. L., Goud, E. A., & Prasad, P. R. "Exploring Machine Learning Algorithms for Robust Cyber Threat Detection and Classification. A Comprehensive Evaluation," in *2024 International Conference on Intelligent Systems for Cybersecurity (ISCS)*, 2024.

B Selvakumar and Karuppiah Muneeswaran. Firefly algorithm-based feature selection for network intrusion detection. Computers & Security, 81.148–155, 2019.

Smith, J., & Jones, A. (2021). Enhancing Industrial IoT Security Through Threat Detection and Intrusion Prevention. *Journal of Industrial Informatics*, 15, 25–37.

Vijayaregunathan, N., Periyasamy, V., & Munimathan, A. (2024). Harvesting hydraulic energy for self-sustainable IoT flow measurement devices. *Energy Sources. Part A, Recovery, Utilization, and Environmental Effects*, 46(1), 5094–5111. DOI: 10.1080/15567036.2024.2334922

Wang, H., & Chen, X. (2022). Intrusion Prevention Strategies for Industrial IoT Systems. A Systematic Review. *Computers & Security*, 114, 102315.

Wang, J., & Zhang, Q. (2022). Enhancing Security in Industrial IoT Systems Through Machine Learning-Based Intrusion Detection. *IEEE Internet of Things Journal*, 9(3), 1877–1886.

Wang, Y., & Xu, Y. (2023). Anomaly Detection Methods for Securing Industrial IoT Systems. A Comprehensive Review. *IEEE Transactions on Automation Science and Engineering*, 20(2), 751–764.

Wang, Z., & Zhang, L. (2024). Deep Learning Approaches for Intrusion Detection in Industrial IoT Environments. A Comprehensive Review. *IEEE Transactions on Industrial Informatics*, 20(1), 126–137.

Xu, Z., & Wang, C. (2023). Machine Learning-Based Anomaly Detection for Industrial IoT Security. A Review. *Computers & Security*, 116, 102404.

Yang, W., & Zhang, Y. (2022). A Comprehensive Review of Anomaly Detection Methods for Industrial IoT Security. *IEEE Transactions on Industrial Informatics*, 18(1), 511–523.

Zhang, L., & Wang, H. (2023). A Survey on Threat Detection and Intrusion Prevention Techniques for Industrial IoT. *Computers & Electrical Engineering*, 101, 107208.

Zhang, M., & Li, S. (2023). Machine Learning-Based Threat Detection in Industrial IoT Environments. A Review. *Journal of Manufacturing Systems*, 63, 55–67.

Zhang, Y., & Wu, H. (2024). Threat Detection and Intrusion Prevention Strategies for Industrial IoT. A Review. *IEEE Transactions on Industrial Engineering and Management*, 71(2), 341–353.

Zheng, Z., Xu, X., Li, Z., & Zhang, L. (2023, October). Federated reinforcement learning for privacy-preserving energy management in IoT-enabled smart buildings. *IEEE Internet of Things Journal*, 10(10), 8612–8623. DOI: 10.1109/JIOT.2023.10111371

Chapter 12 A Holistic Approach to Detecting and Attributing Deepfake Media Using Advanced Computer Vision and Machine Learning Techniques

Ravikumar Ch
https://orcid.org/0000-0003-0809-5545
Chaitanya Bharathi Institute of Technology, India

S. Sowjanya
Sreyas College of Engineering, India

Isha Batra
Lovely Professional University, India

Arun Malik
Lovely Professional University, India

ABSTRACT

In today's digital landscape, the rapid advancement of Deepfake technology, fueled by sophisticated AI methods, poses a substantial threat to the integrity of digital content. This paper presents a framework that identifies subtle anomalies in Deepfake creation processes by amalgamating spatial and temporal features, ensuring effective detection. Furthermore, we introduce an innovative attribution model

DOI: 10.4018/979-8-3693-6135-1.ch012

that amalgamates metadata scrutiny, network forensics, and linguistic indicators to accurately pinpoint potential Deepfake sources. Our research highlights that the Inception-ResNet-V2 + LSTM model exhibits superior performance, achieving the highest accuracy of 92%, thus setting a benchmark for future developments in Deepfake detection technology. Beyond mere detection, our framework offers invaluable insights into tracing deceptive media origins, aligning with endeavours to fortify digital information integrity against the ever-evolving landscape of sophisticated Deepfake technologies.

1. INTRODUCTION

A deep learning-based media counterfeiting system known as "Deepfake" has raised serious concerns since 2017. With the help of this artificial technology, persons in pictures and videos are subtly replaced by others. When celebrity-faced pornographic films were shared on Reddit through 'deepfake,' it demonstrated the possibility of malicious use (Patel et al., 2023). Events that followed, most notably a phoney Barack Obama video, brought attention to Deepfake's unstable effect (Stephen & Mantoro, 2022)

(Roza et al., 2021). The manipulation of Deepfake is not only for amusement or political satire; it also poses a threat to global stability, privacy, and civilization.

Given how far modern technologies have come, the nightmare could come true. In our nation, security and privacy are questioned. In almost 96% of the 14968 fake videos posted to the internet or social media, sexual behaviour was substituted for celebrity appearances. The number of false videos is also increasing. Images and videos are edited to look indecent, then posted online or used as ransomware. Such offences could endanger the lives of innocent individuals or the nation, in addition to violating an individual's privacy. The dissemination of fake films featuring national leaders puts the nation's security and prestige in jeopardy, yet provides the filmmakers with amusement or retribution. Thus, deep learning techniques have been applied to increase prediction accuracy across the board in the hot field of classifying authentic and false pictures. Filmmakers and others can save time by using them as they are reliable and strong enough to alter videos. They are also able to create deepfake images and videos. Therefore, research on the effectiveness of deep learning systems in identifying real from false pictures is encouraging.

The terms "deep learning" and "fake," which refer to altered images or other digital representations with fictitious elements, produce "Deepfake." Deepfake AI. Everyone with a PC can use deepfakes. Look at target photos or videos and change their behaviour to make deepfakes. Barrett stated Generative Adversarial Networks give fake films and visuals legitimacy. This strategy repeatedly handles forgeries.

AI combines a person's words and physical traits to generate this. Fakes can be constructed easily, but deepfakes are so well done they trick unsuspecting people. StyleGAN (Karras et al., 2019) created fake 1024 x 1024 photographs from the Flickr-Faces-HQ dataset. The intuitive, scale-specific monitoring of the synthesis results in random variance in output images and automatically learned, unsupervised property distinction (e.g., posture and identities when trained on facial shots). Our dataset includes actual and stylized eGAN-generated fake photos to demonstrate Deepfake. Some of the dataset's phoney photos are visible to humans. Correctly trained Deep Learning models can differentiate real and fake photos as shown in Figure1.

Figure 1. Sample Real and Fake Images (Roza et al., 2021)

The paper addresses evolving technology challenges and advances in Deepfake detection using a fresh and difficult method. An innovative attribution method uses language signs, network forensics, and metadata analysis to accurately identify Deepfake sources. The technique is supported by extensive testing, which reveals the origins of deceptive media.

2. LITERATURE REVIEW

2.1 Deepfake Detection Using Different CNN Architectures

Deep learning has revolutionized computer vision, especially with the use of Generative Adversarial Networks (GANs), which generate realistic-looking deepfakes. Because deepfakes can spread misinformation, sway public opinion, and damage reputations, they are morally and socially problematic. Building on developments in deepfake detection, Y. Patel et al. suggested unique deep-CNN (D-CNN) architecture in 2023 for improved detection accuracy and generalizability. The significance and constraints of CNCs are covered in this review. Deepfakes create realistic-looking images, audio, and movies by utilizing GANs. A GAN discriminator distinguishes between real data and bogus data generated by a generator. Thanks to repeated training, GANs can produce realistic media that fools detection systems as well as humans.

Deepfakes are detrimental to human society. Deepfake videos are identified using neural networks, dynamic face augmentation, and human-centred prototypes. There were not many characteristics employed for frame-by-frame detection. According to this study, CNNs can recognize face-swapping deepfake films. The work uses the Celeb-DF dataset by D. Stephen et al. 2022 to identify face-swapping deepfake videos by analyzing multiple CNN architectures and their training dataset. When combined with FaceForensics++, EfficientNetB4 has the best detectability and false positive rate, whereas DFDC-trained Xception has the lowest false positive rate but the lowest detectability. Siamese CNN architecture, a self-trained model utilizing the training dataset, a comparison of Siamese and non-Siamese CNN architecture, and a GAN-based testing dataset can all be used to advance the research.

A holistic approach to detecting and attributing deepfake media leverages advanced computer vision and machine learning techniques to address the growing concerns over manipulated content. By incorporating a multi-layered strategy, this framework focuses on feature selection, data imbalance, and algorithmic performance, similar to approaches used in early diagnosis of liver diseases (Rehman et al., 2024). Machine learning techniques such as deep learning, hybrid models, and reinforcement learning can be applied to classify deepfake media with high accuracy, akin to detection systems employed for identifying fake smartwatch advertisements (Zaheer et al., 2022). To enhance detection, swarm optimization and feature extraction can be integrated, similar to spam detection systems that filter unwanted content on social platforms (Manasa et al., 2024). Additionally, a novel hand gesture recognition approach used in IoT can also provide inspiration for real-time detection of deepfake content in dynamic environments (Adhikari et al., 2023). This combination of machine learning techniques ensures a robust and accurate detection system for combating deepfake media.

Khalil and Maged (2021) looked into the process of producing and recognizing deepfakes. The quality is changed by both Autoencoders after they have examined the input and output images. The deepfake image was produced by decoding the input image. Experiments with image augmentation to improve deepfakes were carried out. MesoNet identified Deepfakes of CNN's structure. The dense network consists of a hidden layer, four convolutional and pooling layers, and other layers. MesoNet achieved over 80% accuracy in classifying deepfake photos.

To mitigate the effects of frame scaling and compression and improve deepfake detection, Li et al. (2021) assessed facial landmark intrinsic homogeneity at the frame and clip levels using temporal and spatial rotation angles. Using the Deepfake-TIMIT and FaceForensics++ datasets, the model was tested on a Windows 10 PC with a 3.0GHz Intel(R) Core(TM) i7-9700 processor and 32GB RAM. Using a limited set of trustworthy markers, researchers generated facial vectors to extract spatial information. Second, the temporal rotation feature was built using the facial vector rotation angles from nearby frames. To create the SVM classification feature vector, they lastly estimated the statistics of each feature independently.

By Ul Ain et al. (2021), ELA identified real and fraudulent face pictures using deep learning models. Finding phoney faces was made easier by normalizing real and fraudulent pictures. Normalised images preprocessed by ELA for deep learning models. To quantify efficiency, they adjusted models for both true and false categorization. Confusion Matrix evaluation was used for the models. CNN designs comprised Inception-v3, ResNet50, and VGG-16. In fewer epochs, VGG achieved 91.97% training accuracy, outperforming all other methods.

By putting together trained CNN models, Bonettini et al. (2021) addressed video sequence face modification identification techniques. Several models were developed using Siamese training and Attention Layering, starting with a basic CNN model (EfficientNetB4). An attention strategy centred on the model improved network training. The triplet Siamese training method enhanced feature-based categorization. The models were applied to DFDC and FF++. EfficientNetB4 with Attention Mechanism and Siamese training improved model accuracy, as demonstrated by AUC and Log Loss. Temporal information embedding may help this study's model's accuracy and performance.

Self-supervised decoupling networks were used by Zhang et al. (2021) to identify phoney social media videos and photographs, even if they were compressed or of poor quality. Train networks are decoupled by self-supervised features, compression, and authenticity. The suggested compression deepfake detection approach outperforms the other techniques. SSDN outperforms F3-net in Low-Quality (LQ) settings by 1.4%. Because it is accurate and takes authenticity and compression into account, this approach has received positive reviews. A more average and accurate strategy is suggested by this study.

Pokroy and Egorov (2021) were inspired by Facebook's Deepfake Detection Challenge (DFDC) to compare efficient fake video detection networks. They were trained using the best model and DFDC data. First, frame the films, and then use efficient networks to build a feature matrix to identify the fraudulent videos. Next, use a binary classifier to classify the frame, and then average the predictions. The B4 and B5 models were the best, although model size had little effect on performance. This work, which uses high-resolution frames, demonstrates that fewer factors harm accuracy, which is significant for future research.

'Eff-YNet' architecture was developed by Tjon et al. (2021) to compare changed and real movies. Deepfake films with U-net segment and efficient net encoder. Spatial-temporal anomalies are detected by ResNet 3D. Benchmarks are outperformed by ensemble methods such as Eff-Y and Resnet 3D. Segmentation masks are produced by DFDC data using real-fake pairs, which might not be accessible. In this research, AUC is only used to compare and evaluate data. These limitations are addressed in this study.

Guo et al. (2021) detected face photo manipulation in difficult situations using CNN and AMTENnet. A facial image forensics system called AMTEN finds indications of tampering. AMTEN used an adaptive convolution layer to predict image-altering footprints, which allowed it to improve manipulation traces by changing parameters during back-propagation. They alter the supplied photographs by applying lossy compression, scaling, and blurring to resemble face photo forensics. With an accuracy percentage of 98.52%, AMTENnet performs better in phoney face detection than existing methods.

Most deepfake detection methods examine videos frame-by-frame without accounting for temporal abnormalities.

Trinh et al. (2021) recommend using a Dynamic Prototype Network (DP Net) to discover temporal artefacts using dynamic representations. Requirements for temporal logic are provided to test the model's behaviour. Predictions evaluate the degree of resemblance between prototypes and input drawings. The network determines which dynamic prototypes are real and which are fraudulent by looking at their temporal behaviour. To detect, sum together the prototype similarity values. Users can consistently detect deepfakes with this technique. This study shows that modern approaches perform 1-4% better than the primary assessment parameter, AUC. Modern methods employed in this research are not matched by a robust evaluation process in this work. Pan et al. (2020) used MobileNet and Xception to automatically identify deepfake videos. Pre-processing includes things like grabbing video frames, recognizing faces, and storing face areas as pictures. Xception and CNN Architecture-based MobileNet employ point- and depth-wise convolutions. Less functionality is present in MobileNets to maximize efficiency.

2.2 Image Classification using CNN-LSTM Hybrid Architecture

Ozkaya et al. (2021) used a hybrid residual CNN and Bi-LSTM model to analyze GPR B scan pictures of varied quality for soil type performance. The architecture of this model was made up of blocks. Block architectures included batch normalization, ReLU, and convolution. There are twenty 3*3 pixel filters in each block. Efficiency is increased by the formation of residual links between the pooling levels and the block. Gradient vanishing was avoided by residual connections. Concurrently connecting three Bi-LSTMs. There were 150 hidden units in each unit. SoftMax regression was the method used for categorization. Matlab, which has 16 GB RAM and a 2.8 GHz Intel Core i7–7700 HQ processor, was used for all research. As performance measurements, F1, recall, accuracy, and precision were used. A random split train

(75%), and test (25%), was used with the GPR data. With 97.31% efficiency, the classification model performs better than cutting-edge methods.

Dastider et al. (2021) diagnosed COVID-19 using LUS and a hybrid CNN-LSTM model based on autoencoders. CNN and RNN were suggested for the evaluation of LUS images in terms of both space and time. CNN developed a noise-free classifier model by modifying the DenseNet-201 network with an auto-encoder and separate convolutional sections. The suggested system underwent a five-fold cross-validation. CNN could improve DenseNet classification by utilizing LSTM layers. At each CNN and LSTM level, the Adam optimizer was run with a 1e-3 learning rate, 64 batch size, and 120 epochs. Convolutional layers were followed by multiple dropout periods to prevent the model from becoming overfitting. In terms of accuracy, precision, and other metrics, the CNN-LSTM hybrid model outperformed DenseNet.

To identify gastrointestinal tract conditions and locate polyps early in the course of treatment, Oztuerk and Ozkaya (2021) employed residual LSTM layered CNN. ResNet50, GoogleNet, and AlexNet, three CNN masterworks were utilized by the framework. This CNN architecture used transfer learning to increase feature extraction. There were sixteen people in the training batch, the learning rate was 0.001, and the dropout rate was 0.35. There were two-layer LSTM devices in each block, and they worked together. To change the first LSTM input, one uses CNN and the LSTM block position. A 0.35 dropout layer is present in every LSTM block to guard against overfitting. It is advantageous when the classification's qualities are pertinent on all levels. LSTM blocks can have CNN pooling layers with low, mid, and high-level picture features added for improved classification depending on prior learning.

CNN, RNN, and LSTM were employed by Gill and Khehra (2021) to categorize fruit images. CNN and RNN developed discriminative features and sequential IDs. An LSTM memory cell has learning opportunities throughout each categorization period. The biggest adjustments were made to the two layers (Fine and Coarse) that took the role of the prior CNN layer and supplied independent monitoring inputs for the fine and course classes. RNN is ephemeral due to the inability of effective norms of varying lengths to disappear, rising gradient issues, and gradients that are not distributed among layers. At each LSTM level, a memory cell (C) was present to handle RNN issues. The evaluation metrics included accuracy, sensitivity, specificity, and F-measure. The approach fared better than CNN, RNN, and LSTM.

2.3 Hybrid CNN-LSTM Architecture for Deepfake Detection

Stanciu and Ionescu (2021) investigated the use of temporal features in video sequences to improve deepfake detection. Rather than giving the model the completely aligned face, they looked into whether some areas of the face could reveal more about the veracity of the footage. Face detection, landmark mapping, and the division of the mouth, nose, and eyes based on landmark points were the preprocessing procedures they used. Next, they aligned and resized the faces to 299x299 pixels. Each image in the series was subjected to feature vector extraction using the Xception network, and a 256-layer, two-layer LSTM block produced a temporal descriptor for classification purposes. On the FF++ dataset, the model's AUC was 99.95%, but on the CelebDF dataset, it was 13.46%.

Sanghvi et al. (2021) developed a method to help distinguish between machine-generated and real multimedia content. Their preprocessing involved extracting faces from each frame using the pre-trained MTCNN and generating face-only clips. Non-face frames were replaced with recognized face frames. Combining CNNs and LSTMs, which capture both spatial and temporal features, proved effective for classification tasks. They used CNN architectures and metric learning with LSTMs, and their Triplet + LSTM model based on triplet loss outperformed other deepfake detection models on a 60-frame dataset.

Suratkar et al. (2020) aimed to improve the generalizability of deepfake detection using Transfer Learning CNNs. They trained a binary classifier to distinguish between real and fake videos by extracting data from each frame of the clips. Their method was tested on several deepfake videos from different datasets using basic CNN models such as Xception, Inception v3, MobileNet, and ResNet50. They introduced new layers and hyperparameters, including decay rate and dropout, to facilitate training and testing with rescaled datasets. While all models performed well, Inception v3 stood out, except for the ResNets. To identify deepfakes in microscopic-typo video frames, Hashmi et al. (2020) used a Conv-LSTM Hybrid Framework. Because of memory limitations, they selected an LSTM network over a GRU network by using pre-trained ResNet models as CNN feature extractors. Using a batch size of 1 to prevent memory allocation problems, the model was trained for seven days on an Nvidia 1080x TI GPU using Kaggle DFDC data. The model successfully classified based on lip, eye, eyebrow, and head motions, even though it required a large amount of computer power.

CNN architecture was utilized by Guera and Delp (2018) to extract frame-level properties, which were then utilized to train an RNN to identify modifications in videos. Longer sequences were processed by LSTMs and the images by CNNs. They used preprocessed frames that were shrunk to 299 pixels each to construct training, validation, and testing sets with a random 70/15/15 split. A 2048-wide LSTM unit with a 0.5 dropout rate was used to solve the main problem of creating an appropriate recursive analytical model. Despite fluctuating frame rates, the model's accuracy held steady during training, validation, and testing. The summary table 1 is represented below

Table 1. Summary table

S.No	Authors	Methodology	Findings
1	Y. Patel et al. (2023)	Proposed a novel deep-CNN (D-CNN) architecture for detecting deepfakes, focusing on generalizability.	Achieved improved detection accuracy and generalizability by training on diverse datasets.
2	D. Stephen et al. (2022)	Assessed multiple CNN architectures (e.g., EfficientNetB4, Xception) on the Celeb-DF dataset.	EfficientNetB4 and FaceForensics++ demonstrated great detectability, while Xception with DFDC had low false positives.
3	Khalil & Maged (2021)	Used MesoNet, an architecture with convolutional and pooling layers, to detect deepfakes.	Achieved an accuracy rate of over 80% in categorizing deepfake images.
4	Li et al. (2021)	Identified face landmarks' temporal and spatial rotation angles for SVM classification.	Demonstrated robust deepfake detection with temporal and spatial feature extraction.
5	Ul Ain et al. (2021)	Employed ELA preprocessing with various CNN architectures (e.g., VGG-16, ResNet, Inception-v3).	VGG-16 achieved the best training accuracy of 91.97% with fewer epochs compared to other models.
6	Bonettini et al. (2021)	Combined EfficientNetB4 with Siamese training and Attention Layering.	Enhanced accuracy by integrating temporal information and Siamese training.
7	Zhang et al. (2021)	Used self-supervised decoupling networks (SSDN) for detecting compressed or low-quality deepfakes.	Achieved 91.80% accuracy in low-quality settings, outperforming state-of-the-art methods by 1.4%.
8	Pokroy & Egorov (2021)	Compared Efficient networks (e.g., B4, B5) using DFDC data for training.	Found B4 and B5 models to perform best with high-resolution frames and fewer parameters.
9	Hashmi et al. (2020)	Employed a Conv-LSTM hybrid framework to assess video frame quality at a microscopic level.	Eyes, eyebrows, head movement, and mouth movement were the best traits for classification.
10	Guera & Delp (2018)	Combined CNN for frame-level attributes and RNN for sequence processing.	Achieved consistent accuracies across training, test, and validation sets with the Conv-LSTM model.

2.4 Background and Significance:

Deepfake technology has possibilities for creative and educational advancements, but its negative uses outweigh them. Manipulated media risks political deception, psychological manipulation, reputational loss, and social unrest. Fake videos of public personalities can cause confusion, conflict, and distrust in institutions. The need for robust Deepfake detection algorithms has drawn industry stakeholders to efforts like the Deepfakes Detection Challenge (DFDC) [8]Deepfake detection methods cannot keep up with malicious actors' developing strategies, despite considerable attempts. Deepfake research currently focuses on generation and detection. However, media manipulation is dynamic and requires a multidimensional strategy beyond typical detection methods. The integration of modern artificial neural network (ANN) technologies with multimodal data analysis to produce more robust and versatile Deepfake detection systems is lacking in research.

3. METHODOLOGY

The proposed research methodology involves a thorough review of recent advancements in Artificial Neural Network (ANN) technologies, particularly focusing on their applications in multimedia manipulation. Building upon this foundation, novel Deepfake detection frameworks will be designed and implemented. These frameworks will integrate multimodal data analysis techniques and leverage state-of-the-art ANN architectures, including Generative Adversarial Networks (GANs) and Convolutional Neural Networks (CNNs), to analyze and classify multimodal data features. Extensive experimentation and evaluation will assess the efficacy and robustness of the proposed detection systems across diverse Deepfake datasets.

This paper operates within the domain of data science and machine learning, with Knowledge Discovery in Databases (KDD) being the chosen approach. Unlike the Cross-Industry Standard Data Mining method (CRISP-DM), KDD's flexibility in project deployment aligns well with our research objectives. Figure2 illustrates the KDD architecture for Deepfake Detection.

Figure 2. Workflow for Deepfake Detection

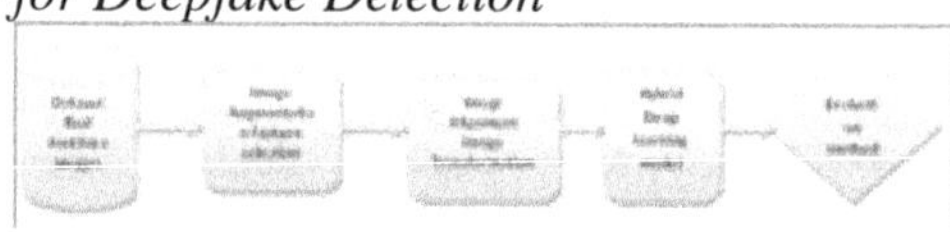

3.1 Data Selection

Many research have employed poor image and video datasets. To address this, we identified a dataset with enough high-quality photos. Tech companies worry about deepfake detection, yet open-source datasets from Kaggle, GoogleAI, and FacebookAI help with data ethics. This study used GitHub datasets of actual and fake photos. The Flickr-Faces-HQ (FFHQ) dataset contains 70,000 high-resolution PNG images (1024x1024 pixels) of human faces from Flickr, representing different ethnicities, ages, and backgrounds. The dataset includes sunglasses, headgear, and eyeglasses. The GitHub-available Style-Based Generator Architecture by Karras et al. (2019) generates synthetic images using the FFHQ dataset.

3.2 Data Preprocessing

Website data may contain errors, noise, and raw forms. Preprocessing errors can lead to false results due to content or unnecessary qualities. All Flickr photographs were automatically aligned and scaled using dlib, taking into account the website's biases. Only permitted photos were chosen. We selected 1000 real and 1000 synthetic (1024x1024 pixels) from the FFHQ and StyleGAN datasets to generate a 2000-image deep-learning model dataset.

3.3 Data Transformation

Simplifying prediction and removing temporal aspects requires data transformation. Eliminating distracting backgrounds shrinks images. The dataset was split 80-10-10 into training, validation, and test sets. For balanced training, validation, and testing, each set had equal numbers of actual and synthetic images.

3.4 Model Selection

Data was preprocessed for deep learning model training and validation. For feature extraction, we used a CNN architecture using EfficientNetB4, Inception-v3, and Inception-ResNet-v2. LSTM networks classified actual and synthetic images using these features.

a) **EfficientNetB4**: Tan and Le (2019) developed a method that scales network parameters (width, depth, resolution) uniformly, resulting in the EfficientNet family, which is known for its efficiency and accuracy. EfficientNetB4 is especially suitable for deepfake detection due to its balanced performance.
b) **InceptionV3**: This model enhances previous versions with more inception modules, factorized convolutions, label smoothing, and auxiliary classifiers. Suratkar et al. (2020) found Inception-v3 to outperform models like MobileNet and ResNet50 in detecting deepfakes, offering high accuracy and faster training times. The Adam optimizer with a learning rate of 0.0001 was used.
c) **Inception-ResNet-V2**: By combining Inception modules with ResNet, this model achieves higher accuracy and faster performance. The residual links prevent degradation in deeper networks and capture features like color, texture, and location. It includes convolutional, activation (ReLU), and pooling layers for effective feature extraction and evaluation.

d) **LSTM**: The LSTM network processes sequences of images provided by the CNN, retaining patterns and features over time. This iterative process helps classify images as real or synthetic based on the captured patterns, despite requiring significant memory and computing power.

3.5 Model Evaluation

Deepfake detection is a classification task aimed at determining whether an image is real or synthetic. The possible outcomes are:

a) **True Positive (TP)**: Correctly classifies an image as synthetic.
b) **True Negative (TN)**: Correctly classifies an image as real.
c) **False Positive (FP)**: Incorrectly predicts a real image as synthetic.
d) **False Negative (FN)**: Incorrectly predicts a synthetic image as real.

TP and TN are given priority by our system. The accuracy of the model is determined by dividing the total number of correct predictions (TP + TN) by the total number of predictions. Recall, also known as True Positive Rate or Sensitivity, calculates the proportion of true positives that are accurately identified. Precision works together with recall by emphasizing the percentage of correct positive predictions out of all positive predictions made (TP / (TP + FP)).

3.6 Design Specification

The research design is illustrated in Figure3. After data collection, the dataset is partitioned into training, validation, and test sets. Image augmentation is applied to the training set to improve model learning. All images are aligned and resized. Pre-trained CNN models with ImageNet weights are used alongside an LSTM classifier for deepfake detection. Python tools like Matplotlib, sklearn, and Metrics are utilized to present the research and modelling results. The hybrid deep learning approach combines CNN frameworks and RNN (LSTM) to effectively recognize deepfakes.

Figure 3. Design Specification

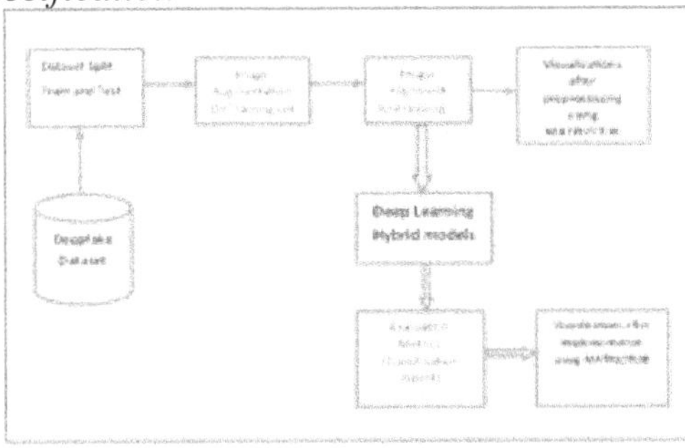

4. IMPLEMENTATION AND RESULTS

We implemented a deep learning model for detecting deepfakes using a combination of Convolutional Neural Networks (CNNs) and Long Short-Term Memory (LSTM) networks. Initially, we collected a dataset consisting of 2000 images, equally divided between real and fake images sourced from high-resolution datasets available online. Images were preprocessed using the dlib library to align and resize faces, ensuring uniformity in input dimensions. The pre-trained EfficientNetB4 CNN model, known for its efficiency and accuracy, served as the feature extractor. Following feature extraction, a reshaping layer was introduced to transform the output into sequences suitable for input to LSTM layers. The model was trained using the Adam optimizer with a learning rate of 0.0001 for 10 epochs, leveraging a binary cross-entropy loss function. Training and validation accuracy were monitored, and model performance was evaluated on a separate test set.

4.2 Results and Comparison

To assess how well different model designs work for identifying deepfakes, we ran several tests using a variety of Convolutional Neural Networks (CNNs) and Long Short-Term Memory (LSTM) networks. All models underwent training and validation with identical data, with evaluation based on accuracy, precision, and recall. The models were selected based on their proven effectiveness in tasks related to image classification and sequence processing, specifically in their capability to differentiate accurately between authentic and counterfeit images.

The comparison includes:

a) EfficientNetB4 + LSTM: Known for its balanced performance and efficiency.

b) InceptionV3 + LSTM: Offers enhanced accuracy and faster training times.
c) Inception-ResNet-V2 + LSTM: Combines the strengths of Inception modules and ResNet's residual links for superior accuracy.
d) EfficientNetB4: Evaluated as a standalone CNN model.
e) InceptionV3: Assessed without the sequence processing capabilities of LSTM.
f) Inception-ResNet-V2: Compared without the LSTM network for sequence retention.

The following table 2 summarizes the results of our experiments, highlighting the accuracy, precision, and recall achieved for each model architecture:

Table 2. Summary of Experimental Results

Model Architecture	Accuracy	Precision	Recall	Comments
EfficientNetB4 + LSTM	89%	High	High	Balanced performance, efficient and accurate.
InceptionV3 + LSTM	91%	Very High	Very High	Outperforms EfficientNetB4 in accuracy and training speed.
Inception-ResNet-V2 + LSTM	92%	Very High	Very High	Highest accuracy, excellent feature capture with residual links.
EfficientNetB4	87%	High	High	Efficient and accurate, but lacks sequence processing.
InceptionV3	89%	Very High	High	High accuracy, and fast training times, but without LSTM's sequence retention.
Inception-ResNet-V2	90%	Very High	Very High	High accuracy and performance, but without sequence processing.

5. CONCLUSION

In addressing the escalating threat posed by Deepfake technology, our research presents advanced detection systems leveraging state-of-the-art techniques from computer vision, machine learning, and forensic analysis. Through rigorous experimentation, we determined that the Inception-ResNet-V2 + LSTM model demonstrated superior performance with the highest accuracy of 92%, very high precision, and recall, underscoring its efficacy in effectively distinguishing between real and fake images. This model's integration of spatial and temporal features, along with the strengths of Inception modules and ResNet's residual links, highlights its robustness and reliability in Deepfake detection, setting a benchmark for future developments in this critical area.

REFERENCES

Adhikari, S., Gangopadhayay, T. K., Pal, S., Akila, D., & Humayun, M. (2023). A novel machine learning–based hand gesture recognition using HCI on IoT-assisted cloud platform. *Computer Systems Science and Engineering*, 46(2), 2123–2140. DOI: 10.32604/csse.2023.034431

Bonettini, N., Cannas, E. D., Mandelli, S., Bondi, L., Bestagini, P., & Tubaro, S. (2021). Video face manipulation detection through an ensemble of CNNs, 2020 25th International Conference on Pattern Recognition (ICPR), pp. 5012–5019.

Ch, R., Sridevi, M., Ramchander, M., Ramesh, V., & Kumar, V. P. (2024). Enhancing Digital Security Using Signa-Deep for Online Signature Verification and Identity Authentication. *International Journal of Systematic Innovation*, 8(2), 58–69.

Chen, B., Ju, X., Xiao, B., Ding, W., Zheng, Y., & de Albuquerque, V. H. C. (2021). Locally gan-generated face detection based on an improved exception. *Information Sciences*, 572, 16–28. DOI: 10.1016/j.ins.2021.05.006

Dastider, A. G., Sadik, F., & Fattah, S. A. (2021). An integrated autoencoder-based hy- brid cnn-lstm model for COVID-19 severity prediction from lung ultrasound. *Computers in Biology and Medicine*, 132, 104296. DOI: 10.1016/j.compbiomed.2021.104296 PMID: 33684688

Gill, H. S., & Khehra, B. S. (2021). An integrated approach using cnn-rnn-lstm for classification of fruit images. *Materials Today: Proceedings*.

Gu¨era, D., & Delp, E. J. (2018). Deepfake video detection using recurrent neural net- works, 2018 15th IEEE International Conference on Advanced Video and Signal Based Surveillance (AVSS), pp. 1–6.

Guo, Z., Yang, G., Chen, J., & Sun, X. (2021). Fake face detection via adaptive manipulation traces extraction network. *Computer Vision and Image Understanding*, 204(5), 103170. DOI: 10.1016/j.cviu.2021.103170

Hashmi, M. F., Ashish, B. K. K., Keskar, A. G., Bokde, N. D., & Yoon, J. H. and Geem,

Hashmi, M. F., Ashish, B. K. K., Keskar, A. G., Bokde, N. D., Yoon, J. H., & Geem, Z. W.Z. W. (2020). An exploratory analysis on visual counterfeits using conv-lstm hybrid architecture. *IEEE Access : Practical Innovations, Open Solutions*, 8, 101293–101308. DOI: 10.1109/ACCESS.2020.2998330

Karras, T., Laine, S. and Aila, T. (2019). A style-based generator architecture for generative adversarial networks.

Khalil, H. A., & Maged, S. A. (2021). *Deepfakes creation and detection using deep learning, 2021 International Mobile, Intelligent, and Ubiquitous Computing Conference*. MIUCC.

Li, M., Liu, B., Hu, Y., Zhang, L., & Wang, S. (2021). Deepfake detection using robust spatial and temporal features from facial landmarks, *2021 IEEE International Workshop on Biometrics and Forensics (IWBF)*, pp. 1–6. DOI: 10.1109/IWBF50991.2021.9465076

Manasa, P., Malik, A., Alqahtani, K. N., Alomar, M. A., Basingab, M. S., Soni, M., Rizwan, A., & Batra, I. (2024, August). Tweet Spam Detection Using Machine Learning and Swarm Optimization Techniques. *IEEE Transactions on Computational Social Systems*, 11(4), 4870–4877. DOI: 10.1109/TCSS.2022.3230823

Ozkaya, U., Oztu¨rk, S., Melgani, F., & Seyfi, L. (2021). Residual cnn+bi-lstm model to analyze gpr b scan images. *Automation in Construction*, 123, 103525. DOI: 10.1016/j.autcon.2020.103525

Oztu¨rk, S., & Ozkaya, U. (2021). Residual lstm layered cnn for classification of gastrointestinal tract diseases. *Journal of Biomedical Informatics*, 113, 103638. DOI: 10.1016/j.jbi.2020.103638 PMID: 33271341

Pan, D., Sun, L., Wang, R., Zhang, X., & Sinnott, R. O. (2020). Deepfake detection through deep learning, *2020 IEEE/ACM International Conference on Big Data Computing, Applications and Technologies (BDCAT)*, pp. 134–143. DOI: 10.1109/BDCAT50828.2020.00001

Patel, Y., Tanwar, S., Bhattacharya, P., Gupta, R., Alsuwian, T., Davidson, I. E., & Mazibuko, T. F. (2023). An Improved Dense CNN Architecture for Deepfake Image Detection. *IEEE Access : Practical Innovations, Open Solutions*, 11, 22081–22095. DOI: 10.1109/ACCESS.2023.3251417

Pokroy, A. A., & Egorov, A. D. (2021). Efficientnets for deepfake detection: Comparison of pretrained models, *2021 IEEE Conference of Russian Young Researchers in Electrical and Electronic Engineering (ElConRus)*, pp. 598–600. DOI: 10.1109/ElConRus51938.2021.9396092

Rehman, A. U., Butt, W. H., Ali, T. M., Javaid, S., Almufareh, M. F., Humayun, M., Rahman, H., Mir, A., & Shaheen, M. (2024). "A Machine Learning-Based Framework for Accurate and Early Diagnosis of Liver Diseases: A Comprehensive Study on Feature Selection, Data Imbalance, and Algorithmic Performance," *International Journal of Intelligent Systems*, vol. 2024. *Article ID*, 6111312, 1–29.

Roza, N. T.. (2021). Comparative Analysis of Deepfake Image Detection Using Convolutional Neural Network. *International Journal of Advanced Research in Computer Engineering and Technology*, 10(5), 182–189.

Sanghvi, B., Shelar, H., Pandey, M., & Sisodia, J. (2021). Detection of machine gener- ated multimedia elements using deep learning, 2021 5th International Conference on Computing Methodologies and Communication (ICCMC), pp. 1238–1243.

Stanciu, D. C., & Ionescu, B. (2021). Deepfake video detection with facial features and long-short term memory deep networks, *2021 International Symposium on Signals, Circuits and Systems (ISSCS)*, pp. 1–4. DOI: 10.1109/ISSCS52333.2021.9497385

Stephen, D., & Mantoro, T. (2022, September). Usage of convolutional neural network for deepfake video detection with face-swapping technique. In 2022 5th International Conference of Computer and Informatics Engineering (IC2IE) (pp. 22-28). IEEE.

Suratkar, S., Johnson, E., Variyambat, K., Panchal, M., & Kazi, F. (2020). Employing transfer-learning based CNN architectures to enhance the generalizability of deepfake detection, 2020 11th International Conference on Computing, Communication and Networking Technologies (ICCCNT), pp. 1–9.

Tan, M., & Le, Q. V. (2019). Efficientnet: Rethinking model scaling for convolutional neural networks, CoRR abs/1905.11946.URL: http://arxiv.org/abs/1905.11946

Tjon, E., Moh, M., & Moh, T.-S. (2021). Eff-ynet: A dual-task network for deepfake detection and segmentation, 2021 15th International Conference on Ubiquitous Information Management and Communication (IMCOM), pp. 1–8.

Trinh, L., Tsang, M., Rambhatla, S., & Liu, Y. (2021). Interpretable and trustworthy deepfake detection via dynamic prototypes, *2021 IEEE Winter Conference on Applications of Computer Vision (WACV)*, pp. 1972–1982. DOI: 10.1109/WACV48630.2021.00202

Zaheer, A., Tahir, S., Humayun, M., Almufareh, M. F., & Jhanjhi, N. Z. (2022, November). A novel Machine learning technique for fake smart watches advertisement detection. In 2022 14th International Conference on Mathematics, Actuarial Science, Computer Science and Statistics (MACS) (pp. 1-5). IEEE.

Zhang, J., Ni, J., & Xie, H. (2021). Deepfake video detection using self-supervised decoupling network, *2021 IEEE International Conference on Multimedia and Expo (ICME)*, pp. 1–6. DOI: 10.1109/ICME51207.2021.9428368

Chapter 13
A Novel FBD Detection Metric:
A Rapid Shield against DDoS Attacks

Shaveta Gupta
https://orcid.org/0009-0008-3776-8247
PGGC-11, Chandigarh, India

Nimit Sachdeva
Ambiente Technologies Pvt. Ltd., Mohali, India

Jimmy Singla
Lovely Professional University, Punjab, India

ABSTRACT

Web and network services have been increasingly targeted by Distributed Denial of Service (DDoS) attacks, which pose a significant threat. To minimize collateral damage and computational requirements, it is crucial to identify DDoS attacks. A new metric called Forward-Backward distance (FBD) is proposed to achieve this objective. FBD can accurately distinguish attacks and normal traffic using just one data point without requiring a minimum data point collection requirement. To achieve FBD, the Random Forest machine learning algorithm is first applied to the training data to detect DDoS attacks. Then, SHAP values are calculated for each data point to understand how the model made predictions. The best feature, which explains the model outcome with the best predictive power, is used to design a metric which can be used as a standalone to identify DDoS attacks. This new metric (FBD) shows a much higher precision (97%), while the recall is lower (39%). This means that it detects ~40% of the DDoS attacks, but out of the detected ones, 97% are the attacks.

DOI: 10.4018/979-8-3693-6135-1.ch013

1 INTRODUCTION

In the current scenario, internet traffic has been growing exponentially. However, this growth brings its challenges. Working on the internet is based on some protocols, and some intelligent but malicious minds know the flaws in these protocols and can easily breach these rules for unscrupulous reasons to misuse them for their benefit. A well-known repercussion of this breach is the Distributed Denial of Service (DDoS) attack (Snehi et al., 2021), as shown in figure 1.

Figure 1. Distributed Denial of Service Attack

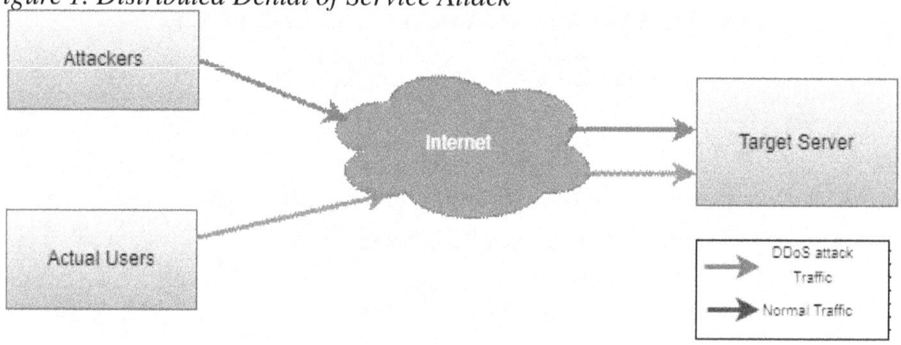

One of the most common reasons for popular websites being inaccessible or web pages not loading for customers is DDoS attacks. A denial-of-service attack intends to render the target server inoperable by bombarding it with more traffic than it can handle within its capacity. To prevent genuine users from being affected, it is crucial to distinguish and filter attack traffic from normal traffic when a website or server is targeted. The primary objective of attack detection methodologies is the same, i.e., to distinguish legitimate traffic and attack traffic. However, there is no foolproof solution now. Although it is nearly impossible to eliminate false positive and false negative detection rates completely, researchers are working towards minimizing them.

There are numerous metrics available nowadays to characterize DDoS/Normal traffic. The most used among them are Entropy (Sachdeva et al., 2014), Renyi's entropy (Behal et al., 2017), Information Distance (Behal et al., 2018), etc. Attackers try to circumvent all the security measures of the network security and mimic normal traffic behavior; hence, the methodology for detection is a bit difficult. Machine Learning algorithms have become a popular method for identifying DDoS attacks in modern times. However, the Machine Learning Model performance depends entirely on the availability of high-quality data and high computation power. To further reduce the dependence on an enormous number of features and sophisticated algorithms, the effort has been made to identify one property/feature of the dataset that can help filter the DDoS attacks most effectively with minimal data and computational requirements.

In the case of DDoS attacks, it is important to note that the forward flow of packets can differ greatly from the backward flow. (Tan et al., 2020). Therefore, this property and the difference between forward and backward flow can indicate a DDoS attack. The current research further explores this property to define a rule that can discriminate between DDoS and normal flow. To identify which features are essential to identify DDoS attacks, we used the Machine Learning model with their associated explainability techniques (SHAP values). These methods are helpful in identifying the features while developing this metric. However, once the metric is defined and threshold optimized in production, it can be used only as a simple rule, with no requirements for advanced methods or computational techniques.

The paper is structured as follows. Section 2 highlights the work related to the detection of DDoS attacks. A detailed description of the proposed metric is presented in Section 3. The results and discussion part are presented in Section 4. Section 5 discussed the comparative analysis of FBD with existing metrics. The proposed work is concluded, and future plans are discussed in Section 6.

2 RELATED WORK

The following section outlines the research conducted to identify and mitigate DDoS attacks. Many authors have reviewed these techniques from time to time. Gupta et al 2018 gave a detailed survey on vulnerability analysis of existing defense frameworks. Reviews presented in these papers helped to understand different dimensions in which defense mechanisms can be thought of.

Prasad et al. 2019 utilized machine learning and Stochastic Gradient Boosting to effectively detect DDoS attacks. To train the model, a hybrid dataset was created by extracting data from three open datasets. The results were then compared with those obtained from other machine learning algorithms. The proposed model was trained on an imbalanced dataset to replicate real-time traffic.

Gupta et al. 2022 proposed a method for detecting DDoS attacks that utilize machine learning and Dimensionality Reduction. The proposed framework seeks to enhance prediction accuracy by identifying the crucial features and minimizing data dimensions. Research findings reveal that utilizing a “lite” model trained on a reduced dataset conserves computational resources and enhances predictive performance. This suggests that reducing the dimensionality of the data can enhance both the model's effectiveness (recall) and efficiency (precision) when compared to using a “full” dataset for training.

Haider et al. 2020 developed a highly effective and scalable deep convolution neural network framework to tackle the problem of detecting the most common and advanced DDoS attacks in Software Defined Networks (SDN). Their approach was tested on a flow-based SDN dataset using benchmarked deep learning ensembles and state-of-the-art hybrid algorithms. The results were compared with a hybrid model called RNNSVM, which combines Support Vector Machine (SVM), Risk-based monitoring (RBM), and Long-Short Term Memory (LSTM) models. The newly developed design proved superior, achieving an accuracy of 99.45%, significantly higher than other versions' accuracy.

Nanda 2016 et al. successfully analyzed an SDN network using a machine learning algorithm to detect hosts that are at risk of being targeted by cyber-attacks. Machine learning algorithms can predict and establish security rules for SDN controllers to prevent malicious network access. The experiment results demonstrate that machine learning algorithms can effectively assist in defining security rules for SDN controllers, with the Bayesian Network achieving an impressive prediction accuracy rate of 91.68%. This equates to the accurate prediction of 254,834 out of 278,598 potential attacks.

Sales 2019 et al. introduced the Smart Detection system, an online method for detecting DoS/DDoS attacks. The sFlow protocol is utilized by this software to collect network traffic data from various network devices, which is then categorized using the Random Forest algorithm. The system successfully identified various types of DoS/DDoS attacks, including TCP flood, UDP flood, and HTTP flood, using three intrusion detection benchmark datasets: CIC-DoS, CICIDS2017, and CSE-CIC-IDS2018. Additionally, the system's effectiveness was compared to recent and comparable approaches.

Polat 2020 et al. introduced a model that uses machine learning techniques such as SVM, KNN, Naïve Bayes, and Neural Networks to detect DDoS attacks. They collected two SDN datasets, one under normal conditions and one during a DDoS attack, and trained and tested both datasets with SVM, NB, ANN, and KNN classification models. The test results revealed that the KNN classifier with wrapper feature selection achieved the highest accuracy rate of 98.3% in detecting DDoS attacks. Using machine learning and feature selection algorithms can improve DDoS attack detection in SDN while reducing processing loads and times.

Research Gaps

- Existing intrusion detection datasets such as KDD-99, DARPA (1988), ISCX (2012), and CAIDA (2007) are old and obsolete, with a lot of inherent problems such as redundancy.

- Many existing systems do not demonstrate threshold selection and its effect on detection accuracy. Collateral damage is more due to attackers' perfect blending of legitimate and attack traffic.
- Existing detection metrics need many features, i.e., many computational requirements.

3 MATERIAL AND METHODS

3.1 Data Set

This research used synthetic datasets produced by (Prasad et al., 2019) simulation-based experiments to confirm its findings. The original data set contains 12794627 rows. Table 1 provides a comprehensive overview of the data set.

Table 1. Dataset Description

Data Set	File Name	Attack Type	File Size
CSE-CIC-IDS2018-AWS	Thursday (15/2/2018) (all-pcaps)	DoS-Slowloris DoS-GoldenEye	46
	Friday (16/2/2018) (all-pcaps)	DoS-Hulk DoS-SlowHTTPTest	47
	Tuesday (20/2/2018) (ML_CICFLOWMETER.csv)	DDoS attacks-LOIC-HTTP	52
	Wednesday21/2/2018 (all-pcaps)	DDoS-HOIC DDoS-LOIC-UDP	76
CICIDS2017	Monday Working Hours.pcap	Benign Traffic	10.8
	Friday Working Hours.pcap	DDoS-LOIC	8.8
		Port Scan	
CIC DoS Dataset (2016)	AppDDoS.pcap	Slowbody2 Goldeneye Slowheaders Hulk Slowloris Rudy	4.6

The data set contains both balanced as well as imbalanced datasets. In an imbalanced dataset, there is a high difference between the number of DDoS attack flows and normal flows. As a result, there is skewed class distribution and poor performance because the machine is not appropriately trained for characterization. So, a balanced data set, as shown in Table 2, has been used in this research work, in which several DDoS and normal rows are comparable; as a result, the machine has enough rows of both types to train itself and, as a result, good performance.

Table 2. Details of Flow in Balanced and Imbalanced Data Sets.

	DDoS Flows	Normal Flows	Total Flows
Balanced Set	6472647	1294529	12794627
Imbalanced Set	6321980	6321980	7616509

3.2 Evaluation Metrics

Regarding machine learning techniques, there are different shapes and sizes to consider. The main question is which one to use for our specific dataset. An effective DDoS security system must prioritize both efficiency and accuracy. To assess the performance of each model, we use a Confusion Matrix that measures the number of False Positives (FPs) and False Negatives (FNs), as described in Table 3.

Table 3. Confusion Matrix

Confusion Matrix		**True Condition**	
		Attack	**Normal**
Predicted Condition	**Normal**	True Negatives (TN)	False Negatives (FN)
	Attack	False Positives (FP)	True Positives (TP)

Regarding our efforts in detecting DDoS attacks, we distinguish between successful DDoS detections, which we call "true positives," and normal detections, which we call "true negatives." If a data point is incorrectly identified as DDoS, it's a "false positive". If it's a DDoS attack but classified as normal, it's a "false negative". To measure the performance of our approach, we use several detection metrics, including accuracy, recall, AUC, f1-score, and receiver operating characteristic (ROC). Accuracy determines how well the test data observed as an attack belongs to one of the attack groups. Conversely, recall is the ratio of detected attacks to the total number of attacks.

- Accuracy= Correct Predictions (TN+ TP)/ All Predictions (TP + FP +FN + TN)
- Precision= TP / (FP + TP)
- Recall =TP/ (FN + TP)

- Receiver Operator Characteristics (ROC): This graph quickly summarizes true positive and false positive rates.
- AUC (Area Under the Curve): The AUC ROC curve is a performance measurement tool for ML models. A higher AUC value indicates better performance.

3.3 Proposed Algorithm

This section presents a detailed description of our proposed metric FBD to detect DDoS attacks. The significant steps followed by our proposed metric are mentioned below, and diagrammatically it is represented in figure 2.

- Data Cleaning & Selection: This first data set that has been described above has been cleaned to remove categorical variables, remove columns having more than 50% missing values, remove rows with irrelevant or negative values, and remove features with matters more than 0.8 in the correlation matrix.
- Features Selection: Under this, those features are selected from a dataset that depicts the forward and backward behaviour of the flow.
- Proposed FBD metric: Selected features were used to calculate the difference between network traffic's forward and backward flow through a subtraction operation.
- Training and Testing: After selecting the features in the previous step, a new column has been added to the data set. To proceed, the next step involves the training and testing of the machine-learning model with these features.

Figure 2. Steps of Proposed Algorithm

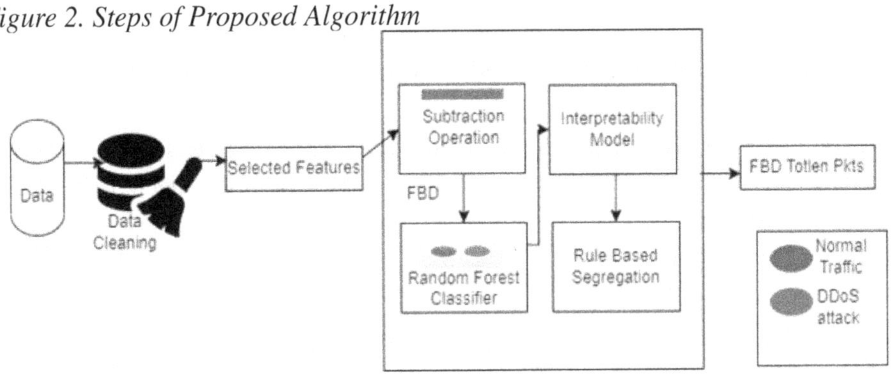

- Interpretability Model: To understand which feature among them contributes the most to the model, this work calculates the SHAP value using the package 'probatus' in Python 3.0 and 'Scikit-learn'.
- Rule-based Segregation: Different threshold values have been tried to arrive at a threshold that can most accurately perform the classification. Finally, the threshold with an optimal tradeoff between precision and recall is selected. The trade-off can be defined differently based on an enterprise's use case and needs.

A description of all the above steps has been given below. The system undergoes a series of steps to prepare a suitable dataset for machine learning algorithms. Only features that provide information about the packet's forward or backward path are selected from a comprehensive list of data elements in this work. The subtraction function captured the difference between the forward and the backflow. Then, interpretability and threshold-based rules were applied to check whether one feature was enough to characterize DDoS attacks and Normal traffic.

3.3.1 Data Cleaning and Selection

It includes the following steps:

- Remove Categorical variables, as these variables do not help characterize DDoS/Normal traffic/Flash Events. IP (internet protocol), Timestamp, and Protocol have been removed.
- Eliminate any columns that contain over 50% missing data.
- Delete any rows that have negative values since they are not relevant.
- Create a correlation matrix that includes all the features. If the modulus of specific features in the correlation matrix is more than 0.8, remove those features, as these features do not make enough impact on the results.

As on the local Linux machines, it is not possible to execute 12794627 flows. To reduce the computational burden of machines, we randomly selected 10% of the data, i.e.,1048576 flows.

3.3.2 Feature Selection

From the exhaustive list of features of the data set, this work picks only the ones that provide information about the forward or backward flow of packets. So, eight features (Fwd Tot Pkts, Bkd Tot Pkts, Fwd Totlen Pkts, Bkd Totlen Pkts, Fwd

Header Len, Bkd Header Len, Fwd IAT Tot, Bkd IAT Tot) have been picked that capture the property of forward and backward flow of packets.

3.3.3 Proposed FBD Metric

Since the subtraction function can best capture the difference between forward and backward flow, four new features have been defined and named as **(Fwd - Bkd) Tot Pkts, (Fwd - Bkd) Totlen Pkts, (Fwd - Bkd) Header Len, (Fwd - Bkd) IAT Tot).** This research work introduces a metric named FBD (Forward-Backward Distance). With the four features using the FBD of the total length of packets, header length, total packets, and total IAT, this study explores the viability of the proposed metric that can complement the existing metrics to improve network security further. To check if these newly defined features can help identify DDoS, this research first applies the machine learning model (Random Forest) to this limited dataset with four columns only.

3.3.4 Training and Testing

Random Forest Machine Learning algorithm has been executed on local Linux machines using Python and the dataset described in Section 3.1. This algorithm has been chosen as it is more accurate on large datasets with few features. Several decision trees are combined in a classifier that predicts dataset accuracy by averaging results. This research work segregates the newly built cleaned data based on the following criteria:

- First, it used the training data to build the machine learning model. The models in the study were trained using 60% of the subset data.
- Second, the trained models have been tested on 40% of the data subset.

Once the machine learning model is trained on four feature sets, the next step is to determine which features contribute more. To achieve this, we have calculated SHAP values for each feature under detailed Artificial Intelligence.

3.3.5 Interpretability Model

We aim to understand how the Machine Learning model identifies DDoS attacks and which features are the most important in that detection. Most Machine Learning models are often referred to as “Black Box” because it is not apparent to end-users how a specific decision was reached by the machine or what characteristics contributed to the decision-making process. (Petch et al.,2022). Interpretability/Explainability is a concept to solve this problem (Petch et al.,2022). This work calculated SHAP values for each data point to better understand feature importance. SHAP value represents the inclination of the data point in predicting one class over the other. In this case, a positive SHAP value means that a given data point in the model led to the prediction being classified as DDoS, while the negative value means the classification of a normal flow. Therefore, this analysis can help us identify which features are most important to select from the dataset for defining the metric, which works as a standalone and a simple rule to filter the attacks.

To achieve this, a library named sci-kit and Probatus has been applied. These libraries recommend prominent features to differentiate DDoS attacks from regular traffic. It also highlights the significance of each feature in identifying DDoS attacks and normal traffic. Interpretability analysis provides the essential feature that can give excellent discriminative power to identify attacks. However, to use this feature as a single metric, a threshold has been defined to classify flow as an attack.

3.3.6 Rule-Based Segregation

Accuracy, Precision, and Recall have all been calculated using various thresholds. One threshold was finally chosen to represent the ideal mix of recall, accuracy, and precision. In this research for threshold selection, we aim to maximize the precision while maintaining a minimum recall. Here, accuracy is given more importance as a performance metric. When this metric is used in production, it should not allow any false detections of normal flow as DDoS attacks because those will be blocked immediately. Whatever is detected as “normal” by this metric can have some DDoS attacks, which more sophisticated methods can further remove.

4 RESULTS AND DISCUSSIONS

The ROC curve, False Negatives, False positives, True Negatives, True Positives, Accuracy, Precision, and Recall results of our proposed algorithm with four feature sets are presented figure 3, table 4, and table 5.

Figure 3. ROC Curve for Random Forest

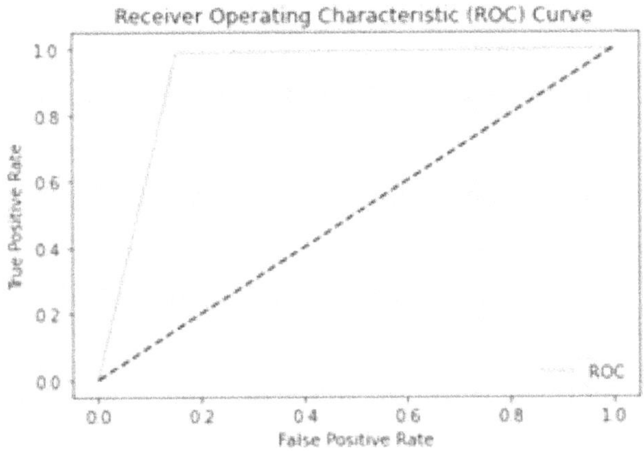

Table 4. TP, TN, FN, FP for Random Forest

True Positives	True Negatives	False Negatives	False Positives
249274	11695	239581	9308

Table 5. Results for Random Forest

S. No	Parameters	DDoS	Normal
1	Precision	0.87	0.99
2	Recall	0.99	0.85
3	f1-Score	0.93	0.91
4	Support	258582	251276
5	AUC	0.9187479651197	
6	Accuracy	0.9177405191959116	

The above results show that the Random Forest model algorithm predicted DDoS attacks fairly well (~92%) even when it used only the Fwd -Bwd flow features. This lends credence to the initial claim that the difference between forward and backward flow is beneficial for detecting DDoS attacks. Then, to understand which feature among them contributes the most to the model, this work calculates the SHAP value using the package 'probatus' in Python 3.0 and 'Scikit-learn'. Results are shown in figure 4 and figure 5.

Figure 4. SHAP Feature Importance

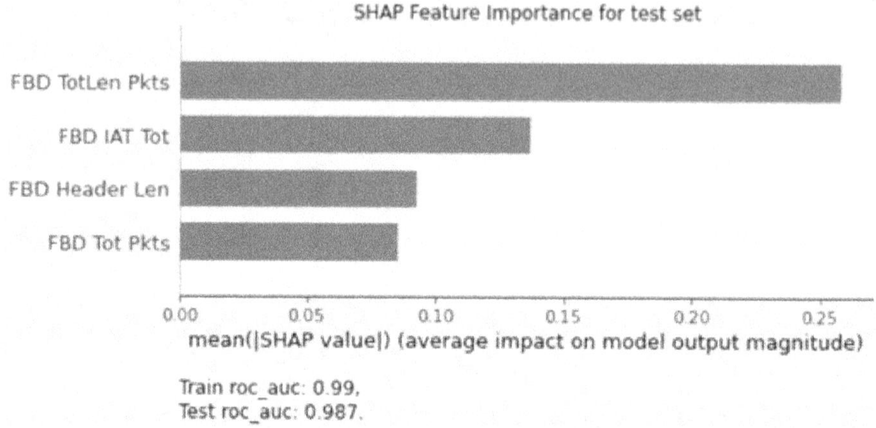

Figure 5. SHAP values for selected features

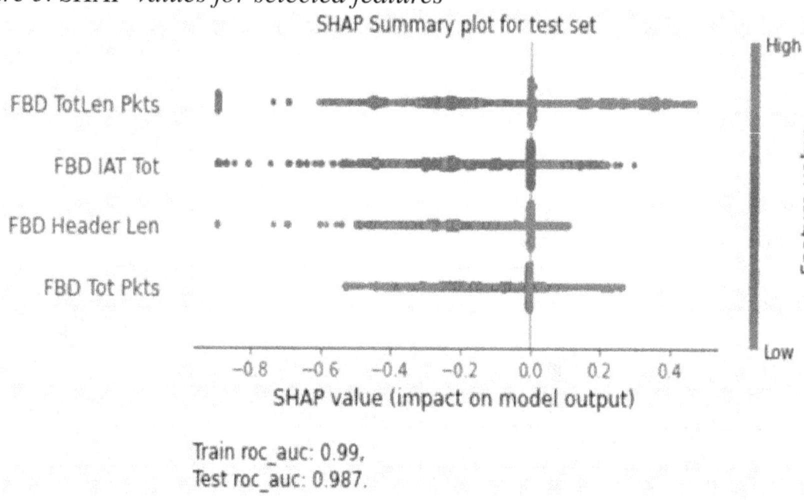

As indicated in figure 4, by SHAP values, FBD TotLen Pkts is the most prominent feature that helps discriminate DDoS attacks and Normal traffic. The FBD TotLen Pkts feature's high value indicates a DDoS attack, while a low value points to normal traffic. The SHAP values for FBD TotLenPkt in Figure 5 are positive for higher values, meaning a DDoS attack. This is consistent with this research work's understanding, as forwarding flow is much higher than the backward flow of packets in case of attack. Higher values of backward flow would mean normal traffic. Although this feature has the highest importance in this model, it is reassuring that other features are consistent with our understanding. For example, a higher FBD IAT tot indicates normal traffic, and a lower value indicates an attack.

The interpretability analysis shows that FBD TotLenpkts alone can give excellent discriminative power to identify attacks. A higher value indicates the attack, but to use this as a single metric, a threshold has been defined to classify flow as an attack.

Different threshold values have been tried to arrive at a threshold that can most accurately perform the classification. The results are provided in table 6.

Table 6. Results of Accuracy, Precision and Recall for different Thresholds

S. No	Threshold	Accuracy	Precision	Recall
1	0	64%	78%	41%
2	100	67.5%	90%	41%
3	200	68.3%	94%	40%
4	**300**	**68.3%**	**97%**	**39%**
5	400	68.1%	97%	39%
6	500	68.3%	98%	38%
7	1000	49.164%	31%	0.00%

It has been concluded that at the threshold of 300, accuracy and precision are at their highest value. Although accuracy does not change much with changing threshold, the choice of threshold as 300 was a conscious choice to balance between precision and recall. So, with only one metric FBD TotLen Pkts and a simple rule, almost 70% accuracy can be achieved. Although the recall is low, extremely high precision in this metric can be an advantage in scenarios where quick filtering/blocking is required and false positives (normal flow blocked wrongly) are expensive. Extremely low false positive rates in this metric can be an essential feature, making it suitable as an initial detection method where the output can be fed to other existing metrics like Entropy, etc. Additionally, this new metric does not need to collect a minimum number of data points as required by the previous metrics (entropy, information distance, etc.). Still, only one data point is sufficient for discrimination. As a result, this novel metric can be used in live situations as a preliminary filter. In this data set, TotLen Pkts is the prominent feature used for discrimination. However, this feature can be different for different scenarios.

5 COMPARATIVE ANALYSIS OF FBD WITH EXISTING METRICS

FBD (Forward Backward Distance) has been compared with the existing metrics (as defined in the references herein), and outcomes are elaborated in table 7. This new metric shows a much higher precision than the current metrics, while the recall is lower. This means that it detects ~40% of the DDoS attacks but out of the detected ones, 97% are the attacks. These results make this metric very useful as the initial check for filtering the attacks, as it needs minimal computational power and is very precise.

Table 7. Comparison of proposed metric with existing metrics

Detection Metric	Recall	Precision	Accuracy Rate
JSD (Bhandari et al., 2020)	94%	76%	88%
Sibson (Tao et al., 2013)	88%	78%	87%
Jeffrey (Cepheli et al., 2016)	86%	79%	86%
Hellinger (Bouyeddou et al., 2018)	82%	81%	83%
Kullback Leible (Bouyeddou et al.,2020)	81%	82%	82%
Total Variation (Monowar et al., 2018)	80%	85%	81%
Proposed FBD (Section 4)	39%	97%	68.3%

6 CONCLUSION

A new metric called FBD can differentiate between regular traffic and DDoS attacks by analyzing only one data point instead of many data points. This metric can be quickly implemented in real-world situations, even in live environments, without requiring significant data collection, storage, or computer power investment.

Experimentation was done with several threshold values to find one that can conduct the most accurate classification between DDoS and normal traffic using FBD. It has been shown that accuracy and precision have their optimal trade-off at threshold 300. Although accuracy does not change significantly as the threshold is adjusted, this work chose 300 as the threshold to strike a balance between precision and recall. We considered precision to be more critical in this case, keeping in mind the live blocking application using this metric, where this can be very effective. In situations where False negatives are expensive (where the requirement is to catch as many attacks as possible in the first filter itself), this metric and the trade-off between precision and recall should be reassessed.

7 FUTURE SCOPE OF WORK

This finding brings up several possibilities for further investigation. The following are a few of them:

Different types of datasets should be provided to the system. In this research work, experiments were conducted on a kind of dataset. However, it is strongly encouraged to supply other datasets from various domains, such as e-commerce, education, healthcare, and so on, to make this solution more generic.

To increase the accuracy using FBD (Forward Backward Distance) multilayer approach can be adopted. In the first layer, this single metric can filter out the DDoS attacks from Normal traffic with 68% accuracy and 98% precision. To increase accuracy, existing algorithms by different researchers can be adopted at the second layer.

REFERENCES

Behal, S., & Kumar, K. (2017). Detection of DDoS attacks and flash events using novel information theory metrics. *Computer Networks*, 116, 96–110. DOI: 10.1016/j.comnet.2017.02.015

Behal, S., Kumar, K., & Sachdeva, M. (2018). D-FACE: An anomaly-based distributed approach for early detection of DDoS attacks and flash events. *Journal of Network and Computer Applications*, 111, 49–63. DOI: 10.1016/j.jnca.2018.03.024

Bhandari, A., Kumar, K., Sangal, A. L., & Behal, S. (2021). An anomaly based distributed detection system for DDoS attacks in Tier-2 ISP networks. *Journal of Ambient Intelligence and Humanized Computing*, 12(1), 1387–1406. DOI: 10.1007/s12652-020-02208-3

Bhuyan, M. H., & Elmroth, E. (2018, December). Multi-scale low-rate DDoS attack detection using the generalized total variation metric. In *2018 17th IEEE International Conference on Machine Learning and Applications (ICMLA)* (pp. 1040-1047). IEEE. DOI: 10.1109/ICMLA.2018.00170

Bouyeddou, B., Harrou, F., Sun, Y., & Kadri, B. (2018, November). An effective network intrusion detection using hellinger distance-based monitoring mechanism. In *2018 International Conference on Applied Smart Systems (ICASS)* (pp. 1-6). IEEE. DOI: 10.1109/ICASS.2018.8652008

Bouyeddou, B., Kadri, B., Harrou, F., & Sun, Y. (2020). DDOS-attacks detection using an efficient measurement-based statistical mechanism. *Engineering Science and Technology, an International Journal, 23*(4), 870-878.

Cepheli, Ö., Büyükçorak, S., & Karabulut Kurt, G. (2016). Hybrid intrusion detection system for ddos attacks. *Journal of Electrical and Computer Engineering*, 2016(1), 1075648. DOI: 10.1155/2016/1075648

Haider, S., Akhunzada, A., Mustafa, I., Patel, T. B., Fernandez, A., Choo, K. K. R., & Iqbal, J. (2020). A deep CNN ensemble framework for efficient DDoS attack detection in software defined networks. *IEEE Access : Practical Innovations, Open Solutions*, 8, 53972–53983. DOI: 10.1109/ACCESS.2020.2976908

Humayun, M., Niazi, M., Jhanjhi, N. Z., Alshayeb, M., & Mahmood, S. (2020). Cyber security threats and vulnerabilities: A systematic mapping study. *Arabian Journal for Science and Engineering*, 45(4), 3171–3189. DOI: 10.1007/s13369-019-04319-2

Lima Filho, F. S. D., Silveira, F. A., de Medeiros Brito, A.Junior, Vargas-Solar, G., & Silveira, L. F. (2019). Smart detection: An online approach for DoS/DDoS attack detection using machine learning. *Security and Communication Networks*, 2019(1), 1574749. DOI: 10.1155/2019/1574749

Nanda, S., Zafari, F., DeCusatis, C., Wedaa, E., & Yang, B. (2016, November). Predicting network attack patterns in SDN using machine learning approach. In *2016 IEEE Conference on Network Function Virtualization and Software Defined Networks (NFV-SDN)* (pp. 167-172). DOI: 10.1109/NFV-SDN.2016.7919493

Petch, J., Di, S., & Nelson, W. (2022). Opening the black box: The promise and limitations of explainable machine learning in cardiology. *The Canadian Journal of Cardiology*, 38(2), 204–213. DOI: 10.1016/j.cjca.2021.09.004 PMID: 34534619

Polat, H., Polat, O., & Cetin, A. (2020). Detecting DDoS attacks in software-defined networks through feature selection methods and machine learning models. *Sustainability (Basel)*, 12(3), 1035. DOI: 10.3390/su12031035

Prasad, M. D., Babu, V. P., & Amarnath, C. (2019). Machine learning DDoS detection using stochastic gradient boosting. *International Journal on Computer Science and Engineering*, 7(4), 157–16.

Ramzan, M. S., Asghar, A., Ullah, A., Jhanji, N. Z., Alsolami, F., & Ahmad, I. (2022). Enhanced Artificial Bee Colony Based Optimization for Mitigating Replication in Large Data for Internet of Things (Iot). *Available atSSRN* 4281666. DOI: 10.2139/ssrn.4281666

Sachdeva, M., & Kumar, K. (2014). A traffic cluster entropy-based approach to distinguish DDoS attacks from flash event using DETER testbed. *International Scholarly Research Notices*, 2014(1), 259831.

Shaveta, S., Grover, D., & Bhandari, A. (2018). Vulnerability analysis of existing distributed denial of service attacks defense frameworks. *Asian Journal of computer science and Technology* 7(3). Gupta, S., Grover, D., AlZubi, A. A., Sachdeva, N., Baig, M. W., & Singla, J. (2022). Machine Learning with Dimensionality Reduction for DDoS Attack Detection. *Computers, Materials & Continua*, 72(2).

Snehi, M., & Bhandari, A. (2021). Vulnerability retrospection of security solutions for software-defined Cyber–Physical System against DDoS and IoT-DDoS attacks. *Computer Science Review*, 40, 100371. DOI: 10.1016/j.cosrev.2021.100371

Tan, L., Pan, Y., Wu, J., Zhou, J., Jiang, H., & Deng, Y. (2020). A new framework for DDoS attack detection and defense in SDN environment. *IEEE Access : Practical Innovations, Open Solutions*, 8, 161908–161919. DOI: 10.1109/ACCESS.2020.3021435

Tao, Y., & Yu, S. (2013, July). DDoS attack detection at local area networks using information theoretical metrics. In *2013 12th IEEE international conference on trust, security and privacy in computing and communications* (pp. 233-240). IEEE. DOI: 10.1109/TrustCom.2013.32

Chapter 14
Progress and Obstacles in Cloud Computing for Healthcare

Abu Jor Al Gefari
Universiti Antarabangsa Albukhary, Malaysia

Imran Hasan
Universiti Antarabangsa Albukhary, Malaysia

Md Amin Ullah Sheikh
Universiti Antarabangsa Albukhary, Malaysia

ABSTRACT

Since the invention of the Internet of Things (IoT), people are seeing a new world in healthcare. The rapid growth of IoT has brought with it solutions to dilemmas and a few challenges with cloud devices. But keeping in mind the benefits of these devices, the challenges need to be solved with efficiency and security. Putting in place cloud storage and analysis for specific periods is very popular in medicine. On the other hand, creating big data, considering the sensitivity, some limitations have to be accepted. The use of latency, throughput, and bandwidth increases the cost of the Internet. Numerous alternative paradigms, most notably edge computing and fog computing, have evolved to solve these shortcomings. Consequently, studies have shown an increase in hybrid solutions based.

DOI: 10.4018/979-8-3693-6135-1.ch014

1. INTRODUCTION

Healthcare means the awareness, monitoring, and maintenance of the health of patients. For the past few years, cloud computing networks have been used to provide services to patients. The global healthcare sector is changing more quickly than it has in the past in an attempt to improve service quality, efficiency, and affordability (Boudlal, Serrhini, & Tahiri, 2022(Alex et al., 2022). Right healthcare looks to smart IT. New technologies to improve the quality of healthcare, reduce costs, and end suffering are positive in everyone's eyes (Sobhy, El-Sonbaty, & Abou Elnasr, 2012), (Alferidah & Jhanjhi, 2020). Along with the benefits of cloud computing come some challenges. Security and legal are one of them. For example, the security of third-party remote data storage, because confidential patient data can be lost or misused, security has become a very important issue (Agapito & Cannataro, 2023), (Alkinani et al., 2021). To contribute to the continuing conversation regarding the revolutionary potential of healthcare cloud computing systems, this research paper will look at the state of the field, analyze the prospects and difficulties, and provide real-world examples. We think that by utilizing the cloud's capabilities, we can establish an ecosystem for healthcare that is effective, easily accessible, and ultimately centered on providing patients with the best care possible. A deeper look into the nuances of healthcare cloud computing and its implications for the delivery of healthcare in the future will be provided in the parts that follow. The field of healthcare is always evolving as a result of improvements in information technology. The state-of-the-art technology for managing healthcare data and saving costs is cloud computing. As more and more medical data moves to the cloud, worries about security and privacy grow. This work creates a new system called TDBNN, which uses a deep learning methodology to identify and classify assaults on cloud data related to healthcare, providing improved security for private patient data in the future of smart cities (Balasubramaniam et al., 2023) (Babbar et al., 2021).

Traditional cloud computing suffers from latency and resource constraints when demand for real-time healthcare applications, such as ECG monitoring, surges. On the other hand, the advent of fog computing offers a possible remedy. To transform real-time healthcare task management, this research investigates a unique Critical Healthcare Task Management (CHTM) paradigm that makes use of multi-agent systems and fog-cloud computing. Comparing our CHTM to pure cloud-based systems, we may achieve considerable gains in network utilization, response time, delay, energy consumption, and cost by addressing the issues of interoperability, resource sharing, scheduling, and dynamic task allocation. Explore this study to see how fog-cloud computing can revolutionize important healthcare task management (Mutlag et al., 2021) (Brohi et al., 2020).

With the help of this research, cloud computing services will enter a new era that will enhance patient care, treatment, and operational effectiveness. Because healthcare cloud computing platforms employ distant servers, anyone with an Internet connection can use the service from any location. First and foremost, the patient's medical record needs to be taken, stored securely and made available to the healthcare professionals. After that, a time slot for the patient's appointment should be set. It is important to make administrative processes more active and to establish a simple communication channel for both sides. Then there is the development and uptake of contemporary telehealth, AI-powered diagnostics, and personalized medical applications.

2. LITERATURE REVIEW

From Paper (Balasubramaniam et al., 2023) (Chesti, Humayun, Sama, & Jhanjhi, 2020), Future Smart Cities: Identifying the Type of Attack in Healthcare Cloud Computing System Using Termite Deep Belief Neural Network (TDBNN). From Paper (Mutlag et al., 2021), The advancements in healthcare technologies have been steadily expanding in practical application during the past ten years. Cloud computing refers to the method by which healthcare applications, such as blood pressure monitoring, heartbeat analysis, and ECG monitoring, communicate with external servers. A variety of technologies, including edge and fog computing, are available under the new cloud paradigm to improve healthcare application performance with the least amount of network latency. Nonetheless, there are a lot of unanswered research questions in the fog-cloud-enabled network for medical applications. Consequently, an ECG dataset is used to design and implement a Critical Healthcare Task Management (CHTM) model in this article. At the fog level, we create a resource scheduling model among fog nodes. It is suggested that a multi-agent system handle network management from the edge to the cloud. By offering interoperability, resource sharing, scheduling, and dynamic task allocation, the suggested approach greatly improves the management of crucial jobs. According to the simulation findings, our strategy considerably lowers network utilization by 79%, response time by 90%, network delay by 65%, energy consumption by 81%, and instance cost by 80% when compared to the cloud.

From Paper (Nasser et al., 2021) (Dogra et al., 2021), A cloud-based and IoT-based smart healthcare system for COVID-19 detection and monitoring. (Hennebelle, Materwala, & Ismail, 2023) (Fatima-Tuz-Zahra et al., 2020) paper talked about the use of clouds to cure diabetes. Diabetes has no permanent cure and is considered one of the leading causes of death worldwide. So, to avoid diabetes, Healthage has invented a cloud system type 2, which will predict diabetes through machine learning technology. Numerical and comparative validation was performed using two datasets on machine learning, RF and LR, where RF gives 6% more accuracy than LR. Using this technology can lead to 2 types of difficulties. Accuracy and limitations, 6% may not seem small but a 6% misdiagnosis can kill a patient. And number 2 is that since diabetes is variable, the nuances of individual cases cannot be determined with statistics alone.

From Paper (Onyebuchi et al., 2022) (Gopi et al., 2021) we got that cloud enterprise data warehousing is a top-tier business. This is a very demanding and profitable business. Data warehousing creates a data warehouse in conjunction with healthcare and receives data from numerous data sources. Currently, the paper has developed an enterprise cloud data warehouse using e-healthcare and treating patients' diseases through e-healthcare data warehouse. The system is expected to improve e-healthcare by creating advanced models using medical software automation. Risk to Data Security: Storing private medical records in the cloud presents serious privacy and security issues. The breach may reveal private information and affect patient confidence. Accuracy & Bias: Prediction models that only consider data may be biased or fail to take into account certain intricacies, which could result in dangerous misdiagnoses. Human in the Loop: Expert judgment in diagnosis and treatment, as well as doctor-patient interaction, should not be substituted by an excessive reliance on technology.

From Paper (M Abd El-Aziz et al., 2022) (Gouda et al., 2022), In many emergencies, patients need immediate treatment. Then getting treatment at the hospital becomes challenging. So, a cloud computing system is proposed to get treatment from anywhere in any condition. In the Healthcare Monitoring-Data Science Technique (HM-DST), initially, an altered data science technique is introduced. This algorithm is known as the Improved Pigeon Optimization (IPO) algorithm, which is employed for grouping the stored data in the cloud, which helps in improving the prediction rate. Next, the optimum feature selection technique for extraction and selection of features is illustrated. A Backtracking Search-Based Deep Neural Network (BS-DNN) is utilized for classifying human healthcare. The proposed system's performance is finally examined with various healthcare datasets in real-time and the variations are observed with the available smart healthcare systems for monitoring. Reliability, accessibility, and human control issues create problems in the use of this technology (Bradley, 2020) (Young, 2021, Fisher, 2018). From Paper (Amanat et al., 2022) (Humayun, Sujatha, Almuayqil, & Jhanjhi, 2022), Patient-physician communication is essential for healthcare. Sharing healthcare records (EHR) security is even more important. Healthcare EHR systems rely on the cloud. Currently, EHR security breaches and meeting system needs have been challenging. A distributed, decentralized ledger technology called blockchain can offer safe, reliable, and unchangeable data-sharing capabilities. Blockchain uses consistent cryptography techniques (hashes) to establish a distributed ledger system that allows distributed actions to be performed without the need for a central authority (Jhanjhi et al., 2021) (Kumar et al., 2021). Because of its immutability, data exploitation in a blockchain network is challenging and visible (Lim et al., 2019) (Nayyar et al., 2021) (Shah et al., 2022). To ensure EHR sharing across various electronic healthcare systems, we present an architecture based on blockchain technology that authenticates the user identity utilizing a Proof of Stake (POS) cryptography consensus method and Secure Hash Algorithm (SHA256). To verify that EHR sensors are assembling and transmitting data to cloud infrastructure, an Elliptic Curve Digital Signature Algorithm (ECDSA) is employed. The findings show that, in terms of power consumption, authenticity, and healthcare record security, the suggested solution outperforms the current ones, which include Proof-Of-Work (POW), Secure Hash Algorithm (SHA-1), and Message Digest (MD5). From Paper (Rani et al., 2022) Healthcare data is the source of information regarding healthcare. Healthcare data sharing enhances the quality of care while also increasing the efficiency of healthcare systems. One of a patient's most precious assets is their healthcare information; it should be owned and controlled by them rather than being dispersed among several healthcare providers (Sharma et al., 2021) Parker, S. (2021). This safeguards privacy and prevents data from being exchanged between healthcare systems. Blockchain has proven to be able to accomplish trusted, auditable computing by combining a public ledger with a decentralized network of peer compromises (Singhal et al., 2020) (Ananna et al., 2023). Access control and cryptographic primitives are not enough to tackle all the privacy and security issues that come with a cloud-based environment, let alone today's cyber threats. The authors of this research suggested a low weight blockchain method for cloud systems that is built on security and privacy for medical data (Azam et al., 2023a) (Oliver, 2019). Both the cost-effectiveness of the data processing methods utilized to encrypt and pseudonymize patient data, as well as the smart contracts within our system, are assessed.

From Paper (Nasser et al., 2021), A cloud-based and IoT-based smart healthcare system for COVID-19 detection and monitoring. Which has worked till covid, now since there is no COVID-19 this technology is not needed.

From Paper (Al-Sheikh & Ameen, 2020), In this project, a wearable, portable, low-power, real-time remote bio signals monitoring system built on the Internet of Things is implemented. A better step in the remote health monitoring field is offered by this approach. The number of people in need of medical attention is rising annually, and traditional bio-signal monitoring systems in hospitals demand that patients be present in person (Azam et al., 2023b) (Miller, 2019). This could result in an ineffective situation when it comes to patient treatment, particularly for those with serious and unstable medical conditions. Thus, contemporary electronic devices in conjunction with internet technology may present potential answers in this area (Riley, 2022) (Roberts, 2020). Taking that into consideration, this project makes use of a mobile application as an Internet of Things platform to remotely monitor a patient's body temperature, heart rate, SPO2, and live ECG signal. Using an Arduino microcontroller-based device, the signals are measured and processed. This paper's primary contribution is the transmission of an electrocardiogram (ECG signal) to a particular smartphone for a physician's observation. This helps diagnose cardiac conditions before the worst-case scenario occurs. Lastly, a smartphone and a personal computer (PC) are used to illustrate the project's outcomes.

According to Paper (Zala et al., 2022), the preservation of private information on open platforms in the present digital era is a serious privacy and security risk. This is especially true for the management of e-health data, where several defined standards must be followed to manage patient health data. The main resources offered by Cloud Service Providers (CSPs) are computation and storage (Zala et al., 2022) (Johnson, 2018). Cloud data security is still a big worry, though. Blockchain technology has saved the CSPs in several cases by encrypting data with special, secret keys, which offer strong protection for the underlying data. As a digital signature to safeguard the data, each network member in Blockchain has distinct secret keys that are directly related to the transaction keys. Still, High workload scenarios cause problems with latency and throughput for blockchain technology. We created a Patient's E-Healthcare Records Management System (PRMS) that prioritizes latency and throughput to get around privacy concerns with e-healthcare records in a third-party cloud. To confirm PRMS's applicability, a thorough performance analysis is conducted on several third-party clouds (Powell, 2018) (Armstrong, 2021). Furthermore, through workload adjustments of up to 10,000 transactions per second, the proposed PRMS system is compared to Blockchain platforms like Hyperledger Fabric v0.6 and Ethereum 1.5.8 in terms of latency and throughput. YCSB and small bank datasets are used to compare the proposed PRMS with the Secure and Robust Healthcare-Based Blockchain (SRHB) method. According to the experimental findings, implementing PRMS on Amazon Web Services decreases System Execution Time (SET) and the Average Delay (AD) time by 2.4%, 8.33%, and 25.15%, 15.26%, respectively. Additionally, deploying PRMS on the Google Cloud Platform decreases System Execution Time (SET) and Average Delay (AD) by 2.27%, 2.4%, and 2.72%, 4.73% AD, respectively. The experimental results confirm the superiority of the PRMS under the high workload scenario over SRHB and its applicability in cloud data centers.

From Paper (Vellela et al., 2023), Cloud computing technology offers new healthcare outsourcing prospects for individuals and organizations seeking to outsource data and processing. Modern information technology has the potential to greatly enhance the healthcare system. apps need environments that are scalable, dependable, and secure, and containerized environments offered the ideal answers as ubiquitous computing for innovative healthcare systems, services, and apps grew increasingly intertwined with Cloud systems. New computer paradigms like cloud computing, which are made possible using eHealth solutions, have the potential to reduce costs and increase the efficiency of storing medical health information. Conventional analysis-based healthcare systems are still in use in impoverished countries. Despite the low adoption rate of computer-based applications among organizations, physicians and government officials were unable to establish a broad network. With the help of the newest cloud computing technology, a heterogeneous network can be constructed to improve the system (Kelly, 2018, Dixon, 2019) (Spencer, 2020). To modernize an outdated healthcare system, a cloud-based application with an integrated strategy and patients has been developed. Massive amounts of Electronic Medical Records (EMR) will be saved daily with this technology. Additionally, this method of eHealth system development guarantees cloud-based patient data protection. This platform can be used to enhance a range of cloud computing infrastructures that offer eHealth system services that are standardized, adaptable, and customized. This analysis's performance is measured in several ways, including specificity, accuracy, and precision. The best results in this analysis will come from an integrated approach that uses a dynamic cloud computing platform to improve the Healthcare System, even though the outcomes for the various strategies vary. From Paper (Talaat, 2022), In a fog computing environment, the efficient prediction and resource allocation technique (EPRAM) for a smart healthcare system.

3. METHODOLOGY

In this research endeavor, the key focus is the challenges, precautions, and the expanding landscape of cloud healthcare, with a specific focus on the efficient prediction and resource allocation in a smart healthcare system within a fog computing environment. The process commenced with an exhaustive literature review aimed at identifying prevailing challenges, discerning trends, and recognizing opportunities at the intersection of cloud computing and healthcare. For this research to be carried out, the following set of research questions were generated:

I. How can cloud computing be optimally utilized in healthcare systems?
II. What challenges and precautions are associated with the integration of cloud computing in healthcare?
III. Which applications stand to benefit most from cloud computing in the healthcare domain?
IV. What security measures are imperative for the successful implementation of cloud-based healthcare systems?

The PubMed database was queried with these structured inquiries, yielding a collection of pertinent manuscripts for our analysis. An internal Python script was employed to sift through the obtained results, extracting title keywords from the manuscripts. Subsequently, we extracted five keywords, excluding articles, prepositions, and adverbs, to identify the prevailing themes and trends within the literature.

Table 1. List of keywords

Keyword
Telemedicine
E-healthcare
Health Informatics
Cloud-based healthcare
Artificial Intelligence in Healthcare

The abovementioned keywords will be generated. The PubMed database will be queried with these structured inquiries and keywords, bringing in a collection of related manuscripts for our analysis. To provide a visual representation of the prominent terms in the analyzed literature, a word cloud diagram (Figure 3) will be generated featuring the extracted keywords. The entire process encompasses the literature review, query formulation, data analysis, paper selection, and subsequent analysis of the chosen paper. The accompanying table not only outlines the queries used but also provides a numerical overview, indicating the number of papers retrieved for each category. This comprehensive methodology serves as a foundation for our exploration into the dynamic realm of cloud healthcare.

Table 2. List of Queries

QueryID	**Query**	**Publication Years Range**	**Number of Papers**
Q1	Cloud Computing & Healthcare	2009–2022	8
Q2	Cloud Computing & Healthcare & Security		6
Q3	Cloud Computing & Healthcare & Challenges		5
Q4	Cloud Computing & Healthcare & Applications		8

Figure 1. Code for PubMed Query

```python
from Bio import Entrez
import pandas as pd

Entrez.email = "saikat@gmail.com"

def fetch_titles(query, years):
    handle = Entrez.esearch(db="pubmed", term=f"{query} AND ({years})", retmax=1000)
    record = Entrez.read(handle)
    handle.close()
    return record["IdList"]

def get_paper_titles(queries, years):
    titles = []
    for query in queries:
        ids = fetch_titles(query, years)
        handle = Entrez.efetch(db="pubmed", id=ids, retmode="xml")
        records = Entrez.read(handle)
        handle.close()
        titles.extend([article["MedlineCitation"]["Article"]["Scoping view of cloud
            computing in healthcare"] for article in records])
    return titles

queries = ["cloud computing & healthcare", "cloud computing & healthcare & security",
           "cloud computing & healthcare & challenges", "cloud computing & healthcare &
               applications"]
years_range = "2009:2022"

titles = get_paper_titles(queries, years_range)
papers_df = pd.DataFrame({"Title": titles, "Query": [q.split("&")[-1].strip() for q in
    queries]})
papers_df.to_csv("pubmed_papers.csv", index=False)
```

Figure 2. Code for Keyword search

```
from Bio import Entrez
import pandas as pd

Entrez.email = "saikat@gmail.com"  # Set your email for PubMed API access

def fetch_titles(query, years):
    handle = Entrez.esearch(db="pubmed", term=f"{query} AND ({years})", retmax=1000)
    record = Entrez.read(handle)
    handle.close()
    return record["IdList"]

def get_paper_titles(keyword, years):
    query = f"{keyword} & healthcare"
    ids = fetch_titles(query, years)
    handle = Entrez.efetch(db="pubmed", id=ids, retmode="xml")
    records = Entrez.read(handle)
    handle.close()
    titles = [article["MedlineCitation"]["Article"]["Cloud Informatics and healthcare"]
        for article in records]
    return titles

keyword = "telemedicine"
years_range = "2009:2022"

titles = get_paper_titles(keyword, years_range)
telemedicine_df = pd.DataFrame({"Title": titles, "Keyword": [keyword] * len(titles)})
telemedicine_df.to_csv("telemedicine_papers.csv", index=False)
```

4. RESULTS

In the investigation into the intersection of cloud computing and healthcare, employing a set of carefully chosen keywords, we unearthed a wealth of information encapsulating the dynamic landscape of modern healthcare technologies. The chosen keywords Telemedicine, E-healthcare, Health Informatics, Cloud-based healthcare, and Artificial Intelligence in Healthcare served as our compass, guiding the exploration of diverse facets within this evolving domain. Telemedicine, as a keyword, led us to a trove of literature encompassing the utilization of digital technologies to provide remote medical services. This exploration unveiled the increasing significance of telemedicine in facilitating healthcare access beyond geographical constraints, allowing patients to receive medical consultations and treatments from the comfort of their homes.

The keyword E-healthcare provided insights into the broader spectrum of electronic healthcare systems. This encompassed the use of digital tools and information technologies to enhance healthcare delivery, showcasing the evolution from traditional healthcare models to more digitally integrated and patient-centric approaches. Our exploration into Health Informatics uncovered a wealth of research dedicated to the application of information technology and data science in healthcare. This includes the management and analysis of health information, contributing to improved decision-making processes and the overall efficiency of healthcare systems. The realm of Cloud-based healthcare emerged as a focal point, addressing the paradigm shift in storing, managing, and accessing healthcare data through cloud computing networks. This transition aimed at enhancing service quality, efficiency, and accessibility, fostering the creation of an effective ecosystem for healthcare delivery. Lastly, Artificial Intelligence in Healthcare proved to be a pivotal keyword, unveiling the transformative potential of AI technologies in diagnostics, treatment, and personalized medicine. The literature delved into the integration of machine learning algorithms and intelligent systems to optimize healthcare delivery, promising advancements in accuracy and efficiency. Throughout our exploration, these keywords collectively formed a narrative that underscored the continuous evolution of healthcare fueled by technological advancements. The synthesis of information gleaned from these diverse keywords not only painted a comprehensive picture of the current state of cloud-based healthcare technologies but also laid the foundation for understanding the challenges, opportunities, and potential future trajectories within this dynamic intersection of healthcare and technology.

The integration of cloud computing in the healthcare sector has witnessed a paradigm shift, offering numerous advantages across various dimensions. Firstly, the scalability and flexibility of cloud infrastructure have facilitated the storage and retrieval of vast amounts of healthcare data. This has significantly enhanced data management, enabling healthcare organizations to efficiently handle electronic health records (EHRs), medical images, and other patient-related information. Additionally, the adoption of cloud computing in healthcare has paved the way for advanced data analytics and machine learning applications, enabling predictive modeling, personalized medicine, and epidemiological research.

The exploration of cloud computing in healthcare, guided by keywords such as Cloud-based healthcare, Telemedicine, E-healthcare, Health Informatics, and Artificial Intelligence in Healthcare, has revealed profound effects on the healthcare landscape, accompanied by unique challenges and promising applications. Despite the potential benefits, the implementation of cloud computing in healthcare is not without its challenges. One notable concern is the interoperability of different healthcare systems and platforms, as data often needs to be shared seamlessly across various entities. Moreover, privacy and security issues pose a significant obstacle, as sensitive patient information must be safeguarded against unauthorized access. This necessitates robust encryption, authentication mechanisms, and adherence to stringent regulatory frameworks such as the Health Insurance Portability and Accountability Act (HIPAA) in the United States (Somani & Trivedi, 2019). Confidential patient data faces the risk of loss or misuse, prompting a critical examination of security measures (Ali et al., 2018). This challenge aligns with real-world scenarios where healthcare institutions grapple with ensuring the robustness of their cloud-based systems to safeguard sensitive patient information. This paper shows a myriad of applications where cloud computing has demonstrated its potential (Griebel et al., 2015). The advent of Telemedicine has seen remarkable advancements, offering healthcare services remotely, thus addressing accessibility challenges. Cloud-based systems enable the seamless storage and retrieval of patient records, facilitating efficient telehealth appointments and creating a patient-centric approach. Furthermore, Health Informatics applications leverage cloud computing to manage vast amounts of medical data, contributing to improved decision-making processes and overall system efficiency (Morais et al., 2022). To mitigate the challenges posed by cloud computing in healthcare, several recommendations emerge. Strengthening security measures through advanced encryption protocols and stringent access controls is paramount. Additionally, fostering collaboration between healthcare institutions, cloud service providers, and regulatory bodies is crucial to developing standardized protocols for data protection and privacy (Mehrtak et al., 2021). Implementing robust risk management strategies and ensuring compliance with data protection regulations will contribute to building a secure foundation for cloud-based healthcare systems.

5. WORD CLOUD ANALYSIS

A comprehensive analysis of the literature, represented visually through a word cloud generated from the keywords, showcases the prominence of these themes in the discourse surrounding the integration of cloud computing in healthcare. The visual representation underscores the significance of these keywords in shaping the narrative of technological advancements in healthcare. The exploration of cloud computing in healthcare in this paper, guided by specific keywords, has provided insights into the transformative effects, challenges, and applications within the healthcare domain. The real-world implications underscore the need for a balanced approach that leverages the benefits of cloud computing while proactively addressing the associated challenges.

Figure 3. Word Cloud of primary and other keywords

6. CONCLUSION

Our discussion on the easy solution through the new process of the cloud has shown the innovative solution of monitoring the use of various medical devices and various processes. Through these tools, we have shown the benefits and challenges of using them. IoT Edge, Fog, and Cloud architectures are proven to be complementary. IoT Edge is capable and advanced in data transformation. Reduces network load in terms of processing which can be considered critical application latency. Cloud computing is more powerful by adding more internal processes, and devices used for decentralization of computing and storage diet, data processing, and analysis offer great flexibility that is closer to IoT devices. In contrast, cloud computing provides vast storage capacity and scalability for managing health data on a broad infrastructure.

Expand and make advanced services accessible. By comparing these managements, we have identified certain advantages and limitations. IoT Edge is ideal for applications requiring low latency and high energy efficiency. On the other hand, cloud computing provides huge storage capacity and scalable infrastructure to manage health data on a big scale and allow access to cutting-edge applications. We have found that, when comparing various architectures, each has unique benefits and drawbacks. Applications needing low latency and high energy efficiency are best suited for IoT Edge. Improved resource management and enhanced resilience against network loss are provided by fog computing. Cloud computing is particularly good at providing centralized services and large-scale storage. Because these designs allow for the real-time processing of health data produced by linked medical devices, they are relevant to the Internet of Medical Things (IoMT) and can lead to more efficient and tailored healthcare services. Connected healthcare systems may be further improved by creative ways to integrate and optimize various structures, as well as by efficient resource management and performance control techniques. It also highlights the general difficulties these systems present, especially when putting the suggested solutions into practice and realizing them. To sum up, this review has helped readers gain a better knowledge of IoT Edge-Fog-Cloud architectures for IoMT and its critical function in the management of health data.

REFERENCES

Abd El-Aziz, M. (2022). R., Alanazi, R., R Shahin, O., Elhadad, A., Abozeid, A., I Taloba, A., & Alshalabi, R. (2022). An effective data science technique for IoT-Assisted healthcare monitoring system with a rapid adoption of cloud computing. *Computational Intelligence and Neuroscience*.

Agapito, G., & Cannataro, M. (2023). An Overview on the Challenges and Limitations Using Cloud Computing in Healthcare Corporations. *Big Data and Cognitive Computing*, 7(2), 68. DOI: 10.3390/bdcc7020068

Al-Sheikh, M. A., & Ameen, I. A. (2020, July). Design of mobile healthcare monitoring system using IoT technology and cloud computing. [). IOP Publishing.]. *IOP Conference Series. Materials Science and Engineering*, 881(1), 012113. DOI: 10.1088/1757-899X/881/1/012113

Alex, S. A., Jhanjhi, N., Humayun, M., Ibrahim, A. O., & Abulfaraj, A. W. (2022). Deep LSTM Model for Diabetes Prediction with Class Balancing by SMOTE. *Electronics (Basel)*, 11(17), 2737. DOI: 10.3390/electronics11172737

Alferidah, D. K., & Jhanjhi, N. (2020). Cybersecurity Impact over Bigdata and IoT Growth. *2020 International Conference on Computational Intelligence (ICCI)*. DOI: 10.1109/ICCI51257.2020.9247722

Ali, O., Shrestha, A., Soar, J., & Wamba, S. F. (2018). Cloud computing-enabled healthcare opportunities, issues, and applications: A systematic review. *International Journal of Information Management*, 43, 146–158. DOI: 10.1016/j.ijinfomgt.2018.07.009

Alkinani, M. H., Almazroi, A. A., Jhanjhi, N., & Khan, N. A. (2021). 5G and IoT Based Reporting and Accident Detection (RAD) System to Deliver First Aid Box Using Unmanned Aerial Vehicle. *Sensors (Basel)*, 21(20), 6905. DOI: 10.3390/s21206905 PMID: 34696118

Amanat, A., Rizwan, M., Maple, C., Zikria, Y. B., Almadhor, A. S., & Kim, S. W. (2022). Blockchain and cloud computing-based secure electronic healthcare records storage and sharing. *Frontiers in Public Health*, 10, 938707. DOI: 10.3389/fpubh.2022.938707 PMID: 35928494

Ananna, F. F., Nowreen, R., Jahwari, S. S. R. A., Costa, E. A., Angeline, L., & Sindiramutty, S. R. (2023). Analysing Influential factors in student academic achievement: Prediction modelling and insight. *International Journal of Emerging Multidisciplinaries Computer Science & Artificial Intelligence*, 2(1). Advance online publication. DOI: 10.54938/ijemdcsai.2023.02.1.254

Azam, H., Dulloo, M. I., Majeed, M. H., Wan, J. P. H., Xin, L. T., & Sindiramutty, S. R. (2023). Cybercrime Unmasked: Investigating cases and digital evidence. *International Journal of Emerging Multidisciplinaries Computer Science & Artificial Intelligence*, 2(1). Advance online publication. DOI: 10.54938/ijemdcsai.2023.02.1.255

Azam, H., Dulloo, M. I., Majeed, M. H., Wan, J. P. H., Xin, L. T., Tajwar, M. A., & Sindiramutty, S. R. (2023). Defending the digital Frontier: IDPS and the battle against Cyber threat. *International Journal of Emerging Multidisciplinaries Computer Science & Artificial Intelligence*, 2(1). Advance online publication. DOI: 10.54938/ijemdcsai.2023.02.1.253

Azam, H., Tajwar, M. A., Mayhialagan, S., Davis, A. J., Yik, C. J., Ali, D., & Sindiramutty, S. R. (2023). Innovations in Security: A study of cloud Computing and IoT. *International Journal of Emerging Multidisciplinaries Computer Science & Artificial Intelligence*, 2(1). Advance online publication. DOI: 10.54938/ijemdcsai.2023.02.1.252

Azam, H., Tan, M., Pin, L. T., Syahmi, M. A., Qian, A. L. W., Jingyan, H., Uddin, M. F., & Sindiramutty, S. R. (2023). Wireless Technology Security and Privacy: A Comprehensive Study. *Preprints.org*. DOI: 10.20944/preprints202311.0664.v1

Babbar, H., Rani, S., Masud, M., Verma, S., Anand, D., & Jhanjhi, N. (2021). Load balancing algorithm for migrating switches in software-defined vehicular networks. *Computers, Materials & Continua/Computers. Computers, Materials & Continua*, 67(1), 1301–1316. DOI: 10.32604/cmc.2021.014627

Balasubramaniam, S., Sankar, K. S., Malar, C. B., Rajasekaran, M. P., Arunkumar, N., & Thilagaraj, M. (2023). Detecting the Type of Attack in Healthcare Cloud Computing System Using Termite Deep Belief Neural Network (TDBNN) for Future Smart Cities. *Journal of Testing and Evaluation*, 51(3), 1421–1437. DOI: 10.1520/JTE20220041

Boudlal, H., Serrhini, M., & Tahiri, A. (2022, May). Cloud Computing for Healthcare Services: Technology, Application and Architecture. In 2022 11th International Symposium on Signal, Image, Video and Communications (ISIVC) (pp. 1-5). IEEE.

Brohi, S. N., Jhanjhi, N., Brohi, N. N., & Brohi, M. N. (2020). Key Applications of State-of-the-Art Technologies to Mitigate and Eliminate COVID-19.pdf. *TECHRxiv*. DOI: 10.36227/techrxiv.12115596.v1

Chesti, I. A., Humayun, M., Sama, N. U., & Jhanjhi, N. (2020). Evolution, Mitigation, and Prevention of Ransomware. *2020 2nd International Conference on Computer and Information Sciences (ICCIS)*. DOI: 10.1109/ICCIS49240.2020.9257708

Dogra, V., Singh, A., Verma, S., Kavita, N., Jhanjhi, N. Z., & Talib, M. N. (2021). Analyzing DistilBERT for Sentiment Classification of Banking Financial News. In *Lecture notes in networks and systems* (pp. 501–510). DOI: 10.1007/978-981-16-3153-5_53

Elhadad, A., Alanazi, F., Taloba, A. I., & Abozeid, A. (2022). Fog computing service in the healthcare monitoring system for managing the real-time notification. *Journal of Healthcare Engineering*, 2022, 2022. DOI: 10.1155/2022/5337733 PMID: 35340260

Fatima-Tuz-Zahra, N., Jhanjhi, N., Brohi, S. N., Malik, N. A., & Humayun, M. (2020). Proposing a Hybrid RPL Protocol for Rank and Wormhole Attack Mitigation using Machine Learning. *2020 2nd International Conference on Computer and Information Sciences (ICCIS)*. DOI: 10.1109/ICCIS49240.2020.9257607

Gopi, R., Sathiyamoorthi, V., Selvakumar, S., Manikandan, R., Chatterjee, P., Jhanjhi, N. Z., & Luhach, A. K. (2021). Enhanced method of ANN based model for detection of DDoS attacks on multimedia internet of things. *Multimedia Tools and Applications*, 81(19), 26739–26757. DOI: 10.1007/s11042-021-10640-6

Gouda, W., Almurafeh, M., Humayun, M., & Jhanjhi, N. Z. (2022). Detection of COVID-19 based on chest x-rays using deep learning. *Health Care*, 10(2), 343. DOI: 10.3390/healthcare10020343 PMID: 35206957

Griebel, L., Prokosch, H.-U., Köpcke, F., Toddenroth, D., Christoph, J., Leb, I., Engel, I., & Sedlmayr, M. (2015). A scoping review of cloud computing in healthcare. *BMC Medical Informatics and Decision Making*, 15(1), 17. Advance online publication. DOI: 10.1186/s12911-015-0145-7 PMID: 25888747

Hennebelle, A., Materwala, H., & Ismail, L. (2023). HealthEdge: A machine learning-based smart healthcare framework for prediction of type 2 diabetes in an integrated IoT, edge, and cloud computing system. *Procedia Computer Science*, 220, 331–338. DOI: 10.1016/j.procs.2023.03.043

Humayun, M., Sujatha, R., Almuayqil, S. N., & Jhanjhi, N. Z. (2022). A Transfer Learning Approach with a Convolutional Neural Network for the Classification of Lung Carcinoma. *Health Care*, 10(6), 1058. DOI: 10.3390/healthcare10061058 PMID: 35742109

Hussain, K., Rahmatyar, A. R., Riskhan, B., Sheikh, M. U., & Sindiramutty, S. R. (2024). Threats and Vulnerabilities of Wireless Networks in the Internet of Things (IoT). *2024 IEEE 1st Karachi Section Humanitarian Technology Conference (KHI-HTC), 2*, 1–8. DOI: 10.1109/KHI-HTC60760.2024.10482197

Jhanjhi, N., Humayun, M., & Almuayqil, S. N. (2021). Cyber security and privacy issues in industrial internet of things. *Computer Systems Science and Engineering*, 37(3), 361–380. DOI: 10.32604/csse.2021.015206

Jun, A. Y. M., Jinu, B. A., Seng, L. K., Maharaiq, M. H. F. B. Z., Khongsuwan, W., Junn, B. T. K., Hao, A. W., & Sindiramutty, S. R. (2024). Exploring the Impact of Crypto-Ransomware on Critical Industries: Case Studies and Solutions. *Preprints.org*. DOI: 10.20944/preprints202409.1325.v1

Kumar, M. S., Vimal, S., Jhanjhi, N., Dhanabalan, S. S., & Alhumyani, H. A. (2021). Blockchain based peer to peer communication in autonomous drone operation. *Energy Reports*, 7, 7925–7939. DOI: 10.1016/j.egyr.2021.08.073

Lim, M., Abdullah, A., Jhanjhi, N., Khan, M. K., & Supramaniam, M. (2019). Link Prediction in Time-Evolving Criminal Network with deep Reinforcement learning technique. *IEEE Access : Practical Innovations, Open Solutions*, 7, 184797–184807. DOI: 10.1109/ACCESS.2019.2958873

Manchuri, A., Kakera, A., Saleh, A., & Raja, S. (2024). pplication of Supervised Machine Learning Models in Biodiesel Production Research - A Short Review. *Borneo Journal of Sciences and Technology*. DOI: 10.35370/bjost.2024.6.1-10

Mehrtak, M., SeyedAlinaghi, S. A., MohsseniPour, M., Noori, T., Karimi, A., Shamsabadi, A., Heydari, M., Barzegary, A., Mirzapour, P., Soleymanzadeh, M., Vahedi, F., Mehraeen, E., & Dadras, O. (2021). Security challenges and solutions using healthcare cloud computing. *Journal of Medicine and Life*, 14(4), 448–461. DOI: 10.25122/jml-2021-0100 PMID: 34621367

Morais, D., Pinto, F. G., Pires, I. M., Garcia, N. M., & Gouveia, A. J. (2022). The influence of cloud computing on the healthcare industry: A review of applications, opportunities, and challenges for the CIO. *Procedia Computer Science*, 203, 714–720. DOI: 10.1016/j.procs.2022.07.106

Mutlag, A. A., Abd Ghani, M. K., Mohammed, M. A., Lakhan, A., Mohd, O., Abdulkareem, K. H., & Garcia-Zapirain, B. (2021). Multi-agent systems in fog–cloud computing for critical healthcare task management model (CHTM) used for ECG monitoring. *Sensors (Basel)*, 21(20), 6923. DOI: 10.3390/s21206923 PMID: 34696135

Nasser, N., Emad-ul-Haq, Q., Imran, M., Ali, A., Razzak, I., & Al-Helali, A. (2021). A smart healthcare framework for detection and monitoring of COVID-19 using IoT and cloud computing. *Neural Computing & Applications*, •••, 1–15. PMID: 34522068

Nasser, N., Emad-ul-Haq, Q., Imran, M., Ali, A., Razzak, I., & Al-Helali, A. (2021). A smart healthcare framework for detection and monitoring of COVID-19 using IoT and cloud computing. *Neural Computing & Applications*, •••, 1–15. PMID: 34522068

Nayyar, A., Gadhavi, L., & Zaman, N. (2021). Machine learning in healthcare: review, opportunities and challenges. In *Elsevier eBooks* (pp. 23–45). DOI: 10.1016/B978-0-12-821229-5.00011-2

Onyebuchi, A., Matthew, U. O., Kazaure, J. S., Okafor, N. U., Okey, O. D., Okochi, P. I., Taiwo, J. F., & Matthew, A. O. (2022). Business demand for a cloud enterprise data warehouse in electronic healthcare computing: Issues and developments in e-healthcare cloud computing. [IJCAC]. *International Journal of Cloud Applications and Computing*, 12(1), 1–22. DOI: 10.4018/IJCAC.297098

Rani, P., Verma, S., Yadav, S. P., Rai, B. K., Naruka, M. S., & Kumar, D. (2022). Simulation of the Lightweight Blockchain Technique Based on Privacy and Security for Healthcare Data for the Cloud System. [IJEHMC]. *International Journal of E-Health and Medical Communications*, 13(4), 1–15. DOI: 10.4018/IJEHMC.309436

Ravichandran, N., Tewaraja, T., Rajasegaran, V., Kumar, S. S., Gunasekar, S. K. L., & Sindiramutty, S. R. (2024). Comprehensive Review Analysis and Countermeasures for Cybersecurity Threats: DDoS, Ransomware, and Trojan Horse Attacks. *Preprints.org*. DOI: 10.20944/preprints202409.1369.v1

Seng, Y. J., Cen, T. Y., Raslan, M. H. B. M., Subramaniam, M. R., Xin, L. Y., Kin, S. J., Long, M. S., & Sindiramutty, S. R. (2024). In-Depth Analysis and Countermeasures for Ransomware Attacks: Case Studies and Recommendations. *Preprints.org*. DOI: 10.20944/preprints202408.2261.v1

Shah, I. A., Jhanjhi, N. Z., & Laraib, A. (2022). Cybersecurity and blockchain usage in contemporary business. In *Advances in information security, privacy, and ethics book series* (pp. 49–64). DOI: 10.4018/978-1-6684-5284-4.ch003

Sharma, R., Singh, A., Kavita, N., Jhanjhi, N. Z., Masud, M., Jaha, E. S., & Verma, S. (2021). Plant disease diagnosis and image classification using deep learning. *Computers, Materials & Continua/Computers. Materials & Continua (Print)*, 71(2), 2125–2140. DOI: 10.32604/cmc.2022.020017

Sindiramutty, S. R., Jhanjhi, N., Tan, C. E., Lau, S. P., Muniandy, L., Gharib, A. H., Ashraf, H., & Murugesan, R. K. (2024). Industry 4.0. In *Advances in logistics, operations, and management science book series* (pp. 342–405). DOI: 10.4018/979-8-3693-1363-3.ch013

Sindiramutty, S. R., Jhanjhi, N. Z., Tan, C. E., Khan, N. A., Shah, B., & Manchuri, A. R. (2024). Cybersecurity measures for logistics industry. In *Advances in information security, privacy, and ethics book series* (pp. 1–58). DOI: 10.4018/979-8-3693-3816-2.ch001

Sindiramutty, S. R., Jhanjhi, N. Z., Tan, C. E., Khan, N. A., Shah, B., Yun, K. J., Ray, S. K., Jazri, H., & Hussain, M. (2024). Future trends and emerging threats in drone cybersecurity. In *Advances in information security, privacy, and ethics book series* (pp. 148–195). DOI: 10.4018/979-8-3693-0774-8.ch007

Sindiramutty, S. R., Jhanjhi, N. Z., Tan, C. E., Yun, K. J., Manchuri, A. R., Ashraf, H., Murugesan, R. K., Tee, W. J., & Hussain, M. (2024). Data security and privacy concerns in drone operations. In *Advances in information security, privacy, and ethics book series* (pp. 236–290). DOI: 10.4018/979-8-3693-0774-8.ch010

Sindiramutty, S. R., Tan, C. E., Shah, B., Khan, N. A., Gharib, A. H., Manchuri, A. R., Muniandy, L., Ray, S. K., & Jazri, H. (2024). Ethical considerations in drone cybersecurity. In *Advances in information security, privacy, and ethics book series* (pp. 42–87). DOI: 10.4018/979-8-3693-0774-8.ch003

Sindiramutty, S. R., Tan, C. E., & Wei, G. W. (2024). Eyes in the sky. In *Advances in information security, privacy, and ethics book series* (pp. 405–451). DOI: 10.4018/979-8-3693-0774-8.ch017

Singhal, V., Jain, S. S., Anand, D., Singh, A., Verma, S., Kavita, N., Rodrigues, J. J. P. C., Jhanjhi, N. Z., Ghosh, U., Jo, O., & Iwendi, C. (2020). Artificial Intelligence Enabled Road Vehicle-Train Collision Risk Assessment Framework for Unmanned railway level crossings. *IEEE Access : Practical Innovations, Open Solutions*, 8, 113790–113806. DOI: 10.1109/ACCESS.2020.3002416

Sobhy, D., El-Sonbaty, Y. and Abou Elnasr, M., 2012, December. MedCloud: healthcare cloud computing system. In 2012 international conference for internet technology and secured transactions (pp. 161-166). IEEE.

Somani, V., & Trivedi, D. M. C. (2019). Utilizing Cloud Computing for Stronger Healthcare Data Security. *Journal of Advanced Research in Dynamical and Control Systems*, 11(11), 60–69. DOI: 10.5373/JARDCS/V11I11/20193169

Talaat, F. M. (2022). Effective prediction and resource allocation method (EPRAM) in fog computing environment for smart healthcare system. *Multimedia Tools and Applications*, 81(6), 8235–8258. DOI: 10.1007/s11042-022-12223-5

Vellela, S. S., Reddy, B. V., Chaitanya, K. K., & Rao, M. V. (2023, January). An Integrated Approach to Improve E-Healthcare System using Dynamic Cloud Computing Platform. In 2023 5th International Conference on Smart Systems and Inventive Technology (ICSSIT) (pp. 776-782). IEEE.

Waheed, A., Seegolam, B., Jowaheer, M. F., Sze, C. L. X., Hua, E. T. F., & Sindiramutty, S. R. (2024). Zero-Day Exploits in Cybersecurity: Case Studies and Countermeasure. *preprints.org*. DOI: 10.20944/preprints202407.2338.v1

Wen, B. O. T., Syahriza, N., Xian, N. C. W., Wei, N. G., Shen, T. Z., Hin, Y. Z., Sindiramutty, S. R., & Nicole, T. Y. F. (2023). Detecting cyber threats with a Graph-Based NIDPS. In *Advances in logistics, operations, and management science book series* (pp. 36–74). DOI: 10.4018/978-1-6684-7625-3.ch002

Zala, K., Thakkar, H. K., Jadeja, R., Singh, P., Kotecha, K., & Shukla, M. (2022). PRMS: Design and Development of Patients' E-Healthcare Records Management System for Privacy Preservation in Third Party Cloud Platforms. *IEEE Access : Practical Innovations, Open Solutions*, 10, 85777–85791. DOI: 10.1109/ACCESS.2022.3198094

Chapter 15
AI in Healthcare Safeguarding Patient Privacy and Confidentiality

Siva Raja Sindiramutty
https://orcid.org/0009-0006-0310-8721
Taylor's University, Malaysia

Noor Zaman Jhanjhi
https://orcid.org/0000-0001-8116-4733
Taylor's University, Malaysia

Navid Ali Khan
Taylor's University, Malaysia

ABSTRACT

In the era of digitization, Artificial Intelligence (AI) integration in healthcare has become a necessity to ensure patient identification & privacy. With the rise of digitalisation in health systems, it has also become increasingly important to have more stringent data protection requirements. This transformation is heavily facilitated by AI-driven technologies that reinforce data security, identify real-time threats and streamline compliance with regulations. By utilizing Machine Learning (ML) algorithms to comb through big data, outliers can be pinpointed and filtered out so that unauthorized access is prevented with the assistance of advanced forms of encryption which protect information while in transit or at rest. But the fast pace of AI development creates as many opportunities as challenges, especially when it comes to marrying data availability and privacy. These ethical concerns, and

DOI: 10.4018/979-8-3693-6135-1.ch015

the necessity for more effective regulatory frameworks, are critical in an evolving ecosystem of AI technologies.

I. INTRODUCTION

A. The Importance of Privacy and Confidentiality in Healthcare

As in any other sphere of healthcare practice, maintaining patient privacy and confidentiality are essential to preserve trust between patients and caregivers and are vital for the effectiveness with which a treatment can be implemented. Healthcare privacy concerns originated around 400 BCE with the principles of the Hippocratic Oath which put secret or private information about patients as a cardinal rule (Burkhardt and Nathaniel, 2019; Gouda et al., 2022). Formal declarations of privacy protections began in the 20th century, with laws such as Medicare and Medicaid (MM) or those included within the Health Insurance Portability and Accountability Act (HIPAA), which was enacted by Congress in 1996 to improve access to health care services. Establishing national standards for patient data security administration guidelines guarantees that sensitive private information is protected from disclosure to unauthorized stakeholders.

Patient trust is on the line, given the gravity of protecting patient information. The sharing of confidential information can cause clients to feel vulnerable, leading them not to share this sensitive information that is pertinent to the care (Conlon, Raeburn and Wand, 2024; Fatima-Tuz-Zahra et al., 2020). This loss of trust can result in reduced health outcomes and a reluctance to use healthcare services. Privacy breaches could similarly have larger impacts across the healthcare ecosystem. They can thus have legal implications, financial ramifications and harm to the reputation of healthcare providers (Pool et al., 2024; Humayun et al., 2022). These vulnerabilities led to high-profile breaches such as the 2015 Anthem data breach that may affect patient data security everywhere. It is not just a question of meeting regulations for patient privacy but ensuring that the trust on which all healthcare delivery rests is nurtured. Despite advances in healthcare practices and technologies, vigilance is necessary over time as privacy challenges come from many directions (Williamson and Prybutok, 2024; Lim et al., 2019). Figure 1 shows the Importance of Privacy and Confidentiality in Healthcare.

B. The Role of AI in Enhancing Data Security

The protection of healthcare data is a high-stakes game and AI plays an important part in it — with all the pros, and cons included. In the past, very limited applications in securing health information were necessary due to manual processes; however as digital technology becomes a key part of healthcare systems and plays a major role now data protection is a top priority (Ibor, Edim and Ojugo, 2023; Gopi et al., 2021). Ensuring that data is maintained and secure, AI tools can detect potential breaches of a system as they begin to occur by detecting an anomaly (Akinola et al., 2024). Since the same capable practices are even more desirable now with breaches in healthcare data on the rise, what has changed?

AI in health is that it brings opportunities on many fronts. Thanks to the AI role, a much larger amount of data can be processed in a shorter duration, leading to generating patterns and predictions that help detect anomalies which help improve patient care and operational effectiveness (Gala et al., 2024; Usman et al., 2023). For example, in medical applications, ML algorithms can help identify diseases early and treat patients with personalized therapies leading to improved health (Kumar et al., 2024; Dogra et al., 2021). This increased usage of AI brings with it its challenges, such as the potential that data can be misused and a requirement for transparency on how AIs process decisions (Chowdhury, 2024; Alkinani et al., 2021). This is key to maintaining that essential trust in AI as "these technologies are supposed to be more secure, the way they operate should make sense and security features work well".

With the mounting quantity of healthcare data and elaborative-natured AI systems, there is a strong necessity for advanced methods that needfully keep privacy in check. This may be overcome by implementing robust methods of encryption as well as legislation that dictates when it is appropriate to use AI in healthcare (Khalid et al., 2023; Chesti et al., 2020). Healthcare organizations can use these strategies to safeguard patient information and get better benefits from AI's capabilities that are improving the quality of care.

Figure 1. Importance of Privacy and Confidentiality in Healthcare

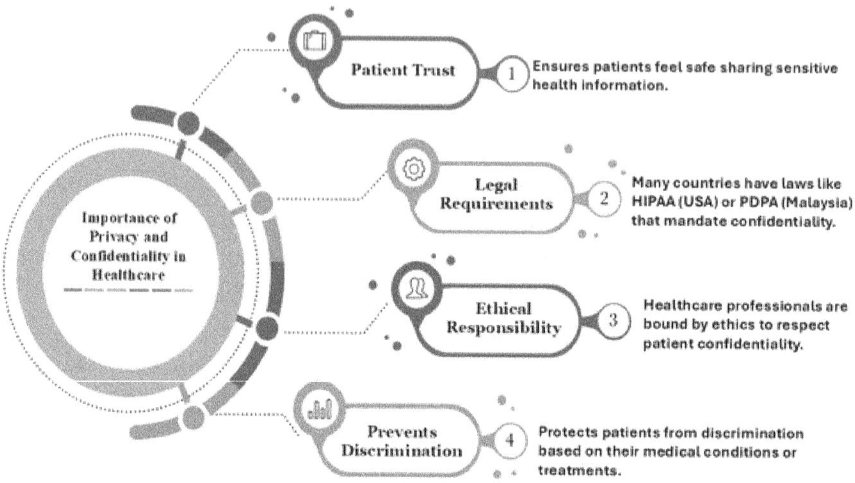

Chapter Contribution

This chapter provides a wide-ranging examination of the interaction between AI and healthcare patient privacy. This chapter delineates the indispensable nature of AI as it augments data privacy and security, furthering discussions related to safeguarding patient confidentiality in an era increasingly dominated by digital. It offers a critical perspective through the case study of how AI methods like anonymization, de-identification & secure data sharing are transforming securing health information (while there also exist notorious lags before breaches could be identified). It also covers the ethical and regulatory issues with AI innovations, suggesting transparency, and accountability while keeping a tab on privacy-related legislation (HIPAA compliant or GDPR compliant).

Not only does the chapter describe how to use AI to hack-proof your organization and prevent unauthorized access, but it also provides example case studies from real-world examples. Through descriptions of where things have gone right and wrong, the book provides useful takeaways for practitioners, builders in healthcare as well and policymakers seeking to use AI judiciously without losing their patients' trust. Finally, this chapter looks ahead to the future of AI-based privacy protection to emerging technologies that may contribute to new forms of patient-centred care while maintaining standards for ensuring confidentiality. In conclusion, this chapter offers essential insights for the harmonization of innovation in AI with ethical and regulatory concerns, representing a valuable theoretical and practical dimension to research provided on healthcare privacy.

Chapter Outline

Section I starts with the importance of privacy and confidentiality in healthcare — it gives a historical perspective on its evolution. Section II explores several common threats to privacy, including data breaches and cyber-attacks, as well as how digital records have made it more difficult to protect our private information. In Section III, we discuss the AI methods used for preserving privacy. Section IV examines the ethical concerns surrounding AI use in healthcare, including a trade-off between technical advancements and obtaining patient consent. Section V Below we summarize the recent common privacy regulations and how can AI systems be engineered to comply with these laws. Lastly, Section VI surveys AI technologies that are still in development and could strengthen safeguards on privacy. In Section VII, three case studies describe how AI is being applied in practice to ensure privacy protection over large healthcare networks and respond to data breaches.

II. UNDERSTANDING PATIENT PRIVACY AND CONFIDENTIALITY

The privacy and confidentiality of the patient are essential components in healthcare as they protect the personal information of an individual and establish trust between a patient and the provider. Privacy refers to the autonomy of controlling personal information, as well while confidentiality is intended to protect this type from illegal access (SEP, 2019). The major difference is that privacy refers to the general concept of granting individuals control over their data, whereas confidentiality denotes the mechanisms used by an organization to protect individual data.

Legislation, such as HIPAA (Health Insurance Portability and Accountability Act) in the US or GDPR (General Data Protection Regulation) of the U.S. Department of Health & Human Services 2020. As part of their certifications to handle and share health information, HIPAA imposes strict rules that patient data is secure from unauthorized access (Terry, 2014) While the GDPR provides similar rights, it affects a much broader category of data in different contexts and places an increased emphasis on consent and transparency (Seiling et al., 2024; Muzafar and Jhanjhi, 2020). Privacy and confidentiality protection of privacy and preservation of confidence underpin all considerations about ethics. Healthcare providers need information to deliver care but also have duties of confidentiality to keep patient data private (Hamad, Jamil and Belkacem, 2024). Issues such as these create an environment where patients are weary and the trust in rehabilitation is broken. If you adhere to ethical practices, only then will patients feel comfortable enough and trust you with the above-mentioned personal information that can be helpful when formulating a good treatment (Zeydan, Arslan and Liyanage, 2024).

Overall, health data privacy regulation has its roots in these two basic principles, and it should be based on them as well. Showing more concern when it comes to patient healthcare data protection, well-established legal frameworks such as HIPAA and GDPR (in the EU) along with ethical practices help protect the information and ensure the integrity of services.

A. Common Threats to Privacy in Healthcare

Data Privacy Threats: Data Breaches Insider Threats Cyberattacks A Data breach is when the data of a person just as his/ her identification, username or password hacker accessed due to loose security settings (Rodrigues et al., 2024). Insider threats are misuse of access to harm the organization or exploit data for personal gain by employees and other trusted individuals (Renaud et al., 2024). Ransomware, phishing scams and other advanced types of cyberattacks are eyeing core system vulnerabilities to compromise information from an organization (Renaud et al., 2024).

Examples from the real world show us just how dangerous privacy breaches can be. For example, the Equifax hack in 2017 exposed the personal information of over 147 million people causing drastic financial losses and significant consumer distrust (Florido-Benítez, 2024; Sindiramutty et al., 2024). The 2021 Colonial Pipeline attack caused fuel shortages and a $4.4 million ransom (Seng et al., 2024). These occurrences illustrate the drastic impact of inadequate security over sensitive information.

The implementation of Electronic Health Records is also a challenge when it comes to maintaining privacy. EHRs while creating ease in maintaining patient records it has increased the risk of breaching data because they are widely used and are integrated across multiple (Adeniyi et al., 2024). Similarly, the rapid transfer of healthcare system information to third parties also hits on footprints of delight and the possibility for unrequired consequences (Shafik, 2024). Figure 2 show Impact on the health system for the potential threat.

Figure 2. Impact on the health system for the potential threat

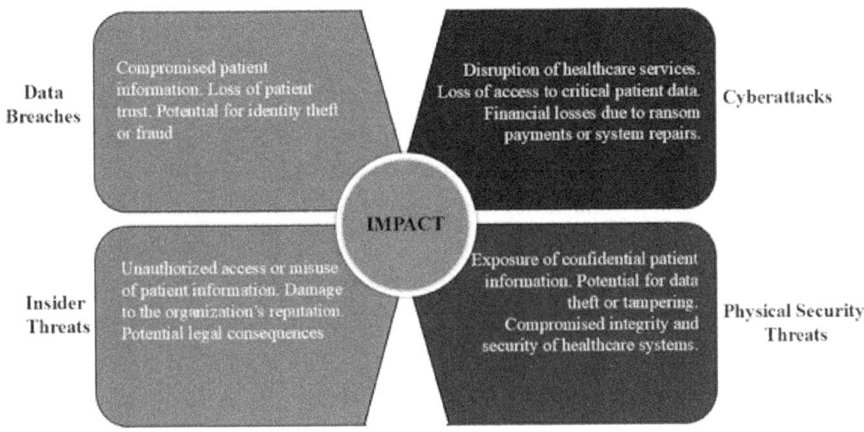

III. AI TECHNIQUES FOR PROTECTING PATIENT PRIVACY

A. AI-Driven Anonymization and De-Identification

How AI Can Anonymize and De-Identify Patient Data to Protect Privacy

Today, AI is used more and more for patient data privacy in methods that involve anonymizing or de-identifying information on patients whenever they send survey forms over the internet. Differential privacy, k-anonymity and data masking are important AI techniques to achieve this goal. For regular data to be differentially private, noise is added to this data which makes it hard for anyone interested in identifying some individual while keeping the collective usefulness of the dataset (Barrientos et al., 2023; Hussain et al., 2024). K-anonymity is responsible for ensuring that every record released does not uniquely identify an individual by simply transforming or suppressing information from said records (Jayapradha *et al.*, 2024; Sindiramutty et al., 2023). Data Masking disguises certain data fields so that use of the information can be made for analytical purposes without revealing individual identity.

The methods of performing anonymization can be improved using AI and ML techniques, as provided by the identification mechanisms for sensitive information being automated (Aboukadri, Ouaddah and Mezrioui, 2024; Manchuri et al., 2024). An example of this is AI models that can find patterns characteristic of sensitive data and, if there are any found apply the proper anonymization methods. Though anonymised it means an individual cannot be identified from the data, so using that for reuse in research or clean analytics does not result in exposure of any individuals.

The evolution of AI also other tools, software and techniques to perform Data anonymization in a more effective & user-friendly manner. In this regard, AI plays a crucial role in ensuring compliance with regulations and gaining patient trust by protecting their data (El Emam et al.

Techniques Such as Data Masking, Generalization, and Perturbation

Data masking inverts and anonymizes sensitive data for instance, names and social security numbers might be replaced by random or masked values to avoid improper access while preserving the data structure for analysis (Chen et al., 2023; Sindiramutty, N. Jhanjhi, et al., 2024). This is a high-quality soft term equivalent to the places where original data does not matter but format and integrity are necessary.

Generalization: Generalizing means replacing specific data values with broader categories instead. For example, precise ages may be changed to age bands like 20–30 years old to minimize the possibilities of leading back an individual (Pfund and Allemand, 2022). While decreasing the granularity that could potentially lead to identification, this method keeps the data valuable for analysis. A perturbation distorts data by, for example, adding noise or slightly changing its values. The idea of this method is to hide the truth in the data and replicate analysis, the most adequate form being Brown et al. (2024). A data set, for instance with edited income numbers to provide the stipulated level of privacy while offering a relevant sense of financial conditions.

Usually, these methods are used together to strengthen privacy. There are tools for masking data or generalization to limit the risk of unmasking with perturbation which would add noise to precision results so attackers could not be able to identify direct values. Every technique still has data utility vs privacy concerns, but together they contribute to a more secure engineered solution for managing this data.

Case Studies Demonstrating the Effectiveness of AI in Data Anonymization

Google Health: Google AI to de-identify health-like medical records for research. At Google Health, trained ML models detected and scrambled personal information to prevent direct identification as researchers mined the data for analysis. This approach involves methods such as data masking and perturbation: it has allowed the maintenance of strict privacy principles related to patient identity while promoting a significant volume of activity health research (Ahmed *et al.*, 2021; George *et al.*, 2023). IBM Watson Health — AI-guided anonymization techniques for health data processing workflows. Using differential privacy techniques, IBM Watson Health designed its data sets to resist de-anonymization. So instead, the Scottish and Welsh health authorities used a process that enabled them to provide important healthcare intelligence to researchers elsewhere (Santosh and Gaur, 2021; Sindiramutty, N. Z. Jhanjhi, Tan, Khan, et al., 2024).

NHS Digital: The UK's NHS Digital agency has employed AI methods in anonymizing patient data for Clinical Practice Research Datalink (CPRD). By employing AI algorithms for generalization and data masking, the patient-identifiable information was kept in sync with each time finding its place to be placed abstracted from real-world meaning that allowed anonymized datasets universally used across the medical community for public health research. By looking at an individual case study on this, we can confidently justify saying AI is more than capable of dealing with sensitive health information in one form or another to aid in many projects, especially within epidemiology studies (Bradley, Lawrence and Carder, 2018). Figure 3 shows AI Techniques for Protecting Patient Privacy

B. AI-Based Access Control and Monitoring

In healthcare, we have seen those constructions relating to the use of AI in managing access to sensitive patient information enhanced security and efficiency. The RBAC can be secured using AI technologies which auto-objective and optimize access of permission so that in no way data goes to any unauthorized entity. AI and RBAC work in tandem as AI continuously monitor access based on user behaviour, role, and data sensitivity (Aboukadri, Ouaddah and Mezrioui, 2024; Stutz et al., 2024)

AI-driven monitoring tools are essential for finding and stopping unauthorized access. ML algorithms for detecting security threats and/or suspicious activities (Dwivedi, Singh and Kushwaha, 2023; Seng et al., 2024). We can take advantage of ML that interrogates massive amounts of data in near real-time to detect anomalous access requests, such as an unauthorized attempt at login or a user going into areas where the s/he does not have permission with sufficient accuracy. The AI automation effort then could result in warnings and lockouts happening without the manual users needing to be aware (Li et al., 2023). This real-time monitoring allows threats to be intercepted, instead of waiting for breaches (Rodrigues, Serrano, Vergara, et al., 2024).

One example of the application of AI within health care includes intelligent access management systems which utilize user credentials, past data and behaviour to prevent unauthorized entry (Sutradhar et al., 2024.) Over the past few years, such systems have entered education with services that can flag or deny a login when behaviour deviates too much from what is normally expected. As an extra function, AI may greatly improve RBAC by on-the-fly modifying access levels dependent upon context — where the individual is or how secure their device is (Cremonezi et al., 2024). Pair with compliance monitoring to generate access logs, and if privileged AI makes possible continuous checks of policy-based monitorization criteria & time-stamped algorithms that create ever-ready audit reports down the line in a near real-time manner. This automation minimizes human error and simplifies the consumption of compliance requirements (Yar *et al.*, 2024; Waheed et al., 2024).

Given the end-to-end capabilities of RBAC, and AI-enhanced monitoring tools for detection, and protection health information can grow significantly when combined with predictive maintenance (Tyagi, 2023) using both proactive as well reactive measures to prevent unauthorized access by any means. As fronts of evolving technology that bolster data security and facilitate compliance, both are central to any meaningful conversation about healthcare data management today.

Figure 3. AI Techniques for Protecting Patient Privacy

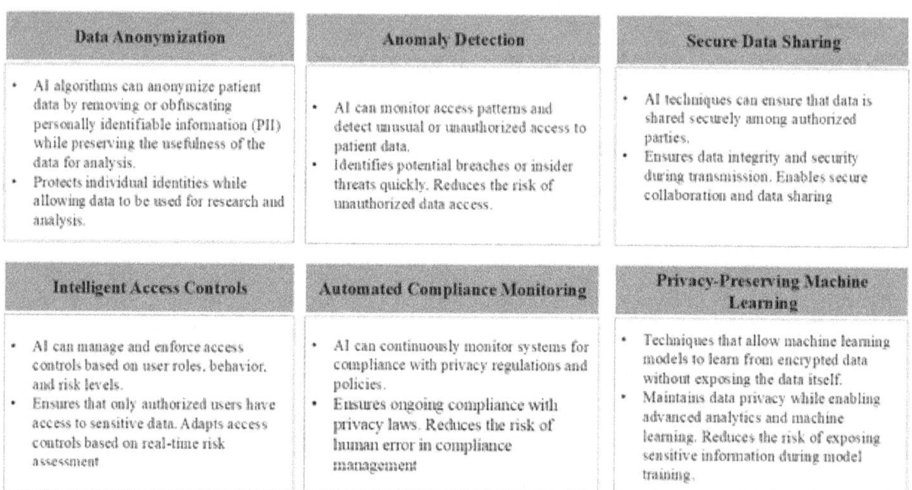

C. Secure Data Sharing with AI

In the healthcare industry, AI has a significant impact on improving data security and interoperability. Since AI-driven solutions use advanced encryption practices, medical professionals can share data quickly and easily with one another. As a result, patient privacy is maintained in the transmission of such sensitive data (Ponnusamy et al., 2022). One example is AI systems that can encrypt data itself so that information when shared, will be decrypted automatically to understand the integrity of confidentially (Zhang et al., 2018).

AI does a great deal to enhance interoperability within healthcare systems. AI software that produces some standardized data AI tools can convert data formats and standards to communicate between fields (Esmaeilzadeh, 2024). For instance, ML algorithms connect different data schemas and present them in a common format which helps to transfer of data (Cong, Yang and Zhao, 2024). AI helps in translating medical terms, and coding systems which subsequently reduces misunderstandings and errors in patient data as well (Lämmermann, Hofmann and Urbach, 2024).

Because the AI does not meet privacy regulations, such as GDPR or HIPAA. Auditing These systems work by monitoring who accesses data, how they access it and what they do with the information — all of which help to provide audit trails for ensuring compliance. AI can also apply role-based access controls to make it so only those with the right permission have restricted data access (Georgiev and Valkanov, 2024; Sindiramutty, Nz Jhanjhi, Tan, Wei, Hamzah, et al., 2024). This reduces the chances of unauthorized data leakage and ensures compliance as required by law.

Thus, AI-powered solutions not only add value in terms of security and interoperability, but they also help to streamline healthcare data management as well. These Tools automate data handling tasks, thereby transferring output smoothly and eliminating manual errors (Sabharwal, Chhabra and Aiden, 2024). Lastly, as current AI tech continues to progress there could be even bigger advancements in data security and system compatibility within research healthcare (Shinde et al., 2023).

IV. BALANCING AI INNOVATION WITH ETHICAL CONSIDERATIONS

A. Ethical Dilemmas in AI-Driven Healthcare

Guarding patient data can pose tough ethical questions, particularly in the realm of AI (Haber et al., 2024). This is where things can get tricky in terms of patient confidentiality, due to the AI having access to so much data it has a large potential cast area. The complexity of ensuring data security during the use of AI to improve health (Aminizadeh et al., 2024). AI systems are designed to collect and process vast amounts of patient data, but this could pose significant risks should unauthorized access or misuse occur (Herzog, Celik and Sulaiman, 2024).

We cannot compromise patient consent and autonomy during our celebration of AI innovation. Patients need to be informed about how their data will be used and have a say in controlling the use thereof. The need to provide a privacy line for people is of primary importance while assessing the scope of AI in providing health care through predictive analysis. Proper Ethical guidelines and ethics committees are indispensable guiding forces behind AI development to ensure developments fall within the boundary of ethical standards (Francés-Gómez, 2023; Alferidah and Jhanjhi, 2020). Most typically, these regulatory bodies oversee establishing guidelines for data security and patient consent (Schuett, Reuel and Carlier, 2024). To prevent the misuse of AI and respect patient autonomy, having clear guidelines is important (Tilala et al., 2024). This guarantees that AI applications are more than just creative but also abide by ethical boundaries.

Developers and healthcare providers need to work hand in glove, adhering to ethical guidelines so as not the lose patient trust yet continue AI technological progress (Banafa, 2024). This partnership is needed to help design AI systems that uphold patient liberties and are used ethically for bettering healthcare practice.

B. Transparency and Accountability in AI Systems

Any AI-driven healthcare system must be transparent to build trust in providers and patients (Sarella and Mangam, 2024). There should be well-defined decision-tracing mechanisms for the solutions built by AI capabilities so that any user can trace back and get insight into how outcomes are generated. Transparent algorithms can be audited by documenting decision processes and inputs, promoting accountability (Cheong, 2024; Brohi et al., 2020). In addition, designing Explainable AI systems can lead to higher user trust in their reliability (Hassija et al., 2023).

Healthcare providers and patients need to be ensured, that the AI systems are reliable (Rana and Shuford, 2024). Regular audits and clear delegation of responsibility for AI decision-making can achieve this (Simbeck, 2023). Together, these can ensure that errors or biases in AI decisions are found fast and corrections to the system improve its performance efficiently (Jarrahi, 2018). These approaches not only help the clinicians to make decisions but also provide comfort for patients that their care is being taken into safe hands.

The trust of patients must be captured through transparent communication regarding the functioning and protective use of their data by AI systems. Strategies include data usage transparency, strong privacy protections and guaranteeing patients access to their health information. It is important not to squander the high levels of trust that patients already have in their healthcare providers because building a trustworthy environment around how information from one patient has been managed and will be used would likely benefit everybody's faith in AI systems. You can verify this and adopt the changes to show confidence that AI systems are well-received by incorporating regular updates, and open dialogues between developers of these digital tools as well as healthcare professionals and patients. Figure 4 balancing ai innovation with ethical considerations.

Figure 4. Balancing AI Innovation with Ethical Considerations

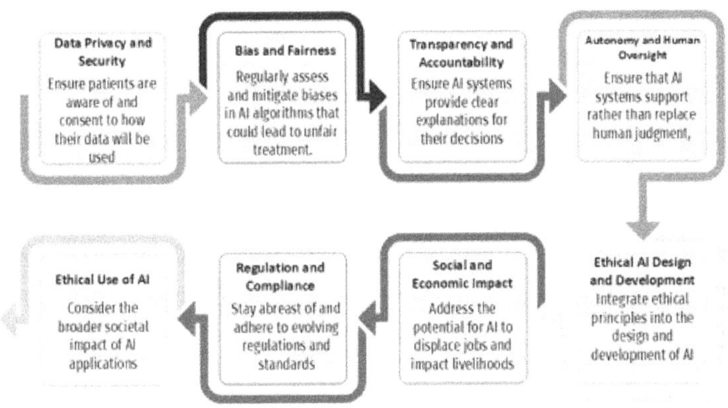

V. REGULATORY COMPLIANCE AND AI

A. Overview of Relevant Privacy Regulations

Legislation such as HIPAA and GDPR play a large role in how AI can be used for health care. The Health Insurance Portability and Accountability Act (HIPAA) are the U.S. standard that sets out general frameworks for good practice, governing how patient health information should be protected in terms of data privacy (Pesapane et al., 2021). GDPR (the General Data Protection Regulation) applies to the EU, and it imposes strict regulations on data processing, which also bind AI in healthcare information (Mesarčík and Hamuľák, 2024; Sharma et al., 2022).

Repeatedly tying hands at evaluating how AI technologies are being built and deployed: strict compliance requirements. On the other hand, protocols such as HIPAA's Privacy Rule which controls how medical professionals and organizations can deal with patient data will also directly influence how AI systems should import or store this information (Ibrahim et al., 2024). The same Data minimization and consent in the case of GDPR makes the structure to build AI systems that treat personal data (Rupp and Von Grafenstein, 2024). Problems can emerge when it comes to making AI systems compliant with these privacy laws. Ensuring data anonymization without degrading the efficacy of AI algorithms is a significant challenge (Dhinakaran et al., 2024). Even if protected or well anonymised, some data can still contain risks when AI systems connect individuals in the database back to their real-world identities. What is more, to protect privacy AI systems have had limitations on how they can be designed and what operations are allowed.

Furthermore, the rapid advancement of AI can quickly outrun more sluggish legislation faster than current regulations adapted to new technologies. As such operational lags can make compliance difficult, though organizations work hard to change their practices in response to new (or refined) standards and legal interpretations. Policy instruments like HIPAA, GDPR etc help shape the landscape but compliance is difficult due to challenges in de-identification and continual policy updates (Farhad, 2024).

B. Designing AI Systems for Regulatory Compliance

Designing AI systems that adhere to privacy regulations involves understanding both global and local requirements and integrating compliance measures throughout development. Key global regulations include the General Data Protection Regulation (GDPR) in Europe and the California Consumer Privacy Act (CCPA) in the United States. These laws require AI systems to ensure data protection, transparency, and user rights (Bauch, 2024; Wen et al., 2023). Local regulations can vary, so it's crucial to stay updated with specific legal requirements in different regions. For instance, Brazil's General Data Protection Law (LGPD) shares similarities with GDPR but has unique provisions (Ferrão et al., 2024). Incorporating these regulations involves designing systems that offer clear data usage policies, robust consent mechanisms, and easy access for users to control their data.

Best practices for integrating compliance into AI development include embedding privacy by design and default principles. This means implementing data protection features from the start rather than as an afterthought (Okon et al., 2024). Regular audits and risk assessments help identify and address compliance gaps early (Ilori,

Nwosu and Naiho, 2024). Additionally, fostering a culture of compliance within development teams can enhance adherence to regulations (Bello, Idemudia and Iyelolu, 2024). Examples of AI solutions that meet regulatory requirements include Apple's Siri, which is designed with features that comply with GDPR and CCPA by providing users with control over their data and transparent privacy settings. Another example is Google's AI tools for healthcare, which comply with HIPAA regulations by ensuring patient data is handled with high standards of privacy and security (Khatiwada et al., 2024).

C. Auditing AI Systems for Privacy Compliance

Ensuring compliance with data protection laws and regulations flows from the auditing of AI systems which allows organizations to perform many "checks." A major step forward is the regular assessment of whether AI systems comply with privacy laws such as GDPR and CCPA (Gambhir et al., 2024). It includes the perception of whether processing operations are consistent with legal performance requirements and consent administration mechanisms. Furthermore, auditing is also done to detect possible data leaks and misuses by reviewing how the data are being saved, processed and shared (Domnik and Holland, 2024).

To ensure compliance is maintained, implementing continuous monitoring over time as regulations evolve or get replaced by new technology (Olawale et al., 2024). Continuous monitoring to address new risks and updating of privacy laws in the protocol (Saeed, Saeed and Ahmed, 2024). Maintaining code updates to address new vulnerabilities to accommodate changing security threats is essential in preserving the integrity and confidentiality of sensitive data (Naguib and Fouad, 2024). Human-in-the-loop architecture one consideration that is already seen when designing AI systems today is the use of third-party audits and certifications to establish trust in models (Benraouane, 2024). Objective evaluation of the organization's compliance with privacy and confidentiality laws/standards by independent entities (Bagheri et al., 2023). These certifications let stakeholders know that the AI systems have been put through objective testing and comply with upholding privacy standards. Additionally, third-party audits may also reveal opportunities for improvement and offer helpful suggestions for attaining best practices for data protection.

To sum up, sound auditing and monitoring practices built into the system as well as third-party evaluations are imperative to ensure compliance with privacy laws and transparency of AI systems. From the security and legal perspective, they help in complying with statutory standards thus also ensuring that our data is far away from already present vulnerabilities. Figure 5 shows Importance of Regulatory Compliance in AI.

Figure 5. Importance of Regulatory Compliance in AI

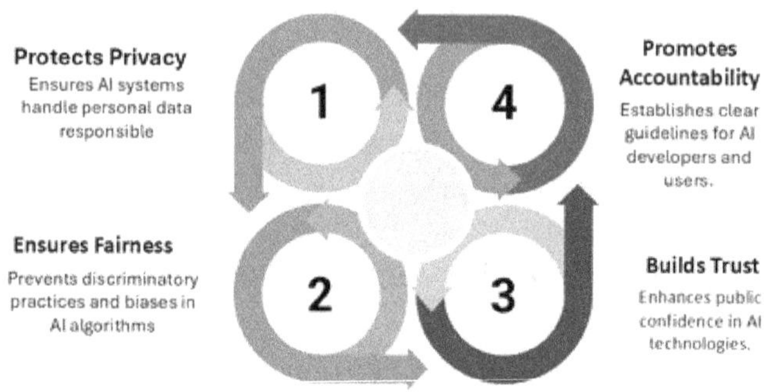

VI. FUTURE TRENDS IN AI-DRIVEN PRIVACY PROTECTION

A. Emerging AI Technologies for Privacy and Confidentiality

Recent advances in AI appear to be an attractive solution for privacy protection, especially in healthcare. So, ML solutions are taking centre stage to protect sensitive patient information, incorporating stronger encryption methods and real-time anomaly detection (Si-Ahmed, Al-Garadi and Boustia, 2024; Azam et al., 2023). The innovations increase privacy by timely detection and correction of unauthorized access to individual health records. Given that the data was anonymized, and we are seeing more AI tools for automating these machine-learning-trained algorithms, privacy is much better. They may strip away personal identifiers but keep data useful for research (Zhao and Zhang, 2024). In addition, AI-led predictive analytics is being used to predict possible breaches and guidelines on how to take care of the patient's privacy before they endanger it (Eid et al., 2024). The implications of AI on healthcare privacy will continue to expand. The next generation of AI models is expected to incorporate more advanced encryption and offer improved access controls, establishing a new bar for data security (Ramos and Ellul, 2024). A secure way of handling patient data, with transparency and traceability, could be expected to draw nearer when AI is merged with the current blockchain technologies (Hemamalini et al., 2023).

Looking forward into the next decade, AI's influence on healthcare privacy will likely be by the widespread introduction of automated systems which helps organizations handle regulations more effectively i.e., compliance to standards (Palaniappan, Lin and Vogel, 2024). In addition, the new system will be driven by AI tools which are likely to advance patient approval control making it a more straightforward and user-pleasant experience (Huynh et al., 2020). These advancements are believed will define how we protect our privacy in healthcare moving forward and foster new standards by which to secure data and encourage patient trust. AI will help advance the security and privacy of patient data by addressing existing challenges and preparing for future ones (Gerke, Minssen and Cohen, 2020).

B. AI and the Future of Patient-Centered Care

In the future where patients reveal the molecular profiles of their diseases, AI could improve patient-centred care by personalizing treatments and outcomes without compromising privacy. Such AI algorithms can comb through mountains of health data and use them in a personalized approach — making healthcare delivery more targeted (Bekbolatova et al., 2024). One such example is the ML model that predicts disease progression and recommends personalized treatment plans for improved patient care (Ahmed et al., 2020). But using data like this invites the spectre of privacy concerns. Preserving the integrity of patient privacy while maximising AI reads is essential both for securing trust and adhering to regulations.

Using AI responsibly and privately will require using intensive encryption down to the pixel where all data can be anonymized (Zhu et al., 2021; Ananna et al., 2023). When AI systems can be created based on de-identified datasets, individual privacy is less at risk (Shahriar et al., 2023). Furthermore, maintaining strict data governance protocols promotes ethical and responsible patient-data utilization (Winter and Davidson, 2022). Future challenges and opportunities for AI in healthcare in the next iterations of AI, this balance will be vital—as AI technology matures and reaches its potential. New regulations are required that can change as well as technology does to better protect patient data. Also, as with other stakeholders—the tech developers and the healthcare providers—an ongoing conversation will need to be had by principals if AI is going to solve our 'privacy problem'.

Overall, AI can transform patient-centric care into a reality by tailoring medicine and enhancing outcomes. Of course, this needs to be predicated against robust privacy rules and ethical guidelines which guarantee patient confidentiality and security. Figure 6 shows future trends in ai-driven privacy protection.

Figure 6. Future Trends in AI-Driven Privacy Protection

VII. CASE STUDIES AND REAL-WORLD APPLICATIONS

A. Case Study 1: AI-Driven Privacy Protection in a Large Healthcare Network

In "Improving Privacy Through AI in a Large Healthcare Network," we highlight how this large healthcare system has incorporated new, more advanced privacy features with the help of AI technologies. The system used AI-driven tools to track and safeguard vital patient information, easing major privacy inhibitions. Growth and fraud were observed with the help of detecting detectors, especially when anomalies, as seen in the use of ML algorithms set up to detect unusual access patterns that will allow unauthorized data locators (Shamshari and Najaf, 2024).

Its results were among the most notable in demonstrating how AI could help detect potential data breaches and improve security. AI systems were able to discover fraud and stop a data breach from occurring (Lysenko, 2024; Camacho, 2024). Using this proactive approach helped not just the protection of data but also compliance with Data privacy regulations (Fayayola, Olorunfemi and Shoetan, 2024). Following the messaging actions, data breach incidents declined significantly and stakeholder confidence in data security increased. Interestingly, more advanced security threats such as in this case must be kept up with by an unending flow of system updates and increased staff training. It is important for the process of change in privacy challenges to be well-adapted through regular assessments of AI performance. The use of AI for this function has yielded advantages to data protection where an appropriate mechanism will be in place that ensures its regular maintenance and review.

B. Case Study 2: AI in Action During a Data Breach

In a recent use case, AI technology was leveraged to help a healthcare provider contain damage from a data breach. The just-launched breach exposed sensitive patient information, leading to the potential for more data losses and a loss of trust. An easily accessible solution was provided by using AI-driven systems to quickly identify and patch vulnerabilities. To detect anomalous activities, ML algorithms examined network traffic for patterns and permitted affected systems to be isolated quickly (Wang et al., 2024). Automated response mechanisms: real-time alerting and incident management allowed to quickly contain the breach (Aminu, 2024).

It also helped to renew patient and stakeholder faith. Advanced analytics were applied to measure the extent of damage caused by hackers and to determine at-risk data. Publicly making clear how their security of details has been secured was a measure that reassured people again. By incorporating AI into monitoring and prevention measures the organization remained capable of anticipating future breaches through a rapidly evolving approach to new threats (Roshanaei, Khan and Sylvester, 2024). AI enabled better communication with the victims Automated updates and notifications addressed any concerns while also putting an end to misconceptions (Semwal, Tripathi and Tyagi, 2024). These efforts not only made a difference in controlling the immediate damage but also went a long way toward restoring community trust.

The successful implementation of AI in these scenarios highlights its utility for breach detection, containment and notification within a time frame that prevents wider damage to the organization from breached data.

C. Comparative Analysis of AI Privacy Solutions in Different Healthcare Systems

These privacy solutions are different from country by country when it comes to AI in health systems. Regulations — The Health Insurance Portability and Accountability Act, HIPAA (US) sets the standard for patients' rights when it comes to their health information; well-established protocols are put in place so that patients' data is protected like fingerprints. The European Union's General Data Protection Regulation (GDPR) provides an even higher standard of protection, especially in terms of data subject rights as well as consent (Calvi, 2024). This is like Canada's

Personal Information Protection and Electronic Documents Act (PIPEDA), which, although centred more around commercial transactions also underscores the importance of consent.

The privacy laws in Australia are regulated by the Privacy Act which includes safeguarding data and its management even for healthcare systems (Kayes et al., 2024). The Personal Information Protection Law (PIPL), in contrast, specifies clear data localization requirements (Grover, Jang and Su, 2024). Japan The Act on the Protection of Personal Information (APPI) is like GDPR but allows for more flexible data transfer mechanisms (Marcén, 2021). Despite this regulation, challenges continue to exist across the globe. U.S., and E.U. data breaches show all is not well with privacy enforcement. A few best practices may consist of strong encryption, frequent audits as well full and thorough training provided to staff. Moreover, is greater transparency and consent process changes essential.

The major areas for improvement include the alignment of regulations globally to enable cross-border data sharing with adequate privacy preserved. Building upon technical advancements in AI and their privacy implications is also important. Such standardisation of privacy practices could dramatically improve healthcare data security across the world. Figure 7 shows AI in Real-World healthcare Applications.

Figure 7. AI in Real-World healthcare Applications

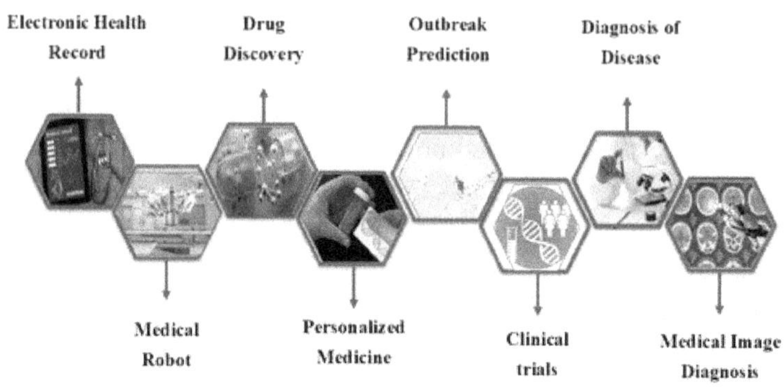

VIII. CONCLUSION

A. Summary of Key Points

In securing vulnerable records to protect patient privacy and anonymity, AI plays a crucial part. The trend of ongoing digitalization in health records has put pressure on traditional data protection methods and mandated AI-driven advanced solutions. It actively tracks and responds to threats (in real-world comparisons, the WatchTower AI would be a band of ornithologists who constantly look for attacks via binoculars). AI-driven systems, in a similar vein, which have the power to monitor data access always are better suited for this kind of work as they will always check variations from the norm and irregularities or unusual patterns that could signal oncoming breaches before they take place. Large volumes of data can be analyzed using ML algorithms to pick out anything anomalous that might have slipped through the net otherwise. In addition to this, AI also bolsters the security encryption methodologies which make sure that data is kept safe while in use, transit or rest thereby protecting it from unauthorized access. Apart from technical defences, AI helps to maintain compliance with an increasing number of privacy laws such as HIPAA and GDPR by automating the audits or access controls healthcare providers need. With healthcare systems leaning more toward electronic health records (EHR), AI plays an important role in safeguarding patient data against ever-advancing cyber threats, securing the data and trust patients must place within their chosen pathway.

AI in healthcare has not only been a technological advancement but an unavoidable innovation of the digital era. With more and more sensitive patient data to sort through, the sheer number of breaches has skyrocketed. The capacity of AI to evolve and respond in real time is what makes it an indispensable tool for securing this data. With the integration of AI in healthcare organizations, patient information stays secure but remains available for its intended essential medical purposes. The complexities and challenges in maintaining digital privacy (GDPR) concern the numerous ways data is at risk, putting these capabilities of AI to work by continually monitoring such breaches, detecting and preventing them from happening. Additionally, AI-powered solutions standardize regulatory compliance lowering the burden on healthcare providers and capturing privacy laws without mitigating effectiveness. That means that when health professionals start using AI, they not only protect patient data but also retain their confidence in the healthcare system as a whole — which encourages patients to provide all necessary information for treatment without fearing infringement of privacy. As such, the ongoing development and disbursement of AI in healthcare are critical to safeguard the confidentiality of this medical information.

B. The Future of AI in Healthcare Privacy

With the growing potential of AI, it will go as far as augmenting patient privacy. As healthcare data has become digital, legacy privacy tools have not been able to keep pace with the proliferation of sophisticated cyber threats. Everything from real-time anomaly detection to ensure tokenization, AI-driven solutions are the most practical approach for healthcare organizations that must act within a new framework of building checks while spotting theft well before the damage is done. Fast-paced advances in AI present both potential opportunities and threats, with the need to strike a balance between making data available for healthcare progression whilst protecting patient privacy. Second development: Personal health data will be enveloped in even tighter digital security thanks to future AI innovations, including more innovative ML models and the merging of blockchain technology with AI. But these new advancements bring with them new ethical dilemmas and require more stringent regulatory pressures. Continued development of AI is dependent upon maintaining transparency, accountability and trust. Although AI offers the most robust means of preserving patient privacy yet, it has an ongoing mission to progress responsibly for patient rights and confidentiality to remain at the heart of healthcare discovery.

There are better days ahead for AI in healthcare and that innovation should persist, as well as cross-industry cooperation. With the healthcare technology landscape becoming more complex, there is an ever-increasing need for advanced AI-based privacy solutions. To advance the power of AI, researchers, clinicians and industry thinkers must collaborate while keeping patient confidentiality at its core. Such initiatives between industries and regulatory bodies can only help in creating AI systems that can protect confidential data or maintain competencies, including security principles along with meeting modern healthcare legal standards. Originality in AI Privacy Safety is anything that extends further than only keeping up with cyber hazards, it entangles about calculating and withdrawing events while making the healthcare sector stable for patients as well as providers. Ultimately, my hope is that by embracing and maintaining a culture of continuous improvement we will be able to fully realize the promise of AI in ensuring patient privacy while fostering trust — helping us not just digitize healthcare but also transform it.

REFERENCES

Aboukadri, S., Ouaddah, A., & Mezrioui, A. (2024). Machine learning in identity and access Management Systems: Survey and deep dive. *Computers & Security*, 139, 103729. DOI: 10.1016/j.cose.2024.103729

Adeniyi, N. A. O.. (2024). The impact of electronic health records on patient care and outcomes: A comprehensive review. *World Journal of Advanced Research and Reviews*, 21(2), 1446–1455. DOI: 10.30574/wjarr.2024.21.2.0592

Ahmed, H., Traore, I., Saad, S., & Mamun, M. (2021). Automated detection of unstructured context-dependent sensitive information using deep learning. *Internet of Things : Engineering Cyber Physical Human Systems*, 16, 100444. DOI: 10.1016/j.iot.2021.100444

Ahmed, Z., Mohamed, K., Zeeshan, S., & Dong, X. Q. (2020). Artificial intelligence with multi-functional machine learning platform development for better healthcare and precision medicine. *Database (Oxford)*, 2020, baaa010. Advance online publication. DOI: 10.1093/database/baaa010 PMID: 32185396

Akinola, O.. (2024). *Artificial Intelligence and Machine Learning Techniques for Anomaly Detection and Threat Mitigation in Cloud-Connected Medical Devices.* International Journal of Scientific Research and Modern Technology., DOI: 10.38124/ijsrmt.v3i3.26

Alferidah, D. K., & Jhanjhi, N. (2020) 'Cybersecurity Impact over Bigdata and IoT Growth,' *2020 International Conference on Computational Intelligence (ICCI)* [Preprint]. DOI: 10.1109/ICCI51257.2020.9247722

Alkinani, M. H., Almazroi, A. A., Jhanjhi, N. Z., & Khan, N. A. (2021). 5G and IoT Based Reporting and Accident Detection (RAD) System to Deliver First Aid Box Using Unmanned Aerial Vehicle. *Sensors (Basel)*, 21(20), 6905. DOI: 10.3390/s21206905 PMID: 34696118

Aminizadeh, S., Heidari, A., Dehghan, M., Toumaj, S., Rezaei, M., Jafari Navimipour, N., Stroppa, F., & Unal, M. (2024). Opportunities and challenges of artificial intelligence and distributed systems to improve the quality of healthcare service. *Artificial Intelligence in Medicine*, 149, 102779. DOI: 10.1016/j.artmed.2024.102779 PMID: 38462281

Aminu, M. (2024) 'Enhancing Cyber Threat Detection through Real-time Threat Intelligence and Adaptive Defense Mechanisms,' *International Journal of Computer Applications Technology and Research* [Preprint]. .DOI: 10.7753/IJCATR1308.1002

Ananna, F. F., Nowreen, R., Al Jahwari, S. S. R., Costa, E. A., Angeline, L., & Sindiramutty, S. R. (2023). Analysing Influential factors in student academic achievement: Prediction modelling and insight. *International Journal of Emerging Multidisciplinaries Computer Science & Artificial Intelligence*, 2(1). Advance online publication. DOI: 10.54938/ijemdcsai.2023.02.1.254

Azam, H., Tajwar, M. A., Mayhialagan, S., Davis, A. J., Yik, C. J., Ali, D., & Sindiramutty, S. R. (2023). Innovations in Security: A study of cloud Computing and IoT. *International Journal of Emerging Multidisciplinaries Computer Science & Artificial Intelligence*, 2(1). Advance online publication. DOI: 10.54938/ijemdcsai.2023.02.1.252

Bagheri, R., Nezhad, M. Z., Rizi, M. H. P., & Sadri, M. (2023). Identifying and evaluating factors affecting user privacy in the smart City using the Meta-Synthesis method and the Fuzzy Dematel technique. *International Journal of Information Technology & Decision Making*, 23(04), 1671–1702. DOI: 10.1142/S0219622023500530

Banafa, A. (2024). *Transformative AI: Responsible, Transparent, and Trustworthy AI systems*. CRC Press. DOI: 10.1201/9781032669182

Barrientos, A. F., Williams, A. R., Snoke, J., & Bowen, C. M. K. (2023). A Feasibility Study of Differentially Private Summary Statistics and Regression Analyses with Evaluations on Administrative and Survey Data. *Journal of the American Statistical Association*, 119(545), 52–65. DOI: 10.1080/01621459.2023.2270795

Bauch, P. (2024) 'Data Privacy and Regulation,' SSRN *Electronic Journal* [Preprint]. https://doi.org/DOI: 10.2139/ssrn.4723359

Bekbolatova, M., Mayer, J., Ong, C. W., & Toma, M. (2024). Transformative Potential of AI in Healthcare: Definitions, applications, and navigating the ethical landscape and public perspectives. *Health Care*, 12(2), 125. DOI: 10.3390/healthcare12020125 PMID: 38255014

Bello, N.H.O., Idemudia, N.C. and Iyelolu, N.T.V. (2024) 'Navigating Financial Compliance in Small and Medium-Sized Enterprises (SMEs): Overcoming challenges and implementing effective solutions,' *World Journal of Advanced Research and Reviews*, 23(1), pp. 042–050. .DOI: 10.30574/wjarr.2024.23.1.1984

Benraouane, S. A. (2024). *AI Management System certification according to the ISO/IEC 42001 Standard: How to Audit, Certify, and Build Responsible AI Systems*. CRC Press. DOI: 10.4324/9781003463979

Bradley, S. H., Lawrence, N. R., & Carder, P. (2018). Using primary care data for health research in England – an overview. *Future Healthcare Journal*, 5(3), 207–212. DOI: 10.7861/futurehosp.5-3-207 PMID: 31098568

Brohi, S. N.. (2020) 'Key Applications of State-of-the-Art Technologies to Mitigate and Eliminate COVID-19.pdf,' *TechRiv* [Preprint]. DOI: 10.36227/techrxiv.12115596.v1

Brown, G., ... (2024) 'Insufficient statistics perturbation: stable estimators for private least squares,' *arXiv (Cornell University)* [Preprint]. https://doi.org//arxiv.2404.15409.DOI: 10.48550

Burkhardt, M. A., & Nathaniel, A. K. (2019). *Ethics & Issues in Contemporary Nursing - E-Book*. Elsevier Health Sciences.

Calvi, A. (2024). Data Protection Impact Assessment under the EU General Data Protection Regulation: A feminist reflection. *Computer Law & Security Report*, 53, 105950. DOI: 10.1016/j.clsr.2024.105950

Camacho, N. G. (2024). The role of AI in Cybersecurity: Addressing Threats in the Digital Age. *Deleted Journal*, 3(1), 143–154. DOI: 10.60087/jaigs.v3i1.75

Chen, M.. (2023). Data anonymization evaluation against re-identification attacks in edge storage, [Preprint]. *Wireless Networks*. Advance online publication. DOI: 10.1007/s11276-023-03235-6

Cheong, B. C. (2024). Transparency and accountability in AI systems: Safeguarding wellbeing in the age of algorithmic decision-making. *Frontiers in Human Dynamics*, 6, 1421273. Advance online publication. DOI: 10.3389/fhumd.2024.1421273

Chesti, I. A., ... (2020) 'Evolution, Mitigation, and Prevention of Ransomware,' *2020 2nd International Conference on Computer and Information Sciences (ICCIS)* [Preprint]. DOI: 10.1109/ICCIS49240.2020.9257708

Chowdhury, N. R. H. (2024). Blockchain and AI: Driving the future of data security and business intelligence. *World Journal of Advanced Research and Reviews*, 23(1), 2559–2570. DOI: 10.30574/wjarr.2024.23.1.2273

Cong, G., Yang, J., & Zhao, Y. (2024). *Machine Learning for Databases: Foundations, Paradigms, and Open problems*. ACM. [Preprint], DOI: 10.1145/3626246.3654686

Conlon, D., Raeburn, T., & Wand, T. (2024). 'Nurses' understanding of their duty of confidentiality to patients in mental health care: A qualitative exploratory study,'. *Collegian (Royal College of Nursing, Australia)*, 31(3), 144–153. DOI: 10.1016/j.colegn.2024.02.002

Cremonezi, B., Vieira, A. B., Nacif, J., Silva, E. F., & Nogueira, M. (2024). Identity management for Internet of Things: Concepts, challenges and opportunities. *Computer Communications*, 224, 72–94. DOI: 10.1016/j.comcom.2024.05.014

Dhinakaran, D., ... (2024) 'Privacy-Preserving Data in IoT-based Cloud Systems: A Comprehensive Survey with AI Integration,' *arXiv (Cornell University)* [Preprint]. https://doi.org//arxiv.2401.00794.DOI: 10.48550

Dogra, V., ... (2021) 'Analyzing DistilBERT for Sentiment Classification of Banking Financial News,' in *Lecture notes in networks and systems*, pp. 501–510. DOI: 10.1007/978-981-16-3153-5_53

Domnik, J., & Holland, A. (2024). On Data Leakage Prevention Maturity: Adapting the C2M2 framework. *Journal of Cybersecurity and Privacy*, 4(2), 167–195. DOI: 10.3390/jcp4020009

Dwivedi, N., Singh, D. K., & Kushwaha, D. S. (2023). A novel approach for suspicious activity detection with deep learning. *Multimedia Tools and Applications*, 82(21), 32397–32420. DOI: 10.1007/s11042-023-14445-7

Eid, M. A. H.. (2024) 'Conceptualizing Ethical AI-Enabled Marketing: Current State and Agenda for Future Research,' *Preprints* [Preprint]. DOI: 10.20944/preprints202404.0786.v1

Esmaeilzadeh, P. (2024). Challenges and strategies for wide-scale artificial intelligence (AI) deployment in healthcare practices: A perspective for healthcare organizations. *Artificial Intelligence in Medicine*, 151, 102861. DOI: 10.1016/j.artmed.2024.102861 PMID: 38555850

Farhad, M. A. (2024). *Consumer data protection laws and their impact on business models in the tech industry*. Telecommunications Policy., DOI: 10.1016/j.telpol.2024.102836

Fatima-Tuz-Zahra, N., ... (2020) 'Proposing a Hybrid RPL Protocol for Rank and Wormhole Attack Mitigation using Machine Learning,' *2020 2nd International Conference on Computer and Information Sciences (ICCIS)* [Preprint]. DOI: 10.1109/ICCIS49240.2020.9257607

Fayayola, N. O. A., Olorunfemi, N. O. L., & Shoetan, N. P. O. (2024). DATA PRIVACY AND SECURITY IN IT: A REVIEW OF TECHNIQUES AND CHALLENGES. *Computer Science & IT Research Journal*, 5(3), 606–615. DOI: 10.51594/csitrj.v5i3.909

Ferrão, S. É. R.. (2024). Towards a taxonomy of privacy requirements based on the LGPD and ISO/IEC 29100. *Information and Software Technology*, 168, 107396. DOI: 10.1016/j.infsof.2024.107396

Florido-Benítez, L. (2024). The types of hackers and cyberattacks in the aviation industry. *Journal of Transportation Security*, 17(1), 13. Advance online publication. DOI: 10.1007/s12198-024-00281-9

Francés-Gómez, P. (2023) 'Ethical Principles and governance for AI,' in *˜The œInternational library of ethics, law and technology*, pp. 191–217. DOI: 10.1007/978-3-031-48135-2_10

Gala, D., Behl, H., Shah, M., & Makaryus, A. N. (2024). The role of Artificial intelligence in improving patient Outcomes and Future of healthcare Delivery in Cardiology: A Narrative Review of the literature. *Health Care*, 12(4), 481. DOI: 10.3390/healthcare12040481 PMID: 38391856

Gambhir, A., ... (2024) 'Beyond the Code: Bridging Ethical and Practical Gaps in Data Privacy for AI-Enhanced Healthcare Systems,' in *Recent Trends in Artificial Intelligence Towards a Smart World*, pp. 37–65. DOI: 10.1007/978-981-97-6790-8_2

George, D. A.S. *et al.* (2023) 'AI-Driven breakthroughs in healthcare: Google Health's advances and the future of medical AI,' Zenodo *(CERN European Organization for Nuclear Research)* [Preprint]. DOI: 10.5281/zenodo.8085221

Georgiev, A., & Valkanov, V. (2024) 'Role-Based Access Control Technique with Trino for Restriction in Hive-Based Data Warehouse,' *2024 59th International Scientific Conference on Information, Communication and Energy Systems and Technologies (ICEST)*, pp. 1–4. DOI: 10.1109/ICEST62335.2024.10639702

Gerke, S., Minssen, T., & Cohen, G. (2020) 'Ethical and legal challenges of artificial intelligence-driven healthcare,' in *Elsevier eBooks*, pp. 295–336. DOI: 10.1016/B978-0-12-818438-7.00012-5

Gopi, R., Sathiyamoorthi, V., Selvakumar, S., Manikandan, R., Chatterjee, P., Jhanjhi, N. Z., & Luhach, A. K. (2021). Enhanced method of ANN based model for detection of DDoS attacks on multimedia internet of things. *Multimedia Tools and Applications*, 81(19), 26739–26757. DOI: 10.1007/s11042-021-10640-6

Gouda, W., Almurafeh, M., Humayun, M., & Jhanjhi, N. Z. (2022). Detection of COVID-19 based on chest x-rays using deep learning. *Health Care*, 10(2), 343. DOI: 10.3390/healthcare10020343 PMID: 35206957

Grover, R., Jang, K., & Su, L. W. (2024). Beyond Digital Protection(ism). *Journal of Information Policy*, 14. Advance online publication. DOI: 10.5325/jinfopoli.14.2024.0005

Haber, Y., Levkovich, I., Hadar-Shoval, D., & Elyoseph, Z. (2024). The artificial third: A broad view of the effects of introducing generative artificial intelligence on psychotherapy (Preprint). *JMIR Mental Health*, 11, e54781. DOI: 10.2196/54781 PMID: 38787297

Hamad, Z. T., Jamil, N., & Belkacem, A. N. (2024). *ChaTGPT's impact on education and Healthcare: Insights, challenges, and ethical consideration*. IEEE Access., DOI: 10.1109/ACCESS.2024.3437374

Hassija, V., Chamola, V., Mahapatra, A., Singal, A., Goel, D., Huang, K., Scardapane, S., Spinelli, I., Mahmud, M., & Hussain, A. (2023). Interpreting Black-Box Models: A review on Explainable Artificial intelligence. *Cognitive Computation*, 16(1), 45–74. DOI: 10.1007/s12559-023-10179-8

Hemamalini, V.. (2023). *Artificial Intelligence–Blockchain-Enabled–Internet of Things-Based Cloud Applications for Next-Generation Society*. Wiley., DOI: 10.1002/9781394213948.ch4

Herzog, N. J., Celik, D., & Sulaiman, R. B. (2024) 'Artificial intelligence in healthcare and medical records security,' in *Advanced sciences and technologies for security applications*, pp. 35–57. DOI: 10.1007/978-3-031-52272-7_2

Humayun, M., Sujatha, R., Almuayqil, S. N., & Jhanjhi, N. Z. (2022). A Transfer Learning Approach with a Convolutional Neural Network for the Classification of Lung Carcinoma. *Health Care*, 10(6), 1058. DOI: 10.3390/healthcare10061058 PMID: 35742109

Hussain, K., ... (2024) 'Threats and Vulnerabilities of Wireless Networks in the Internet of Things (IoT),' *2024 IEEE 1st Karachi Section Humanitarian Technology Conference (KHI-HTC)* [Preprint]. DOI: 10.1109/KHI-HTC60760.2024.10482197

Hussain, K., ... (2024) 'Threats and Vulnerabilities of Wireless Networks in the Internet of Things (IoT),' *2024 IEEE 1st Karachi Section Humanitarian Technology Conference (KHI-HTC)* [Preprint]. DOI: 10.1109/KHI-HTC60760.2024.10482197

Huynh, E., Hosny, A., Guthier, C., Bitterman, D. S., Petit, S. F., Haas-Kogan, D. A., Kann, B., Aerts, H. J. W. L., & Mak, R. H. (2020). Artificial intelligence in radiation oncology. *Nature Reviews. Clinical Oncology*, 17(12), 771–781. DOI: 10.1038/s41571-020-0417-8 PMID: 32843739

Ibor, A., Edim, E. and Ojugo, A. (2023) 'Secure Health Information System with Blockchain Technology,' *Journal of the Nigerian Society of Physical Sciences*, p. 992. .DOI: 10.46481/jnsps.2023.992

Ibrahim, A. M., Abdel-Aziz, H. R., Mohamed, H. A. H., Zaghamir, D. E. F., Wahba, N. M. I., Hassan, G. A., Shaban, M., EL-Nablaway, M., Aldughmi, O. N., & Aboelola, T. H. (2024). Balancing confidentiality and care coordination: Challenges in patient privacy. *BMC Nursing*, 23(1), 564. Advance online publication. DOI: 10.1186/s12912-024-02231-1 PMID: 39148055

Ilori, N. O., Nwosu, N. N. T., & Naiho, N. H. N. N. (2024). Advanced data analytics in internal audits: A conceptual framework for comprehensive risk assessment and fraud detection. *Finance & Accounting Research Journal*, 6(6), 931–952. DOI: 10.51594/farj.v6i6.1213

Jarrahi, M. H. (2018). Artificial intelligence and the future of work: Human-AI symbiosis in organizational decision making. *Business Horizons*, 61(4), 577–586. DOI: 10.1016/j.bushor.2018.03.007

Jayapradha, J., Muttashar Abdulsahib, G., Ibrahim Khalaf, O., Prakash, M., Uddin, M., Abdelhaq, M., & Alsaqour, R. (2024). Cluster-based anonymity model and algorithm for 1:1 dataset with a single sensitive attribute using machine learning technique. *Egyptian Informatics Journal*, 27, 100485. DOI: 10.1016/j.eij.2024.100485

Kayes, A. S. M.. (2024) 'Safeguarding Individuals and Organisations from Privacy Breaches: A Comprehensive Review of Problem Domains, Solution Strategies, and Prospective Research Directions,' *TechRxiv* [Preprint]. DOI: 10.36227/techrxiv.171328715.51528864/v1

Khalid, N., Qayyum, A., Bilal, M., Al-Fuqaha, A., & Qadir, J. (2023). Privacy-preserving artificial intelligence in healthcare: Techniques and applications. *Computers in Biology and Medicine*, 158, 106848. DOI: 10.1016/j.compbiomed.2023.106848 PMID: 37044052

Khatiwada, P., Yang, B., Lin, J.-C., & Blobel, B. (2024). Patient-Generated Health Data (PGHD): Understanding, requirements, challenges, and existing techniques for data security and privacy. *Journal of Personalized Medicine*, 14(3), 282. DOI: 10.3390/jpm14030282 PMID: 38541024

Kumar, N. D.. (2024). Machine learning's role in personalized medicine & treatment optimization. *World Journal of Advanced Research and Reviews*, 21(2), 1675–1686. DOI: 10.30574/wjarr.2024.21.2.0641

Lämmermann, L., Hofmann, P., & Urbach, N. (2024). Managing artificial intelligence applications in healthcare: Promoting information processing among stakeholders. *International Journal of Information Management*, 75, 102728. DOI: 10.1016/j.ijinfomgt.2023.102728

Li, Y. *et al.* (2023) *Development of Situational Awareness enhancing system for AV-to-Manual handover and other tasks.* .DOI: 10.5703/1288284317730

Lim, M., Abdullah, A., Jhanjhi, N. Z., Khurram Khan, M., & Supramaniam, M. (2019). Link Prediction in Time-Evolving Criminal Network with deep Reinforcement learning technique. *IEEE Access : Practical Innovations, Open Solutions*, 7, 184797–184807. DOI: 10.1109/ACCESS.2019.2958873

Lysenko, S. (2024). The role of Artificial intelligence in cybersecurity: Automation of protection and detection of threats. *Economic Affairs*, 69(1s). Advance online publication. DOI: 10.46852/0424-2513.1.2024.6

Manchuri, A. *et al.* (2024) 'pplication of Supervised Machine Learning Models in Biodiesel Production Research - A Short Review,' *Borneo Journal of Sciences and Technology* [Preprint]. .DOI: 10.35370/bjost.2024.6.1-10

Marcén, A. G. (2021) 'The new personal data protection in Japan: Is it enough?' in *Bristol University Press eBooks*, pp. 101–120. DOI: 10.51952/9781529213386.ch003

Mesarčík, M., & Hamuľák, O. (2024) 'General Data Protection Regulation: current challenges and future directions,' in *Contributions to political science*, pp. 117–133. DOI: 10.1007/978-3-031-56045-3_9

Muzafar, S., & Jhanjhi, N. Z. (2020) 'Success stories of ICT implementation in Saudi Arabia,' in *Advances in electronic government, digital divide, and regional development book series*, pp. 151–163. DOI: 10.4018/978-1-7998-1851-9.ch008

Naguib, A., & Fouad, K. M. (2024) 'Database Security: Current Challenges and Effective Protection Strategies,' *2024 6th International Conference on Computing and Informatics (ICCI)* [Preprint]. DOI: 10.1109/ICCI61671.2024.10485182

Okon, S. U., Olateju, O. O., Ogungbemi, O. S., Joseph, S. A., Olisa, A. O., & Olaniyi, O. O. (2024). Incorporating Privacy by Design Principles in the Modification of AI Systems in Preventing Breaches across Multiple Environments, Including Public Cloud, Private Cloud, and On-prem. *Journal of Engineering Research and Reports*, 26(9), 136–158. DOI: 10.9734/jerr/2024/v26i91269

Olawale, N. O.. (2024). RegTech innovations streamlining compliance, reducing costs in the financial sector. *GSC Advanced Research and Reviews*, 19(1), 114–131. DOI: 10.30574/gscarr.2024.19.1.0146

Palaniappan, K., Lin, E. Y. T., & Vogel, S. (2024). Global Regulatory Frameworks for the use of Artificial intelligence (AI) in the healthcare services sector. *Health Care*, 12(5), 562. DOI: 10.3390/healthcare12050562 PMID: 38470673

Pesapane, F., Bracchi, D. A., Mulligan, J. F., Linnikov, A., Maslennikov, O., Lanzavecchia, M. B., Tantrige, P., Stasolla, A., Biondetti, P., Giuggioli, P. F., Cassano, E., & Carrafiello, G. (2021). Legal and Regulatory Framework for AI Solutions in Healthcare in EU, US, China, and Russia: New Scenarios after a Pandemic. *Radiation*, 1(4), 261–276. DOI: 10.3390/radiation1040022

Pfund, G. N., & Allemand, M. (2022). Correlated change between personality traits and perceived social support in old age. *Personality and Social Psychology Bulletin*, 50(2), 167–181. DOI: 10.1177/01461672221120493 PMID: 36149032

Ponnusamy, V.. (2022). *AI-Driven Information and Communication Technologies, Services, and Applications for Next-Generation Healthcare System*. Wiley., DOI: 10.1002/9781119762010.ch1

Pool, J., Akhlaghpour, S., Fatehi, F., & Burton-Jones, A. (2024). A systematic analysis of failures in protecting personal health data: A scoping review. *International Journal of Information Management*, 74, 102719. DOI: 10.1016/j.ijinfomgt.2023.102719

Ramos, S., & Ellul, J. (2024). Blockchain for Artificial Intelligence (AI): Enhancing compliance with the EU AI Act through distributed ledger technology. A cybersecurity perspective, [Preprint]. *International Cybersecurity Law Review*, 5(1), 1–20. Advance online publication. DOI: 10.1365/s43439-023-00107-9

Rana, M., & Shuford, J. (2024). AI in Healthcare: Transforming Patient Care through Predictive Analytics and Decision Support Systems. *Deleted Journal*, 1(1). Advance online publication. DOI: 10.60087/jaigs.v1i1.30

Renaud, K., Warkentin, M., Pogrebna, G., & van der Schyff, K. (2024). VISTA: An inclusive insider threat taxonomy, with mitigation strategies. *Information & Management*, 61(1), 103877. DOI: 10.1016/j.im.2023.103877

Rodrigues, G. A. P., Serrano, A. L. M., & Lemos, A. N. L. E.. (2024). Understanding Data Breach from a Global Perspective: Incident Visualization and Data Protection Law Review. *Data*, 9(2), 27. DOI: 10.3390/data9020027

Rodrigues, G. A. P., Serrano, A. L. M., Vergara, G. F., Albuquerque, R. O., & Nze, G. D. A. (2024). Impact, compliance, and countermeasures in relation to data breaches in publicly traded U.S. companies. *Future Internet*, 16(6), 201. DOI: 10.3390/fi16060201

Roshanaei, M., Khan, M. R., & Sylvester, N. N. (2024). Enhancing Cybersecurity through AI and ML: Strategies, Challenges, and Future Directions. *Journal of Information Security*, 15(03), 320–339. DOI: 10.4236/jis.2024.153019

Rupp, V., & Von Grafenstein, M. (2024). Clarifying "personal data" and the role of anonymisation in data protection law including and excluding data from the scope of the GDPR (more clearly) through refining the concept of data protection. *Computer Law & Security Report*, 52, 105932. DOI: 10.1016/j.clsr.2023.105932

Sabharwal, S. M., Chhabra, S., & Aiden, M. K. (2024) 'AI and Blockchain for Secure Data Analytics,' in *Blockchain technologies*, pp. 39–81. DOI: 10.1007/978-981-97-1249-6_3

Saeed, M. M. A., Saeed, R. A., & Ahmed, Z. E. (2024) 'Data security and privacy in the age of AI and digital twins,' in *Advances in business information systems and analytics book series*, pp. 99–124. DOI: 10.4018/979-8-3693-1818-8.ch008

Santosh, K. and Gaur, L. (2021) *Artificial intelligence and machine learning in public healthcare, SpringerBriefs in applied sciences and technology*. .DOI: 10.1007/978-981-16-6768-8

Sarella, P. N. K., & Mangam, V. T. (2024). AI-Driven Natural Language Processing in Healthcare: Transforming Patient-Provider communication. *Indian Journal of Pharmacy Practice*, 17(1), 21–26. DOI: 10.5530/ijopp.17.1.4

Schuett, J., Reuel, A.-K., & Carlier, A. (2024). How to design an AI ethics board, [Preprint]. *AI and Ethics*. Advance online publication. DOI: 10.1007/s43681-023-00409-y

Seiling, L., Gsenger, R., Mulugeta, F., Henningsen, M., Mischau, L., & Schirmbeck, M. (2024). Beware: Processing of Personal Data—Informed consent through risk communication. *IEEE Transactions on Professional Communication*, 67(1), 4–25. DOI: 10.1109/TPC.2024.3361328

Semwal, R., Tripathi, N., & Tyagi, P. K. (2024) 'Safety first,' in *Advances in hospitality, tourism and the services industry (AHTSI) book series*, pp. 445–466. DOI: 10.4018/979-8-3693-7898-4.ch021

Seng, Y. J.. (2024) 'In-Depth Analysis and Countermeasures for Ransomware Attacks: Case Studies and Recommendations,' *Preprints* [Preprint]. DOI: 10.20944/preprints202408.2261.v1

Seng, Y. J.. (2024) 'In-Depth Analysis and Countermeasures for Ransomware Attacks: Case Studies and Recommendations,' *Preprint* [Preprint]. DOI: 10.20944/preprints202408.2261.v1

SEP (2019). https://plato.stanford.edu/eNtRIeS/it-privacy/

Shafik, W. (2024) 'Shaping the next generation smart City ecosystem: an investigation on the requirements, applications, architecture, security and privacy, and open research questions,' in *S.M.A.R.T. environments*, pp. 3–52. DOI: 10.1007/978-3-031-59846-3_1

Shahriar, S., Allana, S., Hazratifard, S. M., & Dara, R. (2023). A survey of privacy risks and mitigation strategies in the Artificial intelligence life cycle. *IEEE Access : Practical Innovations, Open Solutions*, 11, 61829–61854. DOI: 10.1109/ACCESS.2023.3287195

Shamshari, A., & Najaf, H. (2024) *Machine learning approaches for anomaly detection in network Security*. http://snmzpublisher.com/index.php/eejmr/article/view/9

Sharma, R.. (2022). 'Plant disease diagnosis and image classification using deep learning,' *Computers, Materials & Continua/Computers. Materials & Continua (Print)*, 71(2), 2125–2140. DOI: 10.32604/cmc.2022.020017

Shinde, R., Patil, S., Kotecha, K., Potdar, V., Selvachandran, G., & Abraham, A. (2023). Securing AI-based healthcare systems using blockchain technology: A state-of-the-art systematic literature review and future research directions. *Transactions on Emerging Telecommunications Technologies*, 35(1), e4884. Advance online publication. DOI: 10.1002/ett.4884

Si-Ahmed, A., Al-Garadi, M. A., & Boustia, N. (2024) 'Explainable Machine Learning-Based Security and Privacy Protection Framework for Internet of Medical Things Systems,' *arXiv (Cornell University)* [Preprint]. https://doi.org//arxiv.2403.09752.DOI: 10.48550

Simbeck, K. (2023). They shall be fair, transparent, and robust: Auditing learning analytics systems. *AI and Ethics*, 4(2), 555–571. DOI: 10.1007/s43681-023-00292-7

Sindiramutty, S.R. *et al.* (2023) 'Applications of blockchain technology in supply chain management,' in *Advances in logistics, operations, and management science book series*, pp. 248–304. .DOI: 10.4018/978-1-6684-7625-3.ch009

Sindiramutty, S. R., Jhanjhi, N., Tan, C. E., Lau, S. P., ... (2024) 'Industry 4.0,' in *Advances in logistics, operations, and management science book series*, pp. 342–405. DOI: 10.4018/979-8-3693-1363-3.ch013

Sindiramutty, S. R., Jhanjhi, N., Tan, C. E., Wei, G. W., ... (2024) 'Sustainability in the digital age,' in *Advances in logistics, operations, and management science book series*, pp. 89–132. DOI: 10.4018/979-8-3693-1363-3.ch005

Sindiramutty, S. R., Jhanjhi, N. Z., Tan, C. E., Khan, N. A., Shah, B., & Manchuri, A. R. (2024). Cybersecurity Measures for Logistics Industry. In Navigating Cyber Threats and Cybersecurity in the Logistics Industry (pp. 1-58). IGI Global.

Sindiramutty, S. R., Jhanjhi, N. Z., Tan, C. E., Tee, W. J., Lau, S. P., Jazri, H., . . . Zaheer, M. A. (2024). IoT and AI-Based Smart Solutions for the Agriculture Industry. In Advances in Explainable AI Applications for Smart Cities (pp. 317-351). IGI Global.

Stutz, D.. (2024). *Enhancing Security in Cloud Computing Using Artificial Intelligence (AI)*. Wiley., DOI: 10.1002/9781394196470.ch11

Sutradhar, S., Karforma, S., Bose, R., Roy, S., Djebali, S., & Bhattacharyya, D. (2024). Enhancing identity and access management using Hyperledger Fabric and OAuth 2.0: A block-chain-based approach for security and scalability for healthcare industry. *Internet of Things and Cyber-Physical Systems*, 4, 49–67. DOI: 10.1016/j.iotcps.2023.07.004

Terry, N. (2014). Health privacy is difficult but not impossible in a Post-HIPAA Data-Driven world. *Chest*, 146(3), 835–840. DOI: 10.1378/chest.13-2909 PMID: 25180726

Tilala, M. H.. (2024). Ethical Considerations in the Use of Artificial intelligence and Machine Learning in Health Care: A Comprehensive review, [Preprint]. *Cureus*. Advance online publication. DOI: 10.7759/cureus.62443 PMID: 39011215

Tyagi, A. K. (2023) 'Blockchain and artificial intelligence for cyber security in the era of internet of things and industrial internet of things applications,' in *Advances in computational intelligence and robotics book series*, pp. 171–199. DOI: 10.4018/979-8-3693-0659-8.ch007

Usman, T. M., Saheed, Y. K., Ignace, D., & Nsang, A. (2023). Diabetic retinopathy detection using principal component analysis multi-label feature extraction and classification. *International Journal of Cognitive Computing in Engineering*, 4, 78–88. DOI: 10.1016/j.ijcce.2023.02.002

Waheed, A.. (2024) 'Zero-Day Exploits in Cybersecurity: Case Studies and Countermeasure,' *preprints.org* [Preprint]. DOI: 10.20944/preprints202407.2338.v1

Wang, S., ... (2024) 'Deep learning-based anomaly detection and log analysis for computer networks,' *arXiv (Cornell University)* [Preprint]. https://doi.org//arxiv.2407.05639.DOI: 10.48550

Wen, B. O. T., ... (2023) 'Detecting cyber threats with a Graph-Based NIDPS,' in *Advances in logistics, operations, and management science book series*, pp. 36–74. DOI: 10.4018/978-1-6684-7625-3.ch002

Williamson, S. M., & Prybutok, V. (2024). Balancing Privacy and Progress: A review of privacy challenges, systemic oversight, and patient perceptions in AI-Driven healthcare. *Applied Sciences (Basel, Switzerland)*, 14(2), 675. DOI: 10.3390/app14020675

Winter, J. S., & Davidson, E. (2022). Harmonizing regulatory regimes for the governance of patient-generated health data. *Telecommunications Policy*, 46(5), 102285. DOI: 10.1016/j.telpol.2021.102285

Yar, M. A., Hamdan, M., Anshari, M., Fitriyani, N. L., & Syafrudin, M. (2024). Governing with Intelligence: The Impact of Artificial Intelligence on Policy Development. *Information (Basel)*, 15(9), 556. DOI: 10.3390/info15090556

Zeydan, E., Arslan, S. S., & Liyanage, M. (2024). *Managing distributed machine learning lifecycle for healthcare data in the cloud*. IEEE Access., DOI: 10.1109/ACCESS.2024.3443520

Zhang, S., ... (2018) 'Genie: a secure, transparent sharing and services platform for genetic and health data,' *arXiv (Cornell University)* [Preprint]. https://doi.org//arxiv.1811.01431.DOI: 10.48550

Zhao, L., & Zhang, J. (2024). *Machine learning based business intelligence security and privacy analysis with gaming model in training complexity application*. Entertainment Computing., DOI: 10.1016/j.entcom.2024.100695

Zhu, T.. (2021). *More than Privacy: Applying differential privacy in key areas of artificial intelligence*. IEEE Transactions on Knowledge and Data Engineering., DOI: 10.1109/TKDE.2020.3014246

Compilation of References

Abd El-Aziz, M. (2022). R., Alanazi, R., R Shahin, O., Elhadad, A., Abozeid, A., I Taloba, A., & Alshalabi, R. (2022). An effective data science technique for IoT-Assisted healthcare monitoring system with a rapid adoption of cloud computing. *Computational Intelligence and Neuroscience*.

Abdelkader, S. *et al.* (2024) 'Securing modern power systems. Implementing comprehensive strategies to enhance resilience and reliability against Cyber-Attacks,' *Results in Engineering*, 23, p. 102647. https.//.DOI: 10.1016/j.rineng.2024.102647

AbdelRaouf, A. (2021). A new data hiding approach for image steganography based on visual color sensitivity. *Multimedia Tools and Applications, 80*(15), 23393–23417. https.//DOI: 10.1007/s11042-020-10224-w

Abdulkadium, A. M., Shekan, R. A. A., & Hussain, H. A. (2022). Application of Data Mining and Knowledge Discovery in Medical Databases. *Webology*, 19(1), 4912–4924. DOI: 10.14704/WEB/V19I1/WEB19329

Abdullah, H., & Zeebaree, S. R. M. (2021). Android Mobile Applications Vulnerabilities and Prevention Methods. A Review. semanticscholar.org. https.//www.semanticscholar.org/paper/Android-Mobile-Applications-Vulnerabilities-and-A-Abdullah-Zeebaree/66f217c39116abdf9ab2f89455d228cd5579f110

Abdullah, A., & Arjunan, T. (2023). Leveraging Advanced Machine Learning Techniques for Enhanced Intrusion and Fraud Detection in NoSQL Database Systems. *International Journal of Applied Machine Learning and Computational Intelligence*, 13(11).

Abdul, S. S. M. (2024). Navigating blockchain's twin challenges: Scalability and regulatory compliance. *Blockchains*, 2(3), 265–298. DOI: 10.3390/blockchains2030013

Aboukadri, S., Ouaddah, A., & Mezrioui, A. (2024). Machine learning in identity and access Management Systems: Survey and deep dive. *Computers & Security*, 139, 103729. DOI: 10.1016/j.cose.2024.103729

Acton, T. and Datta, P.M. (2024) 'Endpoint cybersecurity. When smart devices turn stupid,' *Journal of Information Technology Teaching Cases* [Preprint]. https.//.DOI: 10.1177/20438869241242142

Adeniyi, N. A. O.. (2024). The impact of electronic health records on patient care and outcomes: A comprehensive review. *World Journal of Advanced Research and Reviews*, 21(2), 1446–1455. DOI: 10.30574/wjarr.2024.21.2.0592

Aderemi, N. S.. (2024). Blockchain in banking: A comparative review of developments in the USA and Nigeria. *International Journal of Science and Technology Research Archive*, 6(1), 108–126. DOI: 10.53771/ijstra.2024.6.1.0034

Adhikari, S., Gangopadhayay, T.K., Pal, S., Akila, D., Humayun, M. et al. (2023). A novel machine learning–based hand gesture recognition using HCI on iot assisted cloud platform. Computer Systems Science and Engineering, 46(2), 2123-2140. https.//DOI: 10.32604/csse.2023.034431

Agapito, G., & Cannataro, M. (2023). An Overview on the Challenges and Limitations Using Cloud Computing in Healthcare Corporations. *Big Data and Cognitive Computing*, 7(2), 68. DOI: 10.3390/bdcc7020068

Ahamad, S. (2022). Smartphone security and protection practices, (PDF) Smartphone Security and Protection Practices | Shahanawaj Ahamad - Academia.edu. Available at. http.//www.academia.edu/70442415/Smartphone_Security_and_Protection_Practices?rhid=28519263243&swp=rr-rw-wc-30094607

Ahmed, D. E. M., & Khalifa, O. O. (2014). Robust and Secure Image Steganography Based on Elliptic Curve Cryptography. *2014 International Conference on Computer and Communication Engineering*, 288–291. https.//DOI: 10.1109/ICCCE.2014.88

Ahmed, S. F., Alam, M. S. B., Afrin, S., Rafa, S. J., Taher, S. B., Kabir, M., ... & Gandomi, A. H. (2024). Towards a secure 5G-enabled Internet of Things: A survey on requirements, privacy, security, challenges, and opportunities. IEEE Access.

Ahmed, A. A., & Alabi, O. O. (2024). Secure and Scalable Blockchain-Based Federated Learning for Cryptocurrency Fraud Detection: A Systematic Review. *IEEE Access : Practical Innovations, Open Solutions*, 12, 102219–102241. DOI: 10.1109/ACCESS.2024.3429205

Ahmed, H., Traore, I., Saad, S., & Mamun, M. (2021). Automated detection of unstructured context-dependent sensitive information using deep learning. *Internet of Things : Engineering Cyber Physical Human Systems*, 16, 100444. DOI: 10.1016/j.iot.2021.100444

Ahmed, S. F., Alam, M. S. B., Afrin, S., Rafa, S. J., Rafa, N., & Gandomi, A. H. (2024). Insights into Internet of Medical Things (IoMT): Data fusion, security issues and potential solutions. *Information Fusion*, 102, 102060.

Ahmed, Z., Mohamed, K., Zeeshan, S., & Dong, X. Q. (2020). Artificial intelligence with multi-functional machine learning platform development for better healthcare and precision medicine. *Database (Oxford)*, 2020, baaa010. Advance online publication. DOI: 10.1093/database/baaa010 PMID: 32185396

Ahvanooey, M. T. (2020) A survey on smartphone security. Software vulnerabilities, malware, and attacks, International Journal of Advanced Computer Science and Applications. Available at. https.//www.academia.edu/43779422/A_Survey_on_Smartphones_Security_Software_Vulnerabilities_Malware_and_Attacks?rhid=28519395220&swp=rr-rw-wc-70442415

Ajakwe, S. O., Saviour, I. I., Ihekoronye, V. U., Nwankwo, O. U., Dini, M. A., Uchechi, I. U., Kim, D.-S., & Lee, J. M. (2024). Medical IoT Record Security and Blockchain: Systematic review of milieu, milestones, and momentum. *Big Data and Cognitive Computing*, 8(9), 121. DOI: 10.3390/bdcc8090121

Ajala, N.O.A. and Balogun, N.O.A. (2024) 'Leveraging AI/ML for anomaly detection, threat prediction, and automated response,' *World Journal of Advanced Research and Reviews*, 21(1), pp. 2584–2598. https.//.DOI: 10.30574/wjarr.2024.21.1.0287

Ajala, N.O.A. *et al.* (2024) 'Exploring and reviewing the potential of quantum computing in enhancing cybersecurity encryption methods,' *Magna Scientia Advanced Research and Reviews*, 10(1), pp. 321–329. https.//.DOI: 10.30574/msarr.2024.10.1.0038

Ajayi-Nifise, N. A. O.. (2024). BLOCKCHAIN IN U.S. ACCOUNTING: A REVIEW: ASSESSING ITS TRANSFORMATIVE POTENTIAL FOR ENHANCING TRANSPARENCY AND INTEGRITY. *Finance & Accounting Research Journal*, 6(2), 159–182. DOI: 10.51594/farj.v6i2.786

Akinola, O.. (2024). *Artificial Intelligence and Machine Learning Techniques for Anomaly Detection and Threat Mitigation in Cloud-Connected Medical Devices*. International Journal of Scientific Research and Modern Technology., DOI: 10.38124/ijsrmt.v3i3.26

Akkem, Y., Biswas, S.K. and Varanasi, A. (2024) 'A comprehensive review of synthetic data generation in smart farming by using variational autoencoder and generative adversarial network,' *Engineering Applications of Artificial Intelligence*, 131, p. 107881. https.//.DOI: 10.1016/j.engappai.2024.107881

Alaba, F., Madu, I. and Musa, H. (2024) 'Attacks, challenges, and countermeasures for an integrated IoT framework,' *Internet of Things and Cloud Computing*, 12(2), pp. 28–39. https.//.DOI: 10.11648/j.iotcc.20241202.12

Al-Afandy, K. A., Faragallah, O. S., Elmhalawy, A., El-Rabaie, E.-S. M., & El-Banby, Gh. M. (2016). High security data hiding using image cropping and LSB least significant bit steganography. *2016 4th IEEE International Colloquium on Information Science and Technology (CiSt)*, 400–404. https.//DOI: 10.1109/CIST.2016.7805079

AL-Dosari, K., Fetais, N., & Kucukvar, M.AL-Dosari. (2024). Artificial intelligence and cyber defense system for banking industry: A qualitative study of AI applications and challenges. *Cybernetics and Systems*, 55(2), 302–330. DOI: 10.1080/01969722.2022.2112539

Alex, S. A., Jhanjhi, N. Z., Humayun, M., Ibrahim, A. O., & Abulfaraj, A. W. (2022). Deep LSTM Model for Diabetes Prediction with Class Balancing by SMOTE. *Electronics (Basel)*, 11(17), 2737. DOI: 10.3390/electronics11172737

Alferidah, D. K., & Jhanjhi, N. (2020) 'Cybersecurity Impact over Bigdata and IoT Growth,' *International Conference on Computational Intelligence (ICCI)* [Preprint]. DOI: 10.1109/ICCI51257.2020.9247722

Ali, A., Naeem, S., Anam, S., & Ahmed, M. M. (2023). A state of art survey for big data processing and nosql database architecture. *International Journal of Computing and Digital Systems*, 14(1), 1–1. DOI: 10.12785/ijcds/140124

Ali, O., Shrestha, A., Soar, J., & Wamba, S. F. (2018). Cloud computing-enabled healthcare opportunities, issues, and applications: A systematic review. *International Journal of Information Management*, 43, 146–158. DOI: 10.1016/j.ijinfomgt.2018.07.009

Aljabri, A., Jemili, F., & Korbaa, O. (2023). Intrusion detection in cyber-physical system using rsa blockchain technology. *Multimedia Tools and Applications*, 83(16), 48119–48140. DOI: 10.1007/s11042-023-17576-z

Al-Janabi, S. (2021). Overcoming the main challenges of knowledge discovery through tendency to the intelligent data analysis. In *2021 International Conference on Data Analytics for Business and Industry (ICDABI)* (pp. 286-294). IEEE. DOI: 10.1109/ICDABI53623.2021.9655916

Alkaabi, S. R., Gregory, M. A., & Li, S. (2024) 'Multi-Access Edge Computing Handover Strategies, Management, and Challenges. A review,' *IEEE Access*, 12, pp. 4660–4673. https.//DOI: 10.1109/ACCESS.2024.3349587

Alkhatib, M., Albalawi, T., & Saeed, F. (2024). Blockchain-Based quality assurance system for academic programs. *Applied Sciences (Basel, Switzerland)*, 14(11), 4868. DOI: 10.3390/app14114868

Alkinani, M. H., Almazroi, A. A., Jhanjhi, N. Z., & Khan, N. A. (2021). 5G and IoT based reporting and accident detection (RAD) system to deliver first aid box using unmanned aerial vehicle. *Sensors (Basel)*, 21(20), 6905.

Alkinani, M. H., Almazroi, A. A., Jhanjhi, N. Z., & Khan, N. A. (2021). 5G and IoT Based Reporting and Accident Detection (RAD) System to Deliver First Aid Box Using Unmanned Aerial Vehicle. *Sensors (Basel)*, 21(20), 6905. DOI: 10.3390/s21206905 PMID: 34696118

Al-Otaibi, N. A., & Gutub, A. A. (2014). 2-leyer security system for hiding sensitive text data on personal computers. *Lecture Notes on Information Theory*, 2(2), 151–157.

Alquwayzani, A. A., & Albuali, A. A. (2024) 'A Systematic Literature Review of Zero Trust Architecture for UAV Security Systems in IoBT,' *preprint.org* [Preprint]. https.//DOI: 10.20944/preprints202403.0349.v1

Alshahrani, S. M. (2024). Disrupting the status quo: Blockchain's potential for overhauling conventional academic systems, [Preprint]. *Arabian Journal for Science and Engineering*. Advance online publication. DOI: 10.1007/s13369-024-09065-8

Al-Sharideh, M., & Alshammari, R. (2020). Business Intelligence and Data Warehouse. A Review of Literature and Future Directions. *International Journal of Business Intelligence Research*, 10(2), 1–18. DOI: 10.4018/IJBIR.2020040101

Al-Sheikh, M. A., & Ameen, I. A. (2020, July). Design of mobile healthcare monitoring system using IoT technology and cloud computing. [). IOP Publishing.]. *IOP Conference Series. Materials Science and Engineering*, 881(1), 012113. DOI: 10.1088/1757-899X/881/1/012113

Alzaabi, F. R., & Mehmood, A. (2024) 'A Review of Recent Advances, Challenges and Opportunities in Malicious Insider Threat Detection using Machine Learning Methods,' *IEEE Access*, p. 1. https.//DOI: 10.1109/ACCESS.2024.3369906

Alzoubi, M.M. (2024) 'Investigating the synergy of Blockchain and AI: enhancing security, efficiency, and transparency,' *Journal of Cyber Security Technology*, pp. 1–29. .DOI: 10.1080/23742917.2024.2374594

Amanat, A., Rizwan, M., Maple, C., Zikria, Y. B., Almadhor, A. S., & Kim, S. W. (2022). Blockchain and cloud computing-based secure electronic healthcare records storage and sharing. *Frontiers in Public Health*, 10, 938707. DOI: 10.3389/fpubh.2022.938707 PMID: 35928494

Amend, J., Troglauer, P., Guggenberger, T., Urbach, N., & Weibelzahl, M. (2023). Facilitating cooperation of smallholders in developing countries: Design principles for a cooperative-oriented decentralized autonomous organization. *Information Systems and e-Business Management*, 22(1), 1–31. DOI: 10.1007/s10257-023-00659-7

Amin, M. M., Salleh, M., Ibrahim, S., Katmin, M. R., & Shamsuddin, M. Z. I. (2003). Information hiding using steganography. *4th National Conference of Telecommunication Technology, 2003. NCTT 2003 Proceedings.*, 21–25. https.//DOI: 10.1109/NCTT.2003.1188294

Aminizadeh, S., Heidari, A., Dehghan, M., Toumaj, S., Rezaei, M., Jafari Navimipour, N., Stroppa, F., & Unal, M. (2024). Opportunities and challenges of artificial intelligence and distributed systems to improve the quality of healthcare service. *Artificial Intelligence in Medicine*, 149, 102779. DOI: 10.1016/j.artmed.2024.102779 PMID: 38462281

Aminu, M. (2024) 'Enhancing Cyber Threat Detection through Real-time Threat Intelligence and Adaptive Defense Mechanisms,' *International Journal of Computer Applications Technology and Research* [Preprint]. .DOI: 10.7753/IJCATR1308.1002

Ananna, F. F., Nowreen, R., Al Jahwari, S. S. R., Costa, E. A., Angeline, L., & Sindiramutty, S. R. (2023). Analysing Influential factors in student academic achievement: Prediction modelling and insight. *International Journal of Emerging Multidisciplinaries Computer Science & Artificial Intelligence*, 2(1). Advance online publication. DOI: 10.54938/ijemdcsai.2023.02.1.254

Anderson, R., & Fuloria, S. (2010) 'Who Controls the off Switch?' *2010 First IEEE International Conference on Smart Grid Communications* [Preprint]. https.//DOI: 10.1109/SMARTGRID.2010.5622026

Anglano, C. *et al.* (2024) 'The HealthTracker System. app and Cloud-Based wearable Multi-Sensor device for patients health tracking,' *Applied Sciences*, 14(2), p. 887. https.//.DOI: 10.3390/app14020887

Anh, L. D., Mutaher, H., & Bijalwan, A. (2024) 'A Robust Authentication Technique for Client–Server Secure Login,' *Wiley*, pp. 123–140. https.//DOI: 10.1002/9781394272303.ch8

Anh, S. P., & Nakamura, Y. (2024) 'A baseline investigation into the evolution and prevalence of Mirai and Hajime utilizing a network telescope,' *IEEE Access*, 12, pp. 103789–103809. https.//DOI: 10.1109/ACCESS.2024.3434555

Annadurai, C., Nelson, I., Devi, K. N., Manikandan, R., Jhanjhi, N. Z., Masud, M., & Sheikh, A. (2022). Biometric Authentication-Based Intrusion Detection Using Artificial Intelligence Internet of Things in Smart City. *Energies, 15*(19), Article 19. https.//DOI: 10.3390/en15197430

Anusha, K., Rajesh, N., Kavitha, M., & Ravinder, N. (2021, April). Comparative Study of MongoDB vs Cassandra in big data analytics. In *2021 5th International Conference on Computing Methodologies and Communication (ICCMC)* (pp. 1831-1835). IEEE. DOI: 10.1109/ICCMC51019.2021.9418441

Aoun, A., Kashmar, N., Adda, M., & Ibrahim, H. (2024). From Bottom-Up towards a completely decentralized autonomous electric grid based on the concept of a decentralized autonomous substation. *Electronics (Basel)*, 13(18), 3683. DOI: 10.3390/electronics13183683

Ari, A.A.A. *et al.* (2019) 'Enabling privacy and security in Cloud of Things. Architecture, applications, security & privacy challenges,' *Applied Computing and Informatics*, 20(1/2), pp. 119–141. https.//.DOI: 10.1016/j.aci.2019.11.005

Arif, H. *et al.* (2024) 'Future Horizons. AI-Enhanced Threat Detection in cloud environments. Unveiling opportunities for research,' *International Journal of Multidisciplinary Sciences and Arts*, 2(2), pp. 242–251. https.//.DOI: 10.47709/ijmdsa.v2i2.3452

Arkko, J., & Nikander, P. (2004) 'Weak Authentication. How to Authenticate Unknown Principals without Trusted Parties,' in *Lecture notes in computer science*, pp. 5–19. https.//DOI: 10.1007/978-3-540-39871-4_3

Arshad, M., Brohi, M. N., Soomro, T. R., Ghazal, T. M., Alzoubi, H. M., & Alshurideh, M. (2023). Nosql: Future of bigdata analytics characteristics and comparison with rdbms. In *The Effect of Information Technology on Business and Marketing Intelligence Systems* (pp. 1927–1951). Springer International Publishing. DOI: 10.1007/978-3-031-12382-5_106

Aruna, E. and Sahayadhas, A. (2024) 'Blockchain-Inspired lightweight dynamic encryption schemes for a secure health care information exchange system,' *Engineering Technology & Applied Science Research*, 14(4), pp. 15050–15055. https.//.DOI: 10.48084/etasr.7390

Arun, J. S., Cuomo, J., & Gaur, N. (2019). *Blockchain for business.* Addison-Wesley Professional.

Asaithambi, S., Ravi, L., Devarajan, M., Almazyad, A. S., Xiong, G., & Mohamed, A. W. (2024). Enhancing enterprises trust mechanism through integrating blockchain technology into e-commerce platform for SMEs. *Egyptian Informatics Journal*, 25, 100444. DOI: 10.1016/j.eij.2024.100444

Ashitha, U., ... (2024) 'Strengthening Cloud Security Through Multi-Factor Authentication. A Comprehensive Integration of Diverse Approaches,' *2024 International Conference on Electronics, Computing, Communication and Control Technology (ICECCC)* [Preprint]. https.//DOI: 10.1109/ICECCC61767.2024.10593923

Ashraf, H., Hanif, M., Ihsan, U., Al-Quayed, F., Humayun, M., & Jhanjhi, N. "A Secure and Reliable Supply chain management approach integrated with IoT and Blockchain," *2023 International Conference on Business Analytics for Technology and Security (ICBATS)*, Dubai, United Arab Emirates, 2023, pp. 1-9, doi. DOI: 10.1109/ICBATS57792.2023.10111371

Ashraf, H., Jhanjhi, N. Z., Brohi, S. N., & Muzafar, S. (2024). A Comprehensive Exploration of DDoS Attacks and Cybersecurity Imperatives in the Digital Age. In *Navigating Cyber Threats and Cybersecurity in the Logistics Industry* (pp. 236–257). IGI Global. DOI: 10.4018/979-8-3693-3816-2.ch009

Ashraf, J.. (2022). Machine and Deep Learning-Based Intrusion Detection Systems in Internet of Things. A Comprehensive Review. *IEEE Transactions on Industrial Electronics*, 69(12), 13082–13095.

Aslam, M. A., Rashid, M., Azam, F., Abbas, M., Rasheed, Y., Alotaibi, S. S., & Anwar, M. W. (2022). Image Steganography using Least Significant Bit (LSB)—A Systematic Literature Review. *2022 2nd International Conference on Computing and Information Technology (ICCIT)*, 32–38. https.//DOI: 10.1109/ICCIT52419.2022.9711628

Atawneh, S., Almomani, A., & Sumari, P. (2013). Steganography in digital images. Common approaches and tools. *IETE Technical Review, 30*(4), 344–358. https.// DOI: 10.4103/0256-4602.116724

Azam, H. Tan, Micheal, Pin, L.T., Syahmi, M.A., Qian, A.L.W., Jingyan, H., Uddin, M.F., *et al.* (2023) 'Wireless Technology Security and Privacy: A Comprehensive Study,' preprints.*org* [Preprint]. DOI: 10.20944/preprints202311.0664.v1

Azam, H., Tan, M., Pin, L. T., Syahmi, M. A., Qian, A. L. W., Jingyan, H., ... & Sindiramutty, S. R. (2023). Wireless Technology Security and Privacy: A Comprehensive Study.

Azam, H., Dulloo, M. I., Majeed, M. H., Wan, J. P. H., Xin, L. T., & Sindiramutty, S. R. (2023). Cybercrime Unmasked: Investigating cases and digital evidence. *International Journal of Emerging Multidisciplinaries Computer Science & Artificial Intelligence*, 2(1). Advance online publication. DOI: 10.54938/ijemdcsai.2023.02.1.255

Azam, H., Dulloo, M. I., Majeed, M. H., Wan, J. P. H., Xin, L. T., Tajwar, M. A., & Sindiramutty, S. R. (2023). Defending the digital Frontier: IDPS and the battle against Cyber threat. *International Journal of Emerging Multidisciplinaries Computer Science & Artificial Intelligence*, 2(1). Advance online publication. DOI: 10.54938/ijemdcsai.2023.02.1.253

Azam, H., Tajwar, M. A., Mayhialagan, S., Davis, A. J., Yik, C. J., Ali, D., & Sindiramutty, S. R. (2023). Innovations in Security: A study of cloud Computing and IoT. *International Journal of Emerging Multidisciplinaries Computer Science & Artificial Intelligence*, 2(1).

Azam, H., Tajwar, M. A., Mayhialagan, S., Davis, A. J., Yik, C. J., Ali, D., & Sindiramutty, S. R. (2023). Innovations in Security: A study of cloud Computing and IoT. *International Journal of Emerging Multidisciplinaries Computer Science & Artificial Intelligence*, 2(1). Advance online publication. DOI: 10.54938/ijemdcsai.2023.02.1.252

Azeem, M., Ullah, A., Ashraf, H., Jhanjhi, N., Humayun, M., Aljahdali, S., & Tabbakh, T. A. (2021). FOG-Oriented secure and lightweight data aggregation in IOMT. *IEEE Access : Practical Innovations, Open Solutions*, 9, 111072–111082. DOI: 10.1109/ACCESS.2021.3101668

Azeroual, O., & Nikiforova, A. (2022). Apache spark and mllib-based intrusion detection system or how the big data technologies can secure the data. *Information (Basel)*, 13(2), 58. DOI: 10.3390/info13020058

B Selvakumar and Karuppiah Muneeswaran. Firefly algorithm-based feature selection for network intrusion detection. Computers & Security, 81.148–155, 2019.

Babbar, H., Rani, S., Masud, M., Verma, S., Anand, D., & Jhanjhi, N. Z. (2021). 'Load balancing algorithm for migrating switches in software-defined vehicular networks,' *Computers, Materials & Continua/Computers. Computers, Materials & Continua*, 67(1), 1301–1316. DOI: 10.32604/cmc.2021.014627

Badertscher, C., Maurer, U., Tschudi, D., & Zikas, V. (2024). Bitcoin as a transaction ledger: A composable treatment. *Journal of Cryptology*, 37(2), 18. Advance online publication. DOI: 10.1007/s00145-024-09493-7

Badjie, B., Cecílio, J. and Casimiro, A. (2024) 'Adversarial Attacks and Countermeasures on image classification-based deep learning models in Autonomous Driving Systems. A systematic review,' *ACM Computing Surveys* [Preprint]. https.//.DOI: 10.1145/3691625

Bagheri, R., Nezhad, M. Z., Rizi, M. H. P., & Sadri, M. (2023). Identifying and evaluating factors affecting user privacy in the smart City using the Meta-Synthesis method and the Fuzzy Dematel technique. *International Journal of Information Technology & Decision Making*, 23(04), 1671–1702. DOI: 10.1142/S0219622023500530

Bajaj, A. and Vishwakarma, D.K. (2023) 'A state-of-the-art review on adversarial machine learning in image classification,' *Multimedia Tools and Applications*, 83(3), pp. 9351–9416. https.//.DOI: 10.1007/s11042-023-15883-z

Bakar, A., & Ahmad, M. (2021). The Role of Data Warehousing in Business Intelligence for Healthcare Organizations. *Journal of Healthcare Engineering*, 2021, 1–9. DOI: 10.1155/2021/8813194

Balasubramaniam, S., Sankar, K. S., Malar, C. B., Rajasekaran, M. P., Arunkumar, N., & Thilagaraj, M. (2023). Detecting the Type of Attack in Healthcare Cloud Computing System Using Termite Deep Belief Neural Network (TDBNN) for Future Smart Cities. *Journal of Testing and Evaluation*, 51(3), 1421–1437. DOI: 10.1520/JTE20220041

Bamashmos, S., Chilamkurti, N. and Shahraki, A.S. (2024) 'Two-Layered Multi-Factor authentication using decentralized blockchain in IoT environment,' *Sensors*, 24(11), p. 3575. https.//.DOI: 10.3390/s24113575

Banafa, A. (2024). *Transformative AI: Responsible, Transparent, and Trustworthy AI systems*. CRC Press. DOI: 10.1201/9781032669182

Bansal, P. and Ouda, A. (2024) 'Continuous Authentication in the Digital Age. An analysis of reinforcement learning and Behavioral biometrics,' *Computers*, 13(4), p. 103. https.//.DOI: 10.3390/computers13040103

Barrientos, A. F., Williams, A. R., Snoke, J., & Bowen, C. M. K. (2023). A Feasibility Study of Differentially Private Summary Statistics and Regression Analyses with Evaluations on Administrative and Survey Data. *Journal of the American Statistical Association*, 119(545), 52–65. DOI: 10.1080/01621459.2023.2270795

BasuMallick. C. (2022). Top 10 Threat Intelligence Platforms in 2022. Retrieved from https://www.spiceworks.com/it-security/vulnerability-management/articles/best-threat-intelligence-platforms/

Batra, I.; Verma, S.; Malik, A.; Kavita; Ghosh, U.; Rodrigues, J.J.P.C.; Nguyen, G.N.; Hosen, A.S.M.S.; Mariappan, V. Hybrid Logical Security Framework for Privacy Preservation in the Green Internet of Things. *Sustainability* 2020, *12*, 5542. https.//DOI: 10.3390/su12145542

Bauch, P. (2024) 'Data Privacy and Regulation,' SSRN *Electronic Journal* [Preprint]. https://doi.org/DOI: 10.2139/ssrn.4723359

Bécue, A., Praça, I. and Gama, J. (2021) 'Artificial intelligence, cyber-threats and Industry 4.0. challenges and opportunities,' *Artificial Intelligence Review*, 54(5), pp. 3849–3886. https.//.DOI: 10.1007/s10462-020-09942-2

Behal, S., & Kumar, K. (2017). Detection of DDoS attacks and flash events using novel information theory metrics. *Computer Networks*, 116, 96–110. DOI: 10.1016/j.comnet.2017.02.015

Behal, S., Kumar, K., & Sachdeva, M. (2018). D-FACE. An anomaly-based distributed approach for early detection of DDoS attacks and flash events. *Journal of Network and Computer Applications*, 111, 49–63. DOI: 10.1016/j.jnca.2018.03.024

Bekbolatova, M., Mayer, J., Ong, C. W., & Toma, M. (2024). Transformative Potential of AI in Healthcare: Definitions, applications, and navigating the ethical landscape and public perspectives. *Health Care*, 12(2), 125. DOI: 10.3390/healthcare12020125 PMID: 38255014

Belenky, A., & Ansari, N. (2003). On IP traceback. *IEEE Communications Magazine*, 41(7), 142–153. DOI: 10.1109/MCOM.2003.1215651

Bello, N.H.O., Idemudia, N.C. and Iyelolu, N.T.V. (2024) 'Navigating Financial Compliance in Small and Medium-Sized Enterprises (SMEs): Overcoming challenges and implementing effective solutions,' *World Journal of Advanced Research and Reviews*, 23(1), pp. 042–050. .DOI: 10.30574/wjarr.2024.23.1.1984

Benraouane, S. A. (2024). *AI Management System certification according to the ISO/IEC 42001 Standard: How to Audit, Certify, and Build Responsible AI Systems.* CRC Press. DOI: 10.4324/9781003463979

Benstead, A. V.. (2022). Entering the world behind the clothes that we wear: Practical applications of blockchain technology. *Production Planning and Control*, •••, 1–18. DOI: 10.1080/09537287.2022.2063173

Bhandari, A., Kumar, K., Sangal, A. L., & Behal, S. (2021). An anomaly-based distributed detection system for DDoS attacks in Tier-2 ISP networks. *Journal of Ambient Intelligence and Humanized Computing*, 12(1), 1387–1406. DOI: 10.1007/s12652-020-02208-3

Bhardwaj, S. and Dave, M. (2024) 'Attack detection and mitigation using Intelligent attack graph model for Forensic in IoT Networks,' *Telecommunication Systems*, 85(4), pp. 601–621. https.//.DOI: 10.1007/s11235-024-01105-w

Bhatia, M.P.S. and Sangwan, S.R. (2021) 'Soft computing for anomaly detection and prediction to mitigate IoT-based real-time abuse,' *Personal and Ubiquitous Computing* [Preprint]. https.//.DOI: 10.1007/s00779-021-01567-8

Bhavani, Y., Kamakshi, P., Kavya Sri, E., & Sindhu Sai, Y. (2022). A Survey on Image Steganography Techniques Using Least Significant Bit. In D. J. Hemanth, D. Pelusi, & C. Vuppalapati (Eds.), *Intelligent Data Communication Technologies and Internet of Things* (pp. 281–290). Springer Nature. https.//DOI: 10.1007/978-981-16-7610-9_20

Bhuyan, M. H., & Elmroth, E. (2018, December). Multi-scale low-rate DDoS attack detection using the generalized total variation metric. In *2018 17th IEEE International Conference on Machine Learning and Applications (ICMLA)* (pp. 1040-1047). IEEE. DOI: 10.1109/ICMLA.2018.00170

BN, C., & SH, B. (2024). Revolutionizing ransomware detection and criticality assessment: Multiclass hybrid machine learning and semantic similarity-based end2end solution. *Multimedia Tools and Applications*, 83(13), 39135–39168.

Böhmecke-Schwafert, M. (2024). The role of blockchain for trade in global value chains: A systematic literature review and guidance for future research. *Telecommunications Policy*, 48(9), 102835. DOI: 10.1016/j.telpol.2024.102835

Bohora, K., Bothe, A., Sheth, D., Chopade, R., & Pachghare, V. K. (2021). Backup and recovery mechanisms of cassandra database: A review. *Journal of Digital Forensics. Security and Law*, 15(2), 5.

Boisrond, K., Tardif, P. M., & Jaafar, F. (2024) 'Ensuring the integrity, confidentiality, and availability of IoT data in Industry 5.0. A Systematic mapping study,' *IEEE Access*, 12, pp. 107017–107045. https.//DOI: 10.1109/ACCESS.2024.3434618

Bolu, T. (2024). " Temporal Data Processing and Retention Strategies in Cassandra-Kafka Integration for Scalable Time-Series Data.

Bonettini, N., Cannas, E. D., Mandelli, S., Bondi, L., Bestagini, P., & Tubaro, S. (2021). Video face manipulation detection through an ensemble of CNNs, 2020 25th International Conference on Pattern Recognition (ICPR), pp. 5012–5019.

Borgogno, O., & Martino, E. (2024). Decentralised autonomous organisations: Targeting the potential beyond the hype. *Law, Innovation and Technology*, 16(2), 1–40. DOI: 10.1080/17579961.2024.2392933

Boudlal, H., Serrhini, M., & Tahiri, A. (2022, May). Cloud Computing for Healthcare Services: Technology, Application and Architecture. In 2022 11th International Symposium on Signal, Image, Video and Communications (ISIVC) (pp. 1-5). IEEE.

Bounfour, A., & Moussa, A. (2022). Big Data Analytics in the Public Sector. A Review of Current Trends. *Journal of Business Research*, 140, 217–229. DOI: 10.1016/j.jbusres.2021.12.018

Bouyeddou, B., Kadri, B., Harrou, F., & Sun, Y. (2020). DDOS-attacks detection using an efficient measurement-based statistical mechanism. *Engineering Science and Technology, an International Journal, 23*(4), 870-878.

Bouyeddou, B., Harrou, F., Sun, Y., & Kadri, B. (2018, November). An effective network intrusion detection using hellinger distance-based monitoring mechanism. In *2018 International Conference on Applied Smart Systems (ICASS)* (pp. 1-6). IEEE. DOI: 10.1109/ICASS.2018.8652008

Bradley, S. H., Lawrence, N. R., & Carder, P. (2018). Using primary care data for health research in England – an overview. *Future Healthcare Journal*, 5(3), 207–212. DOI: 10.7861/futurehosp.5-3-207 PMID: 31098568

Brohi, S. N.. (2020) 'Key Applications of State-of-the-Art Technologies to Mitigate and Eliminate COVID-19.pdf,' *TechRhiv* [Preprint]. DOI: 10.36227/techrxiv.12115596.v1

Brotherston, L., Berlin, A., & Reyor, W. F.III. (2024). *Defensive Security Handbook*. O'Reilly Media, Inc.

Bui, H. T., Aboutorab, H., Mahboubi, A., Gao, Y., Sultan, N. H., Chauhan, A., Parvez, M. Z., Bewong, M., Islam, R., Islam, Z., Camtepe, S. A., Gauravaram, P., Singh, D., Ali Babar, M., & Yan, S. (2024). Agriculture 4.0 and beyond: Evaluating cyber threat intelligence sources and techniques in smart farming ecosystems. *Computers & Security*, 140, 103754. DOI: 10.1016/j.cose.2024.103754

Burkhardt, M. A., & Nathaniel, A. K. (2019). *Ethics & Issues in Contemporary Nursing - E-Book*. Elsevier Health Sciences.

Buttar, A. M., ... (2024) 'Decentralized Identity Management using Blockchain Technology: Challenges and solutions,' in *Signals and communication technology*, pp. 131–166. DOI: 10.1007/978-3-031-49593-9_8

Caballero-Gil, C. *et al.* (2023) 'Research on smart-locks cybersecurity and vulnerabilities,' *Wireless Networks*, 30(6), pp. 5905–5917. https.//.DOI: 10.1007/s11276-023-03376-8

Calvi, A. (2024). Data Protection Impact Assessment under the EU General Data Protection Regulation: A feminist reflection. *Computer Law & Security Report*, 53, 105950. DOI: 10.1016/j.clsr.2024.105950

Camacho, N. G. (2024). The role of AI in Cybersecurity: Addressing Threats in the Digital Age. *Deleted Journal*, 3(1), 143–154. DOI: 10.60087/jaigs.v3i1.75

Canavese, D. *et al.* (2024) 'Security at the edge for Resource-Limited IoT devices,' *Sensors*, 24(2), p. 590. https.//.DOI: 10.3390/s24020590

Carpenter, J., & Hewitt, E. (2022). *Cassandra: The Definitive Guide, (Revised).* O'Reilly Media, Inc.

Carreira, F., Cunha, P. R., Barata, J., & Estima, J. (2024). Tamper-Proof Blockchain-Based Contracts for the Carriage of Goods by Road. *AIS*, 26. Advance online publication. DOI: 10.62036/ISD.2024.105

Carter, S., & Nielsen, M. (2017). Using artificial intelligence to augment human intelligence. *Distill*, 2(12), e9. DOI: 10.23915/distill.00009

Cavedon-Taylor, D. (2024) 'Deepfakes. a survey and introduction to the topical collection,' *Synthese*, 204(1). https.//.DOI: 10.1007/s11229-024-04634-8

Cepheli, Ö., Büyükçorak, S., & Karabulut Kurt, G. (2016). Hybrid intrusion detection system for ddos attacks. *Journal of Electrical and Computer Engineering*, 2016(1), 1075648. DOI: 10.1155/2016/1075648

Cervantes, J., Garcia-Lamont, F., Rodríguez-Mazahua, L., & Lopez, A. (2020). A comprehensive survey on support vector machine classification: Applications, challenges and trends. *Neurocomputing*, 408, 189–215. DOI: 10.1016/j.neucom.2019.10.118

Chakraborty, S. (2023). AI and ethics: Navigating the moral landscape. In *Investigating the Impact of AI on Ethics and Spirituality* (pp. 25-33).

Chan, C.-K., & Cheng, L. M. (2004). Hiding data in images by simple LSB substitution. *Pattern Recognition, 37*(3), 469–474. https.//DOI: 10.1016/j.patcog.2003.08.007

Chander, B. *et al.* (2024) 'Toward trustworthy artificial intelligence (TAI) in the context of explainability and robustness,' *ACM Computing Surveys* [Preprint]. https.//.DOI: 10.1145/3675392

Chauhan, S., Arora, R., & Kaur, G. (2024) 'Recent Industry-Defined and Domain-Specific IoT Architectures,' *Wiley*, pp. 117–140. https.//DOI: 10.1002/9781119905202.ch8

Chawla, S., Sachdeva, M., & Behal, S. (2016). Discrimination of DDoS attacks and flash events using Pearson's product-moment correlation method. *International Journal of Computer Science and Information Security*, 14(10), 382.

Chen, H. and Babar, M.A. (2024) 'Security for Machine learning-based Software Systems. A survey of threats, practices, and challenges,' *ACM Computing Surveys*, 56(6), pp. 1–38. https.//.DOI: 10.1145/3638531

Chen, B., Ju, X., Xiao, B., Ding, W., Zheng, Y., & de Albuquerque, V. H. C. (2021). Locally gan-generated face detection based on an improved exception. *Information Sciences*, 572, 16–28. DOI: 10.1016/j.ins.2021.05.006

Chen, J., & Zhang, X. (2023). Cybersecurity Challenges in Business Intelligence. A Comprehensive Study. *Journal of Cybersecurity and Privacy*, 3(1), 156–171. DOI: 10.3390/jcp3010009

Chen, M.. (2023). Data anonymization evaluation against re-identification attacks in edge storage, [Preprint]. *Wireless Networks*. Advance online publication. DOI: 10.1007/s11276-023-03235-6

Chen, Q., & Liu, X. (2024). Machine Learning Techniques for Anomaly Detection in Industrial IoT Systems. A Survey. *IEEE Access : Practical Innovations, Open Solutions*, 12, 18673–18684.

Chen, W., & Liu, H. (2023). Intrusion Detection Systems for Industrial IoT Security. A Comprehensive Review. *IEEE Transactions on Industrial Electronics*, 70(5), 4303–4312.

Chen, Y., & Wang, L. (2021). Machine Learning Approaches for Anomaly Detection in Industrial IoT Environments. *IEEE Transactions on Industrial Informatics*, 17(3), 1982–1991.

Cheong, B. C. (2024). Transparency and accountability in AI systems: Safeguarding wellbeing in the age of algorithmic decision-making. *Frontiers in Human Dynamics*, 6, 1421273. Advance online publication. DOI: 10.3389/fhumd.2024.1421273

Cherbal, S. *et al.* (2023) 'Security in internet of things. a review on approaches based on blockchain, machine learning, cryptography, and quantum computing,' *The Journal of Supercomputing*, 80(3), pp. 3738–3816. https.//.DOI: 10.1007/s11227-023-05616-2

Chesti, I. A., ... (2020) 'Evolution, Mitigation, and Prevention of Ransomware,' *2020 2nd International Conference on Computer and Information Sciences (ICCIS)* [Preprint]. DOI: 10.1109/ICCIS49240.2020.9257708

Chew, C.J.W. *et al.* (2024) 'Real-time system call-based ransomware detection,' *International Journal of Information Security*, 23(3), pp. 1839–1858. https.//.DOI: 10.1007/s10207-024-00819-x

Chhabra, A.. (2024). *Navigating the Maze: Exploring blockchain privacy and its information retrieval.* IEEE Access., DOI: 10.1109/ACCESS.2024.3370857

Chhotaray, P., ... (2023) 'Enhancement of Manufacturing Sector Performance with the Application of Industrial Internet of Things (IIoT),' in *CRC Press eBooks*, pp. 1–19. https.//DOI: 10.1201/9781003346623-1

Chiu, T.K.F. *et al.* (2022) 'Creation and evaluation of a pretertiary Artificial Intelligence (AI) curriculum,' *IEEE Transactions on Education*, 65(1), pp. 30–39. https.//. DOI: 10.1109/TE.2021.3085878

Cho, J.-H. *et al.* (2020) 'Toward Proactive, Adaptive Defense. A survey on moving target defense,' *IEEE Communications Surveys & Tutorials*, 22(1), pp. 709–745. https.//.DOI: 10.1109/COMST.2019.2963791

Choithani, T., Chowdhury, A., Patel, S., Patel, P., Patel, D., & Shah, M. (2022). A comprehensive study of artificial intelligence and cybersecurity on Bitcoin, crypto currency and banking system. *Annals of Data Science*, 11(1), 103–135. DOI: 10.1007/s40745-022-00433-5

Choubisa, M. (2024) 'IoT Devices,' *Wiley*, pp. 141–156. https.//DOI: 10.1002/9781119905202.ch9

Choucri, N., Madnick, S. and Ferwerda, J. (2013) 'Institutions for Cyber Security. International responses and global imperatives,' *Information Technology for Development*, 20(2), pp. 96–121. https.//.DOI: 10.1080/02681102.2013.836699

Chowdhury, N. R. H. (2024). Blockchain and AI: Driving the future of data security and business intelligence. *World Journal of Advanced Research and Reviews*, 23(1), 2559–2570. DOI: 10.30574/wjarr.2024.23.1.2273

Ch, R., Sridevi, M., Ramchander, M., Ramesh, V., & Kumar, V. P. (2024). Enhancing Digital Security Using Signa-Deep for Online Signature Verification and Identity Authentication. *International Journal of Systematic Innovation*, 8(2), 58–69.

Christodoulou, I., Rizomyliotis, I., Konstantoulaki, K., Nazarian, A., & Binh, D. (2024). Transforming the remittance industry: Harnessing the power of blockchain technology. *Journal of Enterprise Information Management*, 37(5), 1551–1577. DOI: 10.1108/JEIM-03-2023-0112

Chuang, S. (2022) 'Indispensable skills for human employees in the age of robots and AI,' *European Journal of Training and Development* [Preprint]. https.//.DOI: 10.1108/EJTD-06-2022-0062

Chukwunweike, N.J.N. *et al.* (2024) 'The role of deep learning in ensuring privacy integrity and security. Applications in AI-driven cybersecurity solutions,' *World Journal of Advanced Research and Reviews*, 23(2), pp. 1778–1790. https.//.DOI: 10.30574/wjarr.2024.23.2.2550

Chung, J.-M. (2024) 'Emerging Cyber-Attacks,' in *Emerging Secure Networks, Blockchains and Smart Contract Technologies*, pp. 1–29. https.//DOI: 10.1007/978-3-031-65866-2_1

Cifuentes, Y., Beltrán, L., & Ramírez, L. (2015). Analysis of security vulnerabilities for mobile health applications. https.//www.semanticscholar.org/paper/Analysis-of-Security-Vulnerabilities-for-Mobile-Cifuentes-Beltr%C3%A1n/6a27e71612 3bb59d24f7a418b2c6fdd3917ed361

Cong, G., Yang, J., & Zhao, Y. (2024). *Machine Learning for Databases: Foundations, Paradigms, and Open problems*. ACM. [Preprint], DOI: 10.1145/3626246.3654686

Conlon, D., Raeburn, T., & Wand, T. (2024). 'Nurses' understanding of their duty of confidentiality to patients in mental health care: A qualitative exploratory study,'. *Collegian (Royal College of Nursing, Australia)*, 31(3), 144–153. DOI: 10.1016/j.colegn.2024.02.002

Cremonezi, B., Vieira, A. B., Nacif, J., Silva, E. F., & Nogueira, M. (2024). Identity management for Internet of Things: Concepts, challenges and opportunities. *Computer Communications*, 224, 72–94. DOI: 10.1016/j.comcom.2024.05.014

Cunningham, P., & Delany, S. J. (2021). K-nearest neighbor classifiers-a tutorial. *ACM Computing Surveys*, 54(6), 1–25. DOI: 10.1145/3459665

Cybersecurity measures for Logistics Industry Framework (no date) *Google Books*. Available at. https.//www.google.com.my/books/edition/Cybersecurity_Measures_for_Logistics_Ind/9r_1EAAAQBAJ?hl=en&gbpv=1&dq=%22A%2BComprehensive%2BReview%2Bof%2BCyber%2BSecurity%2BVulnerabilities%2C%2BThreats%2C%2BAttacks%2C%2Band%2BSolutions%22%2Bby%2BElectronics%2BJournal&pg=PA65&printsec=frontcover

Dash, N.B. and Ullah, N.S. (2024) 'Quantum-safe. Cybersecurity in the age of Quantum-Powered AI,' *World Journal of Advanced Research and Reviews*, 21(1), pp. 1555–1563. https.//.DOI: 10.30574/wjarr.2024.21.1.2640

Dastider, A. G., Sadik, F., & Fattah, S. A. (2021). An integrated autoencoder-based hy- brid cnn-lstm model for COVID-19 severity prediction from lung ultrasound. *Computers in Biology and Medicine*, 132, 104296. DOI: 10.1016/j.compbiomed.2021.104296 PMID: 33684688

Datta, S., & Namasudra, S. (2024). Blockchain-Based smart contract model for securing healthcare transactions by using consumer electronics and mobile edge computing. *IEEE Transactions on Consumer Electronics*, 70(1), 4026–4036. DOI: 10.1109/TCE.2024.3357115

Daudén-Esmel, C., Castellà-Roca, J., & Viejo, A. (2023). Blockchain-based access control system for efficient and GDPR-compliant personal data management. *Computer Communications*, 214, 67–87. DOI: 10.1016/j.comcom.2023.11.017

De Cremer, D., & Kasparov, G. (2021). AI should augment human intelligence, not replace it. *Harvard Business Review*, 18(1).

De Hoog, J., Anwar, A., Reiter, P., Mercelis, S., & Hellinckx, P. (2023). Metamodelling of Noise to Image Classification Performance. *IEEE Access, 11*, 47994–48006. IEEE Access. https.//DOI: 10.1109/ACCESS.2023.3273530

Denbigh-White, C. (2024). Identifying risk when using Generative AI Tools. Retrieved from https://www.nextdlp.com/resources/blog/ai-security-questions

Deng, Y. *et al.* (2021) 'Deep Learning-Based Autonomous Driving Systems. A survey of Attacks and Defenses,' *IEEE Transactions on Industrial Informatics*, 17(12), pp. 7897–7912. https.//.DOI: 10.1109/TII.2021.3071405

Desai, H. V. (2012). Steganography, Cryptography, Watermarking. A Comparative Study. *Journal of Global Research in Computer Sciences*. https.//www.semanticscholar.org/paper/Steganography%2C-Cryptography%2C-Watermarking%3A-A-Study-Desai/1ddf3b6ed9275b760c2726dccdd8e0821b649b6e

Desai, T. (2024). Cybersecurity Faces Transformation from Generative AI. Retrieved from https://www.globalxetfs.com/cybersecurity-faces-transformation-from-generative-ai/

Deshmukh, P. U., & Pattewar, T. M. (2014). A novel approach for edge adaptive steganography on LSB insertion technique. *International Conference on Information Communication and Embedded Systems (ICICES2014)*, 1–5. https.//DOI: 10.1109/ICICES.2014.7033807

Dey, S., Abraham, A., & Sanyal, S. (2007). An LSB Data Hiding Technique Using Prime Numbers. *Third International Symposium on Information Assurance and Security*, 101–108. https.//DOI: 10.1109/ISIAS.2007.4299758

Dhanaraj, R. K., Kamila, N. K., Pani, S. K., Balusamy, B., & Rajasekar, V. (2024). *ARTIFICIAL INTELLIGENCE FOR FUTURE INTELLIGENT TRANSPORTATION: Smarter and Greener Infrastructure Design.*

Dhanaraj, R. K.. (2024). *Artificial intelligence for future intelligent transportation. Smarter and Greener Infrastructure Design.* CRC Press.

Dhar, S. *et al.* (2023) 'Securing IoT devices. A novel approach using blockchain and quantum cryptography,' *Internet of Things*, 25, p. 101019. https.//.DOI: 10.1016/j.iot.2023.101019

Dhar, S., & Shamir, L. (2022). Systematic biases when using deep neural networks for annotating large catalogs of astronomical images. *Astronomy and Computing*, 38, 100545. DOI: 10.1016/j.ascom.2022.100545

DHS study on Mobile Device Security -April2017-final. Available at. https.//www.dhs.gov/sites/default/files/publications/ DHS Study on Mobile Device Security - April 2017-FINAL.pdf

Díaz-Rodríguez, N. *et al.* (2023) 'Connecting the dots in trustworthy Artificial Intelligence. From AI principles, ethics, and key requirements to responsible AI systems and regulation,' *Information Fusion*, 99, p. 101896. https.//.DOI: 10.1016/j.inffus.2023.101896

Din, S. N. U., Muzammal, S. M., Bibi, R., Tayyab, M., Jhanjhi, N. Z., & Habib, M. (2024). Securing the Internet of Things in Logistics. Challenges, Solutions, and the Role of Machine Learning in Anomaly Detection. In *Digital Transformation for Improved Industry and Supply Chain Performance* (pp. 133–165). IGI Global. https.//DOI: 10.4018/979-8-3693-5375-2.ch007

Diro, A., Kaisar, S., Vasilakos, A. V., Anwar, A., Nasirian, A., & Olani, G. (2024). Anomaly detection for space information networks: A survey of challenges, techniques, and future directions. *Computers & Security*, 139, 103705. DOI: 10.1016/j.cose.2024.103705

Dissanayake, G. N. (2020). A study on real-time database technology and its applications.

Dogan, A., & Birant, D. (2021). Machine learning and data mining in manufacturing. *Expert Systems with Applications*, 166, 114060. DOI: 10.1016/j.eswa.2020.114060

Dogra, V., ... (2021) 'Analyzing DistilBERT for Sentiment Classification of Banking Financial News,' in *Lecture notes in networks and systems*, pp. 501–510. DOI: 10.1007/978-981-16-3153-5_53

Dogra, V., Singh, A., & Verma, S., Kavita, Jhanjhi, N. Z., & Talib, M. N. (2021). Analyzing DistilBERT for sentiment classification of banking financial news. In Intelligent Computing and Innovation on Data Science: Proceedings of ICTIDS 2021 (pp. 501-510). Springer Singapore.

Dogra, V., Verma, S., Verma, K., Jhanjhi, N. Z., Ghosh, U., & Le, D.-N. (2022). A comparative analysis of machine learning models for banking news extraction by multiclass classification with imbalanced datasets of financial news: challenges and solutions.

Domnik, J., & Holland, A. (2024). On Data Leakage Prevention Maturity: Adapting the C2M2 framework. *Journal of Cybersecurity and Privacy*, 4(2), 167–195. DOI: 10.3390/jcp4020009

Doshi, J., Patel, T., & Bharti, S. K. (2019). Smart Farming using IoT, a solution for optimally monitoring farming conditions. Procedia Computer Science, 160, 746–751. https.//DOI: 10.1016/j.procs.2019.11.016

Duan, Y., & Xiong, Y. (2021). Exploring Business Intelligence and Data Warehouse Technologies in E-Government. *Journal of Information Technology*, 36(1), 52–68. DOI: 10.1177/0268396220903170

Duary, S., ... (2024) 'Cybersecurity Threats Detection in Intelligent Networks using Predictive Analytics Approaches,' *2024 4th International Conference on Innovative Practices in Technology and Management (ICIPTM)* [Preprint]. https.// DOI: 10.1109/ICIPTM59628.2024.10563348

Durakovskiy, A. P., Gavdan, G. P., Korsakov, I. A., & Melnikov, D. A. (2021). About the cybersecurity of automated process control systems. *Procedia Computer Science*, 190, 217–225. DOI: 10.1016/j.procs.2021.06.027

Dwivedi, A.D. *et al.* (2021) 'Blockchain and artificial intelligence for 5G-enabled Internet of Things. Challenges, opportunities, and solutions,' *Transactions on Emerging Telecommunications Technologies* [Preprint]. https.//.DOI: 10.1002/ett.4329

Dwivedi, N., Singh, D. K., & Kushwaha, D. S. (2023). A novel approach for suspicious activity detection with deep learning. *Multimedia Tools and Applications*, 82(21), 32397–32420. DOI: 10.1007/s11042-023-14445-7

Editorial. (2024). Cybersecurity Spending Set to Soar: Over $200 Billion Projection for 2024. Retrieved from https://thecyberexpress.com/cybersecurity-spending-trends-2024/

Eid, M. A. H.. (2024) 'Conceptualizing Ethical AI-Enabled Marketing: Current State and Agenda for Future Research,' *Preprints* [Preprint]. DOI: 10.20944/preprints202404.0786.v1

Elhadad, A., Alanazi, F., Taloba, A. I., & Abozeid, A. (2022). Fog computing service in the healthcare monitoring system for managing the real-time notification. *Journal of Healthcare Engineering*, 2022, 2022. DOI: 10.1155/2022/5337733 PMID: 35340260

Elmasri, R., & Navathe, S. (2021). *Fundamentals of Database Systems* (7th ed.). Pearson.

Erwin, A., Zubair, A. B., & Sherali, Z. (2022). Artificial Intelligence for Cybersecurity: Offensive Tactics. *Mitigation Techniques and Future Directions.*, 1(1), 1–23. DOI: 10.5604/01.3001.0016.0800

Esmaeilzadeh, P. (2024). Challenges and strategies for wide-scale artificial intelligence (AI) deployment in healthcare practices: A perspective for healthcare organizations. *Artificial Intelligence in Medicine*, 151, 102861. DOI: 10.1016/j.artmed.2024.102861 PMID: 38555850

Ettalibi, A., Elouadi, A., & Mansour, A. (2024) 'AI and Computer Vision-based Real-time Quality Control. A Review of Industrial Applications,' *Procedia Computer Science*, 231, pp. 212–220. https.//DOI: 10.1016/j.procs.2023.12.195

Fahd, K., Venkatraman, S., & Hammeed, F. K. (2019). A comparative study of NoSQL system vulnerabilities with big data. *International Journal of Managing Information Technology*, 11(4), 1–19. DOI: 10.5121/ijmit.2019.11401

Familoni, N.B.T. (2024) 'CYBERSECURITY CHALLENGES IN THE AGE OF AI. THEORETICAL APPROACHES AND PRACTICAL SOLUTIONS,' *Computer Science & IT Research Journal*, 5(3), pp. 703–724. https.//.DOI: 10.51594/csitrj.v5i3.930

Fan, J., Li, R., Zhang, C. H., & Zou, H. (2020). *Statistical foundations of data science*. Chapman and Hall/CRC. DOI: 10.1201/9780429096280

Farhad, M. A. (2024). *Consumer data protection laws and their impact on business models in the tech industry*. Telecommunications Policy., DOI: 10.1016/j.telpol.2024.102836

Fatima-Tuz-Zahra, N., ... (2020) 'Proposing a Hybrid RPL Protocol for Rank and Wormhole Attack Mitigation using Machine Learning,' *2020 2nd International Conference on Computer and Information Sciences (ICCIS)* [Preprint]. DOI: 10.1109/ICCIS49240.2020.9257607

Fayayola, N. O. A., Olorunfemi, N. O. L., & Shoetan, N. P. O. (2024). DATA PRIVACY AND SECURITY IN IT: A REVIEW OF TECHNIQUES AND CHALLENGES. *Computer Science & IT Research Journal*, 5(3), 606–615. DOI: 10.51594/csitrj.v5i3.909

Fernández-Iglesias, M. J., Von Eitzen, C. D., & Rifón, L. A. (2024) 'Efficient Traceability Systems with Smart Contracts: Balancing On-Chain and Off-Chain Data Storage for Enhanced Scalability and Privacy,' *Authorea(Authorea)* [Preprint]. https://doi.org/DOI: 10.22541/au.172465854.45833346/v1

Ferrão, S. É. R.. (2024). Towards a taxonomy of privacy requirements based on the LGPD and ISO/IEC 29100. *Information and Software Technology*, 168, 107396. DOI: 10.1016/j.infsof.2024.107396

Florido-Benítez, L. (2024). The types of hackers and cyberattacks in the aviation industry. *Journal of Transportation Security*, 17(1), 13. Advance online publication. DOI: 10.1007/s12198-024-00281-9

Francés-Gómez, P. (2023) 'Ethical Principles and governance for AI,' in *˜The œInternational library of ethics, law and technology*, pp. 191–217. DOI: 10.1007/978-3-031-48135-2_10

Frédéric, T. (2024) *AIS Electronic Library (AISEL) - PACIS 2024 proceedings: Better than Ever? Analyzing the impact of change in consensus mechanism on market liquidity for ethereum*. https://aisel.aisnet.org/pacis2024/track02_blockchain/track02_blockchain/1/

G, J. K. (2023). Generative AI Tech Stack Breakdown | A Comprehensive Guide. Retrieved from https://www.xenonstack.com/blog/generative-ai-tech-stack-breakdown

Gala, D., Behl, H., Shah, M., & Makaryus, A. N. (2024). The role of Artificial intelligence in improving patient Outcomes and Future of healthcare Delivery in Cardiology: A Narrative Review of the literature. *Health Care*, 12(4), 481. DOI: 10.3390/healthcare12040481 PMID: 38391856

Gambhir, A., ... (2024) 'Beyond the Code: Bridging Ethical and Practical Gaps in Data Privacy for AI-Enhanced Healthcare Systems,' in *Recent Trends in Artificial Intelligence Towards a Smart World*, pp. 37–65. DOI: 10.1007/978-981-97-6790-8_2

García, C. R., ... (2023) 'Quantum-resistant transport layer security,' *Computer Communications*, 213, pp. 345–358. https.//DOI: 10.1016/j.comcom.2023.11.010

Garcia, E. V. (2024) 'The technological leap of AI and the Global South. deepening asymmetries and the future of international security,' in *Edward Elgar Publishing eBooks*, pp. 370–387. https.//DOI: 10.4337/9781800377400.00028

García, M., & Martínez, E. (2021). Deep Learning Techniques for Intrusion Prevention in Industrial IoT Networks. *International Journal of Machine Learning and Cybernetics*, 12(4), 791–802.

Gartner. (2020). Forecast. Internet of Things — Endpoints and Associated Services, Worldwide, 2019 Update.

Gaur, L., ... (2021) 'Disposition of youth in predicting sustainable development goals using the Neuro - fuzzy and random forest algorithms,' *HCIS* [Preprint]. https.// repository.usp.ac.fj/12807/

Gaur, L., Jhanjhi, N. Z., Bakshi, S., & Gupta, P. (2022). *Analyzing Consequences of Artificial Intelligence on Jobs using Topic Modeling and Keyword Extraction.* Paper presented at the 2022 2nd International Conference on Innovative Practices in Technology and Management (ICIPTM). DOI: 10.1109/ICIPTM54933.2022.9754064

Gaur, L., Solanki, A., Wamba, S. F., & Jhanjhi, N. Z. (2021). *Advanced AI techniques and applications in bioinformatics.* CRC Press. DOI: 10.1201/9781003126164

Gautam, A., ... (2024) 'Passwords are meant to be secret. a practical secure password entry channel for web browsers,' *arXiv (Cornell University)* [Preprint]. https./// arxiv.2402.06159.DOI: <ALIGNMENT.qj></ALIGNMENT>10.48550

George, D. A.S. *et al.* (2023) 'AI-Driven breakthroughs in healthcare: Google Health's advances and the future of medical AI,' Zenodo *(CERN European Organization for Nuclear Research)* [Preprint]. DOI: 10.5281/zenodo.8085221

Georgiev, A., & Valkanov, V. (2024) 'Role-Based Access Control Technique with Trino for Restriction in Hive-Based Data Warehouse,' *2024 59th International Scientific Conference on Information, Communication and Energy Systems and Technologies (ICEST)*, pp. 1–4. DOI: 10.1109/ICEST62335.2024.10639702

Gera, J., & Battula, B. P. (2018). Detection of spoofed and non-spoofed DDoS attacks and discriminating them from flash crowds. *EURASIP Journal on Information Security*, 2018(1), 1–12. DOI: 10.1186/s13635-018-0079-6

Gerke, S., Minssen, T., & Cohen, G. (2020) 'Ethical and legal challenges of artificial intelligence-driven healthcare,' in *Elsevier eBooks*, pp. 295–336. DOI: 10.1016/ B978-0-12-818438-7.00012-5

Ghadge, N. (2024). Machine Learning: Enhancing Intelligent Search and Information Discovery. *Computer Science & Information Technology (CS & IT)*, 235-243.

Ghadi, Y. Y., Mazhar, T., Shahzad, T., Amir khan, M., Abd-Alrazaq, A., Ahmed, A., & Hamam, H. (2024). Author Correction: The role of blockchain to secure internet of medical things. *Scientific Reports*, 14(1), 21337. Advance online publication. DOI: 10.1038/s41598-024-71990-3 PMID: 39266649

Gharbi, R., & Ben Khedher, S. (2020). Evaluating the Performance of Business Intelligence Systems. An Empirical Study. *Information Systems Frontiers*, 22(3), 609–620. DOI: 10.1007/s10796-018-9820-7

Gill, H. S., & Khehra, B. S. (2021). An integrated approach using cnn-rnn-lstm for classification of fruit images. *Materials Today: Proceedings.*

Gill, S. H., Razzaq, M. A., Ahmad, M., Almansour, F. M., Haq, I. U., Jhanjhi, N. Z., & Masud, M. (2022). Security and privacy aspects of cloud computing. a smart campus case study. *Intelligent Automation & Soft Computing*, 31(1), 117–128. DOI: 10.32604/iasc.2022.016597

Gill, S. S., Xu, M., Ottaviani, C., Patros, P., Bahsoon, R., Shaghaghi, A., & Abraham, A. (2022). AI for next generation computing: Emerging trends and future directions. *Internet of Things : Engineering Cyber Physical Human Systems*, 19, 100514. DOI: 10.1016/j.iot.2022.100514

Gilson, C., & Bouraga, S. (2024). Enhancing the democratic nature of voting processes within decentralized autonomous organizations. *Digital Policy Regulation and Governance*, 26(2), 169–187. DOI: 10.1108/DPRG-09-2023-0126

Gimenez-Aguilar, M., de Fuentes, J. M., Gonzalez-Manzano, L., & Arroyo, D. (2021). Achieving cybersecurity in blockchain-based systems: A survey. *Future Generation Computer Systems*, 124, 91–118. DOI: 10.1016/j.future.2021.05.007

Goel, S., Gupta, S., & Kaushik, N. (2015). Image Steganography – Least Significant Bit with Multiple Progressions. In S. C. Satapathy, B. N. Biswal, S. K. Udgata, & J. K. Mandal (Eds.), *Proceedings of the 3rd International Conference on Frontiers of Intelligent Computing. Theory and Applications (FICTA) 2014* (pp. 105–112). Springer International Publishing. https.//DOI: 10.1007/978-3-319-12012-6_12

Gong, C., & Sarac, K. (2005, May). IP traceback based on packet marking and logging. In *IEEE International Conference on Communications, 2005. ICC 2005. 2005* (Vol. 2, pp. 1043-1047). IEEE. DOI: 10.1109/ICC.2005.1494507

Gong, W., Wang, Y., Chen, H., & Wang, D. (2021). Anomaly Diagnosis for Navigation Sensors of Unmanned Autonomous Vehicles Based on Deep Learning. *Jixie Gongcheng Xuebao. Jixie Gongcheng Xuebao*, 57(24), 268–278. DOI: 10.3901/JME.2021.24.268

Gong, Y., Yu, B., Yang, L., Meng, F., Liu, L., Hu, X., & Xu, Z. (2024). Toward next-generation networks: A blockchain-based approach for core network architecture and roaming identity verification, [Preprint]. *Digital Communications and Networks*. Advance online publication. DOI: 10.1016/j.dcan.2024.08.008

Gopi, R., Sathiyamoorthi, V., Selvakumar, S., Manikandan, R., Chatterjee, P., Jhanjhi, N. Z., & Luhach, A. K. (2021). Enhanced method of ANN based model for detection of DDoS attacks on multimedia internet of things. *Multimedia Tools and Applications*, 81(19), 26739–26757. DOI: 10.1007/s11042-021-10640-6

Gouda, W., Almurafeh, M., Humayun, M., & Jhanjhi, N. Z. (2022). Detection of COVID-19 based on chest X-rays using deep learning. [). MDPI.]. *Health Care*, 10(2), 343. PMID: 35206957

Govea, J., Gaibor-Naranjo, W. and Villegas-Ch, W. (2024) 'Transforming Cybersecurity into Critical Energy Infrastructure. A Study on the Effectiveness of Artificial Intelligence,' *Systems*, 12(5), p. 165. https.//.DOI: 10.3390/systems12050165

Grafiati. (2020). App Security. Retrieved from https.//www.grafiati.com/en/literature-selections/app-security/

Grand View Research. I. (2023). Global Ai In Cybersecurity Market Size & Outlook. Retrieved from https://www.grandviewresearch.com/horizon/outlook/ai-in-cybersecurity-market-size/global

Grandin, A., & Eriksson, M. (2021) *International Payments, Trade Finance & Blockchain : A qualitative study about the impact of blockchain implementation*. https://www.diva-portal.org/smash/record.jsf?pid=diva2%3A1571481&dswid=-4406

Griebel, L., Prokosch, H.-U., Köpcke, F., Toddenroth, D., Christoph, J., Leb, I., Engel, I., & Sedlmayr, M. (2015). A scoping review of cloud computing in healthcare. *BMC Medical Informatics and Decision Making*, 15(1), 17. Advance online publication. DOI: 10.1186/s12911-015-0145-7 PMID: 25888747

Grover, R., Jang, K., & Su, L. W. (2024). Beyond Digital Protection(ism). *Journal of Information Policy*, 14. Advance online publication. DOI: 10.5325/jinfopoli.14.2024.0005

Gu¨era, D., & Delp, E. J. (2018). Deepfake video detection using recurrent neural net- works, 2018 15th IEEE International Conference on Advanced Video and Signal Based Surveillance (AVSS), pp. 1–6.

Guembe, B. *et al.* (2022) 'The emerging threat of AI-driven cyber attacks. a review,' *Applied Artificial Intelligence*, 36(1). https.//.DOI: 10.1080/08839514.2022.2037254

Gui, B., Sam, L. and Bhardwaj, A. (2024) 'From roofs to renewables. Deep learning and geographic information systems insights into a comprehensive urban solar photovoltaic assessment for Stonehaven,' *Elsevier*, 1, p. 100006. https.//.DOI: 10.1016/j.energ.2024.100006

Gul, S., Bano, S., & Shah, T. (2021). Exploring data mining: Facets and emerging trends. *Digital Library Perspectives*, 37(4), 429–448. DOI: 10.1108/DLP-08-2020-0078

Guo, Z., Yang, G., Chen, J., & Sun, X. (2021). Fake face detection via adaptive manipulation traces extraction network. *Computer Vision and Image Understanding*, 204(5), 103170. DOI: 10.1016/j.cviu.2021.103170

Gupta, M. K., & Chandra, P. (2020). A comprehensive survey of data mining. *International Journal of Information Technology : an Official Journal of Bharati Vidyapeeth's Institute of Computer Applications and Management*, 12(4), 1243–1257. DOI: 10.1007/s41870-020-00427-7

Gupta, S., & Grover, D. (2021, March). A comprehensive review on detection of DDoS attacks using ML in SDN environment. In *2021 International Conference on Artificial Intelligence and Smart Systems (ICAIS)* (pp. 1158-1163). IEEE. DOI: 10.1109/ICAIS50930.2021.9395987

Gupta, S., Grover, D., AlZubi, A. A., Sachdeva, N., Baig, M. W., & Singla, J. (2022). Machine Learning with Dimensionality Reduction for DDoS Attack Detection. *Computers, Materials & Continua*, 72(2), 2665–2682. DOI: 10.32604/cmc.2022.025048

Gupta, S., Grover, D., & Bhandari, A. (2018). Vulnerability analysis of existing distributed denial of service attacks defense frameworks. *Asian Journal of Computer Science and Technology*, 7(3), 62–67. DOI: 10.51983/ajcst-2018.7.3.1895

Gupta, V., & Sharma, A. (2022). Adopting Cybersecurity Measures in Business Intelligence Systems. A Systematic Review. *Journal of Information Security and Applications*, 67, 103149. DOI: 10.1016/j.jisa.2022.103149

Habbal, A., Ali, M.K. and Abuzaraida, M.A. (2024) 'Artificial Intelligence Trust, Risk and Security Management (AI TRiSM). Frameworks, applications, challenges and future research directions,' *Expert Systems With Applications*, 240, p. 122442. https.//.DOI: 10.1016/j.eswa.2023.122442

Haber, Y., Levkovich, I., Hadar-Shoval, D., & Elyoseph, Z. (2024). The artificial third: A broad view of the effects of introducing generative artificial intelligence on psychotherapy (Preprint). *JMIR Mental Health*, 11, e54781. DOI: 10.2196/54781 PMID: 38787297

Habib, M., Hussain, A., Rehman, E., Muzammal, S. M., Cheng, B., Aslam, M., & Jilani, S. F. (2023). Convolved Feature Vector Based Adaptive Fuzzy Filter for Image De-Noising. *Applied Sciences, 13*(8), Article 8. https.//DOI: 10.3390/app13084861

Haider, N., ... (2019) 'Cybersecurity of medical Devices. past, present, and future,' in *Springer eBooks*, pp. 811–820. https.//DOI: 10.1007/978-3-030-12281-2_100

Haider, S., Akhunzada, A., Mustafa, I., Patel, T. B., Fernandez, A., Choo, K. K. R., & Iqbal, J. (2020). A deep CNN ensemble framework for efficient DDoS attack detection in software defined networks. *IEEE Access : Practical Innovations, Open Solutions*, 8, 53972–53983. DOI: 10.1109/ACCESS.2020.2976908

Halboos, E. H. J., & Albakry, A. M. (2022). Hiding text using the least significant bit technique to improve cover image in the steganography system. *Bulletin of Electrical Engineering and Informatics, 11*(6), Article 6. https.//DOI: 10.11591/eei.v11i6.4337

Hall, O. J., Shiaeles, S., & Li, F. (2024). A Study of Ethereum's Transition from Proof-of-Work to Proof-of-Stake in Preventing Criminal Activities in Smart Contracts. *Network (Bristol, England)*, 4(1), 33–47. DOI: 10.3390/network4010002

Hamad, Z. T., Jamil, N., & Belkacem, A. N. (2024). *ChaTGPT's impact on education and Healthcare: Insights, challenges, and ethical consideration.* IEEE Access., DOI: 10.1109/ACCESS.2024.3437374

Hameleers, M., Van Der Meer, T.G.L.A. and Dobber, T. (2023) 'They would never say anything like this! Reasons to doubt political deepfakes,' *European Journal of Communication*, 39(1), pp. 56–70. https.//.DOI: 10.1177/02673231231184703

Hamid, H. R. M. H., ... (2023) 'Two factor authentication. voice biometric and Token-Based authentication,' in *SpringerBriefs in applied sciences and technology*, pp. 27–35. https.//DOI: 10.1007/978-3-031-47727-0_4

Han, H. *et al.* (2024) 'Quantum communication based cyber security analysis using artificial intelligence with IoMT,' *Optical and Quantum Electronics*, 56(4). https.//. DOI: 10.1007/s11082-023-06185-7

Harmening, J. (2025) 'Security Management Systems,' in *Elsevier eBooks*, pp. 433–439. https.//DOI: 10.1016/B978-0-443-13223-0.00025-4

Hashmi, E., Yamin, M.M. and Yayilgan, S.Y. (2024) 'Securing tomorrow. a comprehensive survey on the synergy of Artificial Intelligence and information security,' *AI And Ethics* [Preprint]. https.//.DOI: 10.1007/s43681-024-00529-z

Hashmi, M. F., Ashish, B. K. K., Keskar, A. G., Bokde, N. D., & Yoon, J. H. and Geem,

Hashmi, M. F., Ashish, B. K. K., Keskar, A. G., Bokde, N. D., Yoon, J. H., & Geem, Z. W.Z. W. (2020). An exploratory analysis on visual counterfeits using conv-lstm hybrid architecture. *IEEE Access : Practical Innovations, Open Solutions*, 8, 101293–101308. DOI: 10.1109/ACCESS.2020.2998330

Hassani, H., Beneki, C., Unger, S., Mazinani, M. T., & Yeganegi, M. R. (2020). Text mining in big data analytics. *Big Data and Cognitive Computing*, 4(1), 1. DOI: 10.3390/bdcc4010001

Hassani, H., Huang, X., & Silva, E. (2018). Banking with blockchain-ed big data. *Journal of Management Analytics*, 5(4), 256–275. DOI: 10.1080/23270012.2018.1528900

Hassija, V., Chamola, V., Mahapatra, A., Singal, A., Goel, D., Huang, K., Scardapane, S., Spinelli, I., Mahmud, M., & Hussain, A. (2023). Interpreting Black-Box Models: A review on Explainable Artificial intelligence. *Cognitive Computation*, 16(1), 45–74. DOI: 10.1007/s12559-023-10179-8

Hatamizadeh, A. *et al.* (2023) 'Do gradient inversion attacks make federated learning unsafe?,' *IEEE Transactions on Medical Imaging*, 42(7), pp. 2044–2056. https.//. DOI: 10.1109/TMI.2023.3239391

Hatem, A. (2024) *Profiling IoT botnet activity - Enlighten Theses.* https.//theses .gla.ac.uk/84102/

Hazra, R., ... (2024) 'Data encryption and secure communication protocols,' in *Advances in web technologies and engineering book series*, pp. 546–570. https.// DOI: 10.4018/979-8-3693-6557-1.ch022

Hemamalini, V.. (2023). *Artificial Intelligence–Blockchain-Enabled–Internet of Things-Based Cloud Applications for Next-Generation Society.* Wiley., DOI: 10.1002/9781394213948.ch4

Hennebelle, A., Materwala, H., & Ismail, L. (2023). HealthEdge: A machine learning-based smart healthcare framework for prediction of type 2 diabetes in an integrated IoT, edge, and cloud computing system. *Procedia Computer Science*, 220, 331–338. DOI: 10.1016/j.procs.2023.03.043

Herzog, N. J., Celik, D., & Sulaiman, R. B. (2024) 'Artificial intelligence in healthcare and medical records security,' in *Advanced sciences and technologies for security applications*, pp. 35–57. DOI: 10.1007/978-3-031-52272-7_2

Holla, S., & Katti, M. M. (2012). Android based mobile application development and its security. *International Journal of Computer Trends and Technology*, 3(3), 486–490.

Hon, W. K. (2024a) 'Attack vectors,' in *Edward Elgar Publishing eBooks*, pp. 158–180. https.//DOI: 10.4337/9781803923918.00018

Hon, W. K. (2024b) 'Public key infrastructure; passwords,' in *Edward Elgar Publishing eBooks*, pp. 207–233. https.//DOI: 10.4337/9781803923918.00020

Hon, B. C. Y.. (2024). Challenger: Blockchain-based massively multiplayer online game architecture. *Lecture Notes in Computer Science*, 14783, 50–66. DOI: 10.1007/978-3-031-67321-4_3

Hong, Z., ... (2024) 'GRIDB: Scaling blockchain database via sharding and Off-Chain Cross-Shard mechanism,' *arXiv (Cornell University)* [Preprint]. https://doi .org//arxiv.2407.03750.DOI: 10.48550

Hoque, S., Aydeger, A., & Zeydan, E. (2024). Exploring Post Quantum Cryptography with Quantum Key Distribution for Sustainable Mobile Network Architecture Design. *ACM DL*, 5, 9–16. DOI: 10.1145/3659997.3660033

Hossain, M. *et al.* (2024) 'A Holistic analysis of Internet of Things (IoT) security. principles, practices, and new perspectives,' *Future Internet*, 16(2), p. 40. https.//. DOI: 10.3390/fi16020040

Hossain, M. M., & Saha, S. K. (2022). Business Intelligence and Cybersecurity. A Strategic Alignment Approach. *Computers & Security*, 122, 102833. DOI: 10.1016/j. cose.2022.102833

Hu, K. *et al.* (2024) 'An overview of implementing security and privacy in federated learning,' *Artificial Intelligence Review*, 57(8). https.//.DOI: 10.1007/s10462-024-10846-8

Huang, M. J., Sung, H. S., Hsieh, T. J., Wu, M. C., & Chung, S. H. (2020). Applying data-mining techniques for discovering association rules. *Soft Computing*, 24(11), 8069–8075. DOI: 10.1007/s00500-019-04163-4

Human verification. (n.d.). https.//www.semanticscholar.org/paper/An-insight -into-the-security-issues-and-their-for-Khandelwal-Mohapatra/2fb9ed0bea 85dc14552199012ac4dd8a4d8f52a2

Human verification. (n.d.-b). https.//www.semanticscholar.org/paper/Security-risks -and-their-prevention-capabilities-in-Michalska-Poniszewska-Mara%C5%84da/ add75ed2c41e18a5500ea021dca45e5083374465

Humayun, M., & Al, E. (2021). Industry 4.0 and Cyber Security Issues and Challenges. *Turkish Journal of Computer and Mathematics Education (TURCOMAT), 12*(10), Article 10. https.//DOI: <ALIGNMENT.qj></ALIGNMENT>10.17762/turcomat.v12i10.4946

Humayun, M., Hamid, B., Jhanjhi, N., Suseendran, G., & Talib, M. (2021). *5G network security issues, challenges, opportunities and future directions: A survey.* Paper presented at the Journal of Physics: Conference Series. DOI: 10.1088/1742-6596/1979/1/012037

Humayun, M. (2021). Industry 4.0 and cyber security issues and challenges. [TURCOMAT]. *Turkish Journal of Computer and Mathematics Education*, 12(10), 2957–2971.

Humayun, M., Niazi, M., Jhanjhi, N. Z., Alshayeb, M., & Mahmood, S. (2020). Cyber security threats and vulnerabilities: A systematic mapping study. *Arabian Journal for Science and Engineering*, 45(4), 3171–3189. DOI: 10.1007/s13369-019-04319-2

Humayun, M., Sujatha, R., Almuayqil, S. N., & Jhanjhi, N. Z. (2022). A transfer learning approach with a convolutional neural network for the classification of lung carcinoma. []). MDPI.]. *Health Care*, 10(6), 1058. PMID: 35742109

Humayun, M., Sujatha, R., Almuayqil, S. N., & Jhanjhi, N. Z. (2022). A Transfer Learning Approach with a Convolutional Neural Network for the Classification of Lung Carcinoma. *Health Care*, 10(6), 1058. DOI: 10.3390/healthcare10061058 PMID: 35742109

Hur, J. B., & Shamsi, J. A. (2017). A survey on security issues, vulnerabilities and attacks in Android based smartphone. *2017 International Conference on Information and Communication Technologies (ICICT)*. DOI: 10.1109/ICICT.2017.8320163

Huseynov, E. (2025) 'Identity Theft,' in *Elsevier eBooks*, pp. 993–1006. DOI: 10.1016/B978-0-443-13223-0.00060-6

Hussain, K., ... (2024) 'Threats and Vulnerabilities of Wireless Networks in the Internet of Things (IoT),' *IEEE 1st Karachi Section Humanitarian Technology Conference (KHI-HTC)*, 2, pp. 1–8. DOI: 10.1109/KHI-HTC60760.2024.10482197

Huynh, E., Hosny, A., Guthier, C., Bitterman, D. S., Petit, S. F., Haas-Kogan, D. A., Kann, B., Aerts, H. J. W. L., & Mak, R. H. (2020). Artificial intelligence in radiation oncology. *Nature Reviews. Clinical Oncology*, 17(12), 771–781. DOI: 10.1038/s41571-020-0417-8 PMID: 32843739

Ibor, A., Edim, E. and Ojugo, A. (2023) 'Secure Health Information System with Blockchain Technology,' *Journal of the Nigerian Society of Physical Sciences*, p. 992. .DOI: 10.46481/jnsps.2023.992

Ibrahim, A. (2024). " *Security Challenges and Solutions in Integrating Cassandra with Kafka* (No. 13852). Easy Chair.

Ibrahim, R., & Al-Haija, Q. A. (2023) 'Blockchain security measures to combat cyber crime,' in *CRC Press eBooks*, pp. 275–293. https.//DOI: 10.1201/9781003404361-15

Ibrahim, A. M., Abdel-Aziz, H. R., Mohamed, H. A. H., Zaghamir, D. E. F., Wahba, N. M. I., Hassan, G. A., Shaban, M., EL-Nablaway, M., Aldughmi, O. N., & Aboelola, T. H. (2024). Balancing confidentiality and care coordination: Challenges in patient privacy. *BMC Nursing*, 23(1), 564. Advance online publication. DOI: 10.1186/s12912-024-02231-1 PMID: 39148055

Ilori, N. O., Nwosu, N. N. T., & Naiho, N. H. N. N. (2024). Advanced data analytics in internal audits: A conceptual framework for comprehensive risk assessment and fraud detection. *Finance & Accounting Research Journal*, 6(6), 931–952. DOI: 10.51594/farj.v6i6.1213

Iqbal, H. S. (2021). AI-Driven Cybersecurity: An Overview, Security Intelligence Modeling and Research Directions. DOI: 10.20944/preprints202101.0457.v1

Iqbal, T., & Qureshi, S. (2022). The survey: Text generation models in deep learning. *Journal of King Saud University. Computer and Information Sciences*, 34(6, 6, Part A), 2515–2528. DOI: 10.1016/j.jksuci.2020.04.001

Isakov, A. *et al.* (2024) *ENHANCING CYBERSECURITY. PROTECTING DATA IN THE DIGITAL AGE.* https.//innoist.uz/index.php/ist/article/view/153.

Ishkov, A. and Krupnov, Y. (2024) 'Application of blockchain technologies for creation of innovative ecosystem in higher education,' *E3S Web of Conferences*, 549, p. 08031. .DOI: 10.1051/e3sconf/202454908031

Islam, Md. R., Siddiqa, A., Uddin, M. P., Mandal, A. K., & Hossain, Md. D. (2014). An efficient filtering based approach improving LSB image steganography using status bit along with AES cryptography. *2014 International Conference on Informatics, Electronics & Vision (ICIEV)*, 1–6. https.//DOI: 10.1109/ICIEV.2014.6850714

Islam, S. (2024) 'FUTURE TRENDS IN SQL DATABASES AND BIG DATA ANALYTICS. IMPACT OF MACHINE LEARNING AND ARTIFICIAL INTELLIGENCE,' *International Journal of Science and Engineering*, 1(4), pp. 47–62. https.//.DOI: 10.62304/ijse.v1i04.188

Izadi, S., Ahmadi, M., & Nikbazm, R. (2022). Analysis of Feature Selection Methods for Network Traffic Classification. In *International Conference on Advanced Intelligent Systems and Informatics* (pp. 65-77). Cham: Springer International Publishing.

Jabbar, K. and Bjørn, P. (2017) 'Infrastructural Grind,' *ACm* [Preprint]. .DOI: 10.1145/3148330.3148345

Jadhav, P. P., Pande, S. D., Joshi, R., Gonge, S., Shelke, M. P., Futane, P., & Ahammad, S. K. H. (2024). CSADF. Ingesting cuckoo search optimization algorithm enabled with fitness function for effective model transformation pertaining to ADF. *Multimedia Tools and Applications*. https.//DOI: 10.1007/s11042-023-17887-1

Jadhav, V., & Jain, R. (2020). Data Warehousing for Business Intelligence. A Survey. *International Journal of Computer Applications*, 975, 16–22. DOI: 10.5120/ijca2020920223

Jadon, S. *et al.* (2024) 'Blockchain in the Electronics Industry for Supply Chain Management. A survey,' *IEEE Access*, 12, pp. 7089–7120. https.//.DOI: 10.1109/ACCESS.2024.3351370

Jagannath, R.O. and Jain, A.K. (2024) 'Browser-in-the-middle attacks. A comprehensive analysis and countermeasures,' *Security and Privacy*, 7(5). https.//.DOI: 10.1002/spy2.410

Jang, J. Y., & Kim, D. (2021). Implementing Data Warehouse for Business Intelligence. An Overview of the Current Trends. *Journal of Business Research*, 128, 811–821. DOI: 10.1016/j.jbusres.2021.01.045

Jarrahi, M. H. (2018). Artificial intelligence and the future of work: Human-AI symbiosis in organizational decision making. *Business Horizons*, 61(4), 577–586. DOI: 10.1016/j.bushor.2018.03.007

Javadpour, A., Ja'fari, F., Taleb, T., Shojafar, M., & Benzaïd, C. (2024). A Comprehensive Survey on Cyber Deception Techniques to Improve Honeypot Performance. *Computers & Security*, 103792, 103792. Advance online publication. DOI: 10.1016/j.cose.2024.103792

Jayakumar, P., Brohi, S. N., & Jhanjhi, N. Z. (2021). Artificial intelligence and military applications: Innovations, cybersecurity challenges & open research areas.

Jayapradha, J., Muttashar Abdulsahib, G., Ibrahim Khalaf, O., Prakash, M., Uddin, M., Abdelhaq, M., & Alsaqour, R. (2024). Cluster-based anonymity model and algorithm for 1:1 dataset with a single sensitive attribute using machine learning technique. *Egyptian Informatics Journal*, 27, 100485. DOI: 10.1016/j.eij.2024.100485

Jebaraj, J. (2016) *An exploratory study on security issues pertaining to smartphone applications, Academia.edu*. Available at. https.//www.academia.edu/30094607/An_Exploratory_Study_on_Security_Issues_Pertaining_to_Smartphone_Applications?rhid=28519166230&swp=rr-rw-wc-39804973

Jeevitha, R., Bhanumathi, P., & Mukherjee, S. (2024) 'Blockchain-Based Financial Systems Deployment and challenges,' in *Advances in finance, accounting, and economics book series*, pp. 120–147. DOI: 10.4018/979-8-3693-1878-2.ch006

Jhanjhi, N. Z., Brohi, S. N., & Malik, N. A. (2019, December). Proposing a rank and wormhole attack detection framework using machine learning. In *2019 13th International Conference on Mathematics, Actuarial Science, Computer Science and Statistics (MACS)* (pp. 1-9). IEEE.

Jhanjhi, N. Z., Brohi, S. N., Malik, N. A., & Humayun, M. (2020, October). Proposing a hybrid rpl protocol for rank and wormhole attack mitigation using machine learning. In 2020 2nd International Conference on Computer and Information Sciences (ICCIS) (pp. 1-6). IEEE.

Jhanjhi, N. Z., Gaur, L., & Khan, N. A. (2024). Global Navigation Satellite Systems for Logistics: Cybersecurity Issues and Challenges. *Cybersecurity in the Transportation Industry*, 49-67.

Jhanjhi, N. (2021). A design of IoT-based medicine case for the multi-user medication management using drone in elderly centre. *Journal of Engineering Science and Technology*, 16(2), 1145–1166.

Jhanjhi, N., Ahmad, M., Khan, M. A., & Hussain, M. (2022). The impact of cyber attacks on e-governance during the covid-19 pandemic. In *Cybersecurity Measures for E-Government Frameworks* (pp. 123–140). IGI Global. DOI: 10.4018/978-1-7998-9624-1.ch008

Jhanjhi, N., Humayun, M., & Almuayqil, S. N. (2021). Cyber security and privacy issues in industrial internet of things. *Computer Systems Science and Engineering*, 37(3), 361–380. DOI: 10.32604/csse.2021.015206

Jiang, Y. *et al.* (2024) 'Pervasive User Data Collection from Cyberspace. Privacy Concerns and Countermeasures,' *Cryptography*, 8(1), p. 5. https.//.DOI: 10.3390/cryptography8010005

Jiang, C., Xu, C., Chen, J., & Chen, K. (2024). Blockchain-based immunization against kleptographic attacks. *Science China. Information Sciences*, 67(7), 172102. Advance online publication. DOI: 10.1007/s11432-023-3883-4

Jimmy, F. (2024) 'Cyber security Vulnerabilities and Remediation Through Cloud Security Tools,' *Deleted Journal*, 2(1), pp. 129–171. https.//.DOI: 10.60087/jaigs.v2i1.102

Jimmy, F. (2024). Enhancing Data Security in Financial Institutions with Blockchain Technology. *Deleted Journal*, 5(1), 424–437. DOI: 10.60087/jaigs.v5i1.217

JJ, L., Singh, K., & Chakravarthi, B. (2024). Digital forensic framework for smart contract vulnerabilities using ensemble models. *Multimedia Tools and Applications*, 83(17), 51469–51512.

Jmila, H., & Khedher, M. I. (2022). Adversarial machine learning for network intrusion detection: A comparative study. *Computer Networks*, 214, 109073. Advance online publication. DOI: 10.1016/j.comnet.2022.109073

Jun, A. Y. M.. (2024) 'Exploring the Impact of Crypto-Ransomware on Critical Industries: Case Studies and Solutions,' *preprint.org* [Preprint]. DOI: 10.20944/preprints202409.1325.v1

Kadhim, I. J., Premaratne, P., Vial, P. J., & Halloran, B. (2019). Comprehensive survey of image steganography. Techniques, Evaluations, and trends in future research. *Neurocomputing, 335*, 299–326. https.//DOI: 10.1016/j.neucom.2018.06.075

Kalid, S., Syed, A., Mohammad, A., & Halgamuge, M. N. (2017, March). Big-data NoSQL databases: A comparison and analysis of "Big-Table", "DynamoDB", and "Cassandra". In *2017 IEEE 2nd International Conference on Big Data Analysis (ICBDA)* (pp. 89-93). IEEE.

Kaluarachchi, B. N., & Sedera, D. (2024) 'Improving efficiency through AI-Powered customer engagement by providing personalized solutions in the banking industry,' in *Advances in marketing, customer relationship management, and e-services book series*, pp. 299–342. https.//DOI: 10.4018/979-8-3693-7122-0.ch016

Kambourakis, G.. (2019). *Botnets. Architectures, Countermeasures, and Challenges.* CRC Press. DOI: 10.1201/9780429329913

Kanth, T. C. (2024). AI-POWERED THREAT INTELLIGENCE FOR PROACTIVE SECURITY MONITORING IN CLOUD INFRASTRUCTURES.

Kant, N. (2021). Blockchain: A strategic resource to attain and sustain competitive advantage. *International Journal of Innovation Science*, 13(4), 520–538. DOI: 10.1108/IJIS-07-2020-0094

Karras, T., Laine, S. and Aila, T. (2019). A style-based generator architecture for generative adversarial networks.

Kashyap, N., Mishra, A., & Mishra, B. K. (2022). Artificial Neural Networks: Fundamentals, Design, and Applications. In *Handbook of Research for Big Data* (pp. 277-295). Apple Academic Press.

Katiyar, N. *et al.* (2024) 'AI and Cyber-Security. Enhancing threat detection and response with machine learning.,' *Educational Administration. Theory and Practice* [Preprint]. https.//.DOI: 10.53555/kuey.v30i4.2377

Kaur, B., & Joseph, K. T. (2024) 'Security Challenges and Solutions in 5G Networks,' *2024 IEEE International Conference on Interdisciplinary Approaches in Technology and Management for Social Innovation (IATMSI)* [Preprint]. https.//DOI: 10.1109/IATMSI60426.2024.10502490

Kaur, J., Rani, R., & Kalra, N. (2023). Attribute-based access control scheme for secure storage and sharing of EHRs using blockchain and IPFS, [Preprint]. *Cluster Computing*. Advance online publication. DOI: 10.1007/s10586-023-04038-2

Kaur, P., Kumar, M., & Bhandari, A. (2017). A review of detection approaches for distributed denial of service attacks. *Systems Science & Control Engineering*, 5(1), 301–320. DOI: 10.1080/21642583.2017.1331768

Kavitha, T.. (2024). *Secure communication in internet of things. Emerging Technologies, Challenges, and Mitigation*. CRC Press. DOI: 10.1201/9781003477327

Kayes, A. S. M.. (2024) 'Safeguarding Individuals and Organisations from Privacy Breaches: A Comprehensive Review of Problem Domains, Solution Strategies, and Prospective Research Directions,' *TechRxiv* [Preprint]. DOI: 10.36227/techrxiv.171328715.51528864/v1

Keller, J. (2024) 'The Disruption of trust and trust networks. Tracing residents' struggles in the housing market,' in *˜The œurban book series*, pp. 101–138. https.//DOI: 10.1007/978-3-031-57758-1_5

Khalid, N., Qayyum, A., Bilal, M., Al-Fuqaha, A., & Qadir, J. (2023). Privacy-preserving artificial intelligence in healthcare: Techniques and applications. *Computers in Biology and Medicine*, 158, 106848. DOI: 10.1016/j.compbiomed.2023.106848 PMID: 37044052

Khalil, H. A., & Maged, S. A. (2021). *Deepfakes creation and detection using deep learning, 2021 International Mobile, Intelligent, and Ubiquitous Computing Conference*. MIUCC.

Khan, A., ... (2024) 'Future Trends and challenges in cybersecurity and Generative AI,' in *Advances in information security, privacy, and ethics book series*, pp. 491–522. https.//DOI: 10.4018/979-8-3693-5415-5.ch014

Khan, A., Jhanjhi, N., Haji, D. H. T. B. A., & bin Haji Omar, H. A. H. (2024). Overview of XAI for the Development and Modernization of Smart Cities: Explainable Artificial Intelligence. In *Advances in Explainable AI Applications for Smart Cities* (pp. 177-198): IGI Global.

Khan, A., Jhanjhi, N., Hamid, D. H. H., Omar, H. A. H. B. H., Amsaad, F., & Wassan, S. (2025). Future Trends and Challenges in Cybersecurity and Generative AI. *Reshaping CyberSecurity With Generative AI Techniques*, 491-522.

Khan, R., Taqi, M., & Afzal, A. (2024) 'Deepfakes in finance,' in *Advances in information security, privacy, and ethics book series*, pp. 91–120. https.//DOI: 10.4018/979-8-3693-5298-4.ch006

Khan, A. R. S., Syed, H. J., Shuja, J., Khan, A., Qamar, F., & Nguyen, Q. N. (2024). Advancing Secure and Efficient Sensor Data Integration in Smart Cities: A Blockchain-Based Approach. In *Preprints*: *Preprints*.

Khan, A., Jhanjhi, N. Z., & Humayun, M. (2022). The Role of Cybersecurity in Smart Cities. In *Cyber Security Applications for Industry 4.0* (pp. 195–208). Chapman and Hall/CRC. DOI: 10.1201/9781003203087-9

Khan, A., Jhanjhi, N. Z., Omar, H. A. H. B. H., & Haji, D. H. T. B. A. (2024). Risk Management and Cybersecurity in Transportation and Warehousing. In *Cybersecurity Measures for Logistics Industry Framework* (pp. 1–35). IGI Global.

Khan, M. A., & Kaur, M. (2022). Emerging Trends in Business Intelligence. Data Governance and Cybersecurity. *International Journal of Information Systems and Project Management*, 10(1), 5–17. DOI: 10.12821/ijispm100101

Khan, N. A.. (2021). 'A secure communication protocol for unmanned aerial vehicles,' *Computers, Materials & Continua/Computers. Materials & Continua (Print)*, 70(1), 601–618. DOI: 10.32604/cmc.2022.019419

Kharche, A., Badholia, S., & Upadhyay, R. K. (2024). Implementation of blockchain technology in integrated IoT networks for constructing scalable ITS systems in India. *Blockchain Research and Applications*, 5(2), 100188. DOI: 10.1016/j.bcra.2024.100188

Khatiwada, P., Yang, B., Lin, J.-C., & Blobel, B. (2024). Patient-Generated Health Data (PGHD): Understanding, requirements, challenges, and existing techniques for data security and privacy. *Journal of Personalized Medicine*, 14(3), 282. DOI: 10.3390/jpm14030282 PMID: 38541024

Khazane, H. *et al.* (2024) 'A Holistic Review of Machine Learning Adversarial attacks in IoT networks,' *Future Internet*, 16(1), p. 32. https.//.DOI: 10.3390/fi16010032

Khurana, P., Sharma, A., & Singh, P. K. (2016). A Systematic Analysis on Mobile Application Software Vulnerabilities. Issues and Challenges. *Indian Journal of Science and Technology*, 9(32). Advance online publication. DOI: 10.17485/ijst/2016/v9i32/100190

Kim, D. H., & Lee, J. H. (2023). Big Data, Business Intelligence, and Cybersecurity. A Study of Their Interconnections. *Journal of Business Research*, 144, 225–239. DOI: 10.1016/j.jbusres.2022.12.028

Kimon, K., Birte, K., & Christopher, S. (2021). AI-Ethics by Design. Evaluating Public Perception on the Importance of Ethical Design Principles of AI. *arXiv: Computers and Society*. Retrieved from https://arxiv.org/pdf/2106.00326.pdf

Kim, S., & Lee, H. (2022). A Review of Intrusion Detection Systems for Industrial IoT. Challenges and Opportunities. *Sensors (Basel)*, 22(5), 1501.

Kizza, J. M. (2024) 'Authentication,' in *Texts in computer science*, pp. 215–238. https.//DOI: 10.1007/978-3-031-47549-8_10

Kizza, J. M. (2024) 'Blockchains, Cryptocurrency, and Smart Contracts Technologies: Security Considerations,' in *Texts in computer science*, pp. 575–600. DOI: 10.1007/978-3-031-47549-8_26

Kok, S. H., Abdullah, A., Jhanjhi, N. Z., & Supramaniam, M. (2019). A review of intrusion detection system using machine learning approach. *International Journal of Engineering Research & Technology (Ahmedabad)*, 12(1), 8–15.

Kolevski, D. and Michael, K. (2024) 'Edge computing and IoT data breaches. security, privacy, trust, and regulation,' *IEEE Technology and Society Magazine*, 43(1), pp. 22–32. https.//.DOI: 10.1109/MTS.2024.3372605

Korobenko, D., Nikiforova, A. and Sharma, R. (2024) 'Towards a Privacy and Security-Aware Framework for Ethical AI. Guiding the Development and Assessment of AI Systems,' *ACM* [Preprint]. https.//.DOI: 10.1145/3657054.3657141

Kumar, A., & Srivastava, S. (2020). Framework for Integration of Cybersecurity in Business Intelligence Systems. *International Journal of Information Management*, 50, 350–358. DOI: 10.1016/j.ijinfomgt.2019.08.002

Kumar, M. S.. (2021). Blockchain based peer to peer communication in autonomous drone operation. *Energy Reports*, 7, 7925–7939. DOI: 10.1016/j.egyr.2021.08.073

Kumar, N. D.. (2024). Machine learning's role in personalized medicine & treatment optimization. *World Journal of Advanced Research and Reviews*, 21(2), 1675–1686. DOI: 10.30574/wjarr.2024.21.2.0641

Kuo, T.-C., Peng, C.-Y. and Kuo, C.-J. (2021) 'Smart support system of material procurement for waste reduction based on big data and predictive analytics,' *International Journal of Logistics Research and Applications*, 27(2), pp. 243–260. https.//. DOI: 10.1080/13675567.2021.1969348

Kuwajima, H., & Ishikawa, F. (2019). *Adapting square for quality assessment of artificial intelligence systems.* Paper presented at the Proceedings - 2019 IEEE 30th International Symposium on Software Reliability Engineering Workshops, ISSREW 2019. DOI: 10.1109/ISSREW.2019.00035

Lad, S. (2024) *Cybersecurity Trends. Integrating AI to combat emerging threats in the Cloud era.* https.//ijstindex.com/index.php/ijst/article/view/60.

Lämmermann, L., Hofmann, P., & Urbach, N. (2024). Managing artificial intelligence applications in healthcare: Promoting information processing among stakeholders. *International Journal of Information Management*, 75, 102728. DOI: 10.1016/j.ijinfomgt.2023.102728

Leahy, E. (2024). *AI-Powered Bitcoin Trading: Developing an Investment Strategy with Artificial Intelligence.* John Wiley & Sons.

Lee, J., ... (2024) 'Optical Air-Gap Attacks. analysis and IoT threat implications,' *IEEE Network*, p. 1. https.//DOI: 10.1109/MNET.2024.3382969

Lee, M. (2024). *Hacks, leaks, and revelations. The Art of Analyzing Hacked and Leaked Data.* No Starch Press.

Leporati, A., & Rovida, L. (2024). *Looking for Stability in Proof-of-Stake based Consensus Mechanisms.* Blockchain Research and Applications., DOI: 10.1016/j.bcra.2024.100222

Li, J.-H. (2018) 'Cyber security meets artificial intelligence. a survey,' *Frontiers of Information Technology & Electronic Engineering*, 19(12), pp. 1462–1474. https.//. DOI: 10.1631/FITEE.1800573

Li, Y. *et al.* (2023) *Development of Situational Awareness enhancing system for AV-to-Manual handover and other tasks.* .DOI: 10.5703/1288284317730

Liang, B. A. (2006). Fade to Black: Importation and counterfeit drugs. *American Journal of Law & Medicine*, 32(2–3), 279–323. DOI: 10.1177/009885880603200207 PMID: 16927613

Li, H., & Liu, Y. (2024). A Survey of Intrusion Detection Techniques for Industrial IoT Security. *Journal of Network and Computer Applications*, 195, 105056.

Lim, W. *et al.* (2024) 'Future of Generative Adversarial Networks (GAN) for Anomaly Detection in Network Security. A review,' *Computers & Security*, 139, p. 103733. https.//.DOI: 10.1016/j.cose.2024.103733

Li, M., Liu, B., Hu, Y., Zhang, L., & Wang, S. (2021). Deepfake detection using robust spatial and temporal features from facial landmarks, *2021 IEEE International Workshop on Biometrics and Forensics (IWBF)*, pp. 1–6. DOI: 10.1109/IWBF50991.2021.9465076

Lima Filho, F. S. D., Silveira, F. A., de Medeiros Brito, A.Junior, Vargas-Solar, G., & Silveira, L. F. (2019). Smart detection: An online approach for DoS/DDoS attack detection using machine learning. *Security and Communication Networks*, 2019(1), 1574749. DOI: 10.1155/2019/1574749

Lim, M., Abdullah, A., Jhanjhi, N. Z., Khurram Khan, M., & Supramaniam, M. (2019). Link Prediction in Time-Evolving Criminal Network with deep Reinforcement learning technique. *IEEE Access : Practical Innovations, Open Solutions*, 7, 184797–184807. DOI: 10.1109/ACCESS.2019.2958873

Li, Q., & Clark, G. (2013). Mobile security: A look ahead. *IEEE Security and Privacy*, 11(1), 78–81.

Liu, R., ... (2024) 'Unstoppable attack. Label-Only model inversion via conditional diffusion model,' *IEEE Transactions on Information Forensics and Security*, 19, pp. 3958–3973. https.//DOI: 10.1109/TIFS.2024.3372815

Liu, Y. *et al.* (2024) 'An overview of blockchain smart contract execution mechanism,' *Journal of Industrial Information Integration*, p. 100674. .DOI: 10.1016/j.jii.2024.100674

Liu, J., Li, P., Zhang, F., & Ren, K. (2024). MonoCash: A Channel-Free payment network via trusted monotonic counters. *IEEE Transactions on Dependable and Secure Computing*, 21(5), 1–14. DOI: 10.1109/TDSC.2024.3354927

Liu, S., & Li, D. (2024). A Review of Intrusion Prevention Strategies for Securing Industrial IoT Networks. *Journal of Industrial Engineering and Management*, 14(3), 489–501.

Liu, W., & Yu, J. (2023). Cybersecurity Measures in Business Intelligence Solutions. Challenges and Opportunities. *Computers & Security*, 123, 103078. DOI: 10.1016/j.cose.2022.103078

Liu, X., Shah, R., Shandilya, A., Shah, M., & Pandya, A. (2024). A systematic study on integrating blockchain in healthcare for electronic health record management and tracking medical supplies. *Journal of Cleaner Production*, 447, 141371. DOI: 10.1016/j.jclepro.2024.141371

Liu, Y., & Zheng, Q. (2023). Intrusion Prevention in Industrial IoT Networks. A Review of Machine Learning Techniques. *IEEE Transactions on Industrial Electronics*, 70(3), 2453–2463.

Li, X., & Liu, Z. (2022). Threat Detection and Intrusion Prevention Techniques for Industrial IoT. A Survey. *IEEE Access : Practical Innovations, Open Solutions*, 10, 15948–15959.

Li, Y., & Zhan, J. (2021). A Comprehensive Study of Business Intelligence and Its Role in Organizational Success. *Journal of Knowledge Management*, 25(2), 424–442. DOI: 10.1108/JKM-04-2020-0291

Ljupco Markuseski, L., Zdravkoski Igor, I. Z., Miroslav, A., & Jovanoska Aleksandra, A. J. (2019). Knowledge discovery databases (kdd) process in data mining. In *INTERNATIONAL CONFERENCE PROCEEDING* (pp. 529–539). Faculty of Economic Prilep.

Lodhi, S.K., Gill, A.Y. and Hussain, I. (2024) 'AI-Powered Innovations in Contemporary Manufacturing Procedures. An Extensive analysis,' *International Journal of Multidisciplinary Sciences and Arts*, 3(4), pp. 15–25. https.//.DOI: 10.47709/ijmdsa.v3i4.4616

López, R. A., & Gonzalez, A. (2020). Business Intelligence Tools. A Study of the Adoption in Small and Medium Enterprises. *Journal of Small Business Management*, 58(4), 651–671. DOI: 10.1111/jsbm.12443

Lysenko, S. (2024). The role of Artificial intelligence in cybersecurity: Automation of protection and detection of threats. *Economic Affairs*, 69(1s). Advance online publication. DOI: 10.46852/0424-2513.1.2024.6

Madine, M. M., Battah, A. A., Yaqoob, I., Salah, K., Jayaraman, R., Al-Hammadi, Y., Pesic, S., & Ellahham, S. (2020). Blockchain for giving patients control over their medical records. *IEEE Access : Practical Innovations, Open Solutions*, 8, 193102–193115. DOI: 10.1109/ACCESS.2020.3032553

Maione, G. (2024) 'Blockchain technology and the quest for decentralized accountability,' in *Emerald Publishing Limited eBooks*, pp. 49–70. DOI: 10.1108/978-1-83797-739-020241004

Maiwada, U.D. *et al.* (2024) 'Security concerns of IoT against DDOS in 5G systems,' *International Journal of Electrical Engineering and Computer Science*, 6, pp. 98–105. https.//.DOI: 10.37394/232027.2024.6.11

Majeed, R. H., & Taha, A. A. D. (2023). 'A survey study of Iraqi auditors' adoption of blockchain technology,'. *Asian Review of Accounting*, 32(3), 521–546. DOI: 10.1108/ARA-01-2023-0015

Malatji, M. and Tolah, A. (2024) 'Artificial intelligence (AI) cybersecurity dimensions. a comprehensive framework for understanding adversarial and offensive AI,' *AI And Ethics* [Preprint]. https.//.DOI: 10.1007/s43681-024-00427-4

Malhotra, P., & Misra, A. (2022). *ACCOUNTABILITY and RESPONSIBILITY of ARTIFICIAL INTELLIGENCE DECISION-MAKING MODELS in INDIAN POLICY LANDSCAPE.* Paper presented at the CEUR Workshop Proceedings.

Malik, A.W. *et al.* (2024) 'Cloud Digital Forensics. Beyond tools, techniques, and challenges,' *Sensors*, 24(2), p. 433. https.//.DOI: 10.3390/s24020433

Malik, J., Muthalagu, R., & Pawar, P. M. (2024) 'A systematic review of adversarial machine learning attacks, defensive controls, and technologies,' *IEEE Access*, 12, pp. 99382–99421. https.//DOI: 10.1109/ACCESS.2024.3423323

Mallikarjunaradhya, V., Pothukuchi, A. S., & Kota, L. V. (2023). An overview of the strategic advantages of AI-powered threat intelligence in the cloud. *Journal of Science and Technology*, 4(4), 1–12. DOI: 10.55662/JST.2023.4401

Manasa, P., Malik, A., Alqahtani, K. N., Alomar, M. A., Basingab, M. S., Soni, M., Rizwan, A., & Batra, I. (2024, August). Tweet Spam Detection Using Machine Learning and Swarm Optimization Techniques. *IEEE Transactions on Computational Social Systems*, 11(4), 4870–4877. DOI: 10.1109/TCSS.2022.3230823

Manchuri, A. *et al.* (2024) 'pplication of Supervised Machine Learning Models in Biodiesel Production Research - A Short Review,' *Borneo Journal of Sciences and Technology* [Preprint]. .DOI: 10.35370/bjost.2024.6.1-10

Mandal, P. C., Mukherjee, I., Paul, G., & Chatterji, B. N. (2022). Digital image steganography. A literature survey. *Information Sciences, 609*, 1451–1488. https.// DOI: 10.1016/j.ins.2022.07.120

Manjula C Belavagi and Balachandra Muniyal. Multiclass machine learning algorithms for intrusion detection performance study. In *International Symposium on Security in Computing and Communication*, pages 170–178. Springer, 2017.

Manthiramoorthy, C., Khan, K.M.S. and A, N.A. (2023) 'Comparing several encrypted cloud storage platforms,' *International Journal of Mathematics Statistics and Computer Science*, 2, pp. 44–62. https.//.DOI: 10.59543/ijmscs.v2i.7971

Marcén, A. G. (2021) 'The new personal data protection in Japan: Is it enough?' in *Bristol University Press eBooks*, pp. 101–120. DOI: 10.51952/9781529213386.ch003

Mardani, A.. (2020). Cybersecurity in Business Intelligence. Challenges and Solutions. *Computers & Security*, 95, 101850. DOI: 10.1016/j.cose.2020.101850

Martínez-Plumed, F., Contreras-Ochando, L., Ferri, C., Hernández-Orallo, J., Kull, M., Lachiche, N., Ramirez-Quintana, M. J., & Flach, P. (2019). CRISP-DM twenty years later: From data mining processes to data science trajectories. *IEEE Transactions on Knowledge and Data Engineering*, 33(8), 3048–3061. DOI: 10.1109/TKDE.2019.2962680

Masum, R. (2023). Cyber Security in Smart Manufacturing (Threats, Landscapes Challenges). *arXiv preprint arXiv:2304.10180.*

Mathur, S., Lal Gupta, S., & Pahwa, P. (2021). Optimizing OLAP cube for supporting business intelligence and forecasting in banking sector. *Journal of Information Technology Management*, 13(1), 81–99.

Matos, T., & Guerreiro, J. (2024, June). Remote Secure Online Voting System Development. In *International Conference on Human-Computer Interaction* (pp. 51-65). Cham: Springer Nature Switzerland.

Matus, P. P. (2022). AI Ethics and Policy. *Future of Business and Finance*, 101-118. DOI: 10.1007/978-3-031-19039-1_5

Maulina, A. and Rasjid, Z.E. (2024) 'Unified Access Management for Digital Evidence Storage. Integrating Attribute-based and Role-based Access Control with XACML,' *International Journal of Advanced Computer Science and Applications*, 15(3). https.//.DOI: 10.14569/IJACSA.2024.01503131

McGraw, G. (2010). *Mobile application security*. McGraw-Hill. https.//www.amazon.com/Mobile-Application-Security-Himanshu-Dwivedi/dp/0071611016

McIntosh, T. *et al.* (2024) 'Ransomware Reloaded. Re-examining its trend, research and mitigation in the era of data exfiltration,' *ACM Computing Surveys* [Preprint]. https.//.DOI: 10.1145/3691340

Mehrtak, M., SeyedAlinaghi, S. A., MohsseniPour, M., Noori, T., Karimi, A., Shamsabadi, A., Heydari, M., Barzegary, A., Mirzapour, P., Soleymanzadeh, M., Vahedi, F., Mehraeen, E., & Dadras, O. (2021). Security challenges and solutions using healthcare cloud computing. *Journal of Medicine and Life*, 14(4), 448–461. DOI: 10.25122/jml-2021-0100 PMID: 34621367

Mehta, D. *et al.* (2022) 'DieRoll. a unique key generation and encryption technique,' *Journal of Applied Security Research*, 19(2), pp. 168–195. https.//.DOI: 10.1080/19361610.2022.2124589

Mejia-Miranda, J., Melchor-Velasquez, R. E., & Munoz-Mata, M. A. (2017). Vulnerability detection in smartphones. A systematic literature review. 2017 12th Iberian Conference on Information Systems and Technologies (CISTI).

Mesarčík, M., & Hamuľák, O. (2024) 'General Data Protection Regulation: current challenges and future directions,' in *Contributions to political science*, pp. 117–133. DOI: 10.1007/978-3-031-56045-3_9

Mgeladze, M. (2024). The legal regulation hurdles of the Blockchain-Based contracts for maritime transport. *European Journal of Commercial Contract Law*, 16(1), 10–24. DOI: 10.7590/187714624X17132716463892

Mims, N. A. (2025) 'The Botnet problem,' in *Elsevier eBooks*, pp. 261–272. https.// DOI: 10.1016/B978-0-443-13223-0.00014-X

Mishra, S., ... (2024) 'Mitigating the Threat of Multi-Factor Authentication (MFA) Bypass Through Man-in-the-Middle Attacks Using EvilGinx2,' *Wiley*, pp. 59–78. https.//DOI: 10.1002/9781394272303.ch5

Mishra, R., Sharma, S., & Agrawal, R. (2010). Vulnerabilities and security for ad-hoc networks. *2010 International Conference on Networking and Information Technology.*

Mobile Application Security (no date) *Google Books*. Available at. https.//books.google.com.my/books?id=Iq11Hs6FFm4C&printsec=frontcover#v=onepage&q&f=false

Mobile OS vulnerabilities (no date) *Google Books*. Available at. https.//www.google.com.my/books/edition/Mobile_OS_Vulnerabilities/fh3EEAAAQBAJ?hl=en&gbpv=1&dq=Mobile%2BOS%2BVulnerabilities%3A%2BQuantitative%2Band%2BQualitative%2BAnalysis%2Bby%2BShafiullah%2BKhan&printsec=frontcover

Mobile phone security and Forensics (no date) *Google Books*. Available at. https.//www.google.com.my/books/edition/Mobile_Phone_Security_and_Forensics/OE4rJk7u5wIC?hl=en&gbpv=1&dq=Mobile%2BApplication%2BSecurity%2Band%2BForensics%3A%2BA%2BPractical%2BApproach%22%2Bby%2BRichardMobile%2BApplication%2BDevelopment%2C%2BUsability%2C%2Band%2BSecurity%22%2Bedited%2Bby%2BSougata%2BMukherjea%2B-%2BHammer%2Band%2BRic%2BMessier&printsec=frontcover

mobile security. (2019) Available at. https.//www.dhs.gov/sites/default/files/publications/2019_mobilesecurity_rd_programguide_vol3.pdf

Morais, D., Pinto, F. G., Pires, I. M., Garcia, N. M., & Gouveia, A. J. (2022). The influence of cloud computing on the healthcare industry: A review of applications, opportunities, and challenges for the CIO. *Procedia Computer Science*, 203, 714–720. DOI: 10.1016/j.procs.2022.07.106

Mueller-Bloch, C.. (2022). Understanding decentralization of decision-making power in proof-of-stake blockchains: An agent-based simulation approach. *European Journal of Information Systems*, •••, 1–20. DOI: 10.1080/0960085X.2022.2125840

Mumtaz, S. L., Syed, H. J., Al-Ani, A., Fatah, S., Al-Ani, A. K., & Khan, A. (2024). *Detection of Botnet in the loT Network*. Paper presented at the ITM Web of Conferences. DOI: 10.1051/itmconf/20246301019

Mungo, J. (2023) 'Self-paced cybersecurity awareness training educating retail employees to identify phishing attacks,' *Journal of Cyber Security Technology*, pp. 1–49. https.//.DOI: 10.1080/23742917.2023.2244210

Muraleedhara, P. (2024). The Need For AI-Powered Cybersecurity to Tackle AI-Driven Cyberattacks. Retrieved from https://www.isaca.org/resources/news-and-trends/isaca-now-blog/2024/the-need-for-ai-powered-cybersecurity-to-tackle-ai-driven-cyberattacks

Murugan, K. C., Samanta, D., & Goswami, M. (2022). *An Approach on Image Steganography Based on the Least Significant Bit Algorithm* [Chapter]. Handbook of Research on Mathematical Modeling for Smart Healthcare Systems; IGI Global. https.//DOI: 10.4018/978-1-6684-4580-8.ch012

Mustafa, G. *et al.* (2024) 'Blockchain-based governance models in e-government: a comprehensive framework for legal, technical, ethical and security considerations,' *International Journal of Law and Management* [Preprint]. .DOI: 10.1108/IJLMA-08-2023-0172

Mutlag, A. A., Abd Ghani, M. K., Mohammed, M. A., Lakhan, A., Mohd, O., Abdulkareem, K. H., & Garcia-Zapirain, B. (2021). Multi-agent systems in fog–cloud computing for critical healthcare task management model (CHTM) used for ECG monitoring. *Sensors (Basel)*, 21(20), 6923. DOI: 10.3390/s21206923 PMID: 34696135

Muzafar, S., & Jhanjhi, N. Z. (2019) 'Success stories of ICT implementation in Saudi Arabia,' in *Advances in electronic government, digital divide, and regional development book series*, pp. 151–163. DOI: 10.4018/978-1-7998-1851-9.ch008

Muzammal, S. M., & Murugesan, R. K. (2021). Enhanced authentication and access control in Internet of Things. A potential blockchain-based method. *International Journal of Grid and Utility Computing, 12*(5–6), 469–485. https.//DOI: 10.1504/IJGUC.2021.120090

Muzammal, S. M., Murugesan, R. K., & Jhanjhi, N. Z. (2021). A Comprehensive Review on Secure Routing in Internet of Things. Mitigation Methods and Trust-Based Approaches. *IEEE Internet of Things Journal, 8*(6), 4186–4210. IEEE Internet of Things Journal. https.//DOI: 10.1109/JIOT.2020.3031162

Muzammal, S. M., Murugesan, R. K., Jhanjhi, N. Z., Humayun, M., Ibrahim, A. O., & Abdelmaboud, A. (2022). A Trust-Based Model for Secure Routing against RPL Attacks in Internet of Things. *Sensors, 22*(18), Article 18. https.//DOI: 10.3390/s22187052

Muzammal, S. M., Murugesan, R. K., Jhanjhi, N. Z., & Jung, L. T. (2020, October). SMTrust. Proposing trust-based secure routing protocol for RPL attacks for IoT applications. In *2020 International Conference on Computational Intelligence (ICCI)* (pp. 305-310). IEEE. DOI: 10.1109/ICCI51257.2020.9247818

Naef, S., Wagner, S. M., & Saur, C. (2022). Blockchain and network governance: Learning from applications in the supply chain sector. *Production Planning and Control*, 35(9), 932–946. DOI: 10.1080/09537287.2022.2044072

Naguib, A., & Fouad, K. M. (2024) 'Database Security: Current Challenges and Effective Protection Strategies,' *2024 6th International Conference on Computing and Informatics (ICCI)* [Preprint]. DOI: 10.1109/ICCI61671.2024.10485182

Naik, K. *et al.* (2024) 'Current status and future directions. The Application of Artificial Intelligence/Machine Learning for Precision Medicine,' *Clinical Pharmacology & Therapeutics*, 115(4), pp. 673–686. https.//.DOI: 10.1002/cpt.3152

Nair, M. M., Deshmukh, A., & Tyagi, A. K. (2023) 'Artificial Intelligence for Cyber Security,' *Wiley*, pp. 83–114. https.//DOI: 10.1002/9781394213948.ch5

Najmi, K. Y., AlZain, M. A., Masud, M., Jhanjhi, N. Z., Al-Amri, J., & Baz, M. (2023). A survey on security threats and countermeasures in IoT to achieve users confidentiality and reliability. *Materials Today: Proceedings*, 81, 377–382. DOI: 10.1016/j.matpr.2021.03.417

Nanda, S., Zafari, F., DeCusatis, C., Wedaa, E., & Yang, B. (2016, November). Predicting network attack patterns in SDN using machine learning approach. In *2016 IEEE Conference on Network Function Virtualization and Software Defined Networks (NFV-SDN)* (pp. 167-172). DOI: 10.1109/NFV-SDN.2016.7919493

Narayan, D. G., Arali, N., & Tejas, R. (2024). DPoSEB: Delegated Proof of Stake with Exponential Backoff Consensus Algorithm for Ethereum Blockchain. *Computer Science Journal of Moldova*, 32(2(95)), 262–288. DOI: 10.56415/csjm.v32.14

Nasrullah, N. A., Sharma, N., & Niazy, M. S. (2023). A Study of Performance Evaluation and Comparison of NOSQL Databases Choosing for Big Data: HBase and Cassandra Using YCSB. *Journal of Computational Engineering*, 25(3), 1–12.

Nasser, N., Emad-ul-Haq, Q., Imran, M., Ali, A., Razzak, I., & Al-Helali, A. (2021). A smart healthcare framework for detection and monitoring of COVID-19 using IoT and cloud computing. *Neural Computing & Applications*, •••, 1–15. PMID: 34522068

Naveed, H. *et al.* (2024) 'Survey. Image mixing and deleting for data augmentation,' *Engineering Applications of Artificial Intelligence*, 131, p. 107791. https.//.DOI: 10.1016/j.engappai.2023.107791

Nayak, R., Pati, U.C. and Das, S.K. (2023) 'A comprehensive review of datasets for detection and localization of video anomalies. a step towards data-centric artificial intelligence-based video anomaly detection,' *Multimedia Tools and Applications*, 83(21), pp. 59617–59674. https.//.DOI: 10.1007/s11042-023-17889-z

Nayyar, A., Gadhavi, L., & Zaman, N. (2021). Machine learning in healthcare. review, opportunities and challenges. In *Elsevier eBooks* (pp. 23–45). https.//DOI: 10.1016/B978-0-12-821229-5.00011-2

Nguyen, T. T., Quoc Viet Hung, N., Nguyen, T. T., Huynh, T. T., Nguyen, T. T., Weidlich, M., & Yin, H. (2024). Manipulating recommender systems: A survey of poisoning attacks and countermeasures. *ACM Computing Surveys*, 57(1), 1–39.

Nofer, M., Gomber, P., Hinz, O., & Schiereck, D. (2017). Blockchain. *Business & Information Systems Engineering*, 59(3), 183–187. DOI: 10.1007/s12599-017-0467-3

Nosrati, M., Karimi, R., & Hariri, M. (2011). An introduction to steganography methods. *World Applied Programming*, 1(3), 191–195.

Novelli, C., Taddeo, M. and Floridi, L. (2023) 'Accountability in artificial intelligence. what it is and how it works,' *AI & Society* [Preprint]. https.//.DOI: 10.1007/s00146-023-01635-y

Nyemba, W. R., Mbohwa, C., & Carter, K. F. (2021) 'Problem- and Industry-Based Learning. Research, theory and practice,' in *EAI/Springer Innovations in Communication and Computing*, pp. 81–105. https.//DOI: 10.1007/978-3-030-70493-3_5

Obi, N.O.C. *et al.* (2024) 'COMPREHENSIVE REVIEW ON CYBERSECURITY. MODERN THREATS AND ADVANCED DEFENSE STRATEGIES,' *Computer Science & IT Research Journal*, 5(2), pp. 293–310. https.//.DOI: 10.51594/csitrj.v5i2.758

Ogungbemi, O. S. (2024). Smart Contracts Management: The interplay of data privacy and blockchain for secure and efficient real estate transactions. *Journal of Engineering Research and Reports*, 26(8), 278–300. DOI: 10.9734/jerr/2024/v26i81245

Okoli, N.U.I. *et al.* (2024) 'Machine learning in cybersecurity. A review of threat detection and defense mechanisms,' *World Journal of Advanced Research and Reviews*, 21(1), pp. 2286–2295. https.//.DOI: 10.30574/wjarr.2024.21.1.0315

Okon, S. U., Olateju, O. O., Ogungbemi, O. S., Joseph, S. A., Olisa, A. O., & Olaniyi, O. O. (2024). Incorporating Privacy by Design Principles in the Modification of AI Systems in Preventing Breaches across Multiple Environments, Including Public Cloud, Private Cloud, and On-prem. *Journal of Engineering Research and Reports*, 26(9), 136–158. DOI: 10.9734/jerr/2024/v26i91269

Olawale, N. O.. (2024). RegTech innovations streamlining compliance, reducing costs in the financial sector. *GSC Advanced Research and Reviews*, 19(1), 114–131. DOI: 10.30574/gscarr.2024.19.1.0146

Olsen, H.P. *et al.* (2024) 'The right to transparency in public governance. freedom of information and the use of artificial intelligence by public agencies,' *Digital Government Research and Practice*, 5(1), pp. 1–15. https.//.DOI: 10.1145/3632753

Oluoch, I. (2024) 'Crossing Boundaries. The ethics of AI and Geographic Information Technologies,' *ISPRS International Journal of Geo-Information*, 13(3), p. 87. https.//.DOI: 10.3390/ijgi13030087

Omolara, A.E. *et al.* (2021) 'The internet of things security. A survey encompassing unexplored areas and new insights,' *Computers & Security*, 112, p. 102494. https.//.DOI: 10.1016/j.cose.2021.102494

Oniani, D., Hilsman, J., Peng, Y., Poropatich, R. K., Pamplin, J. C., Legault, G. L., & Wang, Y. (2023). Adopting and expanding ethical principles for generative artificial intelligence from military to healthcare. *npj. Digital Medicine*, 6(1), 225. Advance online publication. DOI: 10.1038/s41746-023-00965-x PMID: 38042910

Onyebuchi, A., Matthew, U. O., Kazaure, J. S., Okafor, N. U., Okey, O. D., Okochi, P. I., Taiwo, J. F., & Matthew, A. O. (2022). Business demand for a cloud enterprise data warehouse in electronic healthcare computing: Issues and developments in e-healthcare cloud computing. [IJCAC]. *International Journal of Cloud Applications and Computing*, 12(1), 1–22. DOI: 10.4018/IJCAC.297098

Oriekhoe, N. O. I.. (2024). BLOCKCHAIN TECHNOLOGY IN SUPPLY CHAIN MANAGEMENT: A COMPREHENSIVE REVIEW. *International Journal of Management & Entrepreneurship Research*, 6(1), 150–166. DOI: 10.51594/ijmer.v6i1.714

Ortega, E., Tran, M., & Bandeen, G. (2023). *AI Digital Tool Product Lifecycle Governance Framework through Ethics and Compliance by Design†*. Paper presented at the Proceedings - 2023 IEEE Conference on Artificial Intelligence, CAI 2023. DOI: 10.1109/CAI54212.2023.00155

Otieno, N.I.A. (2024) 'Extensive review of quantum computing and network security,' *World Journal of Advanced Engineering Technology and Sciences*, 12(2), pp. 770–807. https.//.DOI: 10.30574/wjaets.2024.12.2.0337

Owino, B. A., & Paschal, M. J. (2023). AI and ethics in education: Implications and strategies for responsible implementation. In *Creative AI Tools and Ethical Implications in Teaching and Learning* (pp. 196-211).

Ozkan-Okay, M., ... (2024) 'A comprehensive survey. Evaluating the efficiency of artificial intelligence and machine learning techniques on cyber security solutions,' *IEEE Access*, 12, pp. 12229–12256. https.//DOI: 10.1109/ACCESS.2024.3355547

Ozkaya, U., Oztu¨rk, S., Melgani, F., & Seyfi, L. (2021). Residual cnn+bi-lstm model to analyze gpr b scan images. *Automation in Construction*, 123, 103525. DOI: 10.1016/j.autcon.2020.103525

Oztu¨rk, S., & Ozkaya, U. (2021). Residual lstm layered cnn for classification of gastrointestinal tract diseases. *Journal of Biomedical Informatics*, 113, 103638. DOI: 10.1016/j.jbi.2020.103638 PMID: 33271341

P. Khurana1, A. Sharma & Pradeep Kumar Singh (2016) *Juit*. Available at. http.//www.ir.juit.ac.in.8080/jspui/bitstream/123456789/8356/1/A%20Systematic%20Analysis%20on%20Mobile%20Application%20Software%20Vulnerabilities%20Issues%20and%20Challenges.pdf

Pal, A., & Saha, S. K. (2022). Integrating Cybersecurity into Business Intelligence. A New Paradigm. *Journal of Business Research*, 144, 117–129. DOI: 10.1016/j.jbusres.2022.03.015

Palakurti, N. R. (2024) 'Challenges and future directions in anomaly detection,' in *Advances in systems analysis, software engineering, and high performance computing book series*, pp. 269–284. https.//DOI: 10.4018/979-8-3693-2909-2.ch020

Palaniappan, K., Lin, E. Y. T., & Vogel, S. (2024). Global Regulatory Frameworks for the use of Artificial intelligence (AI) in the healthcare services sector. *Health Care*, 12(5), 562. DOI: 10.3390/healthcare12050562 PMID: 38470673

Pan, D., Sun, L., Wang, R., Zhang, X., & Sinnott, R. O. (2020). Deepfake detection through deep learning, *2020 IEEE/ACM International Conference on Big Data Computing, Applications and Technologies (BDCAT)*, pp. 134–143. DOI: 10.1109/BDCAT50828.2020.00001

Papastergiou, S., Mouratidis, H., & Kalogeraki, E. M. (2021). Handling of advanced persistent threats and complex incidents in healthcare, transportation and energy ICT infrastructures. *Evolving Systems*, 12(1), 91–108. DOI: 10.1007/s12530-020-09335-4

Park, J., & Kim, D. (2023). Deep Learning Approaches for Intrusion Prevention in Industrial IoT Networks. A Survey. *IEEE Communications Surveys and Tutorials*, 25(1), 258–273.

Pastorek, A. and Tundis, A. (2024) 'Navigating the landscape of IoT security and associated risks in critical infrastructures,' *ACM* [Preprint]. https.//.DOI: 10.1145/3664476.3669979

Patel, B., & Makaryus, A. N. (2021) 'Cardiac implantable electronic devices and cybersecurity,' *Expert Review of Medical Devices*, 18(sup1), pp. 69–77. https.//DOI: 10.1080/17434440.2021.2007075

Patel, Y., Tanwar, S., Bhattacharya, P., Gupta, R., Alsuwian, T., Davidson, I. E., & Mazibuko, T. F. (2023). An Improved Dense CNN Architecture for Deepfake Image Detection. *IEEE Access : Practical Innovations, Open Solutions*, 11, 22081–22095. DOI: 10.1109/ACCESS.2023.3251417

Pawar, V., & Sachdeva, S. (2023). ParallelChain: A scalable healthcare framework with low-energy consumption using blockchain. *International Transactions in Operational Research*, 31(6), 3621–3649. DOI: 10.1111/itor.13278

Penso, C., Frenkel, L. and Goldberger, J. (2024) 'Confidence Calibration of a Medical Imaging Classification System That is Robust to Label Noise,' *IEEE Transactions on Medical Imaging*, 43(6), pp. 2050–2060. https.//.DOI: 10.1109/TMI.2024.3353762

Peral-García, D., Cruz-Benito, J. and García-Peñalvo, F.J. (2024) 'Systematic literature review. Quantum machine learning and its applications,' *Computer Science Review*, 51, p. 100619. https.//.DOI: 10.1016/j.cosrev.2024.100619

Persson, S. (2024) *Empowering Subcontractors in Swedish Construction with Blockchain Technology for Automated Payment Processes*. https://odr.chalmers.se/items/dc2762af-9520-4b0a-b784-53dee3319e88

Pesapane, F., Bracchi, D. A., Mulligan, J. F., Linnikov, A., Maslennikov, O., Lanzavecchia, M. B., Tantrige, P., Stasolla, A., Biondetti, P., Giuggioli, P. F., Cassano, E., & Carrafiello, G. (2021). Legal and Regulatory Framework for AI Solutions in Healthcare in EU, US, China, and Russia: New Scenarios after a Pandemic. *Radiation*, 1(4), 261–276. DOI: 10.3390/radiation1040022

Petch, J., Di, S., & Nelson, W. (2022). Opening the black box: The promise and limitations of explainable machine learning in cardiology. *The Canadian Journal of Cardiology*, 38(2), 204–213. DOI: 10.1016/j.cjca.2021.09.004 PMID: 34534619

Pfund, G. N., & Allemand, M. (2022). Correlated change between personality traits and perceived social support in old age. *Personality and Social Psychology Bulletin*, 50(2), 167–181. DOI: 10.1177/01461672221120493 PMID: 36149032

Pokroy, A. A., & Egorov, A. D. (2021). Efficientnets for deepfake detection: Comparison of pretrained models, *2021 IEEE Conference of Russian Young Researchers in Electrical and Electronic Engineering (ElConRus)*, pp. 598–600. DOI: 10.1109/ElConRus51938.2021.9396092

Polat, H., Polat, O., & Cetin, A. (2020). Detecting DDoS attacks in software-defined networks through feature selection methods and machine learning models. *Sustainability (Basel)*, 12(3), 1035. DOI: 10.3390/su12031035

Ponnusamy, V.. (2022). *AI-Driven Information and Communication Technologies, Services, and Applications for Next-Generation Healthcare System*. Wiley., DOI: 10.1002/9781119762010.ch1

Pool, J., Akhlaghpour, S., Fatehi, F., & Burton-Jones, A. (2024). A systematic analysis of failures in protecting personal health data: A scoping review. *International Journal of Information Management*, 74, 102719. DOI: 10.1016/j.ijinfomgt.2023.102719

Popoola, O. *et al.* (2024) 'An optimized hybrid encryption framework for smart home healthcare. Ensuring data confidentiality and security,' *Internet of Things*, 27, p. 101314. https.//.DOI: 10.1016/j.iot.2024.101314

Pradhan, A., Sekhar, K. R., & Swain, G. (2018). Digital Image Steganography Using LSB Substitution, PVD, and EMD. *Mathematical Problems in Engineering, 2018*, e1804953. https.//DOI: 10.1155/2018/1804953

Prasad, M. D., Babu, V. P., & Amarnath, C. (2019). Machine learning DDoS detection using stochastic gradient boosting. *International Journal on Computer Science and Engineering*, 7(4), 157–16.

Putra, M. A. P., Alief, R. N., Rachmawati, S. M., Sampedro, G. A., Kim, D.-S., & Lee, J.-M. (2024). Proof-of-authority-based secure and efficient aggregation with differential privacy for federated learning in industrial IoT. *Internet of Things : Engineering Cyber Physical Human Systems*, 25, 101107. DOI: 10.1016/j.iot.2024.101107

Quan, G., Yao, Z., Si, X., Zhu, W., & Chen, L. (2024). A data sharing model for blockchain trusted sensor leveraging mimic hash mechanism. *Electronics (Basel)*, 13(8), 1495. DOI: 10.3390/electronics13081495

Qureshi, S.M. *et al.* (2024) 'Deepfake forensics. a survey of digital forensic methods for multimodal deepfake identification on social media,' *PeerJ Computer Science*, 10, p. e2037. https.//.DOI: 10.7717/peerj-cs.2037

Radanliev, P. (2024a) 'Cyber diplomacy. defining the opportunities for cybersecurity and risks from Artificial Intelligence, IoT, Blockchains, and Quantum Computing,' *Journal of Cyber Security Technology*, pp. 1–51. https.//.DOI: 10.1080/23742917.2024.2312671

Radanliev, P. (2024b) 'Digital security by design,' *Security Journal* [Preprint]. https.//. DOI: 10.1057/s41284-024-00435-3

Radhakrishnan, S., & Travieso-Gonzalez, C. M. (2024). *Biometrics and Cryptography*. BoD – Books on Demand. DOI: 10.5772/intechopen.107597

Rafique, A., Van Landuyt, D., Beni, E. H., Lagaisse, B., & Joosen, W. (2021). CryptDICE: Distributed data protection system for secure cloud data storage and computation. *Information Systems*, 96, 101671. DOI: 10.1016/j.is.2020.101671

Rahman, R. U., Singh, K., Tomar, D. S., & Musheer, R. (2024). Building Resilient Digital Forensic Frameworks for NoSQL Database: Harnessing the Blockchain and Quantum Technology. In *Sustainable Security Practices Using Blockchain, Quantum and Post-Quantum Technologies for Real Time Applications* (pp. 205–238). Springer Nature Singapore. DOI: 10.1007/978-981-97-0088-2_11

Ramos, S., & Ellul, J. (2024). Blockchain for Artificial Intelligence (AI): Enhancing compliance with the EU AI Act through distributed ledger technology. A cybersecurity perspective, [Preprint]. *International Cybersecurity Law Review*, 5(1), 1–20. Advance online publication. DOI: 10.1365/s43439-023-00107-9

Ramya, R. (2024) 'Analysis and applications finding of wireless sensors and IoT devices with Artificial Intelligence/Machine Learning,' in *Advances in computational intelligence and robotics book series*, pp. 77–102. https.//DOI: 10.4018/979-8-3693-0786-1.ch005

Ramzan, M. S., Asghar, A., Ullah, A., Jhanji, N. Z., Alsolami, F., & Ahmad, I. (2022). Enhanced Artificial Bee Colony Based Optimization for Mitigating Replication in Large Data for Internet of Things (Iot). *Available atSSRN* 4281666. DOI: 10.2139/ssrn.4281666

Rana, M., & Shuford, J. (2024). AI in Healthcare: Transforming Patient Care through Predictive Analytics and Decision Support Systems. *Deleted Journal*, 1(1). Advance online publication. DOI: 10.60087/jaigs.v1i1.30

Rani, A., ... (2024) 'Role and Significance of Internet of Things (IoT) in Industry 4.0,' *2024 3rd International Conference on Power Electronics and IoT Applications in Renewable Energy and Its Control (PARC)* [Preprint]. https.//DOI: 10.1109/PARC59193.2024.10486519

Rani, P., Verma, S., Yadav, S. P., Rai, B. K., Naruka, M. S., & Kumar, D. (2022). Simulation of the Lightweight Blockchain Technique Based on Privacy and Security for Healthcare Data for the Cloud System. [IJEHMC]. *International Journal of E-Health and Medical Communications*, 13(4), 1–15. DOI: 10.4018/IJEHMC.309436

Ranjan, J. (2020). Business Intelligence. A Managerial Perspective on Analytics. *Journal of Business Research*, 115, 268–276. DOI: 10.1016/j.jbusres.2020.01.026

Ranjan, J., & Prakash, A. (2023). Challenges in Implementing Business Intelligence. A Study in Emerging Markets. *International Journal of Information Management*, 68, 102321. DOI: 10.1016/j.ijinfomgt.2023.102321

Rao, I. S., Kiah, M. L. M., Hameed, M. M., & Memon, Z. A. (2024). Scalability of blockchain: A comprehensive review and future research direction, [Preprint]. *Cluster Computing*, 27(5), 5547–5570. Advance online publication. DOI: 10.1007/s10586-023-04257-7

Rashmi, S., Siwach, V., Sehrawat, H., Brar, G. S., Singla, J., Jhanjhi, N., . . . Shorfuzzaman, M. AI-Powered VM Selection: Amplifying Cloud Performance with Dragonfly Algorithm. *Heliyon*.

Ravichandran, N.. (2024) ‘Comprehensive Review Analysis and Countermeasures for Cybersecurity Threats: DDoS, Ransomware, and Trojan Horse Attacks,’ *preprint.org* [Preprint]. DOI: 10.20944/preprints202409.1369.v1

Ravikumar, C., Naresh, B., Prasanna, P. L., Goud, E. A., & Prasad, P. R. “Exploring Machine Learning Algorithms for Robust Cyber Threat Detection and Classification. A Comprehensive Evaluation,” in *2024 International Conference on Intelligent Systems for Cybersecurity (ISCS)*, 2024.

Rebello, G. A. F.. (2024). *A survey on Blockchain Scalability: From Hardware to Layer-Two Protocols*. IEEE Communications Surveys & Tutorials., DOI: 10.1109/COMST.2024.3376252

Reda, A., & Ahmed, A. (2021). Trends in Data Warehousing. A Review and Future Research Directions. *International Journal of Business Intelligence Research*, 12(1), 1–21. DOI: 10.4018/IJBIR.2021010101

Rehan, H. (2024) 'AI-Driven Cloud Security. The future of Safeguarding Sensitive data in the Digital Age,' *Deleted Journal*, 1(1), pp. 132–151. https.//.DOI: 10.60087/jaigs.v1i1.89

Rehman, A. U., Butt, W. H., Ali, T. M., Javaid, S., Almufareh, M. F., Humayun, M., Rahman, H., Mir, A., & Shaheen, M. (2024). “A Machine Learning-Based Framework for Accurate and Early Diagnosis of Liver Diseases: A Comprehensive Study on Feature Selection, Data Imbalance, and Algorithmic Performance,” *International Journal of Intelligent Systems*, vol. 2024. *Article ID*, 6111312, 1–29.

Renaud, K., Warkentin, M., Pogrebna, G., & van der Schyff, K. (2024). VISTA: An inclusive insider threat taxonomy, with mitigation strategies. *Information & Management*, 61(1), 103877. DOI: 10.1016/j.im.2023.103877

Repetto, M. (2023). Adaptive monitoring, detection, and response for agile digital service chains. *Computers & Security*, 132, 103343. DOI: 10.1016/j.cose.2023.103343

Reshi, I. A., & Sholla, S. (2024). *Blockchain-based internet of things. Opportunities, Challenges and Solutions*. CRC Press. DOI: 10.1201/9781003407096

Richardson, M. (2020). *Blockchain technology: Learn Step by Step Smart Contracts, Monero, Blockchain Wallet, Bitcoin, Zcash, Ethereum, Ripple, Dash, Mining, Litecoin*. IOTA.

Rock, L.Y., Tajudeen, F.P. and Chung, Y.W. (2022) 'Usage and impact of the internet-of-things-based smart home technology. a quality-of-life perspective,' *Universal Access in the Information Society*, 23(1), pp. 345–364. https.//.DOI: 10.1007/s10209-022-00937-0

Rodrigues, G. A. P., Serrano, A. L. M., & Lemos, A. N. L. E.. (2024). Understanding Data Breach from a Global Perspective: Incident Visualization and Data Protection Law Review. *Data*, 9(2), 27. DOI: 10.3390/data9020027

Rodrigues, G. A. P., Serrano, A. L. M., Vergara, G. F., Albuquerque, R. O., & Nze, G. D. A. (2024). Impact, compliance, and countermeasures in relation to data breaches in publicly traded U.S. companies. *Future Internet*, 16(6), 201. DOI: 10.3390/fi16060201

Roshanaei, M., Khan, M. R., & Sylvester, N. N. (2024). Enhancing Cybersecurity through AI and ML: Strategies, Challenges, and Future Directions. *Journal of Information Security*, 15(03), 320–339. DOI: 10.4236/jis.2024.153019

Roza, N. T.. (2021). Comparative Analysis of Deepfake Image Detection Using Convolutional Neural Network. *International Journal of Advanced Research in Computer Engineering and Technology*, 10(5), 182–189.

Rupp, V., & Von Grafenstein, M. (2024). Clarifying "personal data" and the role of anonymisation in data protection law including and excluding data from the scope of the GDPR (more clearly) through refining the concept of data protection. *Computer Law & Security Report*, 52, 105932. DOI: 10.1016/j.clsr.2023.105932

Russell, B., & Van Duren, D. (2018). *Practical internet of things security. Design a security framework for an Internet connected ecosystem* (2nd ed.). Packt Publishing Ltd.

S., M. (2023). Rewards and Risks: What Generative AI Means for Security. Retrieved from https://cxotoday.com/specials/rewards-and-risks-what-generative-ai-means-for-security/

Sabharwal, S. M., Chhabra, S., & Aiden, M. K. (2024) 'AI and Blockchain for Secure Data Analytics,' in *Blockchain technologies*, pp. 39–81. DOI: 10.1007/978-981-97-1249-6_3

Sachdeva, M., & Kumar, K. (2014). A traffic cluster entropy-based approach to distinguish DDoS attacks from flash event using DETER testbed. *International Scholarly Research Notices*, 2014(1), 259831.

Saeed, M. M. A., Saeed, R. A., & Ahmed, Z. E. (2024) 'Data security and privacy in the age of AI and digital twins,' in *Advances in business information systems and analytics book series*, pp. 99–124. DOI: 10.4018/979-8-3693-1818-8.ch008

Saeed, M.M. and Alsharidah, M. (2024) 'Security, privacy, and robustness for trustworthy AI systems. A review,' *Computers & Electrical Engineering*, 119, p. 109643. https.//.DOI: 10.1016/j.compeleceng.2024.109643

Saeed, S., Jhanjhi, N., Naqvi, S. M. R., & Khan, A. (2022). Analytical Approach for Security of Sensitive Business Cloud. *Deep Learning in Data Analytics: Recent Techniques, Practices and Applications*, 257-266.

Saeed, S. (2019). The serverless architecture: Current trends and open issues moving legacy applications. IJCDS. *Scopus.*

Saeed, S., Abbasi, F. A., Dahri, K., Shaikh, Z. A., Nizamani, M. A., & Memon, M. A. (2024). Improved Hybrid K-Nearest Neighbours Techniques in Segmentation of Low-Grade Tumor and Cerebrospinal Fluid. *The Asian Bulletin of Big Data Management, 4*(02). *Science*, •••, 4.

Saeed, S., Abdullah, A., & Jhanjhi, N. Z. (2019). Implementation of fourier transformation with brain cancer and CSF images. *Indian Journal of Science and Technology*, 12(37), 37. DOI: 10.17485/ijst/2019/v12i37/146151

Saeed, S., Abdullah, A., Jhanjhi, N. Z., & Malaysia, T. (2019). Analysis of the lung cancer patient's for data mining tool. *IJCSNS*, 19(7), 90.

Saeed, S., Abdullah, A., Jhanjhi, N. Z., & Malaysia, T. (2019). Analysis of the lung cancer patients for data mining tool. *IJCSNS*, 19(7), 90.

Saeed, S., Abdullah, A., Jhanjhi, N. Z., Naqvi, M., & Nayyar, A. (2022). New techniques for efficiently k-NN algorithm for brain tumor detection. *Multimedia Tools and Applications*, 81(13), 18595–18616. DOI: 10.1007/s11042-022-12271-x

Saeed, S., & Haron, H. (2021). Improve correlation matrix of discrete Fourier transformation (CM-DFT) technique for finding the missing values of MRI images. *Mathematical Biosciences and Engineering*, •••, 1–22.

Saeed, S., Haron, H., Jhanjhi, N. Z., Naqvi, M., Alhumyani, H. A., & Masud, M. (2022). Improve correlation matrix of discrete fourier transformation technique for finding the missing values of mri images. *Mathematical Biosciences and Engineering*, 19(9), 9039–9059. DOI: 10.3934/mbe.2022420 PMID: 35942748

Saeed, S., & Humayun, M. (2019). Disparaging the barriers of journal citation reports (JCR). IJCSNS. International Journal of Computer Science and Network Security, 19(5), 156-175. *ISI-Index.*, 1, 5.

Saeed, S., & Humayun, M. (2019). Disparaging the barriers of journal citation reports (JCR). IJCSNS: International Journal of Computer Science and Network Security, 19(5), 156-175. *ISI-Index*, 1, 5.

Saeed, S., Jhanjhi, N. Z., Abdullah, A., & Naqvi, M. (2018). Current trends and issues legacy application of the serverless architecture. *International Journal of Computing and Network Technology*, 6(3), 100–108. DOI: 10.12785/IJCNT/060304

Saeed, S., Jhanjhi, N. Z., Naqvi, M., & Humayun, M. (2019). Analysis of software development methodologies. *International Journal of Computing and Digital Systems*, 8(5), 446–460.

Saeed, S., Jhanjhi, N. Z., Naqvi, M., Malik, N. A., & Humayun, M. (2019). Disparage the barriers of journal citation reports (JCR). *International Journal of Computer Science and Network Security*, 19(5), 156–175.

Saeed, S., Shaikh, A., Memon, M. A., Memon, M. H., Abassi, F. A., & Naqvi, S. M. R. (2017). Implementation of failure enterprise systems in organizational perspective framework. *International Journal of Advanced Computer Science and Applications*, 8(5). Advance online publication. DOI: 10.14569/IJACSA.2017.080508

Saeed, S., Shaikh, A., Memon, M. A., & Naqvi, S. M. R. (2018). Impact of data mining techniques to analyze health care data. *Journal of Medical Imaging and Health Informatics*, 8(4), 682–690. DOI: 10.1166/jmihi.2018.2385

Safitra, M. F., Lubis, M., & Fakhrurroja, H. (2023). Counterattacking cyber threats: A framework for the future of cybersecurity. *Sustainability (Basel)*, 15(18), 13369. DOI: 10.3390/su151813369

Sahu, H., Choudhari, S., & Chakole, S. (2024). The use of blockchain technology in Public Health: Lessons learned, [Preprint]. *Cureus*. Advance online publication. DOI: 10.7759/cureus.63198 PMID: 39070517

Salam, A. (2024) 'Internet of Things for Sustainability. Perspectives in privacy, cybersecurity, and future trends,' in *Internet of things*, pp. 299–326. https.//DOI: 10.1007/978-3-031-62162-8_10

Salim, M.M., Rathore, S. and Park, J.H. (2019) 'Distributed denial of service attacks and its defenses in IoT. a survey,' *The Journal of Supercomputing*, 76(7), pp. 5320–5363. https.//.DOI: 10.1007/s11227-019-02945-z

Samizadeh, R., & Tafahomi, S. (2022). Web mining based on word-centric search with clustering approach using MLP-PSO hybrid. *International Journal of Business Intelligence and Data Mining*, 20(1), 35–55. DOI: 10.1504/IJBIDM.2022.119980

Sánchez, R. A. G., Bernal, D. J. M., & Parada, H. D. J. (2021, September). Security assessment of Nosql Mongodb, Redis and Cassandra database managers. In *2021 Congreso Internacional de Innovación y Tendencias en Ingeniería (CONIITI)* (pp. 1-7). IEEE.

Sanderson, C., Douglas, D., Lu, Q., Schleiger, E., Whittle, J., Lacey, J., Newnham, G., Hajkowicz, S., Robinson, C., & Hansen, D. (2023). AI ethics principles in practice: Perspectives of designers and developers. *IEEE Transactions on Technology and Society*, 4(2), 171–187. DOI: 10.1109/TTS.2023.3257303

Sanghvi, B., Shelar, H., Pandey, M., & Sisodia, J. (2021). Detection of machine gener- ated multimedia elements using deep learning, 2021 5th International Conference on Computing Methodologies and Communication (ICCMC), pp. 1238–1243.

Santosh, K. and Gaur, L. (2021) *Artificial intelligence and machine learning in public healthcare, SpringerBriefs in applied sciences and technology*. .DOI: 10.1007/978-981-16-6768-8

Santos, N., Ghita, B., & Masala, G. (2023). Medical Systems Data Security and Biometric Authentication in Public Cloud Servers. *IEEE Transactions on Emerging Topics in Computing*.

Santra, A., Komar, K., Bhowmick, S., & Chakravarthy, S. (2022). From base data to knowledge discovery–A life cycle approach–Using multilayer networks. *Data & Knowledge Engineering*, 141, 102058. DOI: 10.1016/j.datak.2022.102058

Sarella, P. N. K., & Mangam, V. T. (2024). AI-Driven Natural Language Processing in Healthcare: Transforming Patient-Provider communication. *Indian Journal of Pharmacy Practice*, 17(1), 21–26. DOI: 10.5530/ijopp.17.1.4

Sarker, I.H. (2024) *AI-Driven cybersecurity and threat intelligence*. https.//.DOI: 10.1007/978-3-031-54497-2

Sarker, I.H. *et al.* (2024) 'Multi-aspect rule-based AI. Methods, taxonomy, challenges and directions toward automation, intelligence and transparent cybersecurity modeling for critical infrastructures,' *Internet of Things*, 25, p. 101110. https.//.DOI: 10.1016/j.iot.2024.101110

Sasikumar, A., ... (2024) 'Blockchain-Assisted Hierarchical Attribute-Based encryption scheme for secure information sharing in industrial internet of things,' *IEEE Access*, 12, pp. 12586–12601. https.//DOI: 10.1109/ACCESS.2024.3354846

Satpathy, S.. (2024). *AI for Climate Change and Environmental Sustainability*. CRC Press. DOI: 10.1201/9781003452393

Sayeduzzaman, Md., ... (2023) 'An Internet of Things-Integrated Home Automation with Smart Security System,' *Wiley*, pp. 243–273. https.//DOI: 10.1002/9781394213948.ch13

Sayegh, E. (2023). Navigating The Cybersecurity Landscape In 2024. Retrieved from https://www.forbes.com/sites/emilsayegh/2023/12/19/navigating-the-cybersecurity-landscape-in-2024/

Schmidt, B., & Hildebrandt, A. (2024) 'From GPUs to AI and quantum. three waves of acceleration in bioinformatics,' *Drug Discovery Today*, p. 103990. https.//DOI: 10.1016/j.drudis.2024.103990

Schreiber, A. and Schreiber, I. (2024) 'Bridging knowledge gap. the contribution of employees' awareness of AI cyber risks comprehensive program to reducing emerging AI digital threats,' *Information and Computer Security* [Preprint]. https.//. DOI: 10.1108/ICS-10-2023-0199

Schuett, J., Reuel, A.-K., & Carlier, A. (2024). How to design an AI ethics board, [Preprint]. *AI and Ethics*. Advance online publication. DOI: 10.1007/s43681-023-00409-y

Schumacher, L. V. (2024). *Technology Choices and Design Options*. Decoding Digital Assets., DOI: 10.1007/978-3-031-54601-3_14

Seghier, N. B., & Kazar, O. (2021, September). Performance benchmarking and comparison of NoSQL databases: Redis vs mongodb vs Cassandra using YCSB tool. In *2021 International Conference on Recent Advances in Mathematics and Informatics (ICRAMI)* (pp. 1-6). IEEE. DOI: 10.1109/ICRAMI52622.2021.9585956

Seiling, L., Gsenger, R., Mulugeta, F., Henningsen, M., Mischau, L., & Schirmbeck, M. (2024). Beware: Processing of Personal Data—Informed consent through risk communication. *IEEE Transactions on Professional Communication*, 67(1), 4–25. DOI: 10.1109/TPC.2024.3361328

Selamat, S. R., Cai, S. Y., Hassan, N. H., & Yusof, R. (2024). An algorithm for Color-Based password authentication to increase security level, [INNOVATICS]. *Innovation in Research of Informatics*, 6(1). Advance online publication. DOI: 10.37058/innovatics.v6i1.10396

Semwal, R., Tripathi, N., & Tyagi, P. K. (2024) 'Safety first,' in *Advances in hospitality, tourism and the services industry (AHTSI) book series*, pp. 445–466. DOI: 10.4018/979-8-3693-7898-4.ch021

Seng, Y. J.. (2024) 'In-Depth Analysis and Countermeasures for Ransomware Attacks: Case Studies and Recommendations,' *Preprints* [Preprint]. DOI: 10.20944/preprints202408.2261.v1

Seol, J., & Kim, J. (2024). Machine learning ensures Quantum-Safe blockchain availability. *Journal of Computer Information Systems*, •••, 1–25. DOI: 10.1080/08874417.2024.2308207

SEP (2019). https://plato.stanford.edu/eNtRIeS/it-privacy/

Shafik, W. (2024) 'Shaping the next generation smart City ecosystem: an investigation on the requirements, applications, architecture, security and privacy, and open research questions,' in *S.M.A.R.T. environments*, pp. 3–52. DOI: 10.1007/978-3-031-59846-3_1

Shah, I. A., Jhanjhi, N. Z., & Laraib, A. (2022) 'Cybersecurity and blockchain usage in contemporary business,' in *Advances in information security, privacy, and ethics book series*, pp. 49–64. DOI: 10.4018/978-1-6684-5284-4.ch003

Shah, I. A., Jhanjhi, N. Z., & Laraib, A. (2023). Cybersecurity and blockchain usage in contemporary business. In *Handbook of Research on Cybersecurity Issues and Challenges for Business and FinTech Applications* (pp. 49–64). IGI Global.

Shahriar, S., Allana, S., Hazratifard, S. M., & Dara, R. (2023). A survey of privacy risks and mitigation strategies in the Artificial intelligence life cycle. *IEEE Access : Practical Innovations, Open Solutions*, 11, 61829–61854. DOI: 10.1109/ACCESS.2023.3287195

Shamshari, A., & Najaf, H. (2024) *Machine learning approaches for anomaly detection in network Security*. http://snmzpublisher.com/index.php/eejmr/article/view/9

Sharma, J., & Jain, S. (2024) 'Healthcare 4.0,' in *CRC Press eBooks*, pp. 126–146. DOI: 10.1201/9781003474524-7

Sharma, T., & Sharma, P. (2024). AI-based cybersecurity threat detection and prevention. In *Perspectives on Artificial Intelligence in Times of Turbulence: Theoretical Background to Applications* (pp. 81-98): IGI Global.

Sharma, A. (2024). *Rust for blockchain application development: Learn to build decentralized applications on popular blockchain technologies using Rust*. Packt Publishing Ltd.

Sharma, M., & Gupta, R. (2022). Role of Data Warehousing in Business Intelligence. A Review of Key Concepts and Applications. *International Journal of Business Intelligence Research*, 12(3), 44–56. DOI: 10.4018/IJBIR.303650

Sharma, P., Jindal, R., & Borah, M. D. (2023). Blockchain-based distributed application for multimedia system using Hyperledger Fabric. *Multimedia Tools and Applications*, 83(1), 2473–2499. DOI: 10.1007/s11042-023-15690-6

Sharma, R.. (2021). 'Plant disease diagnosis and image classification using deep learning,' *Computers, Materials & Continua/Computers. Materials & Continua (Print)*, 71(2), 2125–2140. DOI: 10.32604/cmc.2022.020017

Shaveta, S., Grover, D., & Bhandari, A. (2018). Vulnerability analysis of existing distributed denial of service attacks defense frameworks. *Asian Journal of computer science and Technology* 7(3). Gupta, S., Grover, D., AlZubi, A. A., Sachdeva, N., Baig, M. W., & Singla, J. (2022). Machine Learning with Dimensionality Reduction for DDoS Attack Detection. *Computers, Materials & Continua*, 72(2).

Shihab, M.A. *et al.* (2024) 'Towards resilient machine learning models. Addressing adversarial attacks in wireless sensor network,' *Shihab | Journal of Robotics and Control (JRC)* [Preprint]. https.//.DOI: <ALIGNMENT.qj></ALIGNMENT>10.18196/jrc.v5i5.23214

Shinde, R., Patil, S., Kotecha, K., Potdar, V., Selvachandran, G., & Abraham, A. (2023). Securing AI-based healthcare systems using blockchain technology: A state-of-the-art systematic literature review and future research directions. *Transactions on Emerging Telecommunications Technologies*, 35(1), e4884. Advance online publication. DOI: 10.1002/ett.4884

Shi, Y., Li, W., Zhu, L., Guo, K., & Cambria, E. (2021). Stock trading rule discovery with double deep Q-network. *Applied Soft Computing*, 107, 107320. DOI: 10.1016/j.asoc.2021.107320

Shoro, S. (2023) *Mobile Computing and its security, (PDF) Mobile Computing and its Security | saima shoro - Academia.edu*. Available at. http.//www.academia.edu/94157460/Mobile_Computing_and_its_Security?rhid=28519263243&swp=rr-rw-wc-30094607

Shu, X., & Ye, Y. (2023). Knowledge Discovery: Methods from data mining and machine learning. *Social Science Research*, 110, 102817. DOI: 10.1016/j.ssresearch.2022.102817 PMID: 36796993

Sicari, S., ... (2014) 'Security, privacy and trust in Internet of Things. The road ahead,' *Computer Networks*, 76, pp. 146–164. https.//DOI: 10.1016/j.comnet.2014.11.008

Sicari, S., Rizzardi, A., & Coen-Porisini, A. (2022). Security&privacy issues and challenges in NoSQL databases. *Computer Networks*, 206, 108828. DOI: 10.1016/j.comnet.2022.108828

Sidi-Mohammed, S., Hichem, S., Jiajia, L., Mubashir Husain, R., & Elias, B.-H. (2020). AI-Driven Cybersecurity Threats to Future Networks [From the Guest Editors]. *IEEE Vehicular Technology Magazine*, 15(3), 5–6. DOI: 10.1109/MVT.2020.3007981

Simbeck, K. (2023). They shall be fair, transparent, and robust: Auditing learning analytics systems. *AI and Ethics*, 4(2), 555–571. DOI: 10.1007/s43681-023-00292-7

Sindiramutty, S. R., Jhanjhi, N. Z., Tan, C. E., Khan, N. A., Shah, B., & Manchuri, A. R. (2024) 'Cybersecurity measures for logistics industry,' in *Advances in information security, privacy, and ethics book series*, pp. 1–58. DOI: 10.4018/979-8-3693-3816-2.ch001

Sindiramutty, S. R., Jhanjhi, N. Z., Tan, C. E., Khan, N. A., Shah, B., & Manchuri, A. R. (2024). Cybersecurity Measures for Logistics Industry. In Navigating Cyber Threats and Cybersecurity in the Logistics Industry (pp. 1-58). IGI Global.

Sindiramutty, S. R., Jhanjhi, N. Z., Tan, C. E., Khan, N. A., Shah, B., Yun, K. J., ... (2024) 'Future trends and emerging threats in drone cybersecurity,' in *Advances in information security, privacy, and ethics book series*, pp. 148–195. DOI: 10.4018/979-8-3693-0774-8.ch007

Sindiramutty, S. R., Jhanjhi, N. Z., Tan, C. E., Tee, W. J., Lau, S. P., Jazri, H., . . . Zaheer, M. A. (2024). IoT and AI-Based Smart Solutions for the Agriculture Industry. In Advances in Explainable AI Applications for Smart Cities (pp. 317-351). IGI Global.

Sindiramutty, S. R., Jhanjhi, N. Z., Tan, C. E., Yun, K. J., ... (2024) 'Data security and privacy concerns in drone operations,' in *Advances in information security, privacy, and ethics book series*, pp. 236–290. DOI: 10.4018/979-8-3693-0774-8.ch010

Sindiramutty, S. R., Jhanjhi, N., & Ray, S. K. (2024). Threat Hunting and Behaviour Analysis. *Utilizing Generative AI for Cyber Defense Strategies*, 235.

Sindiramutty, S. R., Jhanjhi, N., Tan, C. E., Lau, S. P., Muniandy, L., Gharib, A. H., Ashraf, H., & Murugesan, R. K. (2024). Industry 4.0. In *Advances in logistics, operations, and management science book series* (pp. 342–405). https.//DOI: 10.4018/979-8-3693-1363-3.ch013

Sindiramutty, S. R., Jhanjhi, N., Tan, C. E., Wei, G. W., ... (2024) 'Sustainability in the digital age,' in *Advances in logistics, operations, and management science book series*, pp. 89–132. DOI: 10.4018/979-8-3693-1363-3.ch005

Sindiramutty, S. R., Prabagaran, K. R. V., ... (2024) 'Security Considerations in Generative AI for web Applications,' in *Advances in information security, privacy, and ethics book series*, pp. 281–332. https.//DOI: 10.4018/979-8-3693-5415-5.ch009

Sindiramutty, S. R., Prabagaran, K. R. V., Jhanjhi, N., & Murugesan, R. K. (2024). Threat Intelligence and Information Sharing. *Utilizing Generative AI for Cyber Defense Strategies*, 191.

Sindiramutty, S. R., Tan, C. E., & Wei, G. W. (2024) 'Eyes in the sky,' in *Advances in information security, privacy, and ethics book series*, pp. 405–451. DOI: 10.4018/979-8-3693-0774-8.ch017

Sindiramutty, S. R., Tan, C. E., ... (2024) 'Ethical considerations in drone cybersecurity,' in *Advances in information security, privacy, and ethics book series*, pp. 42–87. DOI: 10.4018/979-8-3693-0774-8.ch003

Sindiramutty, S. R., Tan, C. E., Shah, B., Khan, N. A., Gharib, A. H., Manchuri, A. R., . . . Jazri, H. (2024). Ethical Considerations in Drone Cybersecurity. In Cybersecurity Issues and Challenges in the Drone Industry (pp. 42-87). IGI Global.

Sindiramutty, S.R. *et al.* (2023) 'Applications of blockchain technology in supply chain management,' in *Advances in logistics, operations, and management science book series*, pp. 248–304. .DOI: 10.4018/978-1-6684-7625-3.ch009

Sindiramutty, S. R., Prabagaran, K. R. V., Jhanjhi, N., Ghazanfar, M. A., Malik, N. A., & Soomro, T. R. (2025). Security Considerations in Generative AI for Web Applications. In *Reshaping CyberSecurity With Generative AI Techniques* (pp. 281–332). IGI Global.

Singamaneni, K. K., & Muhammad, G. (2024). *A novel integrated Quantum-Resistant cryptography for secure scientific data exchange in ad hoc networks.* Ad Hoc Networks., DOI: 10.1016/j.adhoc.2024.103607

Singh, N.J. *et al.* (2023) 'Botnet-based IoT network traffic analysis using deep learning,' *Security and Privacy*, 7(2). https.//.DOI: 10.1002/spy2.355

Singh, R.K. and Vishwakarma, L.P. (2023) 'Application of Blockchain Technology in agri-food supply chains: Opportunities and challenges,' in *Elsevier eBooks*, pp. 101–117. .DOI: 10.1016/B978-0-323-89963-5.00014-9

Singh, S. *et al.* (2017) 'Advanced lightweight encryption algorithms for IoT devices. survey, challenges and solutions,' *Journal of Ambient Intelligence and Humanized Computing* [Preprint]. https.//.DOI: 10.1007/s12652-017-0494-4

Singh, V. K. (no date) *Blockchain Technology and election transparency: An application ofE-Voting Mechanism - ProQuest.* https://www.proquest.com/openview/6d95fc6f1b45392e98f741bed9837479/1?pq-origsite=gscholar&cbl=7065076

Singh, K., Rahman, R. U., & Pathak, D. (2023, November). A New Forensic Framework for NoSQL Databases: Wide-Column as Case Studies. In *2023 Seventh International Conference on Image Information Processing (ICIIP)* (pp. 79-84). IEEE. DOI: 10.1109/ICIIP61524.2023.10537755

Singh, P., & Prasad, A. (2021). Cybersecurity Considerations in Business Intelligence Implementation. *Journal of Cybersecurity*, 7(4), 121–138. DOI: 10.1002/cybs.2099

smartphone security threats (no date) *ResearchGate*. Available at. http.//www .researchgate.net/publication/345772225_Smartphone_Security_Threats

Smith, J., & Jones, A. (2021). Enhancing Industrial IoT Security Through Threat Detection and Intrusion Prevention. *Journal of Industrial Informatics*, 15, 25–37.

Snehi, M., & Bhandari, A. (2021). Vulnerability retrospection of security solutions for software-defined Cyber–Physical System against DDoS and IoT-DDoS attacks. *Computer Science Review*, 40, 100371. DOI: 10.1016/j.cosrev.2021.100371

Snoeren, A. C., Partridge, C., Sanchez, L. A., Jones, C. E., Tchakountio, F., Schwartz, B., & Strayer, W. T. (2002). Single-packet IP traceback. *IEEE/ACM Transactions on Networking*, 10(6), 721–734. DOI: 10.1109/TNET.2002.804827

Sobhy, D., El-Sonbaty, Y. and Abou Elnasr, M., 2012, December. MedCloud: healthcare cloud computing system. In 2012 international conference for internet technology and secured transactions (pp. 161-166). IEEE.

Somani, V., & Trivedi, D. M. C. (2019). Utilizing Cloud Computing for Stronger Healthcare Data Security. *Journal of Advanced Research in Dynamical and Control Systems*, 11(11), 60–69. DOI: 10.5373/JARDCS/V11I11/20193169

Soni, R., & Sharma, A. (2020). Challenges and Opportunities in Data Warehouse and Business Intelligence. *International Journal of Data Warehousing and Mining*, 16(1), 1–15. DOI: 10.4018/IJDWM.2020010101

Sontan, N.A.D. and Samuel, N.S.V. (2024) 'The intersection of Artificial Intelligence and cybersecurity. Challenges and opportunities,' *World Journal of Advanced Research and Reviews*, 21(2), pp. 1720–1736. https.//.DOI: 10.30574/wjarr.2024.21.2.0607

Soobia, S., Afnizanfaizal, A., & Jhanjhi, N. Z. (2022). Hybrid graph cut hidden Markov model of k-mean cluster technique. *CMC-Computers. Materials & Continua*, 72(1), 1–15.

Sreedharan, R. (2024). *The Role of Blockchain in Healthcare*. Quantum and Blockchain-based Next Generation Sustainable Computing., DOI: 10.1007/978-3-031-58068-0_7

Stanciu, D. C., & Ionescu, B. (2021). Deepfake video detection with facial features and long-short term memory deep networks, *2021 International Symposium on Signals, Circuits and Systems (ISSCS)*, pp. 1–4. DOI: 10.1109/ISSCS52333.2021.9497385

Stefanescu, D.. (2024). *Smart contract powered framework for the next generation industry 4.0 business model.* Deleted Journal. [Preprint], DOI: 10.1145/3686167

Stephen, D., & Mantoro, T. (2022, September). Usage of convolutional neural network for deepfake video detection with face-swapping technique. In 2022 5th International Conference of Computer and Informatics Engineering (IC2IE) (pp. 22-28). IEEE.

Stutz, D.. (2024). *Enhancing Security in Cloud Computing Using Artificial Intelligence (AI).* Wiley., DOI: 10.1002/9781394196470.ch11

Sukhwinder, S. (2023). The Rise of Generative AI in Reinforcing Cyber Defense. Retrieved from https://medium.com/@sukhwinder.s/the-rise-of-generative-ai-in-reinforcing-cyber-defense-4c512fbb8968

Sullivan, C., & Burger, E. (2017). E-residency and blockchain. *Computer Law & Security Report*, 33(4), 470–481. DOI: 10.1016/j.clsr.2017.03.016

Suomalainen, J., ... (2024) 'Cybersecurity for tactical 6G networks. Threats, architecture, and intelligence,' *Future Generation Computer Systems*, p. 107500. https.// DOI: 10.1016/j.future.2024.107500

Suratkar, S., Johnson, E., Variyambat, K., Panchal, M., & Kazi, F. (2020). Employing transfer-learning based CNN architectures to enhance the generalizability of deepfake detection, 2020 11th International Conference on Computing, Communication and Networking Technologies (ICCCNT), pp. 1–9.

Surianarayanan, C., Kunasekaran, S. and Chelliah, P.R. (2023) 'A high-throughput architecture for anomaly detection in streaming data using machine learning algorithms,' *International Journal of Information Technology*, 16(1), pp. 493–506. https.//.DOI: 10.1007/s41870-023-01585-0

Sutheekshan, B., ... (2024) 'Evolution of Malware Targeting IoT Devices and Botnet formation,' *2024 IEEE International Conference on Computing, Power and Communication Technologies (IC2PCT)* [Preprint]. https.//DOI: 10.1109/IC2PCT60090.2024.10486705

Sutradhar, S., Karforma, S., Bose, R., Roy, S., Djebali, S., & Bhattacharyya, D. (2024). Enhancing identity and access management using Hyperledger Fabric and OAuth 2.0: A block-chain-based approach for security and scalability for healthcare industry. *Internet of Things and Cyber-Physical Systems*, 4, 49–67. DOI: 10.1016/j.iotcps.2023.07.004

Sworna, Z. T., Mousavi, Z., & Babar, M. A. (2023). NLP methods in host-based intrusion detection systems: A systematic review and future directions. *Journal of Network and Computer Applications*, 220, 103761. DOI: 10.1016/j.jnca.2023.103761

Talaat, F. M. (2022). Effective prediction and resource allocation method (EPRAM) in fog computing environment for smart healthcare system. *Multimedia Tools and Applications*, 81(6), 8235–8258. DOI: 10.1007/s11042-022-12223-5

Tan, L., Pan, Y., Wu, J., Zhou, J., Jiang, H., & Deng, Y. (2020). A new framework for DDoS attack detection and defense in SDN environment. *IEEE Access : Practical Innovations, Open Solutions*, 8, 161908–161919. DOI: 10.1109/ACCESS.2020.3021435

Tan, M., & Le, Q. V. (2019). Efficientnet: Rethinking model scaling for convolutional neural networks, CoRR abs/1905.11946.URL: http://arxiv.org/abs/1905.11946

Tan, T. M., & Saraniemi, S. (2022). Trust in blockchain-enabled exchanges: Future directions in blockchain marketing. *Journal of the Academy of Marketing Science*, 51(4), 914–939. DOI: 10.1007/s11747-022-00889-0

Tao, Y., & Yu, S. (2013, July). DDoS attack detection at local area networks using information theoretical metrics. In *2013 12th IEEE international conference on trust, security and privacy in computing and communications* (pp. 233-240). IEEE. DOI: 10.1109/TrustCom.2013.32

Tao, C., Guo, H., & Huang, Z. (2020). Identifying security issues for mobile applications based on user review summarization. *Information and Software Technology*, 122, 1–13. DOI: 10.1016/j.infsof.2020.106290

Tayebi, S., & Amini, H. (2024). The flip side of the coin: Exploring the environmental and health impacts of proof-of-work cryptocurrency mining. *Environmental Research*, 252, 118798. DOI: 10.1016/j.envres.2024.118798 PMID: 38555086

Tayyab, M., Hameed, K., Jhanjhi, N. Z., Zaheer, A., & Qamar, F. (2024). Digital Safeguards: Navigating Cyber Threats in the Logistics Industry Framework. In *Navigating Cyber Threats and Cybersecurity in the Logistics Industry* (pp. 258-299): IGI Global.

Tayyab, M., Mumtaz, M., Jhanjhi, N. Z., & Muzammal, S. M. (2024). Industry 4.0. The Digital Revolution Unleashing Sustainable Supply Chains. In *Digital Transformation for Improved Industry and Supply Chain Performance* (pp. 54–69). IGI Global. https.//DOI: 10.4018/979-8-3693-5375-2.ch003

Tayyab, M., Marjani, M., Jhanjhi, N., Hashem, I. A. T., Usmani, R. S. A., & Qamar, F. (2023). A Comprehensive Review on Deep Learning Algorithms: Security and Privacy Issues. *Computers & Security*, 131, 103297. DOI: 10.1016/j.cose.2023.103297

Teig, J., & Eiken, A. (2024). *Use of Generative AI in Offensive Cybersecurity: A case study using PentestGPT with GPT-4 and Dolphin2. 5.* NTNU, van Geest, R. J., Cascavilla, G., Hulstijn, J., & Zannone, N. (2024). The applicability of a hybrid framework for automated phishing detection. *Computers & Security*, 139, 103736. DOI: 10.1016/j.cose.2024.103736

Terry, N. (2014). Health privacy is difficult but not impossible in a Post-HIPAA Data-Driven world. *Chest*, 146(3), 835–840. DOI: 10.1378/chest.13-2909 PMID: 25180726

Teutsch, J., & Reitwießner, C. (2023). *'A scalable verification solution for blockchains,' in Lecture notes series.* Institute For Mathematical Sciences., DOI: 10.1142/9789811278631_0015

The Mobile Application Hacker's handbook (no date) *Google Books.* Available at. https.//www.google.com.my/books/edition/The_Mobile_Application_Hacker_s_Handbook/5gVhBgAAQBAJ?hl=en&gbpv=1&dq=The%2BMobile%2BApplication%2BHacker%27s%2BHandbook%22%2Bby%2BDominic%2BChell%2C%2BTyrone%2BErasmus%2C%2Band%2Bothers%2B-&printsec=frontcover

Tilala, M. H.. (2024). Ethical Considerations in the Use of Artificial intelligence and Machine Learning in Health Care: A Comprehensive review, [Preprint]. *Cureus.* Advance online publication. DOI: 10.7759/cureus.62443 PMID: 39011215

Tiwari, N., Ranjan, P., Biswal, P. K., Barde, C., & Sinha, N. (2024). 'Survey and analysis of blockchain technologies with respect to: Properties, algorithms, architecture, models, evolution and framework,' [Preprint]. *Multimedia Tools and Applications.* Advance online publication. DOI: 10.1007/s11042-024-19580-3

Tiwari, R., & Kumari, S. (2022). Implementing Cybersecurity Best Practices in Business Intelligence Solutions. *Journal of Information Security and Applications*, 66, 103192. DOI: 10.1016/j.jisa.2022.103192

Tjon, E., Moh, M., & Moh, T.-S. (2021). Eff-ynet: A dual-task network for deepfake detection and segmentation, 2021 15th International Conference on Ubiquitous Information Management and Communication (IMCOM), pp. 1–8.

Tong, Z.. (2024). *The ESG Path to Low-Carbon Footprint: Recommended Practices and Lessons Learnt from Electrifying Recovery of the Giant Shale-Gas Basin in China.* OnePetro. [Preprint], DOI: 10.2118/219111-MS

Trinh, L., Tsang, M., Rambhatla, S., & Liu, Y. (2021). Interpretable and trustworthy deepfake detection via dynamic prototypes, *2021 IEEE Winter Conference on Applications of Computer Vision (WACV)*, pp. 1972–1982. DOI: 10.1109/WACV48630.2021.00202

Trizna, D. (2022). *Quo Vadis. Hybrid Machine Learning Meta-Model based on Contextual and Behavioral Malware Representations.* http.//128.84.4.34/abs/2208.12248

Tuladhar, A., Rogerson, M., Engelhart, J., Parry, G. C., & Altrichter, B. (2024). Blockchain for compliance: An information processing case study of mandatory supply chain transparency in conflict minerals sourcing. *Supply Chain Management*, 29(4), 755–777. DOI: 10.1108/SCM-11-2023-0585

Tyagi, A. K. (2023) 'Blockchain and artificial intelligence for cyber security in the era of internet of things and industrial internet of things applications,' in *Advances in computational intelligence and robotics book series*, pp. 171–199. DOI: 10.4018/979-8-3693-0659-8.ch007

Tyagi, A. K., Kumari, S., & Richa, N. (2024) 'Artificial Intelligence-Based Cyber Security and Digital Forensics,' *Wiley*, pp. 391–419. https.//DOI: 10.1002/9781394303601.ch18

Tyagi, A.K. *et al.* (2024) 'Role of Blockchain Technology in Smart Era: A review on possible smart applications,' *Journal of Information & Knowledge Management* [Preprint]. .DOI: 10.1142/S0219649224500321

Tyagi, A. K., & Seranmadevi, R. (2024). *Blockchain for Enhancing Security and Privacy in the Smart Healthcare.* Wiley., DOI: 10.1002/9781394303564.ch16

Uddin, M. (2021). Blockchain Medledger: Hyperledger fabric enabled drug traceability system for counterfeit drugs in pharmaceutical industry. *International Journal of Pharmaceutics*, 597, 120235. DOI: 10.1016/j.ijpharm.2021.120235 PMID: 33549813

Usman, T.M. *et al.* (2023) 'Diabetic retinopathy detection using principal component analysis multi-label feature extraction and classification,' *International Journal of Cognitive Computing in Engineering*, 4, pp. 78–88. https.//.DOI: 10.1016/j.ijcce.2023.02.002

Vaibhav, A. (2020). *International Research Journal of Innovations in Engineering and Technology*. Proquest. [Preprint], DOI: 10.47001/irjiet

Vallabhaneni, R. (2024) 'Effects of Data Breaches on Internet of Things (IoT) Devices within the Proliferation of Daily-Life Integrated Devices,' *Engineering and Technology Journal*, 09(07). https.//.DOI: 10.47191/etj/v9i07.13

Van Vulpen, P., Siu, J., & Jansen, S. (2023). Governance of Decentralized Autonomous Organizations that Produce Open Source Software. *Blockchain Research and Applications*, 5(1), 100166. DOI: 10.1016/j.bcra.2023.100166

Vanmathi, C.. (2024). *The role of blockchain in transforming industries beyond finance*. IEEE Access., DOI: 10.1109/ACCESS.2024.3468611

Vellela, S. S., Reddy, B. V., Chaitanya, K. K., & Rao, M. V. (2023, January). An Integrated Approach to Improve E-Healthcare System using Dynamic Cloud Computing Platform. In 2023 5th International Conference on Smart Systems and Inventive Technology (ICSSIT) (pp. 776-782). IEEE.

Vemuri, N., Thaneeru, N., & Tatikonda, V. M. (2024). Adaptive generative AI for dynamic cybersecurity threat detection in enterprises.

Vijayalakshmi, S. *et al.* (2024) *Artificial intelligence for cyber defense and smart policing, Chapman and Hall/CRC eBooks*. https.//.DOI: 10.1201/9781003251781

Vijayaregunathan, N., Periyasamy, V., & Munimathan, A. (2024). Harvesting hydraulic energy for self-sustainable IoT flow measurement devices. *Energy Sources. Part A, Recovery, Utilization, and Environmental Effects*, 46(1), 5094–5111. DOI: 10.1080/15567036.2024.2334922

Vittala, K. R. P., ... (2024) 'Emerging technology adoption and applications for modern society towards providing smart banking solutions,' in *Advances in medical technologies and clinical practice book series*, pp. 315–329. DOI: 10.4018/979-8-3693-5261-8.ch018

Vysakh, S., & Binu, P. K. (2020) 'IoT based Mirai Vulnerability Scanner Prototype,' *2020 Third International Conference on Smart Systems and Inventive Technology (ICSSIT)* [Preprint]. https.//DOI: 10.1109/ICSSIT48917.2020.9214099

Wachsmuth, G. (2007). Metamodel Adaptation and Model Co-adaptation. In E. Ernst (Ed.), *ECOOP 2007 – Object-Oriented Programming* (pp. 600–624). Springer. https.//DOI: 10.1007/978-3-540-73589-2_28

Waheed, A.. (2024) 'Zero-Day Exploits in Cybersecurity: Case Studies and Countermeasure,' *Preprint.org* [Preprint]. DOI: 10.20944/preprints202407.2338.v1

Wang, G. G., & Shan, S. (2006). Review of Metamodeling Techniques in Support of Engineering Design Optimization. *Journal of Mechanical Design, 129*(4), 370–380. https.//DOI: 10.1115/1.2429697

Wang, H., & Chen, X. (2022). Intrusion Prevention Strategies for Industrial IoT Systems. A Systematic Review. *Computers & Security*, 114, 102315.

Wang, J., & Zhang, Q. (2022). Enhancing Security in Industrial IoT Systems Through Machine Learning-Based Intrusion Detection. *IEEE Internet of Things Journal*, 9(3), 1877–1886.

Wang, Y., & Xu, Y. (2023). Anomaly Detection Methods for Securing Industrial IoT Systems. A Comprehensive Review. *IEEE Transactions on Automation Science and Engineering*, 20(2), 751–764.

Wang, Z., & Zhang, L. (2024). Deep Learning Approaches for Intrusion Detection in Industrial IoT Environments. A Comprehensive Review. *IEEE Transactions on Industrial Informatics*, 20(1), 126–137.

Waqar, A., Hannan Qureshi, A., Othman, I., Saad, N., & Azab, M. (2023). Exploration of challenges to deployment of blockchain in small construction projects. *Ain Shams Engineering Journal*, 15(2), 102362. DOI: 10.1016/j.asej.2023.102362

Washizaki, H., Fukumoto, S., Yamamoto, M., Yoshizawa, M., Fukazawa, Y., Kato, T., Ogata, S., Kaiya, H., Fernandez, E. B., Kanuka, H., Kondo, Y., Yoshioka, N., Okubo, T., & Hazeyama, A. (2016). A Metamodel for Security and Privacy Knowledge in Cloud Services. *2016 IEEE World Congress on Services (SERVICES)*, 142–143. https.//DOI: 10.1109/SERVICES.2016.30

Weichbroth, P., & Łysik, Ł. (2020). Mobile security: Threats and best practices. *Mobile Information Systems*, 2020(1), 8828078.

Wei, Y., Xu, Q., & Peng, H. (2024). An enhanced consensus algorithm for blockchain. *Scientific Reports*, 14(1), 17701. Advance online publication. DOI: 10.1038/s41598-024-68120-4 PMID: 39085315

Wen, B. O. T., ... (2023) 'Detecting cyber threats with a Graph-Based NIDPS,' in *Advances in logistics, operations, and management science book series*, pp. 36–74. DOI: 10.4018/978-1-6684-7625-3.ch002

Westerkamp, M., Victor, F., & Küpper, A. (2019). Tracing manufacturing processes using blockchain-based token compositions. *Digital Communications and Networks*, 6(2), 167–176. DOI: 10.1016/j.dcan.2019.01.007

Williamson, S. M., & Prybutok, V. (2024). Balancing Privacy and Progress: A review of privacy challenges, systemic oversight, and patient perceptions in AI-Driven healthcare. *Applied Sciences (Basel, Switzerland)*, 14(2), 675. DOI: 10.3390/app14020675

Wingreen, S. C., & Samandari, A. (2024). *Information Technology security and risk management. Inductive Cases for Information Security*. CRC Press. DOI: 10.1201/9781003264415

Winter, J. S., & Davidson, E. (2022). Harmonizing regulatory regimes for the governance of patient-generated health data. *Telecommunications Policy*, 46(5), 102285. DOI: 10.1016/j.telpol.2021.102285

Wright, S. A. (2020). *AI in the Law: Towards Assessing Ethical Risks.* Paper presented at the Proceedings - 2020 IEEE International Conference on Big Data, Big Data 2020. DOI: 10.1109/BigData50022.2020.9377950

Xiao, Q. *et al.* (2023) 'Securing NextG networks with physical-layer key generation. A survey,' *Security and Safety*, 3, p. 2023021. https.//.DOI: 10.1051/sands/2023021

Xie, Y., Zhou, X., & Shekhar, S. (2020). Discovering interesting subpaths with statistical significance from spatiotemporal datasets. [TIST]. *ACM Transactions on Intelligent Systems and Technology*, 11(1), 1–24. DOI: 10.1145/3354189

Xiong, X., Guo, L., Zhang, Y., & Zhang, J. (2022). Cyber-Security Enhanced Network Meta-Model and its Application. *2022 6th International Conference on Cryptography, Security and Privacy (CSP)*, 80–85. https.//DOI: 10.1109/CSP55486.2022.00023

Xu, Z., & Wang, C. (2023). Machine Learning-Based Anomaly Detection for Industrial IoT Security. A Review. *Computers & Security*, 116, 102404.

Yalli, J. S., Hasan, M. H., & Badawi, A. (2024) 'Internet Of Things (IOT). Origin, Embedded Technologies, Smart Applications and its Growth in the Last Decade,' *IEEE Access*, p. 1. https.//DOI: 10.1109/ACCESS.2024.3418995

Yamamoto, Y., Fukushima, A. and Yamaguchi, S. (2024) 'Implementation of White-Hat Worms Using Mirai Source Code and Its Optimization through Parameter Tuning,' *Future Internet*, 16(9), p. 336. https.//.DOI: 10.3390/fi16090336

Yampolskiy, R.V. (2024) 'On monitorability of AI,' *AI And Ethics* [Preprint]. https.//.DOI: 10.1007/s43681-024-00420-x

Yan, S., Wang, J., & Liang, J. (2024, May). Big Data Storage and Analysis System for Space Application. In *2024 27th International Conference on Computer Supported Cooperative Work in Design (CSCWD)* (pp. 1764-1769). IEEE. DOI: 10.1109/CSCWD61410.2024.10580324

Yang, X., Liu, X., Zhang, H., Fu, L., & Yu, Y. (2023). Meta-model-based shop-floor digital twin architecture, modeling and application. *Robotics and Computer-Integrated Manufacturing, 84*, 102595. https.//DOI: 10.1016/j.rcim.2023.102595

Yang, W., & Zhang, Y. (2022). A Comprehensive Review of Anomaly Detection Methods for Industrial IoT Security. *IEEE Transactions on Industrial Informatics*, 18(1), 511–523.

Yan, Z.. (2024). *Blockchain-driven Decentralized Identity Management: An Interdisciplinary Review and Research Agenda*. Information & Management., DOI: 10.1016/j.im.2024.104026

Yar, M. A., Hamdan, M., Anshari, M., Fitriyani, N. L., & Syafrudin, M. (2024). Governing with Intelligence: The Impact of Artificial Intelligence on Policy Development. *Information (Basel)*, 15(9), 556. DOI: 10.3390/info15090556

Yoon, Y. (2021). Discovering knowledge in corporate databases. In *Handbook of Data Management* (1999 Edition, pp. 783–794). Auerbach Publications.

Zaheer, A., Tahir, S., Humayun, M., Almufareh, M. F., & Jhanjhi, N. Z. (2022, November). A novel Machine learning technique for fake smart watches advertisement detection. In 2022 14th International Conference on Mathematics, Actuarial Science, Computer Science and Statistics (MACS) (pp. 1-5). IEEE.

Zala, K., Thakkar, H. K., Jadeja, R., Singh, P., Kotecha, K., & Shukla, M. (2022). PRMS: Design and Development of Patients' E-Healthcare Records Management System for Privacy Preservation in Third Party Cloud Platforms. *IEEE Access : Practical Innovations, Open Solutions*, 10, 85777–85791. DOI: 10.1109/ACCESS.2022.3198094

Zeydan, E., Arslan, S. S., & Liyanage, M. (2024). *Managing distributed machine learning lifecycle for healthcare data in the cloud*. IEEE Access., DOI: 10.1109/ACCESS.2024.3443520

Zhang, J., Ni, J., & Xie, H. (2021). Deepfake video detection using self-supervised decoupling network, *2021 IEEE International Conference on Multimedia and Expo (ICME)*, pp. 1–6. DOI: 10.1109/ICME51207.2021.9428368

Zhang, L., & Wang, H. (2023). A Survey on Threat Detection and Intrusion Prevention Techniques for Industrial IoT. *Computers & Electrical Engineering*, 101, 107208.

Zhang, M., & Li, S. (2023). Machine Learning-Based Threat Detection in Industrial IoT Environments. A Review. *Journal of Manufacturing Systems*, 63, 55–67.

Zhang, Y., & Wu, H. (2024). Threat Detection and Intrusion Prevention Strategies for Industrial IoT. A Review. *IEEE Transactions on Industrial Engineering and Management*, 71(2), 341–353.

Zhao, C., Zhang, S., Wang, T., & Liew, S. C. (2024). Bodyless block propagation: TPS fully scalable blockchain with pre-validation. *Future Generation Computer Systems*, 163, 107516. DOI: 10.1016/j.future.2024.107516

Zhao, L., & Zhang, J. (2024). *Machine learning based business intelligence security and privacy analysis with gaming model in training complexity application.* Entertainment Computing., DOI: 10.1016/j.entcom.2024.100695

Zhao, Y.. (2021). Impact of Cybersecurity on Business Intelligence Solutions. *Journal of Business Research*, 128, 103–112. DOI: 10.1016/j.jbusres.2021.01.042

Zheng, Z., Xu, X., Li, Z., & Zhang, L. (2023, October). Federated reinforcement learning for privacy-preserving energy management in IoT-enabled smart buildings. *IEEE Internet of Things Journal*, 10(10), 8612–8623. DOI: 10.1109/JIOT.2023.10111371

Zhou, Z., ... (2024) 'Securely Fine-tuning Pre-trained Encoders Against Adversarial Examples,' *2024 IEEE Symposium on Security and Privacy (SP)*, pp. 3015–3033. https.//DOI: 10.1109/SP54263.2024.00244

Zhu, T.. (2021). *More than Privacy: Applying differential privacy in key areas of artificial intelligence.* IEEE Transactions on Knowledge and Data Engineering., DOI: 10.1109/TKDE.2020.3014246

Zolotova, A., & Goryunova, O. (2023). Business Intelligence and Cybersecurity in the Digital Economy. *Digital Transformation and Global Society*, 3(1), 1–10. DOI: 10.35654/dtgs.2023.0101

About the Contributors

Khalid Hussain is working as a Professor in the School of Computing and Informatics at Albukhary International University Alor Setar Kedah Malaysia, In addition to this he is also a member of the Senate and a member of the Board of Governor at Albukhary International University. Before this he was working as a Professor of Cyber Security at Superior University Lahore and Campus Director at National Superior Institute of Science and Technology (NSIST) Islamabad, previously he had served as Dean of the Faculty of Computer Science and Campus Director in Barani Institute of Sciences ARID Agriculture University, for the last one and half years. He also served at The University of Lahore as Dean Faculty of Computer Science and Information Technology for three years. Dr. Khalid has vast university/industry experience. During his tenure in the industry, he served in defense-related projects, and in recognition of his services, he has been awarded commendation certificates by multiple government agencies. He joined academia in 2008 as a full-time faculty member. In addition to his teaching role, he has been involved in numerous research projects, ICT training, seminars, and workshops, especially in the domain of cybersecurity. He helps set up a pioneer setup for information/ network security certification in Pakistan. He also introduced EC Council certification under the first academia-industry partnership. That project started from a one-room office and has grown into a fully functional campus of RIPHAH University. He did his Ph.D. from Malaysia, under a fully funded UTM / HEC scholarship. Up till now, he published 141 papers, out of which 98 are ISI Indexed Impact Factor, 23 are in HEC-approved journals and 20 are in IEEE and ACM conferences. Except for this, he also has 17 book chapters and three books in his credit. His Cumulative Impact Factor is 83.032. He has completed six applied research projects in the domain of Information Security funded by NESCOM and other funding agencies. Currently, he has won three projects, one from the Fundamental Research Grants Scheme (FRGS), One Matching Grant, and One from the Selangor Research Grant. Up till now 21 MS and 03 Ph.D. students completed their research thesis under his supervision. Currently, he is supervising 13 MS and five Ph.D. students. In reward for his contribution towards Information Security SATHA awarded him, the Gold Medal, in 2015.

***

Md. Farman Ali is a final-year Bachelor of Computer Science student focusing on Data Science. He is passionate about data analysis, statistical methodologies, and software development and is committed to using data science techniques to solve complicated problems. Throughout his academic career, Farman has been seeking opportunities to improve his skills and knowledge, including projects that apply theoretical principles to real-world scenarios. He is currently vice president of SCI committee (School of computing and Informatics). Farman aims to contribute to significant research and innovation in data science. His ambition is to develop a successful profession that promotes data-driven decision-making and innovative technology. He aspires to make a significant contribution to the world of data by committing to continual learning and issue resolution.

Noor Zaman Jhanjhi is a highly esteemed Senior Professor of Computer Science, specializing in Artificial Intelligence and Cybersecurity. He currently holds the position of Professor at the School of Computer Science at Taylor's University, Malaysia, and serves as the Program Director for Postgraduate Research Degree Programmes as well as the Director of Research Center. With a career marked by academic leadership and groundbreaking research, Prof. Jhanjhi has been pivotal in advancing research and education in computer science. Recognized globally, Prof. Jhanjhi has been ranked among the world's top 2% research scientists for three consecutive years (2022, 2023, and 2024). In Malaysia, he is ranked among the top three computer science researchers and was honored with the Outstanding Faculty Member award by MDEC Malaysia in 2022, as well as the Vice Chancellor's Best Research Citations Award from Taylor's University in 2023. His impressive academic portfolio includes over 70 research books edited or authored with prestigious publishers such as Springer, Elsevier, Taylor & Francis, Wiley, and IGI Global USA. His research has garnered more than 1000 points in impact factor, reflecting the depth and breadth of his contributions to the field. A dedicated mentor, Prof. Jhanjhi has supervised and co-supervised 38 postgraduate students to successful graduation and has served as an external examiner for over 60 Ph.D. and Master's theses globally. In addition to his academic accomplishments, Prof. Jhanjhi holds Associate Editor and Editorial Board positions with several high-ranking journals, including PeerJ Computer Science, CMC Computers, Materials & Continua, and Frontiers in Communication and Networks. He was also recognized as an Outstanding Associate Editor for IEEE ACCESS. His contributions to research and innovation are further demonstrated by his successful management of over 40 internationally funded research grants. A sought-after keynote speaker, Prof. Jhanjhi has delivered over 70 invited talks at international conferences and has chaired numerous sessions. His commitment to academic excellence and accreditation extends to his involvement with ABET, NCAAA, and NCEAC over the past decade.

Syeda Mariam Muzammal holds a PhD in Computer Science from Taylor's University in Malaysia. With a passion for academia and a wealth of industry experience, Dr. Syeda has made significant contributions to the field through teaching and research. As a seasoned educator, she imparts knowledge to both undergraduate and postgraduate students. In research, her focus spans various cutting-edge domains. A trailblazer in the Internet of Things (IoT), Dr. Syeda explores the intricacies of IoT systems and their applications. Cybersecurity and Network Security are integral aspects of her research, where a profound understanding of threats and defenses is cultivated. Routing protocols, an essential component of network communication, are a subject of expertise for her. In the ever-evolving landscape of technology, Dr. Syeda is at the forefront of research in Machine Learning, trust-based security, and Blockchain. She has overall 10 years of professional, academic, and research experience, with a number of research publications in well-reputed journals and conferences.

Satyanarayana Nimmala completed his Ph.D. (CSE) from Osmania University, Hyderabad, and Telangana in 2020. He did his B. Tech. from Kakatiaya University, Kothagudem, Telangana, India in 2007. He did his M.Tech. From JNTUH, Hyderabad in 2010, India. Presently he is working as Professor in the Department of CSE (Data Science), CVR College of Engineering, Hyderabad, Telangana, India. His research interests are Data Mining, Bioinformatics, and Machine Learning and Artificial Intelligence. He has authored 30+ research papers published in reputed international journals and has around 100+ citations; he also has credit of 5 patents and 3 book chapters. He has more than 18 years of teaching experience, and he has taught a wide variety of subjects like Advanced Data Structures through C++, Core Java, Python, problem-solving through C, DS through C, DBMS, OS, DWDM, etc. he has guided several B.Tech.and M.Tech. Projects during his teaching career.

Soobia Saeed is currently lecturer at the School of Computer Science, Taylor's University, Malaysia. Prior to joining Taylor's University, she also worked as a research assistant in the neurosurgical unit in Medicare Cardiac and General Hospital (MGCH) under the supervision of Dr. Mohsin Qadeer (Consultant Neurosurgeon. She served as the Director of the Office of Research, Innovation, and Commercialization (ORIC) at Sohail university formerly Jinnah Medical and Dental College (JMDC). Additionally, she held the position of Assistant Professor at Sohail University. During her tenure at JMDC, Dr. Saeed was instrumental in leading the Ethical Review Committee and spearheaded several industrial and pharmaceutical projects, demonstrating her leadership and expertise in bridging academia with industry. Dr. Saeed earned her Ph.D. in Computer Science from Universiti Teknologi Malaysia (UTM), where her doctoral research focused on the application of Artificial Intelligence (AI) in healthcare. Her Ph.D. thesis made significant contributions to the field, particularly in integrating AI into medical practices, enhancing clinical decision-making, and improving patient outcomes. With a strong research background, Dr. Saeed has authored over 96 impactful articles that span the frontiers of Machine Learning, Artificial Intelligence, Computational Neuroscience, Software Engineering, Bioinformatics, and Computing. Her work is particularly concentrated in the areas of machine learning and computational neurosciences, where she has developed innovative solutions to complex challenges in healthcare. These contributions have been published in journals indexed in the Science Citation Index (SCI), underscoring the clinical relevance and significant impact of her research within the medical domain. Dr. Saeed's dedication to advancing knowledge in AI and its applications in healthcare continues to influence both academic and clinical settings, positioning her as a key figure in the intersection of technology and medicine.

Abdullahi Adewole Zakariyah is a second-year student at Albukhary International University, pursuing a degree in computer science. With a passion for data analytics, he has been actively involved in various clubs and associations, currently serving as the treasurer of the Nigerian Student Association (NISCO). Committed to his career goals, Abdullahi aims to leverage his education and leadership experience to make a meaningful impact in the field of technology.

Index

A

B

C

D

E

F

H

I

L

M

P

R

S

T

V

www.ingramcontent.com/pod-product-compliance
Lightning Source LLC
LaVergne TN
LVHW080349011026
849161LV00009B/2238
* 9 7 9 8 3 6 9 3 6 1 3 5 1 *